Most published histories of institutions of higher education are full of trivia from fading yesterdays designed primarily to address the nostalgic interests of loyal alumni. Unfortunately, such books feature little of value for "outsiders" or guidance for a better future. Not so with Wallace Thornton's *When the Fire Fell*. To be sure, he recounts a fascinating past that the school's alumni will treasure; but he also adds to his work important biographical, historical, and theological dimensions that go far beyond any provincial exercise in institutional public relations. Thornton's several strands of recollection and analysis are skillfully woven together to produce a well-told and richly documented story of personal journey, holiness vision, evangelistic passion, publishing ministries, and sometimes clashing perspectives within the Holiness movement, all leading to educational innovation in Cincinnati that clearly has been honored by the Spirit of God. ... Under this historian's careful guidance, watching the Bible's holiness message flourish on the "Mount of Blessings" is itself a fresh blessing that holds potential for discovering God's intentions for the church's tomorrows. Here is a book to be read with minds alert and hearts open to what God has done and will yet do among faithful Christian people.
— Barry L. Callen, Editor of the *Wesleyan Theological Journal*

Thornton has written a compelling account, showing how Martin Wells Knapp through revival meetings, a publishing company and a periodical created a network of evangelists and grassroots support that led to the founding of the most significant holiness educational institution at the turn of the twentieth century. ... A must read for anyone interested in the history of the Holiness Movement and the impact it had on American culture in the first half of the twentieth century.
— D. William Faupel, Professor of the History of Christianity
Wesleyan Theological Seminary, Washington, D. C.

The holiness movement had a deep and lasting impact on all of North American evangelicalism, yet it may be the least-understood of America's major religious movements. *When the Fire Fell* is just the kind of in-depth study—intelligent, well-researched, and judiciously-argued—of a key holiness institution that will be welcomed by all who seek a better understanding of the movement.
— Mike Hamilton, Professor of History, Seattle Pacific University

In this new book, Wallace Thornton, Jr., brings to bear the same analytical skills that made *Radical Righteousness* such a valuable work. With the same attention to detail and nuance, he perceptively brings to life the vivid personalities and issues that surrounded the launching of God's Bible School, which emerged from the nineteenth century holiness revival as the conservative Holiness Movement's leading college, and one of its vital centers of influence.
— R. Stanley Ingersol, Denominational Archivist, Church of the Nazarene

The Asbury Theological Seminary Series in Christian Revitalization Studies

This volume is published in collaboration with the Center for the Study of World Christian Revitalization Movements, a cooperative initiative of Asbury Theological Seminary faculty. Building on the work of the previous Wesleyan/Holiness Studies Center at the Seminary, the Center provides a focus for research in the Wesleyan Holiness and other related Christian renewal movements, including Pietism and Pentecostal movements, which have had a world impact. The research seeks to develop analytical models of these movements, including their biblical and theological assessment. Using an interdisciplinary approach, the Center bridges relevant discourses in several areas in order to gain insights for effective Christian mission globally. It recognizes the need for conducting research that combines insights from the history of evangelical renewal and revival movements with anthropological and religious studies literature on revitalization movements. It also networks with similar or related research and study centers around the world, in addition to sponsoring its own research projects.

Here we present Wallace Thornton's inspired and definitive account of a critical figure in the history of the Wesleyan Holiness movement whose influence far exceeds his life and times. The author presents his subject, Martin Wells Knapp, in a well-developed narrative interfacing biographical, historical and theological perspectives, designed to elucidate what an authentic manifestation of Pentecost wrought in world Christianity in the early twentieth century. It is the story of his life and witness, in relation to a plethora of ministries launched from this revival. These included God's Bible School, *The Revivalist* magazine, the Pilgrim Holiness Church, and the One Mission Society, all expressions of the profound impact of the holiness revival that reverberated through his ministry, influencing major figures and movements around the world. Thornton's study shows Knapp to be a key figure in the rise of the modern holiness and Pentecostal movements. This volume is presented in the Pietist and Wesleyan Studies subseries of the general series in Revitalization Studies.

J. Steven O'Malley
General Editor
The Asbury Theological Seminary Series
in Christian Revitalization Studies

When the Fire Fell

*Martin Wells Knapp's Vision of Pentecost
and the Beginnings of God's Bible School*

Wallace Thornton, Jr.

Asbury Theological Seminary Series in Pietist/Wesleyan Studies

EMETH PRESS
www.emethpress.com

When the Fire Fell:
Martin Wells Knapp's Vision of Pentecost and the Beginnings of God's Bible School

© 2014 God's Bible School and College
Printed in the United States of America on acid-free paper

All rights reserved. No part of this book may be reproduced, or stored in a retrieval system or transmitted in any form or by any means, electronic, mechanical, photocopying, recording, scanning or otherwise, except as permited by the 1976 United States Copyright Act, or with the prior written permission of God's Bible School and College.. Requests for permission should be addressed to: President's Office, God's Bible School and College, 1810 Young Street, Cincinnati, OH 45202.

Emeth Press has been given special permission by God's Bible School and College to publish this work as part of The Asbury Theological Seminary Series in World Christian Revitalization Movements in Pietist/Wesley Studies.

Library of Congress Cataloging-in-Publication Data

Thornton, Wallace, 1968-
  When the fire fell : Martin Wells Knapp's vision of Pentecost and the beginnings of God's Bible School / Wallace Thornton, Jr.
     pages cm
ISBN 978-1-60947-069-2 (alk. paper)
1. Pentecostalism. 2. Knapp, Martin Wells, 1853-1901. 3. God's Bible School and Missionary Training Home. I. Title.
  BR1644.T46 2014
  289.9'4--dc23
                                   2013046613

Cover design by Kevin Moser

Contents

"Back to the Bible" by C. B. Widmeyer   ix

"Back to the Bible" quotes from Lettie Cowman and M. G. Standley   x

Acknowledgments   xi

Foreword   xiii

Preface by William C. Kostlevy   xv

Introduction   xvii

Chapter 1: Catching the Vision: Forging a Foundation   1

Chapter 2: Unveiling the Vision: Claiming the Mount   51

Chapter 3: Completing the Vision: Winning the World   97

Chapter 4: Conquests for the Vision: Claiming the Victory   127

Chapter 5: Securing the Vision: The Quest for the Mantle   171

Chapter 6: Pushing the Battle: Continuing the Conquest   195

Chapter 7: Holding a Steady Course: Advocates and Adversaries   229

Chapter 8: Broadening the Base; Defending the Basics   261

Chapter 9: Storming the Fort: Advancing the Cause   297

Appendix A: Dedicatory Prayer by Seth Rees, September 27, 1900   337

Appendix B: Bibliographical Essay   339

"Back to the Bible."

Dedicated to God's Bible School and Missionary Training Home, Cincinnati, Ohio.
C. B. W. REV. C. B. WIDMEYER.

1. "Back to the Bi-ble," 'tis the mot-to we'll o-bey, "Back to the Bi-ble," hear the call of God to-day: Go preach the Gos-pel to a lost and ruined race, Tell them of Je-sus, who will save them by His grace.
2. "Back to the Bi-ble," let us weep and watch and pray, "Back to the Bi-ble," till we find the "nar-row way;" Walk in the foot-steps of the meek and lowly One, Till we shall reach our home, where there's no setting sun
3. "Back to the Bi-ble," let us preach with one ac-cord, Back to the teachings of our bless-ed ris-en Lord; Back to the days when men had Pen-te-cos-tal pow'r, Trust-ing the prom-is-es, we'll tri-umph ev-'ry hour.
4. "Back to the Bi-ble," lift the Word a lit-tle higher, "Back to the Bi-ble," to the God who sends the fire; Con-quer thro' Je-sus' blood, then trust His sov'reign grace, Watching till He re-turns and shows His smiling face.

CHORUS.

"Back to the Bi-ble," o-bey it one and all, Preach "full sal-va-tion," that saves from sin's dark pall; "Back to the Bi-ble," we'll sing this sweet re-frain, Je-sus is com-ing, He's com-ing back a-gain.

Copyright, 1915, by "God's Revivalist" Office.

My soul was greatly blessed and refreshed as I read the story of that rare life which burned out for God, and when I laid down the book one thought clung with tenacity; his life seemed to say to me one thing; it had but one message—"*Back to the Bible.*"

– Mrs. Charles E. Cowman, upon reading *A Hero of Faith and Prayer: The Life of Martin Wells Knapp* in "Back to the Bible," *Revivalist* (March 22, 1928), 1, original emphasis.

Our motto is 'Back to the Bible,' and we are getting back just as quickly as possible; but we need, even now, to march double quick.... I am pleading more and more for the burning zeal and love of God, and the simplicity of a pilgrim of the Cross—simplicity in everything we do. The reason we are trying to impress on hearts the need of humility and simplicity is that we ought to save money to reach over a billion unevangelized souls!... I want to die *knowing* that I have put in my best for God Almighty!

– M. G. Standley, reported in "The Jubilee Service in God's Bible School Tabernacle," *Revivalist* (April 19, 1928), 5-6 (original emphasis).

Acknowledgments

I am indebted to God's Bible School and College who paid for the research and writing of this book, and to the administration, staff, alumni and constituents of God's Bible School and College for their wealth of information and insight. Among them were Dr. Michael Avery, Rev. Glenn Black, Dr. Sam Deets, Rev. Wesley Humble, Dr. Bence Miller, Mr. Kevin Moser, Rev. Larry Smith, Dr. Leonard Sankey, and Dr. Kenneth Stetler.

I am especially indebted to Dr. William Kostlevy—who has been mentor, resource person, invaluable critic, and, most importantly, supportive friend. He frequently went beyond the call of duty in providing access to the extensive collection of Asbury Theological Seminary. His perspectives on the development of the holiness movement have informed many of the author's own perceptions and have helped to "make sense" of many of the complexities of the following story. Without the many hours dedicated to this project by Dr. Kostlevy, this book would have been severely lacking.

Appreciation is also extended to Ms. Stacy Thompson and her colleagues in the Hamilton County Clerk of Courts office, who spent many hours assisting me in locating and copying relevant court records. The library staff of Albion College provided access to microfilm copy of The Michigan Christian Advocate. Cincinnati Public Library staff facilitated my research through hundreds of newspaper articles. Rev. James Lanham, former pastor of the Eastside Church of the Nazarene in Covington, Kentucky, provided helpful information regarding John Franklin Knapp. Rev. Gary E. Bowell provided copies of helpful primary resources regarding the MCA.

Invaluable assistance was rendered by Dr. Charles E. Jones, distinguished historian and bibliographer of the holiness and Pentecostal movements, and the late Rev. Roger G. Price, indefatigable researcher of the radical holiness tradition. Special appreciation for accommodating this work is also extended to the church in Moberly, Missouri, that I served as pastor during much of the time that this project was in process.

I remain indebted beyond words to my wife, Janice, and to our children, Janna, Charista, William, and Josiah, as well as to our extended family, for their encouragement and assistance throughout the project. Ultimately, I wish to give thanks to God for His grace and benevolence which have favored the school bearing His name, and which, I trust, are reflected in this book as well.

Foreword

On September 27, 2000, God's Bible School and College celebrated its centenary. This momentous milestone elicited retrospection by alumni and other constituents and prompted several initiatives. Among these was the commissioning of Wallace Thornton to produce the official history of God's Bible School. After some time, it became obvious that the scope of this project called for more than one volume. The significant influence that Martin Wells Knapp had on the holiness movement through the *God's Revivalist*, the Salvation Park Camp Meeting, the Holiness Union and the beginning years of God's Bible School was a story all its own. *When the Fire Fell* tells that remarkable story!

Thornton has produced a well-researched, scholarly work that speaks eloquently the praise and gratitude appropriate to God and His people who have fulfilled the dream of Martin Wells Knapp. At the same time, he presents an honest exploration of the various ideologies and principles that shaped the institution and the movements with which it has been associated.

For all of us who love this school and have a profound respect for its history, Wallace Thornton has given us a priceless treasure. May every reader find both inspiration and instruction in this amazing story of the work of God and His people through the school that bears His Name.

Michael R Avery, President
God's Bible School and College

Preface

The publication of a scholarly history of a relatively small Bible college may surprise even some of God's Bible School's (GBS) most dedicated supporters. Interestingly it will not surprise academic specialists in the burgeoning field of American religious studies. In the last decade university press studies of the American Holiness Movement have been published with increasing frequency. Most focus on a single group, such as the Salvation Army, and often fail to touch on central figures of the broad international movement that made holiness churches the fastest growing denominations in the United States and around the world during the first five decades of the twentieth century. Other scholars reduce the Holiness Movement's significance to its role as the alleged incubator of Pentecostalism. Wallace Thornton, Jr.'s *When the Fire Fell* does much more. It faithfully and accurately recounts God's Bible School's role in the world wide spread of Evangelical Christianity. In the process it tells how the college shaped and was shaped by such remarkable spiritual leaders as Martin Wells Knapp, W. B. Godbey, Lettie Burd Cowman, and innumerable others.

In the tradition of the Old Testament chroniclers, whose faithfulness to the truth did not allow them to hide the sins of the powerful, Thornton provides a detailed and fair, warts and all history of the beginnings of GBS. Scholars will appreciate this work's four particular contributions to the study of the history of twentieth-century Evangelicalism. First Thornton clearly delineates the role of God's Bible School in the early twentieth century Holiness Movement. Building on the landmark studies of Donald W. Dayton, Thornton shows how the emergence of the four-fold gospel of Jesus as savior, sanctifier, healer and coming king impacted GBS and how GBS in turn spread this message around the world. Especially valuable in this regard is the role of GBS in the origins and spread of the Pilgrim Holiness Church, the Church of the Nazarene and later churches aligned with the Inter Church Holiness Convention. Equally important is the new information we learn about such central figures of the Holiness Movement as Meredith G. Standley, George B. Kulp and beloved GBS professors such as Robert McNeil and Nettie Peabody.

Secondly, this book, even more than the official histories of such bodies as OMS international, helps us see how God's Bible School shaped the message and strategies of many of the most effective missionaries and national leaders in Asia, Africa and South America. Many have heard of Juji Nakada, the Japanese Moody, but few appreciated fully how his lifelong ministry was shaped by GBS, Charles and Lettie Burd Cowman, W. B. Godbey and his time spent in Cincinnati at GBS with his friend Oswald Chambers. Further, this work is especially important for students of the Holiness Movement in Korea where the Korean Evangelical Holiness Church has continued to thrive even as it has faithfully spread the four-fold gospel throughout Asia.

Thirdly, GBS is one of the primary shapers of modern Evangelical spirituality. It is simply inconceivable to imagine Evangelicalism without the writings of Oswald Chambers and Lettie Burd Cowman. As the authors of the two best-selling evangelical devotional books of the twentieth century, they have nurtured the devotional lives of countless Christians who desire to serve God fully with their hearts, minds, souls and bodies. We know less about the impact of others shaped by the spiritual vision of the Mount of Blessings, such as the dream of F. M. Messenger to place the Scriptures in every home through his Scripture Text Calendar, or countless others who merely sought to serve God in their own neighborhoods. They too are the heirs of the GBS tradition.

Finally Thornton highlights the adaptive power of the holiness message and GBS over its first century. Like its parent Methodism, the holiness message thrives in very different settings, such as in urban rescue missions, seaside resorts, jungles and among common people seeking the Lord around the world. GBS, itself, has not remained unchanged. It has moved from being closely tied to the Methodism of its founder to being a key institution of the Conservative holiness Movement. But, as Thornton demonstrates, change can be deceptive. God's Bible School remains absolutely dependent upon its Lord and its self-sacrificing faculty, staff, administrators, students, alumni and supporters. In a fundamental sense it has never ceased being a faith venture dependent on God and God's people.

William Kostlevy
Director of Brethren Historical Library and Archives

Introduction

Well over a century has passed since "the fire fell" and ignited a passion within the heart of Martin Wells Knapp to see Pentecost recreated in his day. This sparked the publication of God's Revivalist and numerous books, pamphlets, and song books; an industrial school for youth in the Appalachian Mountains; and a camp meeting and Bible School in Cincinnati, Ohio. The flame quickly spread and resulted in a world-wide spiritual conflagration with such institutional legacies as the Pilgrim Holiness Church, One Mission Society, and the Korea Evangelical Holiness Church. Broader still, much of the modern holiness and Pentecostal movements locate their roots in the ideals and intensity of the little man who sought to bring the church "Back to the Bible" and "Back to Pentecost."

This book does not attempt to provide a full-fledged history of God's Bible School or the *Revivalist* constituency. Rather, it focuses on the developments leading up to and surrounding the beginnings of God's Bible School. The rationale for devoting such extensive attention to the precursor developments to the school and its formative period derives from their foundational character; for as Lloyd Day observed, "The pattern for God's Bible School and Missionary Training Home, after two years of its existence, had been made."[2] In a profound sense, what has transpired at God's Bible School in the last century can be properly understood only in the context of the vision of Martin Wells Knapp and his colleagues.

The interpretive framework which guides our journey through the school's formative days is suggested by the school's motto—"Back to the Bible." On the one hand, it indicates an overarching faithfulness to scriptural Christianity, with the Bible serving as the centerpiece of the educational system. On the other hand, it would come to reflect diverse nuances throughout the history of the school, implying such concepts as primitivism and fundamentalism. Indeed, the development of these nuances gives substance to much of the school's history.

In tracing these foundational developments, an attempt is made to be objective and thorough while remaining sympathetic and charitable. The aim here is to avoid hagiography and triumphalism on the one hand and exposé on the other. Although embracing the conviction that the history of God's Bible School reflects divine intervention and blessings in human affairs, this work still acknowledges that, as with any institution, the school has known its dark days and less than noble persons. Rather than obfuscate the truth, the goal is to present the "truth in love," casting everyone and every event in the light of Christian love. Such love "thinketh no evil" and "hopeth all things," thus a genuine effort to place the best construction on apparently negative situations is maintained. Such love also "rejoiceth not in iniquity, but rejoiceth in the truth" (I Corinthians 13:6). Readers will hopefully recognize that any probing into the past, uncovering good or ill, has been done out of love for the institution and its constituents.

Perhaps this approach sounds foreign to the work of an objective historian. Yet, in a sense, no historian is truly objective, for we all have our biases—our perspectives that mold the way we depict events and persons. George Marsden has said it well: "Inevitably one's point of view will shape one's work. Since it is impossible to be objective, it is imperative to be fair."[3] Timothy L. Smith similarly asserts that "a reasonably objective estimate of the facts is no less possible for historians who write from a viewpoint sympathetic to their subject than for those who approach it from the outside."[4]

Obviously, as an alumnus of God's Bible School who cherishes its heritage, this author writes from within the school's tradition. Yet, I have striven to be fair and honest in the following account. May our readers find both inspiration and instruction in our story of the work of God and His people through the school that bears His Name.

Wallace Thornton, Jr.

Notes

¹ Lloyd Raymond Day, "A History of God's Bible School in Cincinnati: 1900-1949," (M. Ed. Thesis, University of Cincinnati, 1949), 11. When Day is cited in notes without a title, the citation refers to his thesis.

² Day, 51.

³ George Marsden, *Reforming Fundamentalism: Fuller Seminary and the New Evangelicalism* (Grand Rapids: William B. Eerdmans Publishing Co., 1987), xi.

⁴ Timothy L. Smith, *Called Unto Holiness: The Story of the Nazarenes: The Formative Years* (Kansas City: Nazarene Publishing House, 1962), 351.

Chapter 1

Catching the Vision: Forging a Foundation

"Martin Wells Knapp ... was a man small in stature but large in love. He was ZEAL INCARNATE."   – Joseph H. Smith

"He was a flaming fire ... Nothing seemed to daunt him."
   – George Kulp[1]

For the casual observer, little distinguishes the southern Michigan city of Albion from the hundreds of other sleepy little college towns that dot the Midwest. Yet, for holiness folk, it holds great significance. For them, it probably remains best known as the location where George Bennard penned the beloved gospel song "The Old Rugged Cross." It also invokes reminiscence of the spiritual and cultural impact of early Wesleyanism on the American frontier, since a small Methodist college still provides its centerpiece. However, even most holiness people are unaware that in an important sense Albion served as the birthplace of one of the holiness movement's most influential and enduring institutions, God's Bible School. For it was here on July 17, 1890, that a visionary young man by the name of Martin Wells Knapp journalized the following inspiration:

> God is blessing book and paper work. He saves me through and through. He is going to do greater things, I believe. A Training-school for gospel workers and an Evangelistic Home is on my heart and in my head. It seems as if God put it there. I had rather be in partnership with Him than any one else, because I know Him better. . . . He knows me better. . . . I agree tonight that if He will give me the building for the Home, to use it for his glory and to put this or a similar statement on it, "This building is a monument of the power and willingness of the loving Christ to answer prayer."[2]

Actually, Knapp had dreamed of starting such a Bible training school about fifteen years earlier while still a student at Albion College; however, as Glenn Black notes, it was at the time of his journal entry that "*faith* began to envision a school."[3] This work seeks to tell the story of how that vision became a reality that has continued now for over a century.

A Divine Surprise

Our story begins with the interaction of Knapp and one of the greatest spiritual forces in Christian history—the holiness movement.[4] This wave of revival swept up Knapp, empowering him to rise above unpromising circumstances. Eventually, it catapulted him to a place of prominence among the holiness ranks, so that Knapp in turn powerfully shaped the movement that had done so much to bring meaning to his own life. The story of these transformations, both individual and collective, set the stage for the realization of Knapp's vision of a Bible training school.

It is doubtful that a better example of the egalitarian impulse or elevating power of holiness could be found than Martin Wells Knapp. His biographer, A. M. Hills, observed as much, terming him "One of God's Surprises."[5] In emphasizing the disadvantages that beset Knapp, Hills compared him to King David and Abraham Lincoln. Like these heroes, Knapp's life began in relative anonymity with his birth on March 27, 1853, in a log house in Calhoun County, Michigan. As a young man, he also possessed few of the characteristics so often associated with great leaders. His youth was beset by illnesses such as sunstroke which were aggravated by a weak constitution apparently inherited from his father. The "fair"[6] education that he acquired was hindered by interruptions to help his ailing father with farm work.[7] In fact, even though he studied intermittently at Albion College from age sixteen to age twenty-three, he was still two years short of graduation when he left school for marriage and ministry.

In addition, Hills observed that Knapp lacked the "physical advantages" beneficial to successful leadership:

> He was only about five feet four or five inches high, and weighed about one hundred and twenty pounds. The proportions of his body were not fine: the various parts and members of his body, in their general effect, seemed as if they had been thrown together or had chanced to come together by some laughable accident of nature. The first impression he made upon a strange audience was always unfavorable.[8]

Undoubtedly self-consciousness of his unattractiveness fostered the excessive timidity which also plagued Martin as a child. This bashfulness drove him to avoid the public, so that he "would rush out of the house, jump over the fence, and break for the woods when he saw a visitor coming to his mother's door." Hills assessed this timidity as "a positive disease" which, "but for all-conquering grace, would have utterly disqualified him for the ministry."[9] Later in life, Knapp "often said of himself that he was a born coward until he was 'born again.'"[10]

Even in spiritual development, the young Knapp seemed destined for failure. Although his father Jared was "an old Methodist class-leader for years—one of the shouting kind" and his mother Octavia a devout lady of "strong character and firm convictions,"[11] Martin "rebelled and tried for a time to be an infidel" while at college.[12]

Despite such an unlikely beginning, Knapp grew to become a religious leader who possessed tremendous spiritual magnetism coupled with exemplary personal piety, so that W. B. Godbey observed, "Though Brother Knapp in his wonderful . . . sweetness in manner . . . reminded me of an angel instead of a man, yet he had a power over the human will which was absolutely and apparently irresistible."[13] Hills similarly described him:

> Nobody that ever knew him in his home and worked with him in literary and religious work during his later years can ever forget that face and those eyes. Brother Knapp, with his pent-up energy and boundless enthusiasm in the work of God, his unfailing love and Christ-like compassion for the sinful, his divine passion for souls driving on his little, overworked body, with his face and eyes flaming with the light of the other world, was to me the best picture of what the Apostle Paul must have been of any man I have ever yet met in public life.[14]

The only explanation for this radical transformation that Hills found satisfactory was "the uplifting, ennobling, and transforming power of the Holy Ghost on a life."[15]

In Hills' estimation, Knapp provided a perfect illustration of the truth of I Corinthians 1:26-29—

> For ye see your calling, brethren, how that not many wise men after the flesh, not many mighty, not many noble, are called: but God hath chosen the foolish things of the world to confound the wise; and God hath chosen the weak things of the world to confound the things which are mighty; and base things of the world, and things which are despised, hath God chosen, yea, and things which are not, to bring to nought things that are: that no flesh should glory in his presence.[16]

Indeed, Hills hoped that his recounting of Knapp's story would inspire others with "natural limitations" to overcome "untoward circumstances and unfriendly environments," with confidence that God could do for them what he had done for Knapp.[17]

The beginning of his transformation came during Knapp's college days and reflected not only a change in Knapp's relationship with God but also Knapp's openness to spiritual formation under the guidance of women, a commitment that marked the rest of his life. Actually, Knapp's "apostasy was short-lived," for he soon "was overcome with introspection about death-bed agonies and funerals."[18] He began to seek God, a quest in which the two most influential human agencies were his mother and a young lady he met at college, Lucy J. Glenn (1855-1890). Martin later wrote that Lucy, "more than any other, was instrumental in my conversion."[19] On another occasion he testified, "In my Egyptian experience mother was my Moses, and [Lucy] my Aaron."[20]

Initially, Lucy had been somewhat reluctant to maintain a relationship with Martin (by correspondence—even though they were both attending Albion College—in compliance with Victorian customs), whom she described as "a careless young man who might be termed 'a scoffer at religion.'" However, she prayed and felt that God would have her correspond with him, not for romantic purposes, but to use her influence to "win him to Christ."[21]

After lengthy self-examination, Martin came up against the seemingly insurmountable obstacle, or "Red Sea," that hindered his conversion. He felt he could fully yield to God in all things save this: he could not bring himself to open the school day with prayer at the grade school in which he then taught. He testified,

> I could get no peace, and whenever I tried to pray that question would rise like a specter before me. I would say, "Anything but that;" but it was God's test question, and he would not be turned away. At this point the impression came: "Now or never! Yield at once, or you will suddenly be cut off and forever lost!" This came like a lightning stroke. I felt as sure of that truth as that I lived. The next Monday morning my school began. Tremblingly I took my Bible, and read one of the shortest psalms I could find, and then my courage failed me. The next and the next morning the same was repeated. Thursday morning I said: "This will do no longer. I will fully obey." God helped, and then I did the best I could, and then it was O so easy to fully trust. And before the sun went down that night the witness of the Spirit was given, and peace—sweet, deep, rich, and inexpressible—was mine.[22]

This conversion was quickly followed by public confession, baptism, and membership in the Methodist Episcopal Church (hereafter, M. E. Church). After this, Martin's and Lucy's relationship took on a romantic tone, and, in 1877, Martin married the young woman to whom he was so greatly indebted spiritually. About the same time, Martin accepted the call to ministry and the young couple began their first pastorate at the Pottersville circuit, which, like all of Knapp's pastoral charges, was in the Michigan Conference of the M. E. Church.

Lucy continued to play a pivotal role in Martin's spiritual development; in fact, extant accounts depict his entrance into ministry and his marriage to Lucy as two parts of a single decision. He always considered Lucy a partner in ministry and used glowing language to describe her significance to their work, as reflected in his lament after her death: "My spiritual mother is gone, the angel of my home has taken her flight. My ministerial co-laborer has been promoted to higher ministry. My office companion henceforth is engaging in brighter companionships."[23]

Upon entering pastoral ministry, Martin faced immediate contention due to some of his natural disadvantages to public work, in addition to his youthfulness. Several parishioners at Pottersville "wanted a more experienced, older man" and felt that the "Conference had imposed upon them" with Knapp's appointment. Shortly before the quarterly meeting, "a cold-heart-ed, beer-drinking, wealthy member of the Quarterly Conference summoned the young man [Knapp] for a talk. It was to warn and prepare him for the lightning stroke that he was hoping soon would leap upon him," namely his removal from the pastorate. Knapp recalled that "it went through [his] heart like a dagger," a burden compounded by Lucy's concurrent battle with typhoid fever.[24]

It appeared that Knapp's ministerial career would end in its infancy, but Martin remained confident that "God was not dead. He had a plan," a truth he believed his opponents had "overlooked." When the quarterly meeting convened, the presiding elder was unable to attend. He sent Knapp's former pastor, a close friend, in his place, ensuring that the "plot" against Knapp was "crushed."[25] Knapp went on to pastor three years at his first charge after surviving this hostility, and his wife recuperated from typhoid, crediting her recovery to divine healing.

Although Knapp received vindication in this first skirmish in ministry, it was not to be the last or most vehement resistance that Knapp would face throughout his ministry. Significantly, even in these early days, opposition to Knapp's ministry was not limited to concerns over his lack of natural advantages. It also involved resistance to his message against the worldliness of such churchgoers as the quarterly meeting member who opposed him at Pottersville: "Always more intent on getting seekers to the mourner's bench than in gaining the praise of prosperous and influential church members, Knapp mercilessly bore down on worldliness." Consequently, his "attacks on the formality, sociability, and fashionability of contemporary Methodism generated opposition in every pastorate he served."[26]

Another characteristic of Knapp's ministry that appeared early was an intense interest in winning souls, especially in foreign fields. In fact, "when he had been in the ministry but a few years, he offered himself to Bishop William Taylor [the famed holiness advocate known as the missionary bishop] to go as a foreign missionary."[27] He and Lucy were disappointed when Martin was rejected as a missionary candidate due to his poor health. However, their zeal for global evangelism continued unabated, as did their high regard for Bishop Taylor. Meanwhile, in an irony of history, it was another Methodist minister also named William Taylor who helped guide Knapp into the most dramatic incident of his life. This experience completed his transformation from bashful, backwoods youth to aggressive soul-winner and holiness advocate—a "divine surprise" indeed.

Sanctifying Power

During his second pastorate, the Duplain circuit, this spiritual crisis took place, forever transforming Knapp and his ministry. He had been struggling for some time with an "inner bent to sinning."[28] After battling with giant "Wrong Views" (thinking that deliverance from "inbred" sin comes in conversion), Martin sought a "second blessing" that would bring complete freedom from this inherited sin nature, an experience commonly termed "entire sanctification." He became convinced of such a need due to "his quick temper, selfish ambitions, and frequent struggles within [which] proved to him that he 'was not possessed with the mind of Christ.'"[29]

To facilitate his seeking, and that of others under his charge, he scheduled three days of special services in June 1882 with a minister named William Taylor (not to be confused with the famous bishop) and his wife. Knapp reported that he "received great help at that time, but not the consciousness that the great work was wrought."[30] He continued avidly reading holiness materials and seeking sanctification. Finally, in November, "the crisis came" after Knapp "had been preaching full salvation, but could lead people no further" than he had gone himself. The testimony he gave regarding this experience provides significant insight into his future ministry and deserves quotation at length:

> In November, 1882, I permitted the Lord to lead me to Kadesh-Barnea, on the borders of the promised land. By his grace I then and there entered the land, receiving the blessed baptism of the Spirit that cleanses from inbred sin and fills with perfect love.
>
> God met me and gave me the promise: "If we walk in the light as He is in the light, we have fellowship one with another, and the blood of Jesus Christ His Son cleanseth us from all sin" [I John 1:7]. The blessed Holy Spirit explained it to my heart, and helped me to take hold of it right then and there. He suggested, "Why not believe on the authority of His Word that God is doing just what He agrees to do just now?" I was conscious that the conditions upon which the promise was based were being met, and could see no reason why I should not, and replied, "Lord, I do." In an instant I was made conscious of my cleansing. The "giants" fled, the "walled towns" crumbled, and Canaan, through Christ, was possessed. To God be all the glory!"
>
> The "fullness" soon followed. I saw then where my trouble had been. I had not dared to venture on the promise and trust in the present tense. I thanked God for the victory given, and asked that, in order with greater confidence I might publicly proclaim and urge the experience, that [sic] He would give me still further unmistakable evidence of its reality. I retired looking for something more. I was not disappointed. Instead of some thing, some One came—the One altogether lovely, even Christ Himself. I had slept about an hour when I was suddenly awakened by what sounded like three distinct knocks on the front door. In an instant I was made just as conscious of the Divine presence as ever man was of the company of an earthly friend. I felt the presence of a gentle, unseen power upon my head. Then a wave of Divine power and love, causing a sensation something like an electric shock, only inexpressibly pleasurable, rolled over my entire being. Then three impressions were made just as vividly as if uttered by an audible voice:
>   1. "This is the added evidence you prayed for."
>   2. "You are healed of your disease [i.e., the results of sunstroke]."
>   3. "A definite call to especial evangelistic work."[31]

Again, far from a fleeting euphoria, this blessing permanently revolutionized Knapp. In fact, his experience reflects, in incipient form, important ideals that characterized Knapp's future ministry, all of which were incorporated into God's Bible School.[32] These features included the importance of literature in propagating the holiness message, the prominence of women in the movement, dependence on biblical allegory and other metaphors, an emphasis on divine healing and other faith works, and an impassioned zeal for evangelistic work, at home and abroad. His testimony also reflects Knapp's indebtedness to the nineteenth-century Holiness Revival, a movement that requires brief summary to put the beginning of God's Bible School in context.[33]

This great revival movement, that swept over much of the English-speaking world and beyond, first surfaced as a resurgence of commitment to the classic Methodist teaching of Christian perfection (one of the many terms for entire sanctification).[34] With American Methodism's preoccupation with upward mobility, exacerbated by its exponential growth and concurrent increase in wealth, dedication to what Wesley termed its "grand depositum" had waned. Indeed, scholars have observed that "in the two decades previous to the Civil War, Wesley's doctrine of Christian perfection was largely neglected and had become little more than a creedal matter among the main Methodist bodies."[35]

Chief among the several voices raised to keep "scriptural holiness" in the forefront of Methodist consciousness was that of Phoebe Palmer (1807-1874), the "mother" of the holiness movement.[36] A convincing advocate of women in ministry,[37] she herself ministered to popular acclaim with tours throughout North America and Great Britain. Palmer also wielded a powerful pen, producing several books and editing a periodical, *The Guide to Holiness*.[37] Her writings were well-received, with the *Guide*'s "circulation rising from thirteen to thirty thousand"[38] during her editorship, and her first book, *The Way of Holiness* (1842), going into "its fiftieth American edition by 1867."[39] Among her many readers was Martin Wells Knapp, who acknowledged his profound indebtedness to her, noting in his journal entry for April 1, 1889, "My heart has burned while reading Mrs. Palmer's works."[40]

In *The Way of Holiness*, Palmer elucidated what became her chief theological contribution, termed "altar theology" or the "shorter way."[41] In this explanation of holiness experience, she appropriated the Old Testament language of sacrifice, admonishing seekers to fully consecrate or lay their all on the altar (Christ) who would in turn sanctify the gift. Regardless of excesses sometimes arising from its application, including the confusion of faith with presumption by some seekers, her altar theology provided the basic understanding of entire sanctification for several generations of holiness people, including Knapp, who followed it when he "dared to venture on the promise and trust in the present tense."[42]

In addition to the "shorter way," posterity primarily remembers Palmer for her leadership in the Tuesday Meetings for the Promotion of Holiness, started by her sister in 1835 at her New York City home. Originally open only to women, many men, including Methodist bishops Hamline, Peck, and Simpson, participated as well, after Thomas Upham, a Congregational minister and college professor, was sanctified in one of the meetings in 1839. The tremendous success of these meetings resulted in their duplication across the country, so that over two hundred similar gatherings were being conducted by 1886, in effect making Palmer's meetings the fountainhead of the holiness revival.[43]

Numerous voices echoed Palmer's testimony of and call to sanctification, including those of fellow Methodists such as the aforesaid bishops, editors Nathan Bangs and George Peck, and hundreds of other ministers, along with thousands of laity.[44] In addition, Methodist dissidents who formed separate denominations, such as the Wesleyan Methodist Connection (1843) and the Free Methodist Church (1860), championed other issues, such as the abolition of slavery, but sought to preserve the "doctrines and usages of primitive Methodism, such as the Witness of the Spirit [and] Entire Sanctification."[45] However, the revival extended far beyond Methodism, as reflected in the broad circle of Palmer's associates, including "Asa Mahan (president of Oberlin College and a colleague of evangelist Charles Grandison Finney), Baptist evangelist A. B. Earle, Presbyterian William E. Boardman, and Quakers Hannah Whitall Smith [author of the best-selling *Christian's Secret of a Happy Life*] and David B. Updegraff."[46]

The holiness revival also intersected the dynamic ministry of C. G. Finney (1792-1875), the "father" of modern revivalism. Though his "Oberlin perfectionism" differed significantly from Wesleyanism, his stress on experiential Christianity, including an insistence on the surrender of the will to the Holy Spirit's leadership and the appropriation of frontier revival techniques in urban ministry,[47] endeared him to many holiness advocates, who downplayed their differences and counted him as one of their own.[48] Thus, after entering revivalism himself, Knapp published excerpts from Finney's *Revival Lectures* and commissioned a biography of Finney by A. M. Hills, who had studied under Finney at Oberlin College.[49]

Finney's and Palmer's efforts both contributed to the Urban Revival (or Layman's Prayer Revival) of 1857-1859, a spiritual awakening which, "in geographical and numerical extent, has probably never been equaled," garnering over two million converts in the United States, Great Britain, and Ireland.[50] In addition, this revival ignited ministries that would challenge generations to come with a call to holiness, including those of William and Catherine Booth, founders of the Salvation Army, A. B. Simpson, founder of the Christian and Missionary Alliance, and Dwight L. Moody, perhaps the greatest lay evangelist in history.[51] In this atmosphere, the ideal of Christian perfection easily came to the forefront. The devout of practically every denomination caught the vision of a "higher life," with many cooperating in "Union Meetings" for the express purpose of promoting holiness.[52] With the Urban Revival, it appeared that the quest for holiness would dominate not only Methodism, but all of American Protestantism.

Although the great division of the country over the slavery issue, culminating in the Civil War, absorbed the attention of the nation and split denominations including the M. E. Church, the revival of holiness continued. Palmer's house-meetings portended a more ambitious organization, the National Camp Meeting Association for the Promotion of Holiness, begun at Vineland, New Jersey, in 1867. Later renamed the National Holiness Association (NHA), this organization, ostensibly inter-denominational but established and led by M. E. Church ministers, represented a new stage in the history of the holiness movement—the era of associations.[53] Under the leadership of John Inskip (1816-1884), and subsequent NHA presidents, this association adapted the time-honored Methodist camp meeting tradition for the specific task of promoting entire sanctification. A series of "national" camp meetings around the country proved an overwhelming success, even attracting the attendance of President Ulysses S. Grant in 1871. The association's accomplishments were mirrored in the election of M. E. Church bishops in 1872, in which half the new bishops were reputed to be promoters of the doctrine of entire sanctification.[54] It appeared the holiness tide would reclaim Methodism, even in the South, which initially received the NHA less enthusiastically due to its Northern origins. In 1870, the address of the Methodist Episcopal South bishops affirmed, "Nothing is so needed at the present time throughout all these lands as a genuine and powerful revival of Scriptural holiness."[55]

However, denominational endorsement of the holiness crusade stopped short of making the NHA an official agency of Methodism, and it soon became apparent that rather than remaking the major Methodist denominations, the holiness revival had birthed a movement with an identity of its own. This movement had Methodist roots, to be sure. However, it embraced a broader scope than one denominational family, as well as a more focused commitment to the experience and life of holiness than the majority of Methodists would embrace.

Several factors contributed to this development. For one, the inclusion of many non-Methodists in the holiness revival meant these folk had little loyalty to Methodism and no desire to be under its bishops' control. For another, many local holiness leaders duplicated the NHA with regional associations; however, these were independent of the NHA and at times featured innovations viewed askance by denominational leaders. In addition, the push for upward mobility and the dominance of German liberalism in Methodist seminaries and colleges resulted in the disaffection of many erstwhile loyal Methodists. Holiness people saw a correspondence in these developments, as Timothy L. Smith put it, "worldliness had begotten spiritual compromise, making the situation favorable to theologies which explained away the call to Christian perfection."[56] Indeed, liberal Methodist theologians such as James Mudge seemed to do just that, as they elevated gradual growth in holiness over the traditional Wesleyan emphasis on the instantaneous attainment of entire sanctification. Stalwart traditionalists like Daniel Steele countered such innovation, and a veritable war of words ensued: "*Entire* and *instantaneous* became battle cries, answered by *progressive* and *gradual*."[57]

The stage was set for schism from Methodism, a development begun in a "first wave" of secession in the early 1880s by "come-out" or "anti-sectarian" leaders such as John P. Brooks and D. S. Warner who decried all denominations as spiritual "Babylon" and urged holiness believers to separate from them and simply be members of the Church of God (though forming different groups using that name).[58] As anti-denominational sentiment swept the movement, particularly in the Midwest, even holiness folks found themselves divided on the "Church Question." Unfortunately, denominational leaders found it convenient to apply the pejorative label of "come-outism" to all holiness advocates, placing pressure on them to desist from their independent activities or to depart from the Methodist fold, in effect producing "put-outers" as well as "come-outers."

The release in 1894 of a statement by the M. E. South bishops reflected the great reversal of their attitude toward the holiness revival since their tacit endorsement in 1870:

> But there has sprung up among us a party with holiness as a watchword; they have holiness associations, holiness meetings, holiness preachers, holiness evangelists, and holiness property... We do not question the sincerity and zeal of these brethren; we desire the church to profit by their earnest preaching and godly example; but we deplore their teaching and methods in so far as they claim a monopoly of the experience, practice, and advocacy of holiness, and separate themselves from the body of ministers and disciples.[59]

This statement made clear the ultimate failure of the holiness cause to win the support of Methodist officialdom; indeed, the emphasis on Christian perfection had come full circle in American Methodism, from obscurity during the early nineteenth century to popularity by mid-century to rejection by the century's end. The bishops' statement was received by holiness advocates as the declaration of a "war of extermination" against them,[60] helping to precipitate a "second wave" of holiness secession from the major Methodist denominations, a phenomenon producing over twenty holiness denominations as well as numerous independent works, and one in which Martin Wells Knapp proved to be a major participant.

However, when Knapp experienced entire sanctification in 1882, the first wave of secession was just beginning, and he "remained scrupulously 'loyal' to the Methodist Episcopal Church" until the late 1890's "like the [NHA] men with whom he worked during those years."[61] In fact, he initially gained positive recognition among the Methodists of Michigan, and even beyond, as his ministry received fresh impetus from the sanctifying power which he had experienced and which he sought to share with others.

From Pastor to Revivalist

This new dynamic resulted in increased effectiveness in revivalistic and evangelistic work[62] and improved reception in Knapp's last two pastorates, at Lyons (1883-84) and Montague (1884-1887), as reflected in a report in *The Michigan Christian Advocate* from one of his parishioners at Lyons:

> The *Rev.* M. W. Knapp, our late pastor, proved himself a man of decided ability; a deep thinker, a clear and forcible reason-er, of unflinching fortitude and unwavering principles . . . He, and his devoted wife, enlisted in a soul-saving work, and in this is their delight. No work, to them, is so preciously sweet as that done for the Master."[63]

Such reputation resulted in many doors opening to the Knapps "for meetings as far as a hundred miles from home."[64] As Martin's energy had already been taxed by his demanding schedule of preaching six times per week, Lucy "herself began to preach and hold revival services, even apart from her husband for a week at a time."[65] Her fairly detailed diary entries from that time recount numerous instances of conversion, sanctification, and deliverance from such worldly vices as tobacco usage, card playing, and theater attendance.[66] Even many who initially rejected their message were won over as the Knapps exemplified the truth they proclaimed.[67]

The couple also augmented their preaching by employing the latest technology—illustrations projected by means of the "magic lantern"—a rudimentary slide projector.[68] Martin's progressive disposition marked his defense of using such methods to reach the masses with concrete expressions of abstract spiritual concepts:

> I have long been convinced that one of the most effective ways of reaching people is through the eyes. Thus the devil is preaching on every side, and often with pictures too disgusting to be seen, polluting all who behold, and helping people hell with victims. Why should we not preach, through the eye, the gospel of the Kingdom?[69]

Behind this logic lay an evangelistic passion which constantly sought a larger audience for the holiness message. This zeal led the Knapps to enter another avenue of ministry—publishing. In retrospect, Martin saw this as inevitable. Not only had holiness literature helped to lead him "like sunshine" until he was "fully sanctified,"[70] but sanctification was the experience that provided him a worthy subject about which to write. In language evocative of Jeremiah 20:9, he confessed, "After I was sanctified . . . God filled me with messages which, like pent-up fire, must find expression . . . I wrote because He filled me so full I could not help it."[71]

Their first project appeared in 1886, a single volume authored by Martin, but published at great sacrifice to the entire family since they were "forced to auction off [their] household goods to finance this venture."⁷² In this work promoting entire sanctification, Knapp asserted that "the great center and mainspring of a holy life is *Christ Crowned Within* without a rival."⁷³ Its wide distribution, with sales surpassing twenty thousand copies by 1898, elevated Knapp to national prominence within the holiness movement and led to evangelistic opportunities far beyond his home state, helping to confirm the "definite call to especial evangelistic work" that accompanied the witness to his sanctification.

This success did not go unnoticed by the Michigan Conference of the M. E. Church. Indeed, it had profited greatly from the work of the Knapps and other revivalists who participated in the conference's Revival Band (its organization of evangelistic itinerants), which witnessed forty-four hundred conversions "through its agency" in just two years.⁷⁴ In 1887, the Michigan Conference formally recognized Knapp's aptitude for such ministry by granting approval of his "location"—freeing him from pastoral work so that he could engage in full-time itinerant evangelism—and imparted a glowing endorsement:

> We believe the Holy Ghost has led him to this step, and knowing the gifts, graces, and usefulness of Bro. Knapp and his wife, we do cordially commend them to the fellowship and cooperation of God's people everywhere, and to the blessings of God in their work.⁷⁵

Publication continued to play a key role in the Knapps' ministry as they entered into full-time itinerancy. Martin's second book, *Out of Egypt Into Canaan* (1888)—further demonstrated the young minister's creative genius as he skillfully detailed a map of "spiritual geography" that explored myriad parallels between the quest for holiness and the history of the Hebrews, particularly from the Exodus to the Conquest.⁷⁶ With metaphors reminiscent of Bunyan's *Pilgrim's Progress*, replete with wilderness pitfalls and battles with giants, and with Canaan representing the sanctified life, this work remains the epitome of holiness typological Bible interpretation.

The positive reception of Martin's first two books, and their sense of God's guidance—"the pillar of fire going before"—led the Knapps to undertake their greatest faith venture thus far in July 1888 with the publication of an eight-page monthly periodical aptly entitled *The Revivalist*. ⁷⁷ As with Knapp's books, this endeavor succeeded famously, claiming at least twenty-five thousand subscribers by the end of 1901.⁷⁸ Making its success even more remarkable is the fact that by 1892 there were at least forty-one non-denominational holiness periodicals being published throughout the United States; however, of these, only *The Revivalist* has endured to the present.⁷⁹

The launching of this "silent preacher" held such far-reaching implications for the future of the holiness movement in general, and God's Bible School in particular, that its significance could hardly be exaggerated. It connected the Knapps and their readers with a frequency and familiarity not afforded by books, wielding them into a cohesive movement—the "Revivalist people"—within the larger holiness movement.[80] Indeed, historians have observed that it was this publication that "established" Knapp's "influence within the holiness movement and provided a support base for the holiness agencies he established during his brief life."[81] Such a base was particularly critical for starting and maintaining the Bible school that Knapp envisioned.

While affording the Knapps the opportunity to update readers on new and ongoing initiatives, and to solicit prayer and financial support for these, the primary purpose of the paper was to encourage "every believer" to "maintain a Revival spirit."[82] To this end, Knapp devoted the front page to revival themes such as "True and Sham Revivals," "Revival Don'ts," and "Sure Cure for False 'Isms."[83] The interior featured similar articles, as well as numerous essays promoting "full salvation." Along with the Knapps, frequent contributors included Beverly Carradine, Seth C. Rees, J. L. Glascock, and W. B. Godbey. In addition, considerable space was devoted to testimonials and "Revival Reports"—many reflecting the impact of *The Revivalist* and related publications as well as the Knapps' pulpit ministry, also underscoring the broad appeal of the holiness movement across denominational lines.[84]

A conspicuous feature that distinguished *The Revivalist* from many other religious, and even holiness, periodicals was the absence of secular advertisements from its pages. To be sure, it was not advertisement free, for it enthusiastically promoted religious activities such as camp meetings and conventions. In addition, holiness literature was prominently marketed, reflecting Knapp's conviction that the "pen and press" provided one of the most effective ways to preach the Gospel.[85] However, Knapp staunchly refused to follow the example of such holiness papers as the *Pentecostal Herald* and the *Christian Witness* that published ads for items ranging from farm seed to hair balsam.

The three-fold logic behind this determination reflects the increasingly radical stance Knapp took and portended the commitments inculcated at God's Bible School. First, Knapp opposed secular ads as being worldly, since they often featured "pictures of actors, baseball catchers, partly-dressed and worldly-dressed people, and kindred cuts."[86] Second, Knapp concluded that even "wholesome" secular ads would detract from the goal of promoting full salvation, prostituting his publishing voice for lesser or even contrary causes. He thus contended, "*The Revivalist* is my pulpit. Its mission is to proclaim the printed gospel . . . hence, I feel that nothing should enter it which does not further it. My commission does not read, 'Go ye into all the world and publish patent pills, and boom bicycles, . . . etc.'"[87]

Knapp's third reason for rejecting secular advertisements stemmed from his commitment to radical faith—a dependence on God to supply the needs for his ministry, whether publishing or otherwise. Knapp felt secular ads would undermine such faith, promoting "distrust" in "God by leading publishers to depend on Egypt [the world] for help instead of on the promises" of God.[88] This failure to trust would in turn undermine his impact on readers, as Knapp questioned, "If I can not have faith in God to help meet the expenses without depending on [worldly advertisements], how can I expect God to use me to inspire faith in other people?"[89]

Such faith became the keystone in Knapp's subsequent endeavors, especially God's Bible School. Indeed, he was willing to live and die by the "faith principle," a resignation that reverberated throughout the holiness movement, as he challenged thousands of others to launch out similarly in faith: "Should the [*Revivalist*] die because of its loyalty to these convictions, it will be a willing martyr to its faith, and can be pointed to as a warning monument of the folly of one who trusted God, with no reliance on the sale of patent pills."[90] Needless to say, his faith was rewarded, and the *Revivalist* continues to this day.

On the Anvil

However, the next couple of years would see Martin's faith tested and stretched beyond anything he had yet experienced, as he faced challenges that threatened to capsize his frail, albeit energetic, vessel. "During 1889-90 Martin W. Knapp went through a two-year 'valley' of ill health, financial crises, and family illnesses."[91] His journal during this period records intense agony—emotional, physical, and spiritual. A typical entry reads, "I have had a feeling of heavy, cutting anguish to-day, such as I have hitherto known but little of."[92]

Dominating the Knapps' other woes was physical illness, which plagued both Martin and Lucy. As a result of weak lungs, Martin was forced for a time to give up preaching and to resign from the superintendency of the Revival Band of the Michigan Conference.[93] This trial was compounded by the feeling (which he attributed to Satanic temptation) that his ministerial brethren did not really appreciate him and thought that he was "in the way of the work."[94] Although he was sometimes self-disparaging, his journal always reflects a submissive tone toward God's will: "O Father, melt and fashion us according to Thy will! Thou art at our helm; steer us where Thou wilt."[95] For Knapp, these sufferings simply indicated that he was being molded "on the anvil" of God's will, as expressed in the old German hymn:

> He kindles for my profit, purely,
> Affliction's glowing, fiery brand;
> For all his heaviest blows are surely
> Inflicted by a Master hand.
> And yet I whisper "As God will,"
> And in his hottest fire hold still.
>
> I will not murmur at the sorrow,
> That only longer lived would be;
> The end may come, and that to-morrow,
> When God hath wrought his will in me.
> And so I whisper, "As God will,"
> And in his hottest fire hold still.[96]

Where this suffering would lead was beyond Martin's comprehension. Anyone familiar with Martin's health record would not have been surprised at his decease, but it was Lucy who succumbed to "La Grippe" (the flu) and passed away on September 5, 1890, leaving Martin with two children, Anna (11) and John Franklin (3). Watching her suffer and die almost crushed Martin, for he steadfastly expected divine healing for Lucy until near the end.[97] When healing did not seem forthcoming, he asserted that "the Lord is going to rebuke unbelief, and raise her up by His own power," contending until near the end that "unbelief . . . defies the restoration of Lucy."[98]

However, her death did not dissuade Knapp's confidence in or surrender to God's will, as he declared, "Again I repeat, God's will be done, with no suggestions from me."[99] Nor did this tragedy shake his faith in divine healing. Rather, he persisted in asserting that if there were a lack, it was not in divine power but in corresponding faith, journaling on the day of her passing, "I trusted to the last that, as at other times, God would interpose, and that she would recover. I thought at times that I, with Anna, [was] praying the prayer of faith for her recovery. I see now that I did not, because there was all the while an 'if' in it and under it."[100] Now, he took solace in the conviction that Lucy had been "glorified" and had "passed into Paradise."[101]

He drew further comfort from his mother and children, especially Anna, who exercised tremendous maturity during this time and was praised for being "effectual in prayer."[102] Martin's journal of this period reveals an intimate portrait of him as a family man, intensely devoted to his "precious, motherless little ones."[103] Later, this strong sense of domestic devotion was incorporated within the institutions begun by Knapp, especially God's Bible School.

The months after Lucy's death found Martin unable to preach, and often even to attend church services, due to continued illness. However, as Day observes, "Knapp never allowed his physical handicaps to hinder his work for the gospel."[104] He simply devoted his energies more fully to print ministry, reporting to *Revivalist* readers that God had shown him that "for the present" publishing was to be his chief work and that "He would bless His Word thus heralded just as much as if published by word of mouth."[105]

In fact, this period of suffering may have been the most productive of Knapp's ministry, excepting the last two years of his life. For one thing, less than two months before Lucy's death, Knapp committed to paper the vision that would bear fruit in the culmination of his life's work, the founding of a "Training-school for gospel workers and an Evangelistic Home."[106] In addition, his prolific writing during this time produced several successful books, including his most enduring and best-selling, *Impressions*.[107] Like many other religious classics, this work presents the lessons the author distilled from his own experience of "trial and testing."[108] Knapp augmented these concepts with wisdom from ancient and contemporary sources to provide a guide enabling fellow pilgrims to differentiate between God's direction and other impressions. Released to immediate acclaim, it remains highly regarded to this day for "its essential biblical and experiential soundness,"[109] endorsed in recent years by

James Dobson of Focus on the Family, who wrote, "This timeless book is the best I have seen on the subject of God's will."[110]

The immediate goal of *Impressions* was to help holiness people "avoid the fanaticisms into which many spiritual movements have fallen because of a failure to 'test the spirits.'" Knapp already observed the holiness landscape of his day littered with "people thus deceived, like wrecked cars on a railroad track."[111] Indeed, *Impressions* presented a message sorely needed in the increasingly fractious holiness movement. In addition, it revealed Knapp to be just the type of leader such times demand, a man possessing the spiritual maturity and sagacity that are acquired only by refinement on the anvil.

At the Crossroads

With *The Revivalist* and related publications drawing nationwide attention, Lucy's death could not have occurred at a more critical juncture. Her loss threatened to unravel the publishing ministry, for, as Martin recognized, "much of [their] success" was due to her "close attention to the business" aspect of their work.[112] However, shortly before Lucy's death, her close friend, Minnie C. Ferle, left her home in Lansing to assist with the office work in Albion, while continuing to bolster Lucy's morale that had already benefited from her comforting letters. After Lucy's passing, Minnie remained, leading Martin to exult to *Revivalist* readers that Lucy's work would go on, at least temporarily, in the hands of this "fully saved worker" who was also "gifted with the pen," believing this to be another way that God "demonstrated that this work [was] His own."[113] While she would never serve as Martin's soul mate or hold his romantic affections to the same degree as had Lucy, he was attracted to Minnie pragmatically as an invaluable help in ministry, leading to their marriage on September 14, 1892.[114]

Six days later, Martin made another transition promising even greater historical import. For some time, he had been considering moving to a more centralized location, such as Chicago. However, several factors led the Knapps to choose Cincinnati, Ohio, instead.[115] Chief among these was the urging of J. L. Glascock, a Methodist evangelist from Cincinnati, with whom Knapp had been affiliated since October 1891.[116] In addition to Glascock, the move to Cincinnati would bring Knapp closer to several holiness advocates with whom Knapp became closely associated, including W. B. Godbey, S. A. Keene, and G. D. Watson. Another possible factor influencing this move was the fact that many of Knapp's books were already being printed in Cincinnati by Cranston and Stowe, publishers for the M. E. Church.[117] In addition, Cincinnati offered several practical advantages of geography and economy to a publisher, particularly with its recent procurement of the Southern Railroad route that insured its dominance over Louisville as the main rail link between North and South.[118] This meant that Knapp's new home would place him at the strategic point where northern and southern holiness advocates would cross the Mason-Dixon Line, indeed, at the veritable crossroads of the holiness movement.[119]

Doubtless this fact was in Knapp's visionary mind when he and his family moved on September 20, 1892 to their first Cincinnati home at 520 Chase Avenue in Cumminsville (now called Northside). Here they wrapped *The Revivalist* for mailing, while Cranston and Stowe continued publishing it, reflecting the continued good will between Knapp and his M. E. colleagues. Martin quickly moved to the forefront of the local holiness ranks, helping to bring order to the movement which had been ravaged by an outbreak of "fanaticism," including one man who "claimed to be Christ incarnated again, and received worship as such."[120] Knapp's sane approach to spiritual discernment, reflected in *Impressions*, made his a welcome presence among such holiness stalwarts as Mary Storey, who considered Knapp's arrival an answer to her prayers and believed that "God had sent Brother Knapp to rebuild the walls of the wasted holiness Zion in Cincinnati and the surrounding country."[121] So successful was Knapp's efforts that just a decade later A. M. Hills opined that "in no city in America is the work of holiness so thoroughly established, so well fortified and organized, and so broad and comprehensive in its plans, and so striking and puissant in its achievements, as it is now in Cincinnati."[122]

To accomplish this stability, Knapp employed methods pioneered decades earlier by Palmer and Inskip. The Knapps' made their new home immediately available for a holiness prayer meeting similar to Palmer's Tuesday Meetings. By September's end, this meeting "had grown into a holiness association" named the Cincinnati Holiness League "organized in [John Street] Methodist Church with Knapp as president."[123] The League provided the *Revivalist* cause with a "nucleus" of local supporters,[124] a vital precursor to the formation of God's Bible School.

The League also afforded Knapp a tool with which to take better advantage of his strategic location. Under his leadership, the League conducted a Union (interdenominational) holiness meeting—the Cincinnati Holiness Convention—in May 1893, with the intent of helping to "bring about the union of believers for which Jesus prayed" in John 17.[125] Advertisement for this event, held at Trinity M. E. Church, promised "something better than the world's fair,"[126] and participants' reports indicated that if not this, it was at least the equal of any other holiness convention.[127] Enthusiasm swelled to the point that the convention crowd decided to organize an even larger association, the Central Holiness League, with J. Wesley Hughes (founding president of Asbury College) as president and Knapp as secretary. This League was envisioned as an umbrella organization for local leagues similar to that started by Knapp in Cincinnati.[128]

Convention announcements strongly stressed the meeting's interdenominational nature, noting that it would be "led by loyal leaders of different churches," including holiness Baptist Edgar Levy.[129] Knapp's role as a bridge-builder also came to the fore as he invited well-known Northern Methodist John Thompson and popular Southern Methodist Beverly Carradine to share the platform. Knapp later rejoiced that here regional tensions, which still loomed large in many quarters, were erased by holiness as "the North and South met and embraced each other."[130] Another traditional boundary was also crossed with the inclusion of African-American Amanda Berry Smith among the speakers. Indeed, the same egalitarian impulse that had helped lift Knapp from obscurity now led him to extend the reach of his ministry as widely as possible—crossing gender, ethnic, regional, denominational, and economic lines.

In particular, Knapp sought to bring the holiness message to the outcasts of society. This passion, coupled with his "long time" desire to "start a Holiness Industrial School for the primary education and Christian training of children," led him to focus attention on the needs of the underprivileged in the foothills of the Cumberland Mountains, issuing in February 1894 a call for prayer regarding such a school to be located near Flat Rock, Kentucky,[131] at a site named Beulah Heights because its "scenery was so beautiful and the atmosphere so delightful."[132] While soliciting *Revivalist* readers with a "pioneer spirit" to relocate there to "educate their children for the King,"[133] Knapp's primary motive was to evangelize and educate the mountain people. He was not only touched that many of these people were illiterate and subsisting in stifling, impoverished conditions, but there were "thousands of souls living in these mountains, many of whom [had] never even heard of Jesus . . ." Indeed, "while the cry from foreign lands [had] been urgent, nothing could be more despairing or more heartbreaking than the cry from the mountains of Virginia, Kentucky and Tennessee."[134]

Knapp's supporters rallied to this cause, and about three hundred total acres were donated, under the condition that "no tobacco or intoxicants were to be raised, made, sold, or used on the property."[135] Classes at Beulah Heights Holiness Primary School began September 9, 1895,[136] with a two-fold purpose: "To instruct the children from the beginning in useful knowledge both mental and spiritual and to open up a place where those who lack opportunity to prepare for their life work may at the call of God come and fit themselves for His service."[137] Accordingly, Bible classes complimented traditional instruction, especially for older pupils. In addition, many students worked at farm chores and other manual labor in exchange for their room, board, and tuition. In these ways, the school at Beulah Heights foreshadowed the establishment of God's Bible School in Cincinnati. In fact, the programs were so similar that after the Cincinnati institution was founded, *The Revivalist* often referred to the older school as "God's Bible School, Beulah Heights."[138]

Another of Knapp's initiatives at Beulah Heights was linked even more directly with developments at Cincinnati. In August 1894, he and the local holiness league began an annual camp meeting at Beulah Heights, with the first meeting featuring the preaching of J. Wesley Hughes, Mary Storey, and Kate Keith.[139] The following year, remarkable results ensued, with over one hundred twenty professing "pardon or entire sanctification."[140] That same year, local leaders relinquished direction of the services to the Cincinnati Holiness League;[141] however, this arrangement was short lived. In 1896, the Cincinnati league withdrew its leadership and sponsored its own "Salvation Park Camp Meeting" at the Hamilton County Fair Grounds in Carthage, Ohio.[142]

The first Cincinnati encampment "attracted hundreds of holiness believers from many states," including such prominent leaders as C. J. Fowler, president of the NHA, who pronounced the camp to be "of as large influence as many that have been established for years" and predicted that "this camp-meeting is a fixture."[143] Excitement among camp attendees was shared by those unable to attend who simply read reports in *The Revivalist*, creating a "great demand for a fuller report of the Salvation Park camp-meeting."[144] Knapp responded by publishing a complete account entitled *Electric Shocks From Pentecostal Batteries; or, Food and Fire From Salvation Park Camp-Meeting*, initiating a popular series that appeared for several years.[145]

Although the Beulah Heights (or Flat Rock) camp and school continued for many years with the promotion of *The Revivalist*, they were no longer "the camp" or "the school" of the *Revivalist* movement.[146] However, the Beulah Heights work gave Knapp invaluable experience in establishing a school and a camp meeting and introduced him to ministry among Appalachians, many of whom were migrating to inner-city Cincinnati, where the Cincinnati league would minister to them through another of Knapp's initiatives that reflected his ongoing commitment to the socially and economically disadvantaged—city missions.

Knapp and his associates sponsored evangelistic meetings at several locations in Cincinnati and Northern Kentucky during the late 1890's,[147] finally renting a former saloon "in a disreputable part of the city" in October 1897 and establishing the Sycamore Street mission.[148] Commencing with a meeting conducted by evangelist W. B. Godbey, this mission's success was phenomenal—seven hundred fifty people professed conversion or entire sanctification in only one year.[149] From the founding of the mission until his death over four years later, Knapp conducted evangelistic services at least once per day at this or other locations.[150] In 1899, these efforts finally led Knapp to rent another location on Sycamore Street (409) where he opened a mission called "Revivalist Chapel."[151] Here, services were held daily at 2:30 p.m. and 7:30 p.m., and this practice continued until the meetings were moved to the campus of God's Bible School. In fact, these services were a direct forerunner of the school that Knapp founded at the crossroads of the holiness movement.

The Voice of Holiness

Knapp's activities in Cincinnati in no way diminished his contribution to the holiness cause beyond the Ohio River Valley. If anything, his success at Cincinnati demonstrated his ingenuity and perspicacity even further to his national audience. Rather than a local enclave, the Cincinnati work became the center of the *Revivalist movement*—an element increasing in size and influence within the global holiness movement. From the years 1895 to 1900, this movement coalescing around Knapp's leadership gathered momentum and new developments occurred with almost blinding speed. Some of these included the launching of the school at Beulah Heights (1895), the beginning of Salvation Park Camp Meeting (1896), the organization of the Holiness Union (1897), the opening of Revivalist Chapel (1899), and the initiation of God's Bible School (1900). However, essential to the success of these ventures was Knapp's continued success as holiness author and publisher.

Indeed, this period witnessed the rapid expansion of Knapp's publishing ministry. His own pen remained active, producing four more books in addition to a steady stream of *Revivalist* articles.[152] Of these books, probably the best-known is *Lightning Bolts from Pentecostal Skies* (1898), the quintessential work setting forth the radical holiness worldview. Its title suggests not only Knapp's increasingly radical views, but also indicates his dynamic communication style, with words "whether written or spoken" that were "lightning-like in brilliancy and power."[153]

Knapp's influence as holiness publisher went far beyond his own writings, which actually made up only a small percentage of Revivalist Press publications by the end of the century. Throughout the 1890's, many other authors looked to Knapp for an avenue to reach the public with their writings. Men such as W. B. Godbey, A. M. Hills, Seth C. Rees, and G. D. Watson, well-known in various regional circles, became fixtures on holiness reading lists and were propelled into a much broader public arena after Knapp had published books they had authored.

In several cases, their books were written upon Knapp's instigation. For example, A. M. Hills wrote *Pentecostal Light* (1898) "at dear Brother Knapp's request," a book which, along with his earlier *Holiness and Power* (1897—also published by Knapp), helped to increase Hills' influence "immeasurably."[154] In fact, Hills gave credit to these books for his invitation to become professor of theology at Asbury College, just one step in his long and noteworthy career as a holiness educator.[155]

The most prolific author discovered by Knapp was W. B. Godbey, whose primary role during the early years of God's Bible School will require further exploration. Although Godbey had already written his famous treatise on *Baptism* (1883),[156] he credited Knapp with inaugurating a "new epoch" of writing ministry in his life: "I must ever glorify God for using Brother Knapp to launch me into authorship."[157] Knapp "succeeded in persuading the beloved teacher to write the commentaries" on the New Testament for which he is best known,[158] but these were joined by innumerable books and booklets (over two hundred), often inspired by the author's "peregrinations" (as he was wont to refer to his travels) to the "Holy Land" and around the world (four times).[159]

Another reflection of the proliferation of Revivalist Press publications in the late 1890's appears in the advertisements for various "libraries" in *The Revivalist*. Readers could choose from "The Better-Way Library" by Beverly Carradine, "The Electric-Light Library" by Godbey, the "Pentecostal Library" by S. A. Keene, "The Bible-Student's Library" by L. L. Pickett, the "Soul Food

Library" by G. D. Watson, and, of course, the "Full Salvation Library" by Knapp.[160] In addition, Knapp offered the "Pentecostal Colportage Library," consisting of booklets of no more than one hundred pages that sold for ten cents each, intended "to undersell and displace the colportage books of a house in another city [Moody in Chicago], that were not sound in their teachings about sanctification."[161] The first work in this series, a daily devotional entitled *Pentecostal Wine from Bible Grapes* (1897), sold over twelve thousand copies, and subsequent issues saw sales soaring into the hundreds of thousands.[162] The cumulative impact of these books on the holiness movement would be difficult to exaggerate.

However, Knapp's publications receiving the widest circulation were not books on devotion or doctrine, or collections of sermons by popular revivalists, but songbooks. In the midst of his other publishing activity, Knapp's heart was filled with melody "such as only God can place there." Soon, he had ideas for several songs and even the title of a songbook. He was thus delighted to form a lasting friendship with L. L. Pickett, "the able musical composer of the Great Salvation Movement South," who assented to supervise the project.[163] The result was *Tears and Triumphs* (1894), soon followed by *Tears and Triumphs, No. 2* (1897).

While containing some traditional songs, these books were filled with new songs, most calculated to present an evangelistic appeal. As the title suggested, they elicited "Tears of Contrition," "Tears of Submission," and "Tears of Soul Burden," while exulting in "Triumphs of Holiness," "Triumphs in Trials," "Triumphs over Satan," and "Triumphs throughout Eternity."[164] Sentiment ran high as congregations sang "The Life-Boat," "The Skeptic's Daughter," "Some Mother's Child," and "The Great Judgment Morning." To facilitate use by the musically illiterate, the books featured a system of round and shape notes designated "music made easy."[165]

Response to these books was overwhelming. *The Way of Faith* reported that about fifty evangelists adopted the first volume for their work and that it had received "several orders for 1,000 copies each, one for 5,000."[166] Altogether, fifty thousand were sold during the first year. By 1898, Knapp could write that "over 200,000 of the two books have come out to sing the devil down and saints heavenward."[167]

This phenomenal reaction underscores the significance of congregational participation, especially through singing, in holiness worship services. It also reflects the foundational role of music in the development of the radical holiness worldview. While Knapp was quick to disparage what he perceived as worldly accoutrements to church music, such as "fashionable choir singing,"[168] he held a deep appreciation for music in ministry, especially evangelism, asserting that "one of the most potent departments of Gospel work is hymnology. The revival movement in every generation has had its hymnologists. Charles Wesley and his songs were as an essential part of the Wesleyan movement as John Wesley and his sermons."[169] Like the Wesleys, Knapp and Pickett imbued their songs with theology, so that their commitments to Pentecostal sanctification, divine healing, and premillennialism may have been better propagated by their music than by any other means. Indeed, such holiness songs have continued to the present to disseminate radical holiness ideology throughout the holiness movement and other evangelical communions, particularly Pentecostalism.[170] In addition, an emphasis on music ministry would characterize God's Bible School throughout its first century and beyond.

Along with the virtual explosion in the number of Revivalist Press books, subscriptions to *The Revivalist* continued to increase at an astounding rate, so that the Knapps "were forced to seek larger quarters."[171] Thus, on October 1, 1895, the address of *The Revivalist* changed from 520 Chase Avenue to Room E, Y. M. C. A. Building, at the corner of Court and Walnut Streets, a spacious location also more conveniently situated with regard to telegraph and post offices.[172] At about the same time, the Knapp family moved to a rental property located on Mount Auburn, thus familiarizing them with the neighborhood destined to become home to God's Bible School.

By 1899, the circulation of *The Revivalist* had reached twenty thousand. Avid readers frequently testified that they held it second in estimation only to the Bible. They, along with friends such as J. L. Glascock, "continually urged" Knapp to make the paper a weekly instead of a monthly.[173] After much prayer, Knapp concluded that the addition of three thousand new subscribers within a short time was God's affirmation,[174] and he responded by transforming *The Revivalist* from an eight-page monthly into a sixteen-page weekly beginning with the January 5, 1899 issue.

In addition to divine benediction, much of the popular reception of Revivalist Press publications can be attributed to Knapp's genius for marketing literature. For one thing, in keeping with his commitments to radical faith and to reaching the economically deprived, Knapp insisted upon sending Revivalist materials gratis to the "worthy poor," even though friends were concerned that such an offer would welcome abuse from "a great many people" who would feign poverty.[175] In addition, premiums, such as one free book per a certain number of new subscriptions to *The Revivalist*, were offered to subscribers.[176]

However, the most crucial ingredient in Revivalist Press marketing was the creation of an extensive international network of "book evangelists." Although financial incentives were offered to book agents, especially college students who were encouraged to become colporteurs during vacations,[177] Knapp's primary appeal for book distributors focused on more spiritual and altruistic aspirations. He thus highlighted the sense of inclusion in the publishing ministry that came to those who might never write themselves, but who could disseminate the writings of others.[178] The response was such that eventually Revivalist Press book depositories and regional offices were established throughout the United States and in several foreign countries. Such missionaries and church leaders as C. E. Cowman (Tokyo), William Hirst (South Africa), Kent White (Denver), and Seth Rees (Rhode Island and Chicago), tied their regional ministries to the Revivalist movement by functioning as distributors of Revivalist Press materials.

By 1900, Knapp's publishing had surpassed even that of such established quasi-official Methodist agencies as Christian Witness, reflecting the increasing dominance of holiness literature by Revivalist Press. Other holiness editors, such as John Thompson of the *Christian Standard* and J. M. Pike of *The Way of Faith*, recognized Knapp's ascendancy, with Pike praising him for "doing more for the circulation of religious literature on *deeply spiritual lines* than any other publisher we know."[179] *The Revivalist*, along with scores of kindred books and booklets, had made Knapp the veritable voice of holiness for much of grassroots America.

Uniting the Forces

Knapp realized that for the radical holiness movement to make further progress, it must be united by more than periodicals, camp meetings, and itinerant preachers—it needed more formal organizational ties. His response to this need began with the various leagues he helped to initiate shortly after his move to Cincinnati. *The Revivalist* provided the forum in which to expand these efforts nationally. By October 1893, Knapp was inviting *Revivalist* readers to join a "Revivalist Prayer League," an informal group committed to "pray twice a day for revivals" and do all they could "to help bring them about."[180] The next issue of *The Revivalist* contained a list of accredited evangelists and a pledge for those who wished to join "The International Revival League."[181] In December, the organization was referred to as the "International Revival Prayer League," and it was reported that pledges in response to the November appeal were "pouring in."[182]

These organizational names reflect the inseparable connection between prayer and revival in Knapp's thinking.[183] The frequency with which the names were modified also indicates the fluidity of the Revivalist movement in the early 1890's.[184] Organizations could be initiated and then abandoned, superseded, or absorbed by another organization, all within the space of a month. However, the net effect of this development was to provide more cohesiveness to the Revivalist family. A sense of belonging was now offered, in which followers were not limited to reading or literature distribution, another crucial development preparing the way for the beginning of God's Bible School.

Knapp's organizational endeavors occurred against the backdrop of the increasingly divisive issue of the "Church Question" or "come-outism." Contrary to Timothy L. Smith's assertion that Knapp continued to "straddle the church question until his death,"[185] Knapp thoroughly evaluated the available options and formulated a carefully nuanced position. At one extreme he found the radical "come-outers" of the "first wave" of holiness secession, particularly the *Gospel Trumpet* people—Church of God (Anderson). While acknowledging that no doubt "many of God's real people" were among such groups, Knapp condemned their leaders for holding a double standard, in fact practicing what they purported to oppose—ecclesiastical dictatorship. He alleged, "While it denounces popery, yet at the same time it exercises it. Its unwritten discipline is more sectarian than some printed manuals . . . It substitutes the dictums of its ministers for the individual liberty of conscience." His devastating critique also charged that it fostered "religious anarchy—its people being accountable to no fixed congregation."[186] He thus labeled the anti-sectarian Church of God option as "anarchistical come-outism" and considered it to be "one of the greatest foes of spirituality and the kingdom of heaven"[187] in general and the *Gospel Trumpet* to be one of the "most strenuous opposers" of *The Revivalist* in particular.[188]

At the other end of the spectrum, Knapp found denominational loyalists in Methodism determined to remain within the "mother" church, even if this meant discarding holiness principles. Knapp certainly appreciated denominational commitment, and emphasized his own loyalty to Methodism, displaying the word "Loyal" prominently on the *Revivalist* masthead. In 1896, he published an article reflecting loyalist leanings in which W. B. Godbey wrote, "I think some of our brethren have made a mistake in leaving the Church. In Methodism I have enjoyed a happy home, without the slightest friction, from my childhood."[189] However, as Methodist suppression of holiness revivalism increased, Knapp and Godbey asserted their independence proportionately, with Godbey eventually declaring, "Though the world has always called me a Methodist preacher, I am no more Methodist than something else."[190]

Knapp came to see inordinate denominational loyalty, especially when it bound people to holiness-fighting leadership, to be as inimical to true spirituality as "anarchistical come-outism." In fact, he accused holiness-rejecting denominationalists of come-outism themselves—that is, of coming out "from God's Church" and "substituting something else in its place"—such as "worldly financial methods" for "Bible giving," worldly amusements for the "joy of the Lord," "unsaved and unsanctified officials" for leaders "full of faith and the Holy Ghost," and "unconverted membership for true believers."[191] In particular, Knapp argued that Methodism had "ceased largely to be a New Testament Church" and had "come-out" of biblical Christianity.[192] For him, official Methodism had become another example of "Protestant popery," especially as it opposed "holiness instead of welcoming and spreading it."[193] To leave such a denomination would not be disloyal, "for true loyalty to the Church is loyalty to Jesus and the Word," not "loyalty to ecclesiasticism," "opinions" of men, or "to committees."[194]

Knapp finally concluded that "anarchistical come-outism" and extreme denominational loyalty were but two sides of come-outism, which he defined as leaving "the real Church of God, and either condemning all organization [anti-sectarianism] or substituting a mere human organization [denominationalism] in its stead."[195] He thus warned, "Two wrecks threaten believers at this crisis in the Pentecostal* movement that is spreading over the earth. One is the wreckage on the rocks of formality and worldly Churchanity;

and the other is the no less perilous wreck of anarchistic come-outism." For him, the only hope for the holiness movement lay in steering "clear of both" and riding "out victoriously on the great ocean of New Testament power, privileges, and practices."[196]

To accomplish this, Knapp sought a third solution to the church question. Many suggestions were proffered by other holiness leaders, but Knapp found some of these almost as unpalatable as the two extremes. For instance, his rejection of the "Hampton" plan for keeping holiness sympathizers within Methodism brought a rift between Knapp and the plan's primary advocate, H. C. Morrison, publisher of *The Pentecostal Herald* and eventual president of Asbury College and founder of Asbury Theological Seminary.[197] Although Knapp and Morrison shared many radical holiness concepts in common, such as divine healing and premillennialism, Knapp believed Morrison's plan to be "too narrow," explaining that

> It is too late in the day now, bless the Lord, ever to be able to corral and confine the holiness movement in the narrow limits of the Methodist Episcopal Church, South. The time was when it seemed that Methodism, as a religious denomination, had a sort of monopoly on the doctrine and experience of entire sanctification; but, praise the Lord! her patent right has expired, and this glorious doctrine and sweet experience has swept out and on until it has reached all denominations, and has become literally an interdenominational movement; and any plan of organization of the movement, to be a success and meet the demands and needs of the case, must of necessity be broader than the confines of any one denomination.[198]

Similar logic led Knapp to reject attempts to organize the holiness movement into a new denomination with entire sanctification as its distinctive doctrine, a plan suggested by Phineas F. Bresee at the General Holiness Assembly in Chicago in May 1901.[199] Although Bresee eventually participated in such an endeavor with the creation of the Pentecostal Church of the Nazarene in 1907,[200] Knapp concluded that such a denomination would

---

* The term "Pentecostal" must be understood in historical context. At the turn-of-the-century, Knapp and many other holiness advocates embraced this label and such related terms as "apostolic faith" and "full gospel." However, after modern Pentecostalism developed in the early twentieth century, the term came to identify those who taught that glossolalia (tongues-speaking) was the evidence of Spirit-baptism. Thus, non-tongues-speaking holiness people, including the leadership of God's Bible School, gradually distanced themselves from the term. For example, in 1919, the Pentecostal Church of the Nazarene dropped "Pentecostal" from its name. Briefly put, such "proto-Pentecostals" as Knapp embraced many of the ideas that were held later by modern Pentecostals, but they did not link tongues-speaking with Spirit-baptism. Knapp's most mature reflection on the gift of tongues reveals that rather than an "unknown language," he considered it tantamount to what later holiness people would call the anointing or "the unction of the Spirit" ("A Dangerous Gift," *Revivalist* (Oct. 3, 1901), 8, 12).

likely fail to accommodate all "members of the New Testament Church, which exist in different denominations, and which probably can never be united in any one denomination, however pure."[201]

Thus, Knapp's resolution of the church question was to chart a middle course between anti-sectarian and denominationalist extremes. This he proposed to do by appropriating an organizational tool almost as old as the holiness movement itself—associationism. Consequently, in September 1897, "Knapp and about a dozen followers met in the parlor of his Mount Auburn home and formed the International Holiness Union and Prayer League,"[202] adopting the motto: "In essentials, unity; in non-essentials, liberty; in all things, charity."[203] "The first officers chosen were: Seth C. Rees, president; Martin Wells Knapp, vice-president; W. N. Hirst, secretary; Byron Rees, corresponding secretary; and C. W. Ruth, treasurer."[204] While its commencement involved a small group, large numbers "were waiting for some such definite action and the Union grew rapidly."[205]

Although the Union had much in common with the leagues that preceded it, undergoing numerous name changes and sharing a common goal to reach "a greater number of people with the gospel of full salvation" and "to carry the work to all parts of the world,"[206] it differed significantly in that it represented Knapp's deliberate attempt to implement the middle solution to the church question. As such, "it was not considered to be a denomination or the beginning of one, but was put forth as 'a fraternal union . . . designed to promote deep spirituality among all believers.'"[207]

The structure of the Union lent itself to the middle course because its genius lay in individual—rather than church—membership, so that denominational members could remain in their church homes while joining the Union whereas "brotherly ties" could also be extended "to those who felt themselves excluded from their churches."[208] Again, this system did not reflect ambiguity, but a studied attempt to preserve and encourage the interdenominational character of the holiness revival, by making denominational affiliation a non-issue, at least in theory.

Accordingly, all holiness people, "irrespective of denominational connections" were welcome to join the Union.[209] In reality, however, Union membership by 1905 consisted of many more "independents" than denominational members. This reflected the *Revivalist* movement's increasing detachment from the Methodist denominations, encouraged by Knapp's promotion of the formation of "independent holiness societies" or missions in areas where local church leaders would no longer tolerate holiness teachings.[210] In effect, the Union "actually helped to draw the loyalists out of the church instead of drawing the drifters in."[211] While far from Knapp's intent, its fostering of independent congregations also sowed the seeds of a new denomination, ultimately bearing fruit in the development of the Pilgrim Holiness Church.[212]

Although his "middle" course failed to provide a lasting solution to the church question, with his own Union providing a major element in the "second wave" of holiness sect formation and eventually adopting Bresee's denominational approach after its founder's death,[213] Knapp's vision of an interdenominational holiness movement would live on, not in an association, but through the publishing and educational ministries he initiated—*The Revivalist* and God's Bible School. Meanwhile, the creation of the Union not only reflected Knapp's brilliance in grappling with the church question, it also strategically united the forces of his colleagues and supporters.

Time to Advance

It appears that by the turn of the century, in light of his publishing and organizational activities, Knapp was the single most influential individual in the holiness movement, prompting A. M. Hills to reflect, "I have considered him for some time the most potential leader and foremost character in the holiness movement."[214] The breathtaking pace at which this "divine surprise" had risen against adversity to such prominence within one of the most dynamic spiritual movements of the nineteenth century bears witness to the power unleashed in that movement—and was taken by friends as incontrovertible validation of "the principle of the Pentecostal enduement of power from on high and the heart-cleansing baptism with the Holy Ghost."[215] Revivalist publications, urban missions, the Salvation Park Camp Meeting, the school at Beulah Heights, and the Holiness Union, along with thousands of supporters, provided a veritable foundation laid in fire for future initiatives. By the turn of the century, the time was right for Knapp to advance and unveil the vision he felt God had given him of what would be the capstone of his life's work—a school specializing in Bible-training and soul-winning.

Notes

[1] "Tributes From His Associates," *Revivalist* (April 14, 1921), 8-9 (original emphasis).

[2] Day, 11. Knapp recounted this commitment shortly after announcing the opening of God's Bible School in June 1900. He concluded, "We see no reason to regret the agreement there made" ("Prophetic," *Revivalist* (July 5, 1900), 10).

[3] Glenn Black, "When Did God's Bible School Really Begin?" *Revivalist* (April 7, 1983), 11 (original emphasis).

[4] For a broad overview of this movement, see Melvin E. Dieter, *The Holiness Revival of the Nineteenth Century* 2nd ed. Studies in Evangelicalism, no. 1 (Lanham, MD: The Scarecrow Press, 1996) and Charles Edwin Jones, *Perfectionist Persuasion: The Holiness Movement and American Methodism, 1867-1936* ATLA Monograph Series, no. 5 (Metuchen, NJ: The Scarecrow Press, 1974). In addition to the works cited in the Bibliographical Essay (Appendix B) by Dayton and Kostlevy, other specialized treatments that contribute helpful insight into the movement at large include Delbert Rose, *Vital Holiness: A Theology of Christian Experience: Interpreting the Historic Wesleyan Message* (Salem, OH: Schmul, 2000); Vinson Synan, *The Holiness-Pentecostal Tradition: Charismatic Movements in the Twentieth Century* 2nd ed. (Grand Rapids: Eerdmans, 1997); Timothy L. Smith, *Called Unto Holiness* and *Revivalism and Social Reform in Mid-Nineteenth Century America* (Nashville: Abingdon Press, 1957); Randall J. Stephens, *The Fire Spreads: Holiness and Pentecostalism in the American South* (Cambridge, MA: Harvard University Press, 2008); and Floyd Cunningham, editor, Stan Ingersoll, Harold E. Raser, and David P. Whitelaw, *Our Watchword and Song: The Centennial History of the Church of the Nazarene* (Kansas City, MO: Beacon Hill Press of Kansas City, 2009);

An invaluable resource for the study of this tradition is Charles Edwin Jones, *A Guide to the Study of the Holiness Movement* ATLA Bibliography Series, no. 1 (Metuchen, NJ: The Scarecrow Press and The American Theological Library Association, 1974), now revised and greatly expanded in a four volume set as *The Wesleyan Holiness Movement: A Comprehensive Guide* ATLA Bibliography Series, no. 50 Vol. One and Vol. Two (Lanham, MD: The Scarecrow Press and The American Theological Library Association, 2005); *The Keswick Movement: A Comprehensive Guide* ATLA Bibliography Series, no. 52 (Lanham, MD: The Scarecrow Press and The American Theological Library Association, 2007); and *The Holiness-Pentecostal Movement: A Comprehensive Guide* ATLA Bibliography Series, no. 54 (Lanham, MD: The Scarecrow Press and The American Theological Library Association, 2008).

For a veritable "Who's Who" among Holiness people, see William Kostlevy, editor, *Historical Dictionary of the Holiness Movement* Second Edition (Lanham, MD: The Scarecrow Press, 2009). For holiness figures who transitioned into Pentecostalism, see Stanley M. Burgess and Gary B. McGee, editors, *Dictionary of Pentecostal and Charismatic Movements* (Grand Rapids: Zondervan Publishing House, 1988), extensively revised and enlarged as Stanley M. Burgess and Eduard M. Van Der Maas, editors, *The New International Dictionary of Pentecostal and Charismatic Movements* Revised and Expanded Edition (Grand Rapids: Zondervan, 2002). Also, see the biographical sketches of key Methodist, Holiness, and Pentecostal figures in Henry H. Knight, III, ed. *From Alders-*

gate to Azusa Street: Wesleyan, Holiness and Pentecostal Visions of the New Creation* (Eugene, OR: Pickwick Publications, 2010), including this author's, "God's Trustee: Martin Wells Knapp and Radical Holiness," 148-157.

A good overview of holiness movement doctrine, history and literature by a scholar affiliated with God's Bible School is Leslie Wilcox, *Be Ye Holy: A Study of the Teaching of Scripture Relative to Entire Sanctification with A Sketch of the History and the Literature of the Holiness Movement* (Cincinnati: Revivalist Press, 1965). A recent anthology of holiness writings is Gene Long, *A Survey of Holiness Literature Vol. 1: Early Church Fathers to 1900* (Salem, OH: Allegheny Publications, 2005) and *Vol. 2: 1901 to Today* (Salem, OH: Allegheny Publications, 2010). Two books focusing on the recent development of the "conservative" Holiness Movement are Brian Black, *Holiness Heritage: The Rise of the Conservative Holiness Movement* (Salem, OH: Allegheny Publications, 2003) and Wallace Thornton, Jr., *Radical Righteousness: Personal Ethics and the Development of the Holiness Movement* (Salem, OH: Schmul, 1998).

[5] A. M. Hills, *A Hero of Faith and Prayer; or, Life of Rev. Martin Wells Knapp* (1902; reprint, Noblesville, IN: Newby Book Room, 1973), 15. Hills' work presents the most complete previous biographical account of Knapp, upon which this portion of our account heavily relies. Other helpful information appears in Knapp's books and *The Revivalist*. Unfortunately, the autobiography that was to be Knapp's next book was never written. The trustees of God's Bible School thus commissioned the prominent evangelist-scholar A. M. Hills to write the biography of a man with whom he admitted that he was not intimately acquainted (11). Furthermore, the work reflects the brevity of time allowed for its preparation, Hills confessing his surprise when the material for the book was sent to him "with the request that [he] have the manuscript in the publisher's hands in seven weeks." Evidently, most of the material was collected by Miss Bessie Queen (later Mrs. M. G. Standley).

[6] Ibid, 41.

[7] Ibid, 37.

[8] Ibid, 38-39.

[9] Ibid, 26. Ironically, Knapp's bashful flights were "especially the case when a minister came."

[10] Day, 7.

[11] Hills, *Hero*, 22-23.

[12] Jones, *Perfectionist Persuasion*, 99-100.

[13] W. B Godbey, *Autobiography of Rev. W. B. Godbey, A.M.* (Cincinnati: God's Revivalist Office, 1909), 367.

[14] Hills, *Hero*, 40-41.

[15] Ibid, 27. Specifically, this involved entire sanctification—"the transforming influence of the sanctifying baptism with the Holy Ghost" (13).

[16] See ibid, 18-19.

[17] Ibid, 27.

[18] Jones, *Perfectionist Persuasion*, 100.

[19] M. W. Knapp, *Pentecostal Letters, Selected from the Correspondence of M. W. Knapp* (Cincinnati: Office of God's Revivalist, 1902), 7.

[20] Hills, *Hero*, 32.

²¹ Ibid, 30.

²² Ibid, 34-35. Knapp's conversion provides an instructive example to modern holiness people of the importance of surrender to God's will in the *conversion* experience, before the complete consecration involved in the later blessing of entire sanctification.

²³ M. W. Knapp, "Glorified," *Revivalist* (Oct. 1890), 3.

²⁴ Hills, *Hero*, 42.

²⁵ Ibid, 43.

²⁶ Jones, *Perfectionist Persuasion*, 100.

²⁷ Day, 8.

²⁸ Lee Haines, "The Co-Founders of the International Holiness Union and Prayer League—Forerunner of the Pilgrim Holiness Church: Martin Wells Knapp [and] Seth Cook Rees," *The Wesleyan Advocate* (July 4, 1977), 10.

²⁹ Day, 8.

³⁰ Hills, *Hero*, 55. This William Taylor should not be confused with the William Taylor who had rejected Knapp as a missionary candidate and was made missionary bishop of Africa in 1884. Although some accounts (Paul Westphal Thomas and Paul William Thomas, *The Days of Our Pilgrimage: The History of the Pilgrim Holiness Church* (Marion, IN: The Wesley Press, 1976), 7 and Haines, "Co-founder," 10) assume that these were the same individual, this must not be the case because the missionary was in Africa during the time Knapp was sanctified. It was David Bundy who first made me aware of this conflation. Also see Melvin E. Dieter, "William Taylor," in the *Dictionary of Christianity in America* Daniel G. Reid, Ed. (Downers Grove, IL: InterVarsity Press, 1990), 1162.

³¹ Ibid, 54-56. This testimony first appeared in Martin Wells Knapp, *Out of Egypt Into Canaan* (1888; Reprint, Salem, OH: Schmul, 2000), 138-144. Knapp's inconsistent use of the term "baptism of the Spirit" to refer at times to entire sanctification and at other times to outpourings of the Holy Spirit subsequent to entire sanctification has evidently confused some scholars as to the occasion of his sanctification. For instance, one scholar wrote that Knapp was "unceremoniously sanctified while reading his Bible April 21, 1889" (Jones, *Perfectionist Persuasion*, 100). Shattuck perpetuates this error in Edward L. Queen II, Stephen R. Prothero, and Gardiner H. Shattuck, Jr. *The Encyclopedia of American Religious History* (New York: Facts on File, Inc., 1996), 297.) What Knapp actually wrote in his diary on April 21, 1889, was that he "received a blessed baptism of the Spirit to-day while reading the Word" (Hills, *Hero*, 39). However, he made no connection of this with his sanctification and used the term likewise to describe other special times of blessing, such as "a blessed baptism of the Spirit that melted wonderfully" which was received on August 31, 1886 (Hills, *Hero*, 75), so that one might say that he had multiple "baptisms" of the Spirit. On the other hand, both Knapp and his associates used the term "baptism of the Spirit" to refer explicitly to the "second blessing" of entire sanctification. See M. W. Knapp, "Pentecostal Baptism," c. 2 in *Lightning Bolts from Pentecostal Skies; or, Devices of the Devil Unmasked*, (Cincinnati: M. W. Knapp, 1898), 13-30 and W. B. Godbey, *Baptism of the Holy Ghost*, (Greensboro, NC: Apostolic Messenger Office, n. d.). It is easy to understand why confusion would result from such usage.

³² A more concise testimony in Knapp's *Pentecostal Letters* (7) also reveals several of these ideals:

Through God-given light from holiness books, papers, meetings, and experiences, aided especially by my wife [who professed sanctification before their marriage] and Brother and Sister William Taylor, two noble pioneer holiness preachers, I finally crossed the Jordan. On a glad night in the old parsonage of Duplain, Michigan, I was fully sanctified, Divinely healed of an old ill, and called to evangelistic work.

[33] While such summary provides necessary context, it also runs the risk of oversimplification, belying the actual complexity of the holiness revival as it impacted various communities at different times and with diverse response. Uniformity of development across the country should not be assumed, as recent scholarship continues to uncover the importance of regional distinctions in the shape the holiness movement assumed (Wesleyan-Holiness-Pentecostal Consultation, Kansas City, MO: October 28-29, 2005). Readers should refer to the resources listed in note 4 for more nuanced accounts of this dynamic movement. Glenn Black also provides a succinct overview of the holiness context in which Knapp's ministry began in "Our Spiritual Heritage" Part I *Revivalist* (January 20, 1983), 11.

[34] Synan (8) notes that Wesley's *A Plain Account of Christian Perfection* was incorporated within the Methodist Discipline from 1788 to 1808, reflecting the concept's fundamental place in early American Methodism. Two of the best scholarly studies of Wesley's views on Christian perfection are Leo George Cox, *John Wesley's Concept of Perfection* (Reprint; Salem, OH: Schmul, 1999) and George Allen Turner, *The Vision Which Transforms: Is Christian Perfection Scriptural?* (Kansas City, MO: Beacon Hill Press, 1964).

[35] William Warren Sweet, *Methodism in American History* (Cincinnati: The Methodist Book Concern, 1933), 341. For in-depth treatment of this decline, see John Leland Peters, *Christian Perfection and American Methodism* (Salem, OH: Schmul, 1995). For an even broader context on Methodist theological change, including changing attitudes toward Christian perfection, see Robert E. Chiles, *Theological Transition in American Methodism: 1790-1935* (Nashville: Abingdon, 1965). For a good summation of various theories as to the forces involved in Methodism's decline, including the decreased emphasis on Christian perfection, see c. 8 in David Hempton, *Methodism: Empire of the Spirit* (New Haven: Yale University Press, 2005), 178-201. Christian perfection still proves problematic for Methodism for, as Colin W. Williams observes, although "modern Methodism has sometimes found the doctrine an embarrassment, [it] is still officially bound to it." *John Wesley's Theology Today* (Nashville: Abingdon Press, 1960), 167.

[36] For a good introduction to Palmer, refer to *Christian History & Biography* Issue 82 (Spring 2004), which features her and the holiness movement. For early biographical information on Palmer, see George Hughes, *Fragrant Memories of The Tuesday Meeting and The Guide to Holiness, and Their Fifty Years' Work for Jesus* (1886. Reprint; Salem, OH: Schmul, 1988). Many of her writings have been reprinted by Schmul Publishing Company or have been collected in an anthology—Thomas C. Oden, ed., *Phoebe Palmer: Selected Writings* (New York: Paulist Press, 1988). For scholarly analysis, see Charles Edward White, *The Beauty of Holiness: Phoebe Palmer As Theologian, Revivalists, Feminist, and Humanitarian* (Grand Rapids: Francis As-

bury Press, 1986), Harold E. Raser, *Phoebe Palmer: Her Life and Thought* (Lewiston, NY: Mellen Press, 1987), and Diane Leclerc, *Singleness of Heart: Gender, Sin, and Holiness in Historical Perspective* (Lanham, MD: The Scarecrow Press, 2001). Also, see Charles Edwin Jones, "The Inverted Shadow of Phoebe Palmer," *WTJ* 31, no. 2 (Fall 1996), 120-131, and "The Posthumous Pilgrimage of Phoebe Palmer," *MH* Vol. 35 (July 1997), 203-213.

[37] See Palmer's book on the subject, *The Promise of the Father; or, A Neglected Specialty of the Last Days* (1859. Reprint; Salem, OH: Schmul, 1981).

[37] This periodical had been started in 1839 by Timothy Merrit as *The Guide to Christian Perfection*, "the first periodical in America devoted exclusively to holiness doctrine" (Synan, 18). It was purchased in 1858 by Phoebe's physician husband, Dr. Walter Palmer.

[38] Jones, *Perfectionist Persuasion*, 3.

[39] Schmidt, Jean Miller, "Holiness and Perfection," *Encyclopedia of the American Religious Experience* Volume II Ed. Charles H. Lippy and Peter W. Williams (New York: Charles Scribner's Sons, 1988), 815. This book is still in print—Phoebe Palmer, *The Way of Holiness With Notes By the Way: Being a Narrative of Religious Experience Resulting from a Determination to Be a Bible Christian* (1867. Reprint; Salem, OH: Schmul, 1988).

[40] Hills, *Hero*, 88.

[41] In response to her own question, "Is there not a shorter way [to be entirely sanctified]"?

[42] William Kostlevy fairly assesses Palmer's "shorter way" by observing that "it did provide a mechanism that allowed people a degree of certainty in the normally subjective realm of personal religious experience"; however, her "teaching remained far more controversial than many students of the Holiness Movement are willing to acknowledge" (*Moving Beyond Phoebe Palmer: Holiness Movement Research Challenges and Opportunities in the 21st Century* (n. p.: Wilmore, KY, n. d.), 4). Knapp and his associates came to recognize some of the short-comings of the "shorter way," as reflected in Knapp's, "Sanctification by Dialogue," *Revivalist* (Jan. 24, 1901), 2 which critiques a typical dialogue between a seeker and an altar worker attempting to encourage the "shorter way." Knapp warned, "it is true that the altar sanctifies the gift when all conditions are met, but not until then; and the wreckage that has come to multitudes professing to believe when the conditions are not met is fearful. Beware of such sophistry!" The *Revivalist* explained further that such presumption was not so much Palmer's fault, but "the trouble has been that so many of her imitators were weak, and followed her a long way off; some of them very much 'off' indeed. As a consequence there are a legion of professed holiness people who are claiming to be sanctified wholly by faith, and yet have not any endorsement of the fact by the Holy Ghost" (Charles Hartley, "Rigmarole or Faith--Which?" *Revivalist* (Feb. 14, 1901), 13.

These articles reflect concern that surfaced among holiness advocates during Palmer's lifetime and has persisted to the present. On the views of one of Palmer's contemporary critics, Bishop Randolph S. Foster, see Foster's *Christian Purity; or, The Heritage of Faith* (1869, Reprint; Salem, OH: Allegheny Publications, 1984) and Dale H. Simmons, "Storm Clouds Over Beulah Land," *MH* Vol. 30 No. 1 (Oct. 1991), 31-41. For a recent critique, see J. Kenneth Grider, *A Wesleyan-Holiness Theology* (Kansas City, MO: Beacon Hill Press of Kansas City, 1994), 404-405.

⁴³ Schmidt, 209-210. Melvin Dieter has suggested that "the subsequent revival of the influence of this doctrine within its home soil of Methodism and out to all of evangelical Christianity in America and around the world flowed chiefly from this 'house-church.' It constitutes one of the most unusual phenomena of American religious history." (*Holiness Revival*, 23).

⁴⁴ The early holiness movement relied heavily on the testimony of its adherent's experiences in proclaiming its message. Such testimonies were standard fare in *The Revivalist* and other holiness periodicals including *The Guide to Holiness* and were compiled in several holiness books, such as *Stars of the First Magnitude* (originally: *Holiness Miscellany. Essays Dr. Adam Clarke and Richard Watson. Experiences of Bishop Foster, Rev. Geo. Peck, D. D., Rev. Alfred Cookman, Rev. J. A. Wood, Rev. E. M. Levy, D. D. [,] D. Steele, D. D)* (1882. Reprint; Salem, OH: Schmul Publishing Co., n. d.); S. Olin Garrison, *Forty Witnesses Covering the Whole Range of Christian Experience* (1888. Reprint; Freeport, PA: The Fountain Press, n. d.); Bernie Smith, ed., *Flames of Living Fire: Testimonies to the Experience of Entire Sanctification* (Kansas City, MO: Beacon Hill Press, 1950); and George Allen Turner, *Witnesses of the Way: The Interior Life of Some Famous Christians* (Kansas City, MO: Beacon Hill Press of Kansas City, 1981).

⁴⁵ Leslie Ray Marston, *From Age to Age a Living Witness: A Historical Interpretation of Free Methodism's First Century* (Indianapolis: Light and Life Press, 1960), 253. While this statement was made of Free Methodism, Wesleyan historians have contended that "from its origin the Wesleyan Methodist Connection was a holiness church" (Ira Ford McLeister and Roy Stephen Nicholson, *Conscience and Commitment: The History of the Wesleyan Methodist Church of America* Fourth Rev. Ed. by Lee M. Haines, Jr. and Melvin E. Dieter, (Marion, IN: The Wesley Press, 1976), 30).

⁴⁶ Schmidt, 814-815.

⁴⁷ Many of the "New Measures" for which Finney became noted, such as "protracted meetings" and "anxious seats," were simply adaptations of time-honored frontier practices, making Finney's evangelism in effect, as Winthrop Hudson termed it, "the camp meeting brought to town" (cited in Malcolm McDow and Alvin L. Reid, *Firefall: How God Has Shaped History Through Revivals* (Nashville: Broadman and Holman Publishers, 1997), 245).

⁴⁸ Finney's difference with Wesleyanism derives from his view of inherited sin as being located totally within the will (as opposed to corrupting the entire person, as in classic Reformed theology). However, early Wesleyan-Holiness proponents often overlooked this, as reflected in the inclusion of Finney by S. B. Shaw in "a 20 inch by 24 inch picture of movement notables suitable for framing. The picture featured sixty evangelists and was titled 'Leaders of the Modern Holiness Movement'" (William Kostlevy, *Holy Jumpers: Evangelicals and Radicals in Progressive Era America* (New York: Oxford University Press, 2010), 95. Some contemporary scholars have continued to minimize the differences between Wesleyan and Oberlin perfectionism, including William Greathouse, who contends "that the difference . . . is more semantic than substantive" (Paul M. Bassett and William M. Greathouse, *Exploring Christian Holiness: The Historical Development* Vol. 2 (Kansas City, MO: Beacon Hill Press of Kansas City, 1985), 311) and Melvin Dieter who describes Finney's view as "within a hair's breadth of Wesleyanism" (*Holiness Revival*, 18).

⁴⁹ A. M. Hills, *The Life of Charles G. Finney* (1902. Reprint; Salem, OH: Schmul, 1991). Knapp felt that other biographies of Finney needed to be augmented by a biography "written by one acquainted with him from the standpoint of holiness" (5).

⁵⁰ Norris A. Magnuson, "Prayer Meeting Revival (1857-1859)," in Daniel G. Reid, *Dictionary*, 922. For scholarly interpretation of this revival, see Timothy L. Smith, *Revivalism and Social Reform* and Kathryn Teresa Long, *The Revival of 1857-1858: Interpreting an American Religious Awakening* (New York: Oxford University Press, 1998). Long questions Timothy L. Smith's assertion that the revival was primarily perfectionist and, while discussing Finney and Palmer's contributions, fails to recognize the numerous other higher life advocates (such as Boardman) contributing to this revival.

There is room for debate as to whose influence was greatest in this movement—Finney's or Palmer's. Wesley Duewel leans toward the former, suggesting that "the instrument . . . God used perhaps most widely in the preparation [for the 1857-1859 revival] was the life, ministry, and writings of Charles G. Finney" (*Revival Fire* (Grand Rapids: Zondervan, 1995), 125). Charles E. White favors Palmer, asserting that her ministry helped to "reintroduce the concept of lay ministry to the church and [thus] touch off the awakening of 1858" ("Phoebe Worrall Palmer," in Daniel G. Reid, *Dictionary*, 861.

⁵¹ McDow and Reid, 265-273.

⁵² In *Revivalism and Social Reform*, Timothy L. Smith traces this fascinating development, as Christians of all denominations worked in tandem for the cause of holiness. For example, "at an all-day union meeting in Baltimore in 1859 prominent pastors of nearly every denomination joined in urging a distinct baptism of the Holy Spirit subsequent to conversion" (136).

⁵³ Since its inception, the association has gone through several name changes—the National Holiness Association, the Christian Holiness Association, and, most recently, the Christian Holiness Partnership. William Kostlevy has observed that the N. H. A. again reflects the significance of women to the holiness movement as a group of Methodist ministers (males) organized an association to propagate the teachings of a lay lady (Palmer). See his article, "Christian Perfection in Pennsylvania Dutch Country: The 1868 Manheim Camp Meeting of the National Holiness Association," in *The Chronicle: Journal of the Historical Society of the Central Pennsylvania Conference of the United Methodist Church* Vol. 9 (Spring 1998), 25-35.

Scholarly histories of the early days of the N. H. A. are Delbert Rose, *Vital Holiness* and Kenneth O. Brown, *Inskip, McDonald, Fowler, "Wholly and Forever Thine," Early Leadership in the National Camp Meeting Association for the Promotion of Holiness* (Hazelton, PA: Holiness Archives, 1999). Helpful early accounts include W. McDonald and John E. Searles, *The Life of Rev. John S. Inskip, President of the National Association for the Promotion of Holiness* (1885. Reprint; Salem, OH: Allegheny Publications, 1986) and George Hughes, *Days of Power in the Forest Temple: A Review of the Wonderful Work of God at Fourteen National Camp-Meetings, From 1867-1872* (1873. Reprint; Salem, OH: The Allegheny Wesleyan Methodist Connection, 1975).

⁵⁴ Timothy L. Smith asserts that "four of the eight new bishops . . . were pronounced friends of holiness: Randolph S. Foster, Stephen M. Merrill, Jesse T. Peck, and Gilbert Haven" (*Called Unto Holiness*, 19).

⁵⁵ Ibid. On the importation of the holiness movement into the South, and its subsequent acceptance and expansion there, see Stephens, *The Fire Spreads*.

⁵⁶ Ibid, 46.

⁵⁷ Frederick A. Norwood, *The Story of American Methodism: A History of the United Methodists and Their Relations* (Nashville: Abingdon Press, 1974), 298. For an excerpt of Mudge's work, *Growth in Holiness Toward Perfection; or, Progressive Sanctification*, see Frederick A. Norwood, ed. *Sourcebook of American Methodism* (Nashville: Abingdon Press, 1982), 388-391. For Daniel Steele's response, see his *Defense of Christian Perfection; or, A Criticism of Dr. James Mudge's "Growth in Holiness Toward Perfection"* (1896. Reprint; Salem, OH: Schmul, 1984).

⁵⁸ Brooks was a Methodist who wrote the "textbook" of come-outism: *The Divine Church: A Treatise on the Origin, Constitution, Order, and Ordinances of the Church; Being a Vindication of the New Testament Ecclesia, and an Exposure of the Anti-Scriptural Character of the Modern Church of Sect* (1891. Reprint; *The Higher Christian Life: Sources for the Study of the Holiness, Pentecostal, and Keswick Movements* Vol. 8 Ed. Donald W. Dayton, New York: Garland Publishing, Inc., 1984). The group he helped organize was the subject of one of the first scholarly histories of a holiness body—Clarence Eugene Cowen, *A History of the Church of God (Holiness)* (Overland Park, KS: Herald and Banner Press, 1949). Warner was a holiness advocate of non-Methodist background—Church of God (Winebrennerian)--who at first cooperated with the N. H. A. but later withdrew because of its involvement with "sects." See Barry L. Callen, *It's God's Church: The Life and Legacy of Daniel S. Warner* (Anderson, IN: Warner Press, 1995) and John W. V. Smith, *The Quest for Holiness and Unity: A Centennial History of the Church of God (Anderson, Indiana)* (Anderson, IN: Warner Press, Inc., 1980).

⁵⁹ Synan, *The Holiness-Pentecostal Tradition*, 40.

⁶⁰ Ibid.

⁶¹ Jones, *Perfectionist Persuasion*, 101.

⁶² *Revivalism* is used here to refer to ministry oriented toward the church, seeking renewal of deep spirituality among professing Christians. *Evangelism* refers to ministry focused on outreach, confronting non-Christians with the gospel. Knapp and many of his colleagues engaged in both types of ministry.

⁶³ "Michigan Methodism," *The Michigan Christian Advocate* (Sept. 27, 1884).

⁶⁴ Jones, *Perfectionist Persuasion*, 100.

⁶⁵ Hills, *Hero*, 59. Shortly after Knapp's sanctification and call to evangelism, his wife, who had been sanctified earlier, also "received a call to the same work" (Ibid, 56).

⁶⁶ Ibid, 65-68. See also Knapp's summary of their work in "Lyons and Muir," *The Michigan Christian Advocate* (Jan. 19, 1884): "Family altars are going up, gold and tobacco are going down, and Pentecostal power is being sought and found."

⁶⁷ Ibid, 69. These included "one influential man" who told Martin "he was doing more harm than good," but who was finally converted.

⁶⁸ Ibid. In addition, they also utilized other visual aids, including "the blackboard, . . . charts and maps" (Haines, *Co-founders*, 10). Ironically, some spiritual heirs of Knapp would absolutely prohibit the use of slide projectors due to their similarity to motion pictures. In some holiness churches, even missions slides were forbidden.

[69] Seth C. Rees, B. Carradine, W. B. Godbey, A. M. Hills, etc., *Pentecostal Messengers*, (Cincinnati: M. W. Knapp, 1898),, 66. For an example of one of Knapp's most popular charts, see the lithograph, "Wrecked or Rescued," reproduced in *God's Clock Keeps Perfect Time: God's Bible School's First 100 Years: 1900-2000* Compiled and Edited by Kevin M. Moser and Larry D. Smith (Cincinnati: Revivalist Press, 2000), 9, and providing the frontispiece of Knapp's book, *Rescued!, or The River of Death, Showing How People Perish In It, and How They May be Rescued*, Rev. Ed. (Cincinnati: Revivalist, 1898). It graphically allegorizes the violation of the Ten Commandments as a "River of Death" with ten tributaries (broken commandments) which are fed by still smaller streams. For example, the "adultery river" is supplied by such tributaries as "brothel/ball room," "theatre and circus," and the "saloon." Below the River of Death are the "Falls of Eternal Despair" which lead into Hell. Above is an "Impenetrable Hedge of Sin" which blocks any escape except through the gate of "Faith" and "Repentance" by which the sinner may reach the "Plains of Regeneration." By entering the gate of "Abandonment" and "Faith," one could even go higher to "Holiness Heights" and, ultimately, to Heaven. Knapp summarizes its purpose (along with that of the book which served as its "key"): "It points vividly to the various ways by which men fall into the River and then shows how by Divine grace they may be rescued, and find a happy spiritual home on Holiness Heights until transferred to the glory realms beyond" (*Pentecostal Messengers*, 67).

[70] M. W. Knapp, *Pentecostal Letters, Selected from the Correspondence of M. W. Knapp* (Cincinnati: Office of God's Revivalist, 1902), 7.

[71] Rees, et. al., *Pentecostal Messengers*, 61.

[72] Haines,10.

[73] Rees, et. al., *Pentecostal Messengers*, 61.

[74] Jones, *Perfectionist Persuasion*, 101. Two-thirds of these converts joined the M. E. Church. Also, see "Mich. State Revival Band," *Revivalist* (Jan. 1890), 2.

[75] Knapp, *Pentecostal Aggressiveness*, 21. See also Hills, *Hero*, 70 and "The Evangelists," *Revivalist* (Jan. 1892), 1.

[76] To the confusion of bibliographers, this book was written and copyrighted in 1887 but was not published until the following year. See my Introduction to the Schmul reprint for the significance of "spiritual geography" to the beginning of God's Bible School.

[77] Rees, et. al., *Pentecostal Messengers*, 64. The phrase "pillar of fire" reflects the popularity of biblical metaphors among holiness advocates. It was institutionalized when Alma White appropriated it as the name for her publication and denomination.

[78] Hills, *Hero*, 81.

[79] Synan, *Holiness-Pentecostal Tradition*, 35. On several occasions, when a periodical in sympathy with *The Revivalist* was discontinued, its publishers would give their subscription list to Knapp and let him complete subscriptions with *The Revivalist*. One notable example of this took place when the *Battle Cry* ceased publication ("To Battle Cry Subscribers," *Revivalist* (Feb. 1, 1900), 16).

[80] Historically, early members of the International Holiness Union co-founded by Knapp were known "as the 'Revivalist people' because of their support of Knapp's school and of [*God's Revivalist*]" (Jones, *Perfectionist Persuasion*, 115). Other holiness people also became identified with such periodicals as the *Gospel Trumpet*, bearing out the truth that in many American indigenous groups, rather than bishops, editors wielded the power.

God's Revivalist was referred to as the "silent preacher" as early as 1912. See "The 'Silent Preacher' A Blessing," *Revivalist* (Jan. 25, 1912), 5.

[81] Melvin Dieter, Ed. *The 19th-Century Holiness Movement* Vol. 4 in *Great Holiness Classics* (Kansas City, MO: Beacon Hill Press of Kansas City, 1998), 371. As later explained, the name of *The Revivalist* was changed to *God's Revivalist and Bible Advocate* with the January 3, 1901 issue.

[82] Martin Wells Knapp, "Aim of *The Revivalist*," *Revivalist* (June 1897), 1.

[83] See *The Revivalist* (Jan. 1890), 1; (April 1890), 1; (Jan. 1892), 1; etc. The last article was a reprint from Finney, again demonstrating his impact on the holiness movement.

[84] For example, a "Brother H." wrote that he was converted, and later "entered into the blessing of Full Salvation" after witnessing the manifestation of "Christ crowned within" the life of Mrs. Knapp (who was shut in at his residence for about a week by a snowstorm) and seeing the Knapps use the chart, "Wrecked or Rescued." (*Revivalist* (May 1890), 4). Another correspondent wrote in response to Knapp's third book, *Revival Tornadoes*, "Have been reading for five days, and the blessed Jesus fills my soul so full of joy and zeal that I laugh, cry, pray, and sing all day long, even when alone" ("A Spiritual Entertainment," *Revivalist* (April 1892), 3). Hundreds of similar accounts, of conversion, sanctification, reclamation, and additional blessing, filled the pages of the *Revivalist*s of the late nineteenth century.

The interdenominational scope of Knapp's outreach is reflected in his quotation from and advertisement of the books of such professional evangelists as Dwight L. Moody and Sam Jones. His approbation of their efforts in the early 1890's also appears in positive reports of their evangelistic activities in several issues of *The Revivalist*. See "Revivalists and Revivals," *Revivalist* (April 1890), 2 for an example. Also, see "Revivals and Prohibition," *Revivalist* (March 1894), 1. Sam Jones was an especially helpful source of illustrations on such subjects as temperance and judgement. See the selection from the *Sermons of Sam Jones* in *The Revivalist* (May 1890), 4. As late as April 1897, Knapp was advertising fifteen of Moody's books, especially emphasizing *Rum, Rags, and Religion; or, In Darkest America and the Way Out* (modeled after William Booth's *In Darkest England and the Way Out*). *Revivalist* (April 1897), 7.

Knapp's frequent attempt to emphasize the trans-denominational dimension of the holiness movement also included holiness testimonies from representatives of diverse denominational backgrounds, such as Edgar M. Levy (Baptist), Francis Ridley Havergal (Episcopalian), David B. Updegraff (Quaker), and Madame Guyon (Roman Catholic). For examples, see *Revivalist* (May 1893), 2 and (Oct. 1895), 6.

[85] Knapp asserted that the three most effective ways of preaching the Gospel are "1st. With our lives. 2nd. With our lips. 3rd. With the pen and press." He went on to extol the third method, observing that "with the pen and press we can preach to multitudes far beyond the reach of our personal presence and also for centuries after 'Our poor lisping stammering tongues lie silent in the grave'" ("Pen and Press Preaching," *Revivalist* (Aug. 1890), 2).

[86] Hills, *Hero*, 82.

[87] Ibid. Knapp further observed that "the Revivalist [was] read largely on the Sabbath and [he] was not clear in thrusting worldly business proposition before readers on that day."

⁸⁸ "Why We Do Not Insert Worldly Advertisements," *Revivalist* (Aug. 1897), 5.

⁸⁹ Hills, *Hero*, 82.

⁹⁰ Ibid, 83.

⁹¹ Haines, 10.

⁹² Hills, *Hero*, 89.

⁹³ Ibid, 87.

⁹⁴ Ibid, 88.

⁹⁵ Ibid, 89.

⁹⁶ "God's Anvil," Hills, *Hero*, 99 (adapted slightly).

⁹⁷ *The Revivalist* updated readers with such reports as the following, "'As this goes to press Mrs. Knapp is balancing between life and death. Her physician says that she must die, but we still look for her to live through the power of Him who beareth our infirmities and carrieth our diseases" ("Editorial Corner," *Revivalist* (Sept. 1890), 2).

⁹⁸ Hills, *Hero*, 96. As late as August 23, he had written, "I still look confidently for her recovery" (Ibid, 97).

⁹⁹ Ibid, 110.

¹⁰⁰ Ibid, 101.

¹⁰¹ "Glorified," *Revivalist*Oct. 1890), 3.

¹⁰² Hills, *Hero*, 96. Knapp's father was evidently in failing health at the time of Lucy's death. His own death took place less than a year later. Little more is known of Anna. She did write several articles for *The Revivalist* throughout the 1890s and evidently had deceased by the time of Octavia Knapp's death in 1909. John Franklin, on the other hand, would go on to figure prominently in the future of God's Bible School.

Martin and his second wife, Minnie Ferle, would have one daughter, named Lucy. As an adult, she apparently had negligible involvement with GBS. At the time of her mother's death, she was married to a lawyer, with the surname of Dennis, in Portland, Oregon. See "300 Bible Students Gather to Pray Before Leader Dies," *The Daily Times-Star* (Feb. 1, 1930), Section D, 18.

¹⁰³ Ibid, 110. For example, shortly after Lucy's death, Knapp wrote: "It seems as if I love the children ten times more than I did" (Ibid, 111).

¹⁰⁴ Day, 11.

¹⁰⁵ "Our Work," *Revivalist* (Aug. 1890), 2.

¹⁰⁶ Day, 11.

¹⁰⁷ M. W. Knapp, *Impressions* (Cincinnati: Revivalist Office, 1892). Though published later, this book was written during the "valley of suffering." Other books produced during this period included *Revival Tornadoes; or, Life and Labors of Rev. J. H. Weber, Evangelist, the Converted Roman Catholic* (Albion, MI: Revivalist,1889) and *Revival Kindlings* (Albion, MI: Revivalist, 1890). The latter book, which consisted primarily of articles reprinted from *The Revivalist*, presented holiness teachings "chiefly from an anecdotal" standpoint. The former created a sensation, in part due to the general popularity of spiritual biographies among holiness people and in light of its subject's phenomenal ministry (*The Revivalist* often reported meetings in which Weber would win several hundred converts), but particularly because of his Roman Catholic background, appealing to the growing anti-Romanism (or "anti-popery") which flourished among Protestants during this period of heavy immigration by Roman Catholics, particularly Irish. "Many Amer-

icans, particularly in the Middle West, viewed with mounting alarm the rapid accretion of Catholic power" (Arthur M. Schlesinger, Sr., *A Critical Period in American Religion: 1875-1900* (Philadelphia: Fortress Press, 1967), 31-32). Fears of Catholic conspiracies against American democracy, lent credence by Irish political machines in the large cities, induced many rural Americans to join such anti-Roman secret societies as the Ku Klux Klan (founded in 1866) and the American Protective Association (formed in 1887). While proscription of secret societies prevented most holiness people from joining organized opposition to Catholicism (like the KKK), appreciation for their anti-Romanist stance was voiced by some radical holiness leaders, most noticeably Alma White, who in the 1920s "aligned herself with the KKK to attack perceived threats to conservative religion from Catholics and to protect the American way of life from the millions of immigrants landing on America's shores" (Susie Cunningham Stanley, *Feminist Pillar of Fire: The Life of Alma White* (Cleveland, OH: The Pilgrim Press, 1993), 5).

Knapp himself reported that "God has clearly and unmistakably shown me that Roman Catholicism is one of the most insidious and deceptive schemes through which Satan is chloroforming souls and peopling hell with victims. It is the apostate harlot described in Revelation, whose sorceries have deceived the nations" (*Pentecostal Letters*, 18). Apparently Knapp's primary offensive against Catholicism depended on encouraging individual conversions and in highlighting them, especially those of people who became holiness ministers, such as Weber, Joseph S. Dempster (author of *From Romanism to Pentecost* and frequent contributor to *The Revivalist*. See "Revival Reports" and "Sermon," *Revivalist* (May 24, 1900), 11, 13-15.), and J. T. Malloy (who assisted W. B. Godbey in evangelism— "Revival Reports," *Revivalist* (Aug. 2, 1900), 11). Testimonies of such converts generated enthusiasm on a par with those of converted drunkards and prostitutes, as evidenced in *The Revivalist* by the many testimonials of the impact of *Revival Tornadoes*, probably more than for any of Knapp's other books except *Impressions*.

[108] Rees, et. al., *Pentecostal Messengers*, 64.

[109] Dieter, Ed. *19th-Century Holiness*, 372. A typical evaluation by a contemporary was that of S. A. Keene, who deemed it "a most instructive, suggestive, and useful book . . . [and] an admirable safeguard" (Hills, *Hero*, 126-127).

[110] Martin Wells Knapp, *Impressions* (Wheaton, IL: Tyndale House Publishers, 1984), front cover. Other endorsers included Paul S. Rees and United Methodist Bishop Emerson S. Colaw, both evangelical leaders with strong GBS ties.

[111] Rees, et, al., *Pentecostal Messengers*, 64.

[112] *Revivalist* (August 1890), 2.

[113] "Not Shut In," and "Mrs. Knapp's Work to Go On," *Revivalist* (October 1890), 3.

[114] In Knapp's journal entry for November 30, 1892, he did record becoming "more and more delighted" with marriage to Minnie (Hills, *Hero*, 128). This was the last of his journal entries that Hills references, unfortunately meaning that most of the Knapps' ministry after their move to Cincinnati does not benefit from this intimate perspective.

[115] Chicago was eliminated as an option at least in part because a large holiness publishing concern (Christian Witness) was already located there.

[116] In December 1891, Knapp reported in his journal that "Bro. Glascock came today, and says he feels that God wants us to go to Cincinnati with our holiness and book work" (Day, 12). For Glascock's account of Knapp's move to Cincinnati, see "The Message,"

Revivalist (April 14, 1921), 4-8 and "Evangelist J. L. Glascock's Influence in Bringing Martin Wells Knapp to Cincinnati to Inaugurate his Work," *Revivalist* (Nov. 3, 1927), 12. Books by Glascock published by Revivalist Press included *Some Grapes From Eschol* (1896), *Revivals of Religion* (1911), and *Wholesome Food for Hungry People* (1913).

[117] Day, 13.

[118] See Walter Havighurst, *Ohio: A Bicentennial History* (New York and Nashville: W. W. Norton and American Association for State and Local History, 1976), 74. Cincinnati was already home to the world's largest publisher, best-known for its McGuffey Readers.

[119] W. B. Godbey often asserted that the holiness movement actually "crossed the river at Cincinnati and entered Dixie-land," fifteen years after he was sanctified in 1868 (*Happy Nonagenarian* (Zarephath, NJ: Pillar of Fire, 1919), 180). By this, he was evidently referring to the ministry of G. D. Watson who pastored a M. E. congregation in Covington, Kentucky. However, Godbey also claimed primacy as pioneer of "the holiness movement from the Atlantic to Mexico through all Dixie-land" (Ibid, 78). At any rate, Cincinnati held a prominent place in the ministry of these and many other holiness advocates, especially after the location of the Revivalist ministries there.

[120] Hills, *Hero*, 130.

[121] Ibid.

[122] Ibid.

[123] Jones, *Perfectionist Persuasion*, 101. To avoid conflict with regular church services, the league conducted its meetings on Sunday afternoons.

[124] Day, 16. Day notes the significance of this early association to GBS: "This appears to be the first organization of Rev. Knapp in Cincinnati which led to the founding of God's Bible School in 1900."

[125] "Holiness Conventions as a Revival Force," *Revivalist* (May 1893), 1.

[126] "Something Better Than the World's Fair," *Revivalist* (May 1893), 1.

[127] "Estimates of the Meeting," *Revivalist* (June 1893), 1. A. D. Hicks, of the *Kentucky Methodist*, gave extravagant praise for this "feast of fat things" in which some of the grapes of Eschol "were so large that it required two men to carry them."

[128] *The Revivalist* appealed for the formation of such local organizations, with the intent that they would sponsor periodic holiness meetings in their community, in addition to supporting Central League activities ("Local Leagues," (June 1893), 3).

[129] "Something Better Than the World's Fair," *Revivalist* (May 1893), 1.

[130] "Cincinnati Holiness Convention Notes," *Revivalist* (June 1893), 1. See Kostlevy's account of this convention in *Holy Jumpers*, 27. "'When I got a clean heart,' Carradine noted, 'it wiped the Mason Dixon line all out.' Carridine [a Southerner], amid shouts and tears of joy, then punctuated his message by hugging convention leader John Thompson [a Northerner]."

[131] "A Holiness Mission Industrial School," *Revivalist* (Feb. 1894), 3.

[132] "Beulah Heights," *Revivalist* (Nov. 14, 1904), 16. Then located in the native county of Knapp's close friend, W. B. Godbey (Pulaski County), this area became part of McCreary County that was formed in 1912 from portions of Pulaski, Wayne, and Whitley Counties. Knapp invitingly described the area to Northern readers as "one of the choicest fruit and garden spots in the State" with "the air so pure and . . . so stimulating that the tired, heavy feeling you had north of the Ohio would soon take its wings and fly away"

(Hills, *Hero*, 134). The enervating environment provided such personal relief for Knapp that he wrote, "Three days on the Heights always makes me feel like a new man" ("Bulah [sic] Heights Holiness School," *Revivalist* (July 1895), 4).

[133] Hills, *Hero*, 134. Evidently, several took his challenge, such as an evangelist in Cincinnati who gave fifty dollars and purchased ten acres there ("Bulah [sic] Heights Holiness School," *Revivalist* (July 1895), 4).

[134] Hills, Hero, 139. Knapp similarly asserted that "there are few places where mental and spiritual training is more needed, or will be better appreciated, than in the mountains of Kentucky" ("Bulah [sic] Heights Holiness School, *Revivalist* (July 1895), 2).

[135] Day, 18. Knapp praised the mountaineers for their desire for a clean school in an environment "uncursed by King Alcohol and King Tobacco and their legions of attending evils" for which Kentucky had become notorious (Hills, *Hero*, 135).

In addition, in keeping with the conviction of many holiness advocates, the raising or usage of pork was also prohibited on the property ("Beulah Heights," *Revivalist* (Nov. 24, 1904), 16). For an extensive holiness treatment of the prohibitions against tobacco and pork, see W. B. Godbey *Swine and Tobacco* (Cincinnati: Revivalist Press, n. d.), a portion of which is reprinted in Adam Clarke, B. T. Roberts, A. M. Hills, and W. B. Godbey, *Chained By A Leaf: The Use and Abuse of Tobacco* (Compilation of reprints; Salem, OH: Schmul Publishing Co., 2001). Godbey and most other holiness opponents of pork usage based their abstinence on a consideration of hygiene, not bondage to Levitical law (2). For a humorous perspective on the "pork issue," see the cartoon reprinted from *Good Health* in the January 10, 1901, *Revivalist*, 8. Complimenting the cartoon is an observation from Oliver Wendell Homes that "men who had eaten largely of pork became swinish in their appearance, and that the hair and beard even became bristly."

[136] Day (19) mistakenly names Madge Duff as the first teacher at the school. She actually did not arrive until 1901, after spending some time at God's Bible School in Cincinnati. Early workers at Beulah Heights included Octavia Knapp (Martin's mother), G. H. Wallace, and Brother John Butler, an Indiana Quaker known as "a splendid, sanctified man, and a practical farmer" ("Beulah Heights," *Revivalist* (Nov. 24, 1904), 16, and Hills 136-141).

[137] "Beulah Heights," *Revivalist* (Nov. 24, 1904), 16.

[138] For example, see *Revivalist* "School Opening," (July 25, 1901), 15 and "Another Member in Heaven," (June 12, 1902), 15.

[139] "Bulah [sic] Heights Holiness Camp-Meeting," *Revivalist* (Aug. 1894), 1.

[140] "Revival Prayers Answered," *Revivalist* (Oct. 1895), 6.

[141] "Bulah [sic] Heights Holiness Camp-Meeting," *Revivalist* (July 1895), 4.

[142] This change was made due to "the distance and inconvenience of getting to Beulah Heights" (Day, 20).

[143] Day, 21 and "Salvation Park Camp-Meeting," *Revivalist* (Sept. 1896), 7. Fowler commended Knapp's choice of a name, "Salvation Park," for the camp, remarking that God certainly made the county fair grounds that, "race-track and all. Where the devil holds high carnival, Jesus came."

[144] "Electric Sparks From Salvation Park," *Revivalist* (July 13, 1899), 13.

[145] *Electric Shocks From Pentecostal Batteries; or, Food and Fire From Salvation Park Camp-Meeting* (Cincinnati: Revivalist Office, 1899). Transcribed prayers, sermons,

testimonies, and even shouts of praise mentally transported readers to the camp. Even altar scenes were included, with the counsel of such men as Seth Rees and C. W. Ruth providing an example to would-be altar workers. These reports were published until at least 1903. For a sermon from the 1899 edition, see "The Will of God" by C. W. Ruth in *Lightning from the Past: Camp Meeting Sermon by Early Twentieth-Century Holiness Revivalists* Compiled and Edited by Wallace Thornton, Jr. (Salem, OH: Schmul Publishing Co., 2001), 158-162.

[146] Although a holiness educational work has persisted at the location, complying with the terms of the deed given to Knapp, it eventually became independent of Cincinnati leadership, becoming "the property of the Beulah Mountain Mission and Orphanage Association" (Day, 71). In the 1950's, the institution, also including an orphanage by this time, was placed under the control of the Bible Missionary Church, which continues to conduct the Beulah Mountain Christian Academy there. See Daniel Ewald, "History of Beulah Mountain Christian Academy," Part One *The Missionary Revivalist* (June 2003), 7. Ewald states that "Knapp began God's Bible School originally at Beulah Heights. For unknown reasons, possibly a lack of ability for students to generate enough income and the difficulty of access to the property, the decision was made to move God's Bible School to Cincinnati." However, I have found no reference in *The Revivalist* or other primary sources to the work at Beulah Heights being called God's Bible School until after the school in Cincinnati had been established, acknowledging the similarity of the two institution's goals.

[147] Day, 21. Among these were the Cincinnati G. A. R. Hall, the Jennie Cassaday Mission, and the Pike Street Mission in Covington, Kentucky.

[148] Hills, *Hero*, 159.

[149] Ibid.

[150] Ibid, 160. In fact, for much of this time, services were held twice or three times daily. For example, when the Cincinnati Holiness meeting moved to the "Gospel Tabernacle" at the corner of Court and John Streets, services where held "every afternoon and evening" ("Cincinnati Holiness Meeting," *Revivalist* (July 13, 1899), 13). Knapp welcomed visiting evangelists to take the Revivalist Chapel pulpit and often left such associates as William Hurst and M. G. Standley in charge while he was traveling.

[151] Jones, *Perfectionist Persuasion*, 103.

[152] *Double Cure* (1895), the smallest of Knapp's monographs, appeared in response to "a flood of correspondence from those seeking light on the subject of Holiness." In it, Knapp attempted to show concisely "what Holiness is and what it is not, from a Bible standpoint, and how to receive and retain it" (Rees, et. al., *Pentecostal Messengers*, 65). *Rescued! or, The River of Death* (1898) provided an exposition of his lithograph, "Wrecked or Rescued." Knapp's last book, *Holiness Triumphant; or, Pearls from Patmos* (1900) was an exposition of the book of Revelation, reflecting Knapp's increasing preoccupation with the premillennial return of Christ.

[153] Martin Wells Knapp, *Pentecostal Letters, Selected From the Correspondence of M. W. Knapp* (Cincinnati: Revivalist, 1902), 3. The term "radical" should not be understood here in a pejorative sense. It is the common adjective used by scholars of the Wesleyan/Holiness tradition "to describe those holiness groups which, through one means or another, departed from the Methodist and other churches of their up-

bringing in the late nineteenth century, usually because of their strict adherence to the centrality of the doctrine and experience of entire sanctification" (Steven Ware, "Restorationism in the Holiness Movement, Late Nineteenth and Early Twentieth Centuries," *WTJ* 34 no. 1 (Spring 1999): 201). The non-radicals who remained within Methodism included the primary participants in the National Holiness Association (until the 1940s). This division is somewhat tenuous, as some Methodist loyalists, such as H. C. Morrison, possessed many characteristics typical of the radicals. Some of the common radical characteristics, in addition to secessionist tendencies, were such emphases as divine healing and premillennial dispensationalism. For more on recent use of the term radical in the holiness movement, see this author's article on "Sweet Radical Holiness" in the *Historical Dictionary of the Holiness Movement*, William Kostlevy, Editor. Second Edition (Lanham, MD: The Scarecrow Press, 2009), 287-288.

[154] Rees, et. al., *Pentecostal Messengers*, 39. In Knapp's biography Hills further expressed appreciation to Knapp: "It was the brotherly kindness of this dear man that introduced this biographer to the holiness public, and started a friendship lifelong, and influences that will flow into eternity" (*Hero*, 145). *Holiness and Power For the Church and Ministry* particularly thrust Hills into the holiness limelight. Richard S. Taylor has opined that "the book is perhaps the most comprehensive collection of [holiness] arguments, exposition, and documentation produced during that time." Well-received in spite of being authored during only fourteen weeks, "in readership and influence the book swept the country and is still in print" (Richard S. Taylor, Ed. *Leading Wesleyan Thinkers* Vol. 3 in *Great Holiness Classics* (Kansas City, MO: Beacon Hill Press of Kansas City, 1985), 335). Hills also acknowledge his debt to Knapp for publishing this book, admitting that "other publishers had turned down the book" before Knapp agreed to risk publishing this book by a new author ("A Man of the Saint Paul Variety," *Revivalist* (April 14, 1921), 10).

[155] On Hills' life, see L. Paul Gresham *Waves Against Gibraltar: A Memoir of Dr. A. M. Hills, 1848-1935* (Bethany, OK: Southern Nazarene University Press, 1992) and *Lightning from the Past*, 97-90.

[156] W. B. Godbey, *Baptism: Mode and Design* (Cincinnati: Elm Street Publishing Co., 1883).

[157] W. B. Godbey, *Autobiography of Rev. W. B. Godbey, A.M.* (Cincinnati: Revivalist, 1909), 365. Further reflecting on Knapp's powers of persuasion, Godbey wrote, "When he undertook to put me out in this great work, I realized that I had come in contact with an irresistible force" (367).

[158] Barry Wade Hamilton, *William Baxter Godbey: Pioneer of the American Holiness Movement* (Ph. D. diss., Drew University, 1993), 52. This dissertation has been revised and published as *William Baxter Godbey--Itinerant Apostle of the Holiness Movement Studies in American Religion* Vol. 72 (Lewiston, NY: The Edwin Mellen Press, 2000). Also, see Barry W. Hamilton, "William Baxter Godbey: Apostle of Holiness," *WTJ* vol. 36 no. 2 (Fall 2001), 144-163.

[159] Although estimates of the number of volumes Godbey produced range as high as three hundred (Minnie Ferle Knapp, "Into the Beautiful Beyond," *Revivalist* (Oct. 7, 1920), 2) and four hundred (Alma White, *The Story of My Life and the Pillar of Fire* Vol.

IV (Zarepath, NJ: Pillar of Fire, 1938), 251), the actual number is likely closer to two hundred, the number estimated by Barry W. Hamilton, "W(illiam) B(axter) Godbey," in Kostlevy, *Dictionary*, 129-130.) This writer has collected over one hundred-sixty original books and booklets by Godbey and has found references to at least thirty more.

Among the books especially dependent on his travels, see *Holy Land* (Cincinnati: Revivalist, 1895), *Footprints of Jesus in the Holy Land* (Cincinnati: Revivalist, 1900), *Around the World, Garden of Eden, Latter Day Prophecies and Missions* (Cincinnati: Revivalist, 1907), and *The Apocalyptic Angel* (Cincinnati: Revivalist, 1914). The autobiographical nature of most of Godbey's writings ensured that many of his smaller works also expounded observations gained during his travels, as did reports in *The Revivalist*, such as J. A. Paine, "Dr. Godbey and Company in the Holy Land," *Revivalist* (Jan. 11, 1900), 12, 14-16.

He was not the only evangelist to use a "travelogue," especially of the "Holy Land," for edification. For example, see A. L. Baldridge, *My Trip to the Holy Land* (Cincinnati: Revivalist, 1937); Beverly Carradine, *A Journey to Palestine* (St. Louis: C. B. Woodward Printing Co., 1891), and Bud Robinson, *My Travels in the Holy Land* (1934? Reprint, Knoxville: The Evangelist of Truth, n. d.).

[160] See "Books for Presents!" *Revivalist* (Nov. 1897), 4.

[161] Hills, *Hero*, 183-184.

[162] Ibid, 185. Its full title was *Pentecostal Wine from Bible Grapes: A Pentecostal Year Book With a Scripture Verse and Apt Comments for Every Day in the Year.* Contributors included Beverly Carradine, W. B. Godbey, Amanda Smith, A. M. Hills, Seth C. Rees, and Martin Wells Knapp. A reprint remains available under the title *Sunrise in Canaan: A Holiness Scripture Verse and Comments for Every Day in the Year with Important Dates in Wesleyan/Holiness History* (Salem, OH: Schmul, 2000).

Earlier (1895), Knapp had initiated a venture similar to the colportage library with the publication of *The Full Salvation Quarterly*, billed as "a glowing Holiness Magazine furnishing choice and sparkling full salvation wine" (*Revivalist* (May 1895), 7), which actually consisted of a series of booklets by Knapp and his colleagues, including Knapp's *Double Cure* (no. 1), Godbey's *Spiritual Gifts and Graces* (no. 2), and S. A. Keene's *Pentecostal Sanctification* (no. 8). Some issues in the series were abridgments of larger works such as Thomas Nelson's *The Midnight Cry* and Beverly Carradine's *The Better Way* while others were compilations of "original articles by several gifted authors" (Ibid and Day, 23).

[163] Pickett was assisted by another composer, Professor John Bryant. Knapp wrote that "songs and tunes came down from heaven into our souls. They flowed from our pens, [and] were sung in our meetings . . ." (Rees, et. al, *Pentecostal Messengers*, 65).

[164] "Tears and Triumphs!" *The Way of Faith* (June 17, 1896), 8.

[165] "Music Made Easy," *Revivalist* (June 1894), 3.

[166] "Tears and Triumphs!" *The Way of Faith* (June 17, 1896), 8. Among the institutions adopting the book for regular use was Asbury College.

[167] Rees, et. al., *Pentecostal Messengers*, 66. These two books were later combined to form one book (Day, 22). Also, see Stephens, 117.

[168] See "How to Reach the Masses," *Revivalist* (May 1892), 1, and the vitriolic "Shots at the Choir," quoted with approbation from the *Ram's Horn* (*Revivalist* (April 1893), 2):

"One reason sometimes why there is not more power in the pulpit, is because there is too much empty sound behind it."

[169] "Revival Hymnology," *Revivalist* (July 1894), 2. In "The Ministry of Music," (*Revivalist* (Feb. 8, 1900), 16), the evangelistic power of music is illustrated by the account of a dying soldier who refused to hear a minister speak of religion, but was converted when the minister sang a gospel song.

[170] Thus, Edith Blumhofer has observed,

When Pentecostalism, after 1901, emerged as an identifiable religious movement, it appropriated much of the idiom of the holiness movement, reinterpreting some of it to nuance its understanding of the baptism with the Holy Spirit. Many of the songs Pentecostals have sung over the years to describe their experience were written before Pentecostalism began, by holiness people intent on describing sanctifying grace" ("The Holiness-Pentecostal Movement," in *The Complete Library of Christian Worship* Vol. 2, *Twenty Centuries of Christian Worship* Robert E. Webber, Ed. (Nashville: Star Song Publishing Group, 1994), 106). For example, one of Aimee Semple McPherson's most frequently used gospel songs was "Come and Dine" by GBS alumni and teacher, C. B. Widmeyer (Edith Blumhofer, "Sister," *Christian History* Vol. 17 No. 2 (Issue 58), 32).

[171] Day, 20.

[172] Ibid. See also, "Removal," *Revivalist* (Oct. 1895), 1.

[173] J. L. Glascock, "The Message," *Revivalist* (April 14, 1921), 7.

[174] Hills, *Hero*, 183.

[175] J. L. Glascock, "The Message," 7.

[176] For example, see "Twenty Premium and Club Offers for the Fall Campaign," *Revivalist* (Dec. 20, 1900), 14.

[177] For example, Knapp sought to recruit at least ten thousand agents to sell S. B. Shaw's *Touching Incidents and Remarkable Answers to Prayer* which sold over two-hundred and fifty-thousand copies ("10,000 Agents Wanted," *Revivalist* (April 1897), 7. This advertisement stated that a thirteen-year-old girl made $7.50 in one day and "a cripple boy made $40.00 in two weeks" by selling this book).

[178] For example, see "Book Evangelism," *Revivalist* (April 1892), 3. Knapp contended that this was a more efficient means of holiness evangelism than engaging in arguments with opponents: "It is not best to scold and get sour over it where holiness is not clearly preached. A much better way is to circulate books that do teach it clearly. Each book will be a settled pastor that will unceasingly preach the whole truth" ("A Better Way," *Revivalist* (Feb. 1893), 3).

[179] "An Important Correction," *The Way of Faith* (Sept. 2, 1896), 4 (original emphasis).

[180] "Revivalist Prayer League," *Revivalist* (Oct. 1893), 3.

[181] "The International Revival League," *Revivalist* (Nov. 1893), 2. Among the "Prayer League Questions" were, "Are you walking in the light? . . . Are you doing your best to circulate the gospel printed, i.e., salvation books and papers? . . . Is I Cor. 13 a picture of your daily life? Are you free from one of the most subtle and fatal snares, compromise with the world? Do you faithfully report to THE REVIVALIST instances of Revival Prayer Answered?" ("Prayer League Questions," *Revivalist* (June 1895), 6. Original emphasis.)

[182] "International Revival Prayer League," *Revivalist* (Dec. 1893), 3.

[183] Knapp persistently insisted that "genuine revivals are always born of *prayer*," contending that in response God would "remove revival opposition" and "give revival victory anywhere this side of hell" ("Prayer for Revivals," *Revivalist* (March 1894), 1 original emphasis). Consequently, *The Revivalist* heading often used for revival reports was "Revival Prayers Answered." Just as this "Hero of Faith and Prayer" had saturated his own life with prayer, particularly in the face of trials and decision, so he admonished his readers to pray. See Hills, *Hero*, 153-154.

[184] These frequent name changes have also led to some confusion among historians. Day mistakenly dates the beginning of the International Revival Prayer League as March 1894. Other historians have evidently adopted his erroneous date (see Jones, *Perfectionist Persuasion*, 101).

[185] Timothy L. Smith, *Called Unto Holiness*, 59.

[186] "Sect-fighting Sectarianism," *Revivalist* (Feb. 21, 1901), 8. Much like Revivalist people, early Church of God (Anderson) adherents were often identified by their leading periodical, the *Gospel Trumpet*, underscoring the significance of publications in the turn-of-the-century holiness movement.

[187] "Come-outism and Revivals," *Revivalist* (April 4, 1901), 1.

[188] "Revival Perils," *Revivalist* (Sept. 12, 1901), 1. Knapp devoted many articles beginning in the early 1890's to exposing come-outism as detrimental to revival and evangelism: "Instead of kindling a fire to melt the ice of formality and worldliness, that is chilling the church, it would destroy the church itself... Instead of seeking to save souls, it would paralyze all organized agencies that are doing that work" ("Come-outism," *Revivalist* (April 1890), 2). Ten years later, he was still asserting that it produced "disunion and demoralization of revival forces" ("Come-Outism and Revivals," *Revivalist* (April 4, 1900), 1). Knapp thus rejoiced when people testified to being "liberated" from "the sectish bondage of such a narrow, iron-bound, unwritten creed, that cuts off every one of God's true people who do not accept their interpretation of what they call truth" ("Liberation," *Revivalist* (July 25, 1901), 8).

[189] "A Mistake," *Revivalist* (Oct. 1896), 6. [193] See his book length discussion, W. B. Godbey, *Come-Outism* (Cincinnati: Revivalist, n. d.) as well as his *God's Ecclesia* (Nashville: Pentecostal Mission Publishing Co., n. d.) and *Christianity and Sectarianism* (Cincinnati: Revivalist, 1911).

[190] W. B. Godbey, *Baptistism* (Cincinnati: Revivalist, n. d.). Although Godbey died in good standing as a member of the Kentucky Conference, such comments were typical of him. See also his, *The Bible* (Nashville: Pentecostal Mission Publishing Co., n. d.) in which he stated, "Though a life-long member of the Methodist Church, I do not belong to it, nor to anything else, but God only" (17). See also, D. William Faupel's preface to *Six Tracts by W. B. Godbey* in *The Higher Christian Life: Sources for the Study of the Holiness, Pentecostal, and Keswick Movements*. Ed. Donald W. Dayton. (New York: Garland Publishing, 1984). He quotes Godbey as writing (in *An Appeal to Postmillennialists*, 5-6):

I was born a Methodist--my father was a Methodist preacher, but when the Lord baptized me with the Holy Ghost and fire in 1868, He cremated the Methodist, along with the Free Mason, the Odd Fellow, the college president and the candidate for the Episcopacy.... If I cannot be a Methodist preacher... and be as free as Gabriel to preach God's word fearlessly . . . and shout the truth of full salvation to the ends of the earth, I will certainly let Methodism paddle its own canoe (i).

[191] "Come-outism," *Revivalist* (Jan. 17, 1901), 13.

[192] "Back to the Bishops," *Revivalist* (March 14, 1901), 8.

[193] "Come-outism," *Revivalist* (Jan. 17, 1901), 13. Knapp and his associates believed its opposition to holiness advocacy marked the beginning of Methodism's march down the long road of spiritual decline that had ultimately produced Roman Catholicism. When church law was successfully maneuvered to mandate pastoral control over holiness meetings, *The Revivalist* countered with an article by Byron J. Rees in which he argued that "a mistaken ecclesiasticism has delegated dangerous authority to its thousands of pastors, and they are given power to 'warn off,' debar, and forbid holiness evangelists of their own denomination whenever they are called to attend and assist in meetings held within the bounds of the pastorate of the antagonistic pastor" ("The Reign of the Petty Pope," (July 5, 1900), 2). After a pastor exercised this power against one of Knapp's associates, Knapp responded, "Verily little popes still live" ("The Whip Cracked," *Revivalist* (Nov. 2, 1899), 8).

[194] "Loyalty to the Church," *Revivalist* (Sept. 1894), 2   To support this position, Knapp used the analogy of a loyal soldier given commands that would prove detrimental to his country: "A soldier who is true to his country will not follow the counsels of men, even if uniformed bright, if he *knows* their orders to be contrary to the declared commandments of His government" (original emphasis).

In response to a question as to the consistency of holiness people withdrawing from a church and calling others hypocrites, Knapp responded, "If the Church is one of Satan's counterfeits, which teaches and lives a sinning religion, a person would certainly be justified in leaving it" ("A Revivalist Subscriber Writes," *Revivalist* (Jan. 4, 1900), 12.).

[195] "Come-outism," *Revivalist* (Jan. 17, 1901), 13.

[196] "Come-Outism and Revivals," *Revivalist* (April 4, 1901), 1.

[197] The Hampton plan was named for the layperson who originated it. However, Morrison appears to have been its chief promoter. On Morrison's disapproval of such independent work as C. B. Jernigan's, see Cunningham, et. al., 131. On Morrison's life, see Jerry Wood, *Pentecostal Holiness: The Life and Preaching of H. C. Morrison* (Salem, OH; Schmul, 2003), Henry Clay Morrison, *Some Chapters from My Life Story*, (Louisville, KY: Pentecostal Publishing Co., 1941), as well as *Lightning From the Past*, 116-119.

[198] "Sectarian Narrowness," *Revivalist* (Jan. 3, 1901), 8. Further alienating Revivalist adherents, Morrison refused in the summer of 1900 to continue publishing articles by Mary McGee Hall in *The Pentecostal Herald*, due to her advocacy of come-outism. Knapp quickly responded by inviting Hall to write articles for *The Revivalist*, in which she explained that she was only "for an exodus from Churches that are dead, and preachers that are backslidden, and fighters of God's truth." She charged Morrison and other holiness evangelists who encouraged holiness people to remain within Methodism with "gross" inconsistency because they traveled over the country making people dissatisfied with their dead churches, and then urged "them to stick to a dead thing" ("To the Holiness People in My Southland," *Revivalist* (Aug. 2, 1900), 13).

The resultant tension helped to stifle the previous good relations between Knapp and the holiness advocates centered at Wilmore, Kentucky, and may help to explain in part why Knapp abandoned his endorsement of Asbury College as "a full salvation school . . . charged with spiritual electricity" and began to work in earnest to begin his own Bible school (See "A Full Salvation School," *Revivalist* (Nov. 1897), 4; "Asbury College," *Revivalist* (July 1894), 3; and "A Full Salvation School," *The Way of Faith* (Oct. 20, 1897), 4). It also explains why two holiness schools were planted so near each other--they reflected different ecclesiologies.

[199] Bresee agreed with Knapp "that the holiness movement in America had reached its zenith under the 'iron-clad government' of Methodism" (Timothy L. Smith, *Called Unto Holiness*, 123). He also rejected anti-sectarian come-outism, but nevertheless felt compelled to withdraw from Methodism, forming an independent congregation, the Church of the Nazarene, in Los Angeles in 1895. At the General Holiness Assembly of 1901 he contended "that the day for a national [holiness] church organization had come" (Ibid, 126) With the blessings of NHA leaders including C. J. Fowler, who saw Bresee and his comrades as "put-outers" rather than "come-outers," Bresee began efforts at consolidation and merger that eventuated in the denomination now known as the Church of the Nazarene. For more on the career of Bresee and the formation of the Church of the Nazarene, see Carl Bangs, *Phineas F. Bresee: His Life in Methodism, the Holiness Movement, and the Church of the Nazarene* (Kansas City, MO: Beacon Hill Press of Kansas City: 1995) and E. A. Girvin, *Phineas F. Bresee: A Prince in Israel: A Biography* in *The Higher Christian Life: Sources for the Study of the Holiness, Pentecostal, and Keswick Movements*. Ed. Donald W. Dayton. (1916, Reprint; New York: Garland Publishing, 1984).

On Bresee's and Morrison's solutions to the Methodist challenge to the holiness movement, see Charles Edwin Jones, "The Holiness Complaint with Late-Victorian Methodism," in *Rethinking Methodist History: A Bicentennial Historical Consultation* Eds. Russell E. Richey and Kenneth E. Rowe (Nashville: Kingswood Books, 1985), 59-64.

[200] This name was adopted at the new denomination's first General Assembly held in October 1907 at Chicago at which time the Association of Pentecostal Churches (primarily an eastern group) merged with Bresee's Church of the Nazarene (primarily a western group). The second General Assembly was held the following year at Pilot Point, Texas, and was marked by merger with the Holiness Church of Christ (primarily a southern group). "The 1923 General Assembly made 1908 the official anniversary date" (R. Stanley Ingersol, "Church of the Nazarene," in Kostlevy, *Dictionary*, 62).

The founders of the Church of the Nazarene attempted to prevent the ecclesiastical abuses many of them had experienced in Methodism by adopting a congregational form of government. Thus, C. W. Ruth explained that the Church of the Nazarene was "nothing in the world but old-fashioned Methodism with a Congregational form of government" (Ibid, 57).

[201] "The Need of Holiness Unions," *Revivalist* (Feb. 8, 1900), 3.

[202] Jones, *Perfectionist Persuasion*, 104. This residence should not be confused with the location of God's Bible School, since the formation of the Union predated the purchase of the "Mount of Blessings" by almost three years. Unfortunately, GBS and Pilgrim Holiness folklore have often perpetuated this mistake, declaring that the Pilgrim Holiness Church (or at least the Union from which it evolved) began on the campus of GBS.

The type of "league" or union organization Knapp created in Cincinnati was not unprecedented among holiness advocates. In 1891, a similar General Holiness League had been formed in New England under the leadership of William McDonald and Joshua Gill. However, the Union effected in Cincinnati was destined to become a truly "international" force, while the league in New England was eventually subsumed by other organizations.

²⁰³ Thomas and Thomas, 15. This motto, borrowed from the Moravian Brethren (*Unitas Fratrum*) was maintained by the Pilgrim Holiness Church.

²⁰⁴ Ibid, 14.

²⁰⁵ Ibid, 13. Seth Rees later described the occasion as "a small affair with a big name" (Ibid).

²⁰⁶ Rees, et. al., *Pentecostal Messengers*, 7. As with the various "leagues" that preceded it, this organization had frequent name changes throughout its history, including "Pentecostal" in some of the names. See *Revivalist* (Nov. 1897), 6 where it is referred to as the Pentecostal Holiness Union and Prayer League. Evidently, the words "prayer league" indicated the absorption of the earlier body by the new organization. On July 3, 1900, the name was changed to "Apostolic Holiness Union." See Seth Rees, "Apostolic Holiness Union," *Revivalist* (Aug. 2, 1900), 12. For practicality, the organization will usually be referred to as the Holiness Union henceforth.

²⁰⁷ Thomas and Thomas, 15-16.

²⁰⁸ Timothy L. Smith, *Called Unto Holiness*, 59.

²⁰⁹ "The Apostolic Holiness Union," *Revivalist* (Aug. 2, 1900), 12.

²¹⁰ In a representative letter to a friend facing denominational opposition, he advised, "If you should be compelled to give up the Church, ought you not, for the sake of the sheep that have been saved, to open right there a Pentecostal Holiness Union Mission?" (Knapp, *Pentecostal Letters*, 25).

In the most succinct statement of his mature position on the church question, Knapp explained to *Revivalist* readers that "while Bible holiness prompts its possessor to be true to the branch of the Church with which he may be identified when that is a branch of the true vine, yet at the same time it may, and usually does, demand a change of relation if identified with a fallen Church" ("Holiness Societies," *Revivalist* (Aug. 2, 1900), 1). He further argued that it was as natural for newly sanctified persons to leave churches that have "apostatized so utterly, and are so completely controlled by the world, the flesh, and the devil, that God has left them," as it was for a new convert to leave Roman Catholicism (See also "Holiness Unions," *Revivalist* (January 3, 1901), 2).

Thus, "while the great object" of the Union was "to form associations composed of believers . . . irrespective of denominational connections, yet in the interests of suffering, ostracized people" who were without denominational homes, the Union favored "the forming of Union Societies wherever it is clear that they will best serve the interests of holiness" ("The Apostolic Holiness Union," *Revivalist* (Aug. 2, 1900), 12).

²¹¹ Timothy L. Smith (*Called Unto Holiness*, 59) made this observation concerning the General Holiness League in New England, but it describes the Holiness Union as well. Jones similarly observes that "by the turn of the century, associationism was fast breaking down as a means of tying the holiness movement to the [Methodist] church" (Jones, *Perfectionist Persuasion*, 104).

²¹² So many organized congregations were in the Union by 1905 that the words "and Churches" were added to the name. Interestingly, a pragmatic consideration involving

one of Knapp's favorite objects for holiness allegory—the railroad—provided impetus for the more churchly organization of the Union. A Manual was developed in 1902 at least in part to enable Union clergy to receive railroad discounts (Thomas and Thomas, 45). After merger with several groups, the transition to denominationalism was complete by 1922, when the name Pilgrim Holiness Church was chosen.

[213] Rees reminisced near the end of his life that Knapp "insisted" that he serve as General Superintendent. At the same time he also remarked that "we all regarded" Martin Wells Knapp "as the founder of our Zion" (Seth C. Rees, *Foundation Principles* Wesleyan Archives, Indianapolis, n. d.).

[214] Hills, *Hero*, 11.

[215] Ibid, 13-14.

Chapter 2

Unveiling the Vision: Claiming the Mount

"God's Bible School will be different from any other in the world."
— Cincinnati Post (August 1, 1900), 6.

From the Pentecostal dynamo there has also burst forth into the spiritual world, light and love and power which is causing multitudes to rush from the old candle-lighted stage-coaches of forms and ceremonies and dry creeds and crooked experiences into the brilliantly lighted, swiftly propelled [railroad] cars of full salvation, which by divine power, are bearing their inmates triumphantly on and up from "glory unto glory."
— Martin Wells Knapp[1]

During the months leading up to and shortly following the inauguration of God's Bible School, Martin Wells Knapp frequently reminded his readership that what was transpiring at this new school was unique. To be sure, Knapp recognized the rich tradition of Christian higher education in America that began with the Puritan establishment of such erstwhile "nurseries of piety" as Harvard and Yale.[2] He was also likely aware of the inception of such Bible schools as New York Missionary Training College (now Nyack College) founded by A. B. Simpson in 1883, and even specifically holiness schools, such as McGee Holiness College founded in 1896 in College Mound, Missouri, that were started with the express purpose of offering a liberal arts program.[3] In addition, he was undoubtedly acquainted with Bible schools that deliberately limited liberal arts offerings (usually termed "general education") to select courses deemed essential for ministerial preparation, of which Moody Bible Institute has been primary.[4] However, what he envisioned for God's Bible School and Missionary Training Home differed significantly from any school yet instituted, for, as Glenn Black has reflected, "God's Bible School is more than just an academic institution."[5]

Indeed, even more than the publishing and organizational advances that preceded it, GBS embodied the spiritual dynamic that characterized Martin Wells Knapp and his associates. It would thus be more accurate to see the early GBS not so much as an educational institution but as the nexus of a new spiritual movement in which academics was only one part of a larger process. Knapp's goal in this process was nothing less than revolutionary, a fact demonstrated by developments directly leading to the school's opening and illuminated in published disclosures of plans for the school.

Miracle of the Mount

Interestingly, Knapp's vision for a Bible school first surfaced in *The Revivalist* in August 1897, almost simultaneously with the formation of the Holiness Union. Here he reported having received "frequent inquiries in regard to a Pentecostal Training School on holiness lines for Christian workers which will direct in the study of the Bible and its doctrines, and at the same time give opportunities for observing and practicing Pentecostal methods in leading people into the experiences of salvation." He then set forth a prescribed reading course that could be undertaken at home, with the additional invitation: "Any student who may wish to take such a course under our supervision in connection with our mission work will be welcome." However, Knapp emphasized that such students should be "dead to everything but God's will, or earnestly seeking so as to be, and . . . called to devote their lives to soul-saving work. No others should apply."[6]

This rudimentary instructional program remained informal and failed to take institutional form. Things solidified somewhat with the announcement in January 1900 of a "Holiness Bible-School" that involved Bible studies conducted daily at 2:30 p.m. at Revivalist Chapel under the auspices of the Cincinnati chapter of the Holiness Union. These classes, "in which the Holy Spirit [was] recognized as the Supreme Teacher and Interpreter" were described as "Pentecostal, and for believers of every name, and evangelical, magnifying holiness as taught in the New Testament."[7] Accordingly, several participants were "wholly sanctified," while others were "reanimated with Pentecostal zeal."[8]

Such success made it apparent that *Revivalist* enterprises, including Knapp's fledgling school, needed more spacious and permanent facilities. In the June 14, 1900, issue of *The Revivalist*, Knapp wrote that he felt "especially impressed to ask . . . readers to pray in regard to the location for the Bible-school and Missionary Training Home and other work which He is comitting [sic] to this movement. Our confidence is in God alone, who, we believe, in answer to the united prayers of His children who are interested, will secure just the donations needed to secure it unencumbered for His work." This confidence was buoyed by the fact that "this work is His, [and] our interests are mutual and one with God's."[9]

Knapp had already explored several options, but believed many of them had been "providentially closed" because God "chidingly showed" him that he had been planning "on too small a scale." He then began looking for a location that could house not only a school, but also the publishing concern, the camp meeting, and eventually, an orphanage—a property "worthy of God and this great movement."[10] Only a week after issuing his request for special prayer, Knapp described such a property to *Revivalist* readers, a plot of almost two acres in Mount Auburn. Situated on "one of the highest points in Hamilton County," Knapp noted that it was centrally located, was "high and healthful," and commanded "a fine view" of "lower Cincinnati, the Ohio

River, [and] the suburban towns in Kentucky."[11] In addition, the property was adjacent to one of the important historic sites in Cincinnati—Filson Overlook—reputedly the "spot from which John Filson, Kentucky historian and surveyor, conceived the plan" for the city of Cincinnati.[12]

Two buildings were already on the lot, a prominent brick mansion facing Young Street and a wooden building behind it which had served as servants' quarters, providing a total of over twenty rooms, sufficient for Knapp's family and workers, "a temporary chapel, and a number of students."[13] There was also ample room for the two dormitories, tabernacle, and orphanage which Knapp planned to add as resources allowed. However, there was a major hurtle to be surpassed before Knapp could secure the property—finances.

An offer of $100,000 had been rejected earlier by the lady who owned the Young Street property, and the situation appeared hopeless. However, the area had recently experienced urban flight, so that it had "greatly depreciated in value for residence purposes."[14] This resulted in the reduction of the asking price to $35,000, a sum still far exceeding Knapp's financial resources. In fact, the only money Knapp initially had for the project was $100 that had been given a couple of years before in circumstances recounted for years in GBS catalogs: "One night God awakened one of His saints in Virginia, 'Mother' [Mrs. E. S.] Duff, and said to her, 'You will soon receive $100.00 by mail. Send it to M. W. Knapp, of Cincinnati, toward the purchase of a Bible School property.'"[15] With only this seed money and with "no capital or backing of any kind, except faith in an almighty, omnipotent God," and confidence that "there is mighty power in prayer," Knapp approached the agents of the owner in late June.[16] What followed caught the attention of even Cincinnati's secular media, as Knapp negotiated a price that "surprised the real estate world."[17]

Before approaching the real estate agents, Knapp believed that "God made it clear and plain that $20,000 was all that we could offer them for it." This Knapp did, and "to the astonishment of the agents themselves," the owner accepted. Taking this as an answer to prayer, Knapp's Cincinnati supporters were encouraged to believe that God would provide the two thousand dollar payment required before the deed could be transferred on July 1.[18] A thousand dollar contribution by Frank Mortimer Messenger, successful New England businessman and radical holiness leader, was followed by numerous smaller gifts so that "before the day of the transfer . . . the money was in." An observer on the night of the transfer recorded that "it just seemed as if the air was weighted with the glory of God" as Knapp "shouted the victory."[19] Such an astounding turn of events persuaded Knapp to name the property the "Mount of Blessings," a name that even the secular media in Cincinnati used for many years to describe the location.

Knapp's family, along with several *Revivalist* workers, soon moved to what would become one of the most famous addresses among holiness people—1810 Young Street. Here they relocated Revivalist Chapel and the *Revivalist* publishing enterprises, except that "an office at the [Y. M. C. A.] was retained as a central place near the Post Office from which shipping and other similar business could be conducted."[20] They also updated *Revivalist* readers weekly on the progress of the "Bible-School Fund" by means of a diagram of blocks representing needed funds which were replaced by Scripture quotations as funds arrived.[21] By school's beginning, over a thousand dollars in addition to the original two had been raised, and by May 1902, the $20,000 goal had been surpassed.

Meanwhile, several challenges other than location and finances immediately confronted Knapp, and their resolution seems almost as incredible as the acquisition of the Mount of Blessings. Primary among these concerns were two obvious, essential factors—faculty and students. Knapp struggled with these issues, battling what Bessie Queen described as a Satanic suggestion, "Now you have gotten that property in your hands, you have got to open the school, and where are your teachers and where are your students?"[22] However, these challenges too were met in good time.

When school began, a well-qualified faculty of three was on hand—Knapp; Beatrice Finney, "a Southern Methodist from Kentucky," and Veda Anderson, "a Baptist from Iowa."[23] Before the year ended, other teachers joined the staff, including Jennie Mitchell, who came to the school "with the highest recommendations . . . from the public schools of Pennsylvania," and Robert Elmer McNeill, who had served as music professor at Albion College.[24] The latter quickly worked to establish a "Bible School Conservatory of Gospel Music."

Recruiting a student body was even less of a challenge than obtaining faculty. *The Revivalist* served as the primary recruitment tool, with "school hints" appearing periodically throughout the summer of 1900.[25] In addition, most of the June 21 issue, bearing the sub-heading "Bible-School Edition," was dedicated to explaining various aspects of the proposed school. The response to this information was rewarding, with "letters . . . from all parts of the country" requesting more details.[26] This positive response encouraged Knapp to begin praying that God would actually limit the students to only those "that ought to be here," asking that God would "close up and block the way for everyone who should not come."[27]

As school got under way, it was clear that Knapp's later prayer was in order, since the seventy-two students who registered throughout the first year crowded the facilities to capacity. The twelve rooms in the wood frame building, which served as the women's dormitory, were filled, and male students were packed into the attic of the mansion. The large parlor, where classes and chapel were conducted, was stretched to its limits, underscoring the need for Knapp's proposed tabernacle. Mealtime also proved problematic; thus, the first building project involved constructing a brick cafeteria between the two original buildings.[28]

One can imagine the eager anticipation in the air as these early witnesses of the "miracle of the Mount" gathered on September 27, 1900, for the opening convention of God's Bible School and Missionary Training Home.

Nor was their expectancy in vain, for the answers to prayer that occurred that summer were only the beginning of a series of remarkable events that would transpire throughout the following century, giving credence to the claim that Malachi 3:10 was "verified daily at this place."[29]

Back to the Bible

Shortly after the end of the first school year, Knapp published a compilation of *Revivalist* articles relevant to the school's beginning, along with a synopsis of its opening convention and first year's highlights, including the sermon and dedicatory prayer by Seth C. Rees (See Appendix A), in a book entitled *Back to the Bible; or, Pentecostal Training*. This book, which was required reading for prospective students in the early days of the school,[30] along with other *Revivalist* publications, provides posterity with detailed insight into Knapp's intentions for the unique educational process to be employed at GBS (God's Bible School). Here we find not only glimpses into what life at the early GBS was like, and how it differed from other schools, but, most importantly, what it was ultimately about.

These sources make it clear that much of Knapp's impetus for starting a new school stemmed from his observance throughout America "of deplorable ignorance" of the Bible, particularly among "ministers of the gospel."[31] He attributed much of the responsibility for this situation to religious educational institutions where so much emphasis was placed on secular studies and methods that "the ordinary course of study . . . involves a great waste of time and money to people who are preparing solely for the work of the kingdom."[32] At best, worldly collegiate education was useless to Christian workers, "cramming the coal-bins of the soul full of the sawdust of secular knowledge instead of the coal of the Word of God."[33] Worse yet, "conformity to the world in a college curriculum" would be just another form of worldliness—"as displeasing to God as in other things that are worldly."[34] At its worst, worldly scholarship became outright idolatry, actually displacing true spirituality, which Knapp saw as symptomatic of the spiritual demise of mainline denominations: "The appalling apostasy which Protestantism has suffered, and under the blight of which it enters the twentieth century, is seen by the following symptoms, which largely prevail: Education is substituted for salvation. College degrees for Pentecostal diplomas . . ."[35]

For these reasons, Knapp would not seek to rejuvenate Christian liberal arts at GBS, refusing "to stuff students with dead languages, higher mathematics, and heathen philosophies" or even "with views of theologians about the Bible." In fact, he pointedly denied any intention for GBS to be, or ever to become, a liberal arts institution, declaring that it was not "a secular school. It does not profess to qualify people for public schools or places in the pulpits of dead churches. It aims at higher things."[36] Instead, GBS would function more as a technical or vocational school, seeking to produce Spirit-filled, Bible-centered soul-winners.

While the radical holiness perspective on education that Knapp represented has been frequently criticized by those within and without the holiness movement as "anti-intellectual,"[37] it actually represented a carefully nuanced worldview that shaped classes and other activities at the early GBS. Morrison's observation regarding early Church of God (Anderson) leaders applies equally well to Knapp and his colleagues: "These leaders were not really 'fighters of education.' Rather than being anti-educationalists, they were 'ultra-supernaturalists.'"[38] That is, a unique form of education developed at GBS, a training that was more experiential than intellectual, focusing more on the spiritual and eternal than the physical and temporal. The primary goal was the attainment of spiritual excellence rather than academic accomplishment. Students came to receive an experience and to learn how to encourage the reception of that experience by others. Knapp thus recruited students to attend GBS so that they might be established "in the gift and gifts of the Holy Spirit" and be provided with "a spiritual equipment that will make them efficient wherever the call of God and the providence of God shall place them."[39]

Central to this equipment was the experience of entire sanctification, or the baptism with the Holy Spirit, which provided the only qualification absolutely necessary for successful Christian workers.[40] However, Knapp believed that this experience must be coupled with grounding in the Bible for the worker to be fully equipped; otherwise, Spirit-baptism without Bible study would leave him or her without substance, liable to "mistakes and blunders" too often characteristic of "unskilled laborers."[41] Further using the analogy of a coal-fueled locomotive, Knapp explained, "The Word of God is the coal which feeds the fire and which keeps him going. The baptism with the Holy Ghost is the fire itself. As the engine soon stops without coal, so the believer can accomplish little unless, like Barnabas, he is 'full of the Scriptures.'"[42] In addition, a thorough and proper understanding of Scripture would alleviate much of the "opposition and confusion in regard to Bible holiness and a full-gospel."[43] Most importantly, Knapp asserted that "Scripture knowledge" remained "essential to revival victory." [44] Accordingly, he chose the motto "Back to the Bible" for GBS, insisting that there the Bible would "be the main book studied, other books being studied only as aids to the mastery of this—a school where it will be honored as the great Mississippi River of research and spiritual culture, into which all others are but tributary streams."[45]

Until his death, Knapp himself served as primary Bible instructor, drawing on his extensive experience in writing and in chart evangelism. Participants were thrilled with his vivid presentations of holiness doctrine, agreeing that "Brother Knapp's method of Bible-study, for accuracy, mental drill, and illustrating and transmitting spiritual truths, can not be surpassed anywhere."[46] Bible principles were further clarified through *Revivalist* books including Knapp's *Impressions* and *Holiness Triumphant*, Hills' *Holiness and Power*, Rees's *Fire from Heaven*, and Carradine's *The Old Man*.[47]

However, Knapp's instruction and collateral books were considered mere tools in divine hands in the process of Bible training at GBS. Knapp informed his readers that only the participation of the Holy Spirit in the learning process would make it successful: "While it is in the student's power to memorize the Word, yet only God can reveal and apply its truths. Hence there must be a united waiting upon God, that the Holy Spirit, who is the Author of the Word, may also act as its Interpreter and unfold its precious meanings."[48] To underscore this dependence upon the Holy Spirit as ultimate teacher, prayer was conducted in class and in private asking for His illumination of Scripture, and students were encouraged "to write out briefly the lessons which God may reveal."[49]

This joint emphasis on magnifying the Bible "above all other studies" and "the Holy Ghost above all other teachers" connected the Bible and the Holy Spirit—the *Word* and the *Fire*—in a unique blend that took the concept of "double-inspiration"—the inspiration of both text and interpreter—"far beyond" that held by Wesley, to the ultimate conclusion that "only the entirely sanctified could properly interpret the Bible."[50]

Knapp thus viewed Spirit-baptism as "the Divine preparation for receiving and understanding the Word of God."[51] Godbey likewise "counseled interpreters to get all the rocks of depravity eliminated from the heart . . . [so that they] could go down into the profound mysteries of revealed truth, be flooded with new spiritual illuminations, and progressively be 'edified by fresh revealments of the Divine attributes in glory, though you never saw a college or inherited Solomonic genius.'"[52]

This wedding of Pentecostal experience to biblical interpretation produced a unique hermeneutic among radical holiness advocates. This way of viewing the Bible joined the assumption that Spirit-baptism was a requisite for correctly understanding Scripture with an insistence that the exclusive purpose of Scripture was to proclaim holiness doctrine and experience. As Knapp put it, "Someone has said that there is a scarlet thread running clear through the Bible, and that this thread is the blood of Jesus. There is another thread running through it . . . the white one of the promise of the Pentecostal outpouring of the Holy Ghost. Of all the promises of the Bible, God exalts this as 'THE PROMISE' of all the ages."[53] Similarly, Godbey asserted that "Holy Bible" meant that the Bible is a "book on holiness" and that "it is a history of God's holiness movement on earth the last six thousand years and the prophetic history of that movement to the end of time."[54]

The application of this interpretive rubric to Scripture resulted in a "hermeneutic of illustration," in which holiness advocates sought to demonstrate the necessity of "second blessing" holiness by finding illustrations of it throughout a wide variety of texts. A brief survey of some ways in which this approach to Scripture was worked out by Knapp and his associates helps to give a feel for what classes at the early GBS offered students. One of the most popular ways the hermeneutic of illustration surfaced was in "spiritual geography," in which "biblical place-names [became] metaphors for spiritual experience,"[55] such as that developed in Knapp's *Out of Egypt Into Canaan*.[56] Canaan imagery became pervasive throughout the holiness movement, informing numerous songs such as "Go Up, Possess the Land," "Dwelling in Beulah Land," and "Good-by Pharaoh!"[57] and innumerable sermons and testimonies such as the following shared by students during the 1901 opening convention at GBS:

> "Praise God, I am living in Canaan now! My State is Kentucky (Covington). I do praise God for full salvation and a clean heart!..."
> "I am in the wilderness, pressing on for Canaan! I am from Indiana."...
> "I am on the victory side! Formerly from Maryland. Living in Canaan, way up on the victory mount—the Mount of Blessings!"[58]

Though finding scriptural justification for their use of the "Egypt to Canaan" allegory by pointing to the typological use of Canaan in relation to the "second rest" in Hebrews 3-4,[59] the creativity of holiness advocates left almost no biblical narrative untouched in the quest to find metaphors for entire sanctification. For example, L. Milton Williams relied on the life of "Jacob the Heelgrasper" to depict "some of God's pictures of the carnal mind,"[60] B. S. Taylor used the account of the Gibeonites (Joshua 9-10) to "make the 'second blessing' plain to common people,"[61] and Beverly Carradine devoted an entire book to *The Second Blessing in Symbol*.[62] G. D. Watson was a master at this type of Bible interpretation, allegorizing accounts of Noah, Isaac, David, and many others to promote such radical holiness themes as premillennialism as well as entire sanctification.[63]

"At times, typology ran unbridled,"[64] as when W. B. Godbey found strong parallels between Job's conversation with his "comforters" and the holiness debate then raging within Methodism.[65] Reflecting his enthusiasm for such typology, Godbey averred, "If I were to notice everything in the Bible setting forth this glorious double salvation, it would take me the balance of my life."[66] In fact, one of the highest compliments that could be paid to a holiness exponent was to be recognized for the ability to find evidence for the second blessing in biblical passages "where few people have ever thought to look for either the doctrine or experience."[67]

While the purpose here is not to give a verdict on the propriety of this extensive use of Bible allegory/typology by GBS teachers and *Revivalist* writers,[68] the practice suggests the energy and originality that marked early GBS classes. More significantly, it reflects the basic approach to life for those espousing the radical holiness mindset. That is, the application of the "hermeneutic of illustration" went far beyond Bible interpretation to influence the way that the early GBS family viewed all the world—history, nature, and personal experience, as well as the Bible.

In other words, classes at GBS were based on the assumption that holiness experience, nature or science, and biblical revelation emanated from the same Source. Unlike some post-moderns who attempt to identify various counter-balancing "sources" of truth (as in Albert Outler's "Wesleyan" quadrilateral[69]), Knapp and his colleagues believed that all "sources" of truth ultimately derived from one source—God—and that they would thus be unified—yielding the same truth.[70] For this reason, all aspects of creation, history, and special revelation were proper subjects to provide analogies for holiness doctrine and experience.

Popular subjects for holiness metaphors included technological innovations in communication, such as the telegraph and radio; and in transportation, especially the railroad system—the rapid growth of which mirrored that of the holiness movement and proved invaluable in the travels of holiness revivalists.[71] The purity and power motifs in Knapp's teaching were often illustrated by dynamite and electricity, as well as such natural cataclysmic forces as earthquakes, cyclones, and lightning.[72] Oswald Chambers found scriptural support for such typology, noting in a *Revivalist* article "how much is said about atmosphere, fire, force and electricity" in the Bible.[73] Knapp concluded, "These figures all proclaim in thunderous tones the destructive power of the Holy Ghost in cleansing the heart from all sin, and filling it with Divine might, to resist the power of the enemy."[74]

History and classic literature provided fertile fields for holiness illustrations, although "carnal fiction" received Knapp's unmitigated condemnation.[75] Without doubt, the most influential literary work inspiring holiness typology was Bunyan's *Pilgrim's Progress*, elements of which were often amalgamated with Canaan imagery as in Knapp's *Out of Egypt Into Canaan*.[76] Songs thus encouraged the "Bloodwashed Pilgrim" on his journey to the "Celestial City," and *Revivalist* articles often presented brief allegories peopled by Bunyan-esque characters like "Pastor Big Head," "Dr. Hate Holiness," and "Dr. Got-it-all-at-Conversion."[77]

History was viewed at the early GBS through the "remnant" schema—holding that throughout history the true Church has usually consisted of a relatively small remnant—the sanctified—whose devotion contrasted sharply with "popular" religion.[78] For this reason, many of the major trends in church history were given scant attention while focus was placed on examples of sanctified lives throughout history, an emphasis borne out in Revivalist Press biographies of persons as diverse as Madame Guyon—Roman Catholic mystic from France, and Lucius B. Compton—"the Mountaineer Evangelist" from western North Carolina.[79]

To bring holiness teachings home to the masses, Knapp and his associates ultimately extended the field of holiness illustrations to commonplace observations. For example, the search for "doubles" in the Bible was complimented by a search for "doubles" in everyday life, with Knapp asserting that the "necessity of a double work" was illustrated on every hand by human anatomy and mass transportation: "Two eyes, two ears, two hands, two feet, are an ever present argument that a double work is in harmony with the divine order. The two rails of the train underneath and the two sets of wheels are further illustrations of the two works of justification and entire sanctification which are essential in traveling to heaven."[80]

In short, commitment to demonstrating radical holiness or "Pentecostal" teaching at GBS went far beyond biblical texts specifically dealing with sanctification to encompass every field of human knowledge. It also went far beyond the classroom and textbooks to touch every aspect of life at GBS, including meals, social activities, and even vacations. This reveals just how extensively the commitment to inculcating Pentecostal experience impacted both individual and community at the early GBS. For, in a profound sense, at the new school on the Mount of Blessings, "Back to the Bible" meant "Back to Pentecost."

Back to Pentecost

To qualify what he meant by going *Back to the Bible* at GBS, Knapp used the subtitle *Pentecostal Training*. A quick perusal of *Revivalist* publications makes it evident that, aside from the term "Holiness" itself, "Pentecostal" was the preferred label worn by participants in the radical holiness movement that Knapp helped to lead.[81] In order to understand adequately what Knapp envisioned for GBS, the question must then be considered, "What did Knapp mean by 'Pentecostal'?"

As already noted, the term did not carry many of the connotations for the Revivalist movement that it does for contemporary Pentecostals. In particular, extant records make no mention of Knapp ever practicing or encouraging *glossolalia* (speaking in "unknown tongues") or identifying such a practice as the evidence of Spirit-baptism, a development that would not take place until after Knapp's death. Yet, Knapp held several commitments which warrant his self-description as a "Pentecostal."

Key among these ideals was the identification of the outpouring of the Holy Spirit on the disciples at Pentecost (Acts 2) as the experience of entire sanctification, a theme incipient in Methodism at least as far back as Wesley's close associate John Fletcher.[82] This concept, receiving one of its fullest expressions in *Lightning Bolts from Pentecostal Skies*, represents the culmination of a shift among many holiness advocates from a Christological (Christ-focused) emphasis to a largely pneumatological (Spirit-oriented) emphasis regarding sanctification.[83] Although this perspective came to dominate most of the holiness movement by 1900, winning the support of such loyal Methodists as Daniel Steele,[84] Leon Hynson observes that "the definition of sanctification through the event of Pentecost reached a crescendo in the preaching of" such revivalists as "Martin Wells Knapp, Seth C. Rees, Charles Stalker and W. B. Godbey"— all closely associated with GBS. In fact, Hynson suggests that "God's Bible School . . . was the geographical center of this new focus."[85]

While Pentecostal sanctification provided the dominant doctrinal distinctive of GBS, the significance of Pentecost for the school went far beyond reception of the second blessing. Indeed, Pentecostal sanctification was the initiation into a new way of living and thinking—a new worldview.[86] This new worldview had Pentecostal sanctification as its foundation, to be sure. However, as application of the "hermeneutic of illustration" has indicated, this worldview dynamically shaped every aspect of life.

Notwithstanding its profound implications, the goal of this worldview was quite straightforward. In short, Knapp's goal in ministry in general, and at GBS in particular, was "nothing less than a restoration of the Jerusalem Pentecost which began the Christian story."[87] As A. M. Hills explained to his Congregationalist associates, "the main issue" of *The Revivalist* was "the multiplication of Pentecosts in all the churches and in individual hearts."[88] Behind this effort was the conviction that just as the Pentecost of Acts 2 ushered in the new dispensation of the Church, Pentecostal sanctification today will initiate a new epoch for both individual believers and the believing community.

This belief imbued numerous holiness songs, such as "Back to Pentecost," "Pentecostal Fire is Falling," and "It Is For Us All Today."[89] It infused *Revivalist* testimonies, such as a report from Texas by pioneer Nazarene leader C. B. Jernigan: "O, glory to God! we are getting back to Pentecost."[90] It informed revivalists' appeals, both to individuals and denominations. For instance, Oswald Chambers pointedly asked individuals, "Have you had a *personal Pentecost?*"[91] while Knapp pled for a denomination-wide "return of Pentecost" to save Methodism.[92]

This appeal for renewed Pentecost gave rise to a unique and potent form of primitivism—the attempt to see the church restored to New Testament standards of purity and power.[93] Although earlier holiness advocates had embraced a primitivist vision, which remained embryonic in Wesley's teachings,[94] Knapp took the theme further with his insistence that the New Testament Church, particularly as described in the book of Acts, provides "a model for the entire dispensation,"[95] elaborating,

> Pentecost and the great revivals which followed it in the primitive Church are the patterns which the Holy Spirit has left for us to follow. They declare in thunder tones that if we would see Pentecostal results, there must be Pentecostal repentance, Pentecostal prayer, Pentecostal sanctification, and conformity to Pentecostal conditions and practices. The great spiritual principles which were magnified by the apostles are the same now as they were then, and insistence upon them will bring similar results.[96]

Simply put, not only could Pentecost be repeated, it *must* be— the very spiritual life of the believer and the church depended on it.

This commitment to the restoration of Pentecost wove together concerns of all three strands of primitivism identified by scholars—ethical, ecclesiastical, and experiential.[97] The ethical focus involved duplicating "apostolic purity and practices for the individual and church"[98] by stressing fidelity to Scripture as the ultimate authority for doctrine and practice. Thus, a supporter explained to a reporter for the *Cincinnati Enquirer* that at GBS, "straight, plain, old-time Bible doctrine, without any of the latter-day interpretations or new-fangled notions, is taught."[99] Knapp's explanation of the motto "Back to the Bible" succinctly captures the thrust of this concern:

> Multitudes of people on every hand have drifted away from the old landmarks, and substituted many other things for the Word of God itself. People, however, are hunting up their Bibles and beginning to study them. The cry is going forth, "To the Word and the testimony." Everything that cannot meet Scripture tests must go. "The Scriptures cannot be broken." Seekers for pardon, for the sanctifying baptism of the Holy Ghost, for Divine healing, for victory over obstacles and circumstances, are demonstrating this fact at the Mount of Blessings; and God is being honored.[100]

Negatively, ethical primitivism involved the denunciation of human authority (as opposed to divine), especially that embodied in creeds. In stunning agreement with his theological arch-enemies in the Stone-Campbell Restoration Movement,[101] W. B. Godbey urged holiness people to accept "no creed but the Bible," warning that "if the Holiness people do not get saved from all the creeds and come back to the New Testament alone, rest assured the Holy Spirit will be grieved. The Bible is a plain book. We need nothing else in the way of doctrine and discipline."[102]

Positively, this strand of primitivism sought to elevate the Bible above all human formulations. Godbey found the initiation of such schools as GBS one of the chief evidences of the holiness movement's success in this matter, contending that "the universal prevalence of Bible schools in the holiness movement is the most prominent vindication and confirmation of her orthodoxy."[103] In particular, students came to GBS "because the school is true to its motto, 'Back to the Bible,' and the dogmas of the Dark Ages are relegated to the background, while New Testament truth and organization are emphasized."[104]

Such organization became the focus of ecclesiastical primitivism in the Revivalist movement. Although Knapp sought to counter Church of God anti-sectarianism with a more balanced approach in the Holiness Union, he actually agreed with much of the "come-outer" assessment of mainline denominations, protesting against the "lack of conformity of denominations to New Testament principles and preachers."[105] Furthermore, those churches unwilling to "repent of their worldly conformity and compromise, and return to New Testament simplicity, principles, and practices" should "cease to be recognized as branches of [God's] Church."[106] In fact, such bodies should simply be considered social "clubhouses."[107]

Since it would be "contrary to the spirit of holiness" for "holiness ministers to exhort believers to identify with such institutions,"[108] Knapp increasingly urged his followers to establish local societies of the Holiness Union, "honoring New Testament principles and proclaiming New Testament Church order and loyalty to the New Testament government."[109] As will be seen, Knapp ultimately heeded his own advice, starting an independent society on the GBS campus in 1901. Godbey explained that "there is nothing here really new on the Church line except the organization of a New Testament Society for the benefit of the students and converts who have no membership in denominational Churches." However, he also acknowledged,

Of course, such a religious society, organized on a *purely New Testament basis*, is, in fact, *a primitive Church*, apostolical and evangelical; but they do not consider it such, nor call it a Church. It is simply an organization on the *New Testament basis*, much after the manner of a holiness band or association . . . [110]

Both the ethical and ecclesiastical dimensions of Pentecostal primitivism were inextricably interwoven with the experiential focus on repeating Pentecost. For this goal to be reached, early GBS constituents believed at least four principles must be embraced. These commitments were known collectively as the "old-time" religion, the "apostolic faith," the "full gospel," and, most descriptively, the "four-fold gospel." The first two elements were regeneration and entire sanctification; the next two, faith for divine healing and in the premillennial Second Coming of Christ.[111] As Donald Dayton has demonstrated in *Theological Roots of Pentecostalism*, this conception of Christ as Savior, Sanctifier, Healer, and Coming King was the informal "creed" binding early Pentecostals together.[112] "No creed but the Bible" really meant no creed but the four-fold gospel.[113]

In other words, rather than disjointed concepts, these ideals provided the irreducible minimum of Pentecostal belief, a four-fold ideological cord that would entirely disintegrate if only one strand were removed.[114] Alone, even "Christ our Sanctifier is not enough."[115] Thus, Seth Rees asserted, "This second chapter of Acts, and the whole book, never was so precious to me as it is in these days, and anybody who would clip out any part of it or take away any portion of it is not in Pentecost, and never had the baptism."[116]

Knapp's arrival at this commitment, particularly the adoption of the last two elements of the four-fold gospel, required careful deliberation before he could overcome being "brought up to believe that things said about divine healing and the return of Jesus were a hindrance to holiness."[117] In fact, several of his colleagues, including W. B. Godbey, L. L. Pickett, and G. D. Watson, preceded him in embracing at least the premillennial focus of the four-fold gospel.[118] This rather swift transition from the postmillennial consensus of the antebellum holiness movement grounded in Methodism to an acceptance of premillennial dispensationalism among most holiness people remains one of the most remarkable aspects of the development of radical holiness or Pentecostal ideology and was widespread by 1898, with W. B. Godbey rejoicing:

What a wonderful flood of light on this subject is inundating the world! Only two years ago Brother [Beverly] Carradine got light on it, and preached it, and Dr. [G. D.] Watson preached his first sermon on it, and there has been a regular revelation on the subject in the last few years. You do not find one sanctified man in a thousand who is not looking for the speedy coming of the Lord.[119]

Scholars have noted various factors influential in this sweeping transformation. It is likely that the four-fold gospel was mediated from A. B.

Simpson to the Revivalist movement especially through Seth Rees, who had served as "president of the Michigan auxillary of Simpson's Christian Alliance while he and his wife, Hulda, pastored the Friend's Meeting at Raisin Valley, Michigan, in 1888."[120] However, since Simpson's premillennialism was apparently more historicist than dispensational,[121] it is likely that a confluence of additional forces led to the holiness movement acceptance of dispensationalism, which was widely popularized through the writings of prophecy teachers like John Nelson Darby and in the Bible Conference Movement promoted by Dwight L. Moody beginning in the 1880's.[122]

For one, the logic and tools used by non-holiness dispensationalists were often parallel to that employed by holiness proponents of the "hermeneutic of illustration."[123] In addition, the shift from post- to premillennialism reflected a growing pessimism toward the dominant culture. While scholars have suggested various causes for this negative outlook,[124] increasing numbers of holiness people concurred with Dr. Godbey's answer to the question, "Is the world growing better?"— "We are constrained, by ten thousand inspired witnesses, to give a negative answer."[125] Evidences of this pessimism in Knapp's thought include his disparaging of the educational establishment and of the Methodist hierarchy—key motivations in his founding a Bible school. In fact, it is likely that Knapp would have never initiated GBS had he not first adopted such an assessment of the larger society.[126]

However, GBS teachers and *Revivalist* writers carefully qualified their pessimism, seeking to maintain the Wesleyan balance between the "optimism of grace" and the "pessimism toward sin."[127] Rather than abandoning the revival and reform impulse of earlier Wesleyanism, Knapp and his associates sought to redirect it into more efficient enterprises. In essence, they despaired of reforming the social order, instead focusing on individual reclamation.[128] As Godbey put it, "Our work is not to tinker with the old ship [the world and popular religion], already hopelessly unseaworthy and condemned by heaven's court of admiralty; but to jump into the life boat, taking everybody with us we possibly can; thus leaving the old bark to her destruction."[129]

In other words, the primary task for GBS and its constituents was to make "bridehood saints" prepared for the imminent return of Christ by getting them entirely sanctified. As C. W. Ruth preached at Salvation Park Camp Meeting, "What is the holiness movement but a call to God's people to put on the wedding garment?"[130] Indeed, *The Revivalist* touted the teaching of premillennialism as "a powerful incentive to holiness."[131]

While such colleagues as Godbey and Pickett undoubtedly influenced his views, Knapp credited his own acceptance of premillennialism and divine healing to Bible study in preparation for classes at Revivalist Chapel in 1898:

> Last year in our Cincinnati meeting, when we began our Bible readings, I told the people I was going to swallow everything that was in the Bible. I found there were over seven hundred references to Christ's coming back to reign on earth. Now, I am trying to make up for lost time in telling

about His coming . . . I made another discovery while reading the Bible at our meetings, and that was that the New Testament magnifies the healing of the body."[132]

Once Knapp embraced these teachings, he threw himself into their promotion wholeheartedly, expanding *The Revivalist* in 1899 with two new full-page features—"Gifts of Healings" and "Behold, He Cometh."[133] In addition, he published many songs proclaiming the imminent return of Christ, as well as several books treating this theme, including his own *Holiness Triumphant; or, Pearls from Patmos* (1900), expounding the Book of Revelation, and Dr. Godbey's New Testament Commentary, distinguished by its "pervasive premillennial orientation."[134] Likewise, Salvation Park Camp was advertised to honor such "spokes" emanating from the "Holiness hub" as "healing" and the "return of Jesus,"[135] with Knapp suggesting that to discard the spokes would also "tear the hub out of the wheel of salvation and ruin it."[136]

The firm commitment of GBS itself to the four-fold gospel from its beginning was reflected in the dedicatory sermon preached by Seth Rees during its opening convention. In this classic exposition of the four-fold gospel, he challenged his hearers to proclaim at home and abroad "All the Words of This Life" (Acts 5:20),[137] particularly emphasizing "the proclamation of the gifts, as well as the gift of the Holy Ghost. A movement that does not proclaim these gifts is a defective movement. A Bible School that does not teach them is not worthy of the name." Specifically, this involved "insisting upon . . . Divine healing" and "the neglected doctrine of the coming of our Lord."

Beyond accounts of healing in Acts and elsewhere in Scripture, the GBS family found biblical support for including divine healing as a provision of Pentecost by locating its fountain in the atonement. Of course, most evangelicals then and now have believed that the atonement provides for the "ultimate redemption" of believers from "physical disease" in the "resurrection into glorified bodies in the next" life.[138] However, by identifying healing as an element of Pentecost along with entire sanctification, many GBS constituents moved the expectation of all but ultimate healing from glorification in the hereafter to the here and now, contending that there was "healing in the atonement along with redemption from sin."[139]

As with the imminent return of Christ, Knapp saw physical healing as an encouragement to holiness, and more than one person came to GBS seeking healing but also finding sanctification.[140] Many others would send requests for prayer for healing to the school, resulting in remarkable testimonies.[141] Consistent with their experiential orientation, such testimonies served, second only to Scripture, as the chief evidence holiness people marshaled to support their promotion of faith healing. Throughout the early years of GBS, Revivalist Press published numerous books recounting divine healing and other miraculous interventions, including *Modern Miracles* by H. T. Davis, *Praying Clear Through* by W. J. Harney, and the perennially popular *Remarkable Incidents and Modern Miracles Through Prayer and Faith* by G. C. Bevington, alumnus and beloved cook at the GBS camp meeting.¹⁴² In addition, innumerable testimonials assured that the column on "Gifts of Healings" never lacked material.

Many testimonies to healing were also shared in chapel at GBS. One can readily imagine how the atmosphere of the parlor-chapel pulsated with excitement just five days after school began, as Mary Storey shared with the campus family how God had once healed her from the results of drinking deadly poison—an accidentally administered dose of tincture of aconite, strong "enough to kill seven men."¹⁴³ Later, the faith of several was undoubtedly bolstered to seek direct divine intervention rather than medical aid when hearing Charles Cowman's testimony to the restoration of his eyesight, so that he was able to discard his eye glasses.¹⁴⁴ Soon, several were experiencing healing on the campus, including teacher Beatrice Finney who was healed from heart disease.¹⁴⁵ Before the first school year ended, so many healings had occurred that the *Revivalist* proclaimed, "God has healed many at the Mount of Blessings."¹⁴⁶

This signaled the fulfillment of Knapp's desire that God's Bible School be a place "where people might be saved and sanctified and healed and a full gospel proclaimed."¹⁴⁷ Indeed, it appeared that the hope for GBS expressed in Rees's dedicatory sermon was transpiring:

> All these years I have said Pentecost ought to return, and yet I have seen nothing anywhere in my evangelistic work that measured up to it; but I trust the Holy Ghost will put Himself upon and in this school, and be so magnified and upheld and consulted that we will get *back to Pentecost*.¹⁴⁸

Notes

¹ Knapp, *Lightning Bolts*, 7.

² For source documents describing the religious foundation of colonial colleges, see Edwin S. Gaustad, Ed. *A Documentary History of Religion in America to the Civil War* Second Ed. (Grand Rapids: Eerdmans, 1993), 201-214. While religious motivations certainly prompted the founding of colonial colleges, Witmer's contention that "the first, Harvard, was essentially a Bible college in its early years" fails to consider the unique role of the modern Bible college as a religious innovation produced in late nineteenth-century America (S. A. Witmer *The Bible College Story: Education With Dimension* (Manhasset, NY: Channel Press, 1962), 27).

³ Begun under the auspices of the Church of God (Holiness), McGee Holiness College and Ministerial Training Institute offered four programs designed to prepare students for secular work, in addition to theological education. "These consisted of a classical course with an A B. degree, a scientific course with a B. S. degree, a literary course with an L. B. degree and a normal course for those preparing to teach in public schools" (Cowen 39). This school evolved into Pauline Holiness College which also made an attempt to prepare students "to enter the American culture as participants in both classical education and the new scientific knowledge" (David Bundy, "Blaming the Victim: The Wesleyan/Holiness movement in American Culture," *WTJ* 32 no. 1 (Spring 1997), 171.

Many other schools began as Bible institutes and evolved into liberal arts colleges as they gradually acquired faculty, constituents, and other resources. In fact, most holiness denominational colleges followed this pattern of development. For example, Anderson University, Olivet Nazarene University, Point Loma Nazarene College, Southern Nazarene University, Trevecca Nazarene University, and Indiana Wesleyan University all had their roots in Bible institutes. It should be noted that in some cases the founders had no intention of starting the nucleus of a liberal arts college but that posterity made adaptations that led to the establishment of such.

⁴ Witmer (37) has identified two general types of Bible colleges: one, focusing on Bible education like Moody, the other, following the pattern of Nyack and including more liberal arts courses. Often, those like Moody offer certificates upon the completion of two- or three-year programs; those like Nyack usually confer traditional degrees.

While Knapp was obviously aware of Moody's Chicago work, having been supportive of Moody's evangelism in the early 1890's, and later developing his Pentecostal Colportage library as an alternative to Moody's, his conception of the ideal Bible college appears to have developed more from holiness/Methodist influences than from influence by Moody. However, an indirect influence from Moody's Bible institute may have come through the involvement of Charles and Lettie Cowman in the beginning of GBS, since Charles had taken classes at Moody's school prior to moving to Cincinnati.

⁵ Glenn Black, "The Story of God's Bible School" *Revivalist* (January 6, 1983), 13.

⁶ "Pentecostal Training School," *Revivalist* (Aug. 1897), 6. Again, it should be noted that Knapp's use of the term "Pentecostal" does not carry many of its modern connotations—most notably that of identification of tongues-speaking and other physical phenomena as evidences of baptism with the Holy Spirit. Rather, its use as the term of choice for self-identification by Knapp and other radical holiness advocates indicates their embrace of a ideology or worldview espousing the attempt to recreate primitive Christianity, not through such phenomena as glossolalia, but through the purity and power resultant from Spirit-baptism which would produce the radical transformation of community and individual life. Our use of the term here results from its historic usage and should not be misconstrued as an anachronistic attempt to identify Knapp and the Revivalist movement with modern Pentecostalism. In fact, later developments indicate that the latter movement represents a departure from (or innovation on) the earlier "Pentecostalism" promoted by Knapp and his colleagues. I am especially indebted to Dr. Charles E. Jones for elucidating this point.

⁷ "The Revivalist Chapel," *Revivalist* (Jan. 25, 1900), 11. Reflecting the importance of the book of Acts as a paradigm for present-day doctrine and practice, one of the first subjects taught was "The Gospel as Taught in the Acts of the Apostles."

⁸ Ibid. Especially noteworthy, "a number of ministers . . . received the baptism with the Holy Ghost, which . . . transformed them into flames of fire."

⁹ "Pray," *Revivalist* (June 14, 1900), 15.

¹⁰ "Worthy of God," *Revivalist* (June 21, 1900), 4.

¹¹ Ibid and "The Location," *Revivalist* (June 21, 1900), 4.

¹² Geoffrey J. Giglierano, Deborah A. Overmyer, with Frederick L. Propas *The Bicentennial Guide to Greater Cincinnati: A Portrait of Two Hundred Years* (Cincinnati: The Cincinnati Historical Society, 1988), 196. In 1909, the Cincinnati Park Board purchased two acres at this location (on the southwest corner of Young and Ringgold Streets) and developed a park named for Filson, who had died shortly after his surveying expedition to the Cincinnati area (which he had named Losantiville). A swimming pool was built in the park shortly after its creation in 1909, no doubt to the consternation of GBS residents who opposed the immodesty associated with "mixed bathing." However, the ball field and gym equipment that were added later have served several generations of GBSers, proving especially beneficial before the completion of the gymnasium in the Miller-Deets Student Center.

¹³ "The Location," *Revivalist* (June 21, 1900), 4. The mansion was part of the "old Peebles property" while the wood structure was on "the Morris homestead" ("School for Bible Study," *Cincinnati Post* (August 1, 1900), 6).

¹⁴ Ibid.

¹⁵ *God's Bible School Catalogue 1931-1932*, 29.

¹⁶ "The Location," *Revivalist* (June 21, 1900), 4; and Hills, 204.

¹⁷ "Wild Scenes in the Tabernacle," *Cincinnati Enquirer* (July 5, 1901), 10.

¹⁸ Hills, 205-206. See also "God's Bible-School and Missionary-Training Home," *Revivalist* (July 12, 1900), 2.

¹⁹ Ibid.

²⁰ Day, 33. Knapp explained the advantage of this move in "Change of Address," *Revivalist* (August 9, 1900), 3.

²¹ Fittingly, the first passage was "Have faith in God." Knapp explained that by paying off the debt within two years, the school would be given a $500 discount. In addition, by early payment, they could avoid paying much of the five percent interest that began on August 1, 1900. Day, 32 and "God's Bible-School and Missionary Training Home," *Revivalist* (Sept. 27, 1900), 14.

²² Hills, 206.

²³ "School for Bible Study," *Cincinnati Post* (Aug. 1, 1900), 6.

²⁴ M. W. Knapp, *Back to the Bible; or, Pentecostal Training* (Cincinnati: M. W. Knapp, 1900), 36.

²⁵ Day, 33.

²⁶ Hills, 206. Day (33) states that "by August of 1900, inquiries concerning the Bible School had been received from twenty different states and two provinces of Canada." By the end of November, almost two hundred inquiries had been received (39).

²⁷ Hills, 206.

²⁸ Day, 40. Day notes that "later, a second story was added above the dining room for school offices."

²⁹ Beatrice Finney, "A Blessing," *Revivalist* (March 7, 1901), 4.

³⁰ "To Prospective Students of God's Bible-School," *Revivalist* (Feb. 20, 1902), 6.

³¹ Knapp, *Back to the Bible*, 13.

³² Ibid, 21. While admitting that "a secular system of education may be needful for people of secular pursuits," Knapp contended that "God has a better course for those who will devote all their time and energies to Him for the interests of His kingdom" (16).

³³ Ibid, 14-15. Knapp's readers were encouraged to dispose of the "chaff" of worldly education that they might be partakers of spiritual "wheat": "Men are usually so full of the first that they elide the second. While those who have the second may utilize the first, if in their possession, yet they have succeeded, and are succeeding, and will succeed without them. The first is simply chaff compared to the wheat of Bible lore and spiritual equipment" ("Chaff and Wheat," *Revivalist* (June 28, 1900), 1).

Knapp also appropriated the image of a bird's useless tail to represent collegiate education in describing the "full salvation bird": "Its right wing is entire consecration and its left wing is complete trust in a complete Savior, while 'mental culture' is simply its tail. As a bird can live, fly and be happy without any tail at all, so if God directs can the full salvation bird without any college drill at all" ("That Full Salvation Bird," *Revivalist* (Sept. 1890), 2).

See "Pentecostal Culture," *Revivalist* (Sept. 20, 1900), 14, and "Reasons Why A College Diploma Should Not Be Made A Condition of Entrance to the Christian Ministry," *Revivalist* (July 4, 1901), 8, in which Knapp provides twenty-two objections including, "The brightest, highest-cultured intellect, if unbaptized with the Holy Ghost, is as powerless in the Christian ministry as a Demosthenes who could not swim would be to rescue men who are drowning. The devil can outwit the mightiest human powers. Only Pentecostal dynamite can dislodge him."

³⁴ Ibid, 16. For example, Knapp compared the vanity of secular education to the ostentation of extravagant dress:

The gospel of Jesus is simple, natural, and beautiful. It banishes all extravagances of dress, speech, and life. Its principles applied to spiritual and intellectual training are the same as when applied to other things. *Higher* music, *higher* mathematics, and other similar studies which encumber many college curriculums, are usually to the Christian worker what jewelry, feathers, and flowers are to the body: needless . . . and totally destitute of Scripture warrant" (original emphasis).

[35] "Appalling Apostasy," *Revivalist* (Feb. 22, 1900), 8. For Knapp, such substitution was nothing short of idolatry, inducing him to compare it with Israel's worship of the golden calf:

Israel provoked the judgment of Jehovah by substituting the 'golden calf' for the true God.

Popular Christianity, with its false preachers, to-day are guilty of a greater blasphemy, in seeking to substitute the golden god of culture in the place of the Holy Ghost. This awful desecration is advertised in the following ways:

Money for universities is magnified above money for evangelizing.

A college diploma is urged above the Pentecostal baptism.

The "elevation of humanity" is emphasized above the salvation of humanity.

Loyalty to the Church and its carnal requirements, above loyalty to Jesus and His commandments.

And, worst of all, "My people love to have it so," and those who loyally protest are counted as cranks and pessimists ("The Golden Calf," *Revivalist* (March 8, 1900), 8).

[36] "God's Bible-School," *Revivalist* (Aug. 30, 1900), 15.

[37] The term "anti-intellectualism" has been used to describe the belief that, in most cases, deep spirituality and higher education are mutually exclusive. Several scholars, notably Mark Noll in his *The Scandal of the Evangelical Mind* (Grand Rapids: Eerdmans, 1994), have followed the lead of Richard Hofstadter's *Anti-intellectualism in American Life* (New York: Vintage, 1962) which "identified 'the evangelical spirit' as one of the prime sources of American anti-intellectualism" (Noll, 11). Noll specifically charges the Pentecostal and Holiness traditions with being major sources of evangelical anti-intellectualism, and of fostering the idea that "in order to be spiritual, one must no longer pay attention to the world" (Noll, 123). Although Noll expresses appreciation for the holiness movement emphasis on "the practical presence of God" as "an essentially Christian goal," he faults what he perceives as the separation of saintliness and scholarship, quoting with approval Martin Lloyd-Jones' indictment of the British Keswick movement: "If you want to be holy and righteous, we are told, the intellect is dangerous and it is thought generally unlikely that a good theologian is likely to be a holy person . . . If you teach that sanctification consists of 'letting go' and letting the Holy Spirit do all the work, then don't blame me if you have no scholars!" (124)

While some Wesleyan scholars have challenged Noll's criticism (See David Bundy, Henry Knight, and William Kostlevy, "Reflections on Mark Noll's *The Scandal of the*

Evangelical Mind (1994)," *WTJ* 32 no. 1 (Spring 1997), 157-192), others, including Barry Callen, editor of the *Wesleyan Theological Journal*, have echoed his indictment, suggesting that Holiness anti-intellectualism "led to a devaluing of art, literature, science, and general culture. Christians by the thousands had virtually retired from the mainstream of society and instead had placed their faith squarely in the authority of their personal experiences with Christ" (Callen, *Guide of Soul and Mind: The Story of Anderson University* (Anderson, IN: Anderson University and Warner Press, 1992), 14).

[38] John A. Morrison quoted in Callen, *Guide*, 7.

[39] "God's Bible-School and Missionary Training-Home," *Revivalist* (June 27, 1900), 3. For a student's perspective highlighting the emphasis on holiness experience, see D. T. Grant, "In God's Bible School: From a Student," *Revivalist* (Dec. 5, 1901), 15.

[40] As early as 1893, Knapp had used a collegiate analogy for this experience, insisting that the "Pentecostal diploma" was the one essential requirement for effective soul-winners:

> There is a diploma that is an indispensable requisite to the most successful Christian life and work . . . Only one college can grant it . . . The founders of the college, where it may be had, hold and disseminate radical holiness views . . . What is the name of the college? Its name is "The College of Pentecostal Power."
>
> Where is it located? Wherever God is and a person who meets the conditions of receiving a diploma.
>
> What are these conditions? Complete devotement to God and present appropriating faith for the baptism of the Holy Ghost.
>
> What are the results? A perpetual revival in the hearts of all who have it, which spreads like a forest fire to the hearts of others; a joyous, fruitful Christian life; a triumphant entrance into heaven, and experiences too rich for present human expression, multiplying throughout eternity ("An Indispensable Diploma," *Revivalist* (Jan. 1893), 1).

[41] Knapp, *Back to the Bible*, 15.

[42] Ibid, 14.

[43] "Deplorable Ignorance," *Revivalist* (June 21, 1900), 2. Knapp believed that many of the objections proposed by antagonists of radical holiness sprang "largely from . . . ignorance of the Word of God."

[44] "Scripture Knowledge Essential to Revival Victory," *Revivalist* (July 5, 1900), 1. Knapp believed that just as Cornelius and his household received the baptism with the Holy Ghost when as "many as heard the Word believed," so revival in the twentieth century "hinged on the proclamation and reception of the word of God." He thus declared that "if believers would have primitive power, there must be a return to primitive ministry of the Word of God and a proclamation of its truths." He even cautioned that the popular holiness practice of encouraging individual testimonials to God's grace had encroached on the place of the Bible in some holiness circles and decried this "tendency to substitute exhortation and testimony in the place of the word of God" writing that

they could no more substitute for the "Word of God itself . . . than a bullet on the battle-field can take the place of the Constitution of the nation."

⁴⁵ "Deplorable Ignorance," *Revivalist* (June 21, 1900), 2. Similarly, Knapp wrote that at GBS the Bible would be "honored as the great Constitution of God's Kingdom, the knowledge of which is essential to intelligent citizenship therein: 'That the man of God may be thoroughly furnished unto all good works'" ("God's Bible-school and Missionary Training-Home," *Revivalist* (July 5, 1900), 1). He contended that "the absolute necessity of the Christian worker being familiar with the Word of God" was derived from its importance for conversion (I Peter 1:23), sanctification (John 17:17), and Christian fruitfulness (Matthew 13:23), its place as the "great central theme of all gospel-preaching and testimony" (Acts 8:25), and its role as the "Divinely-ordained instrument for the upbuilding of God's people" (Acts 20:32)--in short, its significance for Christian experience (Knapp, *Back to the Bible*, 9-10).

⁴⁶ Beatrice M. Finney, "A Blessing," *Revivalist* (March 7, 1901), 4.

⁴⁷ Other textbooks included Smith's *Old and New Testament History*, D'Aubigne's *History of the Reformation*, and *Binney's Theological Compend*.

⁴⁸ Knapp, *Back to the Bible*, 34.

⁴⁹ Ibid, 35.

⁵⁰ Stephen J. Lennox, "Biblical Interpretation in the American Holiness Movement: 1875-1920," *WTJ* Vol. 33 No. 1 (Spring 1998), 19, 27. Lennox sharply criticizes such holiness movement leaders as Godbey for departing from Wesley by imposing a more restrictive view of Christian experience on biblical interpretation. That is, Wesley agreed with Godbey in considering "Christian experience the proper stance for accurate biblical interpretation." However, holiness interpreters often limited Christian experience to "entire sanctification, narrowly defined in terms of what it was, how it was received, and what it would produce." For more extensive critique, see also his dissertation: Stephen J. Lennox, *Biblical Interpretation in the American Holiness Movement: 1875-1920* (Ph. D. diss., Drew University, 1992).

Another study which evaluates the fidelity of the holiness movement to Wesley's theological position (in regard to sanctification) is Bruce E. Moyer, *The Doctrine of Christian Perfection: A Comparative Study of John Wesley and the Modern American Holiness Movement* (Ph. D. diss., Marquette University, 1992). Moyer concludes that, although minor deviations from Wesley's teaching on Christian perfection have appeared in the American holiness movement, the movement has remained faithful to the essence of his position.

⁵¹ Knapp, *Back to the Bible*, 34. Knapp explained that "the birth of the Spirit and the baptism with the Spirit are essential to knowing the Word. It is only those who 'do God's will' who shall 'know His doctrine' (John 7:17)." Oswald Chambers also embraced this position, opening his *Studies in the Sermon on the Mount* with the observation that, "in order to understand the Sermon on the Mount, it is necessary to have the mind of its preacher, and this knowledge can be gained by anyone who will receive the Holy Spirit (see Luke 11:13; John 20:22; Acts 19:2). The Holy Spirit alone can expound the teachings of Jesus Christ" (Grand Rapids: Discovery House Publishers, 1995), 9.

For a contemporary Holiness appraisal of the role of the Holy Spirit in Bible interpretation, see Richard S. Taylor, "The Hermeneutical Objective" in *Hearing God's*

Voice: Biblical Authority and Christian Faith (Salem, OH: Schmul, 2000), 52-53. Taylor contends that "men without the Spirit can never become accurate biblical interpreters, for only Spirit-taught persons will have eyes to perceive spiritual meanings (2 Peter 1:20-21)." Of course, this falls short of saying a person must be entirely sanctified to accurately interpret the Bible. However, it reflects the continued significance of Spirit-guided interpretation for the holiness movement in the twentieth century.

[52] Lennox, "Biblical Interpretation," 27. Barry Hamilton has also observed the prominence of entire sanctification in Godbey's hermeneutic, and for the entire preaching exercise, as well: "According to Godbey, the preeminent qualification for preaching is the experience of entire sanctification. His prooftext for this assertion is Hebrews 1:7, 'He maketh his ministers a flame of fire.' This qualification relieves the minister from the need for a 'collegiate education, extensive travel, nor any other thing.' Godbey acknowledges the potential usefulness of education and other cultural attainments, but declares them to be 'positive hindrances' when they become substitutes for the experience of entire sanctification" (Barry W. Hamilton, "Preaching the 'Narrow Way': William B. Godbey's Homiletical Agenda for the Early Holiness Movement," *MH* Vol. 38 No. 1 (Oct. 1999), 48). Godbey testified of the impact of entire sanctification on his own preaching and Bible intepretation: "Then and there God radically revolutionized my ministerial character, burning up all my sectarian idols and manufactured sermons, which I had made by the power of my intellect and education, as I knew nothing about 'preaching with the Holy Ghost sent down from Heaven'" (I Pet. 1:12) (W. B. Godbey, *Paganization of the American Church* (Cincinnati: Revivalist, 1909), 41).

[53] Knapp, *Lightning Bolts from Pentecostal Skies*, 13 (original emphasis). For earlier emphasis on the centrality of holiness in Scripture, see Jesse T. Peck, *The Central Idea of Christianity* (1856; Reprint, Salem, OH: Schmul, 1999).

[54] W. B. Godbey, *Holiness or Hell?* (Louisville: The Pentecostal Publishing Co., 1899), 5. Godbey claimed that only one scripture was needed to "prove" this assertion, Hebrews 12:14. See the discussion of the radical holiness tendency to narrowly describe the experience of entire sanctification in stereotypical fashion, and impose this reading of the experience on Scripture, in Al Truesdale, "Reification of the Experience of Entire Sanctification in the American Holiness Movement," *WTJ* Vol. 31 No. 2 (Fall 1996), 95-119. Holiness proponents critiqued here include H. C. Morrison, Beverly Carradine, M. W. Knapp, W. B. Godbey, E. E. Shelhamer, and Phoebe Palmer. Truesdale quotes Godbey's claim in his *Christian Perfection* that "every New Testament writer is a perfectionist. The Bible is perfectionism" (109).

[55] Hamilton, "Preaching in the 'Narrow Way,'" 49.

[56] Other popular authors exploring the Egypt-to-Canaan analogy included Beverly Carradine in *Beulah Land* (1904; Reprint, Salem, OH: Allegheny Publications, 1998) and Seth Rees in *The Ideal Pentecostal Church* (Cincinnati: Revivalist, 1897), 57-66 (cc. 17-19). A more recent treatment is found in E. W. Black, *Living Messages from the Canaan Journey* (N. P.: n. p., 1948) with an Introduction by holiness scholar J. A. Huffman.

In addition to this analogy, holiness advocates found symbols of Christian development in various cities, rivers, and mountains. For example, such evangelists as Godbey and "Bud" Robinson found particular edification in the study of biblical mountains. Robinson asserted that "the great events of the Bible took place on the mountains" and that "the meaning of these great events is that you and I are to have a mountain top experience" (*A Pitcher of Cream* (1906; Reprint, Salem, OH: Schmul, 1996), 51) giving the theme a book-length treatment in his *Mountain Peaks of the Bible* (1913; Reprint, Salem, OH: Schmul, 1994). Godbey utilized the mountain analogy to characterize his preaching, noting that he would always start a meeting with the Sinai Gospel--what he described as "'hellfire-and-damnation' preaching which aimed to kindle conviction of sin in unbelievers" (Hamilton, "Preaching in the 'Narrow Way,'" 49). He then moved to the Calvary Gospel--calculated to lead sinners to conversion, from thence to Mount Zion, where he delivered the Pentecost Gospel--encouraging believers to be sanctified, and only then would he proceed to expound the promise of glorification--symbolized by the Mount of Transfiguration (W. B. Godbey, *Salvation and Glory* Compiled by Roger G. Price and Wallace Thornton, Jr. (Reprint of *Plan of Salvation*, n. d. and *Glorification*, 1902; Salem, OH: Schmul, 2000), 30-81). J. B. Chapman explains that the "'mountaintop experience' is the experience of Bible holiness. The figure pictures one who has by grace arisen from the plains of the justified life to the holy mount of entire sanctification" (J. B. Chapman, *The Terminology of Holiness* rev. ed. (Kansas City, MO: Beacon Hill Press of Kansas City, 1968), 86).

[57] These appear in R. E. McNeill, J. F. Knapp, and M. G. Standley, Editors, *Praise of His Glory Songs* (Cincinnati: Revivalist, 1922), numbers 42, 44, and 114 respectively. See Jones, *Perfectionist Persuasion*, c. 5, 35-46 for an enlightening discussion of the Egypt-to-Canaan theme's occurrence in holiness hymnody.

[58] "Bible-School Opening Testimonies," *Revivalist* (Oct. 10, 1901), 4. Both Godbey and Knapp had sermons published under the same title as Knapp's book *Out of Egypt Into Canaan*. Godbey's sermon appears in *Lightning From the Past*. Knapp's sermon, preached at Salvation Park Camp Meeting in 1898 appears in the first issue of *Electric Shocks from Pentecostal Batteries* (72-84).

[59] See Godbey's *Commentary on the New Testament* Vol. 2. (Cincinnati: M. W. Knapp, 1897), 46-60. For more recent examples of writers associated with GBS who have intepreted this passage to teach entire sanctification, see T. M. Anderson, *The Truth for the Times* Vol. 1 (N. P.: n. p., n. d.), 91-121, and Marlin R. Hotle, *Points to Ponder from Hebrews* (Salem, OH: Schmul, 1999), 27-30. See also George Allen Turner, *The New and Living Way* (Salem, OH: Schmul, 1992), 79.

Knapp also defended his use of typology on the title page of *Out of Egypt Into Canaan* by quoting Romans 15:4, "For whatsoever things were written aforetime were written for our learning, that we through patience and comfort of the Scriptures might have hope." Similarly, in his sermon on the subject he cited I Corinthians 10:11, "All these things happened unto them for ensamples: and they are written for our admonition." He then opined, "They are recorded here for us. They are put in the believer's text-book, and we are to learn the lessons . . . Holy Ghost men brought these pictures out and painted them and hung them in the gallery of the Word for us to learn from them and profit by them . . ." (Knapp, *Electric Shocks*, 73).

[60] L. Milton Williams, *Jacob the Heelgrasper or Some of God's Pictures of the Carnal Mind* (Oskaloosa, IO: L. Milton Williams, 1907). In his most popular book, *Where*

Art Thou? Or Spiritual Earthquakes for Saints and Sinners (Cincinnati: Revivalist, 1905), Williams allegorized such biblical narratives as the treachery of Cain and the resurrection of Lazarus to expound holiness teachings. See also his *Walking Before God or Saved Through Obedience* Vol. 2 of Old Testament Characters (Cincinnati: Revivalist, n. d.) in which he focuses on Hezekiah and Abraham.

[61] B. S. Taylor, *Bible Readings and Spiritual Essays* Vol. 3 *The Gibeonites. The Canaanites. Death, Hell, and Judgment* (Cincinnati: Rev. M. W. Knapp, n. d.).

[62] Beverly Carradine, *The Second Blessing in Symbol* (1893; Reprint, Copper Hill, VA: K. & L. Bookroom, n. d.).

[63] See especially Geo. D. Watson, *Love Abounding and Other Expositions on the Spiritual Life* (1891; Reprint, Cincinnati: Revivalist, n. d.) and *God's First Words* (Cincinnati: Revivalist, n. d.), as well as *Coals of Fire: Being Expositions of Scripture on the Doctrine, Experience, and Practice of Christian Holiness.* (1886; Reprint, Salem, OH: Schmul, 1976). See also G. D. Watson, *The Seven Overcomeths* (1889; Reprint, Jamestown, NC: Newby Book Room, n. d.) for an allegorical interpretation of the Book of Revelation in which entire sanctification is the focus and G. D. Watson *Steps to the Throne* (1898; Reprint, Hampton, TN: Harvey and Tait, 1980) for an interpretation of the same in which premillennialism is the object. Lennox has noted the similarity of logic used in interpreting Scripture to support the doctrine of entire sanctification and the doctrine of a premillennial return of Christ (Stephen J. Lennox, "The Eschatology of George D. Watson," *WTJ* Vol. 29 Nos. 1 and 2 (Spring-Fall 1994), 116-117). For instance, although Watson's friend W. B. Godbey found David's reign to symbolize regeneration while "Solomon symbolizes the sanctified experience" (*Thirty-five Old Testament Biographies* (n. d., Reprint; Salem, OH: Allegheny Publications, 1993), 168), Watson used the two kings to represent dispensational periods: "the reign of David was a type of Christ in the suffering dispensation of the church age. Then the reign of King Solomon was a type of the reign of Christ in the Millennium" (Lennox, 116).

[64] William E. McCumber, *Holiness Preachers and Preaching* Vol. 5 *Great Holiness Classics* (Kansas City, MO: Beacon Hill Press of Kansas City, 1989), 206. Even so, McCumber concludes that "the interpretation was generally sound."

[65] Godbey, *Old Testament Biographies*, 284-285. He characterized Eliphaz, Bildad, and Zophar as "leading preachers in the Uz conference" who "proceeded to castigate [Job] for the sin of presumption in professing Christian perfection." The resultant holiness debate between Job and his friends raged on until "God came in the whirlwind and took the debate into hand and turned it into a holiness meeting, calling those three big anti-holiness preachers to the altar while Job prayed for them . . . Job is down by them on his knees praying for them importunately. And Elihu, shouting jubilantly, patting them on the head and saying, "Go for it, I got it that way."

Bud Robinson evidently adopted Godbey's interpretation of Job, further popularizing it in his *Sunshine and Smiles: Life Story, Flash Lights, Sayings and Sermons* (1903; Revised, Shoals, IN: Old Paths Tract Society, 1986), 63.

Godbey also saw Job's account as illustrative of entire sanctification more generally. He asserted that "in the book of Job, the Christian learns the divine philosophy of the second death. This is the crucial test of the Sanctified. Those who stumble here will make ship-wreck. Those who survive it will shine as the stars forever and ever" (*Holy Land*).

⁶⁶ Lennox, "Biblical Interpretation," 28. Godbey's statement was made in *Holiness or Hell*, 139-140. Citing Carradine, Godbey, and Watson, Lennox summarizes the practice:

> They found holiness proof-texts in the prohibition of wearing a garment mixed with wool and linen, the process of cleansing the leper, and many other places . . . Wherever Scripture spoke of two of anything or when something occurred twice, this was seen to teach a second definite work of grace. Passages like the second cleansing of the temple by Jesus, the two sisters of Lazarus, the two elements which flowed from Christ's side, and the double touch on the eyes of the blind man were all treated as holiness texts.

⁶⁷ This commendation was extended to G. D. Watson by William McDonald in the Introduction to Watson's *Coals of Fire*, 3. McDonald observed that "Christians are beginning to believe that the subject [of entire sanctification] is webbing all through Revelation. It is the great truth which glows upon every page of the Holy Book; the great law of all worlds and all ages,--'Thou shalt love the Lord thy God with all thy heart.'"

⁶⁸ At this point it is appropriate to observe that one may agree wholeheartedly with the basic tenets of holiness doctrine, yet disagree with specific incidents of allegorizing by some of its proponents. Many holiness scholars would argue that the holiness position could be substantiated easily without resorting to typology/allegory, agreeing with Dunning that "it needs to be emphasized that scriptural support is not lacking for the authentic holiness message" (H. Ray Dunning, "Christian Perfection: Toward a New Paradigm," *WTJ* 33 no. 1 (Spring 1998), 155). In fact, none of the "thirty texts of Wesley" on which he primarily "based his teaching of entire sanctification" lent themselves to allegory, with only one coming from the Old Testament (Ezekiel 36:25, 26, 29). See *The Wesley Bible: New King James Version: A Personal Study Bible For Holy Living*. Albert F. Harper, General Ed. (Nashville: Thomas Nelson, 1990), 1951-1952.

For further discussion of holiness allegorization, see Charles Edwin Jones, "Beulah Land and the Upper Room: Reclaiming the Text in Turn-of-the-Century Holiness and Pentecostal Spirituality," *MH* vol. 32 no. 4 (July 1994), 250-259; and "Symbol and Sign in Methodist Holiness and Pentecostal Spirituality," in Timothy Miller, ed. *America's Alternative Religions* (Albany, NY: State University of New York, 1995), 23-32. See also Richard S. Taylor, *Preaching Holiness Today* (Kansas City, MO: Beacon Hill Press of Kansas City, 1968) in which Taylor warns of the dangers of reading "spiritual or allegorical meaning into the *events of biblical history*" (104—original emphasis). On the other hand, Taylor encourages the responsible use of "holy history" as a subject for typology (156-160).

⁶⁹ Most of Lennox' criticism of American holiness biblical interpretation is based on its "departure" from Wesley's use of the quadrilateral (Scripture, tradition, rea-

son, and experience) in interpreting Scripture. However, much current dialogue concerning the quadrilateral involves an attempt to re-fashion the quadrilateral for contemporary hermeneutics, thus often assuming shapes quite different from its use in early Methodism. Abraham has shown that much of the current debate over the quadrilateral is as much over Outler's use of the device as Wesley's. "The debate involves the matter of receiving and evaluating the legacy of Albert Outler in Wesley Studies" (William J. Abraham, "Keeping Up With Jones on John Wesley's Conception and Use of Scripture," *WTJ* 33 No. 1 (Spring 1998), 5-13. For Outler's views, see *Essays of Albert C. Outler: The Wesleyan Theological Heritage* Ed. by Thomas C. Oden and Leicester R. Longden (Grand Rapids: Zondervan, 1991) and Albert C. Outler, "The Wesleyan Quadrilateral--In John Wesley," *WTJ* 20 No. 1 (Spring 1985), 7-18. Among the extensive literature dealing with the quadrilateral, see other articles in the same volume of the *Wesleyan Theological Journal*, as well as W. Stephen Gunter, Scott J. Jones, et. al. *Wesley and the Quadrilateral: Renewing the Conversation* (Nashville: Abingdon, 1997), Randy L. Maddox, *Responsible Grace: John Wesley's Practical Theology* (Nashville: Kingswood Books, 1994), Thomas C. Oden, *John Wesley's Scriptural Christianity: A Plain Exposition of His Teaching on Christian Doctrine* (Grand Rapids: Zondervan, 1994), and Donald A. D. Thorsen, *The Wesleyan Quadrilateral: Scripture, Reason, and Experience as a Model of Evangelical Theology* (Nappanee, IN: Francis Asbury Press, 1997).

[70] I am indebted to William Kostlevy for clarifying this point. It is supported by Knapp's quotation of G. D. Watson in *Impressions* (54): "The Holy Ghost never guides us contrary to the Word. The Word never guides us contrary to Providence, and Providence does not guide us contrary to the Word or Spirit. So, these three elements of divine guidance are always harmonious."

[71] For a typical lesson in technological metaphor, see Rev. C. E. Cowman, "Lessons from the Telegraph," *Revivalist* (March 14, 1901), 3.

Many transportation analogies involved the motif of the journey to heaven, which obviously invited comparison with the travels of holiness itinerants. Nautical themes were common, with Godbey finding "crossing the ocean like entire sanctification" (*Holy Land*, 8). Charles and Lettie Cowman edified *Revivalist* readers with spiritual insights inspired by their journey to Japan, observing such lessons in everything from the weather to flying fish ("From Brother and Sister Cowman," *Revivalist* (April 4, 1901), 9). Taking nautical analogies even further, G. D. Watson devoted an entire book to exploring spiritual truths inspired by a sea voyage and the types of ships observed therein, vividly depicting "row boat" Christians, "Steamboat" Christians, etc. (*Spiritual Ships: An Allegory of Religious Characters and Experiences* (1902; Reprint, Salem, OH: Schmul, 1996)).

The railroad's dramatic expansion (over 600% in the fifty years after the Civil War) and clergy passes made it the transportation of choice for holiness revivalists. In addition to offering a convenient analogy for Pentecostal power, the railroad captured Knapp's interest due to his evangelistic zeal for railroad travelers and workers. He thus experimented with a "railroad edition" of *The Revivalist* in 1896, drawing lessons from railroad work. See "Railroad Edition," "Another Railroad Edition," and "Especial Attention," *Revivalist* (April 1896), 1. Although no future railroad editions appeared, the metaphor resurfaced frequently, often blended with Canaan imagery, as in Knapp's *Out of Egypt into Canaan*, where people in various stages of the journey were symbolized by train engines in various situations (133-134).

The theme was reflected in testimonies in *The Revivalist* (for example, "I Have My Ticket," (Oct. 25, 1900), 15, and "Revival Prayer Answered," (April 1896), 6). It lent itself to graphic charts such as "The Two Railroads Into Eternity" which illustrated one of Knapp's revival handbills (See "Revival Hand Bills," *Revivalist* (Jan. 1892), 3 and a copy of the diagram in *The Revivalist* (Aug. 10, 1899), 15). It also appeared in such holiness songs as "The Glory-Land Train," "Get a Transfer," and "The Great Excursion" (numbers 10, 89, and 13 respectively in McNeill, et. al., *Praise of His Glory Songs*).

On the ironic melding of industrial metaphor, particularly the railroad, with the older pilgrim motif, see Charles Edwin Jones, "The Railroad to Heaven," *North Dakota Quarterly* Vol. 40 (Aug. 1972), 69-72. On the impact of the railroad, both as a tool for transportation and as an allegorical device, also see Daniel Woods, *"Spiritual Railroading": Trains as Metaphor and Reality in the Holiness and Pentecostal Movements*, Paper Presented to the Joint Meeting of the Wesleyan Theological Society and the Society for Pentecostal Studies, Asbury Theological Seminary, Wilmore, Kentucky, March 21, 2003.

[72] For example, see "The Greatest Revival Hindrance," *Revivalist* (Jan. 11, 1900), 1. Dr. Godbey gave exegetical support for using dynamite as a metaphor from the Greek, noting that the word for "power" in Acts 1:8 was *dunamis* from which the English word "dynamite" is derived. He thus rendered the "literal reading" of Acts 1:8 to be, "You shall receive dynamite of the Holy Ghost having come on you." He then expounded, "If you will receive the Holy Ghost as a personal, indwelling Sanctifier and abiding Comforter, He will supply you with all the dynamite you need to blow all sin out of you and to qualify you to blow up the Devil's kingdom wherever you go, and enjoy an everlasting victory in your heart and life" (*Commentary on the New Testament Vol. V. Acts-Romans: Paul, The Champion Theologian* (Cincinnati: Revivalist Office, 1899), 12-13). See also Seth C. Rees, *Ideal Pentecostal Church*, 16 and Stephens, 113.

[73] Oswald Chambers, "Spirit-Baptized Humanity. No. 2," *Revivalist* (Oct. 7, 1909), 2-3. Chambers also expounded the instantaneous nature of holiness by describing electricity as "fire and force, working instantaneously."

[74] "The Greatest Revival Hindrance," 1.

[75] Knapp contended that "one of the sure signs of the alarming apostasy that is upon the Churches and of the holiness people falling from their first love is the publication and reading of carnal fiction" ("Facts or Fiction," *Revivalist* (Dec. 27, 1900), 2). He further lamented, "We are deeply pained to see some holiness writers and publishers becoming parties to this wrong . . ." but qualified his position by adding, "we do not refer to allegories like "Pilgrim's Progress," and a very few works which belong to that class, but to fictitious stories . . . which are being imported into Christian homes under the sheepskin of a profession of religion and sometimes of holiness teaching" ("Craze for Fiction," *Revivalist* (May 10, 1900), 8).

Godbey similarly encouraged *Revivalist* readers to "make kindling wood out of every" worldly novel they could, but commended Bunyan's works as ranking "second only to the Bible" and insisted "that all who desire the good of their souls [should] read them, and re-read them, learning the grand truths, so wonderfully revealed to that eminent prophet by the Holy Ghost" ("Question-Drawer," *Revivalist* (April 24, 1900), 12). He further opined that "Bunyan's writings are so ample that they are enough to satisfy all our predilections for fiction." If not, Revivalist publications could fill the gap. For instance, A. M. Hills suggested that Godbey's *Commentary* was "as interesting as a novel" ("From Pentecostal Preachers," *Revivalist* (July 5, 1900), 15.).

[76] See Jones, *Perfectionist Persuasion*, 35, on the connections made between "the pilgrimage of Bunyan's Christian and the Exodus . . . and between the experience of entire sanctification or perfect love and the believer's residence in the Promised Land ..." Holiness writers recognized Bunyan as the author who popularized "Beulah Land" as "a figurative term for the sanctified estate" (Chapman, *Terminology*, 85). Chapman emphasizes that Bunyan located Beulah Land "this side the River of Death" but far beyond "Doubting Castle and the Slough of Despond," a point intended to support the Wesleyan emphasis of entire sanctification attainable in this life. The same point is emphasized in "Beulah Land," *Revivalist* (Nov. 9, 1899), 3.

[77] See "The Revival at Tough Town: An Allegory," (July 1890), 3; "Opposed to the Camp-Meeting," (May 10, 1900), 7, and "Tragedy of the Easter Bonnet," (April 12, 1900), 8. Also, note the graphic illustration in *Lightning Bolts*, 189, that depicts the fate of Dr. Compromise, Dr. Formality, Dr. Culture, and Dr. Fearful and Knapp's cartoon, "Fallen Holiness and the World: Married at Last," *Revivalist* (Feb. 7, 1901), 8.

[78] Following this approach, holiness teachers, including Godbey, Steele and Joseph H. Smith, traced a "slender line of piety" throughout history, identifying such groups as the Lollards, Mystics, and Waldensians as the "real apostolic succession" which championed "the conscious incoming of the Paraclete into the heart" (Lennox "Biblical Interpretation," 25, and Daniel Steele, *Milestone Papers: Doctrinal, Ethical, and Experimental, on Christian Progress* (1876. Reprint, Salem, OH: Schmul, 1984), 154-155. See also, Joseph H. Smith, "The Remnant--Isaiah 1:9," *Revivalist* (May 31-June 7, 1928), 2). Negatively, church history became the story of the persecution of this remnant by the worldly-compromised church (For example, see David Budensiek, *Lessons on Apostasy from Church History* (Salem, OH: Salem Bible College, n. d.).

[79] Abbie Morrow, Ed. *Sweet Smelling Myrrh; The Autobiography of Madame Guyon* (Cincinnati: Revivalist, 1898) and John C. Patty, *Life of Lucius Bunyan Compton: The Mountaineer Evangelist* (Cincinnati: Revivalist Press, 1914). In addition to the profusion of individual biographies, an abundance of books compiling short testimonies/biographies illustrating holiness experience has been published throughout the century, indicating the continued popularity of the genre. For example, see J. O. McClurkan, *Chosen Vessels: Twenty-one Biographical Sketches of Men and Women, most of whom have been used of God in Pioneering Some Great Pentecostal Movement* (1901; Reprint, Salem, OH: The Allegheny Wesleyan Methodist Connection, 1978); Clara McLeister, *Men and Women of Deep Piety* Ed. E. E. Shelhamer (1920; Reprint, Salem, OH: Allegheny Publications, n. d.); Anita K. Brechbill, *20th Century Spiritual Giants* Vol. 1 (Salem, OH: Allegheny Publications, 1999); and numerous similar works published by Harvey Christian Publishers.

Lennox notes that "unlike Wesley who valued the church Fathers because they came so close to the fountain, holiness authors preferred more contemporary heroes such as Madame Guyon, John Bunyan, John Fletcher . . ." (Lennox, "Biblical Interpretation," 25). It is not surprising then that the first major church history book used at GBS was a history of the Reformation. Unfortunately, even then, the tendency to spiritualize source material meant that historical settings were often ignored or distorted, as when John Franklin Knapp took Martin Luther to represent the sanctified and Ulrich Zwingli to represent the carnal, totally disregarding the vital theological issues over which the two reformers contended ("Sanctification vs. Carnality," *Revivalist* (May 18, 1899), 2).

[80] M. W. Knapp, "Notes By the Way," *Revivalist* (Sept. 21, 1899), 2.

[81] Knapp's self-appropriated designation was "publisher of Pentecostal literature," an epithet underscored by such book titles as *Pentecostal Aggressiveness* (Knapp), *Pentecostal Light* (Hills), *Pentecostal Sanctification* (Keene) and *The Ideal Pentecostal Church* (Rees) (See the front cover of *Pentecostal Messengers*).

From 1901 to 1952, the masthead of each issue of the Revivalist informed readers that the paper was "Pentecostal," and its statement of purpose also described it as "Pentecostal and inculcative of Biblical principles, and upholding Bible practices" ("The Revivalist for 1901 Will Be," *Revivalist* (Jan. 3, 1901), 13 (original emphasis)). The words "Pentecostal," "Missionary," "Holiness," and "Unsectarian" were dropped from the masthead beginning with the April 3, 1952 masthead, likely not signaling a change in ideology so much as an attempt to provide a less "cluttered" look.

[82] Much of the debate has centered on how much (if any) credit can be given to John Wesley for this equation, how much should be attributed to other early Methodists such as Charles Wesley, John Fletcher, and Joseph Benson, and how much derives from American religious developments. For an award-winning treatment of the issue, see Laurence W. Wood, *The Meaning of Pentecost in Early Methodism*, (Lanham, MD: Scarecrow Press, 2002). In addition, see his *Pentecostal Grace* (Wilmore, KY: Francis Asbury Press, 1980) and important discussions in such books as Donald W. Dayton's *Theological Roots of Pentecostalism* (Peabody, MA: Hendrickson, 1987), Leo Cox's *John Wesley's Concept of Perfection*, and Kenneth Grider's *A Wesleyan-Holiness Theology*, as well as in numerous articles in the *Wesleyan Theological Journal*, a partial list of which indicates the complexity and endurance of the debate: Herbert McGonigle, "Pneumatological Nomenclature in Early Methodism," 8 (1973), 61-72; Donald W. Dayton, "Asa Mahan and the Development of American Holiness Theology," 9 (1974), 60-69; John A. Knight, "John Fletcher's Influence on the Development of Wesleyan Theology in America," 13 (1978), 13-33; Robert W. Lyon, "Baptism and Spirit-Baptism in the New Testament," 14 no. 1 (Spring 1979), 14-26; Alex R. G. Deasley, "Entire Sanctification and the Baptism with the Holy Spirit: Perspectives on the Biblical View of the Relationship," ibid, 27-44; J. Kenneth Grider, "Spirit-Baptism the Means of Entire Sanctification: A Response to the Lyon View," 14 no. 2 (Fall 1979), 31-50; Timothy L. Smith, "How John Fletcher Became the Theologian of Wesleyan Perfectionism, 1770-1776," 15 no. 1 (Spring 1980), 68-87; Victor P. Reasoner, "The American Holiness Movement's Paradigm Shift Concerning Holiness," 31 no. 2 (Fall 1996), 132-146; Laurence W. Wood, "Pentecostal Sanctification

in John Wesley and Early Methodism," 34 no. 1 (Spring 1999), 24-63; and Kenneth J. Collins, "The State of Wesley Studies in North America: A Theological Journey," 44 no. 2 (Fall 2009), 7-38. Several articles examine Wesleyan hymnody for clues to this problem, underscoring the significance of hymnody as theology in the Wesleyan tradition. Among these are Timothy L. Smith, "The Holy Spirit in the Hymns of the Wesleys," 16 no. 2 (Fall 1981), 20-47; T. Crichton Mitchell, "Response to Dr. Timothy Smith on the Wesley's Hymns," ibid, 48-57; and one by former GBS faculty member, Ken Bible, "The Wesleys' Hymns on Full Redemption and Pentecost: A Brief Comparison," 17 no. 2 (Fall 1982), 79-87.

[83] Charles Jones notes that "Knapp's book titles mark stages of his thought" in regard to this transition (*Perfectionist Persuasion*, 100). For instance, *Christ Crowned Within* depicts entire sanctification as the coronation of Christ "the Conqueror" who ascends "the heart-throne to cleanse from every rebellious impulse, glorify with His presence, and direct by His unerring counsels" (23). On the other hand, *Lightning Bolts from Pentecostal Skies* stresses "the purifying fire of the Holy Ghost [which] eliminates all the dross of inbred sin, expels the seed of sin's disease, ejects the 'old man' of indwelling evil, and fully sanctifies the soul" (16-17). Even though Knapp recognized the place of Jesus in administrating the baptism with the Holy Ghost (*Lightning Bolts*, 33), the emphasis on the role of the Spirit among radical holiness adherents was such that by 1900, one writer observed that "much has been said and written on the subject of the baptism of, or more properly in, the Holy Spirit; but how rarely is reference made to the Baptizer" ("Christ, the Baptizer with the Holy Ghost," *Revivalist* (Sept. 13, 1900), 2—reprinted from a periodical entitled, *Rest and Reaping*). See William Kostlevy's incisive analysis of *Lightning Bolts* in *Holy Jumpers*, 30-32.

[84] Donald Dayton notes that even moderate leaders associated with the NHA "fell in line" with this understanding of holiness (*Theological Roots*, 92). William Greathouse considers Daniel Steele, the scholarly champion of the NHA, to be "the first major Methodist theologian to embrace the Pentecostal position . . .," citing Steele's *Love Enthroned* to support his conclusion. Steele's *Gospel of the Comforter* did much to affirm the radical holiness contention that Pentecost was not an isolated, "solitary event," but "a perpetual dispensation of grace and power, . . . absolutely necessary to the perfection of the Christian evidences" ((1897, Reprint; Apollo, PA: The West Publishing Company, n. d.), 59).

However, Steele evidently held some reservations about using Pentecostal language, as Deasley has observed that Steele found "himself under repeated pressure to qualify" the equation of Spirit-baptism with entire sanctification. He notes Steele's assertion in *A Defense of Christian Perfection* that "none of our standard theologians ground the doctrine of Christian perfection" on the baptism with the Holy Spirit and "that the phrase 'baptism or fulness of the Spirit' may mean something less than entire sanctification" (Deasley, 28-29).

[85] Leon O. Hynson, c. 6 in "They Confessed Themselves Pilgrims, 1987-1930," in Wayne E. Caldwell, Ed. *Reformers and Revivalists: The History of the Wesleyan Church* (Indianapolis: Wesley Press, 1992), 227.

[86] A worldview or ideology refers here to a set of assumptions (usually unquestioned) that inform the choices one makes. The axioms contained in a worldview are

non-negotiable, providing the point of reference by which all other beliefs and opinions are evaluated. Most discussions of worldviews concentrate on the evangelical Christian worldview in contrast to non-Christian worldviews (e. g. James W. Sire, *The Universe Next Door, A Basic World View Catalog* (Downers Grove, IL: InterVarsity Press, 1988), a textbook used for several years at GBS). However, it is important to note that even the major worldviews can (and do) contain competing worldviews. Within Christianity, for example, a strong case can be made for viewing Pentecostalism and the Reformed tradition as competing worldviews.

[87] Richard T. Hughes, "Christian Primitivism as Perfectionism: From Anabaptists to Pentecostals," in Stanley M. Burgess, ed. *Reaching Beyond: Chapters in the History of Perfectionism* (Peabody, MA: Hendrickson Publishers, 1986), 243.

[88] "Open Letter to Congregationalists," *Revivalist* (May 18, 1899), 14. This assertion is repeated in "The Main Issue," *Revivalist* (May 3, 1900), 1. In the late 1890s, this "Spirit-baptized Congregationalist" still exercised considerable influence in his home denomination, drawing other Congregationalists to Knapp's Revivalist work through a series of meetings in Cincinnati in 1897. See reports to the "Pentecostal Holiness Union and Prayer League (International)," *Revivalist* (Nov. 1897), 6.

One of the most poignant appeals for a return to Pentecost was published by the Revivalist Press in 1902 and remains in print—A. M. Hills, *Pentecost Rejected and the Effect on the Churches* in *Holiness Classics No. 2* (Salem, OH: Allegheny Publications, 1995). A major lament of this work concerns the substitution of cultured education for the baptism of the Holy Spirit.

[89] For the words and music of "Back to Pentecost" by Mrs. C. H. Morris see Dayton, *Theological Roots*, 86. The others are numbers 151 and 192 in *Praise of His Glory Songs* Ed. R. E. McNeill, J. F. Knapp, and M. G. Standley (Cincinnati: Revivalist Press, 1922). "Pentecostal Fire is Falling" is also by George Bennard. Although not as widely known as his "The Old Rugged Cross," this remained a favorite song at GBS for decades and was recorded by the college choir in the late 1970's. "It Is For Us All Today" was written by L. L. Pickett.

[90] "Revival Prayer Answered," *Revivalist* (Aug. 29, 1901), 11. Jernigan further exulted, "Believers went the death route, and got the old-time Pentecost on their souls." For Jernigan's association with the Holiness Union, see Cunningham, et. al., 130-132. Also, see C. B. Jernigan, *Pioneer Days of the Holiness Movement in the Southwest* (1919; reprint, Bethany, OK: Arnett Publishing Co., 1964). E. A. Fergerson similarly reported from a meeting in Illinois, "The flood-gate is lifted. Glory! God is giving us a Pentecost here" ("Revival Prayer Answered," *Revivalist* (April 11, 1901), 11).

Such testimonies from Revivalist Chapel were also common, as one from Knapp's sister-in-law, Elizabeth Ferle, "The Lord gave us a Pentecost last night. He let a landslide down into my soul" ("The Revivalist Chapel," *Revivalist* (Jan. 25, 1900), 11). See also, "Pentecostal Services," *Revivalist* (Jan. 24, 1901), 15, and "Sparks from Revivalist Chapel," *Revivalist* (Jan. 4, 1900), 4.

[91] O. Chambers, "The Apostle Paul's Ways in Christ," *Revivalist* (Jan. 17, 1907), 11 (original emphasis). For additional excerpts from this article, see Moser and Smith, *God's Clock Keeps Perfect Time*, 47. See also, A. M. Hills, "Pentecost the Need

of the Individual," *Revivalist* (Nov. 3, 1904), 3 which argues, "This is the universal need of man,--this sanctifying baptism with the Holy Ghost."

[92] "Perilous Paralysis," *Revivalist* (May 9, 1901), 13. Knapp wrote, "See how our D. D.'s have been trying to account for the depletion in the life-blood of Methodism! O, my God, why don't they strike the true secret, and recognizing it, fall upon their faces all along the line, and cry out for a return of Pentecost . . . !" Hills similarly wrote in *Pentecost Rejected* that, after they looked everywhere else, he "devoutly hoped" that denominational leaders would find the cause of the churches spiritual demise in "Pentecost rejected, sanctification despised, and a grieved Holy Spirit!" (23)

[93] Primitivism or restorationism has taken many forms in America, but all rest on the belief that "there is a *fundamental discontinuity*, historical and spiritual, between the church as it is described in the New Testament and the church as it is today--that there has been a fall, and the church is thus in need of restoration" (Garry D. Nation, "The Restoration Movement," *Christianity Today* Vol. 36 no. 6 (May 18, 1992), 28—original emphasis). Thus, the primary task of primitivists is purifying the church and restoring it to the apostolic order, a job they believe only partly accomplished (if even that) by the Protestant Reformation (See Nathan O. Hatch, *The Democratization of American Christianity* (New Haven: Yale University Press, 1989), 167). As Hatch notes, this attempt at restoration "has been a recurring phenomena in the history of the church, and its manifestations among the early immigrants to North America had been particularly intense" (169). Its influence has continued to be so pervasive throughout American Christianity that scholars have recognized primitivism as "perhaps 'the most vital single assumption underlying the development of American Protestantism'" (Charles W. Nienkirchen, *A. B. Simpson and the Pentecostal Movement: A Study in Continuity, Crisis, and Change* (Peabody, MA: Hendrickson Publishers, 1992), 25).

On the broad impact of the restorationist or primitivist theme, see the *Journal of the American Academy of Religion* Vol. 44 (March 1976) which includes several articles on the subject. See also the several works written or edited by Richard T. Hughes treating this theme, including (ed.) *The American Quest for the Primitive Church* (Urbana: University of Illinois, 1988), and *The Primitive Church in the Modern World* (Urbana: University of Illinois Press, 1995). Practically all indigenous religious fellowships in America, most notably the Mormons and Disciples of Christ, trace their roots to this impulse. Although Alexander Campbell's heirs remain "the best known restorationist movement," no group holds a monopoly on this theme, which "is broader than the history of a single movement" (*A Documentary History of Religion in America to the Civil War*, 364, 410).

[94] Primitivism strongly impacted Methodism, with Francis Asbury contending "that the Methodists, more than any other church, had restored the 'primitive order' of the New Testament" (Hatch, 82). Several scholars have argued that Methodist primitivism was incipient in the thought of John Wesley so that "when Wesley's followers . . . exhibited strong primitivist tendencies, 'they were merely taking their cue from Wesley himself'" (Melvin E. Dieter, "Primitivism in the American Holiness Tradition," *WTJ* Vol. 30 no. 1 (Spring 1995), 82, citing Luke Keefer). This should come as no surprise, as one way of viewing primitivism is to see it as a form

of community perfectionism--an attempt "to perfect the *church*"--providing a natural compliment to the Wesleyan emphasis on individual perfection or sanctification (Hughes in Burgess, *Reaching Beyond*, 213). However, American Methodists took the concept much further and "were distinctive and uniquely apostolic in Asbury's view because their entire organizational structure, from bishop to circuit rider, was resolutely committed to an apostolic order of sacrifice and itinerancy" (Hatch, 82). See also, John H. Wigger, *Taking Heaven By Storm: Methodism and the Rise of Popular Christianity in America* (New York: Oxford University Press, 1998); Nathan O. Hatch and John H. Wigger, editors, *Methodism and the Shaping of American Culture* (Nashville: Kingswood Books, 2001); and John Wigger, *American Saint: Francis Asbury and the Methodists* (New York: Oxford University Press, 2009).

As the itinerancy and perfectionist emphasis declined within Methodism, advocates of Christian perfection became leading voices in the quest for primitive purity and practice. Among these were British Methodist William Arthur who penned perhaps the most popular antebellum holiness book, *The Tongue of Fire; or, the True Power of Christianity* Thomas O. Summers, ed. (1856; Reprint. Louisville, KY: The Pickett Publishing Co., 1900) ix (my emphasis), which was precipitated by his "desire to lessen the distance painfully felt to exist between [his] own life and ministry and those of the *primitive Christians*." Similar sentiments were shared by Phoebe Palmer whose best-selling *Way of Holiness* was subtitled "a narrative of religious experience resulting from a determination to be a Bible Christian." Ecclesiastical restorationism was taken to its extreme by anti-sectarian Church of God groups. For scholarly treatment of the influence of primitivism on the Wesleyan/Holiness and Pentecostal traditions, also see Steven Ware, "Restorationism in the Holiness Movement," 200-219 which is a distillation of his dissertation, "Restoring the New Testament Church in the Holiness Movement of the Late Nineteenth and Early Twentieth Century," Ph.D. diss. Drew University, 1999.

[95] "The New Testament Church," *Revivalist* (Oct. 1897), 1. He continued, "While its methods may vary, the principles governing it are the same." See Dieter, *The Holiness Revival*, 251.

[96] "Our Revival Model," *Revivalist* (Dec. 6, 1900), 1. Also, see Knapp's theme for "The Revivalist for 1900," (*Revivalist* (Jan. 4, 1900), 1), where he asserted "that the apostles' doctrine and fellowship (Acts ii, 42) should be the standard of God's people now as at Pentecost, and that a return to primitive principles and practices would precipitate primitive power."

[97] Richard Hughes identifies and explains these three areas: "*ecclesiastical primitivism*, wherein the forms and structures of the apostolic church are of paramount concern; *ethical primitivism*, wherein the lifestyle of the ancient Christians is the chief concern; and *experiential primitivism*, wherein the apostolic gifts of the Spirit are of ultimate concern" (Burgess, *Reaching Beyond*, 213). Steven Ware suggests replacing the "ethical" category with the broader term, "spiritual primitivism," so as to include "restorationist aspirations on matters of spirituality, piety, and faith" (208). However, none of these categories should be construed as mutually exclusive, as Hughes observes that "typologies are always approximations at best, and there are certainly ways in which these categories overlap one another in various combinations" (Burgess, *Reaching Beyond*, 213).

⁹⁸ "A God-Given Mission," in Knapp, *Pentecostal Messengers*, Advertisements, 10.

⁹⁹ "Wild Scenes in the Tabernacle," *Cincinnati Enquirer* (July 5, 1901), 10. Knapp reacts to this article in "As Others See Us," *Revivalist* (July 11, 1901), 15. See also the letter by J. B. Martin in defense of Knapp (after his arrest), in which he states, "I am a Methodist, and, having studied the doctrines and Discipline of my Church, together with my Bible, I consider myself quite orthodox and capable of judging of what is orthodox; and I want to say that the religion taught by Mr. Knapp is not a 'new religion,' as the papers have styled it, but the religion of the fathers--the whole gospel in its purity" ("'Mount of Blessings' Case," *Revivalist* (July 25, 1901), 12).

"A 'New Religion,'" *Revivalist* (Sept. 5, 1901), 15, emphatically denies the creation of a "new" cult or sect at GBS, instead insisting that the teaching and practice there was "simply the old religion of the Bible and of the fathers . . . being expressed." In addition, the school was seen as true to pristine Methodism: "Our meetings, though sometimes mis-represented [sic], are on the old-time full salvation lines of early Methodism and primitive Christianity" ("Our Cincinnati Meetings," *Revivalist* (Nov. 2, 1899), 14). At times, this claim involved a negative contrast with official Methodism: "Primitive Methodism welcomes holiness preachers; counterfeit Methodism opposes them, sometimes demanding their credentials" ("Pikeville, Ky." *Revivalist* (Dec. 5, 1901), 12).

¹⁰⁰ "Back to the Bible," *Revivalist* (March 7, 1901), 13.

¹⁰¹ Godbey reserved some of his most vitriolic polemics for the "Restoration Movement"—which he termed Campbellism—especially due to its view of baptism which he condemned as the materialistic imposition of the "water god" in the place of the Holy Spirit: "Campbellism is all materialism. The true religion is all spirituality" (W. B. Godbey, "An Error Exposed," *Revivalist* (June 1895), 2). See also his *Baptism: Mode and Design*; *Baptism Paganized and Demonized* (Greensboro, NC: Apostolic Messenger, n. d.); *Immersionism* (Cincinnati: Revivalist, 1911); and the only extant transcript of a debate between Godbey and a Disciples minister--Leroy McWherter, *Godbey-Maupin Debate: Outline on a Debate on Water Baptism and the Baptism with the Holy Ghost Between Rev. W. B. Godbey, D. D. and Rev. Wm. Maupin* (Cincinnati: Revivalist, n. d.).

However, Godbey recognized his indebtedness to this movement in his booklet on *Campbellism* (Cincinnati: Revivalist, n. d.), 1: "In this writing I am frank to confess that I am close to home, as I was born and reared in the hot-bed of Campbellism, and the first twenty years of my life, . . . I heard them preach five times as much as all other denominations." He actually sympathized deeply with many of its primitivist commitments, especially anti-creedalism.

¹⁰² *The Bible* (Nashville: Pentecostal Mission Publishing Co., n. d.), 19. Much of the opposition to creeds voiced in the *Revivalist* stemmed from Daniel Steele's appeal to such creeds as the Nicene and Apostles in his opposition to premillennialism. For example, see Rev. Lucius Hawkins, "The Creeds vs. the Bible—I," *Revivalist* (Sept. 20, 1900), 7.

For an important statement of the radical holiness position, including anticreedalism, see W. B. Godbey, "An Encyclical Letter to the Holiness People of Every Land," *Revivalist* (July 11, 1901), 12—

I am sorry to see the Holiness people now making creeds and going into denominationalism which owes its origin to human creeds, and would have perished long ago had it not been for the support of the creeds . . . if they had never adopted any creed but the New Testament, all proclaiming it as their only authority, the Protestant distinctions would not have lasted long, and the devil would have suffered a thousand signal defeats where he now has won ten thousand victories.

In other words, one should "beware of human creeds [because] if they agree with the New Testament they are useless; if they are out of harmony with it they are the work of Satan . . ." This was not to argue that creeds had no merit, for Godbey admitted that "you will find much edifying truth in all the creeds, which you should receive to your profit, as they are all founded on the Bible; but the danger of following them consists in the fact that no human creed is really a summary of all Bible truth. Hence their tendency to warp and disproportionately develop you, making you one-sided . . ." That is, at best creeds were redundant caricatures of the New Testament, at worst they were heretical interpretations.

Oswald Chambers concurred in his *Sermon on the Mount*: "A Christian is to be consistent only to the life of the Son of God within, not consistent to hard and fast creeds. People pour themselves into creeds, and God Almighty has to blast them out of their prejudices before they become devoted to Jesus Christ" (38). Knapp himself rejected such creeds as the Nicene and Apostles in part due to their association with Roman Catholicism ("Objections to the So-Called Apostles' Creed," *Revivalist* (Nov. 15, 1900), 7). Ironically, Knapp's reasoning mirrored that of his opponents in the Church of God (Anderson). See Barry L. Callen, *Contours of a Cause: Theological Vision of the Church of God Movement (Anderson, Indiana)* (Anderson, IN: Anderson University School of Theology, 1995), 64-74 in which he characterizes this movement as "convictional" rather than "creedal."

[103] Godbey, *The Bible*, 20-21. He added that "the Bible School phenomenon is an inseparable concomitant of the New Testament Church in all lands, Christian and heathen." In his report on the "Salvation Park Camp-Meeting, 1909," he similarly stated that "the Bible Schools and Holiness Camps are the crystalization of the great Holiness movement. In these we must stick to the old landmarks; learn how to pray God down from Heaven, and have Him with us in Spirit and the power all the time, or before we are aware "Ichabod" (the glory is departed) will be written on our escutcheon" (*Revivalist* (July 8, 1909), 6).

[104] F. L. P. "Why People Come to God's Bible-School," *Revivalist* (Oct. 14, 1901), 13.

[105] "A Revival Sign," *Revivalist* (March 21, 1901), 1. Knapp further explained his opposition to mainline churches by accusing them of adopting, at least in some degree, the errors of Romanism--evidence that "Protestantism has drifted far away from Bible moorings, and must be reformed or damned." He thus asserted that "Methodist Churches are lapsing into High Church Episcopalianism, Episcopal Churches into Catholicism, and Catholic Churches into hell" ("Back to the Bible," *Revivalist* (Aug. 15, 1901), 1). He similarly rebuked Friends leaders for bringing

their members into bondage on the subject of the ordinances ("Popery Among Quakers," *Revivalist* (Nov. 28, 1901), 4).

The cause of this drift into "ritualism" was the aspiration of "ambitious men" who destroyed the independence of local churches in defiance of the New Testament pattern. The *Revivalist* argued, "No fact is more clearly set forth in history than the independence of the apostolic churches and the simplicity of their organization; yet, with few exceptions, modern Churches pattern after Rome in their general plan of government" (David Parker, "The Primitive Church," *Revivalist* (Sept. 13, 1900), 15). For this reason, Knapp ultimately opposed efforts at church restoration which sought to find the redeeming value of church tradition throughout the centuries (such as that represented by Thomas Oden today), rather than focusing on the apostolic church as normative.

This logic strikingly parallels that of John P. Brooks (Church of God-Holiness), who argued in his *The Divine Church* that there is a "dissimilarity between the Church of scripture and the . . . Church of history, which is the Church of sect, [and] cannot therefore be the true Church" (v). D. S. Warner and H. M. Riggle(Church of God-Anderson) also heralded this theme, encouraging "the cleansing of the sanctuary" by separation from denominations encrusted by the barnacles of human tradition (*The Cleansing of the Sanctuary or, The Church of God in Type and Antitype, and in Prophecy and Revelation* (1903, Reprint; Guthrie, OK: Faith Publishing House, 1967)). As Callen has indicated, this first wave of come-outers signaled a transition from the early holiness movement attempt at *reforming* the church to a latter attempt at *recreating* the church along apostolic lines—thus abandoning the mainline denominations (Barry L. Callen, "Daniel Sydney Warner: Joining Holiness and All Truth," *WTJ* vol. 30 no. 1 (Spring 1995), 92-110.)

[106] "Anti-Revival Influences," *Revivalist* (May 2, 1901), 1.

[107] Knapp admitted that "in the folds of many counterfeit Churches there doubtless are people who are members of the New Testament Church, but who are identified with no visible Church, having mistaken a social club for such a body" ("The New Testament Church," *Revivalist* (Dec. 27, 1900), 1). However, by the following spring, he had concluded in "Anti-Revival Clubhouses," *Revivalist* (May 23, 1901), 1, that

> The Scripture command to 'be not unequally yoked together with unbelievers' applies to the union of God's true people with these so-called Church clubhouses as really as worldly societies that do not carry the mask of Christianity . . .
>
> God's Revivalist is the organ of God's people, and of New Testament societies of every name, yet it protests against such clubhouses being recognized as Christian Churches, and against the criminal silence or open complicity of Christian ministers with such agencies of the pit.
>
> See also, Bessie [Queen], "Beware of 'Clubs,'" *Revivalist* (Jan. 10, 1901), 8.

[108] Ibid. See Knapp's graphic condemnation of "Pentecostal Imposters" in the last chapter (13) of *Lightning Bolts from Pentecostal Skies*, 264-307.

[109] "A Revival Camp-Meeting," *Revivalist* (June 6, 1901), 1. However, in this article, Knapp continued "warning of the anarchistical Come-outism which 'despises dominion.'"

[110] Hills, *Hero*, 33 (my emphasis). Godbey continued, "It is, upon the whole, simply an integral part of the great holiness movement, built up strictly on the *New Testament lines*--i.e., an effort to drop back to *first principles* . . ." Knapp wrote that it was a "lie that we are ambitious to start a new denomination, and to be at the head of a new ecclesiasticism. This is untrue. In fact, we believe that the New Testament Church had little ecclesiasticism" ("Lies Forgiven," *Revivalist* (Jan. 17, 1901), 8. See Hills, *Hero*, 226).

[111] Day, 166.

[112] In *Theological Roots*, Dayton traces the ascendancy of the last three elements of the four-fold gospel among Wesleyan/Holiness people, frequently noting the contributions of the Revivalist movement to these developments. In particular, see pages 91-92, 165-167, and 173-175.

[113] Thus, when Godbey proclaimed "the Bible's my creed," he often did so in context of a defense of the four-fold gospel—particularly the premillennial return of Christ (W. B. Godbey and Seth C. Rees, *The Return of Jesus* (Cincinnati: Revivalist, n. d.), 50). Again, as this book reflects (note "His Return Symbolized," 26-39), such defenses employed the same hermeneutic of illustration relied on to support the doctrine of entire sanctification, reflecting the growing significance of the last two elements of the four-fold gospel at GBS.

[114] Martin E. Marty ("Foreword," Dayton, *Theological Roots*, 11) aptly observes, "to pull at any one of the four has an effect on the other three and on the whole." These ideals make "up a single whole, which possesses 'its own inner logic.'" In fact, tongues-speaking was an accretion not essential to the "inner logic" of Pentecostalism, as Marty asserts that Pentecostalism "is much more than and indeed something other than 'speaking in other tongues.'" For an excellent intellectual history of Pentecostalism briefly reflecting on its holiness roots, see Grant Wacker, *Heaven Below: Early Pentecostals and American Culture* (Cambridge: Harvard University Press, 2001).

[115] "The Four-Fold Gospel," *The Way of Faith and Neglected Themes* (Dec. 23, 1896), 3 (reprinted from *The Christian Alliance*). This article added "that the four-fold gospel requires all the folds to give any one its true emphasis and proportion."

[116] Seth C. Rees, "Pentecost," *Revivalist* (Jan. 23, 1902), 3. Here, Rees unwittingly provided the logic which later generations of Pentecostals would use to insist on tongues-speaking as the evidence of baptism with the Holy Spirit. One must embrace every element of Pentecost in order to realize its distinguishing experience—Spirit-baptism. For Rees and Knapp, this did not include tongues-speaking, but several of their associates would later make this connection. On the contribution of Knapp and his colleagues to the rise of Pentecostalism, see Stephens, 224.

[117] "Facts about the Revivalist," *Revivalist* (Aug. 31, 1899), 15.

[118] Melvin E. Dieter, in c. 4, "The Post-Civil War Holiness Revival: The Rise of the Camp Meeting Churches," in Caldwell, 178, writes that "L. L. Pickett of Louisville, Kentucky, was the most ardent proponent of the position." See L. L. Pickett, *The Blessed Hope Of His Glorious Appearing* (Louisville: Pentecostal Publishing Co.,

1901) and *Why I Am A Premillennialist* (Louisville: Pentecostal Publishing Co., 1927).

[119] Godbey and Rees, *Return of Jesus*, 16. See Dayton, *Theological Roots*, 166 and Kostlevy, *Holy Jumpers*, 174, who concludes that "the decisive year in the transition from post- to premillennialism appears to be 1896 ..." G. D. Watson (*Steps to the Throne*, 3) explains that his conversion to premillennialism involved repudiation of postmillennialism as an "old Roman Catholic notion" and, in early 1896, the unfolding in his mind by the Spirit of "Scriptures on the pre-millennial coming of Christ." Also, see Lennox, "The Eschatology of George D. Watson," 112.

For a recent critique of the shift from a postmillennialist perspective, see Vic Reasoner, *The Hope of the Gospel: An Introduction to Wesleyan Eschatology* (Evansville, IN: Fundamental Wesleyan Publishers, 1999) and my review of this work in the *WTJ* vol. 38 no. 1 (Spring 2003), 260-263. For critique contemporaneous with Knapp, by a well-known holiness advocate who never accepted premillennialism, see Daniel Steele, *A Substitute for Holiness: Antinomianism Revived: The Theology of the So-Called Plymouth Brethren Examined and Refuted* (1887; reprint, Salem, OH: Schmul Publishing Co., 2003). Also, see "About Dispensationalism," c. 8 in W. T. Purkiser, *Security: the False and the True* Rev. ed. (Kansas City, MO: Beacon Hill Press of Kansas City, 1974), 52-55. For a concise overview of various forms of millennial teachings, see Raymond Ludwigson, *The End of Time: A Simplified Survey of Prophecy and Its Various Interpretations* (1951, *Simplified Classroom Notes on Prophecy*; reprint, Salem, OH: Schmul Publishing Co., 2005).

[120] Dieter, in Caldwell, 150. "Later he personally associated with Simpson at Old Orchard, Maine, where the Alliance was formed," and served as evangelist in several Alliance meetings." Rees could maintain a Friends pastorate and Alliance presidency simultaneously because the Alliance originated as an interdenominational fellowship similar to the many interdenominational associations started by Wesleyan exponents of holiness. See also, Paul Rees, *Seth Cook Rees: The Warrior Saint* (1934; Reprint; Salem, OH: Schmul, 1987).

Simpson's writings, as well as those of other Christian and Missionary Alliance writers, frequently appeared in the *Revivalist*. On his influence on holiness leaders' embrace of a divine healing emphasis, as well as the influence of other non-Wesleyans such as Charles Cullis, A. J. Gordon and Andrew Murray, see Richard M. Riss, *A Survey of 20th-Century Revival Movements in North America* (Peabody, MA: Hendrickson Publishers, 1988), 18-23; Dieter in Caldwell, 175-176, and P. G. Chappell, "Healing Movements," in Burgess and McGee, *Dictionary of Pentecostal and Charismatic Movements*, original edition, 353-374. Also, see A. B. Simpson, *The Four-Fold Gospel: The Fullness of Jesus* (Brooklyn, NY: The Christian Alliance Publishing Co., n. d.) and *The Gospel of Healing* (London: Morgan and Scott LD., 1915); A. W. Tozer, *Wingspread: Albert B. Simpson—A Study in Spiritual Altitude* (Harrisburg, PA: Christian Publications Inc., 1943); S. B. Shaw, *Touching Incidents and Remarkable Answers to Prayer* (Reprint; Salem, OH: Schmul, 1997), 236-238; and Andrew Murray, *Divine Healing* (Reprint; Springdale, PA: Whitaker House, 1982), as well as "Books on Divine Healing," *Revivalist* (Nov. 7, 1901), 10 and Andrew Murray, "Persevering Prayer and Healing," *Revivalist* (Oct. 17, 1901), 10.

[121] Nienkirchen, 21. Most fundamentalists went beyond historic premillennial-

ism to embrace "dispensational premillennialism." While historic premillennialists accepted the teaching of a literal thousand year reign of Christ on earth before the final consummation, dispensationalists developed a rather elaborate scheme for correlating Bible prophecy and human history, in which history is viewed as a series of periods of God's work among humans, each being "independent and completed in its own linear time and order." Dispensationalists believe that "when Israel rejected Christ, . . . the Kingdom promise was suspended until the time of Christ's second coming." Consequently, the Church age or "age of Grace" is a "parenthetical" period in which God's mercy is particularly bestowed on Gentiles. While Wesleyan proponents of dispensationalism sometimes adapt this scheme, particularly in making the dispensations parallel to individual Christian experience, they seem to follow essentially the lead of non-Wesleyan dispensationalists, retaining the same basic view of history (Marlin R. Hotle, *A Layman's Guide to Wesleyan Terminology* (Salem, OH: Schmul, 1995), 21). John Fletcher, who predated such Calvinistic dispensationalists as Darby and Scoffield, provided precedent for a "dipensational" view of holiness experience by seeing such experience as a mirror of history. Thus, while Calvinistic dispensationalists usually hold a "sabbatical" view of history with seven periods, many Wesleyans follow Fletcher's delineation of three periods--that of the Father (until the baptism of Jesus by John--symbolizing conversion), that of the Son (from His baptism to Pentecost--symbolizing entire sanctification), and that of the Spirit (from Pentecost to the Second Coming--symbolizing glorification).

[122] The beginning of this trend has been traced to the popularization of the dispensational teachings of an eighteenth-century monk, Manuel de Lacunza, by John Nelson Darby and the denomination which he helped to organize in England during the 1830's—the Plymouth Brethren. In addition to the Bible Conference Movement, one of the most effective tools popularizing dispensationalism was the notes incorporated within C. I. Scofield's study Bible (originally published in 1909 by Oxford University Press).

Among the plethora of scholarly works dealing with the development of millennarianism and dispensationalism, see George Marsden, *Fundamentalism and American Culture: The Shaping of Twentieth-Century Evangelicalism: 1870-1925 (New York: Oxford University Press, 1980)*; Ernest R. Sandeen, *The Roots of Fundamentalism: British and American Millennarianism 1800-1930* (Chicago: University of Chicago Press, 1970); and Timothy P. Weber, *Living in the Shadow of the Second Coming: American Premillennialism, 1875-1925* (New York: Oxford University Press, 1979). Several articles in the *Wesleyan Theological Journal* Vol. 29, nos. 1 and 2 (Spring-Fall 1994) address various aspects of the subject. See also, James H. Moorehead, "The Erosion of Postmillennialism in American Religious Thought, 1865-1925," *Church History* Vol. 53 (1984), 61-77.

[123] For instance, it was a natural step to go from Knapp's charts promoting holiness teaching to diagrams designed to convey "dispensational truth." For non-Holiness examples of such diagrams, see Clarence Larkin, *Dispensational Truth or God's Plan and Purpose in the Ages* (Philadelphia: Rev. Clarence Larkin Est., 1918) and *The Book of Revelation: A Study of The Last Prophetic Book of Holy Scripture* (Philadelphia: Rev. Clarence Larkin Estate, 1919). See also, "Enraptured With Order: How fundamentalists strove

mightily to make sense of history," *Christian History* (Issue 55), 40-41.

For examples of Revivalist Press publications presenting such charts, see Knapp, *Lightning Bolts*, 135; E. G. Marsh, *Simple A B Z's of the Second Coming* (1929), and Paul D. Beck, *Chronology of the Book of Revelation* (1992).

[124] William Kostlevy has suggested that among these may be the "decisive defeat of Populism in the 1896 presidential election" and the financial panic of 1893-1897 ("The Dispensationalists: Embarrassing Relatives or Prophets Without Honor: Reflections on Mark Noll's *The Scandal of the Evangelical Mind*," *WTJ* vol. 32 no. 1 (Spring 1997), 191). Ironically, the latter was precipitated by a series of railroad bankruptcies, thus marring one of Knapp's favorite metaphors for holiness. The result was the demise of 150 banks, 200 railroads, and 15,000 small businesses, with unemployment reaching twenty-five percent. Regardless the social and economic factors, by the turn-of-the-century, holiness radicals had rejected the "myth of progress" promulgated by liberal thinkers (William Kostlevy, conversation with author, December 1, 2000). See also, Christopher Lasch, *The True and Only Heaven: Progress and Its Critics* (New York: W. W. Norton and Company, 1991).

[125] W. B. Godbey, "Question Drawer," *Revivalist* (July 11, 1901), 5. Seth Cook Rees agreed, "I am not pessimistic, and yet I pity the man who feels forced to be an optimist in these days of thickening gloom" (*Miracles in the Slums; or, Thrilling Stories of Those Rescued From the Cesspools of Iniquity, and Touching Incidents in the Lives of the Unfortunate* (Chicago: Seth C. Rees, 1905), 15).

Knapp questioned how people could "talk about the world getting better and better, when the truth is there are more murders, more rapes, more suicides ... committed, and the people of the United States are drinking just double the amount of whisky they did twenty years ago. The wicked are in power ... in Church as well as in State" ("Comfort Ye My People," *Revivalist* (April 18, 1901), 13).

Also, see H. C. Morrison, *Is the World Growing Better; or, Is the World Growing Worse?* (Louisville: The Pentecostal Publishing Co., 1932) and Stephens, 168.

[126] Supporting this assertion is Dayton's observation that Wesleyans with an optimistic view of the society at large (generally postmillennialists) tended to found liberal arts colleges whereas evangelicals with a more negative view of the larger society (generally premillennialists) tended to found Bible colleges and institutes (Donald W. Dayton, "Dispensationalism and the Emergence of Fundamentalism among American Baptists," (Keynote Address for the Wesleyan Holiness Studies Center 1995 Conference: Methodism and the Fragmentation of American Protestantism: 1865-1920, Asbury Theological Seminary, Sept. 29, 1995), 11.

[127] W. B. Godbey ridiculed the charge of pessimism against premillennialists, leveled by such opponents as Daniel Steele (*Jesus Exultant* (1898; reprint, Schmul Publishing Co., 1972), preface), suggesting "The cry of '*pessimism*,' is the Shiboleth of the ignoramus." He later concluded, "I am an optimist on grace and a pessimist on sin" (*Signs of His Coming* (Nashville: Pentecostal Mission Publishing Co., n. d.), 49 original emphasis). John L. Peters and Donald Dayton are among scholars who suggest that the balance was actually lost among Wesley's heirs (Peters, 66 and Dayton, "Dispensationalism . . .," 11). For a more sympathetic scholarly perspective, see Douglas Strong, "Sanctified Eccentricity: Continuing Relevance of the Nine-

teenth-Century Holiness Paradigm," 1999 Wesleyan Theological Society Presidential Address *WTJ* vol. 35 no. 1 (Spring 2000), 16.

Among radical holiness advocates, this dichotomy of outlook meant they were optimistic about the cause of Holiness Pentecost, but were less than enthusiastic about the future of Western society. For example, while Godbey was jubilant over the "great holiness movement girdling the globe," he also observed "black clouds and dense fogs which emanated from the bottomless pit, responsively to the great victory which Satan won over the human race in the Eden War, . . . hovering over us" (*My Triennial Circuit* (Cincinnati: Revivalist, n. d.), 23-24).

[128] On the correlation of a shift in eschatological views to involvement in social reform efforts, see Dayton, "Dispensationalism . . .," 11 and Rodney Layne Reed, *Holy With Integrity: The Unity of Personal and Social Ethics in the Holiness Movement, 1880-1910* No. 3 in "Radical Righteousness: Studies in Evangelical and Wesleyan Theology, Ethics, and History" Eds. William Kostlevy and Wallace Thornton, Jr. (Salem, OH: Schmul, 2003), especially his conclusions on "Eschatology and Ethics," 270-273.

[129] W. B. Godbey, *An Appeal to Postmillennialists* (Nashville: Pentecostal Mission Publishing Co., n. d.), 24. In *The Anchored Soul* (Greensboro, NC: Apostolic Messenger Publishing Co., n.d.), Godbey applied this metaphor specifically to Methodism, blaming its decline on its tremendous growth—"But the millions poured in; she took them on board, the ship began to sink, the cry roaring out, "Life boat! Life boat!" In Godbey's scheme, God's response was the holiness movement, starting with Free Methodism and, later, Wesleyan Methodism.

[130] Dayton, *Theological Roots*, 167, citing *Electric Shocks from Pentecostal Batteries* (1899), 122. W. B. Godbey similarly asserted that "the great work of the holiness movement of to-day is to get the bride ready for the glorious time when the Lord shall come to take her away to the marriage supper of the Lamb" ("The World's Evangelization," *Revivalist* (Oct. 28, 1909), 8). For a book length treatment of this application of the remnant schema to eschatology, insisting that "the Bride must not only be saved but sanctified in the most thorough degree" (7), see G. D. Watson, *The Bridehood Saints: Treating of the Saints Who Are the "Selection from the Selection"—Those Saints Who Are to Make Up the Bride of Christ* (Cincinnati: Office of God's Revivalist, 1913).

[131] Seth C. Rees, "An Incentive to Holiness," *Revivalist* (Jan. 25, 1900), 7. See also, W. B. Godbey, "Does Preaching the Coming of the Lord Impede Revivals?" *Revivalist* (June 13, 1901), 1, in which he gives "a most emphatic negative" and Knapp in "The Coming and Holiness," *Revivalist* (June 13, 1901), 7, in which he contends, "any doctrine that will promote holiness must be true, and should be preached. We claim the right to press the thought of His near coming on this ground."

[132] "Facts about the Revivalist," *Revivalist* (Aug. 31, 1899), 15.

[133] Knapp explained this expansion, "In devoting the space we at present do to 'Healing' and the 'Return of Jesus' is to place them before our readers in their Scriptural light. Jesus and the apostles mightily emphasized them, and a ministry that elides them preaches a fractional gospel . . . " ("Our Object," *Revivalist* (May 4, 1899), 10). Seth Rees exulted after Knapp's death, "thank God, He opened Brother Knapp's eyes, and through Him has opened the eyes of many to see that Pentecost means a full gospel" (Seth C. Rees, "Pentecost," *Revivalist* (Jan. 23, 1902), 2).

¹³⁴ Koslevy, *Holy Jumpers*, 174. As Kostlevy notes, a unique feature of Godbey's commentary, which reflects its eschatological focus, is its beginning in volume one with Revelation and working back to the Gospels.

In addition to *Holiness Triumphant*, Knapp devoted c. 10 of *Lightning Bolts* to the "Pentecostal Expectancy of Christ's Return," 136-161. Godbey augmented his commentary with numerous smaller books on eschatological themes, several enumerating signs of Christ's soon return, many enriched by Godbey's wide grasp of history and by observations during his travels, such as *Signs of His Coming, Prophecies Fulfilled* (Greensboro, NC: The Apostolic Messenger Office, n. d.), and *Omens of His Proximity* (Cincinnati: Revivalist, n. d.). Hamilton asserts that Godbey became a world traveler instead of confining his travels to Palestine primarily to amass evidence that would confirm premillenialism ("William Baxter Godbey: Pioneer," 53-54). See also Hamilton, "Preaching the 'Narrow Way,'" 44-45.

¹³⁵ "Our Camp-Meeting Wheel," *Revivalist* (June 14, 1900), 15. See also, "A Revival Camp-Meeting," *Revivalist* (June 6, 1901), 1.

¹³⁶ "The Hub of the Gospel Wheel," *Revivalist* (June 1897), 2. This article and the accompanying illustration hint that Knapp was at least open to the four-fold gospel before 1898. The diagram used here varied somewhat from the "Camp-Meeting Wheel," most notably in that it does not mention healing.

¹³⁷ Knapp, *Back to the Bible*, 45-52.

¹³⁸ Richard S. Taylor, *God's Integrity and the Cross* (Nappanee, IN: Francis Asbury Press, 1999), 117.

¹³⁹ Dieter in Caldwell, 177. Dieter recalls his father debating this issue with R. G. Flexon, long-time Pilgrim Holiness general leader who also served GBS for several years, with Flexon taking the position that healing is a provision of the atonement and Dieter taking the counterpoint. Key texts cited to prove healing in the atonement were Isaiah 53:5 and Matthew 8:17. See Madge Duff, "Healing in the Atonement," *Revivalist* (Nov. 12, 1903), 10; Emma Dolloff, "Healed by Faith," *Revivalist* (Feb. 11, 1904), 9; and W. B. Godbey, "Divine Healing in the Atonement," c. 3 in his *Divine Healing* (Greensboro, NC: Apostolic Messenger Office, 1909), 13-20. For other scriptural support for healing, see the texts listed in Seth Rees, *Ideal Pentecostal Church*, 53-54 and in "Back to the Bible," *Revivalist* (May 16, 1901), 10. The logic behind teaching "healing in the atonement" is well represented by Mary McGee Hall, "Divine Healing," *Revivalist* (Dec. 13, 1900), 10. To summarize, sickness is of the devil. The blood of Jesus is for redemption from all the work of the devil. Therefore, the saints should have power over sickness. Interestingly, Hall later became associated with John Alexander Dowie's work.

Knapp seemed to distance himself from making healing a special provision of the atonement by writing, "Divine healing is in the atonement, the same as all general blessings are. Every good gift is in it." However, he hastened to add, "I know of no Bible authority for putting an 'if' in for healing" (*Pentecostal Letters*, 42). Both he (*Lightning Bolts*, 128) and Godbey qualified their teaching on the present privileges of faith healing, as Godbey put it, "we must remember that the perfect healing of the body is not reached in this life unless we, in the providence of God, should be honored with a translation" (*Divine Healing*, 15). For an account of Godbey's own healing from cancer, see his *Leprosy* (Cincinnati: God's Revivalist Press, n. d.), 7-8.

On the distinction between divine or faith healing, mental healing, and medical healing, see W. B. Godbey, *Psychology and Pneumatology* (Cincinnati: God's Revivalist Press, n. d.) and John R. Church, *Divine Healing* (Louisville: Pentecostal Publishing Co., n. d.), the latter being a sermon preached by the author at the Bentleyville (PA) Camp Meeting, July 16, 1954.

See also, Nancy A. Hardesty, *Faith Cure: Divine Healing in the Holiness and Pentecostal Movements* (Peabody, MA: Hendrickson Publishers, 2004).

[140] "Bible-School Notes," *Revivalist* (Jan. 17, 1901), 15 tells of a United Brethren minister and a Quaker who had this experience. Knapp quoted with approbation the assertion of the *Christian Standard* that "divine healing of the body is one confirming proof of the divine ability to pardon the sins of the soul (Matt. 9:2) and brings glory to God (v. 8) . . . It is God's outward work proving God's inward work" ("Gifts of Healing," *Revivalist* (May 4, 1899), 10).

[141] For example, see A. L. Harris, "To Him Be All the Glory," *Revivalist* (Sept. 30, 1909), 10 and Bud Robinson, *My Hospital Experience* (Reprint; Noblesville, IN: Newby Book Store, n. d.), 22. The school still receives such requests to this day.

[142] H. T. Davis, *Modern Miracles* (Cincinnati: God's Revivalist Office, 1901); W. J. Harney, *Praying Clear Through* (Reprint; Jamestown, NC: Newby Book Room, 1983); and G. C. Bevington, *Remarkable Incidents And Modern Miracles Through Prayer and Faith* (Cincinnati: God's Bible School and Revivalist, n. d.). One of the first references to Bevington in *God's Revivalist* is a brief testimony in the June 27, 1901 issue (4): "Saved, sanctified, and healed. Hallelujah!" See also his testimony the following year, *Revivalist* (May 8, 1902), 5. On Harney, see "Healing of W. J. Harney," *Revivalist* (Jan. 18, 1900), 10 and "Healing of an Evangelist," *Revivalist* (Feb. 22, 1900), 10.

[143] "Proof Against Poison," *Revivalist* (Oct. 18, 1900), 10—subtitled "Experience of Evangelist Mary Storey, related at God's Bible-School Chapel October 2d" with the text "If they drink any deadly thing it shall not hurt them!" [Mark 16:18]. In those days, aconite—made from the dried, poisonous root of the monkshood flower, was used to relieve fever or gastrointestinal pain. However, it was apparently mistaken by a doctor for another remedy when administered to Storey in an excessively high dosage. See also, "Questions Answered," *Revivalist* (July 5, 1900), 16, which refers to Storey's healing—"Only those can drink deadly things without harm, as in primitive times, who have the primitive faith."

[144] C. E. Cowman, "Don't Tell It," *Revivalist* (Jan. 24, 1901), 10. Also, see "Divine Healing: Bible Reading by Bro. Cowman at God's Bible School, Oct. 14, 1904," *Revivalist* (Nov. 3, 1904), 2. For a similar healing, see the testimony of Laura Davis, "Bible-School Student," "God's Power to Heal," *Revivalist* (July 4, 1901), 10.

Such GBS leaders as W. B. Godbey assured the GBS family that God used medicine as well as direct intervention in healing ("Drugs and Divine Healing," *Revivalist* (May 10, 1900), 10 and "Question-Drawer," *Revivalist* (March 1, 1900), 12). Regardless, several in the Revivalist family came to view any medical assistance askance. See "Medical Science 'Falsely So Called;' Or, What Doctors Say About Drugs," *Revivalist* (Jan. 11, 1900), 10. J. B. Mitchell provided a representative testimony:

When I consecrated my all to God I was sanctified, and when I took a dose of medicine I felt like I had broken my consecration. I knew nothing of Divine healing, but I knew if God could save a sinner like me, He could heal me, so I laid aside medicines and trusted Jesus for all. I have nine in my family, and it has been three years since a dose of medicine was taken. Jesus heals us all ("God's Witnesses," *Revivalist* (Oct. 24, 1901), 4).

[145] Beatrice M. Finney, "Heart Disease," *Revivalist* (Jan. 31, 1901), 10.

[146] "Healing Promises," *Revivalist* (March 7, 1901), 10. For representative testimonies, see Mary A. Ward, "Healed at the Bible-School," *Revivalist* (Jan. 24, 1901), 10; Mrs. Jennie Riley, "Healed at the Bible-School," *Revivalist* (Feb. 21, 1901), 10; and Bessie [Queen], "Bible-School Notes," *Revivalist* (Oct. 10, 1901), 15.

[147] Knapp, *Back to the Bible*, 53.

[148] Knapp, *Back to the Bible*, 50-51 (my emphasis).

Chapter 3

Completing the Vision: Winning the World

The plan which God is giving us for this school is different from that of any school with which we are acquainted. In the first place, God Himself is recognized as the President and Proprietor, working through such agents as He may select.
— *Martin Wells Knapp[1]*

From this place beams of fire are to go to kindle fires all over the world.
— *Seth Cook Rees[2]*

The uniqueness of GBS stemmed largely from the commitment to repeating Pentecost. Under Knapp's leadership, the four-fold gospel was expanded to apply to every facet of life—thus justifying its designation as a worldview. Perhaps the best way to view this pervasive application of Pentecostal principles is to see it as the addition of a fifth "fold" to the four-fold gospel, represented in the formulation of Jesus as "Savior, Sanctifier, Doctor, *Banker*, and Coming King."[3] This formulation took elements of the other four strands of Pentecost and wove them into a powerful theme—*God as Proprietor*, emphasizing both divine possession and provision. Thus, the Healer became the Supplier of every need, the coming King became present Superintendent, and the Sanctifier's presence and power extended far beyond entire sanctification.

God Over All

This understanding resulted from the radical application of the early Wesleyan emphasis that "we are stewards, not proprietors, of possessions."[4] Knapp contended in *Lightning Bolts*, "NEW TESTAMENT GIVING IS BASED ON STEWARDSHIP, NOT OWNERSHIP." Interpreting the parable of the talents (Matthew 25:14-30) as "a graphic picture of two classes of people, i.e., believers who practice the principle of Pentecostal stewardship, and those who decline to," he suggested that this meant that everything should be submitted to God for His disposal, not just the tithe—"not one-tenth for Him and the balance for themselves, but all for Him."[5] He further explained,

> New Testament stewardship is not like renting a farm or store and paying the owner a per cent, [sic] of rent and doing the work in our own way and

under our own name, and expending the profits for ourselves, but just the opposite. It acknowledges the proprietorship of Jesus Christ, labors solely under His instructions, and renders all to Him who owns it, with the explicit understanding that all profits above actual economic expenses of food, raiment, shelter, needful stock, etc., shall be given "in His name," as near as can be estimated, as Christ, the Proprietor Himself, would give it were He personally present.[6]

Knapp thus concluded that the *"accumulation of property for self is absolutely prohibited,"* citing Matthew 6:19.[7] Other scriptural support for this view again came from the book of Acts, in which Knapp found "that under the influence of the Pentecostal Baptism of the Holy Spirit, early Christians sold their possessions and distributed their resources as needs arose."[8]

The 1898 publication of *Lightning Bolts* indicates that Knapp was firmly committed to proclaiming God as Proprietor well before GBS began. By the next year, he was determined to demonstrate this principle through Revivalist ministries, thus "God was formally listed as the proprietor of the *Revivalist*."[9] In January 1901, "God Over All" was prominently proclaimed above the names of the editorial staff, including Knapp, and the periodical's name was expanded to *God's Revivalist and Bible Advocate*.

However, it was at GBS itself that the recognition of God as Proprietor reached its pinnacle. This was most obvious in the school's name, a choice defended in response to several letters "not approving of thus using the Divine appellation":

> 'It *is God's Revivalist*. It is God's Bible-school and Missionary-training Home.' Do not men name buildings and institutions after themselves, thus taking the honor to themselves[?] Why not let God have the honor for what is truly His? As long as the work is kept pure and clean and has the Divine approbation and benediction resting upon it, we want to give honor where it is due. I want people to know that there is one place, one paper, one school where God is honored as the chief Head, and where the work belongs absolutely to Him. It is not a Knapp work, or a Rees movement, or any other man's, but God's. We are simply God's agents that He in his providence has permitted to carry on the work for a time.[10]

This was not merely pious posturing. In a very literal sense, Knapp believed that God's Bible School was God's enterprise, just as surely as the Church belonged to God. He again appealed to the precedent of the apostolic Church: "All through the New Testament, the Church is called God's Church; and if it be true with the whole organized body of believers, the same principle would apply to any section of it, such as this school is."[11]

His earnest desire that God indeed own the new school was reflected in a step that Knapp took when he procured the property at 1810 Young Street that would both inspire and perplex future generations of constituents, jurists, and community leaders—*he deeded the property to God*! Knapp was simply listed as trustee. To further assure that this trusteeship would not become a family inheritance without regard for God's selection of successors, Knapp had the following declaration drawn up—possibly the most significant notice the *Revivalist* ever carried—

Not for Personal Profit.
Cincinnati, Ohio, July 18, 1901.
I hereby certify that I examined the deed conveying the Mount of Blessings property, Corner Ringgold and Young Streets, Mt. Auburn, to M. W. Knapp as trustee for God's Bible-school and Missionary-training Home, and to his successors in office, and that said deed debars the heirs of said Knapp, and holds the property solely and forever to the uses and trust declared in it.
Thomas T. Heath,
Attorney at Law, Cincinnati, O.[12]

Divine possession of the school meant that God was also expected to provide direction, whether on the general administrative level or in intimate personal details.[13] As Knapp put it, God was not only "Proprietor," He was also "President" of God's Bible School.[14] (In fact, Knapp never considered himself the president of the school, although he was referred to as superintendent as well as trustee.) Beatrice Finney exulted, "It certainly is God's school. The Holy Ghost is recognized by all as the General Superintendent. He has complete right of way, and the atmosphere is so charged with His presence that it is suffocating for sin . . . Carnality can not abide here."[15] Frequently, it was publicized that God was the One in charge of conventions and camp meetings, as when "it was announced that the 'Holy Ghost Himself,' with the assistance of Rees, had been invited to conduct the fall Holiness Convention at God's Bible School in 1900."[16]

Many early campus guidelines can be properly understood only in light of God's proprietorship. For instance, several rules reflect concern for "hygienic" holiness—maintaining the purity of the body as the "temple of the Holy Ghost" (I Corinthians 6:19-20). While this purity was firstly a matter of the heart, it would necessarily affect behavior, for "the interior work of grace calls for an outer expression."[17] As Seth Rees asserted, "Those who have received their Pentecost live pure, holy lives. They never practice unclean habits, whether secret or known. They do not have unclean thoughts, unchaste desires, or unholy passions. They do not use wine, beer, tobacco, snuff, or opium."[18]

Serious consequences would follow disregard for God's proprietorship of the body; thus John Franklin Knapp advised that the "way to keep in good health is to mind the checks of the Holy Spirit. If you ride over them, the rational result to be expected is that you will be sick."[19] Many suggestions for maintaining optimal health filled the *Revivalist* features on "Winning and Warning" (oriented toward new converts and unbelievers) and "Reformation" (oriented toward the church).[20] Among these "health hints" were protests against such potentially harmful practices as oyster eating (a source of bacterial infection) and gum chewing (due to pepsin from pork),[21] along with calls for moderation in the use of such stimulants as coffee and tea.[22] Many years later, similar concerns kept soda vending machines off the GBS campus long after they had become common place in most public facilities.[23] The temple's purity also required carefulness in what the mind absorbed and how the believer presented him/herself. Diversions from work would be Spirit-directed, as with reading "holiness and reform books and papers" rather than "sensational novels and periodicals."[24] GBS students were informed in class that "if we are God's children, the world will know it by the way we talk, act, and dress."[25]

GBS constituents were reminded that stewardship of finances was an added concern involved in radical holiness opposition to many practices considered "un-hygienic." For instance, Godbey criticized coffee as being "worthless and expensive."[26] Likewise, tobacco was not only "filthy," it was also "expensive," making its user "a THIEF, robbing God of means that might be used for His glory."[27] Knapp questioned, "How can people calling themselves Christians waste their money for tobacco, chewing gum, theaters, novels, jewelry, fine clothes, and pleasure trips, in the light of soon meeting the smile or scorn before the great judgment throne?"[28]

Such waste as Americans spending twenty-two million dollars annually on chewing gum was viewed as especially tragic in light of the tremendous needs to which such resources could be applied, such as the "twenty million heathen in India . . . about to starve to death."[29] Indeed, such waste diametrically opposed the very purpose of God's Bible School, reflected in Knapp's challenge to his *Revivalist* audience:

> Reader, do you love Jesus enough to deny yourself, and plan to save for the rescue of earth's dying millions? The aim of our Bible-school and Missionary-training Home is to fit men and women to carry the Bread of Life to these people, and it is evidently a part of this great movement to reach them in the least possible time, with the greatest amount of spiritual food with the least possible expense.[30]

With this commitment in mind, school regulations insisted that "dress should be plain, neat, and unworldly."[31] In addition, students circulated tracts on *Dress and Jewelry*, contending that "people prompted by the Spirit in this matter will not dress gayly or gaudily, nor dudishly, nor extravagantly, but simply, humbly, modestly, and economically."[32] Children in the *Revivalist* family were recruited to a life of self-denial for foreign missions by participation in the "Do-Without Band," which was featured with regular reports in Minnie Ferle Knapp's column "For the Young." *Revivalist* readers and people attending services at GBS who possessed jewelry were urged to contribute it so that it could be melted down and sold, the proceeds going to various areas of ministry.[33] By November 1900, William Hirst reported that "the response to this appeal has been surprisingly large. Earrings, breastpins, watchchains, charms, rings, lockets, etc., have been sent in, turned into gospel booklets, and sent out preaching."³⁴ Knapp expressed the motivation for such giving squarely in terms of stewardship:

> Is it best to wear jewelry, or to transform it into money that will fly upon missions of love and mercy to a lost world? Is it best to use God's money for tea, coffee, tobacco, and other indulgences, or use it to awaken, convict, convert, sanctify and edify in the shape of salvation books and papers? Of which way does God approve? Which course will bring His kingly approval, "Well done, thou good and faithful servant; thou hast been faithful over a few things, I will make thee ruler over many things; enter thou into the joy of the Lord" [Matthew 25:23]?³⁵

Beyond finances, this accountability was extended to include practically every human resource, no matter how common or basic. Accordingly, the *Revivalist* announced in December 1901 that it would remain steadfastly committed to warning "God's people against needless waste of time and money for personal adornment and luxuries," refusing to "be even a silent partner to any evil that is robbing God or His people of time, money, influence, strength, or health."³⁶

This same concern pervaded GBS, as students were taught in Bible class that one of the lessons of John 6:9-19 was that "holiness makes its possessor careful to gather up the fragments: time, energy, talents, pennies and everything that can be used for God's glory."³⁷ In particular, they were to "avoid stealing God's time"³⁸ by vigilantly following a strict schedule, a practice further necessitated by their crowded quarters. Among the school rules were the admonitions, "Waste no time, 'redeeming the time because the days are evil' . . . Punctuality and promptness are indispensable to success." Accordingly, time for social visits was limited to 4:30 p.m. to 5 p.m., and even this was discouraged as all of a student's time was "needed for the work at hand."³⁹ In addition, breakfast and dinner were combined to allow "better work in better health, at a great saving of time."⁴⁰ To avoid the disruptions of schedule changes, "the term was to be forty-weeks in length with no vacations."⁴¹

In keeping with Knapp's conviction that vacations were "unPentecostal,"⁴² holidays were observed by outreach to the poor and special services, not by reducing the workload. Several school activities were tangible fruit of the belief that "God's people should utilize every opportunity to make the holidays contribute to soul-winning and the advancement of God's kingdom."⁴³ Most notable of these was the famous Thanksgiving Dinner and Convention begun in 1901, inspired by Seth Rees's mission work in Chicago and in keeping with Knapp's conviction that "God absolutely forbids" the common custom of gathering with family and friends to observe Thanksgiving Day, in which people are "sacrilegiously mocking the very God who they profess to be praising," because Jesus commanded his disciples having a feast to "call not thy friends, nor thy brethren . . . nor rich neighbors" but to "bid the poor, the maimed, the lame, the blind."⁴⁴ The first such dinner at GBS fed three hundred of Cincinnati's poor and resulted in "over seventy-five people" seeking "pardon or sanctification,"⁴⁵ confirming Knapp's contention that "such feasts may be made the occasion of blessed, soul-winning victories."⁴⁶

Likewise, the summer months were to be invested fully for God's work with students often opting to participate in "book evangelism" throughout the country or to remain in Cincinnati for "special evangelistic courses" involving street meetings and rescue work. In short, "students were expected to give themselves wholly to their studies, to the meetings, and Christian work connected with the school."⁴⁷

The Faith Principle

God's proprietorship not only demanded faithfulness in stewardship from the saints, it conversely privileged them to put complete trust in the faithfulness of God to meet their every need—divine *possession* assured divine *provision*. This went beyond health needs, for at GBS faith healing was only part of a larger commitment to the life of radical faith—the "faith principle"—which, as with all Pentecostal principles, was applied on both the institutional and individual levels.

In establishing GBS as a "faith work" or "faith school," Knapp found tremendous inspiration in the example of George Muller, who operated an orphanage as a faith work in Bristol, England, not only to assist orphans, but just as importantly to strengthen the faith of God's people "by giving them proof of the unchangeable faithfulness of the Lord."⁴⁸ Knapp announced before property for the school had even been acquired, "We feel that God's plan for His School and Missionary Training-home is that it should be a 'work of faith and a labor of love.'"⁴⁹ His understanding of GBS as such a faith work is succinctly summarized in the definition of a "faith school" by Henry Shilling, a GBS alumnus who went on to found another faith institution, Transylvania Bible School:

> It is a school brought into existence by the direct will of God to perform a definite task and follow a definite leadership of the Holy Spirit. Being such as this, the school can look into God's face at any given moment and ask for the supply of its needs and have its needs adequately, definitely supplied so that the school may continue along the given line for which God has called it.⁵⁰

This meant that many popular means of religious fund-raising would be rejected at GBS, for "a true faith school need not depend upon public appeal . . . a business project . . . any individual's wealth . . . [or] any church's support . . . for support immediately forestalls the fundamental principles upon which a faith institution must be run."⁵¹ This commitment explains in part Knapp's opposition to camp meeting gate admissions, his condemnation of church fairs and festivals, and his refusal to publish "worldly" advertisements in the *Reviv-*

alist.⁵² It also informed some of the *Revivalist*'s most vitriolic protests, which were leveled against ministers stipulating set salaries, who were condemned as "bound by salary," as "hirelings," and as disciples of Judas.⁵³

Knapp's commitment to faith support rather than set salaries extended back to the dark days of his first wife's terminal illness when he received "a vision of the future work": "One of the promises he made God that night was that, no matter how much He should bless and increase and multiply the work, he would trust God to supply his needs, and take no salary, and that all workers would do the same, giving their services as a love-offer to Jesus."⁵⁴ Knapp adhered to this conviction, announcing near the beginning of the second school year, "No one in connection with the school receives any salary; but all trust God to supply their needs. Our bank check is our Savior's promise, 'Seek first the kingdom of God and his righteousness, and all these things shall be added to you,' and 'My God will supply all your need, according to His riches in glory by Christ Jesus.'"⁵⁵ Another "key verse around God's Bible School was Matthew 20:4, 'Go ye also into the vineyard, and whatsoever is right I will give unto you.'"⁵⁶

The no-salary stipulation made the acquisition of early faculty members quite remarkable, especially in light of the relatively stable positions that several of them previously held. Nonetheless, they accepted the condition as "the Savior's instructions to His ministers, 'Gratuitously ye have received, gratuitously give,' literally" taking "delight" in pouring "out their life and strength as He did to bless others and welcome[d] the test of their faith, which His kind of service brings."⁵⁷

This selfless commitment on the part of school workers resulted in an extraordinary policy regarding the cost of schooling for GBS students—while they were expected to "pay $3 a week board,"⁵⁸ tuition was "absolutely free." Although this practice was intended to assure that no potential student would be denied admission due to "lack of means or faith,"⁵⁹ it by no means relieved them of financial obligations: while school leadership exercised faith for meeting the "expense of planting and maintaining this school," all students were expected "to exercise the faith to pay the expense of their own meals, light, heat, and bedding; otherwise their faith [would] be dwarfed, instead of helped."⁶⁰ Along with the example of faculty and staff, as well as the operation of the institution itself, this requirement was intended to promote one of the chief goals of the school—"to inculcate the faith principle of support in God's work." ⁶¹

In other words, students were to implement the "faith principle" during their time at GBS, which would prepare them for further exploits in faith after graduation. Knapp thus maintained, "No worker will ever be able to inspire much faith in others until he has first learned to pray down his own personal expenses."⁶² His young charges rose to the challenge, with students like G. C. Bevington praying in groceries, shoes, and other necessities, not only for themselves, but for the poor of Cincinnati.⁶³ Many alumni can remember that even after GBS had passed well beyond the half-century mark, students continued to pray in money for books, toothpaste, and postage stamps. This was only one way that students applied the faith principle at GBS. Another was "a weekly free-will offering" that was collected instead of tuition "to help meet the heavy incidental expenses, and at the same time help cultivate the gift of faith among the students."[64] In addition, students often contributed toward offerings for special causes such as missions projects and the Thanksgiving Dinner.

Knapp's confidence that the "faith principle" would prove successful at GBS was not only grounded in trust in God, but also in the faithfulness of His people to be good stewards and, consequently, good givers. Again, this was expected to be a natural result of Pentecost: "Pentecostal revivals loosen the purse-strings. Stinginess and holiness are as antagonistic as water and fire. One of the marks of the people who are in the real experience of Bible sanctification, [sic] is that they love to pour out their lives and all they have for Jesus."[65]

The Revivalist and even secular sources indicate that this confidence was rewarded frequently in the early days of the school, only beginning with the astounding acquisition of the Mount of Blessings property. Indeed, the liberality of the saints was demonstrated repeatedly through offerings for missions, for outreach to the poor, and for special projects on the Mount of Blessings. This generosity figured largely in the Revivalist movement's claim to validity: "One of the proofs of the divinity of this movement is the way that God sends in means to meet its needs."[66] In other words, the reward of faith at GBS was considered one sign of repeated Pentecost—that at GBS it was indeed "God Over All."

God's Tabernacle

A demonstration of Pentecost in action, especially the faith principle, that particularly inspired the campus community and captured the attention of onlookers was the events following Knapp's prayer for a facility in which to conduct the Salvation Park Camp Meeting on the Mount Auburn campus. As early as the 1900 camp meeting, still conducted at the Hamilton County fair grounds, congregants were urged to pray "that God would open up a consecrated spot where the meetings could be annually held."[67] Knapp had this in mind when searching for a location for the Bible school.[68] By housing both the school and the camp meeting on the same campus, Knapp intended to make the camp an integral part of the students' experience at GBS, marking the end of the school year, a practice that has continued to the present.[69]

However, with a significant amount of indebtedness remaining on the campus property itself, this dream seemed far from reality during the 1900 Thanksgiving service when a student, M. G. Standley, received "the gift of faith for $1,000 for the tabernacle." Then, during the New Year evening service, as Knapp was sharing his vision for the new work, "a man handed him one dollar. Mr. Knapp held it up and cried out, 'Here's God's witness for the tabernacle!' and like an electric shock a thrill seemed to go through the whole congregation."⁷⁰ When the subsequent, "joyful, free-will offering service, prompted by the Holy Ghost," was concluded, "over $1,300 in a little while" had been "gladly offered" for the tabernacle.⁷¹

The actions of one contributor illustrate the dynamic alteration of priorities that Pentecostal sanctification rendered. Madge Duff, whose mother had sent the initial $100 toward the Mount of Blessings property, had been sanctified earlier that day. As the offering progressed, she "stood up and said, 'In the bank at my home I have $700. I was saving it to use for myself: but I have spent my time and my money up to this time for the world and worldly things, and now, this evening, I want to make God a love-offering of that $700.'" Holy pandemonium erupted, as the saints repeatedly sang "Praise God, from whom all blessings flow"; and students "jumped and waved their handkerchiefs. You could scarcely hear anything but 'Glory to God! Glory to God!'" Further sealing her consecration, Madge, who had previously "prided herself on rich, costly apparel," exchanged her "rich silk dresses" for "the neat simple garments that 'becometh women professing godliness.'"⁷² The permanence of this transformation was reflected the following fall, when Madge, who had several years of experience teaching in Virginia public schools, took charge of the school at Beulah Heights, serving on the faith-basis.⁷³

Such contributions in reward to faith were responded to with Knapp not coincidentally marking his forty-eighth birthday (March 27, 1901) by applying for a building permit.⁷⁴ The next day, he ordered lumber and published plans in the *Revivalist* for a sixty-by-eighty structure, "capable of seating, comfortably, seven hundred persons" with one side opening to accommodate several hundred more, at a cost of $5,000 for the foundation and inclosing the structure (excluding plumbing and finishing).⁷⁵

April 1 proved to be "an auspicious day at the Bible-school" with supporters and students gathering at 6 a.m. for "'breaking sod' services for the tabernacle." As they marched to the building site singing "We're Marching to Zion," several handed offerings for the project to Knapp.⁷⁶ A little over two weeks later, on April 16, an even larger service occurred featuring the laying of the tabernacle cornerstone. After both Knapp and Seth Rees had prayed, several items representative of the Revivalist work were deposited in the cornerstone—including a Bible; a volume of Godbey's commentary; a copy of Knapp's *Back to the Bible: or, Pentecostal Training*; and the *Constitution and By-laws of the International Holiness Union*. Two lists of names were also enclosed—firstly, those of the GBS family present "since the school first opened" and secondly, those of the *Revivalist* family, "about 16,000 of them." Lastly, an issue of *God's Revivalist* was placed within the stone.⁷⁷

Revivalist subscribers seemed especially touched at the inclusion of their names in the cornerstone of this great faith venture, and offerings proliferated as the building neared completion for camp meeting. They were frequently updated through the *Revivalist* by photos of construction progress and by reports of contributions that demonstrated to the world and to a sleeping Church that He is till the same prayer-hearing, prayer-answering God that He was in the days of the apostles, and that His work can be done and the expenses of His kingdom can be met without fair, festival, begging, telling jokes, and kindred modern methods of tickling money out of people; but by the glad free-will offering of His saints."[78]

Excitement intensified until June 28, the beginning day of camp meeting, arrived. Although the boys' dormitory with its thirty rooms above the auditorium was not finished, the sanctuary was complete in time. About fifteen hundred attended throughout the week, with about one hundred sixty people anointed for healing. Many of those healed responded to the "manifestation of the power of God" by weeping, laughing, shouting, jumping, and "skipping like children."[79] In addition, about five hundred people were "saved or sanctified in the ten days."[80] Seth Rees reported one of the most dramatic conversions—that of a police officer, sent by authorities to keep an eye on the proceedings—"God put him under conviction, and when that tall man rushed down the long aisle of the tabernacle and fell at the altar the congregation almost went wild with delight. And when God saved his soul, all heaven took up the glad song, and gave glory to God."[81]

The highlight of the camp was the dedication service of "God's Tabernacle," conducted on July 4, which even the *Cincinnati Enquirer* described in superlative terms: "It surpassed anything of the kind ever witnessed before in Cincinnati."[82] The platform was "crowded with preachers" including the camp workers, all "men of prevailing prayer"—Seth Rees, described by the *Enquirer* as "the eloquent Quaker evangelist"; W. B. Godbey, "victor on hundreds of camp-meeting battlefields"; E. A. Fergerson, "the fire-baptized railroad man"; Charles F. Weigle, the "singing evangelist"; and Andy Dolbow "one of God's Great Salvation Miracles."[83] As with the school's beginning, Rees had the privilege of delivering the dedicatory message, an "excellent" sermon from the text "Who then is willing to consecrate his service this day unto the LORD?" (I Chronicles 29:5).[84] What then transpired was likened by Bessie Queen to "the dedication of the temple of old":

> As [Rees] closed, he said, "Let all who just now consecrate themselves anew bow their heads in silent prayer." A great hush fell on all the people. Brother Rees then prayed that God would accept the tabernacle, built solely for His glory; take possession of the basement, the auditorium, the sleeping-rooms above, all, all His. He then said, "All who will just now renew your covenant of yourself to God raise you[r] right hand and repeat, 'Holy Ghost, I accept you just now.'" As that murmur, like the surging of the sea, broke in on the hush, the very glory of God filled the place, the people wept and shouted and cried. Yea, God had accepted the offering.[85]

In this atmosphere, Rees "asked the assembly what God wanted them to do in the way of a free-will offering for His work, and told them that there was a present need of about $3000."[86] Knapp took his place, eraser in hand, near a blackboard covered by squares representing one hundred dollars each, eager to erase them as funds were pledged. What followed was headlined in the *Cincinnati Enquirer* as "Wild Scenes in the Tabernacle," in which "women threw away all their jewelry," one woman gave a piano, and another gave a "summer cottage and lot that she owned on the Atlantic Coast."[87] In addition, "Mother" Duff and Madge agreed to pledge $5000 from the sale of a farm in Texas.[88] When the service had concluded, about $20,000 had been given and pledged, above the jewelry and other non-cash items.[89] Not only had the funds for God's Tabernacle been supplied, much of the indebtedness for the campus property had been covered as well. Knapp exulted in this "proof that the people who have real Holiness are a liberal people . . . To God's people be thanks; to Him be the praise!"[90]

From the Mount to the World

The events of this first camp meeting on the Mount of Blessings were taken as confirmation that Knapp's goal for GBS and the Revivalist movement—the repetition of Pentecost—was becoming reality. This conclusion was reflected in the glowing assessments of such participants as W. B. Godbey, who described it as "a veritable Pentecost from beginning to end," and Seth Rees, who reported that "this camp was the nearest 'back-to-Pentecost' of anything we have ever witnessed."[91]

The healings, spiritual victories, and spontaneous offerings were just a few of the marks of Pentecost which characterized the camp. Among the others was "a surprising and inspiring pre-eminence in the interest of missions,"[92] in keeping with Knapp's contention that "the Pentecostal experience brings a missionary spirit. When a man is really sanctified wholly he is cut loose from the world and ready for anything God may call him to."[93] When Knapp preached a missionary sermon on the last Sunday of the camp, not only did the congregation "gladly" offer over $2,600, but "more than forty young people came inside the altar, and with radiant faces" they "volunteered for the foreign field, all without salary."[94]

The foundational role of missions at GBS motivated the second part of its name, "Missionary-training Home," intentionally added to magnify "the *missionary* feature of the gospel." Knapp explained that "whether the work be a mission in home or foreign fields, the object of this school is to help clarify the calling and equip for the work."[95] This clarification sometimes involved a change in the intended field of service, as with Mother Duff, who planned to go to India but instead remained at GBS where she became matron of the rescue home.[96] Similarly, Nettie Peabody, a graduate of the Louisiana State Normal College, attended the 1901 camp meeting at about twenty-eight years of age and enrolled as a student for the fall semester, intending to engage in foreign missions thereafter. Instead, she joined the GBS faculty the following year, remaining as a Bible and theology teacher until her retirement in 1965, thus distinguishing her as the longest-tenured teacher in the school's history. Toward the end of her career she acknowledged that instead of confining her ministry to one foreign field, the Lord had permitted her through her students to reach "nearly every country and many of the islands of the sea."[97]

The examples of Duff and Peabody were illustrative of the GBS family's acceptance of the view of missions pioneered by Knapp's hero, Bishop William Taylor, who "argued that there was no qualitative difference between ministry in the USA or overseas. Accidents of geography were just that! In the divine economy, all were equal."[98] Accordingly, Cincinnati and its suburbs were viewed as a "needy and responsive field for home-mission work" that would provide an ideal proving ground in which all GBS students were expected to work as missionaries.

Before the school began, Knapp outlined a plan for taking advantage of this living laboratory for training in soul-winning, using such methods as house-to-house visitation, tract distribution, open-air meetings, and witnessing at Fountain Square and other places where crowds frequently gathered—techniques he and his associates had mastered in connection with their work at Revivalist Chapel and elsewhere.[99] Many of the "Bible-school Notes" in the *Revivalist* reported the exploits of students during these forays into the city, describing encounters with everyone from inquisitive police officers to belligerent drunks.[100]

A particular burden for "fallen girls," about 1,600 of which were estimated to be in Cincinnati, gripped the hearts of the GBS family, and appeals were made to begin a rescue home on the Mount of Blessings.[101] Although this vision only became reality after Knapp's death, several of the female students took their message of full salvation to the hospital ward where such women received medical care.[102] Other students, like G. C. Bevington, frequently visited the homes of the poor, helping them to procure food, clothing, and jobs, as well as salvation.[103] These activities again underscore the radical holiness emphasis on countering societal ills by reforming individuals, as opposed to political action.[104]

While numerous GBS alumni would continue to employ the lessons learned in Cincinnati in similar home mission ventures throughout the United States and Canada, the *Revivalist* family's imagination was captured by foreign mission endeavors. Although the *Revivalist* had featured a missionary column for several years, its foreign mission thrust intensified almost concurrently with the beginning of GBS. In fact, the same convention which witnessed the school's inauguration was concluded with a farewell service for the first Revivalist-sponsored missionaries to a foreign field—William and Mabel Hirst, who set sail for Capetown, South Africa, with their daughter Miriam, on October 10, 1900.[105]

A few months later, beginning in January 1901, the Revivalist movement launched a unique mission endeavor, the "Round-the-World" tour of Charles H. Stalker, holiness Quaker evangelist, who sought not so much to establish new missions as to persuade missionaries already on the field, regardless of their denomination, to accept the Pentecostal message, through a series of holiness conventions. Frequent updates in the *Revivalist* traced Stalker's journey through India, China, Japan, and Africa. Readers were enabled to support the tour financially by giving to the "Go-or-Send Fund."[106]

Although these first ventures into foreign fields had mixed results, with Stalker's partner Byron Rees abandoning their tour before its completion and the Boer War (1899-1902) putting a damper on outreach in South Africa,[107] they reflected two important precedents for GBS missions already incorporated within the school itself: *independent work* and *faith support*. While these stemmed from the previously explained commitments to ecclesiastical primitivism and to the faith principle, they again illustrate the indebtedness of GBS to Bishop Taylor's philosophy of "Pauline Missions." David Bundy explains this approach, which practically combined the above commitments:

> Any church (congregation of Christians) anywhere in the world is the equal of all others. If the people trust in God, are led by the Holy Spirit and work to make Christ known, they are a church with all of the duties and responsibilities of a church. They should not be directed by mission boards and bishops, but by the Holy Spirit. The results of missionary work should be self-supporting, self-propagating, and self-governing.[108]

In essence, radical holiness missionaries were not so much "sent out" by supporting groups as they "went forth" following divine leadership.[109] Whereas traditional missionaries depended on salaries from sponsoring denominations or organizations, the Hirsts and other missionaries serving under the auspices of the Holiness Union had no guaranteed stipend, but depended on the faithfulness of God and his people to supply finances through such *Revivalist* campaigns as the "Africa Mission Fund." They were thus tied to the Mount of Blessings as "the center of a world-wide work" through faith rather than contracts or other human devices.[110]

The Hirsts were ideal candidates to lead the Revivalist movement in taking this approach to the foreign field, for they were already experienced practitioners of the faith principle, since William had served as Knapp's bookkeeper for several years. During the GBS chapel service the morning before he left Cincinnati for Africa, Hirst told the students, "The Lord so richly blessed my soul when I promised I would never again work for a salary, but would serve Him from the heart; and, beloved, I would rather starve on this line than to get $10,000 a year." His wife likewise testified, "How glad I am to be going on the self-supporting line. I feel so much closer to God by going this way than if we went with a salary to depend on."[111]

Through the alumni of GBS and their converts, this approach to missions would have far-reaching repercussions that Knapp probably never imagined in his wildest dreams. A case in point is the ministry of Charles and Lettie Cowman. After accepting the call to the mission field, Charles, who had advanced rapidly in his career as a telegraph supervisor with Western Union in Chicago, and his wife planned to go under the Methodist Mission Board to Japan, where they were to be high school teachers.[112] However, before making this move, the Cowmans, like many others who would enroll at GBS, learned of Knapp's work through a *Revivalist* issue, this one a sample sent at the request of an anonymous friend.[113] Already confirmed in "the experience of old-fashioned Wesleyan holiness," they were impressed by the "deeply spiritual tone" of the paper and became regular subscribers.[114] They determined to visit its editor before leaving for Japan, and arrived in Cincinnati on September 25, 1900. Here they became the first students to enroll in the new school.[115] Having already studied extensively at Moody Bible Institute, they likely functioned more as Knapp's colleagues than regular students, as Lettie's biography of Charles intimates.[116]

Regardless, their few weeks on the Mount of Blessings had a monumental impact on the couple, with Charles commenting, "In the five years' training at Moody's Institute I have never received such deep spiritual truths as I have in the two months I have been in this place."[117] Most significantly, their time at GBS led them to completely revise their mission to Japan in terms of the faith principle, an ideal with which they were almost immediately confronted, for "within a week's time of [their] arrival . . . God began to speak to [them] about going out in the old apostolic way."[118] Their account of the ensuing turning point remains classic in the annals of holiness missions:

> When we told [Knapp] of our plan to go under a regular Missionary Board, he merely answered, "Go to your room and pray." As we waited before God, a burden that was almost unbearable came upon our hearts and held us in fasting and prayer for three days, when God spoke clearly through Matthew 20:4. We understood by this that the Holy Ghost meant we should go out trusting only in the Lord for all our needs. We immediately told Brother Knapp, and he said, "Thank God, He has heard my prayer!" And thus our work in the Orient, like the great work in Cincinnati, has held together these years on purely faith lines, and God has never failed to keep His part of the contract."[119]

Charles noted in his diary that day, "I made an unreserved, an unconditional, cheerful, and eternal surrender of myself to God. I do not feel the least bit of anxiety about my future path. I want only to be holy."[120]

With this commitment settled, the Cowmans and their friends at GBS eagerly awaited God's response to their faith. Just "three weeks later," the "desired token came" that confirmed their faith that the "Heavenly Banker" would supply their needs—a gift of twenty-five cents.[121] During the Cowmans' stay at GBS, a Presbyterian farmer who visited the school was led "into Canaan" by Charles. After returning home to Iowa, he sent the $300 tithe from the sale of a farm to pay for their steamer fare to Japan.[122] Knapp recalled the excitement on campus when Charles received the check:

> I shall never forget his cry as he swung the check in the air. "O Japan! Japan! Glory to God! Japan!"

His wife, hearing the cry, ran to him, "Charlie, what is it?" "Look," was the only answer. By this time a number of students had gathered, and such a time of rejoicing! Sister Cowman crying, Brother Cowman laughing and shouting. God knows how to answer.[123]

In the *Revivalist* for November 15, 1900, the Cowmans exulted, "We believe this is but the 'first-fruits' of a great harvest."[124] Indeed, the harvest that followed is incalculable by human standards. Out of this seed emerged the Oriental Missionary Society (later OMS International, now One Mission Society), which had grown by 1999 to include "450 missionaries in partnership with 3,530 churches, with membership exceeding one million."[125] In addition, OMS provided the roots of the Korea Evangelical Holiness Church, now one of the world's largest holiness denominations, with about one million members."[126]

OMS retained strong ties with GBS for over twenty years, with the school supplying numerous missionaries to the organization throughout the next half century. In addition, the *Revivalist* featured the Cowmans' work in the "Missionary" column and the Cowmans' relied on GBS as one of their forwarding addresses for supporters, in effect making GBS "one of its home offices."[127] In turn, the Cowmans proved a blessing to *Revivalist* readers through Lettie's contributions in the column, "Thoughts for the Quiet Hour." Many of these, penned during the dark years between Charles' forced retirement in 1918 due to a severe heart attack and his death in 1924, were collected and released in book form in 1925 as the best-selling devotional, *Streams in the Desert*, which "was recently listed among the 20 most widely-read books of all time."[128]

And to think! All of this sprang from a young couple's embrace of the radical faith which they encountered and found exemplified at God's Bible School and Missionary Training Home. In fact, the Cowmans' story aptly illustrates the twofold manner in which Knapp planned for GBS to fuel the flames of Pentecostal holiness around the world. Firstly, Knapp aspired, like many Americans from John Winthrop to John Humphrey Noyes, to propagate his spiritual vision by establishing GBS as a "city set on a hill." He thus admonished his supporters: "As Mt. Zion was situated high above Jerusalem, and looked down upon it, and became the mighty center of a great movement that was a blessing to all Israel, so let our readers pray that the Mount of Blessings may be to this city and to God's Israel of every name and nation."[129]

In a sense, GBS was to be the primary laboratory for Knapp's grand Pentecostal experiment, demonstrating to the world the veracity of Holiness Pentecostal claims. Again, far from a merely academic enterprise, GBS was to provide a proving ground and boot camp where Pentecostal ideals would not only be lectured but also be implemented by students and staff. Ultimately, in this community in which holiness was the rule, Pentecostal principles could be tested and verified for all to witness.[130] Although in the midst of the urban "wilderness" of Cincinnati, GBS would provide a spiritual oasis where students and other holiness people could find "the inexpressible rapture that is to be experienced by redeemed souls in holy communion in a modern Eden that is like unto the Eden of antiquity."[131]

However, this experiment was not conceived as one of creating an isolated or insulated community. On the contrary, everything done at GBS was calculated in terms of missionary motive. Even the Pentecostal successes obtained at GBS that directly benefited the school and its sponsored ministries, such as the gift for the Cowmans' passage to Japan and the donations for God's Tabernacle, became instructional, not just for students, but also for the ever-growing constituency who would read reports of these faith exploits in the pages of the *Revivalist*. In addition, the accounts of healing of bodies and souls and evangelistic endeavors, especially among the poor, were calculated to stimulate similar activity throughout the holiness movement. Simply put, GBS was to be a missionary community, modeling Pentecost in action for the world.[132]

Secondly, Knapp expected GBS to play a crucial role in the promulgation of radical holiness ideals through its alumni, who would leave and engage in ministries that would emulate what they had learned at GBS, effectively replicating Pentecost around the globe. This not only meant the general implementation of the faith principle and other Pentecostal precepts in local churches, missions, and orphanages at home and abroad; it also specifically meant duplicating the Cincinnati center in a series of other "God's Bible Schools" located at strategic points throughout the world.

For example, the article describing the Cowmans' farewell service from GBS indicated their plan to join forces with Juji Nakada, a Methodist Japanese minister who had been sanctified while in Chicago in 1897, at about the time he met the Cowmans.[133] A dynamic communicator whose father was a samurai and who himself was expert in judo,[134] Nakada's persuasive preaching earned him the appellation of the "Moody of Japan."[135] Nakada was eagerly awaiting the Cowmans' arrival so that they could "open a Bible-school," which, like the Cincinnati school, was envisioned "not to cram the mind of the Japanese with secular knowledge, but to evangelize, teach, and exemplify a full gospel."[136] In reporting on their first ten days in Japan, Charles Cowman reiterated this vision "to start a Biblical training-school" patterned after what Knapp was "doing in Cincinnati."[137] By early April 1901, classes had begun with a regimen reminiscent of that on the Mount of Blessings.[138]

While it appears that the Orient eventually assumed the dominance in early GBS interest in missions, with the first international student at the Cincinnati campus being an eighteen-year-old Japanese boy, Shoji Murakami,[139] the Cowmans' plan was paralleled on other fields. In fact, "by September 1902, *The Revivalist* displayed the pictures of three overseas 'God's Bible Schools' – one in Capetown, Africa, carried on by W. N. Hirst; one in Japan, under Charles Cowman; and another in India, conducted by Gorham Tufts."[140] In addition, in both the US and abroad, numerous other schools, not so closely tied organizationally to GBS, also looked to the Mount of Blessings as their model. For example, a Pilgrim Holiness historian has asserted that all the early Pilgrim Holiness regional colleges in the US were "but miniatures of God's Bible School."¹⁴¹ Indeed, as Harry Plank has observed, one of the great contributions of GBS to the holiness movement has been its "mothering influence to other Bible schools."¹⁴²

Furthermore, the schools that followed the GBS paradigm frequently spawned spin-offs as well, again following the pattern of the "mother" school. For example, after two Korean men named Bin Chung and SangJun Kim "began to be burdened for the Holy Ghost," they learned of the "God's Bible School" in Tokyo. In 1905, they journeyed there, even though they did not speak Japanese or English. However, they quickly learned and soon found their heart's desire, receiving the "experience of complete deliverance from sin, and the abiding Holy Ghost." They then returned to Korea, accompanied by Charles Cowman and E. A. Kilbourne, and organized the work of OMS in Seoul. Late the following year (1908), their passion to share the holiness message with other Koreans led to the establishment of a Bible training school. There, just as in Cincinnati, students experienced "God's mighty power as they did on the Day of Pentecost."¹⁴³ Soon, rapid growth forced them to seek larger facilities, beginning a long-time trend. In fact, this school was the precursor to Seoul Theological Seminary, now "one of the largest graduate schools of theology in the world."¹⁴⁴

The replication of Bible schools after the fashion of GBS remained one of the most significant indicators of Pentecost's return for Knapp and his supporters. As W. B. Godbey rejoiced,

> The Bible School phenomenon is the sunburst of the holiness movement, throughout all Christendom this day. So fast as this Holy Ghost revival spreads over the earth, these Bible Schools invariably spring up in its track, thus fortifying its converts, holding the fort and drilling the soldiers for aggressive movements against the powers of darkness, radiating out to every point of the compass.¹⁴⁵

In other words, the schools inspired by the Mount of Blessings, ranging from the Greensboro Bible and Literary School led by Winifred Cox in Greensboro, North Carolina,¹⁴⁶ to the Seoul Bible School, were not competitors with GBS in Cincinnati. Rather, they simply extended the Pentecostal flames even further, thus fulfilling Knapp's plans and prayers to see Pentecost spread from the Mount of Blessings around the world.

Notes

[1] "God's Bible-School," *Revivalist* (July 26, 1900), 14.

[2] Cited in M. W. Knapp, *Back to the Bible*, 53.

[3] Beatrice M. Finney, "My Call to Africa," *Revivalist* (Dec. 19, 1901), 11 (my emphasis).

[4] Robert M. Mussman, *A Candle of the Lord: The Ethical Teachings of John Wesley* (Salem, OH: Schmul, 1992), 63. Wesley thus wrote of "God, the proprietor of all" with regard to careful stewardship in procuring apparel (John Wesley, *The Works of John Wesley* 3rd ed. Vol. 7 (*Sermons*) (1872; reprint, Peabody, MA: Hendrickson Publishers, 1986), 20. See Wallace Thornton, Jr., *Radical Righteousness*, on stewardship's role as an underlying principle guiding Wesleyan/Holiness behavioral standards.

[5] *Lightning Bolts*, 88 (original emphasis). Also, see F. L. P., "After the Tenth," *Revivalist* (June 6, 1901), 8 and "God's Financial Plan," Part IV of Knapp, *Back to the Bible*, 58-66.

[6] Ibid, 89. Knapp continued, "What an honor to be thus associated with the King of Heaven in the distribution of His goods! What perfidy to betray this sacred trust and expend them on ourselves or friends, or to 'lock them up' for selfish purposes in banks, or stocks, or lands! Such riches is robbery, and every dollar thus devoted will prove a weight to sink some soul to hell unless it be restored." Also, see Kostlevy, *Holy Jumpers*, 32.

[7] Ibid, 91 (original emphasis).

[8] Kostlevy, *Holy Jumpers*, 32.

[9] Ibid.

[10] Hills, *Hero*, 332-333 (original emphasis). This defense was penned by Bessie Queen. See a similar defense by Knapp in *Pentecostal Letters*, 79-80. For thinly veiled criticism of appropriating God's name for such enterprises as the *Revivalist*, see Beverly Carradine, *A Box of Treasure* (1910; reprint, Salem, OH: Allegheny Publications, 2000), 111-112:

If a religious paper should call itself "God's Witness and Advocate of Bible Holiness," the legitimate inference would be that it was not only God's special organ, but God's only organ in the world for teaching and spreading holiness. All other papers by this title would be but imitators, and standing in secondary and remote degrees from the Throne. The same would not only be an impertinence, but a direct insult to all other holiness papers published. It would be attempted Divine monopoly.

Knapp's response to such protests was straightforward, "This name does not imply that it is the only paper which is God's, no more than the fact that you, reader, claim to be God's man or God's woman indicates that no other person is" (Hills, *Hero*, 230.)

[11] "God's Bible-school and Missionary-training Home," *Revivalist* (July 5, 1900), 1.

[12] "Not for Personal Profit," *Revivalist* (August 1, 1901), 15. See also, "School for Bible-Study," *Cincinnati Post* (Aug. 1, 1901), 6, which announced in its sub-title: "Property 'Bought for God' To Be Paid For in Two Years."

[13] One of the reasons for the school's name, in fact, was to help procure divine guidance, for "one of the conditions of obtaining His guidance is that He should be

thus acknowledged" ("God's Bible-school and Missionary-training Home," *Revivalist* (July 5, 1900), 1).

[14] "God's Bible-School," *Revivalist* (July 26, 1900), 14.

[15] Beatrice M. Finney, "A Blessing," *Revivalist* (March 7, 1901), 4. See also Belle Staples, "Bible-School Notes," Revivalist (May 23, 1901), 15, "Our superintendent, Brother Knapp, has been absent the past week; but the great General Superintendent—the Holy Ghost—was present, performing His office work . . ."

[16] Kostlevy, *Holy Jumpers*, 32. See typical announcements in Moser and Smith, 37 and 60.

[17] "Holiness Attire," *Revivalist* (Jan. 17, 1901), 3.

[18] Seth Rees, *The Ideal Pentecostal Church*, 13.

[19] J. F. Knapp, "Health Hints," *Revivalist* (Dec. 19, 1901), 11.

[20] Like the departments for "Gifts of Healings" and "Behold, He Cometh," these were regular features of the expanded *Revivalist*.

[21] "Oyster Facts," *Revivalist* (Dec. 27, 1900), 8, and "That Gum Business," *Revivalist* (Sept. 13, 1900), 8. Readers were warned that "when you are chewing gum, if there are cancer microbes in the hog, you'll get your full share of them."

Other health hints acquainted holiness people with potential hazards ranging from poor posture and lack of proper ventilation to dirty cellars and underdone bread (See "Vitalizing Breathing," *Revivalist* (July 26, 1900), 8, and "Health Hints," *Revivalist* (Sept. 27, 1900), 8). In addition, although "bodily exercise profiteth little" (I Timothy 4:8), regular exercise was promoted, especially for those with desk jobs who were promised, "Take a brisk walk every day, and you will get a new life."

[22] Dr. Godbey commented that "coffee is not comparable with rum, tobacco, or opium, but a comparatively mild stimulant, not involving any sin if used in moderation." Yet, he personally practiced abstinence, remarking, "I am glad that I do not know the taste of it . . . I am glad that Jesus has broken every yoke off from my neck, and I am not willing to wear any, even though it be so innocent as coffee, which certainly does capture and yoke its votaries. It is glorious to be free in every respect" ("Question Drawer," *Revivalist* (Nov. 28, 1901), 6. Likewise, he refused to drink tea (See his *Absinthe and the Drink Demon* (Cincinnati: Revivalist, n. d.), 4.

[23] Author interviews of Robert and Marilyn England (March 8, 1999) and Leonard Sankey (February 22, 1999). For an early perspective on soda, see F. L. P., "Soda Water or Souls?," *Revivalist* (June 6, 1901), 7.

[24] "Counteracting Influences," *Revivalist* (July 1892), 3.

[25] "Gleanings from Bible-School Lessons," *Revivalist* (March 28, 1901), 4. These lectures were based on John 4:19-28. Students had earlier confirmation of this point when two persons confessed "in a Bible-school meeting that they had grieved the Spirit greatly and lost their experience by disobedience in regard to dress" ("Holiness Attire," *Revivalist* (Jan. 17, 1901), 3. Similarly, Elizabeth Ferle testified that the way she wore her bangs was "the first and hardest thing that [she] had to lay aside" before being sanctified "Experience of a Cincinnati Mission Worker," *Revivalist* (April 11, 1901), 4.

[26] Godbey, "Question Drawer," *Revivalist* (Nov. 28, 1901), 6. Knapp also condemned their use as "A Needless Waste," *Revivalist* (Nov. 28, 1901), 4, also sug-

gesting that "these stimulants, as Dr. Godbey teaches, become a substitute for the indwelling of the Holy Ghost and the inspiration which He brings."

[27] "Seventeen Shots from a Tobacco State," *Revivalist* (Jan. 1896), 5 and "Tobacco Users," *Revivalist* (March 9, 1899), 8 (original emphasis). Scriptural support for this position was seen in Isaiah 55:2: "Wherefore do ye spend money for that which is not bread?" ("The Tobacco God," *Revivalist* (March 7, 1901), 8). The high percentage of tobacco users in the M. E. Church was considered particularly objectionable to Knapp, considering that "their aggregate outlay [for tobacco] is just about double what the entire church pays for pastoral support" ("A Revival Hindrance," *Revivalist* (May 1890), 8).

[28] "The Starving Millions," *Revivalist* (Aug. 2, 1900), 9. See also, "Holiness Economy," *Revivalist* (Dec. 13, 1900), 2.

[29] "That Gum Business," 8. See also, "Anti-Revival Waste," *Revivalist* (Dec. 5, 1901), 2, in which Knapp argues, "If money thus wasted could be turned into New Testament channels and used in the promotion of revivals of religion on the New Testament basis, the gospel would soon be preached to every creature, earth's impenitent millions warned of their impending peril, and the Bride made ready for the marriage supper of the Lamb." Such selfishness was also regarded as a cause of backsliding "of many who [had] been saved and sanctified," but had failed to "'seek first the kingdom' of heaven 'and its righteousness.'"

[30] "The Starving Millions," *Revivalist* (Aug. 2, 1900), 9.

[31] Knapp, *Back to the Bible*, 39.

[32] "Holiness Attire," *Revivalist* (Jan. 17, 1901), 3. Modesty was another strong rationale for proscribing fashionable dress at GBS. Those who chose to "adorn themselves with the foolish trumpery of fashion" would find that "God hates the haughty" and condemns "the fallen daughter of Zion to-day" just as "those of old" (Isaiah 3:16-24) ("Fruits and Punishment of Pride," *Revivalist* (Sept. 20, 1900), 8).

[33] Revivalist readers were encouraged to send their solid jewelry to GBS, because "plated jewelry is worthless." Knapp admitted that this process would only yield "a fraction of its original cost," but contended that this smaller amount used for God "is worth a hundred-fold more than if borne upon the person or hidden away in a drawer." "Which Is Best?," *Revivalist* (Dec. 13, 1900), 14.

[34] W. N. Hirst, "Consecrated Jewelry," *Revivalist* (Nov. 29, 1900), 8. For reports from some who sent in their jewelry, see Mrs. M. W. Knapp, "Trinkets or Souls," *Revivalist* (Jan. 11, 1900), 8, and "Jewelry Transformed," *Revivalist* (Nov. 29, 1900), 3. In May, 1901, Mrs. Knapp reported that "almost every week for the past six months the writer has carried jewelry to the refiners, sometimes six and seven different parcels ("A Thank-Offering," *Revivalist* (May 23, 1901), 3). Also, see *Pentecostal Letters*, 119.

[35] "Which is Best?" *Revivalist* (Dec. 13, 1900), 14. Also see "Ten Reasons Why Keepsakes Should Be Transformed Into Jewels for the King's Crown," *Revivalist* (Dec. 5, 1901), 13, and Mrs. M. W. Knapp, "Where Is Your Gold?" *Revivalist* (June 6, 1901), 8, in which she admonishes those who have laid their jewelry aside to get rid of it by contributing it for God's work, instead of "holding them" for memory's sake.

[36] "God's Revivalist for 1902," *Revivalist* (Dec. 5, 1901), 1.

[37] Beatrice M. Finney, ed. "Lessons from Bible-Class--Mount of Blessings," *Re-

vivalist (April 11, 1901), 2.

[38] "A Marked People," *Revivalist* (June 28, 1900), 2. As with money, time was put clearly in context of stewardship: "Thirty minutes in indolence or snoozing three hundred days in a year, would amount to fifteen days in a whole year. Can God say, 'Well done, good and faithful servant,' to those who have thus squandered their time?"

[39] Knapp, *Back to the Bible*, 39.

[40] Ibid, 38. For biblical agreement with the practice of only two meals per day, see Abbie C. Morrow, "No Breakfast--Is It Scriptural?" *Revivalist* (April 25, 1901), 8.

[41] Day, 37.

[42] Knapp proclaimed that "the modern craze for vacations is unpentecostal . . . The past year has been one of the busiest and most blessed in all my life . . . My only vacation has been a series of summer camp-meetings, in which a change of labor has proved a blessing to both soul and body, and which I have reason to believe has proved a blessing to multitudes. To God be all the praise. I have learned the blessed secret that the best vacation is found in spreading a glorious gospel of full and free salvation" ("Notes By the Way," *Revivalist* (Sept. 21, 1899), 2).

[43] "Holiday Revival Hints," *Revivalist* (Nov. 7, 1901), 1. Revivalist family members unable to attend such functions at GBS were encouraged at least to give "soul-winning books" and the *Revivalist* for holiday presents. Knapp asserted that "one of the Pentecostal peculiarities of God's people is that of giving soul-winning papers and books for wedding, birthday, and holiday presents" ("Beautiful Gift Cards," *Revivalist* (Sept. 19, 1901), 4).

[44] "Thanksgiving Revivals," *Revivalist* (Nov. 28, 1901), 3. Also, see "Another Commandment," *Revivalist* (Nov. 21, 1901), 13. Likewise, Rev. O. L. Markman implored holiness people to give gifts to Christ's work rather than to friends and family at Christmas, for "it is utterly preposterous to celebrate the birth of Jesus by spending the day in a gluttonous feast and giving our presents only to each other" ("Christmas Presents," *Revivalist* (Dec. 19, 1901), 14). Also see Bessie [Queen], "God's Presents," *Revivalist* (Dec. 5, 1901), 13. On the inspiration provided by Rees's Chicago work, see Day, 44 and Harold R. Crosser, *A History of Education in the Pilgrim Holiness Church* (University Park, PA: Pennsylvania State College, 1953), 17.

[45] "Christmas Dinner," *Revivalist* (Dec. 19, 1901), 12. So successful was the first GBS Thanksgiving Dinner that Knapp planned a similar Christmas dinner, which was supervised by Seth Rees. See also, Belle Staples, "Bible-School Notes," *Revivalist* (Dec. 12, 1901), 14-15 and "Overflowing Blessings," *Revivalist* (Dec. 12, 1901), 12.

[46] "Thanksgiving Revivals," *Revivalist* (Nov. 28, 1901), 3. See also, "Thanksgiving Revival," *Revivalist* (Dec. 12, 1901), 1.

[47] Knapp, *Back to Bible*, 38.

[48] George Muller, *The Autobiography of George Muller* (Reprint; New Kinsington, PA: Whitaker House, 1984), 73. In the preface to the abridgement which he published, Knapp wrote, "There is no book in the whole realm of spiritual literature which has proven such a faith tonic to the writer as the *Life of George Muller*, which he read early in his ministry" (Abbie C. Morrow, ed. *The Work of Faith Through George Muller* (1899; reprint, Salem, OH: Allegheny Publications, 2005), 3. *The Revivalist* also highlighted excerpts from Muller's writings, such as "Early Rising," (March 29,

1900), 15 and "Believing God," (February 25, 1909), 15. See also "George Muller's Work," *Revivalist* (March 8, 1900), 9 and W. N. Hirst, "Lessons from George Muller," (July 5, 1900), 3.

[49] "A Work of Faith," *Revivalist* (June 21, 1900), 5.

[50] Henry Shilling, *Seven Years of Faith; or, Explorations in the Realm of Prayer* (Freeport, PA: The Fountain Press, n. d.), 174. Shilling incorporated many of the principles he imbibed at the Mount of Blessings in Transylvania Bible School. Though he subsequently attended several other institutions after GBS, including Asbury College, Grove City College, and Westminster College, Shilling professed great indebtedness to GBS, especially its emphasis on the Bible—"There I learned what my heart hungered to know. I wanted to know the Book" (22). "The only honest, real, worth-while Bible study I have ever had, I received at [God's] Bible School" (24). "My experience at God's Bible School grounded me firmly in holiness background and doctrines. It gave me a firm hold on the promises of God" (27).

[51] Ibid, 174-175.

[52] See "Camp-Meeting Gate Fees," *Revivalist* (Aug. 22, 1901), 13; "One Hundred Facts About Church Finances," *Revivalist* (May 1895), 5; and "Why I Don't Insert Worldly Ads in The Revivalist" in Hills, *Hero*, 49-50.

[53] See "Preachers' Salaries," *Revivalist* (Aug. 29, 1901), 8, where it is argued that "in no place in the Bible is a stipulated salary for preachers indorsed. The principle is wrong and its fruits are evil." This condemnation included both "salary-seeking among pastors" and "stipulating financial consideration on the part of evangelists" ("Cause of Revival Decline," *Revivalist* (March 1, 1900), 1). Also, see "Bound Preachers," *Revivalist* (Jan. 23, 1902), 13; G. A. Fergerson, "Preachers vs. Hirelings," *Revivalist* (March 8, 1900), 8; W. B. Godbey, *Judas and His Apostles* (Cincinnati: God's Revivalist Press, n. d.), 24-25; Rev. Arthur Greene, "Souls or Money?" *Revivalist* (Sept. 12, 1901), 14; and M. W. Knapp, "Wrecked Humanity and Hirelings," *Revivalist* (Feb. 28, 1901), 1. Rev. John Pennington, "Faith vs. Begging," *Revivalist* (Feb. 27, 1902), 3, puts the issue in perspective of motivation, suggesting that a minister receiving a salary can be "a man of faith" while one supposedly "living by faith" may "be a consummate beggar and miser."

[54] "Pray! Pray! Pray!" *Revivalist* (Jan. 23, 1902), 11.

[55] "Bible-School Opening," *Revivalist* (Aug. 8, 1901), 15. Also, see "A Faith Work," *Revivalist* (June 6, 1901), 15 and Thomas and Thomas, 34-35.

[56] Thomas and Thomas, 34.

[57] "Bible-School Opening," *Revivalist* (Aug. 8, 1901), 15.

[58] "School for Bible Study," *Cincinnati Post* (August 1, 1900), 6.

[59] "A Weekly Free-Will Offering" *Revivalist* (Aug. 8, 1901), 15.

[60] "Faith for Personal Expenses," *Revivalist* (Aug. 8, 1901), 15.

[61] "God's School," *Revivalist* (Sept. 13, 1900), 15.

[62] "Faith for Personal Expenses," *Revivalist* (Aug. 8, 1901), 15.

[63] See Bevington, *Remarkable Incidents*.

[64] "A Weekly Free-Will Offering," *Revivalist* (Aug. 8, 1901), 15.

[65] "Revival Liberality," *Revivalist* (July 11, 1901), 1. See also A. Sims, "Giving," *Revivalist* (Aug. 2, 1900), 15, M. W. Knapp, "Pentecostal Giving," Revivalist (April

11, 1901), 16, and Seth Rees, *The Ideal Pentecostal Church*, 30-32.

[66] Ibid.

[67] "Salvation Park Meeting," *Revivalist* (May 23, 1901), 2.

[68] "Worthy of God," *Revivalist* (June 21, 1900), 4 and "The Location," *Revivalist* (June 21, 1900), 4.

[69] "An Evangelistic Training-School," *Revivalist* (June 27, 1901), 13 explains, "The Bible-school program embraces and incorporates the Salvation Park meeting as a part of its course in evangelistic training, affording its students priceless advantages in this way." Also, see "The Closing Exercises of the Bible-school," *Revivalist* (June 17, 1901), 1.

[70] Hills, *Hero*, 208 Also, see Moser and Smith, 16-17 for Minnie Ferle Knapp's version of events leading up to the dedication of "God's Tabernacle."

[71] "Bible-school Chapel," *Revivalist* (Jan. 10, 1901), 11.

[72] Hills, *Hero*, 208-209.

[73] "School Opening," *Revivalist* (July 25, 1901), 15.

[74] "Bible-School Diary," *Revivalist* (April 4, 1901), 15.

[75] Ibid and "Salvation Park Tabernacle," *Revivalist* (March 28, 1901), 12.

[76] "The Sod Broken," *Revivalist* (April 11, 1901), 12.

[77] "The Laying of the Corner-Stone," *Revivalist* (April 25, 1901), 12. Other books placed in the stone included Rees's *Fire from Heaven*; Godbey's *Return of Jesus*; Knapp's latest book, *Holiness Triumphant*; and *Tears and Triumphs*, the latter to let posterity know that the Revivalist family not only preached and testified a full gospel, "but sang it." The service concluded with a stirring sermon by Rees from the text, "Holiness becometh Thine house, O Lord, forever" (Psalm 93:5).

[78] "God's Tabernacle," *Revivalist* (June 13, 1901), 15.

[79] Seth Rees, "Salvation Park Camp-Meeting," *Revivalist* (July 18, 1901), 12. However, Rees observed that "by no means was this camp one of mere emotion. True, the intoxication of the Spirit was so great at times that no one could preach, and it would seem as if almost the whole congregation would go into the clouds. But when they would come down they always lit on their feet, running in the way of practical Christianity."

[80] Seth C. Rees, "God's Camp-Meeting," *Revivalist* (July 12, 1900), 5.

[81] Seth Rees, "Salvation Park Camp-Meeting," *Revivalist* (July 18, 1901), 12.

[82] "Wild Scenes in the Tabernacle," *Cincinnati Enquirer* (July 5, 1901), 10.

[83] Ibid and announcement of "Salvation Park Meetings," *Revivalist* (June 27, 1901), 13 and "Camp-Meeting Personals," *Revivalist* (July 18, 1901), 1. Charles F. Weigle's name appears with variant spellings in the *Revivalist*, including Wiegele and Weigele. Some of his most enduring songs include "I Love to Walk with Jesus," "No One Ever Cared for Me like Jesus," and "Living for Jesus," numbers 206, 410, and 479 respectively in the hymnal, *Sing to the Lord* (Kansas City, MO: Lillenas Publishing Co., 1993).

Kostlevy gives helpful characterizations of Fergerson and Dolbow in *Holy Jumpers*, 66-68. Also, see "God Answering By Fire; or, The Great Chicago Revival," *Revivalist* (May 30, 1901), 1-4. For representative sermons by Rees, Fergerson, and Weigle, see *"The Last Prayermeeting" or Eternal Verities* (Cincinnati: Revivalist, 1904).

Also, see E. A. Fergerson, *Gold From God's Mint* (Cincinnati: Revivalist, 1914).

[84] Ibid.

[85] Bible-School Notes," *Revivalist* (July 18, 1901), 14.

[86] Seth Rees, "Salvation Park Camp-Meeting," *Revivalist* (July 18, 1901), 12.

[87] "Wild Scenes in the Tabernacle," *Cincinnati Enquirer* (July 5, 1901), 10.

[88] Hills, *Hero*, 210.

[89] Knapp, "Salvation Park Camp-Meeting," *Revivalist* (July 18, 1901), 1 and Seth Rees, "Salvation Park Camp-Meeting," *Revivalist* (July 18, 1901), 12.

[90] Ibid.

[91] W. B. Godbey, "Salvation Park Camp-Meeting," *Revivalist* (Aug. 15, 1901), 11 and Seth C. Rees, "God's Camp-Meeting," *Revivalist* (July 12, 1900), 5.

[92] Godbey, ibid.

[93] "Shall We Send Them," *Revivalist* (Jan. 5, 1899), 9. See also, "A Missionary Church," *Revivalist* (Dec. 27, 1900), 9; "The Bible Idea of Missions and Missionaries," *Revivalist* (April 18, 1901), 9; and "Reports," *Revivalist* (Aug. 15, 1901), 11; where Knapp asserted, "God's true people are a missionary people, and any type of holiness which lacks this stamp is not the Bible kind, but a damning counterfeit."

[94] Seth C. Rees, "God's Camp-Meeting," *Revivalist* (July 12, 1900), 5 and W. B. Godbey, "Salvation Park Camp-Meeting," *Revivalist* (Aug. 15, 1901), 11.

[95] God's Bible-school and Missionary-training Home," *Revivalist* (July 5, 1900), 1.

[96] Hills, *Hero*, 210. For her testimony describing her early experience, see Mrs. E. S. Duff, "Victory Through the Blood," *Revivalist* (July 18, 1901), 2 and Mrs. E. S. Duff, *Redeemed by the Blood* (Cincinnati: Office of "God's Revivalist," 1905).

[97] Florence Carlson, "God's Bible School Loses Longtime Teacher and Friend," *Revivalist* (Oct. 7, 1971), 1, 5. Only a brief absence due to illness ("for seventeen months, beginning in the fall of 1952") interrupted Peabody's service to the school. She left GBS on Sept. 30, 1965, and spent her retirement years in a Brownsfield, Texas, nursing home where she shared a room with her sister. She died on August 28, 1971.

[98] David Bundy, "From Cincinnati to the World: The Beginnings of the Missionary Vision of God's Bible School," *Revivalist* (Winter 2001), 9, 25.

[99] "Cincinnati as a Mission Field," *Revivalist* (June 21, 1900), 5. Also, see "Our Cincinnati Center," *Revivalist* (March 7, 1901), 9, 11; "Slum Work in Cincinnati," *Revivalist* (March 21, 1901), 14; "Open-Air Revival-Meetings," and "Revival Street-Preaching," *Revivalist* (Oct. 3, 1901), 1. W. B. Godbey suggested that such ministry was true proof of "Apostolic Succession," *Revivalist* (June 13, 1901), 3—"The Holy Ghost is calling for a round million to volunteer on this primitive apostolic-line of street and household preaching."

[100] For example, see "Bible-school notes," *Revivalist* (June 27, 1901), 15.

[101] See "The Rescue Home," *Revivalist* (July 25, 1901), 15; Bessie [Queen], "Bible-School Notes," *Revivalist* (Oct. 10, 1901), 15; and the regular updates on the "Rescue Home Fund."

[102] Bessie [Queen], "Bible-School Notes," *Revivalist* (Nov. 21, 1901), 15 and "Our Sisters," *Revivalist* (Feb. 20, 1902), 13.

[103] See G. C. Bevington, *Remarkable Incidents*. Also, see "Rescue the Perishing,"

Revivalist (Nov. 21, 1901), 9, which appeals for food and clothing for the indigent in Cincinnati, Chicago (Rees's work), and Denver (Kent and Alma White's work).

[104] Although such holiness leaders as W. B. Godbey encouraged their followers to support the Prohibition party ("Question Drawer," *Revivalist* (Aug. 9, 1900), 12), *The Revivalist* expressed caution regarding holiness alliances "with the world to reform any evil," citing II Corinthians 6:14-18. It observed that neither Jesus "nor the early Bible Church formed any parties against any one or two evils . . . but instead of teaching reformation on any line, they taught repentance and salvation from all sin." It then contended that

> Even some holiness people are wasting much precious time, and perhaps grieving the Holy Spirit, by entering so much into politics and Government reform. These reform parties often act as snares to get the true people out of the narrow way into a work that never saves a soul from all sin. If all the money, energy, and even praying, that has been expended on political reform and liquor prohibition had been used in getting souls saved, sanctified, and ready for His coming, and in sending the gospel into heathen lands, it would have brought in much richer returns and a greater consciousness of God's leading" (C. Leslie Smith, "Unholy Combinations," *Revivalist* (Dec. 27, 1900), 8).

Also, see Stephens, 171.

[105] See Knapp, *Back to the Bible*, 70-71; "Going!" *Revivalist* (October 4, 1900), 9; and "Gone!" *Revivalist* (October 18, 1900), 9.

[106] See Byron J. Rees, "World-Wide Evangelism: Providence and En Route," *Revivalist* (Jan. 10, 1901), 13, and "The Journey Begun," *Revivalist* (Jan. 31, 1901), 9, on the beginning of this endeavor. Numerous reports appear in the "Missionary" column of *The Revivalist* throughout the following months. See also, Charles H. Stalker, *Twice Around The World With The Holy Ghost or The Impressions and Convictions of the Mission Field* (Columbus, OH: Charles H. Stalker, 1906).

[107] Byron J. Rees, son of Seth and Hulda Rees, apparently spearheaded the "Round-the-World" tour ("The Whole World for Jesus," *Revivalist* (Oct. 4, 1900), 9 and Byron J. Rees, "World-Wide Holiness Evangelism," *Revivalist* (Dec. 6, 1900), 14). However, he and Stalker evidently went their separate ways after their visit to India (Rees to Australia, Stalker to China), with Rees returning home earlier, where he eventually abandoned the holiness movement (See "Missionary" column, *Revivalist* (July 18, 1901), 9 and Kostlevy, *Holy Jumpers*, 83, 181).

The Boer War began about a year before the Hirsts departure for Capetown and pitted the Dutch colonists of South Africa against the British government. Though the British triumphed with the signing of the Treaty of Vereeniging on May 31, 1902, the conflict hampered Revivalist missionary efforts in Africa, delaying the sending of teacher Beatrice Finney and Knapp's sister-in-law, Elizabeth Ferle, to join the Hirsts. See "The War in South Africa," *Revivalist* (March 1, 1900), 9; "The Situation in Africa," *Revivalist* (Oct. 3, 1901), 14; and "A Missionary Meeting," *Revivalist* (Oct.

17, 1901), 3. *The Revivalist* expressed disapproval of the war, depicting it as a tragic waste of resources in light of impoverished conditions elsewhere in the British Commonwealth: "England is pouring out her treasure to murder men in Africa, while her subjects in India are starving for food" (W. N. Hirst, "India's Famine," *Revivalist* (March 22, 1900), 15. Hirst also asserted that one of the "greatest hindrance[s]" to evangelism in South Africa was "the indifference or opposition of whites to any missionary effort" ("News from Africa," *Revivalist* (March 22, 1900), 15).

[108] David Bundy, "From Cincinnati to the World," 9, 25. Also, see Jones, *Perfectionist Persuasion*, 50-51.

[109] Thomas and Thomas, 29.

[110] "A World-Wide Movement," *Revivalist* (Aug. 1, 1901), 14.

[111] "Gone!" *Revivalist* (Oct. 18, 1900), 9.

[112] On the Cowmans' ministry, see Lettie B. Cowman, *Charles E. Cowman: Missionary Warrior* (1928, reprint; Greenwood, IN: OMS International, 1976) and Robert D. Wood, *In These Mortal Hands: The Story of The Oriental Missionary Society: The First 50 Years* (Greenwood, IN: OMS International, 1983).

[113] Charles and Lettie Cowman, "Beginning of Our Association," *Revivalist* (April 14, 1921), 9. See also Lettie Cowman, "The *Revivalist* Sample That Changed The World" in Moser and Smith, 24-25, excerpted from her article, "How We Became Acquainted with You," *Revivalist* (June 10-17, 1920).

[114] Ibid and Cowman, *Missionary Warrior*, 106.

[115] "Farewell Service of Brother and Sister Cowman," *Revivalist* (Dec. 6, 1900), 9.

[116] Cowman, *Missionary Warrior*, 106-107. Also, see Wood, 43. Kenneth Brown states that "in the fall of 1900, the Cowmans helped Martin Wells Knapp found God's Bible School" ("Cowman, Charles E(lmer)," in Kostlevy, *Dictionary*, 80).

[117] "Farewell Service of Brother and Sister Cowman," *Revivalist* (Dec. 6, 1900), 9.

[118] Mr. and Mrs. C. E. Cowman, "Called to Japan," *Revivalist* (Nov. 15, 1900), 9.

[119] "Beginning of Our Association," *Revivalist* (April 14, 1921), 9. See also the riveting account in Cowman, *Missionary Warrior*, 107-111 and Wood, 43-44.

[120] Cowman, *Missionary Warrior*, 109.

[121] "Called to Japan," *Revivalist* (Nov. 15, 1900), 9; Wood, 44; and Thomas and Thomas, 37.

[122] Cowman, *Missionary Warrior*, 111-112. The confusion on the time of this gift, possibly an indication that "Mrs. Cowman's memory may have faltered at this point" (Wood, 44), is clarified by the statement in "Called to Japan," *Revivalist* (Nov. 15, 1900), 9: "Yesterday, at noon, we were overjoyed in receiving a letter from a friend of missions, saying, 'Inclosed bank draft for $300, the means for you and Mrs. Cowman to go to Japan to work in His vineyard.'" Obviously, this does not mean November 14, but some point prior to it, making it well before the Christmas Convention referred to by Cowman in *Missionary Warrior*, 111.

[123] Knapp, ed. *Electric Shocks No. III*, 70, cited by Thomas and Thomas, 38.

[124] "Called to Japan," *Revivalist* (Nov. 15, 1900), 9.

[125] Kostlevy, "OMS International," in *Dictionary*, 192.

[126] Kostlevy, "Korea Evangelical Holiness Church," *Dictionary*, 157-158. The only larger holiness denominations are the Church of the Nazarene and the Salvation

Army. A 1961 split from the KEHC, the Korea Jesus Holiness Church represents another sizeable product of the Cowman legacy, with about 400,000 members in 1995. See Sung H Kim, *History of the Korea Evangelical Holiness Church* Edited by the History Compilation Committee of the Korea Evangelical Holiness Church, Translated by Chun-Hoi HEO and Hye-Kyung HEO (Seoul: Living Waters, 1998) and Myung Soo Park, "Mission, Independence, and New Cooperation(?): The Change of Relationship Between the OMS International and the Korea Evangelical Holiness Church," *WTJ* vol. 40 no. 1 (Spring 2005), 138-171.

[127] Don Davison, Larry Smith, and Jon Plank, *Discover GBS! A Self-Guided Campus Tour* (Cincinnati: God's Bible School and College, 2000), 9. This was also one of the addresses most often used by the Cowmans' during their frequent returns to the United States (Wood, 67). Although Charles Cowman and his colleague E. A. Kilbourne began their own paper, *Electric Messages*, in 1902 to publicize their work, the *Revivalist* remained a key factor linking them to supporters.

[128] Lettie Cowman and Ed Erny, *The Story Behind Streams in the Desert* (Greenwood, IN: OMS International, 1994), back cover. *Streams in the Desert* "has gone through more than 120 editions in English alone and remains a best-seller in Spanish, Chinese, and other languages." Though a prolific author, Lettie recognized that this book, which like Knapp's *Impressions*, emerged from a heart crushed by suffering, was different. She commented, "*Streams in the Desert* was born. My other books were written."

[129] Knapp, *Back to the Bible*, 28.

[130] This can be seen as the logical end of the "hermeneutic of illustration." Knapp and his associates not only sought for analogies to support holiness teaching, they sought their ultimate support in demonstration—experience.

[131] J. L. McKay, "A Picture of the Great Camp, From the Camera of My Soul," *Revivalist* (August 2, 1923), 8. The "Eden" motif was a primitivist concept that has proven popular among Americans since the days of the Pilgrim fathers. It holds that in the pristine wilderness of the "New World," God was once more providing humanity with an "Eden" of sorts, a place to recreate the simplicity of primitive Christianity. The forces of democratization further encouraged many Americans to view their country as a laboratory allowing religious freedom in which the abuses and ills of the Old World could be remedied. Steven Ware aptly observes that "a natural corollary to the popularity of restorationist attitudes toward the church was the widespread assumption of a close relationship between evangelical Protestant Christianity and the surrounding American culture. The assumption was that the United States held a special place in God's redemptive plan for humanity" ("Restorationism in the Holiness Movement," 206). For example, G. D. Watson opined that "there must be a special mission in God's providence for the American nation to perform in the history of the world" ("Isaiah's Vision of America: written during the [First] World War," in Eva M. Watson, *Glimpses of the Life and Work of George Douglas Watson* (1929; reprint, Salem, OH: Schmul, 2001), 114 (originally published by Revivalist Press).

In essence, this was the spiritual impetus behind the concept of Manifest Destiny, with missionaries, circuit riders, and Sunday school organizers providing the vanguard of Westward expansion. In addition, it informed much of the efforts at social reform which preoccupied progressives in the late nineteenth and early twentieth centuries.

[132] While pessimism toward popular culture led Knapp to despair of reforming the society at large, his optimism of grace led him to implement a vision comparable to that propounded by Stanley Hauerwas, who has called for the church to be a "community (of character) capable of showing the world what a redeemed community looks like and by extension revealing to the world its own sinfulness" (*A Community of Character: Toward a Constructive Christian Social Ethic* (Notre Dame: University of Notre Dame Press, 1981), 3, 10-12, cited in Reed, *Holy With Integrity*, 287.

[133] Wood, 38.

[134] Kostlevy, "Nakada, Jugi," *Dictionary*, 184. See also "Juji Nakada's Testimony," *Revivalist* (May 30, 1907), 5, 13.

[135] E. A. Kilbourne, "The Revival in Japan," *Revivalist* (Aug. 20, 1901), 12.

[136] "Farewell Service of Brother and Sister Comwan," *Revivalist* (Dec. 6, 1900), 9.

[137] "From Brother Cowman," *Revivalist* (April 11, 1901), 9—letter addressed March 5, 1901.

[138] Cowman described their routine, "At the Bible-school we rise between five and six, and have our first lesson from nine to ten; English, ten to eleven, and Bible, eleven to twelve. In the afternoon, music and study, and later our gospel wagons and Bible women will work in the afternoon and evening" ("From Brother and Sister Cowman," *Revivalist* (May 16, 1901), 9—letter addressed April 8, 1901).

[139] See Bessie [Queen], "Bible-School Notes," *Revivalist* (May 16, 1901), 14. One of the highlights advertised for the 1901 Salvation Park Camp Meeting was the privilege of seeing Shoji "dressed in native costume" ("Salvation Park Items," *Revivalist* (June 6, 1901), 12). See his photo in the June 13, 1901 *Revivalist*, 6. "Mrs. Knapp's Letter," on the same page "For the Young" explains that Shoji was not only coming to study the Bible but to teach Japanese to John Franklin Knapp who was then thirteen. For Shoji's description of his journey to GBS and appraisal of the school, see Shoji Murakami, "Past One Year," *Revivalist* (May 15, 1902), 7.

[140] Thomas and Thomas, 42. Also, see the photo of the Bible school in Japan in "From Brother and Sister Cowman," *Revivalist* (June 27, 1901), 9. The Japanese work seemed to quickly outpace the African, and, in addition to the Boer War and resistance by white nationals, a significant hindrance may have been the lack of organization among the numerous holiness missionaries who flocked to the southern part of the African continent after the war ended. Various works were begun during this time, some of which were absorbed by other works or simply faded into oblivion. On differences between the Japanese and African works, see "From Brother Hirst," *Revivalist* (Nov. 14, 1901), 9 in which he compares evangelism in Japan to catching fish that swim in schools (like tuna) and evangelism in Africa to catching solitary fish (like bass or trout), with the exception of work in such cities as Johannesburg. Also, see "God's Bible-School in Africa," *Revivalist* (April 10, 1902), 9.

Tufts associated with GBS after severing his connection with the *Gospel Trumpet*—Church of God (Anderson), which was announced in the *Revivalist* (June 27, 1901), 13. He moved quickly after his return to India to establish a "Bible school and Missionary Home" in Calcutta ("From Brother Tufts," *Revivalist* (Nov. 7, 1901),

9—letter dated Sept. 27, 1901). Also, see "Our Work in India," *Revivalist* (July 25, 1901), 10. This school was also referred to as "The Apostolic Bible-School," *Revivalist* (March 6, 1902), 9. The problems revolving around the "World-wide" mission fund after Knapp's death apparently resulted in the dissolution of association between Tufts and GBS and the Holiness Union.

[141] Crosser, 18.

[142] Harry Plank, remarks at The Centenary Celebration of God's Bible School, College, and Missionary Training Home (Sept. 27-30, 2000).

[143] Mrs. C. E. Cowman, "How the Korean Work Began," *Revivalist* (Oct. 7, 1909), 10.

[144] Kostlevy, "Korea Evangelical Holiness Church," *Dictionary*, 157.

[145] Godbey, *The Bible*, 20-21. Godbey further noted,

> In the last seven months, in my tour of ten thousand miles, twice crossing the continent, I have not only found the Bible Schools everywhere, but actually seen them spring up in my presence, like mushrooms in the night. We should all shout night and day over these thrilling manifestations of God's mighty work in our midst. This looks like getting truly and heroically in line with our wonderful Founder, who spent His entire earthly life in teaching His disciples.

[146] The Greensboro school was "in a very true sense the predecessor of the Southern Pilgrim College at Kernersville, North Carolina" (P. W. Thomas, "A Brief History of the Bible Schools and Colleges of the Pilgrim Holiness Church," unpublished paper (April 18, 1967), 2). It was "the first local Bible school established under the auspices of congregations affiliated with the International Apostolic Holiness Union" in 1903. It experienced "rapid growth" under the leadership of Cox, who also published the *Apostolic Messenger* (Crosser, 18). This publishing concern may have actually published more of W. B. Godbey's works than any other publisher, including Revivalist Press.

Chapter 4

Conquests for the Vision: Claiming the Victory

It opened auspiciously, September 27, 1900. The Convention accompanying it was one of unction and power. People were at the altar and claiming victory at every service.
God is setting His seal upon this movement in a more wonderful way than ever. Our main answer to those who oppose us is the fire that is falling. We have never been so sensible of God's leading and blessings in our own souls and in our work as at the present time.
— *Martin Wells Knapp*[1]

While the flames of Pentecost were flaring up worldwide, many considered GBS to be the center of this holy conflagration, agreeing with W. B. Godbey's later assessment: "The brilliancy, fervor and glory shining out from this mountain really manifests more gorgeous splendor and permanent fire than elsewhere in all the earth."[2] However, numerous observers of the new school started by Knapp took issue with this positive appraisal, comprising a wide range of people, including fringe religious leaders, the Methodist establishment, some prominent holiness proponents, and several neighbors of the school.

Fighting Falsehood and Fanaticism

Of course, Knapp was no stranger to controversy, having felt the bitter pangs of conflict from the days of his first pastorate. In addition, his trenchant pen had never avoided controversy when the cause of scriptural holiness was at stake. The pages of the *Revivalist* and Revivalist Press books frequently presented arguments against "gradualism" and other "spurious" or inadequate views of holiness, especially "suppression" or "counter-action" as espoused by Higher Life advocates associated with the Keswick Convention in England.[3]

Knapp and his associates at GBS also admonished fellow holiness advocates who, in their estimation, had fallen into fanaticism. Again, the avoidance of this pitfall had been a major motivation behind the publication of *Impressions*. Likewise, the *Revivalist* was committed not only to "no compromise with worldliness, ecclesiastical slavery, dead Churches and preachers," but also to no compromise with "fanaticism."[4] In his controversial "Encyclical Letter to the Holiness People of Every Land," published in the July 11, 1901 *Revivalist*, W. B. Godbey warned that fanaticism "is a fond device of the devil for the seduction and ruin of the Holiness people" and defined it as "leaning too far to the spiritual side, claiming to follow the Holy Ghost into all sorts of foolish extravagances."[5] This excess could be prevented by trying the spirits (I John 4:1): "you can always detect the evil spirit by his disharmony with the Word of God."

While "anarchistic come-outism" was one brand of extremism that GBS stood against, the most intense conflict pitting GBS against "fanaticism" was that with John Alexander Dowie, a healing evangelist whose popularity climaxed about the time GBS was founded. A native of Scotland who grew up in Australia, Dowie traveled to the United States in 1888 where reception of his healing ministry was so positive that he remained, organizing the "Christian Catholic Church" in 1895 and the utopian community of Zion City near Chicago in 1900.[6] Dowie's emphasis on healing was initially welcomed by such radical holiness leaders as J. M. Pike,[7] and Knapp himself referred to Dowie as "the man whom God has so signally used in Chicago for the past few years in the ministry of Divine healing, and in boldly standing for God . . ."[8]

However, by early March 1900, Knapp began to detect discrepancies between biblical principles and Dowie's beliefs and practices, beginning with the "worldly, costly, fashionable attire" of Dowie's wife and daughter and with Dowie inciting his followers to seek riches.[9] Stronger denunciations followed, with several articles in the March 22, 1900, issue of the *Revivalist* devoted to exposing the heretical practices and concepts espoused by Dowie.[10] It was here that Knapp first used an analogy that he would later expand and find useful in other controversies as well—that of "Poison in the Pan."[11] This line of reasoning suggested that Satan was using Dowie's teachings in much the same way that rat poison worked—"a little strychnine" was mixed "in a big lot of meal." Thus, the "Zion pan" contained a generous quantity of good meal—gospel truth—but it was laced with the poisons of "future probation," of "no eternal punishment," of "popery," and of "blasphemy."[12]

Particularly hateful to Knapp was Dowie's extremely combative stance against those who refused to endorse his ministry, including "virtually every other significant American exponent of divine healing."[13] For instance, the *Revivalist* noted that A. B. Simpson was "the object of [Dowie's] most bitter aversion."[14] In addition, while Knapp himself took issue with D. L. Moody's promotion of "suppressionism," he found it appalling that Dowie would suggest that Moody, who had spoken against Dowie's aberrant teachings, had "died because cursed by Zion"[15] and that other opponents should "desist or come to the same end."[16]

Unsurprisingly, Dowie's organization soon counted the holiness movement, and GBS in particular, as an opponent, with Knapp himself receiving a "warning from one of [Dowie's] agents."[17] Doubtless this was provoked by the defection of several of Dowie's followers to the holiness movement with Knapp's encouragement.[18] These reported Dowie's hostility to the doctrine of entire sanctification and Dowie's "forbidding" his followers to associate with holiness agencies.[19] In fact, one GBS student who had been affiliated with "Zion" received "an admonitory letter" from "Zion's overseer-at-large" which pointedly rebuked him for "attending Mr. Knapp's Bible-school" and attacked Knapp for teaching "many of the most absurd doctrines ever inaugurated by the adversary [Satan]."[20]

The abatement of this conflict was hastened by a startling proclamation made by Dowie, on June 2, 1901, during the height of his popularity. He declared that he was in fact, "Elijah the prophet, who appeared first as Elijah himself, second, as John the Baptist, and who now comes in me, the restorer of all things."[21] Ironically, this claim appears to have marked the beginning of Dowie's decline, with several followers immediately defecting, just as Knapp anticipated.[22] Thereafter, Dowie spiraled downward through a maze of financial mismanagement and grandiose schemes, amidst accusations of sexual debauchery, until his death in 1907, which found him disgraced and alienated from his wife and son and most of his one-time followers.

Pentecostal Aggressiveness

Knapp's conflict with Dowie provides important context for other struggles that bear much more obvious significance for GBS, particularly by reflecting Knapp's conviction that "a gospel minister, and specially the editor of a paper, has to preach against sin wherever it is found, and if [he] did not warn the people of the poison . . . 'in the pan' referred to, [he] would not be doing [his] duty."[23] Knapp took this responsibility to apply not only to charlatans like Dowie, but also to compromised or corrupt members of socially respectable religious bodies. This was particularly true of Methodism, as already apparent in the development of the ecclesiastical primitivism that proved essential to Knapp's response to the "Church question."[24]

Less than a month after exposing the "Poison in the Zion Pan," Knapp focused attention on "Revival Poison in the Methodist Pan," bewailing the replacement of the passion for evangelizing lost souls and for the sanctification of believers that had characterized primitive Methodism with social programs and education and charging modern Methodists with "complicity" with "the tobacco evil," "liquor-traffic," and "worldliness." His professed intent here was not to write "in a spirit of censoriousness," but with the hope that the article would "be one of the trumpet-blasts which God is sending that will help to rouse [Methodism] from her awful lethargy . . ."[25]

This, while perhaps the most poignant, was but one of many articles that Knapp published around the turn of the century reflecting his increasing disaffection with Methodist officialdom.[26] As many Methodist leaders became more vocal in depicting such holiness advocates as Knapp as "come-outers" and "fanatics," Knapp counter-charged that, in reality, he and his associates were the faithful Methodists. One supporter expressed a growing sentiment when he pointed "up to the Mount of Blessings" and said, "That is all there is left of Methodism in Cincinnati."[27] Furthermore, Knapp contended that the actual "fanatics" in Methodism were not the proponents of biblical holiness but those who call "loyalty to New Testament principles and practices 'fanaticism.'"[28] As a former student put it, "it is not fanaticism to trust God, honor the Son, obey the Spirit, keep under the blood, and believe all of His Word. This is what God's Bible-school stands for."[29]

Knapp's controversy with Methodism had already neared the boiling point in the fall of 1898, when the Michigan Conference of the M. E. Church censored him for conducting a Bowens, Maryland, camp meeting "under the auspices of the Chesapeake Holiness Union, a branch of Knapp's own International Holiness Union," against the protests of an area pastor and the local presiding elder.[30] Knapp presented his case to his fellow conference members (and the public at large) in a booklet characteristically entitled *Pentecostal Aggressiveness*.[31] "Undaunted" by his opponents, he returned to preach at the same encampment the following year, even before his appeal to the conference had been heard.[32] His eventual exoneration by the Michigan Conference ameliorated the situation temporarily. However, Knapp felt keenly this heavy-handed blow of "Protestant popery," and this helps to explain why he began to more energetically encourage other holiness advocates under such oppression to form independent holiness societies.[33]

Although he had earlier cautioned the newly sanctified about severing their former church relations, his critique of Methodism resulted in his recognition of three types of churches within its ranks—

1. The New Testament Church, consisting of all truly converted people . . . and children who have not sinned away salvation.
2. Bogus churches, consisting of people who were never converted, or who have apostatized.
3. Mixed Churches, consisting of people of both classes.

His final conclusion on this state of affairs was that "the command to 'come out from among them and be ye separate,' applies to all who find themselves in bogus Churches, *and in mixed Churches whose control is hopelessly in the hands of worldlings*."[34] In other words, Methodism had "fallen so low from the Bible standard that in many places those who would be loyal to real Methodism [were] compelled to form new societies on old-time religious lines, or be disloyal to Jesus Christ and the principles of Methodism."[35]

Ultimately, such logic led Knapp to consider his variance with the Methodist establishment irremediable; indeed, in his estimation Methodism had "crossed the dead-line as a Pentecostal New Testament Church."[36] This conclusion prompted a decision that reverberated throughout the holiness movement. A brief article in *God's Revivalist* for January 10, 1901, made the announcement:

Church Relation Changed.
The editor of the Revivalist has reached a point in his experience where he is clearly led of God to change his Church relation. As soon as certain the time had come, he sent the following to the proper Church authority:

"I hereby withdraw from the ministry and membership of the Methodist Episcopal Church, the same to take effect January 1, 1901. Will deliver parchments and any statements that I may desire to make to next Conference."

M. W. Knapp[37]

The following week, Knapp elaborated on his reasons for this decision in "Why I Withdrew from the Methodist Episcopal Church," primarily distilling points he had earlier made in "Revival Poison in the Methodist Pan." His concluding lament sums up the passion shared by many of his fellow holiness advocates within Methodism:

> O Methodism! Methodism! how oft some of thy sons would have restored thee to thy former power and to primitive purity, but ye would not. Behold thy commission is taken from thee and given to others (Holiness Churches), who are bringing forth fruit unto holiness. O, that thou hadst been true to God and to the work of spreading Scriptural holiness which He committed unto thee! Then had thy peace been as a river, and thy righteousness as the waves of the sea.[38]

Knapp now needed an ecclesiastical home in order to be consistent with his own middle solution to the Church question. This need was supplied by following the course he had already advocated for many others—establishing an independent holiness society. This "New Testament Society of God's Church" was organized on the GBS campus by February 1901; and, reminiscent of the superintendency of GBS, "Jesus Christ" was acknowledged as the "great Head" and "Chief Shepherd" and the "Holy Ghost" as the "officiary of God's societies."[39]

Against the charge of come-outism, Knapp continued to protest that he was "still an old-time Methodist," with the "real fact" being that he had "not come out of Methodism" but that nominal Methodists were the true come-outers: "Modern Methodism largely has 'come out' from primitive Methodism and of God's Church, and is simply a social club posing as a church. To leave such a club is no more 'come-outism,' in a bad sense, than to leave a worldly lodge."[40] Indeed, he contended, Methodism "has left me, not I her. When she returns to her 'first love' I will be with her."[41] In addition, he professed that "he never loved the Methodist Church and Methodist ministers . . . more than at the present time."[42] Further distancing his ministry from anti-sectarianism, Knapp emphasized that his change in church relations did nothing to change the *Revivalist*'s mission to "readers of every name [denomination]," including the "many true children of God" which he acknowledged to still remain within Methodism.[43]

W. B. Godbey reaffirmed this commitment shortly after Knapp's death, emphatically denying that a new denomination was being formed with the "Mount of Blessings" as its center:

> All religious denominations are connected with this work. It is avowedly and practically and unconditionally interdenominational, and not, as some have supposed, undenominational [anti-sectarian], as nearly all the students and workers are members of some branch of the great Protestant church. The idea that some entertain of a new denomination started here is utterly untrue.[44]

Godbey's own case served to illustrate his point—he promoted and worked with the Union while maintaining his Methodist credentials.

Such disclaimers notwithstanding, Knapp's relinquishment of his Methodist credentials provoked criticism from many quarters, with A. M. Hills suggesting that this move "probably cost Brother Knapp more pain than anything else he ever did. People will always be divided in their opinion about the wisdom of it . . ."[45] While Methodist leaders accused him of "hardness" and "prejudice" and questioned the scriptural warrant for his appeal "back to Pentecost,"[46] it was from many of his erstwhile holiness comrades, particularly those committed to the National Association for the Promotion of Holiness, that Knapp received the sharpest criticism for his Pentecostal aggressiveness.

Brotherly Contention

Knapp had forged strong ties with the National Association during his ministry in Michigan. These had remained solid in the early years after his move to Cincinnati, as indicated by National president C. J. Fowler's glowing endorsement of the first Salvation Park Camp Meeting. Attesting to the harmony of the "National" with Revivalist ministries was the fact that all three of the featured speakers involved in the first Cincinnati Holiness Convention maintained close identification with the National Association for many years. In addition, Knapp continued to support National activities, promoting their camp meetings and books in *The Revivalist*. Fowler reciprocated by inviting Knapp to serve as an evangelist at a National camp meeting as late as 1897.[47]

However, as the radical holiness movement coalescing around GBS gained momentum, cooperation between Knapp and National leadership waned.[48] By the late 1890's, it appeared that the Methodist-dominated National was attempting to "Methodize" the holiness movement, whereas Knapp was increasingly looking to non-Methodists such as A. M. Hills and Seth C. Rees for inspiration and support. National leaders also fretted as their influence within Methodism and throughout the independent holiness groups weakened simultaneously with the Revivalist movement's gain in strength, as reflected by the phenomenal escalation of *Revivalist* subscriptions.[49]

They tended to look askance at such developments as the change of the *Revivalist*'s name, the launching of *God's* Bible School, and, even earlier, the organization of the Holiness Union, which they perceived as a direct attempt at competition with the National Association.[50] The National's supporters also considered Knapp's radical trajectory to be divisive and imbued with a "sectarian spirit," especially due to his increasingly vocal advocacy of independent holiness societies.[51] Shortly after Knapp withdrew from the Methodist Episcopal Church, the *Christian Witness* published a flat denial of any endorsement of "the Knapp-Revivalist movement" by the National Association, suggesting that "the fact that a separate association [the Union] was organized to further that movement would indicate that there is in the new movement that which the National Association would not indorse."[52]

Undoubtedly, chief among the elements of the Holiness Union and GBS which the National Association "would not indorse" were the second two aspects of the four-fold gospel. In fact, with the possible exception of the "Church question" itself, more ink was spilled over the matters of divine healing and the Second Coming than any other controversy within the turn-of-the-century holiness movement. On the one hand, National leadership considered healing and premillennialism to be "side issues," or, in railroad parlance—"sidetracks," detracting from "the main thrust of holiness evangelism."[53] Isaiah Reid went so far as to suggest that an emphasis on such themes often served to cover a fall "from the blessing and advocacy of holiness."[54]

On the other hand, Knapp contended, "These truths, instead of being 'sidetracks,' are great feeding branches of the Grand Trunk-line of Bible Holiness, and can not be left unoperated or to the manipulation of fanatics without loss."[55] W. B. Godbey concurred with Knapp that "our holiness brethren who would confine our investigations and elucidations to sanctification make a great mistake," particularly because this would stifle "progress beyond our predecessors, whereas the school of Christ is the most progressive institution in all the world."[56] Both he and Knapp moved to co-opt the term "sidetracks," delineating their own lists of "fatal sidetracks" used by Satan to "ditch all who are on the Great Holiness Railway." Knapp's list included,

1. "Suppression of Demonstration."
2. "Loyalty to Leaders."
3. "Loyalty to the Church."
4. "Compromise."
5. "Fighting Divine Healing and the Return of Jesus."[57]

Knapp made clear his steadfast commitment to these issues by announcing under the "Publisher's Notes" in every issue of *God's Revivalist* that here readers would find "The 'Main Line' magnified, and 'Feeding Branches' honored." Isaiah Reid responded to the prominence afforded these themes in the *Revivalist* by labeling it a "semi-holiness" paper which many people ignorantly took to represent "the real holiness movement."[58]

In a sharp rejoinder, Knapp asked, "Is the Bible a semi-holiness Book because of the like position which it takes on these subjects?" and "If that be true, what kind of papers are those which . . . advertise patent medicines, Sabbath-breaking railroads, fashionably-dressed women, and other worldly wares?"[59]

Even more damaging, Knapp suggested that his opponents in the National Association were compromising the holiness movement by bowing to the constraints of denominational ties and traditional dogmas. In February 1900, he suggested that a rift was developing between the "holiness movement" and a true "Holy Ghost movement": "Facts have demonstrated that a holiness movement may be one thing, and a Holy Ghost movement quite another. There may be a so-called holiness movement, split up into jangling factions, embittered by internal jealousies, and in bondage more or less to creeds and ecclesiastics big and little."[60]

Unsurprisingly, "Poison in the Holiness Pan" appeared a little over a year latter. Here Knapp suggested that some key poisons that Satan sought to "artfully conceal" in the holiness movement were those of "mutilating the gospel by substituting a fractional gospel" for the full gospel; "the poison of strife and division" which he believed was precipitated by "opposition to a full-fledged Pauline gospel"; "the poison of alliance with the world . . . its fashions, its fraternities, its carnal advertisers"; and the "poison of neglect"—abandoning those newly converted or sanctified in holiness services to "backslidden, worldly societies" and anti-holiness ministers so that many of the converts were eventually lost to the holiness cause.[61]

The latter issue had proven in fact to be one of Knapp's chief reasons for leaving the M. E. Church and establishing the New Testament Society of God's Church on the GBS campus. He explained to one correspondent,

> Right here in my work in this city [Cincinnati] I can point out many, many who were either saved or sanctified at our altars, and afterward entered some worldly Church here, with the result that to-day they are cold, formal, deceived Church members. My heart aches for them . . . God showed me clearly that I could no longer advise his children to go into an iceberg where they would be frozen to death, on one hand, and pray and work for them on the other.[62]

Furthermore, Knapp saw this not only as a personal conviction but as a principle that applied to other holiness advocates: "For holiness ministers to exhort believers to identify themselves with such institutions is contrary to the spirit of holiness, and as contrary to the Word of God as darkness is to light."[63]

At this point, the divide within the holiness movement between the Methodist loyalists associated with the National Association and the radical proponents of the four-fold gospel centered at GBS seemed irreconcilable. Its intensity, which was reached during God's Bible School's first year, was portrayed by Knapp as one front of the "revival war" in which the Mount of Blessings was under siege by the "Mount of Jealousy."[64] Other voices that joined in the conflict were those of Daniel Steele, Beverly Carradine, and Charles Fowler on the side of the *Christian Witness* and the National Association versus Seth Rees and L. L. Pickett on the side of the *Revivalist*, GBS, and the Holiness Union. Books and articles espousing each side's respective views on divine healing and the Lord's return proliferated. Charges and counter-charges frequented the periodicals representing both sides.⁶⁵ As the debate waxed hotter, it became clear that this struggle was for nothing less than the future course of the holiness movement.⁶⁶

"God Answering By Fire"

A showdown was inevitable; the disparate positions were too polarized to allow otherwise. Its setting was Chicago. Its significance for the role of GBS in the future of the holiness movement was such that it could be argued that the most important event in the first year of God's Bible School (aside from the founding of the school itself) took place in Chicago, rather than Cincinnati. The developments leading to and involving it were quite complex and reflect the fluidity of the holiness movement at this critical juncture in its history.⁶⁷

The confrontation was precipitated by both the radicals and the Nationals planning special meetings in Chicago in the spring of 1901. Chicago had already been the special focus of radical endeavors through the ministries of Duke Farson, a wealthy banker-turned-preacher who pastored the Metropolitan Methodist Church, and Edwin L. Harvey, Sunday school superintendent of the same church. This church was the location of a missionary convention in December 1900 which helped launch two of GBS's pioneer missionary thrusts. The close of the convention was marked by the ordination of Charles and Lettie Bird Cowman, leading Pilgrim Holiness historians to claim Charles Cowman as the first minister ordained in the Holiness Union.⁶⁸ Among those laying their hands on the newly commissioned couple were Martin Wells Knapp, Seth C. Rees, Byron J. Rees, and Charles Stalker. After the convention, the latter two made their way to New York to begin their "Round-the-World" tour while the Cowmans traveled to San Francisco, from which they sailed to Japan. Knapp returned to Cincinnati, deeply impressed with the leaders of the Metropolitan Church, who likely figured prominently in his decision to withdraw from the M. E. Church less than a month later.⁶⁹

This new camaraderie ensured that Knapp and Rees would be involved in the holiness convention sponsored by the Metropolitan Church Association that had been chartered in 1899 by Farson and Harvey. Seth C. Rees, then one of the most fruitful holiness evangelists with an average of "two thousand conversions per year," was recruited by Farson in January 1901 to be, "under God," leader of the MCA, while he still retained the presidency of the Holiness Union, reflecting the close bond between the two organizations. Rees quickly moved to rent, "for one year, a large meeting room in the First Methodist Episcopal Church in the center of the city for noon holiness meetings." He then "announced that the MCA would host a holiness convention from 1-10 March," in which attention would be given to such subjects as "'slum work,' 'demonstrations,' and 'women's work.'"⁷⁰

Among the workers for this meeting were several who would be involved in the first camp meeting on the Mount of Blessings later that year, including Andy Dolbow, E. A. Fergerson, Seth Rees, and M. W. Knapp. Other speakers included John T. Hatfield, "the Hoosier evangelist"[71] and "a virtually unknown Methodist minister from Texas, Reuben A. (Bud) Robinson," a "converted cowboy and ex-moonshiner" whose prominence in this convention began him on a journey that would end with his being recognized as perhaps "the most important figure in the twentieth-century holiness movement."[72]

However, before Rees, Farson, and Harvey began to arrange quickly for their March meeting, "NHA stalwarts were carefully laying plans for a 'General Holiness Assembly' to convene at the First Methodist Episcopal Church in Chicago on May 3, 1901," well after the scheduled conclusion of the radical holiness convention. Engineered by S. B. Shaw, "a Chicago-based Holiness evangelist and Movement ecumenist," the announced purpose of the proposed assembly was "to pray for revival, encourage cooperation in evangelistic endeavors, remove prejudice against holiness teaching arising from 'extreme, erroneous and fanatical positions assumed by some so-called holiness workers,' and create an international holiness union." In addition to NHA leaders, the assembly was endorsed by "representatives of more than twelve evangelical denominations including six bishops of the Methodist Episcopal Church," giving the appearance of widespread support. However, representation of the fastest growing segment of the holiness movement, the radical element centered at GBS, was conspicuously lacking from the list of endorsers of the call for the assembly. Significantly, one of the few signers "with ties to the radicals, A. M. Hills, was an avowed postmillennialist."[73]

Indeed, Knapp and Rees and most of their colleagues could not endorse the General Holiness Assembly, for they perceived it as nothing less than an attempt "to suppress holiness radicalism and to preserve the loyalty of holiness adherents to what were, in their eyes, apostate denominations."[74] As Rees explained,

> The editors of the [*Revivalist*] have not refused to sign this call because they object to a general assembly of the holiness people throughout the world. On the contrary, we would be delighted to attend such an assembly if it were called and held on a Bible platform [i.e. the four-fold gospel].
> . . . . .
> We insist that it is grossly inconsistent to call it a "General Assembly" when the contents of the so-called "Official Call" rules out more than two-thirds of the holiness people.

Radicals found especially offensive the condition that "all side-issues . . . will be necessarily excluded from the discussions of the assembly." Rees protested, "If the committee wanted a general assembly, why did they not issue the call and leave the assembly to plan its own work and to say for itself what should or should not be excluded from its discussions."[75]

If the radical convention and the General Assembly had gone as originally scheduled, the future of the holiness movement may have been quite different. As it turned out, however, the MCA convention, under the "unrestricted and unquestioned authority and control" of the Holy Spirit expanded far beyond its original conception. It would take an entire book to fully recount what transpired as the meeting broke out in revival. "Conversions and sanctifications were witnessed not by scores but by hundreds. The daily papers took notice and their reporters, both by serious news items and by comic caricatures, gave many columns of free advertising."[76] Converts included numerous preachers who "made the discovery that they had never been regenerated, . . . saloon-keepers, missionaries and thieves, Church members and tramps, Sunday-school superintendents and gamblers, policemen and Salvation Army officers, business-men and thugs, bums and soaks, and women from high life and from the haunts of vice."[77]

The convention proper culminated with "a spectacular ordination service" in which the ordinands were Bud Robinson, Andy Dolbow, E. L. Harvey, and George Kulp. The service concluded as the evangelists "shouted blessings and hallelujahs while the congregation repeatedly sang" a song composed early during the convention, which also became its theme song—"The Pearly White City"—with lyrics clearing expressing the premillennial vision of the radicals, who looked forward to a place beyond time, with "no envy and strife" and where, finally, "the saints are all sanctified wholly" and "live in sweet harmony."[78]

So tremendous was the response to the convention, its organizers determined to continue their meetings, at noon at the First M. E. Church, and during evenings at other evangelical churches. This they did for another sixty-five days with remarkable results. Indeed, history records it as "one of the most fruitful (at least numerically) evangelistic campaigns of the postbellum holiness revival" with "an estimated 2,200 seekers" during the seventy-five day period.[79]

This meant that when the General Holiness Assembly began in May, the MCA meetings were still going strong. In addition, the noon meetings were still being held in the same building (First Methodist) where the assembly delegates gathered. As this august assembly began its deliberations, it became clear that the enthusiasm it portended, and the few converts it garnered, paled in comparison with the radicals' revival. Several delegates "dutifully attended and supported both the General Assembly and Rees' noon meetings." Others transferred their allegiance outright to the radical cause, among whom was W. E. Shepard, later prominent in the MCA and then in the Church of the Nazarene, and Alma White, who was among the "daughters, as well as sons . . . invited to prophesy [preach]," demonstrating that "woman's place in this Convention was honored."[80]

Knapp and other participants in the revival interpreted its success as divine vindication of the four-fold gospel. After the initial convention, he suggested that

> it seemed as if God selected the city of Chicago, and the Holiness Convention just closed, as a Mount Carmel to vindicate His truth. Repeatedly and continuously, the revival fire fell from the skies, until preachers and people were compelled to feel "The Lord He is God," and that a full gospel is the gospel of the Bible.[81]

In other words, the revival fire at Chicago was viewed as "a continuation of the great revival that broke out at Pentecost, and prove[d] that where Pentecostal conditions are met Pentecost will be repeated."[82]

In addition, the radicals received further vindication when the General Assembly leadership capitulated to popular pressure and included endorsements of divine healing and premillennialism, removing them from stigma as "side issues."[83] Furthermore, the assembly gave tacit approval of Knapp's ecclesiological vision, by "giving firm support to those who, in various parts of the country, had found it necessary to organize independent churches."[84] This really did signal the triumph of the radical emphases among holiness leadership, which finally came to accept the fact already apparent to Knapp's associates—the majority of holiness people now embraced the radical holiness ideals propounded by GBS and the *Revivalist*.[85] Although "the extent of the radicals' triumph only gradually became evident" with a few skirmishes remaining (especially over eschatology),[86] it was obvious enough to prompt W. B. Godbey to rejoice, "I am so glad the Chicago Assembly buried the hatchet. Let all say Amen! and turn our swords instead always against the devil."[87]

Knapp's victory in the conquest for the movement's vision reaffirmed his claim on Jeremiah 1, especially verses 17-19,[88] and confirmed him as a prophetic figure throughout the movement, for he had predicted in March 1901:

> Holiness people and papers who have been opposing the formation of independent holiness societies will soon turn their guns in their favor, or suffer.
> . . . . .
> The holiness people and papers that have been deriding the preaching of the full gospel as a compromise with "side issues" will soon see their folly and correct their mistake, or else lose.[89]

Indeed, a new day had dawned in the holiness movement. The old guard tied by the NHA to Methodist officialdom had lost its bid to "Methodize" the movement and its constructs were "largely superseded, even among Methodists, by a new far more radical movement . . . centered at God's Bible School in Cincinnati and committed to the four-fold gospel."[90]

Pentecostal Demonstration and Persecution

While the radical triumph at Chicago assured Knapp's status as "the most potential leader and foremost character in the holiness movement,"[91] it by no means signaled the cessation of opposition to his work. In fact, one of the most controversial aspects of Knapp's work was frequently displayed at "the Great Chicago Revival"—demonstrative worship, including "Holy Ghost demonstrations of shouting, leaping, and rejoicing."[92] As with other Pentecostal practices, "Knapp's apologetic, rooted in the book of Acts, suggested that such displays were normative for those seeking [and finding] entire sanctification."[93] That is, "Pentecostal experience brings with it Pentecostal manifestations."[94] Indeed, "true revivals" will be marked by "the shouting and rejoicing of new-born souls mingled with the songs of mighty triumph and victory."[95]

Such demonstrations were frequent during GBS services and ranged from the exuberance demonstrated during the dedication of God's Tabernacle to what modern Pentecostals would call being "slain in the Spirit."[96] Even meal times became occasions for testimony, as "one after another [would] rise and tell his latest answer to prayer, or how God [was] leading and guiding," with "every testimony . . . greeted by a volume of 'Amens!' 'Lord bless you!' . . ."[97]

Knapp further suggested that such demonstrations would at times be accompanied by another mark of Pentecostal revival—"persecution against its promoters."[98] As Seth Rees had observed during the Chicago Convention, "No one has ever yet been greatly used of God but what the world has first despised them."[99] Indeed, Knapp expected the holiness "testimony against all sin and worldliness and the Pentecostal freedom which we allow believers in shouting, testifying, etc." to arouse "opposition." He blamed this factor for making "it difficult to get or keep a suitable place" for his meetings before moving the Revivalist operations to the Mount of Blessings.[100] So, it came as little surprise to the GBS family when the accusation was circulated that "the teaching of the Bible-school 'unsettles' people in their experiences"[101] or when some Cincinnati residents labeled Knapp's associates as the "Knappites" and "Sons of God," lumping them together in the popular imagination with Dowieites, Mormons, and other fringe sects.[102]

However, on July 11, 1901, the opposition reached a new level. Martin Wells Knapp, founder and superintendent, under God, of God's Bible School, was arrested by a Cincinnati police officer and charged with "disorderly conduct" in connection with the noisy services that extended late into the evening during the first camp meeting conducted in the new tabernacle on the Mount of Blessings.[103] A. M. Hills, who described Cincinnati as "a quiet little city," explained the situation: "The noise of people seeking God and finding Him and getting sanctified and shouting about it until ten o'clock at night was too much for people unused to such late hours and wholly unaccustomed to noise and excitement!"[104]

Elijah B. Coombe, a retired tailor portrayed by Hills as a "sober-minded Presbyterian," swore out the warrant for Knapp's arrest, complaining that he had been deprived of sleep, which was "out of the question when the faithful . . . steam up." Coombe said "he stood it as long as he could, but it became unbearable, and he was forced to seek the aid of the law in his effort to find relief from the noise which he likened unto that produced by a tribe of Sioux Indians engaged in the sun dance."[105] Although Coombe later attempted to withdraw the warrant and instead obtain an injunction forcing the meetings to close earlier, inefficient communication prevented the chief of police from intercepting the warrant before it had been served. Thus, the superintendent of God's Bible School was taken into custody and booked at the Eighth District Station House, where he was released on his own recognizance to await trial.

Immediate reaction among the students, staff, and camp meeting guests at God's Bible School, as well as Knapp's personal response, likely provided quite a shock for the police and Mr. Coombe. Upon receiving notice of his imminent arrest, Knapp called for a prayer meeting in his office. There he told God that "'he did not feel worthy to go to prison for Him,' and asked Him to glorify Himself in this [situation.] He then went down to the dining-room to meet the waiting policeman, assured that if God wanted him to lay in jail it was for His glory." Meanwhile, quite a celebration broke out on the campus. "Instead of crying, Sister Knapp and others laughed and praised God." By the time Knapp was escorted away by the police officer, the students "had heard of it, and were all gathered about him; but no crying, only 'Glory to God!' 'Hallelujah!' 'Amens!' from all."[106]

Knapp's supporters from Washington state to Washington, D. C., and Michigan to Florida responded similarly after reading of the arrest in *God's Revivalist*, deluging his office with letters of encouragement and applause, including the following:

> Kindly allow me to add my mite to the many congratulations you are receiving, for I feel truly that it is more a time for congratulation than condolence. – New York
>
> In this your hour of trial, consider me a bosom companion. We stand together for primitive truth and doctrine. – Massachusetts
>
> I send my heartiest congratulations that you are counted worthy to suffer with your dear Lord, even in imprisonment, persecution, etc. – Indiana
>
> How I wish I could change locations with some of those who are being disturbed by your God-blessed meetings. I have just to read about you all, and the Spirit tingles through me, and while I try to write this my eyes are blinded with tears. – Kansas[107]

Seth Rees, who had left the camp meeting for other evangelistic campaigns, wrote back to encourage Knapp, commenting that if he had any regrets about the situation, it was that Knapp did not actually have the privilege of incarceration so that he could "edit the Revivalist behind the bars."[108]

While onlookers may have been amazed at this rather jubilant response to Knapp's arrest, the *Revivalist* simply explained it by observing that "the Word of God declares that he who will live godly in Christ Jesus shall suffer persecution" and that Jesus commanded His followers "to rejoice and be exceeding glad when thus wronged, which we were graciously enabled to do."[109] Furthermore, it reasoned, "Pentecostal revivals always awaken similar opposition," and "Jesus and His real apostles in all the ages have . . . welcomed the badge of persecutionary reproach."[110]

However, while Knapp and his associates rejoiced in this opportunity to suffer publicly for the cause of holiness, they also capitalized on the situation to challenge their opponents in several issues of the *Revivalist*. They predicted dire consequences to befall those opposed to "Pentecostal revivals," averring that "unless our souls be harmonized with the demonstrations of the Holy Spirit here, they can have no part in the victorious acclamations [at the Marriage Supper of the Lamb]."[111] In a similar vein, they bluntly warned, "People who characterize Pentecostal demonstrations as 'howling meetings' here, unless they repent, will howl themselves hereafter."[112]

Revivalist writers also took opportunity to compare Knapp's trial to religious persecution throughout history.[113] For instance, they likened it to Charles Wesley's condemnation by a grand jury as "a person of illfame [sic], a vagabond, and a common disturber of his majesty's peace."[114] Even more poignantly, Bessie Queen compared Knapp's situation to that of Christ before Pilate: "Brother Knapp, who, for the love of souls, pours out his life early and late, who cares for the sick and suffering, who fasts and weeps and prays for men . . . , in his gentleness and humility, reminded me so of that other judgment-day, when Jesus stood in His purity and innocence to answer the false charge."[115]

Even the Cincinnati newspapers lent some credence to this image of martyrdom, depicting Knapp's appearance for arraignment "with his Bible clasped to his breast and eyes uplifted in silent communion."[116] However, unlike Christ's disciples, Knapp's supporters did not abandon him when the day of trial arrived. Rather, "hundreds of Knapp's disciples," including students and witnesses, such as Bessie Queen, Mary Storey, and James and Jessie Hundley, accompanied him to the courtroom, attired in "dark garb" and carrying "Bibles under their arms."[117] In addition, Knapp was joined by his defense counsel, an Attorney Williams and General Thomas Heath, a well-known attorney who volunteered his services, asking only for "the prayers of God's people."[118]

Here Knapp's entourage faced Judge Lueders of the Police Court, who was joined "behind the bench" by "Judge Ferris of the Probate Court, Mayor Julius Fleischmann, and Chief of Police Deitsch," a delegation that helps to convey the importance of the event on the Cincinnati civic scene.[119] Mr. Coombe had attempted to marshal the opposition as well, producing a statement purportedly signed by "70 property holders to the effect that the noise which emanated from the meetings was not conducive to sleep."[120] Clearly, both sides were out to win in this legal showdown.

At first, it appeared that Knapp would be victorious. Attorney Heath gave an eloquent defense, and Knapp, "one of the quietest men in the holiness movement," was exonerated from a personal charge of disorderly conduct.[121] In fact, testimony from both sides made it clear that the primary source of noise that had induced Coombe's complaint was crowds outside the tabernacle and seekers at the altar, both groups obviously beyond Knapp's control. Furthermore, Judge Lueders had already instructed Knapp to "close his evening services at 9 o'clock" and "refrain as far as practicable from making undue noise." In turn, Knapp had agreed to comply "as far as possible."[122]

In addition, the Judge's finding began with complimentary remarks concerning God's Bible School and Knapp's ministry.

However, when the final decision was handed down, the judge found Knapp guilty and fined him the court costs, which he then remitted, in effect letting Knapp go unpunished except for the stigma of the verdict. Still claiming innocence, Knapp declared that "he would have gone to jail before paying."[123] He and his followers also maintained their confidence that regardless of the Police Court ruling, Knapp would obtain "complete vindication of the charge of 'disorderly conduct' before the great white judgment throne, when the 'Judge of all the earth' will 'do right.'"[124]

This conclusion reflects a foundational element of the radical holiness/Pentecostal worldview. Ultimately, opposition and persecution were believed to have their source in the supernatural dimension, and Satan himself was the instigator, for, as Knapp put it, "Satan hates Spirit-filled men and women, and will do all he can to silence or kill them."[125] In particular, Knapp contended that "Satan is bitterly opposed to God's School. He has done what he could to delay it and can be depended upon to oppose." Among the reasons for such intense opposition, Knapp noted the school's staunch commitment to full salvation and its practical results— "holy being, holy living, and holy activity against the kingdom of sin and Satan," its attempt "to stimulate interest in the foreign-mission fields," and its role as a "living monument, conspicuous to all the world, of the power of God to answer prayer and reward the faith of his children."[126]

Eventually, even opposition would simply serve to advance God's cause at GBS, as Knapp averred, "The more the dogs of criticism bark at us, the more God seems to bless us."[127] For one thing, God's protection was guaranteed, for He "protects His own people."[128] With each battle engaged and won, the faith of the campus family only increased. In addition, such attempts as Coombe's to restrain activities on the Mount of Blessings often boomeranged, by providing even more publicity in the secular press. Knapp thus observed that God "is taking the wrath of man to praise Him, and the remainder He is restraining." In fact, such results of Pentecostal persecution were viewed as only a few of the many "unmistakable tokens of His presence and co-operation" in GBS and its related ministries.[129]

Pentecostal Explosion

Another characteristic of the radical holiness movement that the GBS family took as an indication of its continuity with Pentecost was its rapid growth: "*It is a growing movement. It is mightily increasing from year to year. Only a few years ago it had but two or three organs, while to-day it is voiced by many. Then a few followers; now they 'girdle the globe with holiness unto the Lord.'*"[130] One example already noted is the phenomenal expansion of the work in Japan and Korea pioneered by Charles and Lettie Cowman. In addition, GBS itself continued to enjoy growth during its early years, with around eighty students enrolled by the time of Knapp's death in December 1901 and some one-hundred-fifty enrolled by the end of the second school year.[131]

While the enrollment of GBS would level off, the quest for repeating Pentecost sparked by Knapp's enterprises on the Mount of Blessings would lay the foundation for "probably the most important Protestant story of the twentieth century"—"the growth of pentecostal churches, and even more striking, *the spread of pentecostal theology*."[132] As Mark Noll observes, "Should the trends of the twentieth century continue . . . events around 1900 that precipitated identifiable Christian movements defined by belief in the special work of the Holy Spirit may loom as one of the most decisive turning points in the recent history of Christianity."[133] Doubtless, one of the most important of these events was the establishment of God's Bible School.

This claim for the role of GBS in the development of the "Third Force in Christendom"[134] should not be anachronistically construed in any way as a link between God's Bible School and tongues-speaking (glossolalia). Indeed, the metaphor of a "divided flame"[135] aptly describes the dissonant trajectories followed by those who would embrace the tongues-speaking phenomenon and the leadership of GBS to the present day.[136] It should be noted that God's Bible School was over half-way through its first decade when the tongues-speaking innovation was popularized through the auspices of the Azusa Street Revival which began in 1906. While school leadership was apparently distracted at the time by internal conflict that had nothing to do with tongues-speaking,[137] the administration and faculty aligned themselves solidly behind the verdict of W. B. Godbey, whom both Pentecostal and Wesleyan/Holiness scholars credit with convincing large segments of the holiness movement to reject the teaching of tongues-speaking as an evidence of Spirit-baptism.[138] In such Revivalist Press booklets as *Spiritualism, Devil-worship, and Tongues* and *Current Heresies*, Godbey characterized this development as the climax of "all the heresies of all ages in the Holiness Movement."[139]

This on-going opposition to tongues-speaking at GBS notwithstanding, the contribution of Martin Wells Knapp and his colleagues at GBS and through Revivalist publications to the formation of early Pentecostalism could hardly be overestimated. For one, as has already been demonstrated, they were at the forefront in laying the ideological foundation for Pentecostalism. In addition, while many of the spiritual descendents of Knapp would continue in the radical Wesleyan/Holiness tradition fostered at GBS under the nurture of such instructors as W. B. Godbey and Nettie Peabody, others would take Knapp's seminal teaching on repeating Pentecost even further, embracing the practice of tongues-speaking as *the* evidence of Spirit-baptism.

Among Knapp's associates following the modern Pentecostal (tongues-speaking) trajectory was Alma White's husband Kent, who had served as a *Revivalist* representative at Denver.[140] Another was Abbie C. Morrow, who served as the first editor of the children's/youth periodical *Sparkling Waters from Bible Fountains* and joined W. B. Godbey in the *Revivalist*'s Sunday School Department, providing "Light from a Pentecostal Standpoint" on International Sunday School Lessons. She also contributed to the popular devotional, *Jesus Only: A Full Salvation Year Book* and edited biographies of Madam Guyon and George Muller that profoundly shaped holiness and Pentecostal commitments to such ideals as faith work.[141]

Foremost among those to whom Knapp's influence has been traced were two of early Pentecostalism's most prominent personalities. One of these was Ambrose Jessup Tomlinson (1865-1943), organizer of the Church of God (Cleveland, Tennessee), "one of the oldest and largest pentecostal bodies in America and very likely in the world" with 1.65 million members in 1986. In addition, from this original group several other fellowships emerged, most notably the Church of God of Prophecy.[142]

As a youth, Tomlinson attended the Union High School in Westfield, Indiana, which was then a seedbed of holiness foment among the Society of Friends.[143] In fact, the Quaker community in the area became the "epicenter of Quaker holiness in America"[144] and the Union High School developed a persistent affinity with Knapp's work at Cincinnati.[145] Tomlinson's marriage in 1889 to Mary Jane Taylor, who had been steeped in the holiness Quaker tradition, ensured his exposure to several key figures with links to both the holiness Quakerism centered at Westfield and the Revivalist movement led by Knapp. Among these were Seth Rees, who grew up near the Tomlinson farm, and Rees's close associates, John Pennington and Charles Stalker.[146]

In fact, young Tomlinson was just one of many Quakers who was powerfully swayed by these men's "commitment to advance the cause of radical holiness within the Society of Friends."[147] Knapp and the ministries he inaugurated would play a critical role in their agenda, with Oxford-published Tomlinson scholar R. G. Robins suggesting that GBS and its related enterprises actually "served . . . as a halfway house for thousands of Quakers on the road to radical holiness."[148]

Among those enterprises that most powerfully impacted Tomlinson was the *Revivalist*, one of the numerous holiness papers of which he became an "avid reader." In addition to acquainting him with the writings of Knapp and other radical leaders, this practice undoubtedly fueled his own inspiration to publish. As a consequence, he became a "prolific writer" himself, beginning with his first periodical—an eighteen-page monthly entitled *Samson's Foxes* (1901-1902).[149]

Claims of Tomlinson's direct connections with GBS contain perplexing ambiguities. For example, his son Homer reported that his father attended GBS in 1899—before the school had officially begun![150] In addition, Pentecostal folklore relates that during his time at GBS Tomlinson quickly earned a reputation as a prayer warrior, with students affixing a sign above his door designating him as "The Prevailer."[151] However, the school's enrollment records show no record of his attendance.[152]

A couple of scenarios may explain the persistent tradition placing Tomlinson at GBS. For one, it is possible that he attended some of Knapp's Bible classes at Revivalist Chapel in downtown Cincinnati before GBS had actually been inaugurated. For another, Tomlinson apparently spent some time in 1903 (between late May and early June) in Cincinnati, while in transit from Indiana to North Carolina. While details regarding any visit at GBS during that time are limited, it is obvious that he had some interaction—for when he left Cincinnati, he took with him $50.00 worth of Revivalist Press literature.[153] Regardless of the exact nature of contact that Tomlinson may have had with GBS leadership, it is almost certain—considering the influence of such GBS-affiliated holiness Quakers as Seth Rees and in light of the impact of the *Revivalist* and related publications—that Tomlinson was heavily indebted to the milieu emanating from the Mount of Blessings in the development of his own pursuit of Pentecost.

Even more significant than Tomlinson for worldwide Pentecostalism was the second character, William Joseph Seymour (1870-1922), recognized as the "leading figure in the Azusa Street Pentecostal Revival in Los Angeles."[154] The significance of this revival for twentieth-century Christianity could hardly be over-stated. From 1906 to 1913, thousands thronged the mission on Azusa Street to witness this movement that was destined "to change the course of church history."[155] These visitors, who often returned home to spread the Pentecostal message, were literally from around the world, including "Chicago, Toronto, New York, London, Australia, Scandinavia, South Africa, and many other places."[156] The impact was such that "today, practically all Pentecostal and charismatic movements can trace their roots directly or indirectly to the humble mission on Azusa Street and its pastor."[157]

Historians have often focused on the influence on Seymour by Charles Fox Parham, who is credited with first teaching the doctrine of tongues-speaking as the initial evidence of baptism with the Holy Spirit in his Bible school in Topeka, Kansas, in 1900-1901.[158] However, it appears that Knapp and GBS had an earlier, but equally important, impact on Seymour. Thus, Seymour biographer Rufus Sanders asserts that "it would be the Holiness ministry of the Cincinnati preacher, Martin Wells Knapp, that would change William's life forever."[159]

The exact nature of Seymour's exposure to Knapp's ministry remains ambiguous, much as with Tomlinson. For example, in his case as well there is no indication of his enrollment as a student in school records. However, strong oral tradition insists that Seymour did attend classes taught by Knapp, "though substantive documentation of his tenure in Cincinnati is still lacking."[160] Since Seymour moved to Cincinnati in late 1899 or early 1900,[161] it is likely that any classes he participated in were at Revivalist Chapel, actually predating the founding of GBS.

Regardless, numerous historians consider Seymour's interaction with Knapp's work to have been a critical juncture in his life, with highly acclaimed Pentecostal scholar Vinson Synan suggesting that it was while attending Knapp's classes that Seymour "deepened his understanding of holiness theology."[162] Harvard-published Nazarene scholar Randall Stephens concludes,

"It certainly seems that Knapp's premillennial theology and radical holiness theories had a strong impact on the wayfaring Seymour."[163] The consequent commitment to radical holiness teachings then provided a foundational persuasion encouraging his "spiritual commitment to become a minister of the Gospel" in 1902.[164]

Seymour, an African-American whose parents were former slaves, would have also appreciated another innovative dimension of Revivalist Chapel worship—integration, reflecting Knapp's conviction that a hallmark of "the Pentecostal movement . . . rolling over the world" was its egalitarian impulse: *"It is a united movement. Though its members are diverse in clime and color and creed and social position, yet they are all baptized by the same Spirit into one body, and bound together with golden links of love."*[165] Accordingly, "Knapp included blacks in his meetings and classes and may have provided Seymour with his first exposure to a racially mixed congregation."[166] The themes of holiness and racial reconciliation heralded at GBS were both incorporated within Seymour's ministry, and became prominent features of the Azusa Revival. In fact, the Pentecostal ideology Seymour proclaimed at Azusa, which subsequently spread around the world, was essentially identical (with the exception of the tongues-speaking innovation) to that proclaimed on the Mount of Blessings by Martin Wells Knapp.

Seymour, Tomlinson, Morrow, and White provide then just a few outstanding examples of how the Pentecostal ideology fostered at GBS would influence literally millions of believers throughout the twentieth century. Indeed, if Martin Marty and Donald Dayton are correct in suggesting that the fourfold gospel represents the core of Pentecostalism, then Pentecostals must look to Young Street, even before Azusa Street, to locate the roots of their worldview. Remarkably, this worldview, pioneered by a humble Methodist minister and employed at the Bible school he began in Cincinnati has grown to claim the allegiance of roughly *one tenth of the world's population*!

"Wake Them Up!"

Knapp did not live to see the radicalization of Pentecostal teaching with the introduction of tongues-speaking. Nor did he observe much more than the beginning surge of the exponential growth that Pentecostal theology would enjoy throughout the next century. In fact, he did not survive to complete the second year of God's Bible School, for on Saturday, December 7, 1901, at about 11 p.m., he "was translated" to the next world.[167]

The immediate cause of death was typhoid fever, which the *Cincinnati Enquirer* reported had broken out in an "epidemic" on the "Mount of Blessings."[168] In reality, six others at GBS contracted the illness, evidently "from the use of hydrant water" or from "drinking water from an old well and old cistern on the premises."[169] Only one other patient died—Mary Koch, a student of about nineteen years of age.[170] The Cincinnati newspapers made much of Knapp's views on divine healing, asserting that "it was plainly evident that the prayers of the members of the household had availed nothing"¹⁷¹ and suggesting that had a physician been called earlier, "Knapp probably would not have died."¹⁷² However, all other patients received a physician's care and one of the doctors who inspected the campus after the Health Department became involved reported being "received with the utmost courtesy" and concluded that "Mr. Knapp was not neglected and received every possible care except the presence of a regular physician," belying the rumor that the "Sons of God" refused their adherents the privilege of proper medical attention.¹⁷³

In fact, Knapp's bout with the illness was relatively short, only about a week, and his condition deteriorated rapidly. While a post-mortem examination confirmed typhoid fever as the cause of death, the physicians also noted that Knapp "was physically worn out," and W. B. Godbey suggested that, "his brain power and nervous energy always having been to[o] great for his physical ability; . . . he did his work, and got away to heaven at the early age of forty-eight."¹⁷⁴ As early as the Chicago Holiness Convention in spring 1901 "it was evident to his friends that he had over-extended himself. His day normally started at five in the morning and lasted until he felt he could lay the work aside, whether that was at ten at night or two the next morning."¹⁷⁵

Until the very end, he was busy employing tried and true methods for reaching the lost in Cincinnati and beyond. His publishing work alone, which saw over one million copies of *God's Revivalist* distributed in 1901, in addition to millions of tracts and leaflets and "more than a half million" books, kept five stenographers "busy all the time" and warranted the claim by Seth Rees that "God used him to push Scriptural holiness in books, booklets, and papers into more homes than any man living." ¹⁷⁶

In addition, his creative mind never ceased innovating new methods of reaching souls, including the Thanksgiving Day Dinner and Convention that concluded just days before his final illness and the Salvation wall calendar, which featured "convictive Scripture verses" listed "between the weeks" to "constantly preach Jesus, not the world or worldly wares."¹⁷⁷ The latter was "one of the last things God gave Brother Knapp" and proved to be a phenomenally successful idea, serving as the likely inspiration behind the perennially popular Scripture Text Calendar which would achieve great commercial success in the hands of F. M. Messenger, who would make it the mainstay of the prosperous Messenger Publishing Company which he founded in 1913.¹⁷⁸

However, the work which likely demanded the most of Knapp's time since its inception was that of God's Bible School. He was not simply an administrator or teacher who kept his distance from the students. Rather,

> God gave him such a wonderful love for the boys and the girls in the school. Both he and Sister Knapp were like a father and mother to each . . . . He was never too busy, never too weary, to hear a confession or the story of some one who had been wronged, or to rejoice with some one who had gained the victory, or to pray with some one who was weary or discouraged

... He loved them every one as if they were his own children, and always spoke of them as "our girls" and "our boys."[179]

His unceasing exertions naturally led the GBS family to regard him as "a martyr to the work here."[180] However, the crown of martyrdom was also considered Knapp's reward due to another factor that doubtless contributed to his weakened condition—the stress of the many battles he had weathered since the opening of God's Bible School, including the conflict with Dowie, his withdrawal from the Methodist Episcopal Church, the struggle with the National Holiness Association culminating in the triumphant campaign in Chicago, and his arrest for "disturbing the peace" during Salvation Park Camp Meeting. Seth Rees described Knapp's death starkly in terms of martyrdom: "They killed him, but God took him. His delicate frame and sensitive nature went down under a shower of stones, not so much from the world as from a fallen Church and from back-slidden holiness; but Jesus rose up to receive him."[181]

A brief respite during the summer for a few days in the "Valley of Blessings,"[182] at Lockwood, Kentucky, near the Big Sandy River, had simply not been enough to replenish the vitality drained by conflict and continuous exertion, and Knapp's "tired body had no resources with which to defend itself" when typhoid fever struck. However, the seriousness of his condition "was recognized only during the last three days."[183] On Wednesday, following apparent improvement, he failed quickly. From Friday night to Saturday night, he suffered excruciating "tortures," bringing to his friends' minds his oft stated wish that "before he went home, he would like to taste the physical sufferings of Jesus." On Friday evening, he requested that "God's Anvil," the song which had meant so much to him during Lucy's final illness, be sung, to which he whispered a soft "Amen" of resignation. The next evening, one of his last wishes was for a student to sing one of the last songs he had penned—"Redeemed by the Blood"[184]—which, like his last book, *Holiness Triumphant*, fittingly drew inspiration from his favorite book of the Bible—Revelation. Indeed, it was "written through the love throbbing in his own soul for the New Jerusalem" and demonstrated his unwavering confidence in the four-fold gospel, even in the face of death.[185]

Throughout his illness he characteristically "talked and preached Jesus, exhorting" his attendants "to be true to Him and a full salvation."[186] In fact, "his ministry continued even on his sickbed . . . as he inquired of the nurses if they were on their way to heaven."[187] On Friday evening, while "suffering the most intense agony," Knapp mustered his strength and exclaimed, "Wake them up, wake them up!" The nurse, thinking perhaps he referred to the students, responded, "Wake whom up, Brother Knapp?" He replied, "Wake up the souls that are going to hell."[188] This man who "had a message, knew it was from God, and must be delivered" was possessed with a passion to reach souls for God until the very end.[189]

This passion had ruled the way he lived, it would rule even in his death. Indeed, even in the funeral services, the desires of this man who had submitted his all to God's proprietorship many years before presented a powerful witness to Cincinnati and the world beyond. Knapp had insisted that there would be "no crapes, nor mourning robes" and that his remains be "cremated"—all reflecting his emphasis on the simplicity that good stewardship demands.[190] While the latter request was complied with "reluctantly" by his family and was still unusual enough among holiness people to warrant an article in its defense by the venerable W. B. Godbey, it undoubtedly stemmed from Knapp's desire that no unnecessary expense be wasted upon him when the resources could be put to better use in reaching the lost with the message of full salvation.[191] Even the Cincinnati press took note, reporting that the services memorializing Knapp would "be impressive because of their simplicity."[192] Little wonder that A. M. Hills regarded him to be "the very incarnation of unselfishness" and Seth Rees esteemed him as "the most unselfish, self-denying man I have ever known."[193]

Just a few weeks before his death, Knapp had preached in God's Tabernacle from a passage beautifully reflective of his selfless surrender to God and aptly prescient of his near passing, depicting to his flock at God's Bible School "what it would be to hear God's 'Well done, thou good and faithful servant; enter thou into the joy of thy Lord.'"[194] Now, as he was remembered with "little ostentation and show," great numbers of his holiness comrades were joined by "hundreds of sympathetic friends" who filed through the parlor of the mansion at 1810 Young Street for a final view of his remains, housed in a "black coffin, severely plain" on which a silver plate bore the inscription, "He being dead, yet speaketh."[195] This refrain was born out repeatedly in the many tributes received from the *Revivalist* family and in the funeral which was conducted at 2 p.m. on December 10 with a congregation of about eight hundred gathered in God's Tabernacle, with "the windows draped in white" to mark Knapp's triumphant home-going (rather than the traditional black for mourning).[196]

The prayer and funeral sermon were fittingly offered by W. B. Godbey, Knapp's theological mentor, and were followed by a tribute from evangelist Mary Storey, one of Knapp's earliest associates in his work in Cincinnati.[197] However, before Godbey spoke, the students of God's Bible School sang "I Have Now No Regrets," a song that Knapp had written in tribute to his colleague S. A. Keene but which A. M. Hills suggested now even "more appropriately" applied to Knapp, which reads in part,

> "I have now no regrets!" for the past is all clear,
> With its labor of love for my Savior so dear;
> On his errands so sweet I have sped with delight,
> All my pleasures by day and my song in the night.
> "I have now no regrets!" bless the Lamb that was slain!
> "If I could I would do it all over again."[198]

Perhaps those words sum up as well as any the life of this "hero of faith and prayer," whom Dr. Godbey eulogized by acknowledging that "other men in the holiness movement greater than he there may be on some lines, but I believe you will all admit with me he was the most aggressive man in go-aheaditive-ness and energy and enterprise—he really was without a peer ... He was a regular incarnation of energy."[199]

Seth Rees further emphasized that this energy was a powerful stimulus to others: "The atmosphere where Brother Knapp lived seemed to be loaded with something which not only encouraged, but electrified, and urged one to do his best."[200] In his biography of Knapp, A. M. Hills agreed with these assessments, but again underscored that Knapp's brilliance and energy were not "natural" endowments but were "supernatural" gifts of divine endowment which in Knapp produced the most remarkable transformation Hills had ever observed: "Of all the men that I ever met—potential men, great men—I consider Brother Knapp the greatest surprise, the most truly Spirit-filled, Spirit-thrilled, Spirit-guided, Spirit-illuminated, and Spirit-empowered man I have known. There was in him relatively the least of the human and the most Divine. There is no other rational solution of his career."[201]

J. L. Glascock observed that this greatness stemmed from Knapp's dependence on God through prayer,

> I never knew a man of such habits of prayer as Brother Knapp was. I could scarcely go in to see him for ten minutes, but what he would say, "Brother Glascock, let's have a moment of prayer." He laid all his plans out before God in panorama, told Him every detail. He never dared to take a step in any direction that he had not first prayed through. He took God absolutely and permanently into partnership. That is the secret of his marvelous success. He took his marching orders from high Heaven. We scarcely can conceive of a man with such backward, timid disposition, going such lengths in daring exploits for the kingdom of Jesus Christ. It was not only the sign of a great soul, but the incontrovertible evidence of a man that knew God, and knew how to prevail with Him.[202]

Hills likewise concluded,

> He lived in the unseen realm, and communed with the Invisible ... He waited on God, and got his mind on his great enterprises, and then he ventured upon schemes that would have seemed to others visionary and chimerical; but to him, who had prayed them through, they were as certain as fate, and success was as sure as the promises of the [eternal] God.[203]

Without doubt, one of the most remarkable of these enterprises was God's Bible School and Missionary Training Home, which began in answer to prayer and remains over a century later as a demonstration of "the power and willingness of the loving Christ to answer prayer" and as a testimony to the Pentecostal passion that not only imbued Martin Wells Knapp but was infused within the ethos of the school he started. Indeed, his remaining colleagues and subsequent generations took heed to the cry of this little man who was wholeheartedly surrendered to God to "Wake them up!" No doubt, Seth Rees spoke for many when he wrote that those words "have stirred my whole being, my very bones are on fire. I am doubling my diligence in waking up 'lost souls on their way to hell.'"[204] Since then, countless students have gone out from the Mount of Blessings to "Wake them up!" by proclaiming a full salvation around the world. Indeed, after more than a century has passed, it appears that the prayer of W. E. Shepard has been honored— "May a double portion of the spirit of Rev. Martin Wells Knapp ever abide upon all who pass through the School!"[205]

Notes

[1] Knapp, *Back to the Bible*, 52.

[2] W. B. Godbey, *Adoption* reprinted in *Godbey on Christian Experience* Compiled by Wallace Thornton, Jr. and Roger Price (Salem, OH: Schmul Publishing Co., 1999), 99.

[3] See M. W. Knapp, "Holiness Catechism," *Revivalist* (Sept. 19, 1901), 2-3; W. B. Godbey, "Gradualism," *Revivalist* (March 22, 1900), 2; and D. B. Strouse, "Humanity and Carnality," *Revivalist* (July 12, 1900), 7, 11. For several years, Knapp offered $10 to anyone who could prove that full sanctification comes by growth.

Keswick views were popularized in America by F. B. Meyer during a series of twelve trips (beginning in 1891) undertaken in response to an invitation by Dwight L. Moody (R. T. Clutter, "Meyer, (F)rederick (B)rotherton (1847-1929)," in Reid, *Dictionary*, 736-737). Moody himself became a major American proponent of holiness as "suppression" (of the carnal nature, as opposed to cleansing or "eradication"). This explains why Knapp desired to displace Moody's colportage library and otherwise draw people away from this inadequate understanding of holiness into the deeper, and more scriptural, concept of eradication. See F. M. Messenger, "Meyer Consistent," *Revivalist* (March 21, 1901), 2; W. B. Godbey, *Keswickism* (Louisville: Pentecostal Publishing Co., n. d.); and A. M. Hills, *Scriptural Holiness and Keswick Teaching Compared* (1910; reprint, Schmul Publishing Co., n. d.). The best-known British opponent of Keswick was Oswald Chambers, who wrote in his first book, published by Revivalist Press: "Jesus teaches that he can alter our mainspring of action. He does not teach us to curb or suppress the wrong disposition, He does not even give us something to counteract it, He gives us a totally new disposition." (*Studies in the Sermon on the Mount: God's Character and the Believer's Conduct* (1915; reprint, Salem, OH: Schmul Publishing Co., 2005), 33-34). For contemporary assessments of the Keswick view of sanctification, see Marlin R. Hotle, *In Search of Sanctification* (Salem, OH: Schmul Publishing Co., 1991) and Melvin Dieter, et. al. *Five Views on Sanctification* (Grand Rapids: Zondervan, 1987). Also, see William Kostlevy, "Keswick," *Dictionary*, 150-151 and Leroy E. Lindsey, Jr. *Radical Remedy: The Eradication of Sin and Related Terminology in Wesleyan-Holiness Thought, 1875-1925* (Ph. D. diss., Drew University, 1996).

[4] "God's Revivalist for 1902," *Revivalist* (Dec. 12, 1901), 1. For a typical example of warnings against fanaticism, see A. E. Stephenson, "Trying the Spirits," *Revivalist* (April 25, 1901), 2. Stephenson, who was converted from Christian Science, argued that "third experience" teachings combined Christian Science ideals with spiritualism and "what remains of a Christian experience." See also, M[adge] Duff, "Fanatics," *Revivalist* (Oct. 26, 1905), 10. For a lengthier work disavowing fanaticism, see A. M. Hills, *Holiness: Not a Modern Fad Run by Cranks*, reprinted as Part V in *Sparks from Seven Hammers: Reflections on the Christian Life by Seven Classic Writers* (Salem, OH: Schmul Publishing Co., 2004). Also, see A. H. Kauffman, *Fanaticism Explained: Symptoms, Cause and Cure* (Grand Rapids: A. H. Kauffman, 1904). For candid descriptions of extremes or "fanaticism" among turn-of-the-century holiness

people, see "Fanaticism," c. 28 in C. B. Jernigan, *Pioneer Days* . . . , 150-154.

⁵ "Encyclical Letter . . .," 13. Godbey then asserted, "The truth of it is, that the Bible does not teach us to follow the Holy Ghost, but Jesus only; meanwhile the Holy Spirit is your faithful Leader and Protector. He does not speak of Himself, but Jesus."

⁶ See E. L. Blumhofer, "Dowie, John Alexander," in Burgess and Van Der Maas, *The New International Dictionary of Pentecostal and Charismatic Movements* Revised and Expanded Edition, 586-587 and D. William Faupel, "John Alexander Dowie: A Brief Introduction to His Life and Ministry," (Paper given in preparation for the second Wesleyan-Holiness-Pentecostal Consultation, Kansas City, MO: October 28-29, 2005).

⁷ See the reprint of his testimony concerning the beginning of his healing ministry in Australia, Rev. John Alex. Dowie, "How I Came to Believe in Divine Healing," *The Way of Faith* (Sept. 23, 1896), 3. Also, see "Leaves of Healing," *The Way of Faith* (May 20, 1896), 3.

⁸ "A New Discovery," *Revivalist* (March 8, 1900), 14. In *Pentecostal Letters* (46), Knapp admits to initially having been "deceived in regard" to Dowie's work, "but God undeceived" him after he heard Dowie speak in Cincinnati, where Dowie's "spirit and presence convinced" Knapp that Dowie was "far from the apostolic spirit."

⁹ Ibid, 15. See also, "Dr. Dowie's Delusion," *Revivalist* (March 15, 1900), 14 in which Dowie is again praised for having "fearlessly fought every form of evil in the godless city of Chicago with a courage that few men possess these days," but then condemned for encouraging his followers "to seek riches, wealth, etc."

¹⁰ Among these articles were "Superficial Revivals," 1; "A Word of Warning," 8; "God's Zion vs. Dowie's 'Zion,'" 9; and "Counterfeit Healers," 10.

¹¹ "Poison in the Pan," *Revivalist* (March 22, 1900), 8.

¹² Ibid. See the expansion of this argument in "Poison in the Zion Pan," *Revivalist* (March 21, 1901), 7 (reprinted in Hills, *Hero*, 199-202 and as a tract). Here, and in "The Chicago 'Zion,'" *Revivalist* (March 22, 1900), 9, Knapp found a similarity between Dowie's ministry and Mormonism, a relationship just now coming under scholarly scrutiny. See D. William Faupel, "Alexander Dowie: Born to Command," in Knight, ed. *From Aldersgate to Azusa Street*, 177-184.

¹³ Blumhofer, "Dowie," 587. See "A Word of Warning," *Revivalist* (March 22, 1900), 8; "Forbear Threatening," *Revivalist* (March 22, 1900), 9; and "The Gospel of Zion vs. the Gospel of Jesus," *Revivalist* (March 29, 1900), 8.

¹⁴ "Dowieism," *Revivalist* (July 5, 1900), 12 (article reprinted from the Australian paper, *Life and Light*). Nienkirchen (19) explains that it was, "ironically, . . . Simpson's avowed commitment to a proportionate emphasis on divine healing under the rubric of his Fourfold Gospel that earned him verbal abuse from . . . Dowie . . . Chagrined by Simpson's refusal to accompany him on a cross-country healing campaign, sometime prior to 1885, Dowie maligned him as a fraud and betrayer of divine healing."

¹⁵ "Fakirism," *Revivalist* (March 29, 1900), 10.

¹⁶ "Forbear Threatening," *Revivalist* (March 22, 1900), 9. Also, see "Dowie's Attack on Moody," *Revivalist* (March 22, 1900), 8. Knapp's death was welcomed

with similar reaction "by some of the Dowie people" who saw his death as "a judgment sent upon him because he spoke against the claim of Mr. Dowie that he was the 'reincarnation of the Prophet Elijah' . . ." (J. B. Martin, "Loyal Unto Death," in Hills, *Hero*, 318).

[17] Ibid.

[18] See "Revival Prayer Answered," *Revivalist* (Aug. 8, 1901), 11, for a report of converts from Dowieism. The holiness movement also suffered several defections to Dowie's ranks, including "the first leaders of the Pentecostal Rescue Mission in Binghamton, New York," although the Binghamton work remained committed to the holiness cause and was the precursor of the Pilgrim Holiness Church of New York, Inc. (see Thomas and Thomas, 17). Particularly embarrassing for GBS leadership was the loss of Mary McGee Hall and her husband, L. C. Hall, to Dowie's camp. Hall had written numerous articles in the *Revivalist*, criticizing H. C. Morrison and other holiness advocates who remained loyal to Methodism and advocating the formation of independent holiness works (For example, see the *Revivalist* (Aug. 2, 1900) for her "To the Holiness People Everywhere," 12 and "To the Holiness People in My Southland," 13. Knapp and Seth Rees had also supported the formation of the independent holiness "temple" that the Halls helped lead in St. Louis. See Mary McGee Hall, "The St. Louis (Mo.) Work in 'The Temple,'" *Revivalist* (Sept. 8, 1900), 15; Seth C. Rees, "Call to St. Louis," *Revivalist* (Nov. 8, 1900), 14; and "The Temple Work at St. Louis," *Revivalist* (Aug. 30, 1900), 12. Understandably, the *Revivalist* gave little fanfare when the Halls defected, but Knapp distanced himself from the enterprise:

> It is a mistake the St. Louis movement was "instigated and carried forward" by us. We have reported it the same as we have any other department of the holiness movement, and have stood for the rights of the St. Louis people and all other people where God so led to form Independent Holiness Churches; but we are in no way responsible for any unscriptural attachments that may have caused its downfall.
>
> .....
>
> It is a mistake that Brother and Sister Hall, of St. Louis, have been "dropped" from our work, as they have never been identified with it, except that Sister Hall visited our camp-meeting, participating in it the same as any other similar visitor, and has contributed a few articles to the Revivalist ("Mistakes Corrected," *Revivalist* (Jan. 17, 1901), 8. See also, Hills, *Hero*, 225-226).

[19] "Dowie's Dismal Swamp," *Revivalist* (June 13, 1901), 8. Also, see *Pentecostal Letters*, 46.

[20] "Rescued from Dowieism," *Revivalist* (July 11, 1901), 8.

[21] "Dowie's Delusion," *Revivalist* (June 27, 1901), 8. Dowie continued,

> Elijah was a prophet, John was a preacher, but I combine in myself the attributes of prophet, priest, and ruler over men. Gaze on me, then; I say it fearlessly. Make the most of it, you wretches in ecclesiastical garb.

I am he that is the living embodiment of Elijah, and my commission to earth a third time has been prophesied by Malachi, by God Himself, by His Son Jesus, by Peter, and three thousand years ago by Moses.

In effect, Dowie was claiming not just to be like Elijah, but the actual reincarnation of Elijah, an idea challenged by W. B. Godbey in the *Revivalist*'s "Question Drawer" (October 24, 1901), 15. See also, "Opinion of Counterfeit Elijah," *Revivalist* (Oct. 31, 1901), 8.

[22] Ibid.

[23] *Pentecostal Letters*, 45. See the several letters "Against Chicago Errors" in this compilation (45-52) which reflect the prominence that the conflict with Dowie held in Knapp's thinking.

[24] Knapp explained why he focused more on Methodism than other "worldly denominations"—"Because Methodism, more than any other worldly denomination, professes to be the genuine conserver and expounder of Bible holiness, while equally; or nearly so, with other worldly denominations, she is betraying it . . ." ("True Methodism and Revivals," *Revivalist* (Nov. 14, 1901), 1).

[25] "Revival Poison in the Methodist Pan," *Revivalist* (April 19, 1900), 1,12-13 (Reprinted in *Hills*, Hero, 185-199). This article, like "Poison in the Zion Pan," was also published in tract form.

[26] Knapp's particular agitation over the distancing of the Methodist hierarchy from the promotion of entire sanctification is reflected in such articles as "Painful Omissions," *Revivalist* (June 28, 1900), 8 and "The Voice of the Methodist Church Seventy-Six Years Ago On Sanctification," *Revivalist* (May 2, 1901), 3. Knapp did acknowledge, however, that some Methodist Bishops, such as Bishop FitzGerald, had attempted to staunch the tide of anti-holiness and anti-revival sentiment ("A Controversy with Methodism," *Revivalist* (Feb. 28, 1901), 8).

[27] "Bible-School Testimonies," *Revivalist* (Nov. 14, 1901), 14. See also, "True Methodism and Revivals," *Revivalist* (Nov. 14, 1901), 1. Knapp argued that "primitive Methodism welcomes holiness preachers; counterfeit Methodism opposes them, sometimes demanding their credentials" ("Pikeville, Ky.," *Revivalist* (Dec. 5, 1901), 12).

[28] "Fanaticism and Revivals," *Revivalist* (Jan. 17, 1901), 10 (reprinted on the front page of the Feb. 14, 1901, *Revivalist*. Both this article, and "Fanatics," *Revivalist* (March 1, 1900), 8 denounce extremism at either end of the religious spectrum, such as "Pre-millennial fanatics, who set the very day of our Lord's return" and "Post-millennial fanatics, who proclaim that 'the world is growing better and better' . . .."

[29] D. T. Grout, "Fanaticism in God's Bible-School," *Revivalist* (Feb. 6, 1902), 12.

[30] Kostlevy, *Holy Jumpers*, 32. For Knapp's letter to the presiding elder, see *Pentecostal Letters*, 63-64. Other letters relevant to the case appear in the same chapter (IX, 63-69).

[31] M. W. Knapp, *Pentecostal Aggressiveness; or, Why I Conducted The Meetings Of The Chesapeake Holiness Union At Bowens, Maryland*, (n. p.: n. p., n. d.).

[32] Kostlevy, *Holy Jumpers*, 32. He also returned in 1900 ("Revival Reports," *Revivalist* (Aug. 16, 1900), 11).

[33] "Holiness Societies," *Revivalist* (Aug. 2, 1900), 1.

34 "Churches—Real, Mixed, Bogus," *Revivalist* (Jan. 11, 1900), 8 (my emphasis).

35 "True Methodism and Revivals," *Revivalist* (Nov. 14, 1901).

36 "Withdrawn," *Revivalist* (Oct. 3, 1901), 8.

37 "Church Relation Changed," 13. The announcement concluded, "He has the assurance that God Himself is leading in this step. Pray that all His will in it may be known and done. Further particulars next week." In *Pentecostal Letters* (134), Knapp indicates that his decision "was the results of testings and prayer for nearly a year (see also the letters from 122-147 related to this decision). Also, see "Withdrawing From The Methodist Church," chapter XV in Hills, *Hero*, 215-235.

38 "Why I Withdrew from the Methodist Episcopal Church," *Revivalist* (Jan. 17, 1901), 8.

39 "Societies of God's Church vs. Worldly Societies and Denominations," *Revivalist* (Feb. 14, 1901), 8. See also in the same issue, "God's Church vs. Worldly Churches," 8, 12; "Church Organization," 12; "Questions about God's Church," 12; and "Membership in the Societies of God's Church," 16. While Knapp considered the name "Church of God" to be the most biblical term for the church, he chose to render it "God's Church" due to "its brevity" and to "distinguish it from the sects which use the other form" ("God's Church—Its Bible Name," *Revivalist* (Feb. 14, 1901), 14). To further emphasize his continued disapproval of "anarchistic come-outism," Knapp concluded in this issue an article on the "Perils of Come-outism," 12.

40 *Pentecostal Letters*, 137. "Remarks," *Revivalist* (Jan. 17, 1901), 8. In fact, Knapp reasoned, "Many of her societies are worse than lodges, in that they add to their worldliness the sin of professing to be the Church of Christ." See also, "Sectarianism," *Revivalist* (Aug. 30, 1900), 8 and "Come-Outism," *Revivalist* (May 23, 1901), 8.

41 "Withdrawn," *Revivalist* (Oct. 3, 1901), 8. See also, George B. Kulp, "A Flame of Fire," *Revivalist* (April 14, 1921), 8-9: "Brother Knapp insisted that he did *not* leave the Methodist Church, *it left him* . . ." (original emphasis).

42 *Pentecostal Letters*, 138.

43 "Remarks," *Revivalist* (Jan. 17, 1901), 8.

44 Cited in Thomas and Thomas, 44. See also, W. B. Godbey, "Salvation Park Camp-Meeting," *Revivalist* (July 18, 1901), 13 where he attempts to vindicate Knapp of the charge of "come-outism."

45 Hills, *Hero*, 216.

46 See "The Rev. M. W. Knapp versus Methodism," an article from the *Pittsburg Advocate* cited in Hills, *Hero*, 232-235.

47 In 1897, Knapp was a worker at the National camp meeting near New Albany, Indiana ("Silver Heights Camp-meeting," *Revivalist* (Oct. 1897), 6). Knapp had also preached at earlier National camp meetings ("At the Camps," *Revivalist* (Oct. 1896), 6).

48 See Jones, *Perfectionist Persuasion*, 103.

49 Dieter, *Holiness Revival* (255) notes various factors in the declining influence of National Association leadership.

50 Kostlevy (*Holy Jumpers*, 30) explains that the founding of the Union "marked the formal separation of the radical champions of divine healing and premillennial

eschatology . . . from the conservative, Methodist-dominated [National Holiness Association]." In an important observation as to the difficulty of tracing the following developments, he notes, "The separation itself was wrought with pain and considerable complexity. Alliances formed in the heat of battle by individuals with heightened millennial expectations were frequently short-lived."

[51] See Isaiah Reid, ed. "Beyond the Mississippi," *Christian Witness and Advocate of Bible Holiness* (Oct. 11, 1900), 4 on the open letter by L. B. Kent to Knapp in which the latter is remonstrated for "his advocacy of the Apostolical Society movement, so called." Also, see Knapp's response to such charges in "But The Revivalist," *Revivalist* (Sept. 6, 1900), 8; "A Pentecostal Platform," *Revivalist* (Sept. 6, 1900), 1; and "Contend," *Revivalist* (Sept. 13, 1900), 1.

[52] Isaiah Reid, ed. "Beyond the Mississippi," *Christian Witness and Advocate of Bible Holiness* (Feb. 14, 1901), 4.

[53] Dieter in Caldwell, 177. Also, see Rose, *Vital Holiness*, 59-60.

[54] "Beyond the Mississippi," *Christian Witness* (Jan. 17, 1901), 4.

[55] "Holiness Hindered," *Revivalist* (April 12, 1900), 10. Here Knapp reflects one of his defenses of proclaiming these issues—to combat fanaticism: "If we as holiness people don't teach the truth in regard to our Lord's coming and the healing of the body as Jesus taught it, why people will come along and teach error, such as we see on every hand." "Facts about the Revivalist," *Revivalist* (Aug. 31, 1899), 15. See also, "The Use of Sidetracks," *Revivalist* (Nov. 1897), 7; "Use of Sidetracks," *Revivalist* (Jan. 4, 1900), 8; "Please Don't," *Revivalist* (Jan. 4, 1900), 16; "Fractional Holiness," *Revivalist* (March 28, 1901), 2; and Thomas and Thomas, 17.

[56] "A Great Mistake," *Revivalist* (Jan. 10, 1901), 10. Here Godbey clearly embraces the concept of progressive revelation that was held not only throughout the Revivalist movement but in other restorationist movements, particularly the Church of God (Anderson).

[57] M. W. Knapp, "Fatal Sidetracks," *Revivalist* (April 19, 1900), 10. See also, W. B. Godbey, "Satan's Sidetracks," *Revivalist* (Jan. 11, 1900), 16 and "Side Tracks," *Revivalist* (Feb. 13, 1902), 4 as well as his "Encyclical Letter" and his *Satan's Sidetracks for Holiness People*, reprinted as Part VI in *Sparks from Seven Hammers*.

[58] "Among The Holiness Periodicals," *Christian Witness* (Oct. 18, 1900), 5. He also wrote, "Many of our people are led astray, not because they do not take a so-called holiness paper, but because they persist in taking one which, while it represents holiness, hitches on something else, so that they really think that the attachment is part of the concern . . . The result that follows is division and the separating of forces that should be united" ("Beyond the Mississippi," *Christian Witness* (Dec. 6, 1900), 4).

[59] "Semi-Holiness Papers," *Revivalist* (Nov. 8, 1900), 8.

[60] "A Holy Ghost Movement," *Revivalist* (Feb. 1, 1900), 1.

[61] "Poison in the Holiness Pan," *Revivalist* (April 18, 1901), 2. Also, see "Kinds of Holiness," *Revivalist* (Nov. 14, 1901), 2.

[62] *Pentecostal Letters*, 133-134.

[63] "Anti-Revival Clubhouses," *Revivalist* (May 23, 1901), 1.

[64] See "The Revival War," *Revivalist* (Dec. 13, 1900), 1 and the accompanying illustration which is reproduced in Moser and Smith, 10. As the illustration makes

clear, Knapp considered this war to have two fronts—one against outright sin, the "City of Sin"—the other against compromised holiness, the "Mount of Jealousy."

⁶⁵ See Kostlevy, *Holy Jumpers*, 33-35. The conflict over millennial views was more intense than that on divine healing, although National associated authors opposed the idea of "healing in the atonement" in such works as William McDonald, *Modern Faith Healing Scripturally Considered: A Thoughtful Examination of Faith Healing in the Light of Scripture and Experience* (1892; reprint, Salem, OH: Schmul Publishing Co., 1999) and George W. Wilson, *Truths As I Have Seen Them or Addresses on the Spiritual Life* (1897; reprint, Salem, OH: Schmul Publishing Co., 1986). See also, Dayton, *Theological Roots*, 132-133 and Dieter in Caldwell, 175-176.

On post- verses pre- millennialism, major spokesmen were Daniel Steele and L. L. Pickett. See Steele's *A Substitute for Holiness* and M. W. Knapp, "Fish Bones," *Revivalist* (March 22, 1900), 7; M. W. Knapp, "Substitutes for Scripture," *Revivalist* (Oct. 24, 1901), 7; and Dayton, *Theological Roots*, 164. Pickett's book, *The Blessed Hope*, contained the charges that "the National Holiness Association forbids the preaching of this truth at its camps. *The Christian Witness*, official organ of that body, refuses to publish anything on the pre-millennial side of this subject . . . They frequently present the post-millennial view as the truth (365). Isaiah Reid responded that Pickett's charge involved "A Serious Misrepresentation," *Christian Witness* (May 24, 1900), 4-5 and insisted that, "as the National Association has been misrepresented in the columns of the Revivalist, we think in all fairness there should be proper correction through the same channel." However, Pickett stuck to his guns, "Was It a Misrepresentation?" *Revivalist* (Oct. 17, 1901), 7 until he believed *The Christian Witness* had "improved" with respect to this issue (editorial comment in *The Blessed Hope*, 365). See also, "A Soul-Winning Theme," *Revivalist* (May 3, 1900), 7; "Jesus Is Coming," *Revivalist* (June 7, 1900), 7; and L. L. Pickett, "Holiness and the Return of Jesus," *Revivalist* (July 20, 1901), 7.

⁶⁶ Donald Dayton ("Dispensationalism and the Emergence of Fundamentalism . . .," 11) states, "The longer I have reflected on these currents I have become more and more convinced of the centrality of this struggle between postmillennialism and premillennialism for understanding a range of questions in the holiness movement."

⁶⁷ It is beyond the scope of this work to give a detailed analyses of this confrontation which has been largely suppressed and forgotten until recently. Fortunately, an excellent scholarly treatment is provided in c. 3 "Pentecost Comes To The White City: The Chicago Revival and the General Holiness Assembly of 1901" in Kostlevy, *Holy Jumpers*, 63-76. Kostlevy suggests that the reason this important chapter in the holiness movement's history, which must be considered to understand adequately the role of GBS in that history, has (until his work) remained largely unreported is "a testimony to evangelicalism's and the Holiness Movement's quest for respectability and their desire to avoid the stigma of fanaticism" (58). Timothy L. Smith also briefly covers the radical convention and General Holiness Assembly in *Called Unto Holiness*, 126-129. Also, see Paul Rees, *Warrior Saint*, 58-59.

⁶⁸ Thomas and Thomas, 38. See "The Chicago Convention," *Revivalist* (Dec. 13, 1900), 12.

⁶⁹ Kostlevy, *Holy Jumpers*, 59.

⁷⁰ Ibid, 59-60 and "Chicago Holiness Convention," *Revivalist* (Feb. 14, 1901), 10.

⁷¹ See John T. Hatfield, *Thirty-three Years a Live Wire* (Cincinnati: Revivalist Press, n. d.). For a synopsis of a sermon preached by Hatfield during the Chicago revival, see "Hell," *Revivalist* (June 13, 1901), 16.

⁷² Kostlevy, *Holy Jumpers*, 68-70 provides important insights into the young Robinson's early radical connections, a factor generally ignored in biographical works produced after his death. As an evangelist in the Church of the Nazarene, Robinson probably shaped the young denomination more than any other single individual, even though he held no administrative or academic appointments. See J. B. Chapman, *Bud Robinson: A Brother Beloved* (Kansas City, MO: Beacon Hill Press, 1943), George C. Wise, *Rev. Bud Robinson* (1946; reprint, Salem, OH: Schmul Publishing Co., 2001), and Bud Robinson, *Sunshine and Smiles: Life Story, Flash Lights, Sayings and Sermons* (1903; revised, Shoals, IN: Old Paths Tract Society, 1986). One reflection of Robinson's continued popularity among a broad spectrum of evangelicals is the reprinting of Chapman's biography in 2000 by Faith Baptist Church Publications, with a glowing endorsement by Curtis Hutson, late editor of *Sword of the Lord*, a leading fundamentalist periodical.

⁷³ Kostlevy, *Holy Jumpers*, 72; see also 81-82. Hills proved to be an anomaly on this point throughout his long career as a holiness educator. When Nazarene leaders insisted that his systematic theology must present the premillennial view as well as his own postmillennial perspective, he engaged J. B. Chapman to write a premillennial section. Hill's postmillennial orientation may have been a factor in his early release from the presidency of Illinois Holiness University—forerunner of Olivet Nazarene University (See Gresham, 144-145). His case certainly provides an excellent illustration of the complex fluidity of the radical holiness constituency—it was no monolith dictated by a hierarchy—individualism flourished. See Dayton, *Theological Roots*, 164 and "Dispensationalism and the Emergence of Fundamentalism . . .," 11.

⁷⁴ Kostlevy, *Holy Jumpers*, 61.

⁷⁵ Seth C. Rees, "Chicago Holiness General Assembly," *Revivalist* (April 4, 1901), 2. See also, M. W. Knapp, "Full-orbed Holiness," *Revivalist* (May 2, 1901), 2, which similarly notes, "It is to be regretted that the brethren making a call for a 'general holiness assembly' to be held in Chicago so worded the call as to exclude the greater part of real holiness people . . . who believe . . . the preaching of a full gospel as declared by Jesus and the apostles to be helpful to holiness . . ."

⁷⁶ Paul Rees, *Warrior Saint*, 58. Actually, the secular papers took an interest before the convention even began, primarily due to a challenge issued by Duke Farson to Chicago area churches in which he offered to give a "conditional subscription" of $500, which he doubled to $1000, toward the salary of the pastor "who could prove that it was impossible to start a revival in his church" (Seth C. Rees, "That Chicago Wager," *Revivalist* (April 11, 1901), 15. The stipulations of what the secular media characterized as a wager included Farson choosing an evangelist to conduct a two-week revival at the church, during which time "no church entertainments, sociables, bazaars, fairs or any worldly amusements" would be permitted. "In return, Farson promised a minimum of fifteen conversions or sanctifications." The pastor of Sheffield Avenue Methodist Church, R. A. Morley, took Farson up on his offer, though

the $1000 condition was later dropped at the insistence of the presiding elder. It proved to be a moot point, for the convention that grew from this "wager" saw seventy-five members added to the Sheffield Avenue M. E. Church roll (Kostlevy, *Holy Jumpers*, 64-65).

[77] Seth C. Rees, "That Chicago Wager," *Revivalist* (April 11, 1901), 15.

[78] Kostlevy, *Holy Jumpers*, 70, 37-38 and Arthur F. Ingler, *The Pearly-white City (The City That's Coming Down)*, no. 444 in Haldor Lillenas, ed. and compiler, *Glorious Gospel Hymns* (Kansas City, MO: Lillenas Publishing Co., 1931). See also, "A 'Tempetuous Ordination,'" *Revivalist* (March 28, 1901), 1.

[79] Kostlevy, *Holy Jumpers*, 63 and "A Great Convocation," *Revivalist* (May 9, 1901), 7.

[80] Kostlevy, *Holy Jumpers*, 74 and "Woman's Place," *Revivalist* (May 30, 1901), 5. One of Shephard's best-known books was published by Revivalist Press, W. E. Shephard, *Sin, The Tell-Tale or Be Sure Your Sin Will Find You Out* (Cincinnati: God's Revivalist Press, n. d.).

On May 10, White preached in the convention revival "with great unction and power from David and Goliath, illustrating the truth with her personal experience. "Woman's Place," *Revivalist* (May 30, 1901), 5. This article reflects on the significance of Knapp's *Out of Egypt Into Canaan* in leading White into entire sanctification. Although associated with the MCA, she was read "out of their fellowship, on the divorce issue" in 1905, whereupon she organized her followers into the Pentecostal Union Church (Pillar of Fire), a denomination committed to such radical practices as shouting and vegetarianism (Smith, *Called Unto Holiness*, 128-129). See Stanley, *Feminist Pillar of Fire* and Mrs. Mollie Alma White, *Looking Back From Beulah* (Bound Brook, NJ: The Pentecostal Union (Pillar of Fire), 1902). She gave her testimony and preached during a visit to GBS shortly after the Chicago revival (June 1901) (Bessie [Queen], "Bible-School Notes," *Revivalist* (June 20, 1901), 15.

[81] "Mt. Carmel Repeated," *Revivalist* (March 28, 1901), 10. See also, "Revival Principles Vindicated," *Revivalist* (March 28, 1901), 14.

[82] "God Answering By Fire; or, The Great Chicago Revival," *Revivalist* (May 30, 1901), 1. This article provides the most extensive extant, contemporary account of the revival, to which such disproportionate space was granted because "of the fact that the principles held by the Revivalist have been mightily magnified in it." Also, see "The Chicago Convention," *Revivalist* (March 21, 1901), 12-13.

[83] See Kostlevy, *Holy Jumpers*, 72 and Smith, *Called Unto Holiness*, 127-128. Seth Rees still disparaged the General Assembly, but conceded that "the one redeeming feature of the Convention was in that the good people rescued it from the hands of those who have insisted that all 'side issues' must necessarily be excluded, however excellent or worthy, and the 'Assembly' declared in favor of 'the personal return of the Lord Jesus Christ for the final redemption of His saints,' 'the healing of the sick through the prayer of faith'" ("The Chicago General Assembly," *Revivalist* (May 30, 1901), 12).

[84] Smith, *Called Unto Holiness*, 126.

[85] Thomas and Thomas (17) note that, "The time came when many holiness people were strongly convinced of the premillennial return of Jesus Christ, but while that

truth came to the forefront, the matter of divine healing receded and in a sense was surrendered to other groups." The "other groups" are identified as "pentecostal" in Paul W. Thomas, "An Historical Survey of Pilgrim World Missions," (B. D. thesis, Asbury Theological Seminary, 1963), 31.

[86] Kostlevy, *Holy Jumpers*, 76. A. M. Hill's career is a good case in point of continued foment over eschatology.

[87] "Reports," *Revivalist* (July 4, 1901), 11. Not quite satisfied with the way the NHA and Assembly gave tacit endorsement without full-fledged support, and recanting their former opposition, Knapp called for them to make an open confession of their erroneous opposition to the four-fold gospel ("Which Will It Be?" *Revivalist* (Dec. 5, 1901), 5). However, while this was not forthcoming, relative silence indicated the new consensus.

[88] "Victory Assured," *Revivalist* (Jan. 17, 1901), 9. Knapp vowed, "I am determined to fulfill the commission in that chapter, proving the virtue of the eighteenth verse and claiming the victory of the nineteenth."

[89] "A Prophecy," *Revivalist* (March 28, 1901), 2.

[90] Kostlevy, *Moving Beyond Phoebe Palmer*, 10.

[91] Hills, *Hero*, 11.

[92] "Secrets of Revival Success," *Revivalist* (March 28, 1901), 1.

[93] Kostlevy, *Holy Jumpers*, 33. Knapp wrote that "the opening up of the Pentecostal dispensation was signaled by a 'sound from heaven,' which filled the house, aroused the city, and heralded the incoming of the Holy Ghost which transforms believers into such a joyous, noisy, shouting band of revival workers as to create the criticism that they were on a drunken spree" ("Revival Noise," *Revivalist* (Jan. 4, 1900), 1). Kostlevy suggests that, "in his decision to equate the 'Baptism of the Holy Ghost' with such physical signs, Knapp was within a whisker of Pentecostalism's later insistence that 'speaking in other tongues' was the initial evidence of the 'Baptism of the Holy Ghost.'" Also, see Charles Edwin Jones, "Tongues-speaking and the Wesleyan-Holiness Quest for Assurance of Sanctification," *WTJ* Vol. 22 No. 2 (Fall 1987), 117-124.

[94] "Pentecostal Demonstrations," *Revivalist* (June 20, 1901), 1.

[95] "True Revivals," *Revivalist* (Aug. 29, 1901), 1). See also, "Revival Demonstrations," *Revivalist* (Jan. 31, 1901), 1, 7; "Scriptural Noise," *Revivalist* (Aug. 1, 1901), 12; "A Demonstrative People," *Revivalist* (Aug. 8, 1901), 9; "Revival Distress and Joy," *Revivalist* (Sept. 5, 1901), 3, 12; and "Revival Demonstration," *Revivalist* (Nov. 21, 1901), 1; for a few of the several articles defending demonstrative worship. To balance this emphasis, Knapp also stressed that, "There are times when the Spirit will draw His people into a holy silence before Him, and when His mighty workings will be felt as much or more than times of noise and demonstration" ("Revival Quietness," *Revivalist* (July 4, 1901), 1).

For a defense of emotional demonstration by a noted author who was a participant in later GBS camp meetings, see "Shouting," c. 27 in Samuel Logan Brengle, *Helps to Holiness* (1896; Reprint, Salem, OH: Schmul Publishing Co., 1977), 130-135. Also, see Seth C. Rees, *Ideal Pentecostal Church*, 46-49.

[96] For example, after one of Knapp's lessons on the Book of Revelation, a "young

girl, who recently came to the school and thought she was sanctified, found out the truth, and came forward, seeking God, when, suddenly, just as if some one had struck her, she fell to the floor rigid. When she came to several hours later, her face shown, and she knew the Holy Ghost had come" (Bessie [Queen], "Bible-School Notes," *Revivalist* (Nov. 28, 1901), 14). For a revival report of a "dance-party . . . ringleader" who was prostrated "for an hour" and then brought "through all bright and clear," see "Reports," *Revivalist* (Nov. 28, 1901), 11. For a later example, see Sister Lasley, "God's Bible School Notes," *Revivalist* (Jan. 6, 1910), 13. See also P. H. Alexander, "Slain in the Spirit," in Burgess and Van Der Maas, *The New International Dictionary of Pentecostal and Charismatic Movements* Revised and Expanded Edition, 1072-1074.

[97] "Bible-School Notes," *Revivalist* (Feb. 13, 1902), 14.

[98] "Marks of Pentecostal Revivals," *Revivalist* (July 25, 1901), 1. Indeed, such revivals would be "bitterly opposed by the world, carnal Church-members, and the devil" ("Marks of Pentecostal Revivals," *Revivalist* (Aug. 22, 1901), 1). Also, see *Lightning Bolts*, 73-74.

[99] Seth C. Rees (Reported by Bessie [Queen] at Chicago Convention), "God's Choice," *Revivalist* (June 13, 1901), 2.

[100] "Our Cincinnati Meetings," *Revivalist* (Nov. 2, 1899), 14. Knapp explained that his services had been conducted "for some time in the [Y. M. C. A.] Building, but the noise disturbed them . . . At another place a certain professor became so distracted that he was instrumental in our removal." This appeared to be part of the impetus in seeking larger quarters which could also house a Bible school.

[101] "Unsettled," *Revivalist* (Nov. 28, 1901), 11. Knapp responded to such charges, "Every experience that can stand the test of the Word of God will rejoice under Bible-school teachings, while those who can not will be shown their defects and pointed to the place where God will so establish as to enable them to stand the tests, not only of the teaching of the full gospel here, but of the judgment-day hereafter."

[102] See "Stricken: 'Mount of Blessings,'" *The Cincinnati Enquirer* (Dec. 8, 1901), 9 reports, "It has been claimed that the Knappites held the same views as the Dowieites in regard to doctors, drugs, and earthly means of relief from sickness. One of the sisters who answered the ring of THE ENQUIRER representative yesterday afternoon at the great, gloomy house on Mt. Auburn denied that the sect was opposed to doctors." Also, see "Reign Of Sadness On Blessings' Mount," *The Cincinnati Post* (Dec. 9, 1901), 6.

[103] For a copy of the affidavit, warrant, and court transcript see the *Revivalist* (Aug. 1, 1901), 1-11. Much of this material is also recorded in Hills, *Hero*, 239-273. However, Hills omitted the testimony of Knapp's opposition (239).

[104] Hills, *Hero*, 238. Hills evidently believed much of the problem was due to a rather somber atmosphere in Cincinnati, commenting further that it never had "any brawls, nor parades, or mobs, nor strikes; nothing to ever break its solemn, funereal stillness!" While this statement surely represents hyperbole, it may indicate the rather sedate nature of the Queen City in contrast to other American cities at the time.

[105] "Leader of the Holiness Union is Arrested on a Warrant Charging Disorderly Conduct," *The Cincinnati Enquirer* (July 12, 1901), 5.

[106] "Brother Knapp Arrested," *Revivalist* (July 18, 1901), 15.

107 "Congratulations," *Revivalist* (Aug. 15, 1901), 14.

108 "Regrets," *Revivalist* (Aug. 1, 1901), 13.

109 "Scripture Fulfilled," *Revivalist* (Aug. 1, 1901), 12.

110 "The Enemies' Tactics," *Revivalist* (Aug. 1, 1901), 13 and "Scripture Fulfilled," *Revivalist* (Aug. 1, 1901), 12. Again, Knapp's arrest was one of "the marks of Pentecost" ("Continued," *Revivalist* (July 18, 1901), 15).

111 "A Noisy Meeting Coming," *Revivalist* (Aug. 1, 1901), 13.

112 "Howling Meetings," *Revivalist* (Aug. 1, 1901), 13. The printed barrage against opponents was evidently accompanied by verbal vituperative as well. During the trial, Coombe testified that some "Knapp followers jeered at him, saying: "Glory to God! There goes the old devil!" ("Rev. Knapp Was Fined The Costs," *The Cincinnati Post* (July 17, 1901), 6). This was countered by derision heaped upon Knapp's associates. For example, when asked during the trial about a particular holiness advocate, one of their opponents responded that "it was not a lady, it was a hunchback." *Revivalist* (Aug. 1, 1901), 4. The same person also admitted to removing a stone from a school wall, which subsequently collapsed.

113 The arrest of Knapp was not a unique experience among holiness advocates. For instance, the Salvation Army particularly became the brunt of intense persecution. A fascinating account of this opposition is given in E. H. McKinley, *Marching to Glory: The History of the Salvation Army in the United States, 1880-1992* 2nd ed. (Grand Rapids: Eerdmans, 1995), 81-86. In addition to the persecution of heckling mobs, which sometimes became life-threatening (five officers were martyred between 1880 and 1886), city governments often joined the wave of anti-Salvationist sympathy, passing legislation specifically designed to curtail Army activity. "Many Army meetings were broken up by police, and many Salvation Army officers and soldiers were arrested--some of them often" (McKinley, 84).

Alma White's Pentecostal Union (Pillar of Fire), a group even closer than the Salvation Army to Knapp's Revivalist movement, also had several members arrested. When a group appeared in a Denver court on February 9, 1903, they carried banners reading "Holiness or Hell, Jesus Is Coming, and Prepare to Meet Thy God" (Stanley, *Feminist Pillar of Fire*, 51).

114 "Revival Reproaches," *Revivalist* (July 25, 1901), 1. Also, see "Charles Wesley Falsely Condemned," *Revivalist* (Aug. 1, 1901), 12.

115 "Opening Convention," *Revivalist* (Aug. 8, 1901), 14.

116 "Holiness Meetings Have to Close," *The Cincinnati Enquirer* (July 13, 1901), 8.

117 "Rev. Knapp Was Fined the Costs," *The Cincinnati Post* (July 17, 1901), 6.

118 "Volunteer Service," *Revivalist* (August 1, 1901), 13. Heath had also gained notoriety as the "inventor of a typesetting machine which bids fair to supersede all in the market and revolutionize the whole printing world."

119 "Rev. Knapp," *Post* (July 17, 1901), 6.

120 Ibid. The *Revivalist* expressed skepticism concerning the reliability of the petition, declaring that "there is evidence that a number of people who were solicited to sign it refused to do so; that, instead of its being spontaneous, a considerable working up attended it. The fact that it was circulated upon the Sabbath-day is all that many will need to know to convince them that it was not born of the skies." "That Petition,"

Revivalist (Aug. 1, 1901), 13.

[121] Hills, *Hero*, 238-239.

[122] "Holiness Meetings Have To Close," *The Cincinnati Enquirer* (July 13, 1901), 8.

[123] "Rev. W. M. [sic] Knapp," *The Cincinnati Enquirer* (July 17, 1901), 12.

[124] "Editorial Comments," *Revivalist* (Aug. 1, 1901), 11.

[125] "Revival Screaming," *Revivalist* (Sept. 26, 1901). Knapp further asserted, "He would be pleased if they would work themselves to death as soon as possible. I know of several that he would like to side-track or kill just now."

[126] Knapp, *Back to the Bible*, 31-32. Knapp similarly warned that "the devil hates holiness and holiness camp-meetings. He evidently makes a specialty of opposing both" ("Opposed to the Camp-Meeting," *Revivalist* (June 14, 1900), 2). For books further demonstrating this aspect of "ultra-supernaturalism," see *Impressions* and W. B. Godbey, *Demonology* (Louisville: Pickett Publishing Co., 1902), which also contains chapters by L. L. Pickett, F. B. Meyer, Andrew Johnson, and J. M. Dustman.

[127] *Pentecostal Letters*, 133.

[128] "A Warning to Holiness Opposers," *Revivalist* (Nov. 28, 1901), 4.

[129] "God's Indorsement," *Revivalist* (Sept. 5, 1901), 11.

[130] "A Mighty Movement," *Revivalist* (Feb. 8, 1900), 2 (original emphasis). This rather ironic note for a "remnant" attempting to restore the Church has been noted by Ware (207) and indicates the tenuous equilibrium involved in wedding the Wesleyan optimism of grace with the primitivistic pessimism toward society.

[131] W. B. Godbey reported that there were "eighty to a hundred" students at the time of Knapp's death ("The Cremation," *Revivalist* (Dec. 26, 1901), 13). Cf. "Bible-School Notes," *Revivalist* (January 30, 1902), 15 which indicated that there "were nearly 100 students" at the same time. Both major Cincinnati newspapers reported an enrollment of eighty in December 1901 (See "Reign of Sadness on Blessings' Mount," *Cincinnati Post* (Dec. 9, 1901), 6 and "Poignant: Sorrow Reigns Supreme: Death of Rev. M. W. Knapp Mourned By Followers," *The Cincinnati Enquirer* (Dec. 9, 1901), 10.

Research in school records by Kevin M. Moser has found that, "A total of 150 students enrolled the second school year between Sept. 1901 and June 26, 1902" (Letter to author dated November 22, 2010.)

[132] David E. Harrell, "David E. Harrell Comments at the Opening of the John Carver Collection," *Wesleyan/Holiness Studies Center Bulletin* vol. 7 no. 2 (Winter 1999), 1.

[133] Mark A. Noll, *Turning Points: Decisive Moments in the History of Christianity* (Grand Rapids: Baker Book House, 1997), 302.

[134] This epithet, placing Pentecostalism third behind Catholicism and Protestantism, was popularized in an article in *Life Magazine* (June 9, 1958). On the rapid growth of Pentecostalism, see Edwin Scott Gaustad and Philip L. Barlow, *New Historical Atlas of Religion in America* (New York: Oxford University Press, 1998), and Tim Dowley, ed. *Atlas of the Bible and Christianity* (Grand Rapids: Baker Book House, 1997).

[135] Howard A. Snyder with Daniel V. Runyon, *The Divided Flame: Wesleyans and the Charismatic Renewal* (Grand Rapids: Francis Asbury Press, 1986).

[136] For example, the "Statement of Doctrine" in the *2000-2002 Catalog* (Cincinnati: God's Bible School and College, 2000), 10-11 emphatically asserts, "We believe that the evidence of this experience [of entire sanctification] is not an external manifestation [such as tongues-speaking], but the inner witness of the Holy Spirit that the heart has been purified from sin."

[137] It is likely that *Revivalist*/GBS leadership was significantly distracted from giving close attention to developments out of Los Angeles in the spring of 1906, for a little over two weeks before the Azusa Street Revival began, Mary Storey died, an event that helped to precipitate conflict over the trusteeship which ultimately led to court action. For the earliest *Revivalist* article I have located repudiating tongues-speaking as "the witness of the Holy Ghost Baptism," see "An Error Regarding Sanctification," *Revivalist* (April 6, 1911), 4.

[138] See Barry W. Hamilton, "Godbey, W(illiam) B(axter)," in Kostlevy, *Dictionary*, 129-130 and Synan, *The Holiness-Pentecostal Tradition*, 146.

[139] W. B. Godbey, *Current Heresies* (Cincinnati: God's Revivalist Office, 1908). This work appeared ten years before Godbey's better known *Tongue Movement, Satanic* (Zarephath, NJ: Pillar of Fire, 1918) and devotes a chapter (V) to "The Tongue Heresy" (20-28). His *Spiritualism, Devil-worship, and the Tongues* (Cincinnati: God's Revivalist Press) is undated. In all three works, his argument remains essentially the same—that tongues-speaking "throws wide open the door of the heart to demoniacal interventions" (*Current Heresies*, 20). See also his description of his visit to Los Angeles "to investigate" for himself, in his *Baptism of the Holy Ghost* (Greensboro, NC: Apostolic Messenger, n. d.), 21-22.

[140] The "tongues issue" was a factor in Kent and Alma's separation—Kent accepted tongues, Alma did not. See Stanley, *Feminist Pillar of Fire*, 70-77 and C. M. Robeck, Jr. "Kent White" in Burgess and Van Der Maas, *The New International Dictionary of Pentectostal and Charismatic Movements* Revised and Expanded Edition, 1194.

[141] See Abbie Morrow, Ed. *Sweet Smelling Myrrh* (Cincinnati: M. W. Knapp, Publisher of Pentecostal Literature, n. d.) and Ed. *The Work of Faith Through George Muller* (Cincinnati: Revivalist, 1899). At least one other holiness writer who developed sympathies for the tongues movement (J. M. Pike) contributed to the devotional: W. B. Godbey, Byron J. Rees, A. M. Hills, M. W. Knapp, etc. *Jesus Only: A Full Salvation Year Book* (Cincinnati: Revivalist, n. d.). This devotional and Morrow's edition of Madam Guyon's and Muller's autobiographies remain in print through Schmul Publishing Company. On the influence of Morrow's version of Muller's story, see R. G. Robins, *A. J. Tomlinson: Plainfolk Modernist* (New York: Oxford University Press, 2004), 268.

[142] C. W. Conn, "Church of God (Cleveland, TN), in Burgess and Van Der Maas, *The New International Dictionary of Pentecostal and Charismatic Movements* Revised and Expanded Edition, 530-534. See also the several other articles in the same work dealing with splinter groups from the Church of God (Cleveland), including H. D. Hunter, "Church of God of Prophecy," 539-542. See also, Synan, *The Holiness-Pentecostal Church*, 74-77, 197-200; E. L. Simmons, *History of the Church of God* (Cleveland, TN: Church of God Publishing House, 1938); Mickey Crews, *The Church of God: A Social History* (Knoxville: The University of Tennessee Press, 1990), and several ar-

ticles in the *Church of God Evangel* 92 No. 5 (May 2002), an issue focusing on "Our Holiness Heritage." One should also consult Tomlinson's own works, especially his *The Last Great Conflict* in *The Higher Christian Life: Sources for the Study of the Holiness, Pentecostal, and Keswick Movements* Donald W. Dayton, ed. (1913; Reprint, New York: Garland Publishing, 1985). This work presents a vivid account of his spiritual development including his practice of tongues speaking.

[143] See Robins, 77-101 and Thomas D. Hamm, *The Transformation of American Quakerism: Orthodox Friends, 1800-1907* (Bloomington: Indiana University Press, 1988).

The influence of Quakerism on the holiness movement still offers much room for scholarly inquiry. For instance, Charles E. Jones has noted that the practice of the Church of God of Prophecy of making decisions based on utterances in tongues reflects the influence of Quakerism, in which decisions were made after members felt the guidance of the Inner Light.

[144] Robins, 88.

[145] This positive relationship between such holiness Quaker institutions at Westfield as Union Bible College (formerly "Seminary" and started in connection with Union Academy in 1911) with GBS has continued to this day, with both colleges now identifying with the conservative holiness movement associated with the Inter-Church Holiness Convention.

[146] Robins, 87-88.

[147] Ibid, 88.

[148] Ibid, 97.

[149] H. D. Hunter, "Ambrose Jessup Tomlinson," in Burgess and Van Der Maas, *The New International Dictionary of Pentecostal and Charismatic Movements* Revised and Expanded Edition, 1143-1144. Also, see H. D. Hunter, "Ambrose Jessup Tomlinson," in Burgess and McGee, *Dictionary of Pentecostal and Charismatic Movements*, original edition, 846-848.

[150] Homer Tomlinson, *The Great Vision of the Church of God* (Queens Village, NY: Tomlinson, 1939), 3. Also, see Robins, 167, 279.

[151] Hunter, "Tomlinson," in Burgess and McGee, *Dictionary*, original edition, 846-847. This account is omitted from the revised edition of the *Dictionary*.

[152] This fact is observed by Robins (167) whose work provides the most definitive biography of Tomlinson.

[153] Robins, 167. For evidence of this interaction, see Tomlinson's entry for May 27, 1903, in his Manuscript Diary, vol. 1, on file at the Library of Congress, Washington, DC, and his checkbook receipt "to Mrs. M. W. Knapp for songbooks, December 10, 1903," on file at the Archives of the Church of God of Prophecy, Cleveland, TN (Robins, 279).

[154] H. V. Synan, "Willaim Joseph Seymour," in Burgess and McGee, *Dictionary of Pentecostal and Charismatic Movements*, original edition, 778. See also, C. M. Robeck, Jr. "William Joseph Seymour," in Burgess and Van Der Maas, *The New International Dictionary of Pentetostal and Charismatic Movements* Revised and Expanded Edition, 1053-1054 and Stephen J. Land, "William J. Seymour: The Father of the Holiness-Pentecostal Movement," c. 19 in Knight, ed. *From Aldersgate to Azusa Street*, 218-226.

¹⁵⁵ Synan, "William Seymour," 18. Also, see Noll, *Turning Points*, 299 and A. Kenneth Curtis, J. Stephen Lang, and Randy Peterson, *The 100 Most Important Events in Christian History* (Grand Rapids: Fleming H. Revell, 1991), 176-179.

¹⁵⁶ Noll, *Turning Points*, 299.

¹⁵⁷ Synan, "William Seymour," 19.

¹⁵⁸ See J. R. Goff, Jr. "Topeka Revival," 1147-1149 and J. R. Goff, Jr. "Charles Fox Parham," 955-957 in Burgess and Van Der Maas, *The New International Dictionary of Pentectostal and Charismatic Movements* Revised and Expanded Edition.

¹⁵⁹ Rufus G. W. Sanders, *William Joseph Seymour: Black Father of the Twentieth Century Pentecostal/Charismatic Movement* (Sandusky, OH: Alexandria Publications, 2001), 52.

¹⁶⁰ C. M. Robeck, Jr. "William Joseph Seymour," in Burgess and Van Der Maas, *The New International Dictionary of Pentecostal and Charismatic Movements* Revised and Expanded Edition, 1054. Also, see C. M. Robeck, Jr., *The Azusa Street Mission and Revival: The Birth of the Global Pentecostal Movement* (Nashville: Nelson, 2006), 31-35. The *Dictionary* entry seems more reliable than the book, which contains such inaccuracies as dating a *Revivalist* advertisement for GBS in 1896 and listing the tuition for a fifteen week course at GBS as $150.

There has been some attempt to discredit the tradition that Seymour participated in Knapp's classes, apparently in an effort to emphasize instead the influence of the Church of God (Anderson). See B. Scott Lewis, "William J. Seymour: Follower of the 'Evening Light,'" *WTJ* vol. 39 no. 2 (Fall 2004), 167-183. However, Lewis demonstrates a flawed understanding of the fluidity that characterized the holiness movement at the turn-of-the-century. His argument rests on the assumption that the Gospel Trumpet (Church of God (Anderson) or Evening Light) and Revivalist movements were so antagonistic as to be mutually exclusive. However, for this argument to preclude Seymour from being involved at GBS assumes a staunch, and static, commitment to the Evening Light teachings from early in Seymour's stay in Cincinnati until he left. This seems highly unlikely, since Seymour ultimately moved beyond the sphere of the Gospel Trumpet/Evening Light movement. It is more reasonable to conclude that Seymour may have been influenced by both the Revivalist and the Gospel Trumpet movements during his days in Cincinnati.

In addition, David Bundy has collected substantial evidence from oral tradition in the African-American community in the Indianapolis area that indicates that Seymour did, in fact, take classes from Knapp at Cincinnati (conversation with author during Wesleyan-Holiness-Pentecostal Consultation, Kansas City, MO: October 28-29, 2005). Craig Borlase, *William Seymour: A Biography* (Lake Mary, FL: Charisma House, 2006), 55, indicates that Seymour's studies in Knapp's classes took place on a "part-time" basis. Also, see Stephens (192) and Jack W. Hayford and S. David Moore, *The Charismatic Century: The Enduring Impact of the Azusa Street Revival* (Nashville: Warner Faith, 2006), 74-75.

¹⁶¹ Robeck, "Seymour," in Burgess and Van Der Maas, 1054.

¹⁶² Synan, *The Holiness-Pentecostal Tradition*, 93. Synan is depending on Douglas Nelson, "For Such a Time as This: The Story of Bishop William J. Seymour and the Azusa Street Revival," Ph. D. diss. (University of Birmingham, U. K., 1981). The

first scholarly reference to Seymour's connection with GBS appears to be "a fragmentary summary of Seymour's life" presented in C. W. Shumway, *A Study of the "Gift of Tongues"* (A. B. thesis, University of Southern California, 1914). See Robeck, "Seymour," in Burgess and Van Der Maas, 1054, 1058.

[163] Stephens, 192.

[164] Sanders, 54. Another factor leading Seymour into preaching ministry was his loss of sight in one eye due to smallpox. See Borlase, 1-6.

[165] "A Mighty Movement," *Revivalist* (Feb. 8, 1900), 2 (original emphasis).

[166] James T. Connelly, "William J. Seymour," in Charles H. Lippy, ed. *Twentieth-Century Shapers of American Popular Religion* (New York and Westport, CN: Greenwood Press, 1989), 381-387. Interestingly, while Seymour could attend classes with whites at GBS, Jim Crow laws forbade him from sitting in class with whites at Parham's school in Texas where he visited in 1905, so he took in the lectures from the hallway (Robeck, "Seymour," in Burgess and Van Der Maas, 1055. On racial integration in early Holiness and Pentecostal settings, see Charles Edwin Jones, "The 'Color Line' Washed Away in the Blood? In the Holiness Church, at Azusa Street, and Afterward," *WTJ* Vol. 34 No. 2 (Fall 1999), 252-265. Also, see Stephens, 82-84.

[167] See Larry D. Smith, "No Black Drapery," in Moser and Smith, 19-21.

[168] "Stricken" *Enquirer*, 9.

[169] "Reign Of Sadness," *Post*, 6 and "Stricken," *Enquirer*, 9.

[170] For an account of her passing, see "Bible-School Notes," *Revivalist* (Jan. 16, 1902), 14 which also relates her experience of entire sanctification and being "knocked down by the power of God" shortly before her illness and her father's conversion in God's Tabernacle while she lay on her deathbed.

[171] "Stricken," *Enquirer*, 9.

[172] "Reign of Sadness," *Post*, 6.

[173] "Poignant: Sorrow Reigns Supreme: Death of Rev. M. W. Knapp Mourned By Followers," *The Cincinnati Enquirer* (Dec. 9, 1901), 10.

[174] W. B. Godbey, "The Cremation," *Revivalist* (Dec. 26, 1901), 12. While relatively young compared with Godbey (then 68), Knapp died only one year short of the average US life expectancy at the time.

[175] Lee Haines, "Co-Founders: Martin Wells Knapp [and] Seth Cook Rees," 12. See Hills, *Hero*, 238 where Hills describes his shock at Knapp's haggard appearance in Chicago: "The moment my eyes fell upon him a shock of pain went through me. He looked five years older than when I saw him less than a year before."

[176] Seth C. Rees, "Bereaved," *Revivalist* (Jan. 16, 1902), 12. For an "exact list of books and booklets published" by Knapp, see "God's Wonders," *Revivalist* (Feb. 6, 1902), 1, 4 and Hills, *Hero*, 334-337.

[177] "Gospel Calendar," *Revivalist* (Dec. 5, 1901), 16. See also, "Preach the Word," *Revivalist* (Jan. 9, 1902), 14 which encouraged the Revivalist family to give the calendars to friends who would not otherwise permit them to share the gospel with them.

[178] "Bible-School Notes," *Revivalist* (Jan. 30, 1902), 14. See Kostlevy, "Messenger, F(rank) M(oritmer)," in *Dictionary*, 175-176.

[179] *Hero*, 276-277.

[180] Bessie [Queen], "Translated," *Revivalist* (Dec. 19, 1901), 1-2.

[181] Seth C. Rees, "A Prince Has Fallen," *Revivalist* (Dec. 26, 1901), 12. See also, Glenn D. Black, "Martin Wells Knapp—A Man Full of Faith," Part II *Revivalist* (March 17, 1983), 10.

[182] This rest was taken by the Knapps at the home of Beatrice Finney's parents. The name "Valley of Blessings" was given because of the residents' openness to the radical holiness message: "The people seemed inclined to give attention to a full gospel, and the thought came to me while there that all this valley needed was Pentecost to make it a veritable 'Valley of Blessings.'" Even though he was there to rest, Knapp still conducted at least two meetings while there ("Reports," *Revivalist* (June 13, 1901), 10). See also, "From a Bible-School Student," *Revivalist* (June 20, 1901), 6.

When L. B. Compton conducted a meeting at Catlettsburg, Kentucky, later in the year, the area was again referred to as the "Valley of Blessings" ("Reports," *Revivalist* (Sept. 12, 1901), 11 and "Reports," *Revivalist* (Sept. 19, 1901), 11).

[183] Haines, "Co-founders," 12.

[184] "Bible-School Notes," *Revivalist* (Jan. 2, 1902), 14.

[185] Hills, *Hero*, 282-283. "Of all the books in the Bible none was to Mr. Knapp more precious than the Book of Revelation. He reveled in it. When the air was thick with the arrows of holiness fighters—those who misjudged and opposed him—he always was calmed and rested by reading Revelation." For the words and music of this song, see the *Revivalist* (Jan. 9, 1902), 13. Day wrote of the last days of Knapp's life, that he "had been living in the Book of Revelation" (46).

[186] "Bible-School Notes," *Revivalist* (Jan. 2, 1902), 14.

[187] Haines, "Co-founders," 12.

[188] Bessie [Queen], "Translated," *Revivalist* (Dec. 19, 1901), 1-2.

[189] George B. Kulp, "A Flame of Fire," *Revivalist* (April 14, 1921), 8.

[190] Bessie [Queen], "Translated," *Revivalist* (Dec. 19, 1901), 2.

[191] See W. B. Godbey, "The Cremation," *Revivalist* (Dec. 26, 1901), 12. Also, see Mrs. M. W. Knapp, "The White Path," *Revivalist* (Feb. 13, 1902), 4.

[192] "Cremated: Will Be Knapp's Body: After Short and Simple Religious Services," *The Cincinnati Enquirer* (Dec. 10, 1901), 12. See also, "Poignant: Sorrow Reigns Supreme: Death of Rev. M. W. Knapp Mourned by Followers," *The Cincinnati Enquirer* (Dec. 9, 1901), 10.

[193] Hills, *Hero*, 423 and Seth C. Rees, "Bereaved," *Revivalist* (Jan. 16, 1902), 12.

[194] Bessie [Queen], "Translated," *Revivalist* (Dec. 19, 1901), 2.

[195] "Cremated," *Enquirer*, 12.

[196] "The Funeral," *Revivalist* (Dec. 26, 1901), 2.

[197] Ibid, 2-5. Seth Rees would have likely had a central part in the funeral, but he was involved in another MCA-related campaign in Boston and was unable to leave this engagement. Instead, he spoke later at a memorial service on December 19. See "Memorial Services," *Revivalist* (Jan. 9, 1902), 1-4. He then deposited the remains of Knapp by the cornerstone of God's Tabernacle, where they remained until the Tabernacle was demolished, after which they were buried at Spring Grove Cemetery in Cincinnati. See Moser and Smith, 21.

[198] Hills, *Hero*, 298. "Shortly before his translation Rev. S. A. Keen, the Pentecostal pastor-evangelist, said: 'They think I have worked too hard; but I have now no

regrets, and if I could I would do it all over again.'" The *Cincinnati Post* reported this "hymn" to be a major "feature of the funeral," and noted its inspiration by "a deathbed utterance by" Keene, "formerly pastor of the Walnut Hills M. E. Church" ("Mrs. Knapp Takes Up Dead Husband's Mantle," (Dec. 10, 1901), 1).

[199] W. B. Godbey, "Sermon," *Revivalist* (Dec. 26, 1901), 4.

[200] Seth C. Rees, "Bereaved," *Revivalist* (Jan. 16, 1902), 12.

[201] Hills, *Hero*, 420.

[202] J. L. Glascock, "The Message," *Revivalist* (April 14, 1921), 4-8.

[203] Hills, *Hero*, 422-423.

[204] Seth C. Rees, "Wake Them Up! Wake Them Up!" *Revivalist* (Jan. 16, 1902), 2. For an example of the inspiring recounting of these words uttered by Knapp on his deathbed, see John and Bona Fleming, *Truth on Fire* (Cincinnati: The Revivalist Press, n. d.), 75.

[205] W. E. Shepard, "He Being Dead, Yet Speaketh," *Revivalist* (April 14, 1921), 11.

Chapter 5

Securing the Vision:
The Quest for the Mantle

Who will his falling mantle wear? – Seth C. Rees[1]

Under God the work will go on just as before. – Mrs. M. W. Knapp[2]

*A great work for women with consecrated means opens in connection with this movement.
– Martin Wells Knapp[3]*

The fact that God's Bible School and Missionary Training Home remains a vibrant institution over a century after its founder died—and that only fifteen months after he had opened the school—remains a powerful testament to the solid foundation Knapp had laid, to the commitment of his successors and other colleagues to perpetuate Knapp's vision, and to belief in the faithfulness of God to guide and provide for those yielded to His proprietorship. These last two factors were reflected in Minnie Ferle Knapp's promise to God to "be true to the trust He had given, and carry it on the same line and in the same way, that there should be no change, that it should be pushed on full gospel lines..."

While Martin Wells Knapp may have been the leading human force in the Revivalist movement, the resilient determination of his associates lent credence to their claim that God, not Knapp, was at the head of God's Bible School and its associated ministries, and that He would "carry it forward and bless it as He never [had]."[4] Indeed, Knapp's passing, while keenly felt and greatly mourned, became the occasion of a challenge to lift up the Pentecostal banner for thousands of his radical holiness comrades.

Implicit within this challenge, however, loomed a question that naturally suggested itself to the GBS/*Revivalist* constituency, voiced poignantly by Seth C. Rees in his poem of tribute, "A General on the Field Has Fallen":

> A general on the field! *Who will*
>   *His falling mantle wear?*
> Whose arm shall wield his keen blade still?
>   What hands his standard bear?
> A double portion, Savior, give,
>   Of power from on high!
> 'T were glorious such a life to live,
>   And such a death to die![5]

Indeed, this question assumed paramount significance, not just at GBS, but throughout the entire holiness movement, still roiling from the dynamic foment that had culminated in the triumph of radicalism at Chicago in the spring of 1901. Even outside observers sensed the urgency of this issue, with the *Cincinnati Enquirer* portraying it in rather bleak terms, "Now that he is gone there is a feeling of the deepest gloom, if not discouragement, for who is there to take his place? . . . The future of the Mount of Blessings is very uncertain."[6] The more hopeful sentiments of many GBS supporters were aptly expressed by James and Jesse Hundley, "May dear Brother Knapp's mantle fall upon the right one to lead the Lord's hosts on to eternal victory! There was only one dear Brother Knapp. His place can not be filled; but God will see that his nobly-begun work will move on till Jesus comes."[7]

Speculation on the question came immediately on the heels of Knapp's death, as newspaper reports reflect. This was no doubt intensified by the fact that, while the Holiness Union had several officers, Knapp had been the only trustee of GBS, criticism of which he had answered by noting that he "did not seek the work, but God thrust it upon" him; that the most prominent financial supporters of the school preferred an arrangement with Knapp as sole trustee; that these included experienced, successful business persons; that the deed was "so worded that the school property must be held for the object for which it was given, my natural heirs being debarred"; that he had learned by "experience . . . that it is difficult to do quick and effective work through big Boards [sic]"; and that "when God intrusts a Spirit-baptized man with the work, He also gives him the confidence of Spirit-baptized people."[8]

As for natural heirs, in his prayer during the funeral, W. B. Godbey expressed hope that John Franklin Knapp, Martin's only son, would one day take up his father's mantle, intoning, "Put Thy hand on his only son, dear Johnnie . . . Do, Lord, inspire him, inspire the saints in his behalf, that Johnnie shall rise up and be 'Brother Knapp' number two!"[9] However, John Franklin was only fourteen when his father died, and was relatively unknown to the *Revivalist* family.[10] In addition, over a year earlier, he had expressed a desire to go to Japan as a missionary, so it was uncertain that he would even remain at GBS after reaching adulthood.[11] Regardless, it was later reported that before his death, Martin had requested that John Franklin "be added to the Trusteeship when he reached age 21," a wish not fulfilled until the summer of 1920.[12] Meanwhile, the GBS family immediately needed mature leadership to advance and preserve the gains made under John Franklin's father, so it was forced to look elsewhere for the present.

Seth C. Rees

Among early conjectures, the *Cincinnati Post* reported Seth C. Rees to be "tipped as the probable successor" to Martin Wells Knapp.[13] In many ways, Rees would have been the logical choice for this position. Knapp's publication of his book, *The Ideal Pentecostal Church* (1897), had introduced Rees to the holiness movement as an author and led to other well-received books including *The Holy War* and *Fire From Heaven*.[14] Knapp's high regard for Rees also led to the latter's appointment as associate editor of *God's Revivalist* and to Knapp's insistence that Rees should be president of the Holiness Union when it was formed in 1897. In fact, Knapp wrote that he considered Rees "probably the strongest man in the holiness movement to-day," and with good reason in light of his colleague's outstanding qualities and prodigious accomplishments.[15]

As already noted, Rees's roots were in the Quaker tradition. He was born in 1854 to Quaker parents in Westfield, Indiana, educated at Quaker-operated Union Academy (like his Westfield neighbor, A. J. Tomlinson), and nourished under such Quaker Holiness pioneers as David B. Updegraff, Calvin Pritchard, and Dougan Clark. However, Rees's fiery brand of evangelism, which led friends to designate him the "EarthQuaker," belied stereotypical images of placid Quaker meetings where congregants sat silently awaiting the Spirit's prompting.[16] Although Rees kept his membership in the Ohio Yearly Meeting (Society of Friends) for years after the formation of the Holiness Union, his experience in 1883 of the "baptism with the Holy Spirit" launched him on a remarkably productive ministry that found him associating increasingly with non-Quaker advocates of holiness.[17]

Aggressive outreach characterized all his endeavors, including mission work among the "Modoc, Cherokee, and Peoria Indians" in Kansas and Oklahoma and "phenomenal success" at pastorates in Ohio, Michigan, and Rhode Island, including a two year period (1894-1896) during which his pastorate at the independent Church of Emmanuel in Providence witnessed "over one thousand" converts. This was followed by itinerant work during which Rees devoted "himself totally to Pentecostal evangelism."[18] A venture that consumed much of Rees's energy about the time of Knapp's death, and was publicized by his book, *Miracles in the Slums*, was rescue work, which began with a home for "fallen" women in Chicago and resulted in similar homes being established at numerous locations throughout the country, from New England to California and from Ohio to Texas.[19] Charles Slater paid tribute to Rees's zealous labors, asserting "I have yet to meet a man who carried a greater burden for souls than did Brother Rees."[20]

If Knapp had been "the most aggressive warrior"[21] the holiness movement had, Rees must have been second only to him, a characteristic leading his biographer-son Paul Rees to dub his father the "warrior-saint." One of his typical reports to the *Revivalist* read, "The devil is still roaring. The fight is hot, but we are in victory."[22] Like Knapp, this aggressiveness often found Rees embroiled in controversies, the best-known being one in 1917 that threatened to split the fledgling Nazarene denomination.[23] However, as with Knapp, Rees's uncompromising stance was "tempered by his love for people, reflected in his advice, 'If you carry a hatchet, don't forget to take your oil.'"[24]

For opposition to ecclesiastical tyranny, commitment to the four-fold gospel, and passion for souls—especially world-wide evangelism—few men could have been more alike than Seth Cook Rees and Martin Wells Knapp. Yet, in other obvious characteristics, two men could have hardly been more different, a fact that had allowed each of the two to compensate for the weaknesses of the other. Whereas Knapp's physique prompted congregations to react negatively, Rees was endowed with impressive looks that naturally drew the approval of crowds. "Large of body, high of forehead, with brown eyes flashingly expressive, his strong, open countenance framed by dark hair roached back on the left side and a Van Dyke beard, he stood, without effort at distinctiveness, a commanding figure with a commanding message."[25]

This physical advantage was coupled with Rees's oratorical abilities, lauded by other holiness pulpit giants of the day, including H. C. Morrison and Beverly Carradine. Morrison wrote that "there is no man in all the holiness movement who preaches with more fervent power, and direct effect on the masses, than Seth C. Rees."[26] Carradine likewise declared that he knew "of no man in the holiness ranks to-day who preaches more convincingly and unctuously."[27] Distinguished appearance and dynamic oratory combined to produce an image "of manliness and Godliness fused into electric effectiveness by the fire of the Holy Ghost."[28] This combination made Rees the natural choice for leadership positions. Morrison opined that he "would attract attention in any pulpit or on any platform, and would be a leader in the United States Senate if he were a member of that body," and Carradine averred that he was "as good a leader as he [was] a preacher."[29]

So, surmises that Rees would be Knapp's successor as superintendent of God's Bible School and editor of *God's Revivalist* were quite understandable. However likely it seemed, this was not to be. Perhaps this was because Rees's natural abilities and aggressiveness were mixed with a restless adventurousness that found him moving from one challenge to another quite rapidly. In fact, at the time of Knapp's death Rees was already engaged in another evangelistic campaign, this time in Boston, similar to the Chicago Convention of spring 1901, only this time "even more spectacular"—if that were possible.[30] Ultimately, it was unlikely that Rees would be willing to settle down in Cincinnati and take up another man's mantle. However, he would continue to play a significant role in supporting God's Bible School and continuing as associate editor of the *Revivalist* until 1905 when "he severed his connection," with his son Paul later explaining that "other tasks were calling."[31]

Metropolitan Church Association

If Rees was out of contention for the mantle, the Metropolitan Church Association, with which he and Knapp had affiliated and had joined forces during the great Chicago revival, offered other possibilities for a successor to Knapp. It is likely that such a choice had held great appeal for Knapp, considering the enormous "influence of the MCA on Knapp at the time of his death."[32] In addition to Rees, the MCA had several leaders with potential to superintend the ministries centered on the Mount of Blessings, including Duke Farson, E. L.

Harvey, and F. M. Messenger. One factor that may have brought these names to the forefront was the fact that MCA adherents, particularly ex-banker Farson and businessman Messenger, who had been a successful textile mill superintendent, had "in many cases" been "the primary financial resources for the entire radical movement" which Knapp had led.[33] Again, it was Messenger who had given $1000 toward the initial sum needed to purchase the Mount of Blessings property.

Harvey's preaching seems to have especially garnered Knapp's enthusiasm.[34] Consequently, Harvey and his wife Getrude were enlisted as special workers for the first Thanksgiving Dinner and Convention at GBS, just a couple of weeks before Knapp's death.[35] The *Revivalist* later reported that before the guests ate their Thanksgiving dinner, "Brother Harvey ... preached to them in the power of the Holy Ghost" so that many of them responded to the altar call and "testified with glad faces that Jesus had pardoned their sins."[36]

Such evangelistic fervor and effectiveness had led Knapp to find in Harvey a kindred spirit. Accordingly, William Kostlevy notes that "Knapp had, in the months before his death, increasingly turned to Harvey for direction. In fact, only a week before his death Knapp had requested that Harvey assume temporary leadership of the Revivalist empire in Cincinnati including direction of the 1902 [Salvation Park] Camp Meeting ..."[37]

However, the increasing radicalism of the MCA, particularly its criticism of "denominational loyalty" and its insistence on Spirit-filled saints displaying physical responses such as "jumping" served to distance it from many other holiness proponents, including key figures in the Revivalist movement. By the time of the 1902 camp meeting, the mantle had largely slipped from the MCA grasp. Although Harvey had been announced as late as March 1902 as an evangelist slated for the impending Salvation Park Camp Meeting, he apparently never participated.[38] While no reasons for his absence were given in the *Revivalist*, the MCA would painfully withdraw its support from GBS and go its separate way over the coming years, launching its own periodical, *The Burning Bush* in May 1902. An obvious factor in this schism was the ultimate possession of Knapp's mantle by other associates of Knapp who were already ensconced on the Mount of Blessings.[39]

Woman's Place

The *Cincinnati Post* broke the suspense concerning Knapp's successor with a front page article on December 10, 1901, just three days after his death, announcing "MRS. KNAPP TAKES UP DEAD HUSBAND'S MANTLE." In contrast with the *Enquirer*'s negative outlook of the previous day, this article's subtitle suggested, "Sorrow, But No Discouragement, Follows Leader's Death at Mount of Blessings." The public was informed that Mrs. Knapp's experience as "the able assistant of her husband" and "fluent speaking" and work as "a leading writer for the Bible School paper" left her well-qualified to assume the reigns of her husband's many enterprises and that, in light of her popularity, she would be "well accepted by all of the followers." Reflecting the cultural bias against women in leadership that was predominant in American society at the time, the paper described her as "a sweet-faced, matronly woman of educational attainments, [who] possesses rare executive ability for a woman." Almost as if in a postscript, the last sentence of the *Post* article stated, "The institution will be under the control of a Board of Trustees, composed of Mrs. Knapp, Miss Mary Storey and Miss Queen, with Mrs. Knapp as General Manager."[40]

No doubt many in the public at large and in the Revivalist family were stunned, for different reasons, with the latter announcement. For the general public, the assumption of such positions by women was still a novelty. However, Knapp's supporters had already been well prepared to accept such developments. For them, the surprise likely came over the identity of the youngest of the trustees and perhaps over the fact that none of the trustees were men.

In addition, numerous people would eventually question the irregularity of the trustees' "semi-secret selection." Later, it was suggested that the trusteeship rested on "scant evidence—a piece of paper with three names on it," which had no independent witnesses to verify its authenticity.[41] Naturally, the *Revivalist* (December 12, 1901) introduction of the trustees made no mention of this, merely reporting that Knapp apparently had a premonition of his impending death about two months before, and then announcing—"About a month ago he named his trustees. He chose only those whom God had tested and proved, and who felt the call of God on them for this work for life. Those chosen were Sisters M. W. Knapp, Mary Storey, and Bessie."[42]

It may have appeared ironic to the public that the administration of a school originally envisioned to be "exclusively for boys" should be left to the care of three women, but the logic lying behind this succession also provided the very reason that God's Bible School had instead been founded as a co-educational institution: "God says, 'He will pour His spirit upon His handmaidens, and they shall prophesy,' and they should have equal training with the 'sons.'"[43] While shocking to then-prevailing prejudices, such decisions were recognized by holiness people as consistent with holiness tradition in general and with Knapp's ministry in particular.

With strong roots in the Methodist approbation of lay exhorters, holiness proponents had long recognized the contribution that such women as Phoebe Palmer and Amanda Smith made to the promotion of holiness. Early leaders such as B. T. Roberts and Luther Lee had joined their voices to those of such women in advocating more visible ministry roles for their sisters in the faith.[44] However, the insistence on extending full ministerial privileges to women reached its apex among those holiness advocates, such as Knapp, who sought to see Pentecost fully replicated.

W. B. Godbey wrote the classic radical holiness defense of women in ministry—*Woman Preacher*—in which he waxed eloquent in praise of women's effectiveness:

Give the women a chance, (and they are taking it), and they will rob Satan of his whisky, confronting him on every ramification of the battle field, fill the saloons and brothels of Christendom, and the jungles of heathendom, with blood-washed and fire-baptized missionaries, march to the music of full salvation to the ends of the earth, belt the globe with the glory of God, and transform a world long groaning in sin and misery into a paradise.[45]

In *Lightning Bolts from Pentecostal Skies*, Knapp concurred, referring readers to Godbey's book and asserting that, not only may "women . . . be Pentecostal preachers," but that "by her divine call to this sacred ministry, by her gifts and graces and fruitage, she has demonstrated the genuineness of her call, and is recognized among the most effective of Pentecostal preachers."[46] At GBS in particular, Knapp noted that "a great work for women with consecrated means opens in connection with this movement."[47] Interestingly enough, however, the Pentecostal logic for women's equality was made no clearer by anyone than Seth Rees, who contended,

> The Ideal Pentecostal Church is without distinction as to the prominence given to the sexes. The women were equally honored with the men when the Spirit was poured out . . . Women, as well as men, are to prophesy when this holy baptism with the Spirit shall be administered . . .
> Originally, woman was not only man's helpmeet but his equal . . . Sin cursed and degraded her, until in dark heathendom we find her as man's slave . . .
> But just in proportion as the grace of God and the light of the Gospel are shed abroad, in that proportion woman is elevated, until at Pentecost she stands, a second Eve, by the side of her husband, sharing in the beatific blessings of the baptism with the Spirit.
> Taking humanity as a whole, it may be said with confidence that more genuine New Testament piety can be found among women than among men. From the days of Pentecost until this hour, whenever Holy Ghost revivals have been produced, holy women have mothered them . . .
> Nothing but jealousy, prejudice, bigotry, and a stingy love for bossing in men have prevented woman's public recognition by the church. No church that is acquainted with the Holy Ghost will object to the public ministry of women. We know scores of women who can preach the Gospel with a clearness, a power, and an efficiency seldom equalled [sic] by men.
> Sisters, let the Holy Ghost fill, call and anoint you to preach the glorious Gospel of our Lord.[48]

Such a stance was amply illustrated throughout Knapp's spiritual journey and ministry, which had both benefited significantly from the influence of women, beginning with the pivotal role that his mother and Lucy Glenn had played in his conversion. While Lucy had been an integral part of the *Revivalist* ministry until her death, Martin's mother also retained an important place in the enterprises her son initiated, even after his death, until her own death on February 11, 1909. Though described by Hills as among "the most retiring of women, reticent and timid,"[49] Octavia Knapp became the matriarch of the GBS/Revivalist family, to whom she was affectionately known as "Grandma" Knapp. With zeal akin to her son's, she ministered in downtown Cincinnati "in the workhouses and homes of the poor" where she gained a reputation as an "angel of mercy," and took a special interest in the work at Beulah Heights which she frequently visited.[50] In addition, she became fully involved in the activities of God's Bible School, even taking Bible classes for "a part of two years" from Nettie Peabody, who often discussed the lessons with her in advance of presentation in the classroom.[51]

As his ministry unfolded, Martin looked as well to other women who surrounded him to provide advice and encouragement and to shoulder significant responsibilities involved in the production of the *Revivalist* and the operation of GBS and the school at Beulah Heights. Hills considered this an outstanding feature of Knapp's life, suggesting that his biography illustrates "the tremendous power of a truly Christian woman's influence"[52] and observing that "throughout his entire career he was nobly appreciative of women, a benediction to women, and a companion of women in the work of his life."[53]

In addition to Knapp's mother and his first and second wives, Hills recognized the two women who joined Minnie Ferle Knapp as the trustees of GBS and its related ministries as particularly "potent forces in the inner life of this receptive and appreciative soul."[54] To understand how Mary Storey and Bessie Queen achieved such influence, it remains necessary not only to consider their own early careers in relation to Knapp's work, but also to examine further the personality and career of Minnie Knapp, who had been designated "General Manager" of GBS.

Minnie Ferle Knapp

Although Minnie had picked up many of the responsibilities carried by Martin's first wife, Lucy, before her death, the two differed in some crucial regards. For one, Lucy was much more than a ministerial colleague to Martin; she was, in fact, his soul mate. Minnie was never to become a spiritual mentor to him in any degree near that of Lucy. Although Martin confessed becoming "more and more delighted" with marriage to Minnie, their relationship was obviously more pragmatically motivated.[55]

This did not mean that Minnie failed to significantly impact the enterprises in which she assisted her husband. In fact, she proved to be a key figure in the initiation of two major emphases of the Revivalist movement that endured throughout the first century of GBS. One of these was a special attempt to reach children and teens with the message of the full gospel. This began to take shape in a *Revivalist* department "For the Youth" which Minnie Knapp edited for years. The popularity of this column ultimately led to the publication of a separate paper for children and youth, *Sparkling*

Waters from Bible Fountains, which began as a weekly "holiness leaflet especially adapted for the Sunday School" but soon developed into a full-fledged periodical.[56] Not coincidentally, although the first issue appeared in January 1902, the announcement of this new paper came during the very month that GBS launched an even better-known effort to reach children and others among the poor—the Thanksgiving Dinner and Convention. In other words, *Sparkling Waters* and the Thanksgiving Dinner were just two expressions of a comprehensive vision for the GBS family to reach the "youth of the nation"[57] beginning with the Cincinnati community, which also included other efforts to "feed the lambs"[58] including special services for children on the Mount of Blessings and the dissemination of books such as A. M. Hills' *Food for Lambs; or, Leading Children to Christ* and, later, M. G. Standley's *The Story of the Christ*.[59]

Although Mrs. Knapp introduced the editor of *Sparkling Waters*, Abby C. Morrow, as "the best and most spiritual writer for children" of whom she was aware, the paper obviously bore the imprint of Martin and Minnie.[60] Practically a *"Revivalist"* for the young, *Sparkling Waters* echoed the emphases of its forbearer, especially in its use of vivid anecdotes and passionate appeals to warn young people against worldliness and such vices as tobacco and alcohol consumption and to stimulate interest in missions among youth.[61]

The focus on missions lay especially near to Minnie's heart and was the other great emphasis to which she notably contributed at GBS and in the *Revivalist*. In fact, the development of a vision for world-wide evangelism as "a central concern" of the Revivalist movement has been traced by David Bundy to the influence of Minnie Knapp, who, in her "For the Youth" column of *The Revivalist*, "began, in December 1896, to devote space to the story of Sammy Morris."[62] This story was followed the next month by a full-fledged "Missionary" department which remained a regular *Revivalist* feature for years. Through articles in this column, Minnie continued to champion the cause of global holiness evangelism. In addition, after Martin's death, she toured extensively in behalf of missions, making an important trip throughout the Caribbean.[63]

However, although Minnie was efficient, reliable, and passionately devoted to the radical holiness cause, her leadership abilities contrasted sharply with Lucy's, who had worked in tandem with Martin as an equal partner. While Lucy's creativity and resilience balanced her husband's, Minnie was more dependent, leaning heavily on Martin's energetic personality. After his death, she suffered from attacks of nervous prostration, forcing the delegation of many administrative details of GBS and Revivalist ministries to others.[64] Had she been more like Lucy, Martin may have named her sole trustee. As it was, he likely realized that she would need to lean on the shoulders of others possessing more stamina and forcefulness. If this were not the case, the history of God's Bible School may have been much different.

Mary Storey

Martin found in Mary Storey and Bessie Queen many of the qualities which naturally commended them as members of an administrative "triumvirate," cooperating with Minnie in guiding the Mount of Blessings enterprises after his death.[65] Miss Mary Storey had already distinguished herself as a loyal supporter of the Knapps' work since their arrival in Cincinnati, being among the first holiness adherents in the city to cast her lot with them. She herself had immigrated to Cincinnati from Ireland at age twenty-one (c. 1873). Here she had joined her brother in business and gained respect throughout the community as a successful manager of his large department store.[66] A faithful Methodist from her early days in Cincinnati, she searched for a deeper spiritual experience than that gained in conversion, even praying "behind the counter in the shop." Soon, she was entirely sanctified while praying in a "Methodist classroom."[67]

The effect of this experience on Mary was remarkable. She became a "zealous and faithful worker in missions and Gospel meetings and house-to-house visitation," even renting a house at one time with "large, double parlors" which was used for "Gospel meetings."[68] She eventually abandoned her lucrative career and entered full-time evangelistic work. Her evangelistic services were soon in demand far beyond Cincinnati, particularly in the states of Indiana, Kentucky, Ohio, and West Virginia.[69]

A typical fiery holiness evangelist, it appeared that God had answered Mary's prayer "to make a 'warrior' out of her." She was known to say often, "I love the fight," and was regarded highly by the Revivalist family for her opposition to "sin, a popular Christianity, formalism, etc."[70] Her reports to *The Revivalist* provide a running account of her fearless exploits through what frequently proved to be hostile territory, denouncing tobacco and liquor in such states as Kentucky and Tennessee in the face of tremendous resistance. She regularly used the language of warfare, as in a report from East Maysville, Kentucky: "This was another hard battle; but God again gave the victory, in convicting, converting, and sanctifying souls, some old gamblers being among the number saved."[71]

Storey also prepared the way for other female evangelists in areas traditionally adverse to women ministers. J. S. Miller, a Methodist Episcopal presiding elder in east Kentucky, noted this result of her ministry, "When she holds a meeting once at a place, it is no more trouble for the people to make arrangements for a woman to preach."[72] After her meeting at East Bernstadt, Kentucky, where around two hundred were converted, one participant said he would not "rest until the Lord sends ten thousand more holy women to save this world, for they have 95 per cent more backbone than the men."[73]

Throwing herself into the Revivalist work in Cincinnati when she was not away representing the Mount of Blessings as "school evangelist,"[74] Storey's vigor as a holiness "warrior" inspired Knapp and their other colleagues. After Knapp's death, "her solid Methodist churchmanship and her unwavering faith in God was an anchor of stability and balance" on the Mount of Blessings, in fact helping to moderate considerably the radical trajectory that had characterized GBS under Knapp's leadership.[75]

Bessie Queen

Bessie Queen was undoubtedly the most surprising choice among the three trustees. At only twenty-one years of age, she astounded friends and foes with her accession to one of the most influential positions in the holiness movement. This was even more incredible considering that, unlike her fellow trustees, she was a relatively new convert. Only three years before, she was, by her own description, a "giddy, careless girl, with no real thought of life or its responsibilities."[76] Spiritual concerns seemed far from Bessie's mind, when her businessman father found her apparently bored one day, and suggested that she, a younger sister, and some friends visit the services being conducted at Knapp's Sycamore Street mission, "to see the circus, to see some fun, and to hear the shouting."[77]

Although initially amused by the proceedings, Bessie became "indignant" at the preacher's (Knapp's) suggestion that she was "on the brink of hell" and determined that she would never go back to the chapel. However, an "impelling force" kept drawing her back, until "the weight of the enormity of her sins" hung over her in deep conviction, and sleep seemed "impossible." Finally, her "proud heart" yielded and she determined that she "would have Jesus if everything and every one else on earth had to go," and she was converted.[78]

"Just about one week later," she was "wonderfully sanctified,"[79] and by October 1898 felt called to work in the Revivalist office, though she admittedly "knew nothing about office work, and not much about any other kind."[80] However, a place was soon made for her in the office, and she became a fixture in the Revivalist work, despite her parents' strong opposition to her new holiness experience and associates, to the extent that they "barred [her] from home" and "threatened to place her in an insane asylum."[81]

(Eventually, M. G. Standley relates, "every one of [Bessie's] family was finally saved. Her father and mother went to Heaven believing in the baptism with the Holy Ghost and fire."[82])

Although she had little hands-on experience, Bessie's family background ideally equipped her for assisting the Revivalist cause. Her father was a respected community leader and member "of one of the best and most prominent families of Kentucky,"[83] who had moved from Maysville, Kentucky, to Cincinnati where he became publisher of *The Western Architect and Builder*, the official organ of the local contractor's association. In addition, her father's political activities had a profound influence on Bessie, for she "and her father had been very close" and "she had gone with him to political meetings and symphonies" and "had discussed elections and candidates until she had a great knowledge of political economy."[84]

Doubtless, this background in publishing and civic leadership drew the Knapps' attention, and Bessie was soon employed in writing numerous articles for the *Revivalist*. Her writing was polished and poignant and quickly assumed prominence, especially through her "Bible-School Notes," a regular feature that kept the Revivalist family abreast of campus developments. In effect, these articles made this enterprising young woman, second only to Martin Wells Knapp, the voice of God's Bible School for most of its constituents, a role that would only be magnified after Martin's passing.

In fact, although the *Cincinnati Enquirer* reflected on Queen's significance at GBS in February 1902 by recognizing this "comely girl" as "the most prominent dweller in the Mount of Blessings" next to Mrs. Knapp,[85] Minnie Knapp heavily relied on the young woman and "allowed Bessie Queen virtually unrestricted authority in the direction of the periodical."[86] For all practical purposes, she held the editorial reigns of the *Revivalist*, a position which under Knapp had become arguably "the single most powerful force in the shaping of the direction of" the radical holiness movement. William Kostlevy thus concludes that "Queen, as defacto editor, more than Storey, Standley, Godbey, or even Seth C. Rees, had inherited the mantle of the fallen leader. It was a remarkable coup for a young woman who three years earlier had cast her lot with the despised holiness people to the horror of her affluent parents."[87]

The "Spiritual Work": Meredith Goslin Standley

While the selection of three trustees provided for the general administration of the Mount of Blessings enterprises, and for the editorial direction of *God's Revivalist* in particular, it left several issues to be addressed. Most remarkably, Knapp failed to clearly "select an immediate successor" to superintended God's Bible School itself.[88] In addition, he named no one to follow him as Bible teacher at the school or as pastor of the New Testament Society of God's Church that he had formed on the campus. Thus, "in one of their first actions, the trustees named Meredith G. Standley as teacher of Bible at God's Bible School,"[89] a move that was later indicated to be in accord with Knapp's wishes.[90] In addition, Standley's position as assistant pastor of the New Testament Society was advanced to that of full pastor by April 1902.[91] Mrs. Knapp assured constituents that "Rev. M. G. Standley, a former student, is here, and has the spiritual work, and is surely God's choice at this time."[92] The January 2, 1902, issue of *God's Revivalist* sought to establish his qualifications by announcing,

> Rev. Meredith Standley, now assistant pastor, will take charge of the Bible-class for the present . . . The same course of study that the Lord gave Brother Knapp will be carefully and earnestly followed. Brother Standley is well fitted for the work—saved, sanctified, and all on fire for God and souls. The Lord has given him wonderful revivals of religion. Broth-

er Knapp was intimately acquainted with him for some years, as he has been in connection with our work here, also being a student himself in the school last year. He believes, teaches, and preaches a full salvation, insisting on all the fundamentals of salvation. He is, like Brother Knapp, a digger of souls.[93]

The last designation aptly described Standley, as will be seen, not only then, but throughout his long career at God's Bible School. Already, Standley had distinguished himself through evangelistic endeavors, returning shortly after Knapp's death from a successful revival campaign in the state of Washington where he was characterized as "a faithful, fearless worker."[94] In addition, even before he became a student at GBS, Standley had preached in Knapp's stead when other responsibilities called the leader away.[95] Fittingly for Bible school work, he also possessed special interest in youth, confessing in his book, *The Story of the Christ*, "I have always said that I would rather talk to a congregation of children than grown people."[96]

Standley's gift for soul-winning combined a creativity reminiscent of that possessed by Knapp with a compassion that was likely deepened by the pathos of his childhood years in the western part of Cincinnati, in which he acknowledged "there were very few happy days," because he "was given to worry."[97] This stemmed primarily from losing his father who had died while attempting to save Meredith "from a runaway horse" when the boy was only six years of age.[98] As a result, he developed an especially strong affection for his mother, for whom he professed that he "would have been glad to die."[99] However, he also "took on [his] mother's worries," which included, in addition to providing for seven children, a terrible burden for Meredith's brother Lew, who had developed a habit of heavy alcohol consumption.[100]

Although his mother was converted during a campaign by Gypsy Smith conducted at the city's Music Hall and the family had begun attending a local Methodist Church, Meredith found that he simply had a religious "profession, but had no real possession."[101] He threw his energies into making life better for his mother, and, while working in a shoe store on Fifth Street, discovered that he had exceptional talent as a salesman.[102] However, his hard work and "clean" living left him unsatisfied until he and some friends began visiting a Methodist mission and he came under conviction.[103] Upon his mother's urging, Meredith went to the altar and as he prayed, someone quoted Isaiah 55:7. When Meredith heard those words, he responded in faith "and realized right then and there that God came into [his] heart; He had heard [his] prayer, and a transformation took place!"[104] Despite strong opposition from co-workers at the shop where he was employed, this young man whose friends predicted would only last a week as a Christian instead lived the rest of his days for Christ, devoting half a century to labors at God's Bible School.[105]

Sometime after his conversion, Meredith, under conviction for a "quick temper," sought entire sanctification as a result of holiness services led by a Brother Keith at a local mission. He subsequently received new faith for the salvation of his brother Lew, who was soon "wonderfully and mightily converted."[106] Sometime afterwards, Meredith experienced a call to preach. Though initially "timid and backward," he began speaking at Pike Street Mission in Covington, Kentucky, where he became a welcome speaker notwithstanding initial opposition to his holiness message.[107]

Martin Wells Knapp soon learned of this young preacher, and invited Meredith to conduct a meeting at Revivalist Chapel on Sycamore Street. After struggling with feelings of inferiority while considering the great preachers who had held services there, Standley received the promise to "be strong and of good courage" (Joshua 1:9) and was filled with boldness that marked a new epoch for him—"a high mark in life's progress."[108] During the meeting, he testified, "And the Lord blessed me so I could not hold it, and 'If the place is full of Knapps and Carradines, and Godbeys, I will get up anyway."[109] The promise of Joshua 1:9 became an encouragement for Standley "to go forward with greater zeal" many times across the ensuing years.[110]

Although he had received training for a year each at two well-established holiness schools—Asbury College and Taylor University—with a benefactor pledging to pay for another year at Taylor, Meredith felt led to instead enroll at Knapp's new school, where he had already assisted in preparing the buildings for the new venture.[111] He threw himself with abandon into campus activities, working at times "ten or twelve hours, all night if necessary" to see that "God's work was to go." This industriousness doubtless won Knapp's approval, so that Standley recorded in his autobiography, "Brother Knapp immediately made me his assistant pastor."[112]

Shortly after Knapp's death, with the responsibilities as GBS Bible teacher and pastor of the New Testament Society weighing heavily upon him, M. G. Standley found that he "was not completely satisfied" with his spiritual state, although he "was not backslidden." So, he journeyed to Beulah Heights "to settle this question." He concluded that he had been "entirely consecrated" but had unwittingly confused it with "entire sanctification." After a short prayer—but "a prayer of faith"—he received the assurance that he was sanctified wholly, and his "doubts, fears, and uncertainties were settled forever."[113] Thereafter, Standley seemed to have a special gift for encouraging others who struggled with insecurity and doubts about their relationship with God.

In fact, the first chapel service after his return to GBS was marked by unusual blessing, with Standley preaching for five hours, an incredible length even for that day! What followed was ten days of "the most marvelous meeting" that Standley ever witnessed, as "God came in his mighty searching power," and "all students who had question marks in their hearts, and longings unsatisfied, began seeking God and He answered." Several seekers benefited greatly from Standley's counsel to help them avoid the extremes of fanaticism, and M. G. Standley emerged from this meeting firmly established as the spiritual leader of God's Bible School, a position he would hold for almost fifty years.[114]

"A Pentecostal Wedding"

Bessie Queen was one of his first colleagues at GBS that early appreciated M. G. Standley's potential as an integral figure in the ongoing success of God's Bible School.[115] So, it came as little surprise to the GBS family when their engagement was announced, which was quickly followed by their wedding, officiated by Seth C. Rees, and conducted on Tuesday, May 13, 1902, "in the presence of the pupils of the school."[116] The service, "using the simple Quaker ceremony,"[117] was described by Rees as "truly a Pentecostal wedding."[118] This designation proved especially fitting considering the reception that was held in the spirit of the principles of Pentecost that Knapp had advocated: "Instead of a wedding dinner for those who were able to return the favor, Rev. and Mrs. Standley invited scores of poor children of the community to God's Bible School, and served them until their appetites were fully satisfied."[119]

While students may have expected this development, the *Cincinnati Enquirer* reported the wedding as yet "another surprise" to "the outside world" and followed with a sensational story which had the former socialite Bessie Queen marrying a converted daredevil, because it confused her groom with a Meredith *Stanley*, who had gained notoriety as a daredevil by jumping from bridges in the Cincinnati area (but was never associated with GBS).[120] The next day's *Enquirer* contained a profuse apology for the "great injustice done to God's Bible School, and Rev. Meredith G. Standley" through this "unfortunate mistake" and suggested that "no one stands higher in the community than Mr. and Mrs. Standley" and praised GBS as "an institution which is doing great good in the world, without any hope of pecuniary gain."[121]

This article marked a turning point in the depiction of GBS in the Cincinnati press, with no more "sensations" on the Mount of Blessings reported for over half a decade. However, the Standleys' marriage remained problematic for many holiness people, in large part due to an article written by none other than Bessie herself. In a rather lengthy essay, published in the November 28, 1901 issue of *God's Revivalist*, just a few days before Knapp's demise, she expressed her commitment to and "union with God's Revivalist work and office" in the strongest possible terms—that of the marriage contract, entitling her article "Why I Am Married." After repeating the story of her conversion, in which she underscored her indebtedness to Knapp and his associates, Bessie enumerated several reasons why she did "so tenderly love" the work and had "given [herself] so fully to it." These factors included such elements of radical holiness/ Pentecostal ideology as the four-fold gospel, God's proprietorship, passion for the lost, and faith support. Ironically in light of later developments, she also stressed the careful stewardship practiced on the campus, with all contributions being "devoted directly to the work in hand, not one cent being taken from such funds for the support of the superintendent or any of the workers, their labors all being given freely as a love-offering to Jesus" and with "no place on the table," for "tea, coffee, candy, pastry, and every needless luxury" and "no money ... wasted on gold and fashionable dress."[122]

As if this article were not sufficient, Bessie reiterated her commitment to the *Revivalist* and GBS work in terms of marriage even more unequivocally just following Knapp's passing: "Two years ago, when [God] sanctified me, unknown to any one, He began talking to me about giving my life to this work, and not getting married, but to marry Jesus alone. I have kept that covenant with him, and, as I told Brother Knapp on Wednesday, I expect to keep it until I meet him again in heaven."[123] While detractors would later point out the apparent discrepancy between this declaration and Bessie's subsequent marriage to M. G. Standley, Bessie was evidently able to reconcile the seeming contradiction within her mind. Perhaps she concluded that since it appeared that M. G. Standley had "taken up the mantle of . . . Rev. M. W. Knapp," as the *Cincinnati Enquirer* put it,[124] she was simply further sealing her commitment to GBS by marrying the man now entrusted with its "spiritual work."

Regardless, the marriage of M. G. and Bessie Standley proved to be one of the most significant developments in the history of God's Bible School, for it consolidated within the hands of this young couple both the editorial direction of the *Revivalist* and the administrative control of the school. This fact had become apparent to GBS constituents by August 1902, likely prompting a rebuttal that appeared in the *Revivalist* against "an impression scattered among the Revivalist family that the superintendency of God's Bible-school has passed out of the hands of Sister Knapp."[125] Despite this assurance that "Sister Knapp is still the superintendent of the Bible-school," Dr. Godbey's explanation of the situation sometime later more closely approximated reality: "When Brother Knapp was translated to heaven, as a normal consequence the management of these great educational and philanthropic institutions devolved on Brother and Sister Standley as the shock wrought so heavily on the nerves of Sister Knapp, as to disqualify her to give them much help."[126]

Indeed, though Meredith Standley was not formally made a trustee until 1906 (after Mary Storey's death), it became obvious after his marriage to Bessie Queen that he and his wife were the true heirs of the mantle laid down by Martin Wells Knapp. It would be under their leadership that Knapp's vision would be translated into action on the Mount of Blessings and far beyond for almost half a century to come.

Notes

[1] Quoted in Hills, *Hero*, 402.

[2] Mrs. M. W. Knapp, "To Every Member of the Dear Revivalist Family," *Revivalist* (Dec. 26, 1901), 2.

[3] "Cincinnati as a Mission Field," *Revivalist* (March 14, 1901), 15.

[4] Mrs. M. W. Knapp, "To Every Member of the Dear Revivalist Family," *Revivalist* (Dec. 26, 1901), 2.

[5] Quoted in Hills, *Hero*, 402 (my emphasis).

[6] "Poignant: Sorrow Reigns Supreme," *Enquirer* (Dec. 9, 1901), 10.

[7] Quoted in Hills, *Hero*, 367.

[8] *Pentecostal Letters*, 144-145. Knapp's experience with unwieldy boards evidently involved his work with the Revival Band of the Michigan Conference of the M. E. Church.

[9] "The Funeral," *Revivalist* (Dec. 26, 1901), 2-4.

[10] "Bible-School Notes," *Revivalist* (Feb. 20, 1902), 14.

[11] "Mrs. Knapp's Letter," *Revivalist* (June 13, 1901), 6 explains that Shoji Murakami, GBS's first international student, was not only coming to study the Bible but to teach Japanese to John Franklin. On John's call to Japan, see also "Farewell Service of Brother and Sister Cowman," *Revivalist* (Dec. 6, 1900), 9 and Bessie [Queen], "Bible-School Notes," *Revivalist* (May 16, 1901), 15. It should be noted that John was quite young and understandably impressed by the excitement surrounding the Cowman's departure for Japan.

[12] Glenn Black, "John F. Knapp: Preacher—Teacher—Writer," *Revivalist* (Nov. 17, 1983), 7.

[13] "Reign of Sadness," *Post* (Dec. 9, 1901), 6.

[14] Two of these are still in print, *The Ideal Pentecostal Church* and *The Holy War* (1904. Reprint; Salem, OH: Schmul, 1995). Revivalist Press also kept *Fire From Heaven* (Cincinnati: Revivalist, 1899) in print until at least mid-century. In addition, Rees contributed to several other books such as *Pentecostal Messengers* and *The Return of Jesus*, co-authored with W. B. Godbey.

[15] Knapp, *Pentecostal Letters*, 14. Knapp felt that at least some of the opposition which Rees and the Revivalist movement faced was because "the marvelous success God has given him has awakened jealousy in some circles."

[16] For an intimate, and yet fairly objective, account of Rees' life, see Paul Rees, *Seth Cook Rees: The Warrior Saint* (1933. Reprint; Salem, OH: Schmul, 1987). Also, see Robins, 91-92.

[17] See Hamm, *The Transformation of American Quakerism*, 145, on the departure of holiness advocates such as Rees from Quaker societies. As with Methodism, this development coincided with the passing of the first generation of Quaker holiness leaders.

[18] Haines, 11, and "Experience of Seth C. Rees," *Revivalist* (Feb. 21, 1901), 4.

[19] In addition to *Miracles in the Slums*, see c. 7 of *The Warrior-Saint*, 64-77. Particularly noteworthy were the homes established at Columbus, Ohio; Kansas

City, Missouri; and Pilot Point, Texas. The first came "under the efficient control of the Society of Friends, and the other two [under] the care of the Church of the Nazarene" (65).

[20] Paul Rees, *Warrior-Saint*, 151.

[21] "The Funeral," *Revivalist* (Dec. 26, 1901), 3.

[22] "Revival Prayers Answered," *Revivalist* (Feb. 28, 1901), 11.

[23] This conflict occurred while Rees was pastor of University Church of the Nazarene in Pasadena, California (1912-1917) and found Rees pitted against the district superintendent who disorganized his church. This led him to form the Pilgrim Tabernacle which became the mother congregation of the Pilgrim Church, the body that merged in 1922 with the International Holiness Church (descended from the Union he and Knapp had started) to create the Pilgrim Holiness Church. Interestingly, the dispute at Pasadena revolved around another holiness college, providing striking similarities to the situation leading to Rees's withdrawal from involvement at God's Bible School. It is described in detail in Timothy L. Smith, *Called Unto Holiness*, c. 12, 272-297; in Kirkemo, c. 3, 38-67; and in Cunningham, et. al., 204-213. See also Mallalieu Wilson, *William C. Wilson: the Fifth General Superintendent* (Kansas City, MO: Nazarene Publishing House, 1995), 84-86.

[24] Paul Rees, *Warrior-Saint*, 141.

[25] Paul Rees, 45. As beards went out of vogue, particularly among holiness preachers, Rees changed this feature.

[26] Ibid.

[27] "Come and Hear Him," *Revivalist* (May 5, 1900), 3.

[28] Paul Rees, 45.

[29] "Come and Hear Him," *Revivalist* (May 5, 1900), 3.

[30] Paul Rees, *Warrior-Saint*, 59. Also, see Kostlevy, *Holy Jumpers*, 78-79.

[31] Ibid, 63.

[32] Kostlevy, *Holy Jumpers*, 80.

[33] Ibid, 83.

[34] For examples of his sermons, see Edwin L. Harvey, *Sermons on Bible Characters* (Waukesha, WI: Metropolitan Church Association, 1909).

[35] "Thanksgiving Services at the Mount of Blessings," *Revivalist* (Nov. 21, 1901), 13 and Bessie [Queen], "Bible-School Notes," *Revivalist* (Nov. 21, 1901), 14-15.

[36] Belle Staples, "Bible-School Notes," *Revivalist* (Dec. 12, 1901), 14-15.

[37] Kostlevy, *Holy Jumpers*, 80.

[38] See the announcement for "Salvation Park Camp-Meeting," *Revivalist* (March 13, 1902), 14. The same issue reports, "E. L. Harvey, of Chicago, spent last Saturday with us. The students keenly enjoyed the message be brought to them in the afternoon." Mrs. M. W. Knapp, "Bible-School Notes," 14-15. There appears to be no subsequent mention of Harvey by name in the *Revivalist*, including reports of the 1902 camp meeting where he is conspicuously absent.

[39] This becomes clear in the protests against GBS leadership that peppered *The Burning Bush* throughout its early years. For example, see E. L. Harvey, "Poison in the Revivalist Pan," *The Burning Bush* (June 25, 1903), 7; "Putting the Patient to Sleep," *The Burning Bush* (August 13, 1903), 9 and the related cartoon on page 1;

and "The Cincinnati Skeleton," *The Burning Bush* (June 1, 1905), 4 and the related cartoon on page 1.

[40] "Mrs. Knapp Takes Up Dead Husband's Mantle," *Cincinnati Post* (Dec. 10, 1901), 1. Apparently, this was the first time that GBS made the front page of a secular paper.

[41] Kostlevy, *Holy Jumpers*, 80.

[42] "Trustees Chosen," (Dec. 19, 1901), 12. See also, Bessie [Queen], "Translated," (Dec. 19, 1901), 1-2; Hills, *Hero*, 286; and "Reign of Sadness on Blessings' Mount," *Cincinnati Post* (Dec. 9, 1901), 6 on Knapp's premonition of his impending death about two months to three weeks before his demise.

[43] *Pentecostal Letters*, 104.

[44] See Dieter, "Women in Leadership," in Caldwell, 178-180 and Hynson, "The Place of Women" in Caldwell, 226. Hynson suggests that "the rationale of Pentecostal authority [for women] to preach differs from the special appeal of feminist thought," with the former based on the egalitarian impulse of Pentecost while the latter lacks such "cohesive logic" and is "louder, strident."

[45] W. B. Godbey, *Woman Preacher*, (Louisville: Pentecostal Publishing Co., 1891), 12.

[46] *Lightning Bolts*, 231.

[47] "Cincinnati as a Mission Field," *Revivalist* (March 14, 1901), 15.

[48] Rees, "Knows No Gender," c. 7 in *The Ideal Pentecostal Church*, 28-29.

[49] Hills, *Hero*, 23.

[50] George Kulp, "Coronation of Octavia N. Knapp," *Revivalist* (March 18, 1909), 5.

[51] Nettie Peabody, "Grandma as a Student," *Revivalist* (March 18, 1909), 4.

[52] Hills, *Hero*, 13.

[53] Ibid, 419. Hills also added of Knapp, that, "yet, withal, he was one of the manliest men I ever met."

[54] Ibid, 13.

[55] Hills, *Hero*, 128. This was excerpted from Martin's last journal entry, date November 30, 1892.

[56] "Sparkling Waters from Bible Fountains," *Revivalist* (Nov. 7, 1901), 4. Also, see "Subscribe for 'Sparkling Waters,'" *Revivalist* (Nov. 7, 1901), 3 and "Sparkling Waters," *Revivalist* (Feb. 6, 1902), 13. *Sparkling Waters* ceased publication in 1962, ending about the same time as the Thanksgiving Dinner (1961), so that their durations were practically concurrent.

[57] Day, 44. See also, "The Salvation of the Children," *Revivalist* (May 2, 1901), 8.

[58] "Sparkling Waters from Bible Fountains," *Revivalist* (Nov. 7, 1901), 4.

[59] On children's services, see "Revival Reports," *Revivalist* (Aug. 9, 1900), 11 and Bessie [Queen], "Bible-School Notes," *Revivalist* (June 6, 1901), 14. See A. M. Hills, *Food for Lambs; or, Leading Children to Christ* (Cincinnati: Revivalist, 1899) and M. G. Standley, *The Story of the Christ* (Cincinnati: God's Revivalist Press, n. d.). The latter was published during the first decade of the school's history. See the advertisement in the March 18, 1909, *Revivalist*, 16, featuring a glowing endorsement by A. M. Hills. Later, the new edition was advertised with an additional endorsement by Oswald Chambers (*Revivalist* (Sept. 27, 1923), 15). For other materials advertised for youth and children, including *A Bunch of Flowers for Girls* and *Beautiful Be's*

for Boys, see "Books for the Young. 'Sparkling Waters' Library," *Revivalist* (Jan. 16, 1902), 7.

⁶⁰ "Mrs. Knapp's Letter," *Revivalist* (Dec. 19, 1901), 7.

⁶¹ See *Sparkling Waters From Bible Fountains* (Jan. 8, 1911), 1, and (July 13, 1912), 4 for typical promotions of temperance (prohibition).

⁶² David Bundy, "From Cincinnati to the World," 9. Minnie Knapp's account of Sammy Morris, son of an African tribal leader who at an early age was converted to Christianity and immigrated to the United States to learn more about the Holy Spirit, where he became a great impetus to revival at Taylor University which he attended until his death at age twenty-one, had an impact that proves difficult to over-estimate. For example, David Bundy has traced its influence through numerous periodicals in Scandinavia and Russia ("The Global Structures of the Holiness Traditions," recording of a presentation given at the 37th Annual Meeting of the Wesleyan Theological Society at Hobe Sound Bible College, Hobe Sound, FL (March 1, 2002). The account continues to inspire holiness people (and other evangelicals) to this day, resurfacing often in Revivalist literature. See its occurrence in Meredith G. Standley, *The Light that Never Fails* (Cincinnati: God's Bible School and Missionary Training Home, 1934), 69-71.

⁶³ Mrs. M. W. Knapp, *Diary Letters: A Missiona[r]y Trip through the West Indies and to South America* (Cincinnati: God's Revivalist Office, 1918).

⁶⁴ Minnie gives her account of this condition and her healing in *Magnify God* (Cincinnati: Mrs. Martin Wells Knapp, n. d.).

⁶⁵ See Glenn D. Black, "Three Women Served As Administrators At God's Bible School From 1901-1911," *Revivalist* (Aug. 4, 1983), 11.

⁶⁶ "Revival Persecution," *Revivalist* (Aug. 1, 1901), 7 and "She Is Not Here," *Revivalist* (April 5, 1906), 1.

⁶⁷ "She Is Not Here," *Revivalist* (April 5, 1906), 2. For Storey's testimony to entire sanctification, see "Sister Mary Storey's Experience," *Revivalist* (Jan. 23, 1902), 5.

⁶⁸ Ibid.

⁶⁹ "Revival Persecution," *Revivalist* (Aug. 1, 1901), 7.

⁷⁰ "A 'Warrior' Crowned," *Revivalist* (April 5, 1906), 8. Storey reflected on her prayer to be a warrior in *The Revivalist* (April 16, 1900), 4, opining that this was the reason God had allowed her to suffer certain hardships.

⁷¹ "Revival Reports," *Revivalist* (March 15, 1900), 11.

⁷² "Revival Reports," *Revivalist* (Jan. 14, 1900), 11.

⁷³ "Revival Prayers Answered," *Revivalist* (Dec. 1896), 6.

⁷⁴ Day, 48.

⁷⁵ Larry D. Smith, "Mary Storey, Servant of God," *Revivalist* (Winter 2000), 15. William Kostlevy refers to Storey as a "Methodist loyalist" who was "less radical in temperament than Knapp." She was thus less favorably disposed toward the MCA and was "critical of the radicals' boycott of the General Holiness Assembly," being "convinced that the radicals' rejection of the Assembly had 'quenched the fire, power, and glory' that had accompanied the Chicago revival" (*Holy Jumpers*, 80).

⁷⁶ Bessie [Queen], "Salvation of a Cincinnati Girl," *Revivalist* (March 14, 1901), 16.

⁷⁷ "Salvation Testimonies," *Revivalist* (May 24, 1900), 16. See also "Cincinnati

Salvation Incidents," *Revivalist* (Feb. 22, 1900), 16.

[78] Bessie [Queen], "Salvation of a Cincinnati Girl," *Revivalist* (March 14, 1901), 16.

[79] Bessie [Queen], "Why I Am Married," *Revivalist* (Nov. 28, 1901), 5. In "Bible-School Chapel Testimonies," *Revivalist* (Dec. 13, 1900), 4, she testified, "I know I am sanctified because selfishness, meanness, and lots of other things are gone."

[80] Bessie [Queen], "Salvation of a Cincinnati Girl," *Revivalist* (March 14, 1901), 16.

[81] "Rev. Knapp Was Fined The Costs," *Cincinnati Post* (July 17, 1901), 6. Although the *Post* mistakenly spells her name "Gwinn," context makes it clear that the article refers to Bessie Queen. When Bessie became ill a couple of months after Knapp's death, several newspaper articles described the ensuing attempts of her mother to have Bessie removed from the Mount of Blessings, to no avail. "Mother Demands A Doctor's Care," *The Cincinnati Enquirer* (Feb. 18, 1902), 12, reported that, "Miss Queen, who is a comely girl of about 22 years, entered into the work of the school with such tremendous zeal that she has broken down under the strain . . . Mrs. Queen has always objected to her daughter's connection with the school although she is a devout Christian herself. She regards the followers of Rev. Knapp as fanatics, and she tried often, but in vain, to induce Bessie to return home to her family." Also, see "Denied Permission To See Her Daughter," *Cincinnati Post* (Feb. 18, 1902), 8 and "Prayed For Sweet Sleep To Come," *The Cincinnati Enquirer* (Feb. 19, 1902), 12. For her account of this illness and her recovery, see Bessie [Queen], "A Miracle," *Revivalist* (March 27, 1902), 10.

[82] Meredith G. Standley, *My Life As I Have Lived It For Christ and Others* (Cincinnati: Meredith G. Standley, 1949), 76.

[83] "Unique Wedding Celebration By Rev. and Mrs. Standley of God's Bible School," *The Cincinnati Enquirer* (May 15, 1902), 7.

[84] M. G. Standley, *My Life*, 73.

[85] "Mother Demands a Doctor's Care," *Cincinnati Enquirer* (Feb. 18, 1902), 12.

[86] Kostlevy, *Holy Jumpers*, 82.

[87] Ibid.

[88] Glenn Black, "Three Women Served As Administrators At God's Bible School From 1901-1911," *Revivalist* (Aug. 4, 1983), 11.

[89] Kostlevy, *Holy Jumpers*, 80.

[90] Day, 48. See also "God's Work," *Revivalist* (May 1, 1902), 1-2, an unsigned article that could have been written by Mrs. Knapp or Bessie that states that Standley, "at Brother Knapp's request was chosen pastor; also teacher of the Bible-class. Brother Knapp loved him, and he desired that he should always remain in the work here" (2).

[91] "Going West," *Revivalist* (April 3, 1902), 1.

[92] Mrs. M. W. Knapp, "To the Revivalist Family," *Revivalist* (Jan. 16, 1902), 2.

[93] "The Bible-School," *Revivalist* (Jan. 2, 1902), 13.

[94] "Reports," *Revivalist* (Dec. 26, 1901), 11. This report from his meeting at Novelty, Washington, indicated that "sixty-six souls have been born again; 10 backsliders reclaimed, and 5 believers sanctified." Also, see "Words from God's Ministers," *Revivalist* (Jan. 16, 1902), 5 and several reports in earlier *Revivalist*s on the campaign.

For examples of the mature Standley's sermons, see his sermons selected by his wife and published in Meredith G. Standley, *The Light That Never Fails*.

[95] For example, Standley preached at Revivalist Chapel when Knapp was conducting the camp meeting of the International Holiness Union at Denton, Maryland, in 1900 ("Revival Reports," *Revivalist* (Aug. 16, 1900), 11).

[96] From the Preface.

[97] M. G. Standley, *My Life*, 13.

[98] Ibid, 12.

[99] M. G. Standley, *The Light That Never Fails*, 134.

[100] M. G. Standley, *My Life*, 13.

[101] Ibid, 14.

[102] Ibid, 15.

[103] Ibid, 16-18.

[104] Ibid, 19.

[105] Ibid, 19-25.

[106] Ibid, 30-34.

[107] M. G. Standley, *My Life*, 35-39.

[108] Ibid, 40-41.

[109] "Sparks from Revivalist Chapel," *Revivalist* (Jan. 4, 1900), 4.

[110] M. G. Standley, *My Life*, 41.

[111] Ibid, 44-51. Standley found his year at Asbury to be especially helpful in preparing him for the self-denial which was expected of all students at GBS.

[112] Ibid, 51.

[113] Ibid, 59-62. Also, see *The Light That Never Fails*, 134-135.

[114] Ibid, 59-63. In particular, "the enemy tried to get some to go to the extreme in fasting."

[115] Interestingly, the first testimony reported from Standley's first meeting at Revivalist Chapel was one from Bessie Queen ("Sparks from Revivalist Chapel," *Revivalist* (Jan. 4, 1900), 4).

[116] "Wedded to Evangelist," *Cincinnati Post* (May 14, 1902), 2.

[117] M. G. Standley, *My Life*, 70.

[118] Seth C. Rees, "A Pentecostal Wedding," *Revivalist* (June 19, 1902), page number unavailable because the copy from which the microfilm was made was mutilated.

[119] Day, 49. The feast was enjoyed by more than 500 children and provided "an abundance of good things, including more than 50 gallons of ice cream." "Unique Wedding Celebration," *The Cincinnati Enquirer* (May 15, 1902), 7.

[120] "Wedding at God's Bible School: Latest Sensation on the Mount of Blessings," *The Cincinnati Enquirer* (May 14, 1902), 12.

[121] "Unique Wedding Celebration," *The Cincinnati Enquirer* (May 15, 1902), 7. This article also contained a retraction of the report in "Prayed For Sweet Sleep To Come," *The Cincinnati Enquirer* (Feb. 19, 1902), 12, that Queen had been "one of the child actresses at the old Museum," an "amusement resort" in Cincinnati.

For M. G. Stanley's account of the "furor" over the *Enquirer* article, and the subsequent apology, which was evidently precipitated at least in part by the outrage of Bessie's parents, see his, *My Life*, 72-76.

122 Bessie [Queen], "Why I Am Married," *Revivalist* (Nov. 28, 1901), 5.
123 Bessie [Queen], "Translated," *Revivalist* (Dec. 19, 1901), 2.
124 "Unique Wedding Celebration," *The Cincinnati Enquirer* (May 15, 1902), 7.
125 "Notice," *Revivalist* (Aug. 23, 1902), 15.
126 W. B. Godbey, "Adoption," in *Godbey on Christian Experience*, 103.

Chapter 6

Pushing the Battle: Continuing the Conquest

Man and man's teachings were nowhere at this blessed Convention, on this veritable "Mount of Blessings." Jesus was glorified. Scores of the saints found God explaining to them the way He had been taking them in the past years. Yes, for some of us at least, we record that this Convention of 1906 was the most blessed one we have ever attended. Glory to His name!

. . . . .

The thoroughly efficient and organized band of workers in the Mission, the splendidly manipulated open air marches, and the literal, massed power of God's Bible School students silenced the devil on the very streets of the awful city. It makes some of us thank God upon the very remembrance of it; and that we were privileged to witness it. Two big feeds (Christmas and New Year's nights) were given to the men in this Mission and many found Jesus as their Savior also. (This is truly Holiness socialism.)

. . . . .

The fourfold truth of God was heralded forth as God witnessed—Salvation, Sanctification, Healing and the Second Coming.
                           – Oswald Chambers[1]

To Him be praise for every day, hour and minute spent in "God's Bible School." I look back without a single regret; but if I could, I would do it all over again. There was not one lesson too hard, or test too great, or a rule to severe. All we took in Him as His divine plan for us.
                           – Irene Blyden[2]

The three trustees to whom Knapp bequeathed his charge promised their constituents that there would "be no stop in any department of the work; but we shall, by the strength and help and wisdom of Jesus, push the battle hotter and harder than ever before."[3] After returning from his evangelistic tour in the Northwest and joining forces with the three trustees, M. G. Standley concurred, "I never felt more like pushing the battle . . ."[4] These were not idle words; the GBS family responded to the challenge with fervor and pressed forward with "renewed vigor on all lines."[5]

Building and Growing

The implications of this sustained advance involved virtually all of the practical emphases that had been stressed under Knapp's leadership, especially faith work, home missions and world evangelism. The new trustees' "first faith venture" was the purchase of a lot "directly back of the main building."[6] The success of this endeavor encouraged them to move the campus building program ahead, a decision reflected in the same article that announced Standley's new role as Bible teacher:

> The girls are crowded for room, but we are praying and expecting the Lord to send the means to immediately build a new dormitory. This building will contain about 30 rooms, a dining-room that will seat about 450 people at a time, also a large kitchen . . . God has the money, and, according to His command, we are stepping out by FAITH IN HIM ALONE.[7]

Soon thereafter, the work began on what was known for the next twenty years or so as the Girls' Dormitory (later known as the "Ten Weeks Building" for the short term course established by E. G. Marsh.) It proved to be a massive undertaking for the school's leadership, with the total cost of building and equipment placed at $40,000, since the project expanded far beyond its original plan, eventually comprising over seventy rooms.[8] In fact, the five-story brick structure located at the south-east corner of the campus and facing Ringgold Street functioned as a multi-purpose facility: "The first floor housed the engine room and laundry facility; the second floor consisted of general offices and a Book Room; the third floor featured the dining room and kitchen; while the fourth and fifth floors contained 50 rooms for a Girls' Dormitory."[9]

The innovative stewardship pioneered by Knapp guided plans for the new building. For example, in a feat of creative engineering, a steam plant was designed that powered the school laundry, a motor to produce electricity, and, eventually, the school printing office, while waste steam was utilized in heating all of the campus buildings. This was accomplished in spite of discouraging predictions as to the effort's impossibility from several steam heating companies. Once again, GBS leadership had successfully overcome an obstacle through faith and their staunch commitment that "everything [be] made to count for God."[10]

M. G. Standley had received a promise that the building would be ready to use for camp meeting (June 20-30, 1902). He publicly proclaimed this, contending that "God's promise to me, for the building, was clear and definite and I believed God, and testified to that fact." This he did, even though advised by friends, including "that illustrious old saint, Dr. Godbey," to "not publicly speak of using the building, as Camp was so near at hand, and if it was not ready, it would dishonor God to testify to a faith that did not materialize." In addition, numerous setbacks plagued the project, including the failure of a retaining wall and the consequent injury of a worker, a strike by the iron workers putting up the girders, and then a strike by the bricklayers, prompting Standley to confess that "it looked as if the very devil had moved earth and hell to keep us from going on."

Finally, it appeared the ultimate blow to any hope of using the building by camp meeting had been delivered when the funds for the project ran out. Rather than admit defeat, however, Standley "called all on the 'Hill' for a day of fasting and prayer, laid the pressing need before them" and received additional assurance that God would answer. Shortly thereafter, a special express parcel arrived at the school office. Mrs. Knapp, the Standleys, and others gathered and opened it together. As the contents were revealed, they were stunned. There was a large bundle of money which had begun to mildew and crumble—"evidently it had been buried, possibly even for some years in the ground." Afraid to handle the fragile currency, the school leaders turned it over to government officials who "forwarded it, without expense, to Washington to be valuated." Meanwhile, there was "a shouting, hallelujah time . . . on the 'Mount of Blessings'!" A few days later, a check came from Washington for over $2,200. No one at the school ever learned where that mysterious bundle of money had been hidden, who unearthed it, or who sent it to GBS, but they rested in the assurance "that *God* put it on the heart of some one to forward it, and *He* sent it just exactly at the time it was needed!" Consequently, work on the building continued, and when camp meeting began, the new dining room was put to use and guests were housed in the new dormitory. Standley exulted in the vindication of his faith, "*God* told me we were going to have that building for Camp, and while the devil did everything possible to stop us, God just quietly moved on and His promise was made a reality."[11]

This major advance in alleviating campus over-crowding encouraged Knapp's heirs to improve the school's services to reach even more students. Of obvious significance was the expansion of the Bible school course of study to a full two years, beginning with the 1902-1903 school year, just the first of numerous steps in the advancement of the school's academic offerings.[12] As the academic program progressed, it took on a more formal tone, with the first student diplomas being granted at the end of the 1908-1909 school year, in a brief evening service prior to the beginning of camp meeting that featured a message from Dr. Godbey and the presentation of diplomas by Mrs. Knapp to the three students who had completed "the full Bible School" course that year—"Sister [Emma] Meredith, and Brothers Emerson Smith and Guy Wilkinson."[13] However, the size of this first "graduating" class belies the phenomenal growth the school experienced during its first few years. During the 1903-1904 year, the enrollment had grown to 243 students representing 31 states and 6 foreign countries.[14] And, by 1914, the school counted its alumni at just over three thousand.[15]

The school's sphere of educational opportunities was further enlarged through promotion of a correspondence program developed by Martin Wells Knapp—"God's Bible-School Home Circle"—which targeted those unable to relocate to Cincinnati.[16] While this initial program lapsed, it was a precedent setting initiative, with similar efforts at distance education re-emerging periodically throughout the following century as significant components of God's Bible School's ministry, especially under the leadership of Oswald Chambers, Nettie Peabody, and Mattie Perry.

Another effort at making GBS studies accessible to the widest possible student base was the beginning of a grade school in the fall of 1902 consisting of "the upper three elementary grades," which was intended, not only to educate campus and neighborhood children, but also "to aid those students who came to God's Bible School with a deficiency in the fundamentals of education," so that they could benefit from remediation before actually enrolling in the Bible School program.[17] This endeavor was particularly dear to M. G. Standley's heart, as he contended that God was "leading to the establishment of New Testament schools for the children" to keep them from going astray.[18] Accordingly, in the fall of 1905, a "Pentecostal school for children" in lower grades was also begun on the campus.[19]

Perhaps most significantly in terms of precedent, the trustees chose to expand the school's work program for students in 1904, allowing many to attend GBS who were otherwise unable financially. This decision also had significant ramifications for Revivalist publications, for it was determined that a primary way to increase work positions was by moving the printing operation to the campus from the Methodist Book Concern (where it had been done "at a cost of $1,000 to $1,500 a month"). "Instead of constructing a building for the machinery, it was decided to partition off one-fourth of the Tabernacle, with an additional floor for the bindery and mailing department placed above the printing area," for a total cost of $250. The boon created for work students was immediate, with about fifty young men having "worked their way through school in this department by January of 1905."[20] This proved to be an omen of things to come, with a high percentage of students throughout the century relying on the campus work program to make their education financially feasible.

Rescuing the Perishing

One of the other great faith endeavors of Knapp's successors also demonstrated the continuing commitment of GBS to reaching society's outcasts. This was their pursuit of Knapp's dream to establish a rescue home on the Mount of Blessings. Initially frustrated in their attempts to follow the founder's plan of building a frame structure for this purpose on the campus,[21] the school's leaders were elated when an old mansion across the street (1817 Young Street) which had been previously valued at $30,000 was offered to them for $10,000, with the owners "donating $2,500 of that, making it $7,500." By May 1902, the building, dubbed "Hope Cottage," was part of the Mount of Blessings campus.

As the trustees and M. G. Standley felt themselves already overextended with their publishing and educational ministries, Seth C. Rees consented to their request for him to become superintendent of the rescue home, while he "would continue to superintend his "Rest Cottage" in Chicago and other rescue homes around the country as they would open.[22] The day-to-day operation of the home rested on the shoulders of the matron, "Mother" Duff, who found there just as fulfilling a mission field as she ever dreamed to find among the lepers of India. She was assisted by a devoted coterie of workers including a Sister Payne and Sister Elizabeth West, who like the rest of their colleagues on the Mount of Blessings, were not "to receive any salary; only such free-will offerings as their needs demand[ed].”[23]

The first "inmate," as the residents were termed, was Julia, who had come to the Mount of Blessings camp meeting from Columbus, Ohio, seeking salvation from a downward spiral that ultimately left her residing in a "house of sin."[24] Accounts of lives like hers touched the hearts of *Revivalist* readers, and they responded with a flood of contributions of such household items as linens and silverware, in addition to financial support, while others donated labor to refurbish the old mansion.[25] On May 5, 1905, the campus family celebrated the lifting of the mortgage from Hope Cottage, and rejoiced in the great successes the home had witnessed.[26] In fact, by that time, Mother Duff had chronicled enough victories and heart-rending stories from wayward women who had found shelter in the rescue home to write a book, which she did, entitling it *Redeemed by the Blood*.[27] Just six years later, Hope Cottage had already "sheltered between six and seven hundred girls."[28]

The work of the rescue home was complimented by the on-going outreach of GBS students and staff to the impoverished areas of Cincinnati and its suburbs. Much of this work centered in the school's rescue mission, considered a necessary compliment to Hope Cottage, as Mother Duff averred, "A rescue mission and a rescue home are both necessities in rescuing the perishing, and how we thank God that He has supplied us with both!"[29] Originally located at 430 Plum Street, where it was pastored by Fred T. Fuge, a GBS alumni and former sailor "from Newfoundland where he had been converted under the Salvation Army,"[30] it was moved in the spring of 1904 to "the blackest part of" Cincinnati—George Street—a veritable "devil's highway" lined with bars and brothels.[31] Early leadership at this location was provided by former GBS students, Brother and Sister Frank Leischer, who garnered a remarkable harvest with as many as thirty converts within the space of four weeks.[32] In fact, "almost every night, souls [were] at the altar crying for mercy,"[33] encouraging the GBS family's expectation of "a constant revival there the whole year through."[34] In 1907, the pastorate of George Street Mission was committed to Lew W. Standley, who could naturally empathize with those bound by alcohol and other vices.[35] Under his leadership over the next thirteen years, the mission continued to feature services where a "full gospel" was preached "every night in the week."[36]

In addition, the mission combined ministry to the soul with that to the body, with meals being provided to the needy, including a popular "free lunch" for men on Thanksgiving Day, not to be confused with the larger dinner provided at the GBS campus, which continued to expand, with about eighteen hundred feasting at the dinner in 1905. At the mission, five hundred men were served three thousand sandwiches that same evening.[37] Demand for this service was so great, that a stampede by the crowd awaiting the "lunch" was barely averted in 1908.[38] A typical recipient was a "thin-faced man" who arrived requesting, not food for himself, but for his wife at home with a sick baby. He ultimately received much more than he asked, leaving the mission "with a basket of food and a heart full of salvation." Follow-up by one of the rescue missionaries found him "happy in the Lord" and having already "established a family altar."[39]

Such follow-up provides just one indication that GBS's aggressive campaign to battle sin and to see its captives freed was not confined within the walls of George Street Mission or Hope Cottage. Indeed, every device imaginable was employed to reach the lost. For example, even the school wagon, pulled for years by a horse named "Old Tom" was pressed into service as an evangelistic tool, with various soul-winning slogans painted on its side and additional placards periodically affixed to advertise such events as camp meeting. As the school modernized, the horse-drawn "Eternity Wagon" was eventually replaced by a motorized delivery truck, which challenged those it passed to consider, "WHERE WILL YOU SPEND ETERNITY?"[40]

In efforts more inclusive of the entire campus family, various visitation and soul-winning activities were organized. For example, "one afternoon of each week [was] devoted to house to house visitation, especially in the slums." During these visits, occupants were "definitely dealt with in regard to their soul's welfare," with numerous resultant conversions. However, care was also taken to note homes "destitute of food and fuel, and almost destitute of clothing," with reports being made to campus leadership. In turn, the school responded by meeting such needs through its "Poor Fund" and barrels and boxes of donated clothing. Students also visited various hospitals, going "cot to cot, talking to the sick and dying" and "holding a public service every Sunday in the dining room" of one hospital. In addition to spiritual help, some patients were also "healed in answer to the prayer of faith."[41] Students also conducted jail services, preached at missions not directly connected with GBS, and took the message of the full gospel to the masses through street-meetings.[42]

The conquest to reach into the "highways and hedges" led to the organization of "slum corps" by June 1902. "Several times a week," these groups would leave the Mount of Blessings late in the evening, when iniquity was at its height, and visit "saloons and brothels, seeking to win some to Jesus."[43] The resultant *Revivalist* reports include stirring accounts of inconceivable suffering and lurid scenes which shocked many of the students who had come from rural backgrounds and were unaccustomed to seeing such debauchery as "painted faces, bare necks and arms, short dresses exposing the person, lewd pictures—such scenes as to make one feel as if they were in the very vestibule of hell, and the winds from the pit were fanning them."[44] An entire book could easily be filled with anecdotes of the forays by these young soul-winners-in-training into places like "Rat Row," so called because of its proximity to the river, so that when the water level went up, its inhabitants had "to move out like rats, and their houses [got] a 'housecleaning' then, through the Ohio River, if at no other time."⁴⁵

In 1903, the GBS family developed a special interest in Shantytown, a shanty boat settlement on the Ohio River in southwest Cincinnati reputed to be "one of the darkest and most destitute places of the city." The work began with three or four students who visited from boat to boat and obtained permission from a poor widow, "Mother Timony," to hold prayer meetings in her boat. They were soon joined by Thomas Wright, who had spent much of his life "along and upon the great rivers" and was given "an intense desire" to share the gospel with the residents of Shantytown.⁴⁶ Prayer for more suitable quarters for the growing work was answered through the benevolence of a supporter in Pennsylvania who donated $150 for the purchase of a mission boat.⁴⁷ By April 1903, "God's Rescue Boat" was "neatly and comfortably" outfitted to accommodate around one hundred people in meetings,⁴⁸ and the "happy salvation crew" embarked under the leadership of Wright.⁴⁹ Within a year, the ministry had won the confidence of the community, leading to the report: "We scarcely ever go down but what we are called on to go and pray with some who are sick, as they all have great faith in the prayers of the Bible School."⁵⁰ By this time, a thriving Sunday School had been established as well, drawing as many as seventy eager young scholars.⁵¹

The souls saved and sanctified and other victories at Shantytown inspired the GBS family to establish a similar ministry in Cincinnati's East End at "Shantyville" by May 1905, with "God's Bible School Salvation Boat" under the leadership of John A. Corrigan.⁵² In addition, by this time, missions had been established at Newport, Kentucky; Covington, Kentucky; and Mt. Washington, Ohio—a town located about twelve miles from Cincinnati.⁵³

The efforts of GBS students to rescue the perishing were not without opposition, both from residents of the slums and from some public officials. Denizens of the "dives and saloons" would sometimes jeer at them, blowing smoke in their faces and taunting them about religion; while reaction from civic leaders ran the gamut from antagonism to cooperation. One hostile village mayor engineered the arrest of a GBS student and two of his friends for open-air preaching. Once behind bars, "instead of whining and crying," the young men "shouted and praised God," counting "it all joy to suffer for Jesus' sake." What followed brings to mind the imprisonment of Paul and Silas at Philippi; in fact, the young evangelists "had not been in ward five minutes until one of the prisoners was gloriously saved." Soon, the mayor followed legal council and had them set free, but not before "the matter had stirred the whole town," with several who had opposed the meeting changing their attitude and offering to pay bail for the preachers, though ultimately none was needed. Determinedly, the same student returned to the village to hold another meeting, this time with a large tent supplied by the GBS trustees.⁵⁴

Indeed, such resistance not only left GBS workers undeterred, it positively inspired them. This tenacious zeal caught the attention of all of Cincinnati in the spring of 1905 when the school conducted its first pre- camp meeting "full salvation campaign" to reach "the masses . . . with the Gospel message." The result of a burden received by M. G. Standley, the campus family soon committed to this massive undertaking to distribute about one-half million tracts and handbills to the city populace (which then numbered about four hundred thousand). To accomplish this task, it was decided to have about two hundred students and workers march in a procession through downtown, with several playing such instruments as cornets, drums, and guitars. Here they would divide into several companies, to better cover the city. On Sunday afternoons, services were to be held at "the Auditorium, one of the large prominent halls of the City," located at the corner of Seventh and Elm Streets. In addition, street meetings were to be conducted at various points each evening until camp meeting commenced.[55]

However, a major obstacle loomed over the proposed campaign—the mayor refused to grant permission for the street meetings, personally threatening to have Standley arrested if the school conducted open-air services.[56] Standley returned from his discussion with the mayor and gathered the campus family in the Tabernacle, where they prayed "and asked God to make His leadings in the matter clear."[57] A vote was then taken, with Standley making it clear, "When you vote, remember that if you vote 'go' then you must be willing to go to jail. If you say it is God's will, and you go with us in the open-air meetings, you pledge yourself to be willing and ready to go to jail, regardless."[58] The almost unanimous conclusion was that "His command, 'Go out into the highways and hedges, and compel them to come in,' was not withdrawn, and that [they] were to obey God rather than man."[59] Thus, after marches into the Kentucky cities of Newport and Covington, the campaign in Cincinnati began on Saturday, May 27, regardless of the mayor's disapprobation. The march began at Liberty and Sycamore and proceeded downtown, through the business district to Government Square where the group dispersed into smaller bands which then conducted the street meetings. In just this one evening, about twenty-five thousand people received a gospel tract, and about fifty "raised their hands for prayer" while several actually knelt for prayer in front of the large crowds that gathered.[60] Such scenes were repeated for a week with great success: "In many instances the crowds seemed held by the power of God, and seemed to loathe to leave when the meetings would close."[61]

As for the mayor's opposition, no arrests were forthcoming, a fact that apparently disappointed some of the students, who had "built themselves up to the place where they were willing to suffer and go to jail for Jesus' sake."[62] In fact, after the campaign had continued a week, in light of the good it had obviously accomplished, such as the restoration of drunkards to sobriety, the mayor withdrew his opposition and, in response to an appeal by Mary Storey and Bessie Standley, issued permits for the street meetings to be conducted for another week.[63] Meanwhile, expectation of persecution was not wholly disappointed; for other challenges confronted some of the street meetings, as when a crowd in a predominantly Catholic neighborhood "jeered and whooped and shot pistols" and made a bonfire with many of the tracts. However, the campaign continued unabated, closing triumphantly on June 11 with an afternoon service in the Auditorium, in which Dr. Godbey prayed, Lew Standley gave his testimony, and "the whole congregation stood and waived [sic] their handkerchiefs as they sang unto the Lord."⁶⁴

Although the outreach ministries of GBS would continue to sporadically face ridicule and opposition, its philanthropic labors ultimately won the admiration and support from several civic leaders. For example, in an ironic twist, Judge Lueders of the Police Court—the very judge who presided over Knapp's trial for disturbing the peace—ended up taking an unusual interest in the rescue work of GBS. He personally escorted (along with a police officer) Mrs. Knapp and other GBS leaders and students "through the worst dives in the city" including "Over the Rhine"—then the German district of Cincinnati.⁶⁵ Later, he sent several young women brought before his court to Hope Cottage, reflecting growing official appreciation for the results of GBS rescue work.⁶⁶

Yet another endeavor that elicited public support and demonstrated the ongoing pursuit by the GBS trustees of its founder's vision of faith-supported personal evangelism and social assistance was the establishment of God's Orphanage, now made urgent by the number of children seeking refuge at Hope Cottage.⁶⁷ Rather than locating it on the Mount of Blessings, as Knapp had planned, the trustees thought children would better benefit from a rural environment, so they purchased a two-hundred acre farm in the vicinity of Milford, Ohio—about twenty-five miles from the GBS campus—for only $20,000.⁶⁸ In addition, they planned on permanently relocating the Salvation Park Camp Meeting (which still taxed the accommodations of the Hilltop) to a beautiful grove on the property, which was "easy of access, right on the line of the 'Cincinnati, Milford and Loveland Traction Co.'"⁶⁹ Although the camp was only conducted there in 1906, the property proved ideal for the orphanage, especially since it already boasted a thirteen-room farmhouse. By October 1902, eleven children had found refuge in the orphanage and their number had doubled by the following year. Older children had various chores around the farm, and they were educated in "the grade school which was conducted at the orphanage," with Coral L. Osborn serving as first teacher.⁷⁰ Of course, emphasis was put on the children's spiritual development, as well as academics, and some went on to enroll as students at GBS.⁷¹

The move of the camp meeting back to the city in 1907 reflects the ongoing commitment of GBS leadership to aggressive outreach to the lost of Cincinnati, with George Kulp suggesting—"Why not have a ten days' meeting in Cincinnati, open air meetings every evening, advertising the services thoroughly, and instead of taking the people out to the camp-grounds have the Camp right in the heart of the city, and give them the full Gospel?"⁷² While the temporary move to the orphanage grounds had appealed to holiness people's desire for a pure and wholesome environment, the *Revivalist* now boldly proclaimed, "This is not a camp-meeting to 'HOLD THE FORT!' This is a camp-meeting to STORM THE FORT . . . This will not be a camp-meeting of religious contemplation; it will be a time of blessed militant fighting on the winning side."[73]

Indeed, the move back to Cincinnati marked the launch of the most ambitious evangelistic campaign undertaken to that time in connection with the camp meeting. The secular press took note, with the *Cincinnati Post* reporting the campaign as an "Open War on Cincinnati's Sin."[74] To assure maximum visibility and accessibility to the public, evening services were held in "the GRAND OPERA HOUSE in the heart of the city" (now known as Music Hall), while day services were conducted on the Mount of Blessings. In addition, promotion of the camp included the admittedly "novel method of 'Salvation Sandwich Board Men'," whom the *Post* likened to crusaders of old, only now replacing chain mail with sandwich signs advertising the meeting and replacing swords with tracts proclaiming full salvation.[75]

Results of the camp met or exceeded expectations. Features included morning meetings with Oswald Chambers and W. B. Godbey, and other workers included E. A. Fergerson, Fred T. Fuge, George B. Kulp, and L. Milton Williams.[76] An extraordinary number of seekers prayed through to receive the Holy Spirit, even though many of them had previously "testified to being saved and sanctified."[77] Visitors were also impressed at "the way the 'boys and girls' of the 'Bible School' worked early and late, so heartily and cheerfully as unto the Lord," even though many of them were only able to get into a few services because of their work load.[78]

Perhaps the most dramatic day of the meeting was the first Saturday, which witnessed the first "hallelujah march" through downtown to the "opera house," this time with no government opposition, with Oswald Chambers observing that "the mayor of Cincinnati practically gave the city over the Bible School at this camp."[79] A band led the marchers, and students and other workers invited the crowds along the route to the service, with hundreds taking up their invitation and following. The scene defies description, as several hundred marchers paraded down the middle of Race Street, marching three abreast, and carrying "salvation banners" while their "mighty chorus of praise and victory rang out upon the evening air:

> 'He brought me out of the miry clay
> He set my feet on the rock to stay,
> He puts a song in my soul to-day,
> A song of praise, Hallelujah!'

When the throng finally reached the "Opera House," the *Revivalist* reported that

> ... the presence of God filled the place and instead of settling down, God's children shouted and danced and sang, and for awhile it looked impossible to have any preaching that night. On the main floor, several were testifying at once, and the fire spread to the gallery, and three or

four were testifying there, and a holy confusion reigned. The Holy Ghost fell on those seated on the platform and they began to march around and suddenly it seemed like fully one-third of the great congregation were shouting and praising God, and having a general jubilee.[80]

The account of the camp that appeared in the *Cincinnati Post* was reminiscent of the secular press's coverage of the first camp meeting conducted by Knapp in God's Tabernacle, with the sub-title: "Wild Scenes of Ecstacy [sic] and Grief Enacted by 'Reclaimed' Sinners at Bible School Revival." Although this article ridiculed the emotional displays that characterized the camp, its depiction does accurately reflect the intensity generated in the services, as some of the congregation groaned, sobbed, and "actually writhed" in agony as E. A. Fergerson brought to a climax his "awful description" of the horrors of hell.[81] However, to the GBS leadership, no amount of derision could outweigh the wonderful harvest of souls reaped by the camp.[82]

Conquests Abroad

The camp meeting campaigns, rescue work, and other means of outreach provided visible evidence of the *Revivalist*'s contention that, on the Mount of Blessings, "The fire of heavenly love is burning brightly in many hearts, and the true missionary spirit . . . is growing more intense as the days go by, and God is honoring the efforts put forth in His name and giving precious souls."[83] Furthermore, this passion for missions at home was matched by a continued thrust for world evangelism.

Africa

This was signaled with the departure of two missionaries from GBS for Africa on January 2, 1902—less than a month after Knapp's death. These were Beatrice Finney, member of GBS's founding faculty, and Elizabeth Ferle, sister to Minnie Ferle Knapp.[84] They joined the William Hirst family in Africa on February 12, 1902 and helped them begin in earnest the work of "God's Bible School" in Africa, which had an enrollment of forty-five within a couple of months.[85] While Finney returned to the United States after a few years where she continued to support GBS,[86] Elizabeth Ferle met and married an Australian immigrant, Charles Rodway, in 1904.[87] They eventually established a work under the auspices of the International Apostolic Holiness Union in 1908 "at Mt. Frere on the Transkei Native Reserve in Cape Province," where a church and "an industrial arts high school for girls was established."[88]

Meanwhile, several other missionaries followed the Hirsts and Ferle and Finney to South Africa over the next few years. Among these were GBS alumni James and Jesse Hundley, who set sail on September 2, 1903, after a tour of deputation during which they were accompanied by Mrs. Knapp.[89] Also sailing with the Hundleys were Rev. and Mrs. Albert A. Miller, and son Paul, missionaries from the Church of Emmanuel in Providence, Rhode Island, where Seth Rees had pastored. The Miller's inclusion in the Hundley's party signaled an important development in GBS/Revivalist mission endeavors, as they were but two of several missionaries from the Church of Emmanuel to benefit from the support of the Revivalist family.[90]

In 1904, a successful revival meeting in Port Elizabeth convinced James Hundley that this was the open door he had been seeking, and this provided the "center for the work" in South Africa by 1907.[91] At this time, Fred T. Fuge, who had been serving as a pastor and evangelist in the United States, was appointed as superintendent of this field.[92] Fuge was a master communicator whom Paul Rees described "as a preacher who had an eye for the unusual, a tongue for the eloquent, and a heart for the immensities."[93] His messages and writings drew from his colorful seafaring and ministerial experiences as well as from a "wide acquaintance with literature, art, history, science, and theology."[94] His ministry in South Africa proved successful almost immediately, with a three-month tent meeting in early 1908 which won numerous converts, seventeen of which "entered into Christian service."[95] Fuge's leadership profoundly influenced the future direction of African holiness missions, particularly Pilgrim Holiness and Nazarene, by inaugurating a new era of organizational advance, so that posterity in the Pilgrim Holiness Church recognized him as "perhaps the man who had the greatest influence in bringing a sense of direction and permanence to the early South African work."[96]

Under Fuge's charge, the number of holiness missionaries in South Africa swelled until, by 1912, "at least twenty-three missionaries were associated with the Port Elizabeth work." While "not all came from God's Bible School," they "were united by common holiness convictions" and GBS alumni were among the most outstanding workers.[97] Several of these ultimately left the mission base at Port Elizabeth and took the holiness message into the interior of the continent

A few of these remain particularly noteworthy, among them being Lula Glatzel. Although Glatzel had received a call to Africa, she felt the need of educational preparation, but this seemed "impossible" until God "opened the way" for her to attend God's Bible School in 1906, strengthening her faith that "His promises are true." Her training at GBS, though only for one school year, left an indelible impression, as she reflected, "The nine months at 'God's Bible School' will never be forgotten."[98]

On May 5, 1907, at only eighteen years of age, she and a party of eight other GBS alumni, including Marietta ("Etta") Innis, set sail from New York city, bound for Africa.[99] Before embarking, they discovered that they were not the only holiness missionaries to take this voyage, and they were joined by Harmon Schmelzenbach from Peniel Bible College in Peniel, Texas.[99] Some of the missionaries disembarked earlier, but Schmelzenbach, Glatzel, and Innis continued on to Port Elizabeth, and joined in the work led by Fred

Fuge,[100] with "Miss Innis preaching among the white people and holding street corner meetings, a thing unheard of for a [woman] to do in those days," but with "a fruitful ministry."[101]

While laboring there, Bible study drew Schmelzenbach's attention to the statement that "one [shall] chase a thousand, and two put ten thousand to flight" (Deut. 32:30). This led him to conclude that "if he were married, his effectiveness as a missionary would be increased 10-fold," so, on June 19, 1908, one year and one day after they arrived in Africa, Lula Glatzel and Harmon Schmelzenbach were united in marriage in his home in Port Elizabeth by Rev. Fuge, to whom they looked as "their spiritual father."[102] Harmon and Lula Schmelzenbach's real passion was for the inland tribes, and "their honeymoon was spent traveling inland to new areas of labor."[103] Their lack of sponsorship by a "recognized denomination" created difficulty with tribal work, so they settled for a time in Natal. While there, Harmon received word that his sponsoring congregation at Peniel had joined the fledgling Nazarene denomination and also received an invitation to "open a mission in Africa under its name," although, consistent with the radical holiness emphasis on faith missions, "no financial support was promised." Harmon readily agreed, having already been "convinced of the inherent weaknesses of independent missions."[104]

With "four donkeys, a small wagon, and basic supplies," Harmon and Lulu set out to establish a Nazarene work in "an area where the gospel had never been preached before."[105] They settled upon Swaziland, which Fuge described as "the darkest and the most needy of all South Africa's mission fields" with natives reputed to be "in filth and immorality . . . lower than the beast of the field," even stooping to "kill their own children and take certain parts of their little bodies to make fertilizer."[106] In December 1910, the Schmelzenbachs, with their infant son David in tow, finally arrived in northern Swaziland, after an exhausting journey of five hundred miles, over treacherous terrain inhabited by the dreaded crocodile and numerous other dangers. Here they were soon joined by Etta Innis, who had also joined the Nazarenes.[107]

The work was established slowly and in the face of monumental difficulties including the deaths of four of the Schmelzenbachs' children and staunch resistance by Swazi witch doctors; in fact, "it was not until 1913 that the Schmelzenbachs won their first converts."[108] However, these pioneer missionaries remained faithful, and by the time of Harmon's death in 1929 the results were astounding—one of the great legacies of holiness missions—with "twenty-four missionaries, located at seven mission stations, plus 143 African workers were preaching, teaching, and nursing for the Lord. There were 110 organized churches with an estimated membership of 3,000. A hospital, several day schools, two Bible schools, and four annual camp meetings in various areas were reaching many thousands of people."[109]

Other notable missionaries to Africa from GBS included the Fred De Weerd family and the Charles Slater family, who "arrived together on February 19, 1909" at Port Elizabeth, and formed "an energetic and effective singing-and-preaching team and were signally blessed in their evangelism among the European peoples." In a move indicative of the model that GBS provided on the African field, "it wasn't long after arriving that they were publishing holiness tracts and books, and a publication was launched under the editorship of the DeWeerds known as *Africa's Revivalist*."[110] In fact, De Weerd credited his success to an event that took place in "those blessed School days" on the "Mount of Blessings"—his experience of entire sanctification, which came after he had been alone with God "for thirty-six hours, waiting, weeping, dying out" and crying "from the depths of [his] heart a final, everlasting Yes."[111]

Charles Slater had also "diligently . . . sought and obtained the experience of sanctification" at GBS, and "manifested a unique singleness of heart the remainder of his happy, useful, victorious life," as well as the flexibility that mission work often requires, even going to the West Indies for a time when that door opened and his chosen field of Africa had been temporarily closed.[112] Eventually leaving Port Elizabeth, he and his wife Maude moved their family to pioneer the International Apostolic Holiness work in Swaziland, settling at a site they called "Ebenezer" on June 28, 1910. Among the hardships they endured was the death of their eight-month old son, Charles Livingston, who had "the first Christian burial in that section of Swaziland.[113]

After several years of faithful service in South Africa, the Slaters returned to the United States just prior to the outbreak of World War I. However, this was hardly the end of Charles' service to missions. Indeed, he became a true "missionary evangelist," conducting extensive campaigns in the Caribbean, as well as meetings in Mexico, Venezuela, Japan, Korea, China, India, Egypt, and England.[114] In addition, he evangelized and represented missions throughout the United States, and helped strengthen the Pilgrim Holiness Church as a "general field secretary" and as an Assistant General Superintendent.[115] However, in large measure his heart remained in South Africa, where he returned for a remarkable evangelistic tour in 1949, which garnered a harvest of at least 6,757 souls and ended with Slater's death, as he collapsed with a coronary thrombosis. Even then, a "wicked man who saw him breathe his last repented on the spot," a fitting memorial to a life devoted to winning the lost.[116]

Not all mission endeavors in Africa by GBS alumni were so closely tied to the alma mater as those of the Slaters and De Weerds, or even those of Glatzel and Innis. Again, in an era when missionaries committed to radical faith often "went out" instead of being "sent out," numerous GBS alumni initiated independent works or missions that were only later (if ever) assumed as denominational works. Perhaps the most outstanding of these was the orphanage begun by Lillian Hunt Trasher in Egypt.

Trasher, a convert from Roman Catholicism, was naturally gifted as an artist, and planned on pursuing a career as an illustrator, but sensed God leading her to devote her life to Christian service. In 1905, at the age of eighteen, she entered GBS where she studied under "godly teachers" for two years.[117] Upon completion of her studies, she traveled to Marion, North Carolina, where she assisted Miss Mattie Perry in her orphanage.[118] At the time, Lillian was engaged to be married to "a fine young minister." Her wedding date was less than two weeks away when "the voice of God spoke to her 23-year-old heart with unmistakable clarity: *I want you to go to Africa.*" Her fiancé "had not heard this call," so Lillian ended the engagement.[119]

She prepared to leave for Africa, "in the face of her family's strong disapproval."[120] Furthermore, although Mattie Perry was supportive with a letter of recommendation, Lillian had no mission board or denominational support; in fact, she began the trip toward Egypt "with only five dollars in her possession."[121] However, several remarkable provisions of funds convinced her that God was in her call (or as she liked to term it, her "permit") to Egypt.[122] On October 8, 1910, the day she set sail from New York, she received additional affirmation when someone suggested that "she open her Bible and ask God for a verse of Scripture appropriate to the hour. She did so and the first verse she saw was Acts 7:34 '. . . I have seen the affliction of my people which is in Egypt, and I have heard their groanings and am come down to deliver them. *And now come, I will send thee into Egypt'*."[123] Indeed, there she would devote fifty-one years, serving without furlough from 1929 to 1954.[124]

Lillian had not arrived in Egypt with plans to establish an orphanage. However, a dying mother left her starving baby in Trasher's keeping, and Lillian realized her training at Perry's orphanage had given her invaluable experience in the much needed care of orphans. So, "she rented a house and started an orphanage in Assiout, Egypt (230 miles south of Cairo)."[125] She depended on God to provide her ministry's needs, claiming Psalm 37:25 and saying, "Lord, You furnish the bread, and I'll care for the children," a plan which never failed.[126]

Within a year, eight children were in her care and the work grew until in 1955, "her family numbered 1,200."[127] Across those years, in which she endured many hardships and threats, including a plan by Arab terrorists to murder her, more than eight thousand children were reared in the orphanage, with many going on to assume "places of responsibility in the government and the professional disciplines."[128] Affectionately known to her "family" as "Mamma Lillian," she became famous world-wide as "the Nile mother"—a title given her by journalist Jerome Beatty, who asserted, *"Egypt is a land of wonders, but to me its greatest is Miss Lillian Trasher."*[129] Perhaps a tribute paid by an Islamic official reflects best the depth of love and high esteem with which the people of Egypt regarded her—"I believe that when she dies, in spite of the fact she is a woman and a Christian, God will take her directly to paradise."[130]

Asia

Although the far-reaching work of Oriental Missionary Society (OMS), initiated before Knapp's death, has already been cited as a prominent example of the success of Knapp's "Pentecostal experiment," this and some other elements of GBS/Revivalist outreach to Asia bear further mention. For one thing, as already briefly alluded, another set of GBS-supported missionaries, E. A. (Ernest Albert) and Julia Kilbourne, joined Charles and Lettie Cowman in Japan in the fall of 1902 and are thus considered co-founders of OMS.[131] They eventually traveled to Seoul where, with the assistance of the John Thomas family from Wales, they helped to establish the Bible Training School which became the nucleus of OMS work in Korea.[132] In 1917, the Kilbournes returned to the United States where he "assumed administrative leadership" of OMS in 1918 "and, following the death of Charles Cowman in 1924, was named president, a position he held until his death."[133]

The Kilbournes' involvement also illustrates the dynamic fluidity of radical holiness missions at the time. While the Bible-School Mission in Tokyo was considered "the Japanese branch of God's Bible School," and the OMS leaders "considered themselves independent missionaries . . . yet E. A. Kilbourne claimed that they became representatives of the International Apostolic Holiness Union."[134] In fact, OMS remained "the missionary outlet for the Orient" for the constituents of both the Union and GBS for many years.[135] Confusion results from anachronistic attempts to separate the loyalties of the missionaries or their supporters among the various organizations at this early date, because in their infancy the Union, GBS, and OMS were simply varying institutional manifestations of the radical holiness evangelistic impulse, and many of their constituents identified with all three (and even more) organizations. It was not until significant conflict and clarification that revolved around the GBS trustees that the organizations and their constituencies began the process of divergence.

Perhaps the most significant methodological contribution to missions made by the GBS/Revivalist supported work in the Far East was the Kilbourne's and Cowman's emphasis on developing a "native" ministry. In 1909, Kilbourne asserted,

> God has already set His seal to the work of the *native* ministry in Korea. Hitherto the foreign missionary has been the evangelist and pastor, but he has discovered how he may multiply himself many times by training the native converts . . . resulting in a creditable addition to the ministry of the Lord's work . . . Korea is ripe for the work of holiness, and the Koreans make good preachers when filled with the Holy Ghost and the Word of God."[136]

Cowman concurred and worked to see other missionaries become "fully convinced that God's plan for the evangelization of the Orient was through her own people."[137] This explains in large part the motivation to duplicate GBS with Bible schools throughout the Far East. It also doubtless proved one of the factors in the phenomenal growth of OMS throughout its first century, particularly in Korea. In addition, the Kilbournes' and Cowmans' emphasis on equipping nationals to establish indigenous works was then a cutting-edge concept that only became standard practice with missiologists decades later, and would prove invaluable in countries eventually closed to missionaries, such as China.

The dawn of radical holiness outreach to Chinese evidently began in Japan as Juji Nakada and the Cowmans evangelized several Chinese who were there for educational purposes.[138] E. A. Kilbourne also carried a burden for evangelizing China, going back to his call to foreign missions, in which he had a vision of "a highway stretching from Chicago to San Francisco, arching across the Pacific to Tokyo, extending from there to Seoul and on to Shanghai. Consequently, he regarded China as God's ultimate destination for the young missionary society."[139] However, the first missionaries to take the radical holiness message to China were not under the auspices of OMS initially.

Elbridge and Minnie Munroe, both GBS alumni, "like the Cowmans (or like Abraham who followed God in blind faith, whose example they felt they had emulated) sailed for China without denominational backing and with no friends to meet them, no knowledge of Chinese, and with 'very little means'."[140] Regardless, upon their arrival in 1903 they established an independent work in Hong Kong, and went on to establish the South China Holiness Mission in Canton, a work that deeply impressed the Cowmans and Oswald Chambers who visited it while traveling together in 1907.[141] Like their OMS counterparts, the Munroes saw the need to prepare native ministers, and soon established the South China Holiness Bible School. Common goals and philosophy eventually led to the "absorption" of the Munroes' work by OMS, with the Cowmans explaining to the *Revivalist* family in February 1909: "Brother and Sister Munroe have desired that their Holiness Mission in China be united with ours, so feeling it to be of God, their work has now become a branch of this."[142] Meanwhile, E. R. Munroe continued to serve as representative of the "China Branch" of *God's Revivalist*, again underscoring the mutual fellowship and support of GBS and OMS.

In addition to the works under OMS auspices, the other focus for Asian missions among the early GBS/Revivalist constituency continued to be India. Gorham Tufts was joined in his work by A. Lee Grey and his family who left GBS for the field in September 1903.[143] Over the next few years they were joined by such GBS alumni as Miriam Miller (1905); Thaddeus L. Vaughan (1905); and Bertha E. Cox (1906).[144] Although "permanent" institutional developments from their endeavors did not result, their ministry played an important part in keeping India before the *Revivalist* constituency.[145]

In particular, Vaughan's brief ministry in India served to inspire the entire GBS/Revivalist family. In many ways he reflected the ideals championed at the school, testifying that it was at GBS that he "received the Holy Ghost, and settled it for time and eternity that God could have His way with" him.[146] It was also at GBS, "during a prayer-meeting which continued about four hours, that he received his call to India." A *Revivalist* writer recalled that though he was "tested and tried at home" before embarking for India, "all we ever heard of him was "VICTORY." However, Vaughan would be immortalized in the annals of GBS missions endeavors as the school's first missionary martyr, perishing of an unnamed ailment that caused him extreme suffering for a week. Shortly before his passing on January 21, 1908, he told a fellow missionary: "I do not know but that I may pass over the river before morning. But if I do, I shall stoop down and take a drink the first thing. I shall drink fresh from the Rock." Little wonder that the GBS family's zeal for souls was kindled further by his example, as the *Revivalist* proclaimed, "His courage and boldness urge us to press harder than ever toward the goal."[147]

The Caribbean and South America

Another region that quickly captured the interest of GBS constituents was the "West Indies." The first GBS-supported missionaries to the area were C. O. Moulton and his wife, who were also sent off in the farewell service in New York in which Beatrice Finney and Elizabeth Ferle were seen off to Africa, with the latter leaving in the morning and the Moultons departing in the evening of the same day. Although the Moultons were "sent out under the Portsmouth (R. I.) Camp-meeting," of which Seth Rees was president, the association with Rees also brought Moulton the support of the International Apostolic Holiness Union and the *Revivalist*.[148]

"Moulton had been a newspaperman in New England and proved to be a 'go-getter' in the West Indies," even though he frequently suffered extreme deprivation, going "without food because of the lack of money . . ."[149] He established a successful work named the "Christian Mission" on St. Kitts and Saba, and encouraged the development of national leadership there and at Barbados, to which he journeyed in 1904. The Christian Mission at Barbados "was indigenous to the core, paid rents and other minor expenses with local offerings, and recognized the ability of the West Indians."

Moulton still realized the need for additional missionaries and gave an appeal at the 1905 Salvation Park Camp Meeting for others to come to his assistance.[150] Among the respondents was young John Corrigan and his wife, who had superintended the work on the mission boat at Shantyville. They sailed for Barbados in December 1907 and were quickly assigned to the work at Georgetown, British Guiana.[151] However, Corrigan's mission term was short-lived, for he succumbed to a tropical fever and died within two weeks of his arrival at Georgetown, becoming the second GBS martyr in the cause of world missions.[152] Then, less than two years later on January 27, 1909, at only thirty-six years of age, Moulton died, reportedly of a "broken heart," and was buried next to Corrigan.[153]

Moulton's influence would linger, especially through his converts, one of the most noteworthy being Irene Blyden, a young lady from the island of Saba.[154] She traveled to GBS, where she studied "from about 1905-1909."[155] While a student, she threw herself into evangelistic outreach, ministering with powerful results at Shantytown and during the 1909 camp meeting, with Oswald Chambers observing that she had "the voice and presence of a good preacher, and [that] the Lord witnessed to her message.[156] Upon graduation, she returned to the Caribbean, pausing before her voyage long enough to pen words of gratitude to Mrs. Knapp, "To Him be praise for every day, hour and minute spent in '*God's* Bible School'. I look back without a single regret; but if I could, I would do it all over again. There was not one lesson too hard, or test too great, or a rule to severe. All we took in Him as His divine plan for us."[157]

This resilient dedication was evident throughout the remainder of Blyden's life. Shortly after returning to her home island, she received a call as a missionary to Nevis, located two islands to the south, and "gave a lifetime of fruitful and respected ministry."[158] Here in 1919 she married Richard Alfred Taylor, an alumnus of GBS, originally from the island of St. Kitts. Both shouldering tremendous responsibilities, they "were always rightfully considered as a part of the missionary staff."[159] After their deaths, they were acknowledged as having been "respected and beloved by more people in Nevis than anyone else known to the present generation." In addition, their four children (Katherine, Ira, Wingrove, and Marie) would grow up to "proclaim Christian holiness across the islands and around the world."[160] Of special import to GBS has been A. Wingrove Taylor, who would later follow in his parents footsteps as a student on the Hilltop.

When Irene Blyden returned home from GBS, she traveled in a missionary party in which Rev. and Mrs. James M. Taylor were also members.[161] He soon became leader of the loyal remnants of Moulton's work which he reorganized, and this became solidly identified with the Holiness Union by the end of 1911, assuring a continued link to GBS for many years.[162] This tie was strengthened by missionaries with strong GBS connections such as O. L. King, as well as several GBS alumni who served in various capacities throughout the Caribbean well past the half-century mark.

Among early alumni contributing to the Caribbean field were missionary evangelists Charles Slater and R. G. Finch, who held numerous campaigns throughout the region.[163] GBS has likely never produced any other graduates more passionate about missions than these two men. Like Slater, Finch received his entire sanctification at GBS, but in a most unusual location—"by a bath tub in the men's dormitory."[164] After a short period of pastoral work, he entered evangelism and proved remarkably effective.[165]

His first tour of the Caribbean was made in 1912 in the company of James Taylor, who persuaded him to become the field's superintendent. The Finch family remained there for several years, enduring severe hardships including the death of their son Daniel in 1919. Following his return from the Caribbean, Finch's passion for missions resulted in his appointment in 1922 as General Superintendent of Foreign Missions in the Pilgrim Holiness Church, a position he held until 1930, when he was appointed "general evangelist," a further recognition of him as "an outstanding spiritual figure."[166] Eventually, concern over cultural accommodation by large segments of the Pilgrim Holiness constituency led Finch to leave the denomination and form the Emmanuel Association; however, his zeal for holiness evangelism and missions never waned. And, he never forgot his indebtedness to GBS, reflecting in a biography, "These days spent at God's Bible School I have never gotten over. My only sorrow is that they were so few . . ."[167]

Crowned with Victory

An apt motif describing the early evangelistic endeavors radiating from the Mount of Blessings would simply be one word—VICTORY. This was not only the fitting epitaph of Thaddeus Vaughan, but also portrays the faith and ambitions of numerous students who left the Hilltop to engage in the battle for souls, not only on foreign soil, but also across the United States. In fact, several alumni from the early years of the school rendered distinguished service to Christ across this country, many as "pastors, evangelists, teachers, slum workers" and as workers in rescue homes, city missions, and orphanages.[168]

Their ministries gave ample evidence of the success of Knapp's Pentecostal experiment, especially reflecting the value of the experience they gained through such enterprises as George Street Mission, of which George Kulp contended, "It is not only a Bible School plant, but it is a real training school for Bible School students where they can work and pray and get an experience as altar workers, that is so much needed . . ."[169]

For example, the Frank Leischers took the practical skills honed in soul-winning work at George Street Mission with them to Denver, Colorado, where Frank pastored the People's Mission Church and was "abundant in labors, 'full of good works,' and won many souls for the kingdom."[170] Likewise, Catherine Stephenson, who had been "a faithful student" while at GBS, found her experience there and later as "an efficient missionary in connection with Hope Cottage" invaluable preparation for both home and foreign evangelistic endeavors as she labored with her husband, Charles Stalker, GBS's "former 'round-the-world' missionary'."[171]

The success of some alumni in the evangelistic field eventually led to ecclesiastical advancement, reflecting the priority placed on effective evangelistic preaching in the early holiness movement. A typical illustration appears in the career of W. B. (Walter) Dunkum (GBS, 1903-06), who periodically reported results of his campaigns, which were often "crowned with victory,"[172] to his alma mater, of which he wrote, "I thank God that He ever permitted me to attend His Bible School."[173] Following the pattern of such evangelists as W. B. Godbey and Bud Robinson, he authored numerous books and booklets, including *Heart Talks from Beulah Land*, *Rolling Shot*, and *"Hot Potatoes with Jackets On."*[174] Before long, Dunkum had a reputation as "a spiritual giant, master theologian, profound thinker and a Biblical preacher."[175] Within a few years after leaving GBS, he began working at the Kingswood Holiness College in Kingswood, Kentucky, where he served as president for a time.[176] Later, he helped pioneer the Wesleyan Methodist Connection in Kentucky, and served as its conference president in 1924-25 and 1931-32.[177]

Other early alumni that entered leadership positions and significantly impacted the development of their ecclesiastical fellowship were George W. Smith (at GBS from 1901 to 1905 and 1908-1909) and Everett A. Keaton (at GBS from 1908-1909). Both men attained prominent positions in the Church of Christ in Christian Union, with Smith serving as editor of the *Church of*

Christ Advocate and secretary of the General Council and Keaton serving for thirty consecutive years as moderator. Keaton also reflects the impact of George Street Mission as a recruiting station for students, for it was as a young convert that he made his way into the mission and experienced entire sanctification after falling under deep conviction, which he passionately described in his testimony published in the *Church of Christ Advocate,*

> It was holiness or hell, sanctification or damnation. . . . I fell at the mercy seat, and poured out my soul to God; but O, how the "old man" does hate to die and give up his place to the "new man." I don't know how long I was praying through, but I was surrounded by a number of noble young men who stayed with me, praying and doing all they could until victory came in sweeping power, completely eradicating the "old man" and filling my soul with "the sanctification" without which I would never have seen a heavenly home."[178]

Such witness was a powerful stimulus for many to accept holiness teaching in the South Ohio Annual Council of the Christian Union, and may have been responsible in part for the formation of the Church of Christ in Christian Union as a distinct holiness body, committed to what some termed "Cincinnati religion" because of its association with GBS.[179]

Several students from this era would also go on, as Nettie Peabody and M. G. Standley had, to provide valuable service to GBS itself. Among these were W. W. (William Webster) Holland (student—1904-06), who became Dean of Theology, Elmer G. Marsh (student—1910-12), who served on the staff 1913-68, including from 1961-65 as president, and C. B. (Charles Brenton) Widmeyer (student—1902-04), who served as instructor from 1945 to 1948. Holland, who arrived at GBS on December 31, 1901, from his home in Maryland, possessed a gift for writing that was soon discovered by the *Revivalist* staff, and he contributed several articles reflective of the typical experiences of a student, from homesickness to answers to prayer, and from "great victories in the lunch stand" during camp meeting to progress at George Street Mission, where he reported, "Victory is on our banners and we are marching on. Hallelujah!"[180]

Prior to his years on the faculty at GBS, Widmeyer had a fruitful and colorful ministry that indicates just how versatile the skills of early GBS alumni often were. After completing his studies at GBS, he formed the evangelistic team of Chaffin, Widmeyer, and DeWare with a couple of fellow students. They sang and played instruments as well as preached, and were privileged to work on occasion with such seasoned evangelists as Seth C. Rees.[181] They also functioned as an informal public relations team for GBS, allowing congregations to witness first-hand some "samples of the School."[182] Congregants soon found that they possessed the same fire for which the Hilltop was known, a fact that some found disquieting, as reflected in a report sent from a meeting in Kansas: "The Lord gave blessed victory despite the prejudice . . . Somebody made this remark, 'I love those boys' singing and playing, but I don't like the hell they preach'."[183]

Widmeyer's subsequent career included teaching at Hutchinson Bible School in Kansas, where he also served as a superintendent in the International Apostolic Holiness Church. He became president of the Hutchinson school in 1909 and about that time joined the Nazarene denomination. This was only the first of several presidencies, including Western Holiness College—1909-1912 (forerunner of People's Bible College), Oklahoma Holiness College—1915-20 (forerunner of Southern Nazarene University), and Pasadena College—1923-26 (now Point Loma Nazarene University). In addition, Widmeyer "served as a pastor and district superintendent in the Church of the Nazarene" and gave twenty-five years of service as a member of the denomination's Board of Education.[184]

Concurrent with much of his other ministry, he taught at several holiness schools. However, the work for which posterity most remembers Widmeyer is his song writing, which produced over four hundred gospel songs, the best known of which are "Come and Dine" and "In the New Jerusalem."[185] In important ways, these songs encapsulate the emphases Widmeyer imbibed at GBS—aggressive soul-winning and expectant faith—both essential elements in the on-going effort to push the battle for victory.

Notes

[1] Oswald Chambers, "A Great and Blessed Season," *Revivalist* (Jan. 17, 1907), 5.

[2] Cited in Belle Staples, "Bible School Notes," *Revivalist* (Nov. 11, 1909), 13 (original emphasis).

[3] "Trustees Chosen," *Revivalist* (Dec. 19, 1901), 12.

[4] "Words from God's Ministers," *Revivalist* (Jan. 16, 1902), 5.

[5] Mrs. M. W. Knapp, "To the Revivalist Family," *Revivalist* (Jan. 16, 1902), 2.

[6] "Our First Faith Venture," *Revivalist* (Jan. 5, 1905), 12.

[7] "The Bible-School," *Revivalist* (Jan. 2, 1902), 13 (original emphasis). On the problem with over-crowding that the new building helped to alleviate, see "Room for All" and "Overflowing," *Revivivalist* (Dec. 12, 1901), 12.

[8] "A Retrospect," *Revivalist* (Aug. 7, 1902), 5.

[9] Black, "Ten Weeks Building," *Revivalist* (May 19, 1983), 10. See also, Day, 49-50. This structure was "demolished in 1974 to make way for the present student center." However, a brick wall inside the entry of the student center was constructed from remnants of the old building (Don Davison, Larry D. Smith, and Jon Plank, *Discover GBS! A Self-Guided Campus Tour* (Cincinnati: God's Bible School and College, 2000), 12.

[10] "The Steam Heating Plant" and "The Engine," *Revivalist* (Jan. 5, 1905), 19-20.

[11] *God's Bible School and Missionary Training Home Catalogue 1933-1934*, 5-7 (original emphases). See also, M. G. Standley, *My Life*, 64-69. While dormitory and dining facilities were available for use by camp meeting as Standley had prayed, the remainder of the building was completed in 1903, with a special service for "the laying of the cornerstone of the engine" held in the spring ("Bible-School Notes," *Revivalist* (June 4, 1903), 15).

[12] "Bible-School Notes," *Revivalist* (June 5, 1902), 15.

[13] "Bible School Notes," *Revivialist* (July 15, 1909), 12. See also Moser and Smith, 61.

[14] "Electric Shocks, No. 6: Salvation Park Campmeeting, 1904," in *Revivalist* (Sept. 15, 1904), 11. This data comes from Mary Storey's "talk" during camp meeting.

[15] Day (73) gives the number as 3014; however, the figure may actually be higher since some "students" who took in classes for a brief time (such as Godbey's lectures before camp meeting) may not have been formally "enrolled."

[16] See Day, 52 and "From God's Bible-School Home Circle," *Revivalist* (April 17, 1902), 15. For just one example of the impact of the early GBS correspondence courses, see Bertha Smith, *How the Spirit Filled My Life* (Nashville: Broadman Press, 1973), 23-24. For Smith, "the Bible became a new book," as she studied one of the courses. Smith went on to become a distinguished missionary with the Foreign Mission Board of the Southern Baptist Convention, going to China in 1917. She served until she was captured by the Japanese who interned her in 1941. "Repatriated in 1942, she returned to China after the war and worked until 1948 when she was forced out by the communists. She then moved to Formosa [Taiwan] to help establish Southern Baptist work there, where she served until her retirement in 1961"

(from book cover).

[17] Day, 68. Although Day indicates this began in 1901, the article cited below indicates that the "New Testament" school for children was to begin in the fall of 1902.

[18] "Bible School Notes," *Revivalist* (June 19, 1902), 15. This article contains a report on a sermon in which Standley unburdened his heart to the GBS family concerning the responsibility to provide Christian education for children.

[19] "One Peep," *Revivalist* (Oct. 19, 1906), 16 and "Bible School Notes," *Revivalist* (Nov. 9, 1905), 13. See also E. H. Lewis, "Children's Pentecostal School at the 'Mount of Blessings'," *Revivalist* (Sept. 19, 1907), 7 and Sister Scott, "Pentecostal School Opening At 'Mount of Blessings'," *Revivalist* (Oct. 10, 1907), 10.

[20] Day, 56. See also Glenn D. Black, "The Old Tabernacle," *Revivalist* (May 19, 1983), 10 and "God's Printing Office," *Revivalist* (Jan. 5, 1905), 23-26. The last article describes the acquisition of a printing press which would sell for $5000 if new for only $1500 in answer to prayer. For a photograph of the printing department personnel, taken around 1908, see "Archives," *Revivalist* (Sept. 1995), 12.

[21] See "Door of Hope," *Revivalist* (Nov. 28, 1901), 12 and a sketch of the proposed structure in the *Revivalist* (Jan. 23, 1902), 16),

[22] "The Rescue Home" (2) and "A Larger Rescue Field" (3), *Revivalist* (May 15, 1902).

[23] "The Rescue Home," *Revivalist* (May 15, 1902), 2.

[24] *Redeemed by the Blood*, 29. Also, see "Mother" Duff, "Julia's Triumphant Home-Going," *Revivalist* (Oct. 18, 1906), 14.

[25] For example, see "Bible-School Notes," *Revivalist* (May 29, 1902), 15, "Bible-School Notes," *Revivalist* (June 26, 1902), 15, "Jubilee Day," *Revivalist* (May 18, 1905), 1-5 and "Thanksgiving Morning at Hope Cottage," *Revivalist* (Dec. 21, 1905), 5.

[26] "Jubilee Day," *Revivalist* (May 18, 1905), 1-5.

[27] Much of her book's material appeared in *God's Revivalist* during the spring of 1905. See the issues beginning with April 6, 1905.

[28] Day, 71.

[29] *Redeemed by the Blood*, 233.

[30] Thomas and Thomas, 69 and "Bible-School Notes," *Revivalist* (Dec. 17, 1903), 15 and "The Missionaries' Farewell," *Revivalist* (Feb. 2, 1911), 8. Also, see "Plum Street Mission Work," *Revivalist* (March 31, 1904), 15.

[31] "Bible School Notes," *Revivalist* (April 21, 1904), 14-15. The mission apparently first relocated to 220 George Street, then later to 330 George Street. For a good photograph of the latter location, see page one of *God's Revivalist* (May 5, 1910).

[32] See "Victory at George St. Mission," *Revivalist* (April 27, 2006), 14 and "God's Bible School Notes," *Revivalist* (April 28, 1909), 11. For typical reports of the mission's successes about this time, see "Salvation Still Flowing at George Street Mission," *Revivalist* (Dec. 29, 1904), 15, and "Report of City Mission," *Revivalist* (March 2, 1905), 14.

[33] "George Street Mission," *Revivalist* (Feb. 9, 1905), 15.

[34] "Do You Want A Share?" *Revivalist* (Sept. 28, 1905), 1.

[35] Lew W. Standley, "God's Bible School Mission on George St --- A Great

Work," *Revivalist* (April 9, 1908), 1.

[36] Lew W. Standley, "George Street Bible School Mission," *Revivalist* (Aug. 26, 1909), 16.

[37] Day, 71-72.

[38] "God's Bible School Mission on George Street," *Revivalist* (Dec. 10, 1908), 6.

[39] "At George Street Mission Thanksgiving Night," *Revivalist* (Dec. 14, 1905), 13-15. See also, "George Street Mission Thanksgiving Evening," *Revivalist* (Dec. 16, 1909), 14 and several articles in the same issue of the Revivalist that deal with GBS Thanksgiving activities, including the dinner on the Mount of Blessings.

For the Holiness synthesis of social and spiritual reclamation, especially in the context of Lew Standley's ministry at George Street Mission, see Larry D. Smith, "Soup, Soap, and Salvation," in Moser and Smith, 145, 150-153. Also, see Rodney Layne Reed, *Holy With Integrity: The Unity of Personal and Social Ethics in the Holiness Movement, 1880-1910*.

[40] As with so many of the techniques used in the early days of GBS, the idea of "wagon evangelism" goes back to the days of Knapp. It appears that the idea originated with an unidentified correspondent with Knapp who initially proposed to take such a wagon, emblazoned with the words "Holiness unto the Lord" and "Scripture texts in golden letters," across the country. While this more ambitious plan was apparently discarded, GBS evidently adapted it for local use. "Gospel-Wagon Evangelism," *Revivalist* (Dec. 13, 1900), 4. For photographs of the original Eternity Wagon and the motorized version, see Moser and Smith, 70-71 and 151, respectively.

[41] "Home Missionary Work," *Revivalist* (Jan. 5, 1905), 27-28.

[42] Day, 73-74.

[43] "Bible-School Notes," *Revivalist* (June 5, 1902), 14.

[44] "Cincinnati Slums at Night," *Revivalist* (May 15, 1902), 12. Such reports missed no opportunity to decry more socially-acceptable forms of worldliness like church socials that might incline young people to start down the path of degeneracy. For a typical report of the economic/social assistance offered to the poor, see "Scene in the West End," *Revivalist* (Jan. 15, 1903), 5.

[45] "Rat and Sausage Rows," *Revivalist* (May 15, 1902), 12.

[46] Thomas Wright, "The Work at Shantytown," *Revivalist* (June 1, 1905), 4.

[47] "Despise Not the Day of Small Things: Sister Storey's Talk; Bible-School Day, at Salvation Park Camp: Reported by B[essie] S[tandley]," *Revivalist* (Aug. 6, 1903), 12.

[48] "Home Mission Work, 1905, 28) For photographs of the boat's interior, see Moser and Smith, 59. For an exterior photograph, see the *Revivalist* (June 1, 1905), 5.

[49] For Wright's testimony, including how he was entirely sanctified at GBS under the influence of W. B. Godbey, see Thomas Wright, "Redeemed," *Revivalist* (June 1, 1905), 10-11.

[50] "Shantytown," *Revivalist* (July 28, 1904), 14.

[51] "Shantytown," *Revivalist* (June 16, 1904), 11. The average attendance of the Sunday School by January 1905 was "about sixty" ("Home Mission . . .") For representative reports from the Sunday School and other Shantytown activities, see Brother Wright, "Victory at Shantytown," *Revivalist* (Dec. 29, 1904), 14; "Hallelujah Testimonies: From Shantytown Sunday School, Feb. 19, 1905," *Revivalist* (March

16, 1905), 5; and Thomas Wright, "Victory Down By the River," *Revivalist* (April 27, 1905), 13. For a description of the Sunday School's schedule, see "Shantytown Sunday-School," *Revivalist* (Feb. 4, 1909), 13.

[52] John A. Corrigan, "East End Mission—Shantyville," *Revivalist* (June 1, 1905), 3-4. Also, see "Shantyville," *Revivalist* (May 4, 1905), 13. For a photograph of this boat, see Moser and Smith, 58.

[53] While George Street Mission was a rescue mission open twenty-four hours per day, other GBS missions tended to be more on the order of store-front churches. For further descriptions of the individual works, see the May 4, 1905 and June 1, 1905 issues of *God's Revivalist*.

[54] "Bible-School Notes, *Revivalist* (June 12, 1902), 14. For a report on the following trial, at which M. G. Standley spoke in defense of the student, see "Bible-School Notes," *Revivalist* (June 26, 1902), 15.

[55] "A Full Salvation Campaign," *Revivalist* (June 1, 1905), 1.

[56] See M. G. Standley's account in *My Life*, 84-88, and, in edited form, in Moser and Smith, 32-33.

[57] "A Full Salvation Campaign," *Revivalist* (June 1, 1905), 1.

[58] M. G. Standley, *My Life*, 86.

[59] "A Full Salvation Campaign," *Revivalist* (June 1, 1905), 1.

[60] "Full Salvation Campaign," *Revivalist* (June 8, 1905), 1.

[61] "God's Bible School Campaign," *Revivalist* (June 22, 1905), 12.

[62] M. G. Standley, *My Life*, 87.

[63] Ibid, 87-88.

[64] "God's Bible School Campaign," *Revivalist* (June 22, 1905), 12.

[65] "Cincinnati Slums at Night," *Revivalist* (May 15, 1902), 12.

[66] M. G. Standley, *My Life*, 131.

[67] "Mother" Duff, "Let Us Rescue Them In Time," *Revivalist* (May 10, 1906), 2-3. Duff noted that boys were not permitted to stay at the rescue home, and "we . . . have to turn the orphan away frequently, and O, how it hurts us!"

[68] Day, 57 and "A History of God's Bible School," *Revivalist* (May 29, 1975), 7 (an article "prepared by the 1975 Annual Staff, Mrs. Elnora Ratcliff, Sponsor").

[69] George B. Kulp, "Salvation Park, God's Answer," *Revivalist* (May 10, 1906), 2. Plans were made to develop the property on a grand scale, including the construction of a tabernacle "seating 5,000" (see the photograph "Grove Scene at "Salvation Park, Ohio," *Revivalist* (May 10, 1906), 1) and "an advanced school of the prophets," to remedy the loss of "young men who desire greater advantages than we now offer" (Kulp, "Salvation Park, God's Answer," 2). Although these developments never materialized, they reflect the aggressive vision maintained by the trustees and their colleagues. Also, see "Salvation Park Camp Ground," *Revivalist* (May 17, 1906), 1 and "Salvation Park," *Revivalist* (June 7, 1906), 1.

[70] Day, 57. See also, Coral L. Osborn, "God's Orphanage Pentecostal School," *Revivalist* (Dec. 12, 1907), 12; "God's Orphanage Notes," *Revivalist* (July 22, 1909), 14; and "Inasmuch," *Revivalist* (Jan. 4, 1912), 8. For examples of touching photographs of the orphans, see "Motherless Children," *Revivalist* (July 25, 1907), 13 and "Our Little Brothers and Sisters," *Revivalist* (May 19, 1910), 8. For photographs of

the orphanage building, see "The Orphanage," *Revivalist* (Nov. 1, 1906), 8-9.

[71] See "A Holy Ghost Revival in God's Orphanage," *Revivalist* (March 4, 1909), 14 and "God's Orphanage Notes," *Revivalist* (Nov. 4, 1909), 12.

[72] George B. Kulp, "God and Cincinnati," *Revivalist* (May 16, 1907), 3.

[73] "Christ's Camp, Cincinnati, City," *Revivalist* (May 30, 1907), 11 (original emphases).

[74] "Open War on Cincinnati's Sin," *Cincinnati Post* (June 24, 1907), reproduced in Moser and Smith, 50.

[75] "Christ's Camp, Cincinnati, City," *Revivalist* (May 30, 1907), 11 (original emphasis) and "Open War on Cincinnati's Sin," reproduced in Moser and Smith, 50. GBS leadership welcomed such innovative methods to draw the masses to camp meeting. An even more novel method was employed in 1910—the use of large black umbrellas with camp advertisements painted on them. See "The Great Umbrella March of 1910" in Moser and Smith, 64-65.

[76] "Some of the Workers at 'Salvation Park' Camp, 1907," *Revivalist* (July 25, 1907), 1. For Chamber's perspective on the camp, see Moser and Smith, 49-50.

[77] "Christ's Camp-Meeting," *Revivalist* (July 25, 1907), 3-4. Early *Revivalists* contain numerous testimonies of individuals who professed sanctification, but after arrival at the Mount of Blessings, discovered that they had not had their "personal Pentecost" and subsequently prayed through. Prominent among these was Nettie Peabody (See Nettie Peabody, "Undeceived," *Revivalist* (May 1, 1902), 13).

[78] Ibid, 4.

[79] Oswald Chambers, "Hungry Beyond Words For the Bible"—Camp Meeting 1907 in Moser and Smith, 49.

[80] "Christ's Camp-Meeting," *Revivalist* (July 25, 1907), 4-5.

[81] "Audiences Are Hypnotized Into Religious Frenzy By Exhorters At The Grand," *The Cincinnati Post* (Friday, June 28, 1907), 9 (reproduced in Moser and Smith, 48).

[82] Although GBS personnel "kept no strict account of the numbers who came to the altars . . . many found God." In one service, there were as many as fifty seekers. See "Christ's Camp-Meeting," *Revivalist* (July 25, 1907), 5.

[83] "Bible-School Notes," *Revivalist* (Nov. 12, 1903), 15.

[84] See Beatrice M. Finney, "My Call to Africa," *Revivalist* (Dec. 19, 1901), 9; "Elizabeth D. Ferle," *Revivalist* (Dec. 26, 1901), 9; "Farewell Missionary Service," *Revivalist* (Jan. 16, 1902), 9-10; "En Route for Africa," *Revivalist* (Jan. 30, 1902), 11-12; and Mrs. M. W. Knapp, "The Farewell Meetings," *Revivalist* (Feb. 6, 1902), 9, 13.

[85] Beatrice M. Finney, "Answered Prayer," *Revivalist* (April 20, 1903), 9 and "Notes from God's Bible School in Africa," *Revivalist* (April 24, 1902), 9. See also, "God's Work in Africa," *Revivalist* (Jan. 28, 1904), 2-5.

[86] Finney had returned by summer 1905, for she spoke briefly on August 25, 1905, at a "Farewell Missionary Service," *Revivalist* (Sept. 7, 1905), 9.

[87] Thomas and Thomas, 74. See Charles and Elizabeth Rodway, "Victory in Africa," *Revivalist* (August 24, 1905), 9.

[88] Norman N. Bonner and Alberta R. Metz, "The Wesleyan Church in Africa," c. 11 in Caldwell, 477. See also, Thomas and Thomas, 74; "Letter from Brother and Sister Rodway," *Revivalist* (Jan. 14, 1909), 7; Charles and Elizabeth Rodway, "Praise

to God from Mt. Frere, Africa," *Revivalist* (Feb. 14, 1918), 5, 9; "Victory in Africa," *Revivalist* (Oct. 20, 1921), 12-13, and Moser and Smith, 86.

[89] "En Route for Africa," *Revivalist* (August 6, 1903), 9.

[90] See the testimony of the Millers in "Experience and Call," *Revivalist* (Aug. 13, 1903), 9. Also, see "Off for Africa," *Revivalist* (Sept. 17, 1903), 9 and Mrs. M. W. Knapp, "The Farewell Missionary Meetings," *Revivalist* (Oct. 1, 1903), 9. On the large number of missionaries from the Church of Emmanuel, see John Pennington, "To the Revivalist Family," *Revivalist* (Sept. 24, 1903), 1.

[91] Bonner and Metz, in Caldwell, 476.

[92] "Off for Africa," *Revivalist* (Aug. 1, 1907), 10. This article describing the Fuges' departure stressed that "the Foreign Missionary Board of 'God's Revivalist and the International Apostolic Holiness Union' recently unanimously appointed them [the Fuge's] as superintendents of the work in Africa." A depiction of the Fuges' reception when they returned to GBS appears in Moser and Smith, 66.

[93] Paul S. Rees in "About the Author" in Fred T. Fuge, *The Vapor-Life Series* Vol. 1 (Cincinnati: The Revivalist Press, 1965), 5.

[94] Roy S. Nicholson in ibid, 6. For other examples of Fuge's sermons and other writings, see his message, "He Shall Preserve Thee," *Revivalist* (Aug. 10, 1905), 2-3; Fred T. Fuge, *The Glorious Christ: Radio Addresses* (N. P.: n. p., n. d.); and Fred T. Fuge, *Thrilling Adventures on Land and Sea* (Cincinnati: M. G. Standley, 1936). The latter work reflects Fuge's personal experiences at sea and on the mission field, as well as tales he compiled. It is but one of the many printing jobs done to "help young men [at GBS] prepare for Christian work and thus further the Gospel." Also, see his autobiography F. T. Fuge, *The Wonder Book of My Life*. Fostoria, OH: Fostoria Daily Review Co., 1955. For an anecdote reflecting Fuge's antics while speaking, see Moser and Smith (67).

[95] Thomas and Thomas, 69. Prominent among these were "G. A. Schoombie and W. H. Reynolds who gave lifelong service to the [Pilgrim Holiness] Church."

[96] Bonner and Metz, in Caldwell, 476.

[97] Thomas and Thomas, 69-70.

[98] Lulu [sic] Glatzel, "Obedience is Better Than Sacrifice," *Revivalist* (Dec. 6, 1906), 5. See also, Moser and Smith, 53.

[99] This college, of which E. P. Ellyson was then president, later merged with Bethany College to become Bethany-Peniel College, a precursor to Southern Nazarene University.

[99] J. Fred Parker, *Into All The World: The Story of Nazarene Missions Through 1980* (Kansas City, MO: Nazarene Publishing House, 1983), 15.

[100] See Harman [sic] Schmelzenbach, "At the New Brighton Station," 10 and Lula Glatzel, "God Is Able," 2, both articles in "The African Missionary Number" of *God's Revivalist* (March 26, 1908).

[101] William C. Esselstyn, *Nazarene Missions in South Africa* (Kansas City, MO: Nazarene Publishing House, 1952), 36. Innis later married Herbert A. Shirley, another missionary who arrived in 1907. They both served with the Schmelzenbachs in Swaziland.

[102] Harmon Schmelzenbach, III, *Schmelzenbach of Africa: The Story of Harmon*

F. Schmelzenbach: Missionary Pioneer to Swaziland, South Africa (Kansas City, MO: Nazarene Publishing House, 1971), 15, 73; and Parker, 15. Also, see Lulu Schmelzenbach, *The Missionary Prospector: A Life Story of Harmon Schmelzenbach: Missionary to South Africa* (Reprint; Salem, OH: Allegheny Publications, n. d.).

[103] Ibid.

[104] Parker, 16.

[105] Parker, 16. See also, Lula Schmelzenbach, "Among People Who Never Heard of Jesus," *Revivalist* (May 13, 1909), 9, 12.

[106] Fred T. Fuge, "Greetings From Africa," *Revivalist* (Jan. 27, 1910), 10.

[107] Esselstyn, 38.

[108] Parker, 19. Also, see Esselstyn, 38-39.

[109] Ibid, 27.

[110] Thomas and Thomas, 70-71. See also Charles L. Slater, "The Missionaries' Arrival and Welcome to the Dark Continent," *Revivalist* (April 22, 1909), 9 and Charles and Maude Slater, "Report from New Brighton, Africa," *Revivalist* (Sept. 2, 1909), 10, 14.

[111] Fred De Weerd, "A Retrospect," *Revivalist* (Nov. 18, 1909), 8. See also, Fred De Weerd, "Called and Going," *Revivalist* (Sept. 3, 1908), 5. For further biographical information on De Weerd, particularly the circumstances of his death, see Mrs. Fred De Weerd, *The Last Mile of the Way* (Fairmount, IN: Mrs. Fred DeWeerd, 1923).

[112] Maude E. Slater, *Missionary Evangelist: A Biography of Charles L. Slater* (N. P.: Mrs. Maude E. Slater, 1951), 13; 21-23. See also Charles Slater, "To the Regions Beyond," *Revivalist* (Nov. 21, 1907), 5. For several photographs of the Slaters, and his testimony from the *Revivalist* (Nov. 21, 1907), see Moser and Smith, 15.

[113] Thomas and Thomas, 73. See Slater, *Missionary Evangelist*, 25-52.

[114] Slater, *Missionary Evangelist*, 56-85.

[115] Thomas and Thomas, 135, 335.

[116] Slater, *Missionary Evangelist*, 126.

[117] Lester F. Sumrall, *Lillian Trasher: The Nile Mother* (Springfield, MO: Gospel Publishing House, 1951), 9. This biography was completed at Trasher's request (viii-x).

[118] See Mattie E. Perry, *Christ and Answered Prayer* (Cincinnati: Mattie E. Perry, 1939), 159.

[119] *Letters from Lillian* (Springfield, MO: Assemblies of God Division of Foreign Missions, 1983), 11 (original emphasis). Sumrall, 12-13.

[120] Scott Shemeth, "Lillian Hunt Trasher" in Burgess and Van Der Maas, *The New International Dictionary of Pentectostal and Charismatic Movements* Revised and Expanded Edition, 1153.

[121] Sumrall, 12. In 1912, Trasher was ordained in the Church of God (Cleveland). Later, during "a trip to America she was impressed by the giving and prayers of the Assembly of God . . . constituency and as a result became part of that organization in 1919" (Shemeth, 1153). Regardless her association with tongues-speaking Pentecostalism, she retained the admiration of holiness people, as reflected in Anna Talbot McPherson, *Vignettes of Holy Lives* (Salem, OH: Allegheny Publications, 2003), 207-208.

[122] Ibid, 12-17 and "Five Dollars Plus God" in Moser and Smith, 52-53.

[123] Ibid, 17-18 (original emphasis).

[124] Shemeth, 1153.

[125] Ibid.

[126] *Letters from Lillian*, 7. Like Martin Wells Knapp, Lillian drew much inspiration for her faith work from the ministry of George Muller (Sumrall, 5).

[127] Shemeth, 1153.

[128] *Letters from Lillian*, 5, 15.

[129] *Letters from Lillian*, 11 (original emphasis).

[130] Shemeth, 1153.

[131] Thomas and Thomas, 38-39. The Kilbournes spent a short time at GBS before the 1902 Salvation Park Camp Meeting, during which they fare-welled. See "On the Way," *Revivalist* (May 8, 1902), 9. While at the school, their two children "took their first lesson in Japanese from Shoji" Murakami. "Bible-School Notes," *Revivalist* (April 17, 1902), 14. Young Edwin, known as "Bud," declared he was "'called' just as much as his father." In fact, he became "an important second-generation OMS leader" (Kostlevy, *Dictionary*, 174). For a photograph of the family, see Moser and Smith, 26.

[132] See E. A. Kilbourne, "The Bible School in Korea," *Revivalist* (Sept. 30, 1909), 9 and John and Emily Thomas, "Korea," *Revivalist* (June 17-24, 1909), 8-9. The Thomas family also had "a stint at God's Bible School" before traveling to Korea (Wood, *In These Mortal Hands*, 78.) They had been trained at Star Hall in Manchester, England.

[133] Kostlevy, *Dictionary*, 174.

[134] Wood, 50.

[135] Thomas and Thomas, 38.

[136] E. A. Kilbourne, "The Bible School in Korea," *Revivalist* (Sept. 30, 1909), 9 (original emphasis).

[137] C. E. Cowman, "Native Ministry in the Orient," *Revivalist* (Nov. 17, 1910), 10. Eventually, OMS projected an indigenous work throughout other world regions as well, with plans "to reach, in cooperation with other evangelical missions, all the Orient and Latin America with the full gospel, through a sanctified, trained, NATIVE MINISTRY" (Day, 102, original emphasis).

[138] Sister Cowman, "Noh; or, Out of Darkness into Light," *Revivalist* (Feb. 4, 1904), 9, 13-14.

[139] Wood, 125. In E. A. Kilbourne, "My Call to Japan," *Revivalist* (May 8, 1902), 9, he described the vision without the inclusion of the Korean and Chinese elements: "It seemed that there was a highway built up, which reached from here, right across America and the Pacific Ocean, to Japan, and across Japan right on up to glory, and it was indicated to me that this was the way I was to travel on my way to heaven."

[140] Wood, 128.

[141] "From Dark China," *Revivalist* (Nov. 30, 1905), 11 and Wood, 126-127. Also, see Brother and Sister Monroe, "South China Holiness Mission," *Revivalist* (Feb. 14, 1918), 10.

[142] Charles and Lettie Cowman, "Another Year In Japan," *Revivalist* (Feb. 4,

1909), 9-10. However, Wood notes that "union, or, more accurately, absorption would not be accomplished from more than 20 years" (127).

[143] Thomas and Thomas, 42-43. See A. Lee Grey and Wife, "En Route for India," *Revivalist* (Dec. 3, 1903), 8 and "God's Work in India," *Revivalist* (Jan. 28, 1904), 12-14.

[144] Ibid, 43. See also Miriam Miller, "A Real Call and I Am Going," *Revivalist* (Aug. 31, 1905), 9, 14; Thaddeus L. Vaughan, "The Result of Simple Consecration," *Revivalist* (Oct. 26, 1905), 9; and Bertha E. Cox, "Yes, Lord, I'll Go," *Revivalist* (August 16, 1906), 5.

[145] Thomas and Thomas, 68-69.

[146] Thaddeus L. Vaughan, "The Result of Simple Consecration," *Revivalist* (Oct. 26, 1905), 9.

[147] "'God's Bible School' Band Increasing in Heaven," *Revivalist* (April 9, 1908), 8 (original emphasis).

[148] "Brother and Sister Moulton," *Revivalist* (April 17, 1902), 9. This article provides a brief biographical sketch as well. See also Thomas and Thomas, 40-42.

[149] Thomas and Thomas, 41, 76.

[150] Thomas and Thomas, 76.

[151] John A. Corrigan and Wife, "Called to the West Indies," *Revivalist* (Dec. 12, 1907), 5.

[152] Thomas and Thomas, 76. Corrigan died on February 17, 1908, just a few weeks after Thaddeus Vaughan's death. See "'God's Bible School' Band Increasing in Heaven," *Revivalist* (April 9, 1908), 8.

[153] Thomas and Thomas, 76-77. The source of Moulton's heartbreak was his sudden ouster as leader at the annual conference. Also, see George B. Kulp, "Translation of Rev. C. O. Moulton," *Revivalist* (April 29, 1909), 11.

[154] See Thomas and Thomas, 76 and Caldwell, 407. It appears that the first mention of Blyden in GBS records is in "Bible-School Notes," *Revivalist* (Nov. 5, 1903), 14-15, which states that "every one was much interested as Brother Moulton [who was then visiting GBS] told of Irene" who was expected "to come to the school as soon as possible."

[155] Wingrove Taylor, "Three Drops of Water" in Moser and Smith, 56-57.

[156] Guy Wilkinson, "God's Blessing Still on Shantytown," *Revivalist* (Jan. 16, 1908), 14 and Oswald Chambers, "Impressions of the 1909 Salvation Park Camp," *Revivalist* (July 8, 1909), 3.

[157] Cited in Belle Staples, "Bible School Notes," *Revivalist* (Nov. 11, 1909), 13 (original emphasis).

[158] Paul L. Swauger, Jr. "Wesleyans South of the United States," c. 10 in Caldwell, 407.

[159] Thomas and Thomas, 76. In fact, "Nevis was never the permanent residence of a North American Wesleyan [Pilgrim Holiness] Missionary." Swauger in Caldwell, 408.

[160] Swauger in Caldwell, 407.

[161] James M. Taylor, "Our Missionary Party," *Revivalist* (Nov. 25, 1909), 15.

[162] Thomas and Thomas, 77.

[163] In addition to their separate campaigns, the two also conducted joint efforts, one campaign in the early 1920s being chronicled in Ralph G. Finch and Charles L. Slater, *Campaigning For God In Southern Waters* (Louisville: Pentecostal Publishing

Co., n. d.).

[164] See *Lightning from the Past: Camp Meeting Sermons by Early Twentieth-Century Holiness Revivalists* (Salem, OH: Schmul, 2001), edited by this author, for a biographical sketch of Finch (64-65). Grateful acknowledgment is made to Schmul Publishing Company to quote from the various sketches in this book and its companion volume, *Sons of Thunder: Camp Meeting Sermons by Post-World War II Holiness Revivalists* (1999).

[165] See "Reports," *Revivalist* (Dec. 23, 1909), 11.

[166] Thomas and Thomas, 140 cited in Thornton, *Lightning from the Past*, 65. Although Wesleyan historians (Hynson in Caldwell, 228) have considered "Finch's role in creating dissension and division in Colorado [producing the Emmanuel Association] . . . the major issue in his ministry," this fails to recognize the important role he played in the development of Pilgrim Holiness missions. One of the most problematic aspects of Finch's teaching was his emphasis on the "death route" preceding the experience of entire sanctification, which Hynson (228) argues was "not typical of the Pilgrim Holiness Church." However, a fair reading of such pioneers as Knapp and Rees reveals a strong emphasis on "dying out" from the earliest days of the Holiness Union. For a typical sermon dealing with the subject by Finch, see R. G. Finch, "Subdued or Dead, Which?" in *Flames of Fire: Sermons by Pilgrim Preachers* (Indianapolis, IN: The General Board of the Pilgrim Holiness Church, n. d.), 72-77. The inclusion of this sermon with others by such Pilgrim authorities as Seth Rees, George Kulp, and Charles Slater in addition to the identity of the publisher seems to belie Hynson's claim. Also, see my *Radical Righteousness*, 95-101.

[167] Rev. Ralph G. Finch, *My Early Years and Five Revival Sermons* (Cincinnati: Published for the Author by God's Bible School and Revivalist, n. d.), 83.

[168] "Bible-School Notes," *Revivalist* (March 11, 1909), 14.

[169] George B. Kulp, "The Bible School Convention," *Revivalist* (Oct. 28, 1909), 15.

[170] "God's Bible School Notes," *Revivalist* (April 28, 1910), 11.

[171] "Off to the Foreign Lands," *Revivalist* (Jan. 28, 1904), 6. Catherine was highly regarded at GBS for being "very successful in the slum work" and for her courageous incursions into brothels to rescue girls, during which "God delivered her from danger again and again." See also the report of Seth C. Rees on the Stalkers' "Pentecostal wedding" in "Reports," *Revivalist* (Dec. 17, 1903), 11.

[172] "Reports," *Revivalist* (Sept. 23, 1909), 14.

[173] W. B. Dunkum, "The Fire Burns, Hallelujah!" *Revivalist* (Aug. 10, 1905), 5. This article also provides his testimony to conversion and entire sanctification.

[174] *Heart Talks from Beulah Land* (Louisville: W. B. Dunkum, n. d.), *Rolling Shot* and *"Hot Potatoes with Jackets On,"* both reprinted by Revivalist Press, 1981. Others of Dunkum's books reprinted by Revivalist Press in 1981 include *Life of Paul*, *Eternity's Night*, and *Temptation*.

[175] J. A. Phillips, "Introduction" to W. B. Dunkum, *Biblical Orations* (Syracuse, NY: Wesleyan Methodist Publishing Association, n. d.).

[176] Bence C. Miller, "Introduction" to W. B. Dunkum, *What We Believe and Teach* (Reprint; Cincinnati, Revivalist Press, 1981), 3. Dunkum alludes to his involvement at Kingswood in "Reports," *Revivalist* (Sept. 23, 1909), 14 and "Reports," *Revivalist*

(Sept. 21, 1911), 14. The school at Kingswood "was a project originally started by J. W. Hughes, founder of Asbury College at Wilmore, Kentucky, for the same reason as Asbury. The project had been taken over by some Pilgrims, and in 1919 was adopted as the general Church school" (Thomas and Thomas, 110).

[177] Miller, "Introduction" to *What We Believe and Teach*, 3. Also, see my *Radical Righteousness*, 214.

[178] "A Letter from Our Publisher Boy," *Church of Christ Advocate* (Oct. 27, 1908) cited in Kenneth Brown and P. Lewis Brevard, *History of the Churches of Christ in Christian Union* (Circleville, OH: Churches of Christ in Christian Union, 1980), 78-79.

[179] Brown and Brevard, 77-79.

[180] Webster Holland, "George Street Mission, Cincinnati," *Revivalist* (July 19, 1906), 16 and Webster Holland, "Great Victories in the Lunch Stand," *Revivalist* (July 14, 1904), 14. In his testimony, Wm. Webster Holland, "The Real Thing," *Revivalist* (May 1, 1902), 15, he reflects on struggles he had after arriving at GBS, including homesickness. Also, see Webster Holland, "God's Bible School George Street Mission, Cincinnati," *Revivalist* (Sept. 13, 1906), 12. For a much later book-length example of Holland's writing, see William W. Holland, *Solace for the Sorrowing: Being a series of Funeral Meditations for the comfort of the bereaved* (Cincinnati: The Revivalist Press, 1946).

[181] See "Reports," *Revivalist* (July 13, 1905), 12-13 and "Reports," *Revivalist* (Sept. 28, 1905), 11. For photographs of Widmeyer and Donald DeWare, who was nicknamed "Western Tornado," see Moser and Smith, 23.

[182] "Reports," *Revivalist* (Sept. 28, 1905), 11.

[183] "Reports," *Revivalist* (July 13, 1905), 12-13.

[184] Glenn D. Black, "Meet Two of Our Earliest Students," *Revivalist* (July 7, 1983), 11 and Ronald B. Kirkemo, *For Zion's Sake*, 64.

[185] Ibid. These songs are numbers 593 and 652 respectively in the hymnal, *Sing to the Lord*.

Chapter 7

Holding a Steady Course: Advocates and Adversaries

"I feel that Dr. Godbey and Oswald Chambers were the two men on earth who came nearest to living the Book. They lived the Sermon on the Mount, if ever I met two men who did."
— M. G. Standley[1]

It is a consolatory fact that amid all the clouds and storms, snow blizzards, icebergs, and flotillas Satan never succeeded in quenching the Pentecostal fire which has wrapped their mountain from the very beginning. The camp meetings throughout lugubrious years of litigation never cooling down; but retaining the Pentecostal flame, unabated which still continues, hotter, stronger, and brighter as the years come and go and His glorious appearing draweth nigh.

... the holiness people are uniting in prayer to God; to run these educational and philanthropic institutions without a break till Gabriel blows His trumpet and the glorious coming King catches his waiting bride.
— W. B. Godbey[2]

While the administrative trustees rallied the troops and alumni led the charge in spreading the flames of radical holiness, much of the credit for the continued ardor of the atmosphere at GBS belongs to the men and women of the faculty who faithfully labored, often at great personal sacrifice, to assure that students would receive solid grounding in God's Word, in practical evangelism, and in other subjects conducive to mastery of the first two areas. In fact, the attention demanded by *Revivalist* publications, by campus improvements, and by rapid expansion of the school's mission outreach, both at home and abroad, meant that much of its academic dimension would rely heavily upon faculty—both full-time teachers and visiting lecturers/evangelists.

Living By the Book: Early Faculty

Consistent with Knapp's egalitarian vision, women continued to play a significant role on the GBS faculty throughout the period of administrative trusteeship and beyond.[3] Nettie Peabody's responsibilities increased as she began to write for the *Revivalist* Sunday School column (in addition to W. B. Godbey's expositions), contributed several other articles, and eventually became registrar—a position she held for many years.[4] She was joined as one of the "regular teachers" in 1904 by Elizabeth West, who also worked in Hope Cottage. West's decision to join the faculty proved remarkable for at least two reasons. For one, she was another highly qualified educator who chose to labor at GBS on the faith line, giving up her relatively lucrative position as superintendent of schools in the city of Camden, New Jersey, where she had taught "with much success for a number of years."[5] For another, she journeyed to Cincinnati shortly after being entirely sanctified, with the intention of visiting "His Bible School to get in touch with the Rescue Work," to which she felt called. So, she arrived at GBS only "expecting to remain six weeks" but, like Peabody and "Mother" Duff, found that God changed her plans.[6] While waiting for an opening elsewhere in rescue work, the door opened for a faculty position at GBS. She thus willingly "took up the work of teaching" on the Hilltop, where she would devotedly labor for the last thirteen years of her life.[7]

Robert Elmer McNeill: Singing with the Spirit and with Understanding

Other "regular" teachers during this formative period included M. G. Standley, R. E. McNeill, W. B. Godbey, and, for a short time, John Pennington. McNeill continued to direct the "Bible School Conservatory of Gospel Music," a work he would maintain until his death in October 1937. This program reflected the ongoing, integral role that music played in GBS ministry, particularly in its evangelistic activities, in keeping with Knapp's conviction that "among the most potent factors in promoting real revivals is Pentecostal singing and songs."[8] In fact, McNeill felt "his calling was to evangelistic-singing and playing." However, this call worked out in his life much like Nettie Peabody's call to missions. Thus, M. G. Standley explained that, rather than McNeill himself being "called out into the evangelistic-field, the Lord let him train young men and women" with "hundreds going out" to proclaim the message of full salvation through music. Indeed, this was McNeill's passion—"his whole heart was wrapped up in getting young people full of music, and so trained that God could use them in singing or playing the glorious gospel!"[9]

Students had numerous opportunities to put their music lessons to work in practical evangelistic settings, and reports from camp meeting campaigns, street meetings, and George Street Mission are replete with references to music which had "the drawing power of the Holy Spirit in it" and the wonderful responses it elicited.[10] This was in keeping with the foundational commitments of the "conservatory": First, the school would offer "only sacred song."[11] Thus, the *Revivalist* announced, "Higher music will not be taught in connection with the school, but attention given to everything that pertains to the thorough mastery of the principles of gospel music, both instrumental and vocal." Second, the music department was inextricably tied to the Bible School, so that, except for unusual cases, students taking music were required to enroll in the Bible course, and were "subject to the rules which govern the school." Third, the department strove for excellence from the beginning, emphasizing that students "would learn to 'sing with the Spirit and with the understanding also'."[12]

William Baxter Godbey: Sanctified Eccentricity

W. B. Godbey's vast influence throughout the holiness movement and in the *Revivalist* family in particular has already been noted through his personal impact on Knapp as spiritual and theological mentor, through his numerous contributions to *Revivalist* publications, and through his frequent appearances as evangelist at Salvation Park Camp Meeting and other GBS venues. However, the pivotal role that Godbey played in shaping GBS during its formative period and beyond requires further scrutiny. In fact, one could hardly exaggerate the impact on God's Bible School of this man who came to profess a love for the Mount of Blessings second only to his love for the Holy Land.[13]

Godbey remains one of the most unique characters in holiness folk-lore. The son of a Methodist circuit-rider in Pulaski County, Kentucky, he testified to experiencing at the age of three "infantile justification" from which he sadly fell, to be converted again in his teen years during a Baptist revival meeting.[14] His penchant for academics quickly surfaced, and he received an excellent classical education, earning both the B. A. and M. A. degrees from Georgetown College. This was followed by a lifetime of informal education, during which Godbey learned at least a dozen languages, acquisition of which was undoubtedly facilitated by his extensive travels. In 1859, he became founding president, as well as professor, of Harmonia College, a rather rudimentary institution, where he served for about ten years.

Godbey also served as Presiding Elder of the Barboursville District of the M. E. Church (1873-1876), as well as several pastoral appointments. However, an event in 1868 assured that his lasting legacy would not be as a pastor, administrator, or even as an educator. This was his experience of entire sanctification, a doctrine that he initially opposed, explaining, "I had no sympathy with the doctrine of sanctification as a distinct blessing, but regarded its advocates as fanatics. I had strong prejudice against noisy demonstrations in religion." However, he experienced "inward conflict" and a "longing desire for holiness" which built to a climax in which he surrendered to be sanctified, as he testified to readers of the *Guide to Holiness*:

> One night, amid the wonderful effusions of the Holy Spirit, while the house rang with shouts, I found myself running round, praising God at the top of my voice.
> That was my Pentecost. I was baptized with the Holy Ghost and with fire. "Refining fire went through my heart, illuminating my soul, scattering life through every part, and sanctifying the whole."

This event totally changed the trajectory of Godbey's ministry, as he noted, "Then and there my ministerial character also underwent a radical revolution. I had never been a revivalist. From that day God began to convert people wherever I labored."[15] Thereafter, Godbey would be the quintessential holiness revivalist. In just the first fifteen years after his sanctification, he counted 5,000 converts in his meetings, in addition to several hundred who were entirely sanctified. Among those profoundly influenced by his ministry, in addition to Martin Wells Knapp, were Alma White, G. D. Watson, H. C. Morrison, Bud Robinson, and John Wesley Hughes, with Dr. Delbert Rose suggesting that "it is a serious question whether Asbury College would ever have been born in Wilmore, Kentucky" had it not been for Godbey's influence on Hughes.[16]

Indeed, Godbey was one of the most influential holiness leaders around the turn-of-the-century—"one of the generally recognized saints of his generation."[17] Although he decried "human leadership" as the "bane of the Holiness Movement," he was not reluctant to bring his authority to bear when he perceived true holiness to be at stake.[18] In fact, he took this as one of his chief responsibilities towards the end of his career, explaining, "The reason that I am traversing all lands and doing my best, by speech and pen, to keep the Holiness people on the Bible line is that so many of them get sidetracked and ruined forever."[19]

His colleagues at GBS especially encouraged him in this task. For instance, when Knapp was grappling with the Church Question, he turned to Godbey for a final word, recognizing in him probably one of the few men at the time with the stature and fortitude to write an "Encyclical Letter to the Holiness People of Every Land."[20] As earlier noted, after the Azusa Street revival broke out in Los Angeles in 1906, it was Godbey who has been credited by scholars with convincing large segments of the Holiness Movement to reject the teaching of tongues-speaking as an evidence of Spirit-baptism.[21] "His arguments, particularly in such Revivalist Press books as *Current Heresies*,[22] apparently proved" so effective within the *Revivalist* movement that little reference to the subject even appeared in the *Revivalist* itself until several years after the Azusa Street revival began, bearing mute testimony to Godbey's influence on the Mount of Blessings and beyond.[23]

The high esteem which Godbey commanded at GBS stemmed from the regard that Knapp held for him, with Godbey reporting that Knapp had actually credited Godbey, "rather than himself," with being the "founder" of GBS.[24] While this claim may at first seem incredible, Knapp may have suggested such since it was Godbey that conducted the meeting that opened Sycamore Street mission—Knapp's first attempt at conducting daily public services in Cincinnati. Regardless, it is certainly consonant with Knapp's estimation of Godbey (published in the *Revivalist* the same month that GBS began) as a leader with "mature experience in the Pentecostal gifts and graces" with "profound knowledge of the New Testament" who had, "more than any other, . . . planted holiness and watered it all over the South."[25]

This regard led Knapp to make two final requests of Godbey at the close of the 1901 Salvation Park Camp Meeting, which Godbey vividly recalled as the last time he saw Knapp alive:

> When I had bid him adieu, he gripped my hand, like a drowning man, observing, "Brother Godbey, I am never going to let go your hand till you make me two promises, the one that you will attend my camp-meeting, the Lord willing, as long as you live, and the other that you will translate the New Testament out of Greek into English and go at it without delay."[26]

Godbey quickly complied with the latter request, having his translation about half completed when Knapp died. Also, though he continued his "peregrinations" abroad and followed a demanding "triennial circuit" of itinerancy throughout the United States, he became a fixture at the GBS camp meeting and frequently conducted extended class sessions for several weeks at a time on the Hilltop, attracting large numbers of special students.[27]

In fact, Godbey left an indelible impress upon the school's academic program and served as its scholarly authority and chief intellectual guide well beyond the time of his death through the influence of his New Testament commentaries and other writings. It was in keeping with his philosophy that, at GBS, "in the place of Greek authors the Greek New Testament was given, and in the place of Caesar and Cicero the Latin New Testament was offered."[28] Faculty, students, and *Revivalist* readers consulted him for the authoritative verdict on subjects ranging from higher criticism and the unpardonable sin to women's hairstyles and teaching children about Santa Claus, with many of his responses appearing in his popular "Question Drawer" *Revivalist* column.[29]

In his teaching, he demonstrated a complexity that posterity has often failed to appreciate. In particular, Godbey had an amazing ability to reconcile positions that many other holiness people have considered to be mutually exclusive. For example, in preparing his New Testament translation (and even in camp meeting preaching) he relied exclusively upon the "Sinaitic manuscript" (actually the critical edition by Hort and Westcott) as "the highest New Testament authority," while staunchly defending the "plenary verbal inspiration of the Scriptures" against the claims of "higher criticism" which he termed "the fatal infidelity of this age."[30]

In addition, Godbey strongly opposed evolutionary theory, suggesting that "the reason why we have Holiness schools and colleges throughout the country, and must have them everywhere, is because the 'Darwinian infidelity,' . . . has made its way into the popular schools."[31] Yet, he did not subscribe to the "young earth" teaching later predominant among fundamentalists, contending that "the days of creation are not limited to twenty-four hours."[32] Likewise, Godbey insisted that sanctification was necessary for entrance into heaven—an idea he publicized widely in his book *Holiness or Hell?*.[33] Yet, he "would not deny admission into heaven for Catholics, Mormons, or adherents of other religions—however, everyone was required to have a 'clean heart'."[34]

Students also looked to Godbey as a model preacher. Even in his sixties, he still awed crowds with a "voice . . . like the Niagara Falls"[35] and an expansive vocabulary that included words of his own manufacture from Latin and Greek stems, with an approach that was at once "dramatic and descriptive as well as personal and direct." He also demonstrated balance in evangelistic topics, generally beginning his campaigns majoring on "God's judgments and wrath," and following "his 'Sinai' blasts . . . with 'Calvary' pleadings" in which he emphasized God's "love and mercy."[36] Of course, to follow through with a mountain metaphor, his preaching moved on to the mounts of Pentecost (entire sanctification) and Transfiguration (glorification).[37]

However, students' regard for Godbey was due not only to his intellectual prowess and preaching ability but perhaps even more so because of his godly demeanor, reflected in an incident in the fall of 1909, related by a Sister Lasley:

> A few weeks ago . . . Brother Godbey surprised us by walking into the room. His presence was a benediction. With hands uplifted in his characteristic way, he paused and invoked the blessing of God upon us, and as he said, "Showers of blessing upon you one and all," the glory of Heaven settled upon us, and we laughed and shouted and praised the Lord. No student in that class will ever forget the time that we had, will ever get over the real fragrance that came into our hearts at the words of prayer of this saint, this prophet of God.[38]

Many other students cherished similar memories of their encounters with Godbey. For example, Matilda Steele remembered that, "during school, Dr. Godbey would come to the dining room at noon and repeat the Hebrew alphabet. He would then say beautiful Hebrew spoken in heaven. He would go out through the kitchen and look in the garbage cans and say people are starving all over the world."[39] In addition to this, Augusta Oakes Guy remembered that Godbey would sometimes "walk the campus with a box of pencils tied to his cane asking students to record his dictation for some future book."[40]

Such practices projected an image for which Godbey became legendary—that of "sanctified eccentricity."[41] Then and now, both admirers and detractors have often noted Godbey's idiosyncrasies, with many unfortunately taking these as cause to dismiss his prodigious accomplishments in shaping the holiness movement. To be sure, Godbey was different than the "average" American of his (or probably any) day—even contrasting sharply with other holiness people, as a couple of encounters indicate.

A writer for the *Church Witness* described his introduction to Godbey at the historic train depot in Moberly, Missouri:

> In connection with meeting Brother Godbey, I think I had one of the strangest experiences of my life. We had noticed an elderly gentleman on the train, considerably burdened with what seemed to be an oversupply of bundles and packages curiously tied together, and depending from over his

shoulder. He wore a broad-brimmed linen hat and a rather antiquated linen duster. . . . The accumulated dust and soot upon his clothes and person, which gave him a somewhat grotesque appearance, bore evidence that he had indeed come from no small distance. . . . His talk seemed incoherent, and his whole appearance was suggestive of an old farmer whose mind was clouded by long travel and loss of sleep. I will not attempt to write all the feelings and thoughts that came to my mind concerning him. Imagine my surprise, however, when he came to us a little later, spoke of hearing us say we were going to camp-meeting, and said, "I am [traveling] from Texas; my name is Godbey." I am certain I was never before so taken down in the conceptions I had formed of a man. And this was Dr. Godbey!—the man who had been twice around the world, and had written so many scholarly works on the Sacred Scriptures. . . . "I really wonder if we should know Jesus when He comes."[42]

On another occasion, Godbey's hosts "discovered that his bed in the guest room had not been used, and his reply to their questions was something like this: 'Well, the bed looked so comfortable that I thought about how Jesus often had no place to lay His head, and I just couldn't sleep in it. I slept on the floor!'"[43]

As this incident reflects, Godbey's eccentricity was not the result of thoughtlessness but actually represented a studied attempt to glorify God in all things, even at the expense of personal comfort and reputation. Thus he exulted, "If I am crazy, it is for the Lord."[44] However, Godbey was far from crazy. In fact, his eccentricity, while genuine rather than contrived, was intentional—not only stemming from personal piety but also calculated to boost evangelistic endeavors. He thus admitted turning the jeers of critics to his advantage, noting that "reports of my craziness, oddities, and eccentricities brought thousands of curiosity seekers to my meetings . . . I made it a rule by the help of God to effect the coupling of curiosity and conviction, so that hundreds who came to mock, stayed to pray."[45]

Undoubtedly, this tactic served Godbey well, for as John R. Church observed, "old Dr. Godbey was rather eccentric . . . but my, how God did use that man!"[46] H. C. Morrison similarly commented in the eulogy he gave at Godbey's funeral, ." . . the innocent and beautiful spirit characterized him, [and] made his eccentricities attractive and amusing rather than offensive. . . . Cursings, abuses, and ridicule neither intimidated, embarrassed, or angered him." Consequently, "his ministry was always unctuous and with power . . . ."[47]

Even his death on September 12, 1920 was a glorious occasion, with Mrs. Knapp writing that "for days before his departure his room was filled with a rare fragrance, a sweetness that cannot be described—the presence of the Father and the angels." After his passing, his District Superintendent reflected the estimation that many held for Godbey by saying, "I would rather go to the Judgment in his shoes than any other man's I know of."[48] Indeed, it is doubtful that any one else has ever come closer to living out the ideals upon which GBS was founded; and certainly, few individuals have impacted the school more greatly than W. B. Godbey.

Scotch Granite and an Old Soldier: Oswald Chambers and George B. Kulp

At GBS, many of the students' most memorable lessons were learned outside the classroom—in rescue work, street meetings, etc., but also in camp services, revival meetings, and conventions, where they heard some of the greatest holiness exponents of their day. In addition, several of these ministers, much like Godbey, would stay for extended periods of time, giving lectures on various topics from the symbolism of the tabernacle to eschatology. The flexibility afforded by such courses allowed GBS students to sit under a wide variety of teachers. Furthermore, some of these visiting lecturers returned with great frequency and had perhaps as profound and lasting an influence upon students as did the "regular" faculty. Among them, two remain especially noteworthy, not only for their teaching at GBS, but also for various other contributions.

Oswald Chambers remains best known to posterity as the author of *My Utmost for His Highest*, the best-selling devotional of the twentieth century (with the possible exception of *Streams in the Desert*) that continues to impact millions, including such world leaders as U. S. President George W. Bush, who "spends some time every day reading the spiritual works of Oswald Chambers."[49] "Ironically, many people reading Chambers work have no idea that they are digesting vintage holiness piety"; however, to be understood best his writings must be read in the context of Chamber's commitment to holiness ideology.[50] In fact, before his tragic death at age forty-three in 1917 (due to complications from appendicitis), Chambers was little known outside the holiness movement, where he was considered, especially among GBS constituents, to be a bright and rising star. Actually, it was not until the 1927 publication of his popular devotional (compiled from his writings by his wife) that Chambers gained wide acclaim, giving a prophetic ring to one of his statements: "I feel I shall be buried for a time, hidden away in obscurity, then suddenly flame out, do my work, and be gone."[51]

Known affectionately to the GBS family as our "Scotch granite brother,"[52] Chambers had grown up near Aberdeen, Scotland, in a Baptist minister's family and was converted as a result of the ministry of Charles Haddon Spurgeon. He early showed exceptional aptitude in artistic and literary endeavors, which was honed by studies at the National Art Training School and the University of Edinburgh. Awards in the fine arts and in writing further encouraged his ambition to follow a career in art, when he felt the Spirit's prompting to enter the ministry, a call with which he struggled until "he seemed to hear the Lord say, 'I want you in My service, but I can do without you'."[53]

Chambers entered the Gospel Training School at Dunoon, Scotland, "a small Baptist college run by faith principles."[54] Here he remained as an instructor after graduation, serving from 1897 to 1906. After hearing F. B. Meyer speak on the "deeper life" at Dunoon, Chambers "'determined to have all God had for him,' and for four years he prayed incessantly for 'the baptism of the

Holy Ghost'." Throughout this time, "he was very oppressed by his sense of inner depravity."⁵⁵ His struggle finally ended in 1902 with a glorious experience of entire sanctification after he contritely confessed "that he had desired the power of the Spirit out of selfish ambition." ⁵⁶ Thereafter, the theme of his ministry—indeed, of his life—was *abandonment to God*, as reflected in a message on "Divine Guidance" that he delivered at GBS:

> Some people are far more concerned about being in earnest than about going God's way, and the devil will twist you about your earnestness. Your crying to God will not save you. There is only one thing, abandoning yourself straight over to Jesus Christ. There is no other way. *Let go*, for pity's sake. It is the *will* that must be surrendered. You may give God everything you like and still be damned. He never asked you to give Him things, but asks you to alter the center of your will.⁵⁷

Chambers had been introduced to the *Revivalist* family by Juji Nakada whom he met in 1905, instantly forming a lasting friendship. They planned on traveling to Japan together, but decided to tour America en route. Of course, one of the places that Nakada felt was a must-see for his Scottish friend was the Mount of Blessings, so they arrived at GBS on January 1, 1907, during the holiday convention. Chambers was immediately enthralled with GBS, particularly its emphasis on "the fourfold truth of God . . . Salvation, Sanctification, Healing and the Second Coming" and its rescue work, of which he proclaimed, "This is truly Holiness socialism."⁵⁸

When he was approached about remaining at the school for the spring 1907 term to teach and write some books, he readily agreed, making Chambers' stay of about six months at GBS the longest of any location he visited in the United States.⁵⁹ In the classroom, he became known as "a demanding teacher who insisted that his students not substitute sentimental piety for serious study."⁶⁰ In fact, "if Chambers had a pet peeve, it was, in his words, 'intellectual slovenliness, disguised by a seemingly true regard for spiritual interests'." And, he believed the cure for this plague to be "extermination by honest, hard-working, sanctified students of God's Word."⁶¹ However, while George Kulp and other colleagues at GBS admired Chambers for being "cultured in the scholarly sense," they also found in him a "spiritual" man "in communion with Him who takes the things of God and reveals them to those who are willing to receive them," making his "Bible readings . . . seasons of refreshing and strengthening."⁶²

Although Kulp expressed the sentiments of many regarding Chambers when he wrote, "we would be glad if God would let him stay on the 'Mount' and teach until Jesus comes," Chambers was on his way to Japan with Nakada by the summer of 1907. However, he returned every year for camp meetings until 1910, giving Bible readings that ranked in popularity with those of W. B. Godbey.⁶³ He also continued to write numerous articles for the *Revivalist* until his death, with the Revivalist Press publishing his first two books, *Biblical Psychology* (1912) and *Studies in the Sermon on the Mount* (1915).⁶⁴

While Chambers made a tremendous impact on the GBS family, the Mount of Blessings also left an indelible mark on him. Though he never returned after 1910, he went on the following year to establish his own Bible Training College in Great Britain that was similar in many respects to GBS. In fact, there was perhaps nowhere else on earth that Chambers found his ideal of abandonment to God so fully realized as on the Mount of Blessings, as reflected in his description of the 1908 camp meeting, during which,

> ... the mourners got slowly but surely delivered from the worshipping of their own earnestness, their own prayers, their own tears, their own fastings, their own everything, and by deciding and *abandoning to the Lord* ... they were taken gloriously through into the embrace of an Almighty Savior who presented them whiter than the driven snow before God, or sanctified them wholly by the blessed, almost unspeakable transaction, of spiritual union with the Lord where the life becomes unmixed and the whole character invaded by divinity.[65]

After the following year's encampment, he asserted, "There is a superior note, an intenser [sic] spiritual reality in the abandonment of these people to God."[66] In particular, Chambers was impressed with the selfless service rendered by GBS students to guests during special events, such as the 1907 camp meeting:

> One thing that will remain with us as long as we live, was not the preaching, not the meetings, nor the marches, nor testimonies, (these were grand), but the splendid, supereffacing service of the boys and girls (students) who waited at tables, washed the dishes, erected tents, pulled them down, and did the drudgery. Their lives for ten days were one unbroken testimony to the blessing of God ... .[67]

Oswald Chambers thoroughly enjoyed the striking variety of colorful personalities associated with GBS in its early days, sharing in his *Revivalist* reports and in personal letters vivid descriptions of such figures as "grand old Dr. Godbey." One leader with whom he was especially impressed was George Brubaker Kulp, whose "promp[t] soldier-like manner" commanded not only Chambers' respect, but that of the entire campus family, many of whom referred to him as "our grand old chief."[68] Such military imagery fit Kulp well, considering his youthful career as well as his later ministry.

Kulp was raised by devout Methodist parents in Philadelphia, Pennsylvania, and was won to Lord by his "father's prayers."[69] He ended his education in the Philadelphia public schools at age sixteen and joined the Union Army, then engaged in the Civil War. "He was a member of the Ninety-First and Ninety-Fifth Pennsylvania Regiments of the Fifth and Sixth Corps of the Army of the Potomac," placing him under General Grant's command so that he was at Appomattox when the war ended.[70] He returned to civilian life in July 1865, having attained the rank of corporal, but was forever stamped by his experience as a soldier, bringing into his ministerial work the vigor of battle along with the organizational skills he learned in the army, in addition to flavoring his sermons with innumerable illustrations from his military experiences.[71]

Kulp was converted in 1869 and studied at Pennington Seminary. He entered the ministry of the M. E. Church, which licensed (1872) and ordained him (1881). After a decade of successful ministry in Philadelphia, including one of the city's largest M. E. Churches, he moved to the Michigan Conference and pastored from 1882 to 1898. Following this, he pioneered a church at Holbrook, Nebraska, where he "had an intense experience of spiritual revitalization that resulted in his decision to leave" the Methodist Church "and cast his lot with Seth C. Rees and Martin Wells Knapp in the International Apostolic Holiness Union."[72] Shortly thereafter, he returned to Michigan where he pastored the Immanuel Holiness Church in Battle Creek, which grew to become one of the most prominent churches in the Holiness Union.

After renewing his "ministerial vows" in 1901 during the MCA-sponsored Holiness Convention in Chicago, Kulp quickly advanced in the ranks of the Holiness Union, becoming general superintendent in 1905, a position he held until 1921. Under his skilled administration, the Union evolved from a loose-knit organization of seventy unions and churches to a full-fledged denomination (then termed the International Holiness Church) with over four hundred churches and numerous mission works around the world.[73]

During this period, his prominence on the Mount of Blessings grew commensurately. For example, although Kulp had written for the *Revivalist* as early as 1900, his articles became more frequent about 1905, and by the end of the decade they were often featured on the front page.[74] In addition, he produced several books that were published by Revivalist Press, including a classic work on prayer—*The Calloused Knees*, a daily devotional—*The King's Allowance*, and several books of sermons, anecdotes, and practical advice for ministers.[75]

At GBS, he became one of the most popular camp meeting evangelists and frequently visited the campus for other occasions. In fact, he often chose the Hilltop as the sight for such Holiness Union functions as assemblies and ordinations.[76] In addition, for well over a decade, his lecture series (consisting of ten-day sessions) were among the most demanded classes at the school, with up to three series offered during a school year.[77] Kulp's preaching and lectures presented a dynamic blend of holiness fire and cultured reflection. As one student put it, "While the lectures are of a high order, yet they are deeply spiritual and help us toward God."[78] Another participant suggested, "The word 'lecture' seems entirely too poor a name for the God-inspired, Heaven-sent messages he has been giving us from day to day. What a vast difference between a 'lecture,' in the common acceptation of the term . . . and one delivered by a God-called, God-sent, Spirit-anointed ambassador of Jesus Christ!"[79]

While Kulp taught several Biblical and theological subjects, his forte was "pastoral theology," and much of his sage advice in this area was distilled in his book by that title.[80] This topic reflected his special interest in young ministers' "thorough preparation for God's service"—through entire sanctification, to be sure, but also through "application to study."[81] This followed through in his role as general superintendent, as he held ministers under his charge to exacting standards, much like a military leader. However, like Francis Asbury with his circuit riders, he did not ask them to make sacrifices that he would not match or even exceed. For instance, Kulp took no salary for his services as general superintendent for almost a decade, instead depending for income on revival stipends and a small pension from the military. In fact, he "paid most of the expenses of the general superintendency out of his own pocket."[82]

W. L. Surbrook, a later Pilgrim Holiness general superintendent, aptly summarized Kulp's leadership qualities: "He possessed a rare combination: on the one hand he had the fearless boldness and daring of a general, while on the other he was a humble, approachable, teachable, tender soul."[83] Kulp would exemplify this balance between zeal and order and between rigid discipline and gentle forbearance as he supported GBS throughout some of its most troubled days.

Administrative Struggles: Organizing the Mission Work

Among the "regular" teachers during the first decade, John Pennington remains remarkable not so much for his teaching as for his role in the school's administration. Pennington, a Quaker like Seth Rees, was "an intimate friend" of the latter, whom he followed as pastor of the Church of Emmanuel in Providence, Rhode Island.[84] During his pastorate, ties between the church and GBS remained strong, as signaled by the *Revivalist*'s support of such missionaries from the church as the Albert Miller and the C. O. Moulton families.[85] It seemed natural then, when the GBS trustees and M. G. Standley felt the need for "another teacher in the School," to extend the call to Pennington.[86] At the 1903 Salvation Park Camp Meeting, "the public announcement that Brother John Pennington would be senior teacher in the Bible-school the coming year was received with great joy."[87] The *Revivalist* noted, "He is a man whom we all dearly love, and expect that God will make him a great blessing . . ." In addition, it indicated that, "Brother Knapp, before he died, while planning for the work, mentioned Brother Pennington as a man whom he believed God might some day call here, and now He has done it."[88]

From this article introducing his new ministry, it was clear that Pennington was more than a teacher: "He will serve as pastor of the New Testament Society of God's Church here at the Mount of Blessings; in the school be senior teacher of the Bible-class, and also counselor in all business appertaining to the work at home or abroad."[89] M. G. Standley later explained that, due to his own writing for the *Revivalist*, fund raising efforts, and "working night and day getting the printing office started," he willingly "gave" Pennington "the pastorate of the tabernacle, the cottage prayer meetings, and so forth . . ."[90]

Pennington's first year at GBS apparently went well, with a *Revivalist* reporter exclaiming in October 1903, "How we praise God for sending Brother Pennington to us! He is a real father to the students—a real shepherd to the flock. We feel that God is going to give a year of great victory."[91] His preaching was well-received, with E. A. Fergerson noting that during one sermon which Pennington preached in the 1904 camp meeting, "many people got victory before they reached the altar." In addition, he, along with M. G. Standley, was noted for his efficient administration during the camp.[92]

However, the ambiguous and rather broad description of Pennington's role as "counselor in all business appertaining to the work at home and abroad" was almost certain to create tensions with the administrative trustees. This unfortunate development took place in the context of one of Pennington's great passions—missions. In particular, foreign missions held a special place in his heart, perhaps even more so after the tragic loss of his young daughter, Eva. A "trained nurse, Eva [had] arrived in China as an Ohio Yearly Meeting missionary in 1903. After about one year of service in which, by her devout and beautiful spirit, she endeared herself to missionaries and Chinese alike, her health broke and she returned" to live with her parents at GBS until her death on September 28, 1904.[93] No doubt this weighed upon her father's mind when he examined GBS's support for missionaries through the "World-Wide Holiness Missionary Fund."

What he discovered was that the GBS trustees had interpreted the term "world-wide" broadly to include home as well as foreign missions. Part of their reasoning was that most of the foreign fields they sponsored had their own separate fund, and "if money came designated for Japan, Africa, China, or elsewhere, it was sent to that field." In addition, the work at Beulah Heights was "in dire need of funds," and the "Trustees contended that this was just as much a world-wide missionary project as if it were in China or any other field." Consequently, "over a period of several years a little over $2,700.00 of this World-wide Mission Fund had gone into home missionary work, most of it into the Beulah Heights Mission Home."[94]

During the 1903 Christmas Convention at GBS, the Holiness Union had "informally" created a "Missionary Board" that included the three GBS trustees, along with John Pennington and Seth Rees.[95] When this board met early in 1905, Pennington shared his opinion that use of "world-wide" mission funds to support Beulah Heights was "misappropriation of funds" and that the funds should only be used to support foreign work. Rees agreed with this conclusion. However, the trustees had "the final say, and they decided that [they] were justified in putting this money into home missionary work, for it was to be used for home and foreign missionary work where most needed, and to be appropriated according to the judgment of the Trustees."[96]

About a week after the meeting, Rees and Pennington both tendered their resignations. As Pilgrim Holiness historians have reflected on the ensuing events, "the record is not complete and judgment must be reserved." However, it is clear that "it was not considered a small matter by Seth Rees; he refused to have any cooperative arrangement with the Revivalist group and their missionary work."[97] Indeed, while his son Paul may have been correct that "other tasks were calling," this issue proved the underlying reason why "he severed his connection" with GBS.[98] It was also likely a "major factor" in his resignation "as general superintendent during the next annual meeting of the Union in 1905."[99]

For their part, the GBS trustees announced in the *Revivalist* for February 16, 1905, that the informal missionary board of which Rees and Pennington had been a part had been disbanded by "the Council of the Union," which had "decided to leave the work in the hands of the God's Revivalist Family, as formerly, and the entire action of 1903 was rescinded." The *Revivalist* also stressed that no funds were kept for administrative costs: "If you send one dollar, a dollar goes to the field." It also announced the intention of making "every six months . . . an itemized statement in God's Revivalist of the funds received and disbursed."[100] This was echoed again in the following issue of the *Revivalist*, along with the assurance that "the money designated for any field is kept distinctly separate for that field, and so forwarded."[101]

The trustees were also forced to deal with several complications brought about by the withdrawal of Rees and Pennington. Of immediate concern, both of these men had already been advertised as featured speakers for the 1905 camp meeting, but were now "refusing to come."[102] It was thought that other evangelists might follow suit and that the crowd could be smaller. Instead, such Salvation Park regulars as W. B. Godbey, E. A. Fergerson, and Lucius B. Compton participated, along with other prominent holiness revivalists including A. M. Hills, L. Milton Williams, and John Butler. Significantly, at least two men who had been close associates of Rees and Pennington and who were obviously great supporters of foreign missions—Charles Stalker and C. O. Moulton—also participated.[103] If anything, the congregations were even larger than the previous year, so large in fact that at times two separate services were conducted simultaneously, to accommodate the estimated five thousand that had gathered at the Hamilton County Fair Grounds for camp meeting.[104] C. O. Moulton proclaimed it to be "the greatest camp-meeting [he] was ever in. Surely God was there. His very presence seemed to pervade the grounds."[105] A. M. Hills, who had counted eight hundred and fifty seekers, concurred, "It was by far the most victorious camp-meeting for spiritual power we have ever seen."[106]

Complications involving the mission work itself were more challenging to resolve. While the work in the Orient, already strongly organized by the Cowmans and Kilbournes, was relatively unscathed and remained firmly allied with GBS, ripples of the disagreement with Pennington and Rees soon reached other fields, particularly India and Africa. As a consequence, earlier gains were largely lost, with Pilgrim Holiness historians observing that "all of the work started in Africa or India before 1905 ended in failure, insofar as the establishing of permanent work was concerned."[107] In India, A.

Lee Grey, one of the most promising missionaries, joined the Methodists and "served a lifetime in India with considerable distinction."[108] In Africa, the work was in turmoil for some time after the new field superintendent, James Hundley, was removed from his position, evidently because agreed with Rees and Pennington's perspective.[109] He was eventually replaced in 1907 by Fred Fuge, who remained loyal to GBS leadership and under whom the work again flourished.

These events signaled several future developments, some of which had implications reaching far beyond GBS-sponsored ministries. In general, it suggested to holiness leaders the need for more careful organization, including appropriate accountability structures. The struggle over the world-wide fund, especially as it unfolded in Africa, may help to explain why missionaries like Harmon Schmelzenbach were ultimately attracted to the more tightly-organized denominational structure of Nazarene missions rather than the loose-knit network of independent missionaries linked to GBS and the Holiness Union.

In particular, the Rees-Pennington departure brought George Kulp's organizational skills into play, for he followed Rees as the Holiness Union's general superintendent and largely assumed Rees's role in connection with GBS as well. Kulp quickly moved to implement his philosophy that "our most aggressive and definite work is done when we are most thoroughly organized."[110] Thus, Mary Storey announced in the January 18, 1906, edition of the *Revivalist* that the Council of the Holiness Union had agreed to form a missionary board, called the "The Foreign Missionary Board of 'God's Revivalist' and 'the International Apostolic Holiness Union.'" Members were the three GBS trustees, M. G. Standley, Lucius B. Compton, L. Milton Williams (secretary), and George B. Kulp (chairman—a position he held until retiring from the general superintendency).[111] Compton's inclusion had double significance—not only was he the assistant general superintendent of the IAHU, he was also personally immersed in home mission work, operating Eliada Orphanage and Faith Cottage (a rescue home for women) in Asheville, North Carolina, enterprises which were supported by the *Revivalist* family and that employed GBS alumni including Edith Van Dusen and Hattie Byers.[112]

This board's "chief work seems to have been the appointment of missionaries," with little financial oversight since "most of the financial support went directly from the donor to the missionaries."[113] However, the board did attempt to establish a rudimentary hierarchy by appointing field officers, such as naming Charles and Lettie Cowman the "General Superintendents for Japan, Korea, and China."[114]

The board's name reflected the ongoing cooperation between the Mount of Blessings and the Holiness Union under Kulp's chairmanship, as the Union's "missionary affairs continued to be interwoven with God's Bible School," which "provided the institutional setting for the [International Holiness] Church's missionary work until 1922."[115] This was due in large part to Kulp holding "strongly to the idea of keeping God's Bible School . . . as the spiritual and intellectual center 'for the holiness movement throughout the world'."[116] Thus, for the time being, Holiness Union and GBS/*Revivalist* missions would remain essentially identical.

On Trial: The Court Case Begins

The conflict over disbursement of mission funds also served as a backdrop to even more intense controversy at GBS which developed following the death of Mary Storey on March 23, 1906. "Now came the question: Who will be the next Trustee?" In his autobiography, M. G. Standley wrote, "Before she went to Heaven she made the request that I should take her place. Mrs. M. W. Knapp . . . had requested it, too; and so had Mrs. Standley."[117] In the *Revivalist*, Lucius B. Compton agreed that "Sister Storey's choice was a good one" and George Kulp gave a glowing endorsement, reporting that Martin Wells Knapp had personally spoken to him about Standley: "I have secured just the man I have been needing so long; the right man for the place; he is a jewel."[118] Mrs. Knapp also explained Standley's selection to the *Revivalist* family: " . . . we looked up to God for *His* choice, seeking only *His* will. . . . He has made us feel that His choice is Brother M. G. Standley, and not only witnessed to us, but to others of His anointed ones."[119]

Not all the GBS family agreed, however, with Standley's selection, particularly in light of continued allegations of financial irregularities. Prominent among these was James Storey, Mary's brother, who had served as GBS's bookkeeper for a number of years. He decided to take action and so began one of the most remarkable sagas in the history of American jurisprudence. On February 20, 1907, Storey's attorneys filed a lawsuit with the Court of Common Pleas of Hamilton County, Ohio, creating a case that would not be ended until April 27, 1982—making it the longest running "court case in Ohio and perhaps in the entire U. S."![120]

Storey filed his suit "on his own behalf" and on behalf of contributors and others affiliated with GBS and its related ministries, naming Mrs. M. W. Knapp, Bessie Standley, and Meredith G. Standley as defendants. In it, he made two primary allegations: (1) That M. G. Standley's placement as trustee was invalid—"without authority and contrary to the laws in such cases." (2) That the Standleys had "misappropriated the funds" of GBS in numerous ways, including financially supporting Meredith's mother and Bessie's father and mother, the last of whom was alleged to have been the recipient of an expensive piano purchased with school funds. An integral argument in Storey's suit was "that no plan for perpetuating the work" of GBS had "been perfected," whereby legal selection of trustees by GBS constituents could be made. Instead, he charged "that defendants claim to have the sole and absolute control of the [property], and that they are amenable to no one 'except themselves and God' . . ." In addition, he suggested that Mrs. Knapp had "neglected and . . . entirely failed to perform the duties resting upon her as

Trustee of said property, and that she [had] been wholly and constantly under the influence of her co-defendants . . ."

Storey's suit also contained two basic petitions: (1) That the court issue an injunction restraining the defendants from "transferring, conveying, incumbering, missapropriating, or wasting the money and property" of GBS and "that a receiver may be appointed of said property." (2) That the court issue an order calling the GBS constituents "to form an organization according to the laws of the State of Ohio, for the purpose of electing a board of trustees . . ."

Of course, the lawsuit was sensationally described in the Cincinnati papers, in part due to the prominence GBS had gained through its aggressive evangelistic and philanthropic enterprises, particularly the Thanksgiving Dinner.[121] In addition, the case "dragged out for days largely through the efforts of Judge Pfleger to have the matter settled amicably out of Court" and the fact that the he "was extraordinarily lenient with both sides upon the question of allowing times and fullness of scope to the hearing of witnesses and the reading of documentary evidence."[122]

When Judge Pfleger finally handed down his ruling, the front page of the *Post* announced,

> The Knapp-Standley rule is overthrown and the government of God's Bible School is placed in the hands of the thousands who support the famous institution . . .
>
> . . . . .
>
> The dynasty established by the will of Martin Knapp, the founder, by which the rulers of the community were to attain to leadership by succession, is broken, and hereafter an annual election will have to be held to decide who are to be the Bible School Trustees.[123]

This made matters for Mrs. Knapp and the Standleys sound much worse than they really were. In fact, as the *Post* briefly noted, the petition for receivership was denied, and the Standleys and Mrs. Knapp were allowed to remain in place as trustees, with the addition of a court-appointed "ancillary trustee"—Frank H. Kemper, until the annual Christmas convention at GBS, during which the first election of trustees by GBS constituents was to be conducted. Kemper was to have charge of all financial books until the election, at which time three trustees were to be selected, one for a three-year term, one for a two-year term, and one for a one-year term, with annual elections mandated for the third Thursday of each December thereafter, so that one trustee would be voted on per year.

In short, the Court had ruled against Storey's first petition—that calling for a receiver—and in favor of his second petition—that calling for elections for GBS trustees. The judge's reasoning for the latter was,

> Martin W. Knapp was authorized and empowered to appoint his successor in trust, but that he failed to exercise the appointing power vested in him previous to his death, and finds further that the attempted ap-

pointment of successors by said Martin W. Knapp prior to his decease by executing a written instrument which was not either a deed or will, was not a formal or valid exercise of said appointing power . . . [so that] the defendants, who had acted as Trustees of said property are not properly appointed Trustees.

In addition, the Court agreed with Storey "that the attempted appointment of Meredith G. Standley as one of the Trustees . . . was not a valid exercise of the appointing power." In other words, the Court had ruled that GBS had been operating for over five years without properly-constituted trustees or administrators!

As to the petition for receivership, the Court considered this an inappropriate and extreme response to the situation, especially since it found no cause to sustain allegations against the Standleys regarding misappropriation of funds or "living in luxury." In dismissing these charges, the judge expressed his evaluation of the character of the trustees, and of their claim to divine approbation. Of the latter, he suggested that "the claim of the Trustees that they considered themselves responsible only to God would be sacrilege if it were not made in all sincerity."[124] He further expressed concern over "Mrs. Knapp's plan of determining important questions by prayer and revelations from God" as "not indicative of a very safe administration of the business affairs of the institution." However, "the Court was of the opinion that the Trustees, including Mrs. Standley, "were honest and godly people . . . and that they [had] attempted in good faith to carry out the principles of the founder M. W. Knapp." In particular, Judge Pfleger expressed confidence in Mrs. Knapp as "a devout woman," excusing any negligence of duty on her part as a result of her recent illness. He further stated that he had "no doubt of the sincerity and good faith of Meredith G. Standley in the work which he has performed." Because the lawsuit's "reflections" were "mainly cast upon Mrs. Bessie Standley," the judge elaborated in his assessment of her role at GBS:

> It is plain, however, that she has taken the leading part in the trust and that she has controlled both Mrs. Knapp and her husband on questions of policy and business. That this was done without reference to the welfare of the institution I cannot and will not believe. She is practically the head and brains of the institution, because of her intimate and practical knowledge of its affairs and indeed of every department.[125]

Here things would rest until December 1907, with the court record ending with a note portending future developments: "This cause is continued and reserved for the future and further consideration of the court upon all questions not herein disposed of and for the purpose of receiving reports from time to time from the ancillary trustee . . ." Little did anyone then realize just how long the case would be continued. For the time being, everyone's attention was riveted on the upcoming elections.

Throughout the intervening months, the GBS trustees faced the accumulation of opposition that had mounted since shortly after Knapp's death. Much of this had surfaced in connection with *The Burning Bush*—publication of the Metropolitan Church Association—then edited by Duke Farson and Edwin L. Harvey and associated closely with F. M. Messenger and W. E. Shepard. MCA concerns regarding GBS were not new; they had emerged soon after the announcement of Knapp's successors had been made. Although their complaints regarding GBS's new leadership were numerous, their primary contention was that the rejection of E. L. Harvey as head of GBS, whom it suggested was Knapp's true choice, removed God's blessing on the *Revivalist* (and, of course, GBS and related enterprises)—"God then raised up the Burning Bush to take up the work where Brother Knapp had dropped it."[126]

The Burning Bush claimed that proof of this could be found in significant changes made in the *Revivalist* under Bessie Queen's (Standley's) direction. In particular, it cited a *Revivalist* editorial that warned against emotional display without corresponding ethical living as "ridiculing Holy Ghost demonstration." It also correctly discerned, and vehemently protested, the fact that "Queen, operating with the full support of [Mary] Storey, Mrs. Knapp and the influential Godbey, . . . [had] immediately moved [after Knapp's death] to moderate the [*Revivalist*'s] strong come-outer sentiment."[127] As proof of this shift, the *Burning Bush* argued that Knapp "had not been in heaven sixty days until the [*Revivalist*] began drifting to the shallows, and inserted an Epworth League column to cater to the Methodists." Interestingly, the column only ran in the *Revivalist* for less than a month, with its discontinuance explained in the *Revivalist* as due to the League's promotion of "the various so-called literary and social attractions that keep young folks from God" and suggesting that "it stands for the most cowardly surrender the Church has made"—language reminiscent of Knapp's protests against Methodism.[128] The MCA claimed responsibility for this abrupt reversal in policy, but were frustrated in their further attempts to "rescue" the Mount of Blessings.[129] Their protests against GBS leadership continued however, and were given renewed impetus by James Storey's lawsuit.[130]

For their part, the GBS trustees wisely chose to refrain from engaging in a war of words with their opponents in the *Revivalist*.[131] However, Mrs. Knapp and the Standleys benefited from the unwavering support of numerous key holiness leaders, a crucial factor for their continued success. Several of these leaders voiced publicly their support, the most vocal in their defense being the venerable Dr. Godbey, who explained his perspective on the lawsuit in his booklet, *Adoption*, where he claimed that the Standley's right to the trusteeship resulted in part from Knapp's "adoption" of Bessie Queen, "an exceedingly brilliant damsel . . . whom he adopted as a daughter, the normal consequence of her extraordinary sufficiency, as a helper in his editorial work." By extension, or as Godbey put it, "on the beautiful hypothesis of matrimonial unification," M. G. Standley became Knapp's adopted son.

Godbey concluded, "This adoption in the good providence of God actually brought them the happy succession of the glorified founder of all these noble institutions which now shine in this holy mountain . . ."[132]

In the same booklet, Godbey further described his role in defending the trustees:

> I was in California when the suit was brought and consequently the prosecution came off in my absence. I was not present in any of the courts though the malcontents tried hard to draw me in. As the charges were all made from the standpoint of maladministration, and while I transacted more business with them than any other person in the world I had never seen anything wrong and was consequently utterly incompetent either directly or indirectly to cooperate with the malcontents, but waited patiently till the litigation was all consummated and taken out of court.
>
> Then I took it on myself to visit the presiding judge in his residence, meet him face to face and receive his personal testimony in reference to the prosecutions, when he told me positively that none of the charges were sustained, and consequently the allegations of maladministrations had all proved effete and the court had fully exonerated the accused, finding no valid testimony for their connection[.]"[133]

Other holiness leaders lent the Standleys and Mrs. Knapp less visible, but just as appreciated, encouragement throughout the crisis. Notable among these was Oswald Chambers, who had insisted the Standleys join him for a "midwinter rest," something they "had never done before," just before they became aware of the lawsuit. Later, Meredith Standley wrote, "That week was exactly what we needed. We didn't know what was coming on, but God knew, so He got us ready by giving us that rest." In addition, Chambers words of advice proved a real consolation to them.[134]

Perhaps the most decisive support the trustees received was from the other members of the "Bible School and Apostolic Holiness Union Foreign Missionary Board"—George B. Kulp, Lucius B. Compton, L. Milton Williams, and E. A. Fergerson. It was these men who broke the silence of the *Revivalist*, "in view of the many conflicting statements, false accusations and misrepresentations of the work and conditions that . . . existed . . . at God's Bible School, and the misinterpretations of the lives and actions of the trustees," and sought to set the record straight. They did this by publishing in the October 31, 1907, *Revivalist* the ruling of the Court of Common Pleas, as well as "the report of the expert selected by the attorneys to make a thorough examination of the books, and a personal letter from the judge to Mrs. M. W. Knapp."[135] While the forthright publication of these documents undoubtedly reassured many constituents of the institution's integrity, the role of Kulp and his associates in their publication especially helped to ensure that the rank and file of the Holiness Union would stand behind GBS.

"All Is Well"

This became evident when the election of trustees was conducted, in accordance with court guidelines, on December 19, 1907. The *Revivalist* had published the required announcements of the election, which was open to "all members of the local Apostolic Holiness Church" which met on campus, "all missionaries and evangelists" who were GBS graduates, and all school employees "other than those receiving a salary, and the teachers thereof who have subscribed to, or will subscribe to the doctrines, principles and teachings of Martin W. Knapp . . ."[136]

The election itself proved to be anti-climatic. According to M. G. Standley's autobiography, Mrs. Knapp was unanimously reelected and he and his wife "were minus two or three votes."[137] What followed; however, truly sealed the triumph of the trustees. For one, the General Assembly of the International Apostolic Holiness Union, also in session at George Street Mission during December 1907, "fully" endorsed "the position and course taken by the Trustees of God's Bible School" and announced "to the public [their] unwavering faith in said Trustees and the great work involved." In addition, the assembly re-elected L. B. Compton as assistant general superintendent but also chose to elect a second assistant general. Their choice was none other than M. G. Standley![138]

While these actions of the Holiness Union bolstered support for GBS and its leadership throughout the holiness movement, further court action helped to solidify the trustees' still tenuous position. In February, 1908, the Court of Common Pleas, in response to M. G. Standley's petition to eliminate the mandated elections because it "would wreck the work," changed its requirement from annual to triennial elections.[139] Then, Standley appealed the issue to the Circuit Court which, while remanding the case to the lower court, did comply with Standley's request and nullify the mandated elections altogether. This meant the Court of Common Pleas still retained responsibility for assuring that the school was properly managed as a charitable trust, but that the election of trustees in December 1907 would be the only such election ever conducted.[140] M. G. Standley exulted, "God Almighty overruled, and established the Trusteeship."[141]

George Kulp and his colleagues in Holiness Union leadership rejoiced that "the enemies of this work are being defeated on every hand and we are proving 'if God be for us, who can be against us'."[142] He was soon admonishing the faithful to support the school as it sought to wipe out its indebtedness, an effort mandated by the court. Kulp then expressed confidence in God's continued ownership of the cause, "We KNOW He will carry forward His own work, and He shall have all the praise and glory for it. Amen!"[143] In the same vein, in 1909, M. G. Standley reported that the Lord awakened him about 4:30 one summer morning "with the command, GO FORWARD!" This, along with the trustees' triumph over their legal opponents, verified to him that "GOD WAS AND IS WITH US!"[144]

Under Standley's leadership the school would indeed continue to "go forward" as he and his colleagues pursued the vision of preparing workers to evangelize the world with the holiness message, so that, in truth, the sun would never set on the students of God's Bible School.

Notes

[1] M. G. Standley, *My Life...*, 119.

[2] Godbey, *Adoption*, 104.

[3] Underscoring the ongoing commitment to woman's place in ministry, "God's Bible School Notes," *Revivalist* (Sept. 22, 1910), 12 (original emphases), proclaimed,

> The Pentecostal Church is without distinction as to the prominence given to the sexes. The women were equally honored with the men when the Spirit was poured out. 'I will pour out My Spirit upon all flesh, and your sons and your DAUGHTERS shall prophesy.' And also upon the servants and upon the HANDMAIDS in those days will I pour out My Spirit.' Women as well as men, are to prophesy when this holy Spirit shall be administered.

[4] For examples of her writing, see Nettie Peabody, "Separation," *Revivalist* (Nov. 20, 1902), 13 and "Compromise," *Revivalist* (Nov. 5, 1903), 4. Also, see her books, *Outline for Bible Study* (Cincinnati: n. p., 1942) and *The Glory of the Son of God* (Cincinnati: God's Bible School and College, 1960).

[5] "Another Member of God's Bible School in Heaven," *Revivalist* (Sept. 27, 1917), 2-4.

[6] Elizabeth West, "Redeemed, and in the Will of God," *Revivalist* (June 15, 1905), 5.

[7] "Another Member of God's Bible School in Heaven," *Revivalist* (Sept. 27, 1917), 2-4. See also, Larry D. Smith, "Elizabeth West: Singing the Reaper's Song," *Revivalist* (April 2000), 19.

[8] "Revival Singing," *Revivalist* (Oct. 24, 1901), 1. See also, "Power of Song in the Home," *Revivalist* (Jan. 25, 1900), 15; "The Ministry of Music," *Revivalist* (Feb. 8, 1900), 16; and "The Importance of Gospel Singing," *Revivalist* (Nov. 22, 1900), 13.

[9] "They Are Crossing, Swiftly Crossing," *Revivalist* (Nov. 11, 1937), 1-2. See also, Larry D. Smith, "There Is Therefore Now No Condemnation," *Revivalist* (Nov. 1998), 23 and Moser and Smith, 22-23.

[10] "Home Missionary Work," *Revivalist* (Jan. 5, 1905), 27-29.

[11] "Bible-School Notes," *Revivalist* (June 5, 1902), 14-15.

[12] "Announcement—Bible-School Conservatory of Gospel Music," *Revivalist* (Nov. 22, 1900), 13. See also, "Gospel Song Lovers, Attention !" *Revivalist* (Feb. 7, 1901), 13.

[13] Centenary Commemorative Edition of *God's Revivalist* (Sept. 2000), 8.

[14] See his *Infantile Christianity*, also published as *Infantile Justification* (Cincinnati: God's Revivalist Office, 1911). For further biographical material which helps inform this work, see *Lightning from the Past*, 73-79. Also, see the works cited earlier by Barry W. Hamilton and, of course, *The Autobiography of Rev. W. B. Godbey, A. M.* (Cincinnati: Revivalist, 1909), along with his *The Happy Octogenarian* (Nashville: Pentecostal Mission Publishing Co., n. d.) and *Happy Nonagenarian* (Zarepath, NJ: Pillar of Fire, 1919).

[15] "Experience of Dr. W. B. Godbey, Evangelist, of Kentucky," *Guide to Holiness*

and Revival Miscellany vol. 65 no. 6 (Dec. 1896), 222-223. See also, "Experience of Rev. W. B. Godbey," *Revivalist* (Aug. 1895), 2.

[16] Delbert R. Rose, "Little Man, Mighty Accomplishments," *The Herald* (Dec. 18, 1968), 7. Hughes was "wholly sanctified" under Godbey's ministry (Joseph A. Thacker, Jr., *Asbury College: Vision and Miracle* (Nappanee, IN: Evangel Press, 1990), 7). Godbey was the first holiness preacher Robinson heard (*Sunshine and Smiles*, 39). In his *The Abundant Entrance* (Greensboro, NC: Apostolic Messenger, n. d.), Godbey refers to Robinson as "my son in the Gospel" (25). Morrison was called to preach under Godbey's ministry (*Lightning from the Past*, 116); Watson was influenced to enter itinerant ministry by Godbey; and White was converted under his ministry, and consecrated by him as bishop of the Pillar of Fire, presumably the first women to attain such a position in the United States (*Lightning from the Past*, 77).

[17] John Paul, "Star Dust and Ashes: Historic Sketches of 'The Movement' and of H. C. Morrison, one of its Bright 'Stars'," *The Pentecostal Herald and Way of Faith* (Aug. 6, 1947), 9.

[18] W. B. Godbey, *Spiritualism, Devil-worship, and the Tongues* (Cincinnati: God's Revivalist Press, n. d.), 29.

[19] Ibid, 28.

[20] *Revivalist* (July 11, 1901), 12-15.

[21] See Barry W. Hamilton, "Godbey, W(illiam) B(axter)," in Kostlevy, *Dictionary*, 130 and Synan, *The Holiness-Pentecostal Tradition*, 146.

[22] See also his *Tongue-Movement, Satanic* and *Baptism of the Holy Ghost*.

[23] It is also likely that *Revivalist*/GBS leadership was significantly distracted from giving close attention to developments out of Azusa in the spring of 1906, for a little over two weeks before the Azusa revival began, Mary Storey died, an event that helped to precipitate conflict over the trusteeship which, as will be seen, ultimately led to court action. For a later article repudiating tongues-speaking as "the witness of the Holy Ghost Baptism," see "An Error Regarding Sanctification," *Revivalist* (April 6, 1911), 4.

[24] Godbey, *Adoption*, 98. See also, W. B. Godbey, "God's Bible School and Missionary Training Home," *Revivalist* (Sept. 7, 1911), 1, which begins, "Our glorified Brother Knapp always called me the founder of God's Bible School and Missionary Training Home." In this article, he also suggests that Harmonia College (where he was president) was the predecessor of Asbury College, so that, in effect, he was the founder of the latter institution as well.

[25] M. W. Knapp, "But the Revivalist," *Revivalist* (Sept. 6, 1900), 8. The latter claim was not greatly exaggerated, with Bishop Roy Short observing that credit was due him, more than anyone else, for "the revival among Kentucky Methodism of the old time Wesleyan emphasis upon sanctification and perfect love" (Roy Hunter Short, *Methodism in Kentucky* (Rutland, VT: Academy Books, published by The Commissions on Archives and History of the Kentucky and Louisville Conferences, The United Methodist Church, 1979), 115.

[26] *Baptism of the Holy Ghost*, 28.

[27] See W. B. Godbey, *My Triennial Circuit* (Cincinnati: God's Revivalist Press, n. d.); Mrs. M. W. Knapp, "Into the Beautiful Beyond," *Revivalist* (Oct. 7, 1920), 2-5;

and "Bible-School Notes," *Revivalist* (April 17, 1902), 14-15.

²⁸ Day, 74.

²⁹ In his *Higher Criticism* (Cincinnati: God's Revivalist Office, 1909), 12-13, Godbey relates how Mary Storey resorted to him for an explanation to students concerning an article in one of the city papers in which an "eloquent" preacher in "one of the largest Protestant churches in the city" was quoted as denying the inspiration of Scripture. Godbey's "explanation was brief." He "simply stated, 'Dr. B— is an infidel'—yet he stands at the head of one of the largest Protestant denominations in America!" Evidently, this terse response satisfied the students. See also, W. B. Godbey, "The Unpardonable Sin," *Revivalist* (Sept. 10, 1903), 16 and "Question Drawer," *Revivalist* (July 13, 1899), 5, (July 26, 1900), 11, and (Sept. 19, 1901).

³⁰ W. B. Godbey, "Wield the Word," *Revivalist* (July 18, 1901), 16 and "Higher Criticism," *Revivalist* (Feb. 10, 1910), 1. Also, see his booklet on *Higher Criticism* and W. B. Godbey, "Question Drawer," *Revivalist* (April 25, 1901), 10.

³¹ W. B. Godbey, *Catholicism* (Cincinnati: Office of God's Revivalist, n. d.), 2. See also his *Regenerated Earth* (Greensboro, NC: Apostolic Messenger, n. d.).

³² W. B. Godbey, *Man the Climax of Creation* (N. P.: n. p., n. d.), 5. See also his *Bible Astronomy* (Louisville: Pentecostal Publishing Co., n. d.). Here he contends that the Hebrew word *yom* "is not to be understood as definite, but an indefinite expression for a long period of time" and "that none of the seven were solar [days]" (7).

This was but one of several theories of origin propounded at GBS across its first century. Increasing identification with Fundamentalism found the school eventually favoring views of origins popular among Calvinistic Fundamentalists. Around mid-century, a favorite view at GBS appears to have been the "Gap" theory, which suggests an indefinite period of time between verses 1 and 2 of Genesis 1, an era during which it is thought that Lucifer was cast out of Heaven (see Isaiah 14) and then threw the earth into chaos, thus necessitating the earth's reconstruction which is thought to be described in the "creation" account (See Kenneth H. Wells, *God's Footstool: Its Creation, Ruin, and Redemption: A Study of the Five Periods of the Earth's History, based on the Statements of Scripture and the Facts of Science* (Whitefish, Montana: Kenneth H. Wells, 1964) and L. Thomas Holdcroft, *The Pentateuch* (Oakland, CA: Western Book Company, 1966), 2, 132). Wells' book, which reflects the ideological connection between the "gap" or "reconstruction" view and premillennial dispensationalism (a connection also evident in some "young earth" works), received a glowing endorsement from William S. Deal, a Wesleyan author who was published frequently in the *Revivalist* and whose books have been used in GBS classes.

For the last several decades, the "young earth" view has been dominant at GBS. Such works as John C. Whitcomb and Henry M. Morris, *The Genesis Flood: The Biblical Record and Its Scientific Implications* (Phillipsburg, NJ: Presbyterian and Reformed Publishing, 1961) have been promoted. Recently, the school has hosted Ken Ham, founder of Answers in Genesis, a "young earth" creationist organization begun in Australia but now headquartered in northern Kentucky (See Kenneth A. Ham, *The Lie: Evolution* (Green Forest, AR: Master Books, 1987) and Ken Ham, Andrew Snelling, and Carl Wieland, *The Answers Book: Detailed answers at layman's level to 12 of the most-asked questions on creation/evolution* (Green Forest, AR: Master Books,

1990). In 2005, GBS also provided the facilities for the production of AIG's Answers Academy curriculum.

For a general analysis of holiness movement reactions to Darwinism, see Ronald L. Numbers "Creation, Evolution, and Holy Ghost Religion: Holiness and Pentecostal Responses to Darwinism," *Religion and American Culture* Vol. 2 (Summer 1992), 127-158. Also, see his *The Creationists: The Evolution of Scientific Creationism* (Berkeley: University of California Press, 1992) and Mark Noll, *Scandal of the Evangelical Mind*, 12-15 and 177-208.

[33] W. B. Godbey, *Holiness or Hell?* (Louisville: The Pentecostal Publishing Co., 1899).

[34] Hamilton, "William Baxter Godbey: Apostle of Holiness," 162. See also, W. B. Godbey, "Question Drawer," *Revivalist* (May 30, 1901), 11, where he asserts "that facts, and not names, are conspicuous with God." See also, his *Mormonism* (Cincinnati: God's Revivalist Press, n. d.) and *Mohammedanism* (God's Revivalist Press, n. d.).

[35] Delbert R. Rose, "Little Man, Mighty Accomplishments," *The Herald* (Dec. 18, 1968), 7.

[36] James McGraw, "The Preaching of William B. Godbey," *The Preacher's Magazine* (March 1956), 9.

[37] See *Godbey on Christian Experience*. For scholarly analysis of Godbey's revivalistic preaching and writing, see Barry W. Hamilton, "Preaching the 'Narrow Way': William B. Godbey's Homiletical Agenda for the Early Holiness Movement," *MH* vol. 38 no. 1 (Oct. 1999), 40-52.

[38] "Bible School Notes," *Revivalist* (Dec. 2, 1909), 12.

[39] Matilda Steele, *To God Be The Glory* (Bridgeport, WV: Matilda S. Steele, 1978), 11.

[40] Augusta Oakes Guy, *Pioneering With God* Rev. ed. compiled by Dan Shaw, Garman Kemmel and Willis Dobson (Bethany, OK: Augusta Oakes Guy, 1983), 146. See the excerpt from this work in Moser and Smith, 107-110.

[41] For a brilliant discussion of this concept, see Douglas M. Strong, "Sanctified Eccentricity: The Continuing Relevance of the Nineteenth Century Holiness Paradigm," c. 13 in Barry L. Callen and William C. Kostlevy, eds. *Heart of the Heritage: Core Themes of the Wesleyan/Holiness Tradition as Highlighted by the Wesleyan Theological Society 1965-2000* (Salem, OH: Schmul Publishing Co., 2001), 311-322 (originally published in the *WTJ* vol. 35 no. 1 (Spring 2000), 9-21).

[42] Cited in "A Railroad Glimpse of Dr. Godbey," *Revivalist* (Sept. 6, 1900), 12.

[43] McGraw, "Preaching of . . . Godbey," 7-9.

[44] "Gold from Godbey," *Revivalist* (May 23, 1901), 14.

[45] Seth C. Rees, et. al. *Pentecostal Messengers*, 20.

[46] John R. Church, *Divine Healing* (Louisville: Pentecostal Publishing Co., n. d.), 34.

[47] Delbert R. Rose, "Little Man, Mighty Accomplishments," *The Herald* (Dec. 18, 1968), 21.

[48] Mrs. M. W. Knapp, "Into the Beautiful Beyond," *Revivalist* (Oct. 7, 1920), 3.

[49] Kenneth T. Walsh, "Once More With Feeling?" *U. S. News and World Report* (Sept. 6, 2004), 28. For an excellent biography of Chambers, see David McCasland, *Oswald Chambers: Abandoned to God: The Life Story of the Author of My Utmost for His Highest* (Nashville: Discovery House, 1993). McCasland also compiled an annotated

edition of *The Complete Works of Oswald Chambers* (Grand Rapids: Discovery House Publishers, 2000). For shorter biographical accounts, see Wesley L. Duewel, *More God More Power: Filled and Transfigured by the Holy Spirit* (Grand Rapids: Zondervan, 2000), 59-62; "Oswald Chambers: Surrounded by God's Presence" c. 4 in Wesley L. Duewel, *Heroes of the Holy Life: Biographies of Fully Devoted Followers of Christ* (Grand Rapids: Zondervan, 2002), 39-51; *Lightning from the Past*, 42-44; and Kostlevy, *Dictionary*, 49-50. On Chambers' affiliation with GBS, see Dorothy Walters, "Life and Work of Oswald Chambers," *Revivalist* (Aug. 17, 1967), 8-9; Glenn D. Black, "Oswald Chambers Served As Instructor At God's Bible School in 1907," *Revivalist* (Aug. 18, 1983), 11, 13; David McCasland, "Oswald Chambers Joins the Faculty at God's Bible School: Part One," *Revivalist* (April 1996), 7-8 and Part Two *Revivalist* (May 1996), 7-8; and Moser and Smith, 40-47.

[50] Kostlevy, *Dictionary*, 50.

[51] Walters, "Chambers as Instructor," 9.

[52] Sister Lasley, "God Exalted Above All," *Revivalist* (Feb. 25, 1909), 5.

[53] Walters, "Chambers as Instructor," 8.

[54] Duewel, *Heroes of the Holy Life*, 40.

[55] Duewel, *More God More Power*, 59.

[56] *Lightning from the Past*, 42.

[57] Brother Chambers (reported by I. M.), "Divine Guidance," *Revivalist* (March 25, 1909), 2-3 (original emphasis).

[58] Oswald Chambers, "A Great and Blessed Season," *Revivalist* (Jan. 17, 1907), 5.

[59] McCasland suggests that "God's Bible School is probably the only institution with which Chambers was associated on an on-going basis in the U. S." Cited in Stephen Hulba, "Religious Tract Was Born Here," *Cincinnati Post* (Sept. 27, 2000), http://www.cincypost.com/news/bible092700.html.

[60] Kostlevy, *Dictionary*, 49.

[61] McCasland, "Oswald Chambers Joins the Faculty," in Moser and Smith, 41.

[62] George B. Kulp, "A Spiritual Watering Place," *Revivalist* (Jan. 17, 1907), 4.

[63] In addition to the references below to the 1908 and 1909 camp meetings, see his report of the 1910 camp, "A 'Golden Wedding' Camp," *Revivalist* (July 21, 1910), 10-11.

[64] The first edition of the latter work was reprinted in 2005 by Schmul Publishing Co. and reflects significant variations from the current Discovery House edition.

[65] Oswald Chambers, "He Doeth All Things Well," *Revivalist* (July 9, 1908), 7 (my emphasis).

[66] Oswald Chambers, "Impressions of the 1909 Salvation Park Camp," *Revivalist* (July 8, 1909), 3.

[67] Oswald Chambers, "'Jesus Only' and 'Saintly Character'," *Revivalist* (July 25, 1907), 16.

[68] Oswald Chambers, "Impressions of the 1909 Salvation Park Camp," *Revivalist* (July 8, 1909), 2-3.

[69] Victor C. Wilson, *A Research Study on the Biography of George B. Kulp* (Term paper, Marion College, 1977), 6. In addition to this material, this section is indebted to *Lightning from the Past*, 104-107 and Kostlevy, *Dictionary*, 181-182.

[70] Thomas and Thomas, 52.

71 For example, see his ordination message in "The Charge To Candidates," *Revivalist* (July 19, 1906), 5-7, 10.

72 Kostlevy, *Dictionary*, 181-182.

73 *Lightning from the Past*, 105. "The name was changed to Pilgrim Holiness Church after the merger with Seth Rees' Pilgrim church in 1922.

74 See George B. Kulp, "Hard on the Stove," *Revivalist* (May 17, 1900), 8, for one of his early articles.

75 George B. Kulp, *The Calloused Knees; or, A Man Sent From God Whose Name Was John* (1909) and *The King's Allowance: A Daily Rate for Every Day* (1917). See also, *Nuggets of Gold, For the Use of Preachers, Teachers, and All Workers. Gathered Here and There, Through Over Thirty Years of Active Ministry* (1908); *Truths that Transfigure: Faith Tonics; Fifteen Sermons for Saints Published at Request of Laity and Ministry* (1927); *A Voice From Eternity; or Soul Searching Sermons* (1909); and *The Departed Lord or, Words That Burn* (n. d.).

76 For examples, see the announcements in *God's Revivalist* (Dec. 7, 1905), 1 and (Dec. 9, 1909), 14.

77 See "Special Notice," *Revivalist* (Oct. 17, 1907), 14. In 1911, Kulp reported that he was in his fifteenth series of lectures conducted during a five year period ("Wanted: Nehemiahs!" *Revivalist* (May 18, 1911), 1).

78 Sister Lasley, "Bible School Notes," *Revivalist* (Dec. 2, 1909), 12.

79 "Bible School Notes," *Revivalist* (March 11, 1909), 14.

80 Republished as *The Making of a Preacher* (along with C. F. Wimberly, *Falling from Grace*) (Salem, OH: Schmul, 1986).

81 Sister Lasley, "Bible School Notes," *Revivalist* (Dec. 2, 1909), 12.

82 Thomas and Thomas, 56.

83 W. L. Surbrook, "Another General Promoted," *Pilgrim Holiness Advocate* (Aug. 10, 1939), 1. Cited in Wilson, *Biography of George B. Kulp*, 11.

84 Standley, *My Life*, 81.

85 In his introductory address to the Revivalist family, Pennington noted the extensive missionary activity of the Church of Emmanuel, which included several rescue workers in the United States and about a half-dozen missionaries abroad (John Pennington, "To the Revivalist Family: Greeting in Jesus' Name," *Revivalist* (Sept. 24, 1903), 1 (letter dated Sept. 14, 1903).

86 Ibid, 80.

87 Seth C. Rees, "The Cincinnati Camp as I Saw It," *Revivalist* (Aug. 20, 1903), 14.

88 "Called of God," *Revivalist* (Sept. 3, 1903), 1.

89 Ibid, also, see Day, 72.

90 *My Life*, 80.

91 "Bible-School Notes," *Revivalist* (Oct. 22, 1903), 15.

92 E. A. Fergerson, "Another Account," *Revivalist* (June 30, 1904), 1.

93 Byron L. Osborne, *The Malone Story: The Dream of Two Quaker Young People* (Canton, OH: Malone College, 1970), 101. Though Eva was dying, she made a deep impression on the campus family with her "beautiful, fragrant, smiling" demeanor. When she died at Christ Hospital as the "result of an operation," the hospital superintendent noted that "she had been beside many deathbeds, but only a few like this.

The room was filled with the glory of God" (Larry D. Smith, "Beautiful, Fragrant, Smiling Eva," *Revivalist* (Nov. 1999), 7, 17).

The Penningtons were not the only members of the campus family mourning the loss of a child during this difficult time. On Valentine's Day of 1905, M. G. and Bessie Standley buried their six month old son Nathaniel, who had died from influenza.

[94] Standley, *My Life*, 80-81.
[95] See "The Foreign Missionary Work," *Revivalist* (Feb. 16, 1905), 1.
[96] Standley, *My Life*, 81.
[97] Thomas and Thomas, 46.
[98] Paul Rees, *Warrior-Saint*, 63.
[99] Thomas and Thomas, 46. See also Hynson in Caldwell, 222.
[100] "The Foreign Missionary Work," *Revivalist* (Feb. 16, 1905), 1.
[101] "The World-Wide Holiness Missionary Funds," *Revivalist* (Feb. 23, 1905), 9.
[102] Standley, *My Life*, 83.
[103] See the photo of some of the camp workers in Moser and Smith, 33.
[104] "What Hath God Wrought!" *Revivalist* (July 13, 1905), 1-3, 10.
[105] C. O. Moulton, "A Happy People," *Revivalist* (July 13, 1905), 6.
[106] A. M. Hills, "Prayed Up and Ready," *Revivalist* (July 13, 1905), 7. E. A. Fergerson wrote, "I think a very conservative estimate of the number of seekers from first to last would be about 900" ("A Great Meeting in Every Respect," *Revivalist* (July 13, 1905), 6).
[107] Thomas and Thomas, 68-69.
[108] Paul W. Thomas, *An Historical Survey of Pilgrim World Missions* (B. D. thesis, Asbury Theological Seminary, 1963), 139-140.
[109] In a lengthy letter to Nazarene General Superintendent R. T. Williams, dated April 22, 1933, James and Jesse Hundley share their perspective on this situation, and the subsequent court case involving GBS. They present a detailed account of how events unfolded in Africa as the conflicting parties dealt with property issues, etc. They also briefly mention Gorham Tuft and his work. This letter is on file in both the Nazarene and Wesleyan Archives, as well as at GBS.
[110] See announcement for the "Apostolic Holiness Convention of Ohio," *Revivalist* (Dec. 7, 1905), 1.
[111] Mary Storey, "The Foreign Missionary Board of 'God's Revivalist' and 'The International Apostolic Holiness Union,'" *Revivalist* (Jan. 18, 1906), 13.
[112] See L. B. Compton, "God's Revivalist and Apostolic Union Work in the Mountains of Western North Carolina," *Revivalist* (Oct. 1, 1903), 14; Lucius B. Compton, "In Direct Answer to Prayer," *Revivalist* (Nov. 30, 1905), 5; Edith Van Dusen, "Orphanage Work in Asheville, North Carolina," *Revivalist* (March 15, 1906), 13; Lucius B. Compton, "Eliada Orphanage and Training Home," *Revivalist* (Dec. 27, 1906), 4; and John C. Patty, *Life of Lucius Bunyan Compton: The Mountaineer Evangelist* (Cincinnati: The Revivalist Press, 1914).
[113] Thomas and Thomas, 68. Thomas, *Pilgrim World Missions*, 140, indicates that "there was very little progress in the matter of having money channeled through regular channels, and so the general leaders had little vital control of the work."
[114] "Foreign Work," *Revivalist* (Feb. 1, 1906), 12.

[115] Thomas, Pilgrim World Missions, 140 and Hynson in Caldwell, 235.

[116] Thomas and Thomas, 111.

[117] M. G. Standley, *My Life*, 116.

[118] Lucius B. Compton, "A Triumphant Pilgrim Is Gone; Another Takes Her Place," and George B. Kulp, "God Calls Men To-day," *Revivalist* (April 5, 1906), 14. Standley later mistakenly attributed Kulp's quote to Compton (*My Life*, 116-117).

[119] Mrs. M. W. Knapp, "God's Choice," *Revivalist* (April 5, 1906), 4 (original emphasis).

[120] "Highlights of the Miller Presidency," *Revivalist* (April/May 1995), 19-20. For most of the material on the court case, see the files in the Cowman Archives at GBS, which are organized chronologically. Where approximate dates are apparent, court records will not usually be cited.

[121] For a partial copy of an article in *The Cincinnati Enquirer* (Feb. 21, 1907), see Moser and Smith, 45.

[122] "Receiver Refused by the Court," *The Cincinnati Enquirer* (April 21, 1907), 3.

[123] "Orders New Deal for God's Bible School," *Cincinnati Post* (April 20, 1907), 1.

[124] Ibid.

[125] "Receiver Refused . . .," *Enquirer* (April 21, 1907), 3.

[126] "God's (?) Revivalist," *The Burning Bush* (Feb. 5, 1903), 6-7. Standley obliquely refers to *The Burning Bush*'s attacks in *My Life*, 122.

[127] Kostlevy, *Holy Jumpers*, 82.

[128] "Epworth League," *Revivalist* (Jan. 30, 1902), 10. This explanation also suggested that "no Christian can keep in touch with God, and have the fire and unction with the power of the Holy Ghost, and be yoked up with such a society." See also, "Epworth League," *Revivalist* (Jan. 2, 1902), 8; J. F. Knapp, "Entering the Kingdom," *Revivalist* (Jan. 9, 1902), 15; and J. F. Knapp, "What is meant by 'The Evangelization of the World?'" *Revivalist* (Jan. 16, 1902), 10.

[129] "God's (?) Revivalist," *The Burning Bush* (Feb. 5, 1903), 6-7. For an example of continued charges against GBS leadership, see "Probing 'God's Revivalist'," *The Burning Bush* (Nov. 17, 1904), 1-3.

[130] See "God's Revivalist School," *The Burning Bush* (Feb. 28, 1907), which reproduces the *Cincinnati Enquirer* (Feb. 21, 1907) article on the lawsuit; "God's Revivalist Under Court Order," *The Burning Bush* (Nov. 14, 1907), 1; and "Seth Rees' Confession," *The Burning Bush* (Dec. 26, 1907), 1. The last article duplicates a letter in which Rees discusses his and John Pennington's separation from the work at GBS. I am indebted to Gary E. Bowell for his kind assistance in locating these articles.

[131] M. G. Standley later wrote, "Never once did we make answer, seek revenge, or use the columns of the paper for anything but that which would be inspiring and edifying to God's people" (*My Life*, 122).

[132] W. B. Godbey, "Adoption" in *Godbey on Christian Experience*, 99.

[133] Ibid, 103.

[134] M. G. Standley, *My Life*, 120-121. See also Moser and Smith, 44-46.

[135] George B. Kulp, Lucius B. Compton, L. Milton Williams, and E. A. Fergerson, "From the Missionary Board," *Revivalist* (Oct. 31, 1907), 1. See also in the same issue of the *Revivalist*, "Decree of the Court," 1-2; "Report of the Expert Accoun-

tant," 2-3; and "A Letter from Judge Pfleger," 3.

[136] "NOTICE," *Revivalist* (Oct. 24, 1907), 15 and "NOTICE," *Revivalist* (Dec. 5, 1907), 14.

[137] M. G. Standley, *My Life*, 125.

[138] J. E. Strong, Secretary, "Hallelujah! Praise the Lord!" *Revivalist* (Jan. 9, 1908), 1-2.

[139] *My Life*, 124-129.

[140] Story V. Knapp et. al. Court of Appeals of Ohio, Hamilton County (Dec. 5, 1927) records by West Group, 1998. M. G. Standley hints that a factor in this decision was friendship between one of the Circuit Court judges and Bessie Standley's father.

[141] *My Life*, 131.

[142] "To the 'Revivalist Family," *Revivalist* (Jan. 9, 1908), 1.

[143] George B. Kulp, "The 'God's Bible School Work," *Revivalist* (July 9, 1908), 10-13, 15 (original emphasis). See also, Meredith G. Standley, "All Is Well," *Revivalist* (July 9, 1908), 1-3.

[144] M. G. Standley, "Things As They Are," *Revivalist* (July 8, 1909), 1, 12 (original emphasis).

[145] "Just in Its Infancy," *Revivalist* (Dec. 21, 1911), 14 (original emphasis).

Chapter 8

Broadening the Base; Defending the Basics

[The GBS camp meeting] is the most like anything that I think Heaven is, that we can get while living down here in this country. This is one place that, of all places I have been, seems holy ground; where denominational lines are forgotten, at least are not in effect; and where God's people meet in common cause, the cause of Holiness—second blessing, Bible, St. Paul, St. John, John Wesley Holiness. People of many denominations were present, but to me they all looked and acted very much alike.
– George Beirnes[1]

Thus the greatest of all the marvelous Camp Meetings on the "Mount of Blessings" passed into history . . . June 3, 1928. We are certain that no one who visited and witnessed the scene that we are talking about could but say with us that it was one of the greatest scenes of spiritual power and one of the greatest answers to the claims of the Modernists and Evolutionists that God is a myth and does not visit the people, answer their prayers, and undertake for them as recorded in the old days in the Bible!
– F. M. Messenger[2]

The leadership of Meredith and Bessie Standley throughout the period of administrative trusteeship (1902-1911) confirms that, in many ways, the "Standley years" actually began shortly after the death of Martin Wells Knapp. Throughout the first decade, their role as Knapp's heirs became more apparent, and their vindication in the court case beginning in 1907 further strengthened their position. It is thus unsurprising that M. G. Standley's appointment as "president" (technically, *chairman* of the Trustees) in 1911 came without fanfare. In fact, little had changed; for all practical purposes, he would simply continue to lead the school much as he had already done, with the able contributions of his wife and the continued cooperation and blessing of Minnie Ferle Knapp.

As Larry D. Smith has observed, it was under M. G. Standley's presidency that GBS matured and "realized much of its founder's vision and became a flourishing focal point for the entire holiness movement."[3] In fact, one of the Standleys' greatest feats may have been the broad consensus they formed with other religious leaders, even beyond the holiness fold, helping to establish GBS as one of the great interdenominational institutions of the evangelical community. This consensus involved the gradual distancing of some old ties, the renewal of some relationships that had been strained during past controversies, and the welcoming of new comrades in the efforts to win the world and to turn the Church "Back to the Bible."

The Pilgrim Connection

Chief among the existing ties nurtured during the early years of the Standley administration were those with the International Apostolic Holiness Union—later International Holiness Church—which merged with the Pilgrim Church of California (headed by Seth Rees) in 1922 to form the Pilgrim Holiness Church. Primarily through the influence of George Kulp, who viewed "the GBS complex of ministries as the heart of the developing movement,"[4] the Mount of Blessings served as the *de facto* "headquarters" of the evolving denomination until Kulp's retirement from the general superintendency of the International Holiness Church in 1921.

It would be difficult to overestimate the influences that GBS and the Pilgrim Holiness Church exerted on each other. In fact, strong evidence indicates that the ethos of the Hilltop remained virtually identical with that of the early Pilgrims. On one hand, Pilgrim leadership continued to have a dynamic influence on GBS, especially through Kulp's spiritual, intellectual, and administrative contributions. In lectures, sermons, and articles advocating such themes as divine healing and opposition to worldliness, he and his "Pilgrim" colleagues helped to assure that at GBS the radical holiness witness remained clear.[5] Kulp also vigorously promoted the primacy of the spiritual at GBS and was the speaker when revival broke out on campus in December 1917, with regular classes being suspended for over two weeks as meetings were conducted in the dining room, which "was often the scene of mighty prevailing prayer." This meeting was characterized by the demonstrative worship for which Pilgrims became known, including "leaping and shouting and praising God" and some participants being "prostrated under the power of God."[6]

On the other hand, GBS and its trustees reciprocated by exerting significant influence on the development of the Pilgrim Holiness Church, with M. G. Standley serving on the denomination's General Council until 1930. Leon Hynson suggests that "the vision of God's Bible School would to some degree be carried through the Church's entire history."[7] For example, the zeal for world-wide evangelism inculcated on the Hilltop would permeate the young Pilgrim denomination and its antecedents, reflected in Seth C. Rees's reminiscence on this commitment as one of the Pilgrims' "foundation principles" and his insistence that

> ". . no one has or can be a true, loyal Pilgrim who is not on fire for missions. It matters not what is professed or what else one may be, he cannot be a consistent, loyal Pilgrim, worthy of the name, if he is not on fire to reach the ends of the earth with this burning Gospel message.
>
> . . . . .
>
> I know the standards of New Testament piety and I know the standards of the Pilgrim Holiness Church. No one has a right to profess to be sanctified wholly who is not an ardent, active promoter of missions."[8]

Beyond the fact that GBS provided "the main center" for the IAHU/ Church, the chief demonstration of GBS's contribution to the strong missional ethos among Pilgrims was the fact that it served "as the training center for most of the early Pilgrims."⁹

In particular, "most of the missionaries before 1930 came from God's Bible School."¹⁰ Just a brief delineation of the careers of a few of them demonstrates their vast contribution to the development of Pilgrim missions:

One of these with deep Pilgrim and GBS roots was Flora Belle Slater, daughter of Charles and Maude Slater. Having received a call to missions at age nine, she trained at GBS and Kingswood College. Reflecting the versatility of her parents, she served in several fields including Mexico, Puerto Rica, Peru, and the Philippines. In the latter country, she directed a Bible college, maintaining it "on a completely self-supporting basis, though many times her faith was put to the acid test."¹¹

In Africa, Clarence Gault Keith and his wife Roberta served with distinction for many years, including an eighteen year stint without furlough. Ethel Jordan, an earlier alumna of GBS, went to Africa in 1928 and served two ten-year terms in Cape Province, Natal, and Northern Rhodezia (now Zambia). Claudie Peyton, who spent four years working at Hope Cottage and God's Orphanage after her graduation in 1926, served in Zambia from 1930 until her death in 1984. Her unstinting labor of love, especially in the establishment and operation of a highly successful orphanage, won the love and respect of the people of Zambia, reflected in 1983 by the Zambian president bestowing upon her the honorific title of Grand Officer of Zambia.¹²

Ruth Bowman, after several years of pastoral and teaching service, including positions on the faculty of Eastern Pilgrim College, Owosso College, and Frankfort College, began pastoral work on the island of Grand Cayman in 1949. Although illness briefly forced her return to the United States, she returned to Grand Cayman in 1953 and made the island her home until her death in January 1991, establishing a reputation as a "straight-forward, straight-laced, strict but gentle and humorous lady" who remained steadfast amidst many changes.¹³ Here her labors helped to establish the holiness movement as a dominant force—contributing much toward making that small island likely the nation with the highest number of holiness devotees per capita.¹⁴ Upon her death she was especially remembered for the "burden of prayer" she carried, not only for "her beloved Island and its people" but also for GBS—"her beloved School and its leaders and students."¹⁵

Other GBS alumni who ministered even earlier in Grand Cayman, as well as at several other locations throughout the Caribbean, were Edward Everett Phillippe and his wife Eunice Leona. In addition to preaching, their fruitful ministry of forty-three years in the Caribbean included Everette's serving in such administrative positions as district superintendent of the Northern Islands District and, ultimately, as Field Superintendent of the Caribbean Area.¹⁶ "Aunt Margaret" Hankins worked as a missionary-evangelist throughout the Caribbean and devoted several years to missions in Jamaica, where her husband, a layman, constructed the buildings of the Caribbean Pilgrim College.

Numerous other Pilgrim leaders also received their education at GBS and left the school's indelible stamp on the denomination. Among these were Robert Heckart—pastor, evangelist, district superintendent, college president, and author; H. D. Dukes—member of the General Board and district superintendent; and William H. Neff—"one of the finest preachers in the [Pilgrim Holiness] Church, virtually without peer." [17]

Neff's enrollment at GBS proved particularly poignant because it was motivated by the death of his brother Wesley, who had attended GBS for one year with aspirations of becoming a missionary to Africa, but who drowned during a visit home. Thereafter, William felt that he was "to take his brother's place" in ministry and thus followed his steps to the Mount of Blessings,[18] where he was equipped for a lifetime of fruitful service, including many years as successful pastor, evangelist, district superintendent, assistant general superintendent, and as general superintendent from 1955 to 1966.[19]

Despite the impact that GBS had upon the Pilgrims through its alumni and through its inspiration of numerous regional Bible schools that were either initiated by or later identified with the Pilgrim Holiness Church, seminal forces gathered strength throughout this period that would eventuate in the cessation of "official organizational ties" between GBS and the Pilgrim denomination.[20] Numerous factors would contribute to this development, including—ironically—the very fact that GBS had helped to mother so many "Pilgrim" schools.[21] In addition, the numerous mergers that rapidly expanded the Union/Church's constituency contributed to the growth of a denominational consciousness that would eventually lead many Pilgrims to favor their own schools over such independent works as GBS. This denominational consciousness was likely encouraged, in another ironic twist of history, by one of GBS's most prominent supporters—George B. Kulp—through his emphasis on organization. Another negative, but powerful, incentive toward increased denominational organization was presented by the Rees/Pennington departure from GBS, an incident that underscored the necessity of better accountability structures, particularly in the context of mission activities.

By 1922, wittingly or not, the GBS trustees had largely turned the supervision of GBS/Revivalist sponsored mission works over to the International/Pilgrim Holiness Church or to such agencies as the Oriental Missionary Society. In this year, the Pilgrims took some decisive actions signaling the organization under their control of the mission work which had been spawned largely by the "Revivalist/Union" movement. Among these was the election of a General Superintendent of Foreign Missions—GBS alumnus R. G. Finch—and the establishment of denominational headquarters at Kingswood College in Kingswood, Kentucky.[22]

This general relationship of continuing cooperation concurrent with increasing independence between GBS and the International/Pilgrim Holiness Church was reflected as well in a development in Cincinnati in 1921. This local parallel to the general trend involved the establishment of an International Holiness Church away from the GBS campus. Located downtown (at Fifteenth and Elm Streets), this congregation was independent from GBS, yet retained strong ties with the school, with its first pastor being John Coleman—one of the "products" of GBS mission work, who had succeeded Lew Standley as pastor of George Street Mission. In fact, M. G. Standley preached and officiated at the church's dedication on August 7, and John Franklin Knapp delivered a sermon as well on the dedicatory day.[23]

These developments did not signal lessened zeal among GBS leaders or constituents with regard to home or foreign missions. Rather, they reflected tacit recognition that the far-flung mission outposts that still enjoyed the support of GBS and *Revivalist* constituents required more oversight than the GBS trustees could adequately provide. It also helped to free the trustees to focus on the publishing and educational ministries of the Mount of Blessings, as well as the social relief and evangelistic ministries concentrated in the Cincinnati area, including Hope Cottage, God's Orphanage, and the annual Thanksgiving Dinner. In this sense, the denominational development of the Pilgrim Holiness Church may have done a great service for GBS, allowing the school to narrow its own mission to more manageable proportions.

Ultimately, it also indicated the divergent trajectories that the Pilgrim Holiness Church and GBS would follow. While the former would go down the path of denominationalism that Martin Wells Knapp had so assiduously avoided, the school and the *Revivalist* remained faithful to his vision, embracing an interdenominational constituency that continued to count numerous Pilgrims among its most loyal members, but reaching a broad spectrum of evangelicals, particularly from other Wesleyan traditions.

Holiness Crossroads

The evangelists who preached in camp meetings, conventions, and revivals on the Mount of Blessings during the Standley era represent one significant area in which the school's constituency was broadened while the school simultaneously retained a symbiotic relationship with the Pilgrim Holiness Church. The latter relationship remained strong as GBS continued to welcome such Pilgrim evangelists and missions speakers as George B. Kulp, Lucius B. Compton, and R. G. Finch. In fact, Kulp remained an integral part of the camp meetings, both as preacher and as "official offering-taker for the Camp," well past his retirement from the general superintendency.[24]

The beneficial influence on and for GBS exerted by evangelist/leaders such as Kulp helps to illustrate the powerful role that evangelists still played in shaping the holiness movement throughout the first half of the twentieth century, a phenomenon shared by virtually all holiness groups. Indeed, the impact of such evangelists as "Bud" Robinson and C. W. Ruth on the Nazarenes and E. E. Shelhamer on the Free Methodists remains incalculable.

Perhaps one of their most significant contributions to the movement was as a unifying factor, tying together divergent groups and denominations through their evangelistic campaigns. This effect was intensified at GBS, as the school provided a platform which united evangelists and congregants from a plethora of backgrounds. Perhaps more powerfully than ever, GBS under the Standley administration served as a sort of crossroads of the holiness movement—where Nazarenes, Free Methodists, Pilgrims, Quakers, Wesleyan Methodists and many others—even Baptists and Presbyterians—put aside their sectarian differences and all rallied to promote radical holiness.[25]

After the 1924 camp meeting, E. (Everett) O. Chalfant, Chicago Central district superintendent in the Church of the Nazarene, who visited the GBS camp meeting each year for over twenty years, exclaimed, "I am more and more convinced that the great interdenominational work carried on on the 'Mount of Blessings' is the greatest spiritual force found in any one place in the world. Those in charge are sticking to the old motto, 'In non essentials liberty, in essentials unity, in all things charity.'"[26] George Kulp likewise assessed the 1925 encampment: "The interdenominational spirit that prevailed was remarkable. It seemed to be a fulfillment of the prayer of our Lord, 'that they all may be one, even as we are one.'"[27]

A cursory reading of camp meeting reports throughout the 1910's and 1920's finds this sentiment reflected repeatedly. In addition, the colorful cadre of preachers, missionaries, and special speakers who graced the platform of God's Tabernacle during this period, proclaiming the message of full salvation through exposition and testimony, lent credence to "Uncle Buddie" Robinson's glowing endorsement:

> It would pay ten thousand preachers and evangelists and Christian workers to stop for ten days and go to the Camp and just feast with the saints. There is not a preacher of any denomination but who would be received as a brother beloved of the Lord, for there is not one drop of sectarian blood on the "Mount of Blessings."[28]

While several volumes would not suffice to describe fully the innumerable company of illustrious preachers and other workers who contributed to and benefited from this ecumenical spirit, no history of God's Bible School would be complete without at least highlighting a few outstanding personalities among them. Several revivalists that were frequent camp meeting and convention speakers at GBS throughout its second and/or third decades had been associated with Martin Wells Knapp during (or even before) the founding days of the school, including J. L. Glascock, W. B. Godbey, John T. Hatfield, John Wesley Hughes, F. M. Messenger, L. L. Pickett, C. W. Ruth, and W. E. Shepard. Others who had an early association with the school and were invited back to minister during this period were L. Milton Williams, who had stood faithfully by the trustees during the Rees-Pennington defection, B. O. Shattuck, a prominent IAHU pastor in Michigan who went on to serve as a district superintendent in that state for the Pilgrim Holiness Church (1927-1930), and John Butler, the Quaker "farmer-evangelist" from Indiana who testified gratefully that, while he and his wife had earlier professed entire sanctification, it was not until their student days at GBS (while Martin Wells Knapp was still living) that they actually attained this grace.[29]

Each in his own inimitable way swayed the campus family and visitors with their unique presentation of holiness truth—both in word and deed. For example, Brother and Sister Hatfield impressed students and other camp attendees with their humble service wherever it was demanded, which found them sometimes alternating "between dishwashing, the platform, and the altar," with both proving "equally efficient in all stations."[30]

Of course, most prominent among those who had been associated with the school's founder (especially through the Chicago revival) was Bud Robinson himself, who drew crowds wherever he went, with as many as three to four thousand congregating on the Hilltop to hear him during the 1920s.[31] Robinson reminisced in 1928 that he had been visiting the Mount of Blessings since 1902 and that he had "often said, in traveling over the United States, that this was probably the *best* one spot on the face of the earth."[32] He suggested that, indeed, "the very ground is sacred because that 'Hill' has been bathed in tears and literally soaked with prayers" with probably "more precious souls . . . saved and sanctified there than on any other spot on the globe" during the school's first twenty-five years.[33]

Other evangelists who had been introduced to the GBS campus during the school's first decade gained much more prominence during its second and third decades. Among these, three remain especially noteworthy. The first was G. D. Watson, who had made his initial appearance at the GBS camp meeting in 1910, coincidentally the last Hilltop encampment attended by Oswald Chambers, with whom he has been favorably compared. Although his writings had long been a staple of *Revivalist* readers, Watson now received reciprocal benefit from what he described as "the peculiar, unspeakable, melting power of the Holy Spirit [that] seemed to pervade, to fill, to overflow and control everything" on the Hilltop. He concluded that at the GBS camp meeting, "The heart of Jesus was being satisfied, and my heart rejoiced in union with His."[34] At the same time, Watson exercised both a stimulating and stabilizing influence at the camp meetings with his profound and creative Scripture readings—providing such mental stimulus that John Wesley Hughes said he had "the 'neck-ache' every day after the Doctor [finished] because he [had] to think so hard and fast to keep up with him" and stability because his teachings helped "to guard against fanaticism and to inspire sane efficiency for the Kingdom."[35]

If Watson helped to stave off fanaticism, two much younger evangelists who were also introduced at the 1910 camp meeting assured that formalism would also be held at bay. These were John and Bona Fleming, variously termed the "Kentucky boys" (by Oswald Chambers), the "Flaming Brothers" (by George Kulp), and "sons of thunder" (by Joseph H. Smith). Prior to being converted, John and Bona were both reputed to be "a terror to the law of the land," and heavy drinking and reckless living were their norm. However, their turn-around was precipitated when W. W. Hankes, a missionary to Africa, felt led by God to return to the United States to the state of Kentucky. He began his work in the mountains of eastern Kentucky by conducting a meeting in the town of Willard, during which the Fleming brothers threatened to "whip" the preacher. However, it was not long until both came under deep conviction and were dramatically converted.

Soon, the Flemings accompanied Hankes to meetings, including Salvation Park Camp Meeting, to share their testimonies as trophies of grace. Both accepted the call to preach, and their personal testimonies remained a central feature of their evangelistic campaigns which garnered phenomenal responses from saint and sinner, with John recording thirty thousand seekers during the first fifteen years of his ministry.[36] Numerous holiness leaders endorsed their dynamic ministry, including Oswald Chambers who expressed enthrallment with the Flemings' "testimony of marvelous deliverance from sin and present personal entire sanctification," asserting that "the liberty, enthusiasm and demonstration of these men . . . was absolutely in the Holy Ghost."[37] Multitudes of GBS camp goers for the next several decades agreed, as Joseph H. Smith expressed it: "The people there always count upon them as among the chief features at this great Feast of Tabernacles on the 'Mount of Blessings'. They never weary of them; in fact, like the OLD, OLD Story itself, 'those that know them best seem hungering and thirsting to hear them like the rest'."[38]

The attraction of the Flemings' testimonies and other messages was twofold. Firstly, their messages, such as Bona's testimony delivered at the 1917 GBS camp meeting, were described as "full of fire and unction."[39] Typically, their sermons were accompanied by shouting, running, jumping and other emotional demonstration. In fact, contemporary attempts to depict their preaching make it clear that the power and demonstration accompanying their ministry defied description. In an assertion reflecting the ongoing pursuit of repeated Pentecost at GBS, Joseph H. Smith suggested that "the power of their ministries proves that the day of Pentecostal Revivals is not yet past."[40]

Secondly, the narrative nature of many of their messages, featuring homespun illustrations devoid of theological sophistication, endeared John and Bona Fleming to common people. For instance, camp meeting crowds at GBS delighted as John took the hermeneutic of illustration to creative extreme—"hanging on his words as he gave fourteen points as to how a Ford auto is like a sanctified person."[41] The impact of such analogies on the grassroots level of the holiness movement proved tremendous. In fact, through their employment of various metaphors, the Fleming brothers may have been the chief promulgators of what has been critiqued by some scholars as a "substantive" view (in contrast with a "relational" view) of entire sanctification, which reputedly holds that original sin (carnality) is a material substance, intrinsic within the fallen human body, remediable only by death or by a "magical" rather than a moral transformation.[42] While it is highly unlikely that the Flemings actually held such a view, which Martin Wells Knapp and other holiness authorities strongly repudiated, some of their analogies may have been misconstrued to result in such "a folk misunderstanding," highlighting the possible pitfall of over-simplification inherent to the hermeneutic of illustration.⁴³

In the 1922 GBS camp meeting, John illustrated the need for and results of entire sanctification by telling about "his nephew, who had a tooth pulled. He asked him if it ached. In reply the nephew said, 'Uncle John, what a foolish question to ask. How can a tooth ache when it is pulled?'" He then "exhorted professors . . . to get carnality taken out of their souls, and then the aching trouble of their lives would be gone."⁴⁴ Likewise, John's own testimony to entire sanctification included what may yet be the most popular imagery associated with the "substantive" view of sanctification. The person who led him to seek the second blessing explained to John that carnality would function much like a stump from a newly felled tree that would sprout branches in the spring. As John recalled it,

> He said, "John, you have a stump in your heart."
> It scared me. He said, "The stump is there. You have had your sins all taken away, but there is a stump. You must have it taken out, or sprouts will come up around your life and pull you back into sin."
> We went in mother's parlor and prayed, "Oh God, take the stump out, take the stump out, take the stump out!" . . .
> I rose to my feet and like a flash the Holy Ghost came and blew that stump out . . ."⁴⁵

This depiction of the "eradication" of carnality powerfully shaped popular conceptions of entire sanctification throughout the holiness movement, particularly among Pilgrims and Nazarenes.⁴⁶ Of course, such imagery was not original with the Flemings, with some proponents contending that it had scriptural precedent in "the root of bitterness" warning in Hebrews 12:15. In fact, Martin Wells Knapp himself had used the "stump" illustration as early as 1899 in the *Revivalist*.⁴⁷ In addition, similar metaphors proved popular throughout the twentieth century among other holiness evangelists, such as Bud Robinson, who relied heavily on narratives in their messages.⁴⁸

The acclaim accorded the Flemings at GBS demonstrates the ongoing emphasis on experiential spirituality on the Mount of Blessings under the Standleys' leadership. In fact, many of the speakers in highest demand throughout these years were those who simply shared personal testimonies—of salvation, healing, and special deliverance. Among them were Bud Robinson's testimony to divine intervention after he was crushed and nearly killed in a street-car accident in 1919; Charles Wireman's testimony to deliverance from the debauched life of a Kentucky mountain outlaw that resulted in the moniker "Bull Dog Charlie"—which he retained even after he became an evangelist; and C. B. Fugett's testimony to radical conversion to *The Sunny Side of Life* from a background similar to that of Wireman and the Flemings.⁴⁹

Perhaps the most popular speaker at GBS in the 1920's was actually a layperson—World War I hero Sergeant Alvin C. York—who in many ways personified the ideal holiness vision that GBS sought to perpetuate. Although renowned in his native Tennessee mountain community as an excellent hunter, York, as a young backwoodsman, would hardly have been envisioned to be a future military hero. In fact, as a committed member of the Churches of Christ in Christian Union, he had no desire to go to war; however, York complied with draft registration and after two days and a night of prayer felt that he had received "assurance direct from God" that he "should go" and that he "would come back without a scratch."[50] Soon, he was in the thick of fighting in the Argonne Forest of France, where, on October 8, 1918, he performed what has been termed "the greatest war feat" by a single person "in the annals of United States history."[51] In a stunning move, in which he employed turkey hunting techniques against the enemy, York took several German machine gun nests, killing at least twenty-five and capturing one hundred thirty-two of the enemy. As a result, almost instant fame was his, with six countries decorating him with honors including the Congressional Medal of Honor.[52]

Needless to say, GBS was just one of many places where York was invited to recount the great victory that he had won, which he insisted, even to hardened military leaders, was due, not to "man power," but to "a higher power."[53] In fact, York's response to popular acclaim may truthfully be the most remarkable "victory" that he won, for he steadfastly resisted the temptations that accompany fame and fortune: "He easily could have become a millionaire by endorsing products and advertising, but he refused"—instead raising money for schools in his home area and similar philanthropic causes.[54] He also regularly used speaking engagements to highlight spiritual themes, downplaying his own spectacular military victory as insignificant compared to victory over sin, telling the 1922 GBS camp meeting crowd that "it was harder to stand the temptations of the world than to enter the battle front" and that "self is the greatest thing we have to battle against."[55]

While he preferred to testify about spiritual victory, with a clear cut testimony to a personal experience of entire sanctification, even his recounting of his military feats had a spiritual motivation—"to show people how God can keep a man, if he will only stay on God's side."[56] This humble spirit endeared York to several generations of the GBS family, which eventually included his own son, George Edward, who enrolled as a student in 1941.[57] Perhaps evangelist Will Huff best summarized the high esteem accorded Sergeant York, not only as a military hero, but as a hero of holiness, on the Mount of Blessings:

> It so refreshing to hear this young man who is absolutely unspoiled, either by his war record or by flattering offers made to him by the moneyed interests of the movies. He knows the grace of Full Salvation, testifies humbly to the same, and is most modest in telling of his war experience . . . This young man will be remembered without having to remind the people of himself.[58]

While the testimonies of such diverse figures as Alvin York and the Fleming brothers became an integral part of the GBS psyche, the campus family was also profoundly shaped by the careful exposition of several of the great holiness evangelists of the day. Foremost among these were William H. Huff and Joseph H. Smith, men who represented another significant development during the first half of the Standley administration—rapprochement with the National Association for the Promotion of Holiness.

Will Huff has failed to receive his just due as a holiness exponent by posterity, probably due to his death at the young age of fifty-three in 1928. However, he was one of the most formidable advocates of holiness during the first quarter of the twentieth century, characterized by B. O. Shattuck as a "mighty preacher of righteousness, whose oratory is set on fire by the Holy Ghost."[59] His dynamic preaching ministry, which made him one of Bud Robinson's favorite evangelistic co-workers, was coupled with a deep concern for the outcasts of society, both in the United States and abroad. In this country, Huff expressed special interest in "the plight of African Americans," from whom he drew many of his riveting illustrations.[60] He also felt a particular passion for Latin America, making five missionary tours there and eventually transferring his membership from the Northwest Iowa Conference of the Methodist Episcopal Church to its South American Conference, led then by his friend Bishop William F. Oldham.[61] Such an inclusive vision for souls, as well as the combination of precise logic and fiery delivery in his preaching, won Huff wide respect among his contemporaries throughout the holiness movement, further heightened by his service as president of the National Association from 1919 to 1921, during which he "helped bring back a sense of stability to the movement."[62] A vital part of this accomplishment involved reaching out to the diverse constituencies of the holiness movement, including that centered on the Mount of Blessings.

Even further aligning GBS with the National Association was Joseph H. Smith, who served as a camp meeting evangelist at GBS every year for over a decade beginning in 1922, with his wife often accompanying him there as a youth worker.[63] For several reasons, Smith stood out as a giant on the landscape of the twentieth-century holiness movement. For one, although Smith was primarily self-educated, he was a teaching preacher, which endeared him to both clergy and lay people.[64] In fact, he was widely considered the "dean of holiness expositors"—garnering such recognition from characters as diverse as Bud Robinson and Dr. Gross Alexander, professor of New Testament at Vanderbilt University and editor of *The Methodist Review*. Interestingly, the "classroom" where Smith focused his educational efforts was the camp meeting—not a forum usually associated with deep scholarship.[65] However, this was consonant with Smith's conviction that the camp meeting was "the 'unit and center' of the Holiness movement."[66] This employment of the camp meeting as a tool for instruction was taken even further in 1897 when Smith's special concern for ministers' continuing education led him to begin an "itinerant institute on evangelism" called the "School of the Prophets" which convened at various camp meetings across the country.[67] This "institute" was introduced to GBS in the 1922 camp meeting, with as many as three thousand gathering to hear his "indescribable" messages that were "profound in thought, deeply spiritual, and transcendently eloquent."[68]

Smith's stature as a holiness leader was also heightened by his unique perspective on the holiness movement's development from the era of associations (he had joined the National Association in 1883) to the development of numerous, distinctly "holiness" denominations, schools, and other institutions. In addition, his popularity on the camp meeting circuit kept him abreast of major currents in the movement for much of its first century. Holiness people thus revered him as "a living link to the past," and treasured his recollections and life's story as well as his deep Bible expositions.[69] In fact, Smith celebrated his seventieth birthday during the 1925 GBS camp meeting, and in a "never-to-be-forgotten" service was requested to share "his life story instead of preaching," with the resulting narrative convincing missionary R. Wingrove Ives that Smith was "a worthy successor to Fowler, Pepper, Thompson, Inskip and others of this great movement."[70]

His superb expository skills, extensive knowledge of the holiness movement's history and development, and passionate but sagacious promotion of the movement's distinctive doctrine, all combined with a warm, self-effacing personality to make Smith one of the most beloved presidents of the National Holiness Association, a position he held from 1925 to 1928.[71] In fact, the Association's membership honored him in 1928 with the designation of "honorary president"—"and referred to him by that title until his death in 1946."[72]

While he poured himself into advancing the holiness cause, Smith was objectively reflective on the movement's shortcomings, candidly assessing these in 1916 in *Things Behind and Things Before in the Holiness Movement*, a brief document that remains remarkably relevant to the contemporary movement.[73] Here, he addressed the movement's general neglect of outreach to African Americans—"a nearby mission field," its *"lack of any disciplinary system"*—which he considered its *"most serious defect,"* and the infection of some of its institutions, particularly schools, by "commercialism."

Perhaps his most devastating critique went straight to the heart of what Smith considered to be the nineteenth-century Holiness Revival's original "commission"—

> The carrying of the truth and testimony and power of holiness into all Christendom. "Till we all come in the unity of the faith and the knowledge of the Son of God unto . . . the fullness of Christ." Till the doctrine of sanctification by faith is established in all the churches as now we have all seen the doctrine of justification by faith.[74]

In other words, the holiness movement had been charged, not only "with the evangelization of the whole world" but also "with the sanctification of the whole church."

Smith charged that rather than fulfilling this call, the holiness movement had "developed the lesser idea of calling a church out from the church instead of calling the whole church out from the world."[75] This had resulted in the formation of the numerous "holiness" denominations, each of which Smith acknowledged had "a mission and a place in the present order and condition of things." This granted, he argued that no one holiness denomination, "nor all together," could "begin to fill the place of the holiness movement!"[76] Smith thus appealed "for seasons of fasting and prayer," that the holiness movement would once again be truly interdenominational and inclusive rather than sectarian and exclusive, imploring holiness leaders:

> Let us, beloved, go down to the depths of humility and bathe our souls together in the fathomless billows of love, till we arise to furnish afresh, not only to the holiness people but to the Church at large, *a demonstration of the answer to the Saviour's prayer that 'they all may be one, ... that the world may believe'.*"[77]

While Joseph H. Smith was arguably the most influential individual in promoting this interdenominational holiness impulse during the first half of the twentieth century, it is doubtful that any institution provided a more congenial reception to this agenda than did God's Bible School. As if the diversity of speakers already delineated here, who were welcomed in God's Tabernacle throughout the 1910s and 1920s, was not enough to establish the school's distinction as a holiness crossroads, they represent but a fraction of the innumerable company of outstanding holiness proponents who graced the campus during this period, to which could be added such names as J. B. McBride, C. H. Babcock, J. D. Drysdale, and J. M. Hames.[78]

In addition to the camaraderie shared by evangelists and congregants at GBS, several other evidences could be marshaled to demonstrate the emphasis on unity in holiness at GBS throughout its second and third decades. Particularly poignant was the return during the 1926 camp meeting of Seth C. Rees to the campus "for a few days." Undoubtedly, the significance of this brief visit was not lost upon the Trustees and those who had intimate acquaintance with the school's early history, especially as Rees, upon the invitation of M. G. Standley, prayed on the same platform for which he had given the dedicatory prayer about a quarter century before, now thanking God "for the great work that had been wrought through this Institution" and indicating the healing of another old wound.[79]

Perhaps the most pronounced evidences of holiness ecumenism at GBS involved the composition of its student body and its relationship to other holiness agencies, including colleges and mission organizations. By 1922, the school had more than thirty denominations represented among its students.[80] However, there was no attempt at GBS to develop a monopoly among holiness schools. In fact, throughout this period, the *Revivalist* and the camp meeting advertised other holiness schools, including Kingswood College, Asbury College, Beulah Park Bible School, Houghton College, Taylor University, John Fletcher College (a precursor to Vennard College), Olivet College (now Olivet Nazarene University), Trevecca College (now Trevecca Nazarene University), and the Wesleyan Methodist College of Central, South Carolina (now Central Wesleyan College).[81] In addition, GBS welcomed to its services music groups from other schools, such as Olivet University's Aeolian Quartette and Asbury College's Glee Club.[82] Likewise, the Standleys welcomed special speakers associated with other colleges, such as Walter Surbrook, while he was president of Kingswood College.[83]

This wholehearted promotion of sister holiness colleges was mirrored by the support of a wide range of mission agencies at GBS. To be sure, mission services often featured alumni, particularly those affiliated with the Pilgrim Holiness Church and OMS. Among the favorite Pilgrim speakers were Charles Slater, R. G. Finch, and O. L. King, the latter of whom had attended GBS for two years and had answered the call to foreign missions in 1917, serving sacrificially and successfully at Antigua—a work that drew such support from GBS that for years it was referred to as "Revivalist island."[84] Among the most popular OMS representatives were Edwin "Bud" Kilbourne, son of OMS pioneers E. A. and Julia Kilbourne, and his wife, Hazel Mae Williams Kilbourne. In fact, coming back to GBS was a homecoming with multiple nuances for the Kilbournes—not only had they trained at the school, they had also met and married there, had been ordained there (in 1915—Bud as an elder, Hazel as a deaconess), and had family there (she was a niece of M. G. Standley).[85] However, the breadth of missionary representation at GBS went far beyond those groups tied closely with the school's origin to encompass practically the entirety of the holiness movement.

Among those organizations represented at GBS during camp meetings and other special events were Free Methodist, Wesleyan Methodist, Church of the Nazarene, Pentecost Bands, and the National Holiness Missionary Society (the missionary arm of the National Holiness Association, which evolved into an independent organization now known as World Gospel Mission).[86] In addition to missionaries, groups often sent prominent organization-wide leaders to represent their mission works. For example, at the 1924 GBS camp meeting, all fields of Nazarene foreign missions were represented by Dr. H. F. Reynolds, one of the denomination's first three general superintendents. Most of the Saturday, June 7, missionary service was devoted to his "very instructive and inspiring message on Giving" which was replete with "vivid illustrations."[87] Among other prominent Nazarenes who participated in the same encampment were veteran evangelist C. W. Ruth and notable song writer Haldor Lillenas and his wife, who "sang about 'Zion's Hill'" so that "many of the saints shouted for joy at the glorious prospects ahead."[88]

The participation at GBS of such high-profile figures from diverse groups throughout the holiness movement, whether as evangelists, mission speakers, or even as representatives of other schools, provides remarkable evidence of the school's development under the early years of the Stanley administration into a seedbed of holiness ecumenism; indeed, the school's base was increasingly broadened during this period to make it a child of the entire holiness movement.

The Fundamentalist Factor

The expansion of the school's influence ultimately extended beyond the holiness movement into the broader evangelical community, particularly through the increasing affinity of GBS with the burgeoning fundamentalist movement. While a full exploration of this development lies beyond the scope of this work, the impact of Fundamentalism on God's Bible School must be recognized to understand accurately the school's subsequent history. In fact, Fundamentalism had demonstrably influenced the understanding of the concept of "Back to the Bible" or "Back to Pentecost" at GBS so that by 1930 the school had evolved in some significant ways since its founding.

This period witnessed the development of Fundamentalism as a distinct religious movement. While the latter half of the nineteenth century had witnessed growing concern among many American Christians over the inroads of liberal scholarship into mainline Protestant denominations, it was during the first couple decades of the twentieth century that this concern led to the coalescence of a vast army of evangelicals into an identifiable movement that transcended denominational borders. While various segments of Fundamentalism would adopt additional agendas, the primary concern of Fundamentalism was militant opposition to the various manifestations of modernism, particularly German higher criticism and Darwinism. To counter such liberal trends, conservatives chose to champion "non-negotiable" tenents of orthodox Christianity—the fundamentals—leading to the movement's designation as "Fundamentalism" by 1920.[89]

In his landmark study of *Fundamentalism and American Culture*, George Marsden aptly describes Fundamentalism as "militantly anti-modernist Protestant evangelicalism"—noting that it bound together forces from many older movements (including the holiness movement) who became "co-belligerents united by their fierce opposition to modernist attempts to bring Christianity into line with modern thought."[90] In historic Fundamentalism, then, adherence to essential Biblical doctrines was not enough; militant opposition to error played an inherent role—a true fundamentalist is "one who interprets the Bible literally and also exposes all affirmations and attitudes not found in the Word of God."[91] To support this militant stance, fundamentalists have quickly pointed to Biblical passages promoting separation (such as Ephesians 5:11) and using the imagery of warfare (such as II Timothy 2:3-4).[92]

This militant thrust was given new fuel by World War 1, as fundamentalists "blamed the war on the effects of German higher criticism and the widespread acceptance of evolutionary thought" and strove to purge such errors from society, beginning with the church.[93] While the devastation of the war may have garnered popular support for the fundamentalist cause, its appeal was undoubtedly dampened by the famous Scopes Trial of 1925, in which Clarence Darrow made the aging William Jennings Bryan and his defense of creationism the object of ridicule in a made-for-media encounter.[94] Although this episode cast aspersions on the credibility of Fundamentalism, it failed to rout the movement, which remained a vital force in religion and politics well past the mid-century mark, as witnessed by the rise of such organizations as Jerry Falwell's Moral Majority in the 1970s.[95]

While a large swath of the holiness movement—particularly the grass-roots—participated in the fundamentalist crusade, this involvement has been largely slighted by historians, who have tended to concentrate on Baptist and Reformed participation.[96] In addition, numerous misconceptions have unfortunately surfaced regarding the links between Fundamentalism and the holiness movement. On the one hand, some scholars have emphasized the holiness movement as an antecedent of Fundamentalism, suggesting far too great a causative relationship between the two.[97] On the other hand, some Wesleyan scholars have suggested that fundamentalist concerns were foreign insertions into the holiness movement (if they were present at all) and that authentic Wesleyans, particularly in early Methodism, would have cared little for the controversies that embroiled twentieth-century fundamentalists and modernists.[98] This position fails to appreciate the fact that prior to the rise of modernism, most holiness people were committed to evangelical orthodoxy and that many also took aggressive—one could say even "militant"—stances against such "errors" of their day as Russellism, Mormonism, and Christian Science.[99]

The truth lies somewhere between these extremes. Popular holiness literature from the first half of the twentieth century is replete with fundamentalist themes. However, important distinctions can be discerned between the Holiness and Calvinist brands of fundamentalism, and no institution provides a better case study for the exploration of these nuances than does God's Bible School.[100]

In fact, higher criticism and Darwinism fell under the condemning eye of holiness leaders associated with GBS in the early years of the school, as already noticed in connection with the career of W. B. Godbey, whose *New Testament Commentary* was lauded in *Revivalist* advertisements for its opposition to "the world and worldly criticism."[101] Remarkably, the establishment of GBS practically coincided with one of the first major volleys in the Revivalist Movement's onslaught against modernism—the June 1900 volume in Knapp's *Pentecostal Holiness Library*, a booklet by H. T. Davis which devoted a chapter to explaining the mutual incompatibility of "the Shining Way of holiness" and "any sympathy whatever with the Higher Criticism."[102]

By the end of the school's first decade, those lending their voices to the crusade against liberalism included such highly-respected figures at GBS as George B. Kulp, Oswald Chambers, and A. M. Hills. Kulp early established and long retained a reputation as "a fundamentalist of the old school, and often said that he had no desire to change from the paths in which his fathers trod."¹⁰³ Chambers expressed his viewpoint unapologetically in a 1910 *Revivalist* article, characterizing higher criticism as "the position [taken toward the Bible] of the unregenerate, cultured people."¹⁰⁴

Hills' opposition to modernism was the most voluminous and vehement of any of the holiness luminaries associated with GBS in its formative years.¹⁰⁵ He considered the teachings of Darwinism and higher criticism to be detrimental to holiness doctrine and practice, complaining that if evolution were true, it undercut not only the Biblical teaching of creation, but also "the sacredness of the marriage relation," the need "for regeneration," the importance of "Christ's atonement," and the doctrine of the "immortality of the soul." Ultimately, for Hills, evolution undercut the concept of the Incarnation itself, so that "the bottom is gone from our Christianity."¹⁰⁶ However, Hills considered especially damaging to the holiness cause the implications of evolution concerning the doctrine of sin—"then the doctrine of the depravity and fall of man is gone. We are falling upward instead of downward."¹⁰⁷ Since Hills argued that this was not the case, he averred that "the new popular Evangelism"—based on the teachings of higher criticism—"offers no cure for depravity, and leaves men to struggle, despair and die."¹⁰⁸ This meant that holiness teachings were superior to modernism, since universal human experience accorded with the Biblical concept of depravity.

In other words, Hills' primary objections to modernism were on moral and experiential grounds.¹⁰⁹ Thus, while they appreciated and frequently appropriated the scholarly work of Reformed fundamentalists which focused on the doctrinal and exegetical flaws of liberalism, Hills and his compatriots at GBS focused on the spiritual decline that they believed to be inextricably linked with modernism. Positively put, holiness fundamentalists found their chief weapons against liberalism to be the fire of God's Presence and the faithful lives of His people. The first factor imbued F. M. Messenger's exultation after the 1928 GBS camp meeting:

> We are certain that . . . it was one of the greatest scenes of spiritual power and one of the greatest answers to the claims of the Modernists and Evolutionists that God is a myth and does not visit the people, answer their prayers, and undertake for them as recorded in the old days in the Bible!¹¹⁰

The second factor informed Madge Duff's 1905 summary of "What God's Bible School Teaches":

> We accept the English Bible as a whole, in spite of the few insignificant flaws due to the errors of the translators. Our motto is, "Back to the Bible," and we apply it to experience as well as doctrine. *We teach "higher living" instead of "higher criticism,"* and endeavor to turn out real theologians in the etymological sense of the word, i. e., those who are familiar with the Word of God.¹¹¹

A telling assertion by H. T. Davis succinctly combined both the elements of Divine Presence and ethical living as antidotes to the doubts fostered by liberalism: "Just in the same ratio that men get near God, and become more and more like Him, does their faith in the plenary inspiration of the Bible increase. They believe the Bible, the whole Bible, the Bible from lid to lid. They believe that Moses wrote the Pentateuch . . . and they believe the story of Jonah." Underscoring the experiential nature of this conviction, Davis also insisted, "Those in the enjoyment of full salvation have had too many of the precious promises of the Bible fulfilled in their own personal experience, and too many positive and direct answers to their own prayers, to doubt for a single moment any part of the Bible."[112]

This experiential and ethical approach to the fundamentalist/modernist controversy tended to be the dominant tactic followed at GBS throughout its first several decades, providing an instructive contrast with the more academic approach of such Reformed fundamentalists as J. Gresham Machen and producing significant results.[113] For example, GBS would find its primary field of engagement with modernism not in the classroom or in the textbook but in open air services and at the mourner's bench. Its main weapons would be not the lectures of learned exegetes but the shouts of victorious saints.

As the fundamentalist/modernist controversy reached fever-pitch during the 1920s, the barrage against liberalism increased in intensity on the Mount of Blessings. By 1922, *Revivalist* literature advertised GBS not only as "interdenominational" and "international," but also as "Fundamental."[114] Such identification remained strong over the next few decades and was proclaimed proudly in the school catalog, such as the notice in 1934-1935, "All members of the faculty of *God's Bible School and Missionary Training Home* are saved and sanctified, pronounced Fundamentalists! Only such are accepted for any services in *God's Bible School*."[115] As recently as 1978, the GBS catalog gratefully acknowledged, "Throughout the life of the School, it has enjoyed the services of some of the finest fundamentalist educators in our country…"[116] In fact, the public understanding of this association with Fundamentalism was well-entrenched as late as 1965 when the *Cincinnati Post Times-Star* referred to GBS as a "Fundamentalist school."[117]

C. W. Troxel, missionary with the National Holiness Missionary Society, rejoiced that in the 1924 camp meeting he discovered—"Praise God, no evolutionists here; no destructive critics in this group!"[118] In fact, such prominent participants in Hilltop activities as Fred Fuge, C. W. Ruth, Bud Robinson, and Joseph H. Smith frequently stressed fundamentalist themes, as when Smith explained "that higher critics want . . . to do away with Moses and his writings because of the way he says the world was started. And they want to do away with Daniel, because of the way he says the world will come to an end."[119]

Other special speakers at GBS who remain particularly noteworthy for their promotion of the fundamentalist agenda were two evangelists who are better known for their connections with the holiness institutions at Wilmore, Kentucky—another bastion of holiness fundamentalism during this period.

The first of these, John Paul, was highly regarded throughout the holiness movement as an educator and writer as well as an evangelist, having served as president of three schools—Asbury College, Taylor University, and John Fletcher College—and as an editorial assistant for H. C. Morrison's *Pentecostal Herald* for twenty-five years and as joint editor of *The Christian Witness* (with G. A. McLaughlin) for ten years.[120]

While Paul was more highly visible as a guest speaker at GBS after 1930, he was a welcome visiting minister at the camp meeting as early as 1923.[121] By this time, he was already a well-established holiness spokesman for Fundamentalism, primarily due to the publication of his book, *What is the New Theology?*, in which he argued against evolution, "modern destructive criticism," and defective views of God, Christ, and the atonement.[122] While unbending in his opposition to these ideas, Paul presented a refreshing corrective to stereotypical images of fundamentalists perpetuated in the media, with a persona that was both "humble and Christlike." Observation of his saintly life led Dr. John R. Church to write, "I never knew him to say or do anything that was out of keeping with what he professed. He was the type of person that you could point to and say, 'That is a sample of true holiness.'" This gentleness did not detract from Paul's pointed opposition to modern errors, but actually appealed to his audience, prompting John L. Brasher to remark that Paul was "the man with a lance so keen yet so anointed that it healed as it pierced."[123]

A second evangelist associated with Asbury College (in fact, one of its prominent alumnus and a board member from 1919-1959) who rallied GBS constituents around the banner of Fundamentalism was Andrew Johnson. Saved under the ministry of H. C. Morrison and sanctified under the ministry of John Wesley Hughes, Johnson was an unabashed advocate of "entire sanctification as a second, definite, distinct work of grace." A "brilliant" communicator, Johnson stood out among holiness proponents as a zealous political activist, himself acknowledging that he was a "natural-born politician," an inclination that led him to run as the vice presidential candidate on the 1928 Prohibition ticket.[124] Regardless his "unique" traits, Johnson's evangelistic career that spanned sixty-five years provides a typical illustration of just how closely the traditional holiness message became interwoven with fundamentalist themes in the 1920s among both the leadership and the grassroots of the holiness movement.

As with John Paul, it was a book that firmly established Johnson's reputation as a champion of Fundamentalism. In Johnson's case, the book was co-authored with L. L. Pickett and entitled *Postmillennialism and the Higher Critics*, reflecting the premillennial orientation of most holiness (and non-holiness) fundamentalists and suggesting that the postmillennial view provided congenial soil for the seeds of higher criticism.[125] Interestingly, this work, which Donald Dayton regards as "the most explicit adoption of fundamentalist rhetoric . . . in the holiness literature," was published in 1923, the same year that Johnson was announced as a special visiting preacher during the GBS camp meeting.[126] Soon, Johnson's was a prominent presence on the

Hilltop, with the Standleys inviting him to write articles on Fundamentalism versus Modernism for the *Revivalist* and to deliver a series of lectures on "The Fundamentals of the Christian Faith" to the entire student body during the spring of 1928. Among his topics were the "Diety and Virgin Birth of Christ, The Plenary Inspiration of the Holy Scriptures, The Earmarks and Mistakes of Modernism, and The Facts of Fundamentalism." In addition, he urged *Revivalist* readers to join the fundamentalist crusade, contending that "God's people all ought to take an active hand in fighting this heresy known as Modernism."[127] Likewise, Johnson was welcomed to bring this crusade to the GBS camp meeting, where he thrilled congregants in 1929 with a "great message on Fundamentalism."[128]

While certainly augmented by such visiting speakers as Paul and Johnson, the fundamentalist cause claimed the vigorous support of resident leaders on the Hilltop as well. In fact, fundamentalist rhetoric at GBS reached a crescendo in the preaching and writing of none other than the founder's son, John Franklin Knapp, who emerged as a leader in his own right on the Hilltop during the 1910s and 1920s, frequently speaking during camp meetings and chapel services and writing numerous *Revivalist* articles, in addition to shouldering several administrative and educational responsibilities. Like Paul and Johnson, J. F. Knapp provides an excellent example of how Pentecostal holiness ideals and fundamentalist themes were wielded together throughout much of the early twentieth-century holiness movement.[129] To be sure, he wholeheartedly embraced the four-fold gospel heralded by his father, praying that this cause would go forward at GBS until "King Emmanuel shall girdle the globe with Full Salvation!"[130] However, without any apparent thought of contradiction, he linked such experiential elements of radical holiness as "the healing of the body by faith" with the fundamentalist opposition to "The Highway Robbery of Our Bible" by "materialism, higher criticism and evolution." For John Franklin, GBS and its alumni were at the vanguard of two inseparable causes—the promotion of holiness and the defense of the fundamentals—in both "standing firm as Gibraltar for the 'faith once delivered unto the saints'."[131]

Ultimately, the flames of fundamentalist passion were fueled throughout the country by numerous GBS alumni, some of whom became quite prominent for their efforts in the battle against modernism. Among these was C. B. Widmeyer would become known in the 1920s for championing the causes of fundamentalism as president of Pasadena College, and would work closely with the Fundamentalist Association as president of the Convention of the Conservative Protestant Colleges of America.[132] Another was U. E. Harding, who had also attended GBS during the school's decade of administrative trusteeship. By the 1920s, he had risen above numerous adversities including "a severe affliction of the eyes" and the death of his mother when he was only ten to become "one of the most influential folk evangelists of the early-20th-century holiness movement."[133] As the nation's first recipient of a successful cornea transplant in 1938 (which gave him limited vision), he received national media attention.[134]

However, long before this, he had earned the respect of holiness people as a church planter, pastor, and evangelist, pastoring some of the Nazarene denomination's most prestigious charges, including Pasadena First Church, and helping to organize fifty-five Nazarene congregations in Indiana, where he served as district superintendent.

In numerous ways, Harding's ministry reflected the emphases he imbibed at GBS. For instance, his outreach efforts earned him recognition as one of the most aggressive Nazarene district superintendents.[135] In addition, posterity has especially remembered Harding as a fiery opponent against what he perceived to be the great evils of his day, including wordliness and modernism. With regard to worldliness, his book *Movie Mad America* has been recognized as the quintessential holiness diatribe against the "Hollywood mind set."[136] With regard to modernism, he collaborated with Basil Miller on a book entitled *Cunningly Devised Fables: Modernism Exposed and Refuted*—"the first extended head-on attack of modernism to come from the Nazarenes." This work, prefaced with "a laudatory introduction by James B. Chapman" and "warmly endorsed" by A. M. Hills in the *Herald of Holiness* relied heavily as well on Harding's reputation for publicity. Its vitriolic language against modernism is indicated by such chapter titles as "Modernism's Mud God, Non-miraculous Universe, Dead Soul and Deified Man," "Modernism's Godless Conversion Through Religious Education," and "Modernism's Satanic Missionary Program."[137]

So dire did Harding's and other holiness fundamentalist's predictions of the impact of modernism on popular culture become that by 1930 even the possibility of repeating Pentecost, GBS's original *raison d'etre*, was being questioned. This shift is nowhere reflected better than in a startling 1926 quote from one of the school's most prominent supporters, in fact, one of its first donors—F. M. Messenger:

> Brethren, we *can* have revivals if we work while the day lasts, but the night cometh when no man can work; and we *must* have revivals or apostatize; we may revive Pentecost to a certain degree, but to repeat it, or to preach that we may repeat it, is to raise a standard which neither the Bible nor experience will substantiate, and one which will discredit what we *can* and *may* do.[138]

Messenger's statement represents significantly revised expectations embodied in the expression "Back to the Bible." In general, this involved an increased focus on individual salvation as opposed to social transformation, a deepening distrust of the emerging popular "Hollywood" culture, and further disillusionment with the religious establishment. Thus, while GBS was broadening its base to reach a wide spectrum of holiness and fundamentalist evangelicals, it was also narrowing its expectations as to the fulfillment of its mission beyond the chosen remnant.

Although this reservation regarding the buoyant optimism of GBS's founding vision reflects an important degree of cultural retrenchment that had begun at the school by the mid-1920s, it should not be overblown. Its full import would only gradually surface throughout mid-century, as the school faced the challenges of the Roaring Twenties, the Great Depression, and the Second World War. Meanwhile, the exuberant optimism that had led to the birth of GBS continued to serve as a powerful corrective to the over-arching pessimism that colored much of American evangelicalism after World War I.[139] In fact, this effervescent enthusiasm infused even F. M. Messenger's report of the 1928 GBS camp meeting, about two years after he had issued his shocking qualifier concerning the possibilities of restored Pentecost.[140] This robust optimism still encouraged many to compare favorably the services at GBS with the outpouring of the Holy Spirit at Pentecost, as in the estimate of the same camp meeting given by an evangelist new that year to the camp meeting (but not new to the school)—E. E. Shelhamer: "Hence the motto over the 'Mount of Blessings' is not a misnomer when it says 'Back to the Bible'—'Back to Pentecost'. It comes the nearest to being the reproduction of Pentecost I have yet seen, and pardon the writer if he says he has seen a great deal."[141]

In summary, while the emergence among holiness people of fundamentalist concerns may have tempered their expectations of repeated Pentecost, the course followed by the school's leadership and its constituents throughout GBS's second and third decades reflects the irrepressible optimism voiced by Shelhamer. This not only appeared in the school's expansion of its role as a holiness crossroads for evangelistic outreach in the United States and beyond, but in numerous advances undertaken in such areas as academics, missions, building, and finances—developments that helped catapult God's Bible School to the height of its influence.

Notes

[1] Geo. Beirnes, "Wednesday, June 6" Camp Report Issue *Revivalist* (July 12, 1923), 7.

[2] "With God," *Revivalist Our Jubilee Issue!* (June 21, 1928), 2, 4.

[3] Larry D. Smith, "M. G. Standley (1911-1950): Strong, Aggressive Leadership," *Revivalist Centenary Commemorative Edition* (Sept. 2000), 9.

[4] Melvin E. Dieter, "Pilgrim Holiness Church" in Kostlevy, *Dictionary*, 238. See also, Thomas and Thomas, 111.

[5] For example, see George B. Kulp, "Divine Health: A Lecture to the Bible School Students," *Revivalist* (May 9, 1912), 2-3 and *Revivalist* (May 16, 1912), 2-3. On opposition to worldliness, see his "Are Holiness People Extremists?" *Revivalist* (Feb. 7, 1918), 1.

[6] Bessie Standley, "Bible School Notes," *Revivalist* (Jan. 31, 1918), 11-12.

[7] Hynson in Caldwell, 235.

[8] Seth C. Rees, "Foundation Principles," Clipping from a foreign missions scrapbook by Paul Wm. Thomas, Wesleyan Archives, Indianapolis, IN: Dec. 4, 1985.

[9] James R. Moore, "A Brief History of Pilgrim Holiness Colleges" (Term Paper, Marion College, 1984), 1.

[10] Thomas and Thomas, 33.

[11] On Slater's career, as well as those of most of the following missionaries, see Annie Eubanks, *These Went Forth: Biographical Sketches of Pilgrim Missionaries* (Indianapolis: Foreign Missions Department Pilgrim Holiness Church, n. d.), n. p.

[12] Bonner and Metz in Caldwell, 498. See Peyton's photo with children from God's Orphanage in Moser and Smith, 185. On Jordan's departure for Africa, see Mrs. M. W. Knapp, "Bible School Notes," *Revivalist* (March 15, 1928), 13.

[13] Genie Dickerson, "And Thou Shalt Be Missed Because Thy Seat Will Be Empty," *Revivalist* (April 1991), 19. See also, Ruth Bowman, "On Holy Ground," in Moser and Smith, 113 and 118-119.

[14] On the strength of the holiness presence in Grand Cayman, see Brian Black, *The Holiness Heritage*, 179.

[15] Dickerson, "And Thou Shalt Be Missed . . . ," *Revivalist* (April 1991), 19. On Bowman's memories of her year at GBS (1920-1921), see Ruth Bowman, "On Holy Ground," in Moser and Smith, 113, 118-119.

[16] See Swauger in Caldwell, 407, 415, 417.

[17] Hynson in Caldwell, 235, 261. Among Heckart's books are *Behold the Lamb of God* (Radio sermons) (Butler, IN: Higley Press, 1959); *The Shepherd Psalm: An Exposition of the Twenty-third Psalm*, and *An Exposition of the Book of Revelation* (N. P.: n. p., n. d.)—the latter dedicated to the memory of Nettie Peabody.

[18] "Bible School Notes," *Revivalist* (Oct. 30, 1921), 10.

[19] On Neff's tenure as general superintendent, see Thomas and Thomas, 258-260.

[20] Melvin E. Dieter, "Pilgrim Holiness Church," in Kostlevy, *Dictionary*, 238.

[21] Hynson suggests that this development caused the significance of GBS for the Pilgrims to diminish "sharply" (in Caldwell, 235).

²² See Thomas and Thomas, 109-111.

²³ "Bible School Notes," *Revivalist* (Sept. 8, 1921), 11. Also, see "Bible School Notes," *Revivalist* (July 22, 1920), 12. In effect, this church was the successor to George Street Mission (See Dorothy Walters, "Her Labors, Not In Vain," *Revivalist* (Jan. 18, 1968), 3). On campus, the school continued to conduct Sunday afternoon services (a testimony meeting at 2:00 and a preaching service at 2:30) for several years. See "A Hearty Welcome," *Revivalist* (May 24, 1924), 16.

Lew Standley, who suffered from nerve problems, entered evangelistic work, in which he continued for several years.

²⁴ Charles Slater, "Tuesday, June First," in "Other Reports of the Great Camp," *Revivalist* (July 22, 1926), 2-3.

²⁵ In 1927, a "Baptist brother from Kentucky" gave a welcome testimony during a platform meeting at which John Fleming had charge. It was noted that he "evidently had the 'fire' with the 'water' as there was a tremendous outburst of steam, and things began to move" (Charles F. Beitzel, "Saturday, May 28 Camp Meeting Reports" *Revivalist* (July 7, 1927), 4). As recent as 1929, Joseph H. Smith exulted in the fact that on the platform during GBS camp meeting were Presbyterian ministers as well as preachers from various Wesleyan denominations ("The Cincinnati Camp Meeting of 1929," *Revivalist* (July 4, 1929), 2).

²⁶ E. O. Chalfant, "Afternoon Services" Friday, June 6 Camp Meeting Reports *Revivalist* (July 17, 1924), 4.

²⁷ George B. Kulp, "A Veritable Mount of Blessings," *Revivalist* (July 16, 1925), 11. This perspective may help to explain why Kulp apparently never attempted to bring GBS under the auspices of the International/Pilgrim Holiness Church.

²⁸ "A Special Letter from Uncle Buddie," *Revivalist* (June 4-11, 1925), 4.

²⁹ Shattuck had participated in Salvation Park Camp Meeting before GBS was started. On the Butlers' experience of entire sanctification at GBS, see Hills, *Hero*, 140-142 and M. G. Standley, "Put on Love," *Revivalist* (Nov. 17, 1921), 3.

³⁰ "Sunday, June 13," 5-6 in "A Pentecostal Diary: The 1915 Camp-meeting Day by Day," *Revivalist* (July 8, 1915), 6.

³¹ For example, see Joseph H. Smith, "The First Great Sabbath of the Camp, June 3," Camp Report Issue *Revivalist* (July 12, 1923), 3.

³² "The Necessity of Vital Salvation: Brother Bud Robinson's Talk in the Tabernacle Monday Morning, May 7, 1928," *Revivalist* (May 24, 1928), 2 (original emphasis).

³³ "A Special Letter from Uncle Buddie," *Revivalist* (June 4-11, 1925), 4.

³⁴ G. D. Watson, "As the Shout of a Great and Victorious Army," *Revivalist* (July 21, 1910), 8. For biographical material on Watson, see "G. D. Watson: Writer and Preacher of Full Salvation," in D. W. Lambert, *Heralds of Holiness* (Burslem, Stoke-on-Trent, United Kingdom: M. O. V. E. Press, 1975); Wallace Thornton, Jr., ed. *Lightning from the Past*, 205-210; and Eva M. Watson, *Glimpses of the Life and Work of George Douglas Watson* (1929, Revivalist Press; reprint, Salem, OH: Schmul, 2001). His testimony also appears in "Experience of Rev. G. D. Watson," *Revivalist* (May 1892), 2.

³⁵ "Wednesday, June 16" in "A Pentecostal Diary: The 1916 Camp-meeting Day by Day," *Revivalist* (July 8, 1915), 10-11. Oswald Chambers found Watson's Bible

readings to be "a grand stimulus, reminding one of 2 Peter 3:16" ("A 'Golden Wedding' Camp," *Revivalist* (July 21, 1910), 10). A. E. Rassman reported that Watson's Bible reading from Psalm 23 "was crammed full of the richest meat we have ever eaten at God's spiritual table" ("Wednesday, June 9," in "The Great Annual Feast on the 'Mt. of Blessings'," *Revivalist* (July 15, 1920), 11).

[36] See Harry F. Woods, "Saturday, June 10," report in "A Glorious and Victorious Camp," *Revivalist* (July 27, 1922), 3. For their testimonies, see John and Bona Fleming, *Truth on Fire* (Cincinnati: The Revivalist Press, 1934). Also, see Wallace Thornton, Jr., *Sons of Thunder*, 76-85 and C. T. Corbett, *Our Pioneer Nazarenes* (Kansas City, MO: Nazarene Publishing House, 1958).

Hankes testified that he had been backslidden years before when he visited GBS and came under "terrible conviction" while Seth Rees was preaching and was reclaimed. Thus, indirectly, the Fleming brothers' salvation was contributed to by GBS. (See "Thursday, June Third," *Revivalist* (July 22, 1926), 11.

[37] Oswald Chambers, "A 'Golden Wedding' Camp," *Revivalist* (July 21, 1910), 10.

[38] Joseph H. Smith, "Commendation" in Fleming, *Truth on Fire*, 3.

[39] "Sunday, June 17," in "Echoes from the Great Revivalist Camp-Meeting June 8-17," *Revivalist* (July 19, 1917), 9.

[40] Joseph H. Smith, "Commendation" in Fleming, *Truth on Fire*, 3.

[41] J. W. Short, "Wednesday, June 6," in "The Great Revivalist Camp of 1923," *Revivalist* (July 12, 1923), 8. He evidently preached the same message at the 1924 camp, with a brief outline given in G. A. Schoombie, "Saturday, June 7," in "A Great Spiritual Feast—the Camp of 1924," *Revivalist* (July 17, 1924), 5:

> The Ford has only two gears; the sanctified man has two works of grace.
> In high gear the Ford is a good puller; so is the person with the second blessing.
> The Ford will pull anywhere; so will a sanctified person.
> The Ford is the hardest car to back; the sanctified man is hard to get to backslide.
> When you have a blowout, everybody in the country knows it; when a sanctified man backslides, everybody knows it.
> Easiest kept; so is the sanctified man.
> Easiest started when hot; sanctified people are easy to get blessed.
> The Ford has four spark plugs: so has the sanctified person—obedience, faith, victory, fire.

[42] Mildred Bangs Wynkoop, *A Theology of Love: The Dynamic of Wesleyanism* (Kansas City, MO: Beacon Hill Press of Kansas City, 1972), 48-50. Wynkoop was at the vanguard of critics of the "substantive" view. The development of the "relational" view which she championed and the resultant conflict within the Church of the Nazarene is traced in Mark R. Quanstrum, *A Century of Holiness Theology: The Doctrine of Entire Sanctification in the Church of the Nazarene 1905 to 2004* (Kansas City, MO: Beacon Hill Press of Kansas City, 2004). Of particular interest to the history of

GBS is Mark Eckart, *A Presentation of Perfection: An Historical Look at Sanctification in the American Holiness Movement and Specifically in the God's Revivalist* (Salem, OH: Schmul, 1993), c. 6, 137-167 in which the author evaluates *Revivalist* articles by a grid dependent on the categories of substantive and relational as well as Christological Purity and Pentecostal Power. Eckart concludes that *Revivalist* articles usually depicted sanctification as substantive and focused on Pentecostal Power.

[43] Richard S. Taylor, "Why the Holiness Movement Died," c. 2 in Keith Drury, et. al. *Counterpoint: Dialogue with Drury on the Holiness Movement* (Salem, OH: Schmul Publishing, 2005), 51. Taylor contends that Wynkoop and her followers have attacked "a straw man," engaging in "a totally misguided battle" and suggests that the so-called "substantive" view of sin "has never been espoused by reliable Wesleyan advocates."

Martin Wells Knapp expressly repudiated the doctrine of "Sin in the Flesh" in several *Revivalist* publications, even devoting a tract to the denunciation of this "error." See his *Holiness Triumphant*, 32, where he expresses particular concern that this teaching could encourage "a sinning religion" and identified it with the "works of the Nicolaitans"—"This error taught that sin resided in the flesh, and hence that it was impossible for people to keep from sinning while in the body." See also, D. B. Strouse, "Teachings of the 'Holiness Movement'," *Revivalist* (Feb. 22, 1900), 2. Strouse explained that holiness people "do not teach, as many hold, that there is, or can be, sin in the human body--mere flesh and bones--but that all sin is in, or comes from, the spiritual part of man, called the heart; that all men are born with a sinful heart, which separates between them and God, and, in addition to this, all have sinned, and come short of the glory of God."

[44] Harry F. Woods, "Saturday, June 10," in "A Glorious and Victorious Camp," *Revivalist* (July 27, 1922), 3.

[45] Thornton, ed. *Sons of Thunder*, 77 citing Fleming, *Truth on Fire*, 18-19.

[46] Bona joined the Church of the Nazarene in 1920 and John followed suit in 1921. Bona had previously been a member of the International Holiness Church (See *Nazarene Evangelists: Pictorial Directory* (Kansas City, MO: Evangelism Ministries—Church of the Nazarene, 1983), 29. For an extensive scholarly treatment of entire sanctification as the eradication of carnality, see Leroy E. Lindsey, Jr. "Radical Remedy."

[47] "Lawn or Locusts," *Revivalist* (Nov. 9, 1899), 3:

> Regeneration cuts them [trees of sin] down, and implants all the fruits and flowers of the Spirit, while the second work of grace, the baptism of the Holy Ghost, which fully sanctifies, kills the trees of sin both root and branch, and takes them out, and transforms the garden into a beautiful paradise, unobstructed by weeds and trees of sin.

Another of Knapp's early associates, C. W. Ruth, succinctly explained, "Justification destroys the 'shoots' of sin. Sanctification destroys the 'roots' of sin" (*Sanctification* (Westfield, IN: Union Bible Seminary, n. d.), 26).

For a defense of such metaphorical imagery in holiness preaching, see J. B. Chapman, *Terminology*, 88. However, Chapman's defense of holiness typology was tempered with caution: "Figures are for illustration, not for proof . . . After the truth of God's Word is established by plain statement, the figures will be found to agree with and to illustrate the truth. It is never safe to found an important doctrine or to establish an important practice upon a type or figure, even though the figure be in the Word of God." For an example of Chapman's own use of Bible allegory, see his "The Second Blessing Symbolized in Jewish History and Worship," *Revivalist* (May 17, 1928), 3, in which he briefly elucidates symbols for two works of grace from the Genesis creation account through the Jewish feasts. In *Terminology* (83-84), Chapman expressly approved of Knapp's use of the Canaan allegory in *Out of Egypt into Canaan*.

[48] For example, in a 1930 sermon preached in the GBS tabernacle, Robinson likened sin to the chaff removed from wheat. He explained that, "until you are sanctified wholly you have something in your bosom that is sin. You get the baptism of fire that burns all the chaff out and you would not give a dollar a bushel for any of it [sinful pleasure]" (Bud Robinson, "God's Double Cure," *Revivalist* (March 20, 1930), 3).

[49] On Robinson's miraculous recovery, see his *My Hospital Experience* and Mrs. E. G. Marsh, "Friday, June 8," in "The Great Revivalist Camp of 1923," *Revivalist* (July 12, 1923), 9-10. On Charles Wireman, see "Echoes From The Great Revivalist Camp-Meeting June 8-17" continued from the previous week *Revivalist* (July 19, 1917), 3; C. L. Wireman, *Kentucky Mountain Outlaw Transformed* (Intercession City, FL: C. L. Wireman, n. d.); and C. L. Wireman, *"Bull Dog" Charlie and the Devil* (El Dorado Springs, MO: The Witt Printing Co., n. d.). On Fugett, see his *The Sunny Side of Life* (N. P.: n. p., 1946), with a foreword by M. G. Standley. Fugett went on to figure prominently in the affairs of GBS during the height of the Standley administration in the 1940s. He, like Wireman and the Flemings, hailed from Kentucky. It appears that preachers from that state were among the favorites at GBS during its early years, perhaps due to the emotional exuberance often associated with them, as in the following report: "After supper came the Preachers' Meeting, and the Kentucky preachers beat it for jumping, shouting, marching" (William Heslop, "Wednesday, June 7," in "A Glorious and Victorious Camp," *Revivalist* (July 20, 1922), 1-3.

[50] R. G. Humble, *Sgt. Alvin C. York: A Christian Patriot* (Circleville, OH: The Churches of Christ in Christian Union, 1966), 22. Also, see Moser and Smith, 139.

[51] Ibid, 29.

[52] See Wesley E. Humble, "Alvin York," in Kostlevy, *Dictionary*, 340-341.

[53] Richard Humble, *Christian Patriot*, 33, shares York's recollection of his tour of the famous battle site with General Lindsey, who "was described as a natural born fighter who could swear just as awfully as he could fight." When the general asked, "'York, how did you do it?' The answer given was, 'Sir, it is not man power. A higher power than man power guided and watched over me and told me what to do.' With bowed head the reply solemnly came, 'York, you are right'."

[54] Brown and Brevard, *History of the Churches of Christ in Christian Union*, 122.

[55] R. S. [R. G. ?] Finch, "Saturday, June 10," in "A Glorious and Victorious Camp," *Revivalist* (July 27, 1922), 3-4. See also, in the same issue, Harry F. Woods, "Saturday, June 10,"2-3. In the *Revivalist* (July, 20, 1922), 8, it is reported that, "Brother York explained that his hardest temptation as a Christian was not while he was in France, as one would naturally suppose, but since the Armistice was signed,

in the form of tempting offers of large amounts of money from worldly concerns for only a few days' service—and this in the face of heavy financial burdens. But he remembered that the Word says, 'What shall it profit a man, if he shall gain the whole world, and lose his own soul?' and was enabled to resist the tempter."

[56] "Friday, June 9," in "A Glorious and Victorious Camp," *Revivalist* (July 20, 1922), 7-8.

[57] See Day, 94. George Edward York became a Nazarene minister. See his photo, along with his parents and President and Mrs. Standley, in Moser and Smith, 263. Interestingly, because of this connection with GBS, students there, who were normally forbidden to attend movies, were given free admission to the 1941 movie entitled *Sergeant York*, starring Gary Cooper (Author interview of Rev. and Mrs. P. Lewis Brevard (Oct. 19, 1999)).

[58] William H. Huff, "Sunday, June 11," in "The Final Day of the Feast," *Revivalist* (July 27, 1922), 4-5.

[59] "Friday, June 17," camp meeting report in *Revivalist* (July 28, 1921), 4.

[60] Kostlevy, "Will H. Huff," in *Dictionary*, 152. Huff "spent a substantial portion of each year ministering in the South under the direction of Methodist Episcopal Church bishop Robert Elijah Jones."

[61] Brown, *Inskip, McDonald, Fowler*, 272. In addition to preaching at the 1922 GBS camp meeting, Huff also gave a missionary message concerning a recent visit to South America. Here he contrasted North America with its southern neighbor, asserting that "the former is the product of a people who came to this country seeking religious freedom, while the latter is the product of a people who came for conquest and gold" (Harry F. Woods, "Saturday, June 10," in "A Glorious and Victorious Camp," *Revivalist* (July 20, 1922), 8.

[62] Ibid, 272. Huff had served as first vice president of the NHA since 1917, and automatically became president upon the death of Charles J. Fowler, who had served as president for twenty-five years. Brown suggests that Huff's "reputation and expertise were just what the association needed . . . and he helped lead the organization through a very difficult time."

[63] In addition to speaking at GBS, "in 1923 [Smith] became a regular contributor to *God's Revivalist*, for which he wrote during the rest of his active life" (Rose, *Vital Holiness*, 100).

For a typical report of "a splendid service with the young people" conducted by Mrs. Smith, see Charles Slater, "Tuesday, June First," in "Other Reports of the Great Camp," *Revivalist* (July 22, 1926), 2-3.

[64] Brown, "Joseph Henry Smith," in Kostlevy, *Dictionary*, 277.

[65] Rose, *Vital Holiness*, 102. J. C. McPheeters, who followed H. C. Morrison as president of Asbury Theological Seminary and editor of *The Pentecostal Herald*, referred to Smith as the "dean of holiness expositors. Alexander asserted that Smith was "one of the greatest expositors of the English Bible in all the world." In *A Pitcher of Cream* (95), Robinson wrote,

> Now, without a doubt, Joseph H. Smith is the greatest Bible teacher in the holiness movement, and I am persuaded that he has not a superior

in the United States, and as far as I know, there is no man on earth that is his equal. He is the giant of America. When it comes to explaining the Scriptures, he just simply stands at the head of the column. He is like Saul, the son of Kish. He is head and shoulders above all in his tribe.

[66] Brown, "Joseph Henry Smith," in Kostlevy, *Dictionary*, 277.

[67] Ibid. On the School of the Prophets, also referred to at times as "The School of Pentecostal Methods" or "Evangelistic Institute," see Rose, *Vital Holiness*, 88-94. Smith also served as director of the School of Theology at the Meridian Male College in Meridian, Mississippi, beginning in 1907. Later, he served for many years as director of Theology and Evangelism at the Chicago Evangelistic Institute (a precursor to Vennard College), a school that was inspired by his School of the Prophets.

Smith's School of the Prophets was apparently the inspiration for the ministerial meetings of the same name begun by H. E. Schmul many years later as a ministry of the Inter-Church Holiness Convention.

[68] J. B. McBride, "Sunday, June 4," in "A Glorious and Victorious Camp," *Revivalist* (July 13, 1922), 4.

[69] Brown, *Inskip, McDonald, Fowler*, 274.

[70] R. Wingrove Ives, "Thursday, June 4," in "Reports by Some of the Preachers, Missionaries and Workers," *Revivalist* (July 16, 1925), 8.

[71] Regardless receiving wide acclaim for his preaching and leadership abilities, Smith persisted in humble rejection of anything "by way of title that would seem in any measure to put him above the majority of his brethren"—refusing at least three honorary doctorates and expressing reluctance to even use the title "Reverend," simply preferring to be known as Joseph H. Smith (Thornton, ed. *Lightning from the Past*, 185-186).

[72] Brown, *Inskip, McDonald, Fowler*, 274.

[73] Joseph H. Smith, *Things Behind and Before in the Holiness Movement* (Chicago: Evangelistic Institute Press, 1916).

[74] Ibid, 40.

[75] Ibid, 40-41.

[76] Ibid, 50. While Smith recognized the spiritual benefit of holiness churches and denominations, he protested against such logic as that used earlier by W. B. Godbey to promote the creation of independent holiness churches, in which he compared established churches (particularly the Methodist) to an "old ship, already hopelessly unseaworthy," and encouraged true believers to "jump into the life boat, taking everybody with us we possibly can; thus leaving the old bark to her destruction" (*An Appeal to Postmillennialists*, 24).

Smith (48-49) instead contended,

> So great is the contrast between the holiness church and the average other church beside it, with the overflowing of spiritual life in the one and the dearth of it in the other, it mighty be easy to esteem the other . . . as but a sinking ship. It would be easy to imagine that our best and

only service for any holiness people within them would be to pull them out and get them into our life boat. But, beloved, if any are really making this mistake we have to analyze it but a little to find that underneath is a subtle spirit of sectarianism. Let us not be beguiled. . . . The truth is, beloved, dead and degenerate, formal and fashionable as the churches are, *I have found none of them yet from which the Holy Spirit has entirely withdrawn His membership* (original emphasis).

⁷⁷ Ibid, 43 (original emphasis).

⁷⁸ See J. B. McBride, *Knowing God: Life Story and Selected Sermons* (Cincinnati: God's Bible School and Revivalist, 1923); C. H. Babcock, *Christ Exalted* (Cincinnati: God's Revivalist, 1926); and John Douglas Drysdale, *J. D. Drysdale: Prophet of Holiness* (London: Lutterworth Press, 1955). Drysdale was an educator and author, serving as founder and principal of Emmanuel Bible College in Birkenhead, England and penning such works as *The Price of Revival* (Birkenhead, Ches., England: Emmanuel, 1946) and *Holiness in the Parables* (1952; reprint, Salem, OH: Schmul, 1984). Hames, well-known Wesleyan Methodist evangelist, was also a prolific author, particularly focusing on the development of Christian character after entire sanctification in such works as *Deeper Things* (Cincinnati: God's Bible School and Revivalist, 1926) and *Beulah Land Saints* (1927; reprint, Salem, OH: Schmul, 2001).

⁷⁹ "Hilltop" Reporters, "The Opening Service," in "A Great Spiritual Feast: God's Revivalist Camp Meeting of 1926," *Revivalist* (July 8, 1926), 3.

⁸⁰ "What Is God's Bible School?" in J. F. Knapp, "Ask for the Old Paths," *Revivalist* (June 8-15, 1922), 13.

⁸¹ See Belle Staples, "Missionary Day: Thursday, June 6," in "A Glorious and Victorious Camp," *Revivalist* (July 20, 1922), 5 and "Holiness Colleges, Academies and Bible Schools," *Revivalist* (August 29, 1929), 12.

⁸² See Harry F. Woods, "Saturday, June 11," in Campmeeting Reports *Revivalist* (July 21, 1921), 7 and "Bible School Notes," *Revivalist* (June 14, 1928), 11.

⁸³ "Bible School Notes," *Revivalist* (June 14, 1928), 11. Surbrook was a son-in-law of E. E. Shelhamer and later served as a general superintendent in the Pilgrim Holiness Church (1933-1946). See Thomas and Thomas, 147-148.

⁸⁴ Finch was described as "one of the most alert, live, earnest zealous, workers and speakers on Missions that we know" by William Heslop, "Wednesday, June 7," in "A Glorious and Victorious Camp," *Revivalist* (July 20, 1922), 2. He was a regular missions speaker at GBS for many years.

Oscar Logan King eventually became superintendent of the Antigua District of the Pilgrim Holiness Church. He was highly regarded for building "up a work of significant credit to himself and to his Lord, and reportedly broke through the stronghold of the traditional Anglican church" (Paul L. Swauger, Sr. "Wesleyans South of the United States," in Caldwell, 410). See "A Great Spiritual Feast—the Camp of 1924," *Revivalist* (July 10, 1924), 2 where King tells that as a student at GBS, "He had no call at that time, but had an open heart." Also, see Mrs. O. L. King, "Saturday, May 30," in "Reports by Some of the Preachers, Missionaries and Workers," *Revivalist* (July 9, 1925), 4-6 and O. L. King, *The Price of a Coconut* (Indianapolis:

Pilgrim Publishing House, 1936).

Other prominent Pilgrim mission representatives at GBS during this period included George Beirnes (British Guiana), William Beirnes (Caribbean), Fred DeWeerd (South Africa), Fred Fuge (South Africa), R. Wingrove Ives (Caribbean), and John Thomas (Korea).

[85] During the 1915 camp meeting, "Bud" and Hazel were ordained to the ministry of the Apostolic Holiness Church, again reflecting the overlapping at the time of GBS, OMS, and what would become the Pilgrim Holiness Church. See "A Pentecostal Diary: The 1915 Camp-meeting Day by Day," *Revivalist* (July 8, 1915), 12. Also, see Mrs. C. E. Cowman, "Sabbath, May Thirtieth," in "A Great Spiritual Feast: God's Revivalist Camp Meeting of 1926," *Revivalist* (July 8, 1926), 4; Mrs. M. G. Standley, "The Children's Meetings," *Revivalist* (July 8, 1926), 16; and Charles Slater, "Tuesday, June First," in "Other Reports of the Great Camp," *Revivalist* (July 22, 1926), 3. Also, see Moser and Smith, 26 and 87.

[86] See L. R. Roberts, "Wednesday, June 4," in "A Great Spiritual Feast—the Camp of 1924," *Revivalist* (July 10, 1924), 9; "General Report of the Great Camp," *Revivalist* (July 16, 1925), 1-3; and Charles Slater, "Tuesday, June First," (2-3) and Ralph G. Finch, "Thursday, June Third," (8-9) in "Other Reports of the Great Camp," *Revivalist* (July 22, 1926). The welcome at GBS of the representatives of the NHMS, such as C. W. Troxel, provided yet another indication of rapprochement between GBS and the National Association. On this organization, see W. W. Cary, *Story of the National Holiness Missionary Society* (Chicago: National Holiness Missionary Society, 1940).

[87] Ejnar Larson, "Saturday June 7," in "A Great Spiritual Feast—the Camp of 1924," *Revivalist* (July 17, 1924), 4. George Kulp rejoiced that Reynold's address "was in the power of the Spirit, and the saints shouted and wept." He also credited it with "an increased offering in the afternoon" ("Simply Indescribable," *Revivalist* (July 17, 1924), 6-7). On Reynold's life, see Amy N. Hinshaw, *In Labors Abundant; a biography of H. F. Reynolds* (Kansas City, MO: Nazarene Publishing House, 1938) and M(ervel) Lunn, *Hiram F. Reynolds: Mr. World Missionary* (Kansas City, MO: Nazarene Publishing House, 1968).

[88] Revivalist Office Reporters, "Saturday, May 31," in "A Great Spiritual Feast—the Camp of 1924," *Revivalist* (July 10, 1924), 3. At the time of his visit to GBS, Lillenas was pastor at Indianapolis First Church of the Nazarene. See Haldor Lillenas, *Down Melody Lane: An Autobiography* (Kansas City, MO: Beacon Hill Press, 1953), 40-41.

[89] T. P. Weber, "Fundamentalism," in Reid, *Dictionary*, 461-465. Also, see G. M. Marsden, "The Fundamentals," in Reid, *Dictionary*, 468-469 and G. M. Marsden and B. J. Longfield, "Fundamentalist-Modernist Controversy," in Reid, *Dictionary*, 466-468. The term "fundamentals" was popularized with the publication of *The Fundamentals* beginning in 1910, a series edited by A. C. Dixon, Louis Meyer, and R. A. Torrey and financed by Lyman and Milton Stewart. The labels "fundamentalism" and "fundamentalist" were adopted in 1920 by Curtis Lee Laws, editor of the *Baptist Watchman-Examiner*.

[90] Marsden, *Fundamentalism and American Culture*, 4. On the origins of this

movement, also see Sandeen, *The Roots of Fundamentalism*.

⁹¹ George W. Dollar, *A History of Fundamentalism in America* (Greenville, SC: Bob Jones University Press, 1973), 283. See also Dollar's definition: "Historic Fundamentalism is the literal exposition of all the affirmations and attitudes of the Bible and the militant exposure of all non-Biblical affirmations and attitudes" (xv). Dollar served as chairman of the church history department of Bob Jones University, which remains at the forefront of Fundamentalist institutions. See also, David O. Beale, *In Pursuit of Purity: American Fundamentalism since 1850* (Greenville, SC: Unusual Publications, 1986).

⁹² See Dollar, 283-286 and "Here We Stand: A fundamentalist historian answers the critics of fundamentalism: An Interview With Mark Sidwell," *Christian History* Vol. XVI, No. 3 (Issue 55), 44-45.

⁹³ Weber, "Fundamentalism," 463.

⁹⁴ See *Christian History* Vol. XVI, No. 3 (Issue 55), which is devoted to "The Monkey Trial and the Rise of Fundamentalism."

⁹⁵ See Ed Dobson, Ed Hindson, and Jerry Falwell, *The Fundamentalist Phenomenon: The Resurgence of Conservative Christianity* Second Ed. (Grand Rapids: Baker Book House, 1986).

⁹⁶ Much the same could be said of Pentecostalism's relationship to Fundamentalism, as Anderson observes in his *Vision of the Disinherited*, 5. For important correctives to this trend, see William Kostlevy's excellent essay, "Historiography of the Holiness Movement," in his *Holiness Manuscripts: A Guide to Sources Documenting the Wesleyan Holiness Movement in the United States and Canada* ATLA Bibliography Series, No. 34 (Metuchen, NJ: The American Theological Library Association and The Scarecrow Press, 1994), 1-40 (especially note pages 38-40). Also, see Douglas M. Strong, "Fighting Against Worldliness and Unbelief: Henry Clay Morrison and the Transformation of the Holiness Movement Within Methodism," (Wesleyan Holiness Studies Center 1995 Conference: Methodism and the Fragmentation of American Protestantism: 1865-1920, Asbury Theological Seminary, Sept. 1995) and Donald Dayton, *Theological Roots of Pentecostalism* and "Dispensationalism and the Emergence of Fundamentalism . . ."

⁹⁷ For example, see Mark Noll, *Scandal of the Evangelical Mind*, 115-117. On Noll's attempt to lay the guilt for fundamentalism's "anti-intellectualism" at the feet of the Holiness and Pentecostal movements, see note 37 in Chapter Two above.

⁹⁸ For example, see Paul Basset, "The Fundamentalist Leavening of the Holiness Movement: 1914-1940," *WTJ* Vol. 13 (Spring 1978), 65-91; Susie Stanley, "Wesleyan/Holiness Churches: Innocent Bystanders in the Fundamentalist/Modernist Controversy" in *Reforming the Center: American Protestantism, 1900 to the Present* Ed. Douglas Jacobsen and William Vance Trollinger (Grand Rapids: Eerdmans, 1998), 172-193; and Al Truesdale, editor *Square Peg: Why Wesleyans Aren't Fundamentalists* (Kansas City, MO: Beacon Hill Press of Kansas City, 2012).

⁹⁹ In such polemicisms holiness advocates could point to precedent in John Wesley, whose "longest writing on a single subject" was his work addressing the Pelagian teachings of Unitarian John Taylor. See Richard S. Taylor, Foreword to John Wesley, *The Doctrine of Original Sin According to Scripture, Reason, and Experience* (Reprint;

Salem, OH: Schmul Publishing, 1999), 4-5.

[100] For an insightful discussion of Fundamentalism in relation to the holiness movement, particularly the conservative holiness movement, see Mark Sidwell, "The Conservative Holiness Movement: A Fundamentalism File Research Report," in the Fundamentalism File of the J. S. Mack Library, Bob Jones University, Greenville, SC, 8-11. As Sidwell indicates, a common theme that undoubtedly attracts adherents of Fundamentalism and the holiness movement to the other movement is the stress on separation.

[101] For example, see "The Chance You Have Been Waiting For," *Revivalist* (Jan. 11, 1912), 12.

[102] H. T. Davis, "The Shining Way," *Pentecostal Holiness Library* Vol. III No. 6 (June 1900), 121.

[103] Thomas and Thomas, 53 citing the daughter of Kulp, Mrs. J. E. Strong, "Ancestry and Activities," *Pilgrim Holiness Advocate* (August 10, 1939), 2-3.

[104] Oswald Chambers, "The Bible and Ideas of the Bible," *Revivalist* (March 17, 1910), 3.

[105] Bassett ("Fundamentalist Leavening . . . ," 69) suggests that "Methodism and the holiness movement did not concern themselves more than very minimally with the issues being raised by the so-called 'higher criticism' in the period 1870-1914, while the reformed tradition was abubble with controversy." However, Hills' fundamentalist convictions were well-established several years before, as indicated by his writings in *God's Revivalist* and by two chapters (cc. 7-8) devoted to "Higher Criticism" in his *Fundamental Christian Theology* (Pasadena, CA: C. J. Kinne, 1931) which, although not published until much later, was primarily written between 1909 and 1915 (see Gresham, 162 and Kostlevy, *Dictionary*, 145—Basset (80) erroneously suggests that Hills began writing this about 1919).

In addition, the writings of such holiness authorities as Chambers and Davis indicate that Bassett's estimation of the strong interest in fundamentalist concerns among holiness people should be revised back at least to 1900.

[106] A. M. Hills, "Bible or Evolution," *Revivalist* (July 6, 1911), 1-2. See also his *Fundamental Christian Theology*, 150-151. While fundamentalist in philosophy, Hills' independent thinking was reflected not only in his postmillennial eschatology, but also in his staunch opposition to the theory of verbal inerrancy (both positions which put him at odds with many other fundamentalists). See his *Fundamental Christian Theology*, 126.

[107] A. M. Hills, "The Trend of Theology in the Universities of Our Land," *Revivalist* (Oct. 14, 1909), 1, 5.

[108] A. M. Hills, "The New Evangelism," *Revivalist* (March 30, 1905), 1.

[109] For another example, see A. M. Hills, "The Effect of Higher Criticism on One of its Own Defenders and Advocates," *Revivalist* (Nov. 7, 1918), 12.

[110] "With God," *Revivalist Our Jubilee Issue!* (June 21, 1928), 2, 4. It should be noted that such polemic was not new for GBS. In fact, it bears a striking parallel to Martin Wells Knapp's response to his detractors among Methodism and elsewhere—"Our main answer to those who oppose us is the fire that is falling" (*Back to the Bible*, 52).

[111] Madge Duff, "What God's Bible School Teaches," *Revivalist* (Oct. 26, 1905), 3 (my emphasis).

[112] "The Shining Way," 121.

[113] For example, see J. Gresham Machen, *Christianity and Liberalism* (New York: Macmillan, 1923).

[114] Advertisement inside back cover of *Praise of His Glory Songs*.

[115] *God's Bible School and Missionary Training Home Catalogue 1934 -- 1935* (Cincinnati: God's Bible School and Missionary Training Home, 1934), 11. Several later catalogs simply stated, "All members of the Faculty are definitely Christian and pronounced Fundamentalists." For example, see *God's Bible School Bulletin 1939-1940* (Cincinnati: God's Bible School and Missionary Training Home, 1939), 9.

[116] God's Bible School and College Catalog 1978-1979, (Cincinnati: God's Bible School and College, 1978).

[117] "'Sister Peabody' Awaits Her 63d Meeting of God's Bible School," *Cincinnati Post Times-Star* (May 28, 1965), 39.

[118] C. W. Troxel, "That Missionary Day," in "A Great Spiritual Feast—the Camp of 1924," *Revivalist* (July 17, 1924), 1.

[119] Charles L. Slater, "Saturday, June 3," in "A Glorious and Victorious Camp: The Story as Told by a Number of the Workers," *Revivalist* (July 13, 1922), 2. See also, C. W. Ruth, "If Modernism Were True: What?" *Revivalist* (March 3, 1927), 12; Fred T. Fuge, *The Old Constitution and Will the Old Book Stand* (Flint, MI: Fred T. Fuge, n. d.); Bud Robinson, "Monkeys and Jawbones," in *Bud Robinson's Religion, Philosophy and Fun* (Kansas City, MO: Beacon Hill Press, 1942), 23-27; and Bud Robinson, *A Pitcher of Cream*, 96-101. In Bud Robinson, *The Moth-Eaten Garment* (Kansas City, MO: Beacon Hill Press of Kansas City, 1961), 26, Robinson argues similarly to A. M. Hills that evolutionists "have denied inbred sin and carnality" and the "big preachers tell us that, when man fell, he fell up instead of down . . ." See the report on one of his diatribes against evolution at GBS in J. F. Knapp, "Tuesday, June 5," in "The Great Revivalist Camp of 1923," *Revivalist* (July 12, 1923), 6.

[120] On Paul, see *Sons of Thunder*, 178-184 which includes a message he preached at GBS. On his career, which included service on the faculty of Meridian College, Asbury Theological Seminary, and Chicago Evangelistic Institute, as well as service as interim president of the NHA in 1925, see Kostlevy, *Dictionary*, 231-232; Brown, Inskip, . . ., 273-274; McCumber, *Great Holiness Classics* Vol. 5, 212-213; and Bernie Smith, *Flames of Living Fire*, 92-93. For his tenure as president of Taylor University, including his ambivalence on the school's relationship with the Methodist Episcopal Church, see William C. Ringenberg, *Taylor University: The First 125 Years* (Grand Rapids: Eerdmans, 1973), 96-104.

[121] See "Camp Meeting" advertisement in *Revivalist* (May 3, 1923), 12.

[122] John Paul, *What is New Theology?* (Wilmore, KY: Asbury College, 1921).

[123] *Sons of Thunder*, 178.

[124] Bernie Smith, *Flames of Living Fire*, 50-51 and Kostlevy, *Dictionary*, 165. See also, *Sons of Thunder*, 149.

[125] Andrew Johnson and L. L. Pickett, *Postmillennialism and the Higher Critics* (Chicago: Glad Tidings Publishing Co., 1923).

¹²⁶ "Dispensationalism and the Emergence of Fundamentalism . . .," 12. Also, see "Camp Meeting" advertisement in *Revivalist* (May 3, 1923), 12.

¹²⁷ Andrew Johnson, "God's Bible School," *Revivalist* (April 26, 1928), 8.

¹²⁸ John Fleming, "The Camp of Camps!" *Revivalist* (June 27, 1929), 1.

¹²⁹ Throughout this work, when the name Knapp is used alone, it usually refers to Martin Wells Knapp unless the context reflects otherwise, as when quotations from the Revivalist refer to John Franklin Knapp as "Brother Knapp."

¹³⁰ In this prayer, offered on Easter, March 27, 1921 (also M. W. Knapp's birthday), in a special memorial service for his father, note his impassioned reference to the "Full Gospel" and his conclusion to the prayer, which he offered "in the name of Jesus Christ, our coming King, our Healer, our Savior, our Sanctifier." See "An Easter Memorial Day," *Revivalist* (April 14, 1921), 2.

¹³¹ J. F. Knapp, "The Highway Robbery of Our Bible," *Revivalist* (August 31, 1922), 1-3. See also, J. F. Knapp, "Ask For The Old Paths," *Revivalist* (June 8-15, 1922), 1, 13 in which he answered the questions "What is God's Revivalist?" and "What is God's Bible School?" by affirming that the former was devoted to "the essential doctrines of all evangelical churches" and the latter was not "a theological seminary where the courses offered and the teachings given attempt to combine ancient religious concepts with modern evolutionary theories."

Also, note the advertisement for "God's Bible School and Missionary Training Home: Fall Term Opens September 18, 1925," *Revivalist* (June 4-11, 1925), 13 which includes in the school's "platform" belief in "The Bible, in both Old and New Testaments, God's only recorded and infallible revelation to man" as well as belief in the Trinity, in regeneration, in the "Wesleyan doctrine of Christian perfection," "a continued life of victory," "Divine healing of the body," the "Second Coming of Christ, imminent and personal," and "the Gospel to be preached in all the world."

¹³² "Announcement," *Revivalist* (April 29, 1926), 13. See also, Kirkemo, 66 and 80-91 (c. 5 "The Great Debate of the 1920s.")

¹³³ *The Nazarene Pulpit: A Collection of Sermons from Some Well Known Preachers* (Kansas City, MO: Nazarene Publishing House, 1925), 64 and Kostlevy, *Dictionary*, 140-141. The introduction to his sermon "The Lost Christ" in *The Nazarene Pulpit* (64-71), states that Harding "was a student at God's Bible School at Cincinnati, for a time." Kostlevy indicates that this was shortly after his conversion in 1902. Evidently, he had completed his studies at GBS by 1909, for he was then engaged in a prolonged evangelistic tour in the South, as indicated by a report in "Revival Prayer Answered," *Revivalist* (March 4, 1909), 11. Although earlier a member of the Free Methodist Church, in 1911 Harding joined the Pentecostal Church of the Nazarene, of which he remained a member until his death in 1958.

¹³⁴ Kostlevy, *Dictionary*, 140-141 and Vivienne E. Hughes, *Seeing Through the Eyes of the Dead* (Portland, OR: U. E. Harding, n. d.). On Harding's life, also see U. E. Harding, *Pen Pictures from Life's Pathway* (Pasadena, CA: The Mission Press, 1938) and *Sons of Thunder*, 134-148.

¹³⁵ See Timothy L. Smith, *Called Unto Holiness*, 336.

¹³⁶ See note 1 on U. E. Harding, *Movie Mad America* (Grand Rapids: Zondervan, 1942) in Charles W. Christian, "Friendship with God and the World: How Far From

Oxford to Hollywood?" *WTJ* Vol. 42 No. 1 (Spring 2007), 120.

[137] Bassett, "The Fundamentalist Leavening . . .," 77. So strong were the denunciations of modernism in this work, Kirkemo recoils in horror from its descriptions of "modernism, liberalism, higher criticism, and evolution as the 'filth of the lowest dregs of vice' . . .," *For Zion's Sake*, 88. See his c. 5 for another typical contemporary Nazarene perspective on the "fundamentalist leavening" of the holiness movement.

[138] F. M. Messenger, "Is the Holy Ghost Withdrawing?" *Revivalist* (April 22, 1926), 4, 13.

[139] Historians often consider the modern era to have commenced about the end of this conflict. For example, see Paul Johnson, *Modern Times: The World from the Twenties to the Nineties* Rev. ed. (New York: HarperCollins, 1991).

[140] "With God," *Revivalist Our Jubilee Issue!* (June 21, 1928), 2, 4.

[141] E. E. Shelhamer, "A Great Camp in Many Respects," *Revivalist* (June 21, 1928), 5.

Chapter 9

Storming the Fort: Advancing the Cause

Oh, it is high time that we cease singing, "Hold the fort, for I am coming," and begin to shout the battle cry: "STORM the fort of sin and Satan, Christ, our Captain, leads us on." and if He is leading, then we are sure of victory.
Beloved, we are praying that instead of having students, God will mightily multiply us, and that we shall have boys and girls filled with the Holy Ghost, on fire for God, going up and down this land, and foreign lands as well, preaching a full Gospel.
– M. G. Standley[1]

In many ways, the achievements of the school's first decade had set the pattern for the duration of the Standley administration—ambitious advances occasionally punctuated by institutional crises. Its successes would propel the school forward so dramatically that later GBS president Samuel Deets would assert that M. G. Standley was "the man whom God used to build this Bible school into a world-renowned organization with spiritual influence far out of proportion to its size."[2] However, this task was not accomplished single-handedly by President Standley. Indeed, his administrative colleagues, dedicated faculty, passionate students, and numerous other constituents took up his rallying cry to "storm the fort" and closed ranks in an all-out effort to broadcast the message of full salvation to the ends of the earth. This effort led them to make several impressive advances throughout the 1910s and 1920s.

Academic Progress: From John Franklin Knapp to Charles W. Carter

Among the tremendous strides taken by GBS's leadership during this period was the significant strengthening of the school's academic programs. At the forefront of this academic advance was John Franklin Knapp, whom M. G. Standley acknowledged as GBS's "educational man."[3] His tireless quest for higher academic ground was pursued on both the individual and institutional levels. Personally, John Knapp's scholarly bent served him well as he completed graduate studies at the University of Cincinnati, where he earned the prestige of membership in Phi Beta Kappa, and at Lane Seminary.[4] In addition, he achieved wide respect as a leader throughout the holiness movement, as evidenced by his service as a vice president for the National Holiness Association in the mid-1920s and by Asbury College granting him the honorary Doctor of Divinity degree.[5]

John Franklin's institutional accomplishments were no less remarkable than his personal achievements. These began with the expansion of the school's offerings in college preparatory studies in 1914 through the creation of an "academy" or high school of which Knapp was the founding principle, a position he held until 1927. Formed in response "to the many urgent requests" the school had received, this department of studies, also designated as the "academic" program, was intended to fill a gap between the elementary grade offerings at GBS and the courses of the Bible school proper. The resultant structure of three programs—preparatory (elementary grades), academic (high school), and theological (Bible school)—remained in place from 1914 until 1931.[6]

From its initial day of classes on October 8, 1914, the high school endeavored to achieve academic excellence. "The subjects that were offered . . . were identical to those offered by the public schools at that time" except that the New Testament texts were used for Greek and Latin (instead of secular classics).[7] Among the subjects taught were rhetoric, physiology, medieval and modern history, music, and geometry. In addition, Bible and Christian worker training was provided through courses in Scripture drill, evangelistic work, and Sidney Collett's *All About the Bible*.[8]

This academic rigor was rewarded in 1922 when John Franklin Knapp represented the school before the Ohio Department of Education in Columbus, just after the completion of the Revivalist Memorial Building, which included an impressive state-of-the-art classroom floor. As a result, GBS received a certificate dated May 22, 1922, "recognizing the High School as the equivalent of a public high school of first grade."[9] Furthermore, this accreditation was accompanied by increased recognition of the high school's academic quality by universities throughout Ohio.[10] This milestone, the most significant educational fete of GBS in its first three decades, assured J. F. Knapp's role as the school's academic leader, with "the trustees . . . glad to give him full and complete control of the educational work . . ."[11]

Complimenting J. F. Knapp's vision was a cadre of dedicated faculty and staff that reflected several of the positive trends established during the school's first decade. Much of this continuity was due to the persistant service of such long-term teachers as R. E. McNeill, who continued to oversee the music department throughout the school's second and third decades. He married in 1915, and was joined on the music faculty by his wife, who had taught piano at Berea College in Kentucky following studies at the Cincinnati Conservatory of Music.[12] Her employment at GBS was just one example of the continued prominence of women on the faculty, with several other new female teachers, including Amy Spaulding, Emily Strong, Elsie Elkhardt, and Edythe Luke, joining long-time stalwarts Nettie Peabody and Elizabeth West (who died in 1917).[13] Another early practice that persisted was that of welcoming guest lecturers, including "outstanding theologians, evangelists, teachers, and Christian leaders," to the campus, with their presentations "given in the chapel at regular intervals" throughout the school year.[14]

In addition to the establishment of the high school, several other new developments transpired during this period, including the expansion of the correspondence course to three years length in November 1917. Completion of this program, which included course work during the school year and reading requirements during the summers, resulted in a diploma "signed by each member of the Bible School faculty."[15] Reflecting how non-traditional studies often set the pace for advances, it was not until the fall of 1928 that the on-campus Bible Course "was extended to include a third year."[16] The same semester also witnessed the introduction of a "One Year Practical Course" comprised of personal devotions, "Bible study and English, personal work in Sunday Schools and missions, cottage prayer meetings, house-to-house visitation, and a course in soul-winning."[17]

The latter course reflects the ongoing stress on the practical aspects of theological education which had been a hallmark of GBS since its inception. While striving "to improve" the school's programs "as Providence and the Holy Spirit may indicate," the administration maintained that the school's "specialty" was not developing "a high degree of mental culture" but preparing "men and women trained and ready to endure hardness as good soldiers of Jesus Christ; men and women who, fearing nothing, [would] give themselves to win men and women to Jesus."[18] If anything, the emphasis on such practical activities as "House-to-House visitation," "Slum Work," "Orphanage Work," and "Rescue Home Work"—all with an eye to winning souls as well as providing economic and social relief—accelerated during this period.[19] In addition, the practical opportunities afforded to the many students in the school work program continued to expand, with seventy-five participants during the 1916-1917 school year alone and over two thousand during GBS's first quarter century.[20]

This pragmatic approach to Christian ministry, coupled with the academic improvements spearheaded by John Franklin Knapp, produced an influx of students leading GBS to ever higher enrollments. In 1914, the school celebrated its largest number of graduates to date: twenty-six (thirteen male, thirteen female). By 1928, this number had increased to seventy—another record. Overall registration from the school's inception until 1931 was 7,333, with 3,233 (44%) of these enrolling in the years from 1921 to 1930. In fact, GBS had 392 students in the 1930-31 school year alone.[21]

A high percentage of these alumni pursued full-time ministry, as with the class of 1923, which saw seventy percent of its forty-eight graduates enter "Christian work as preachers, missionaries, colporteurs, etc."[22] In addition, several alumni of the period went on to exemplify in their ministries the fusion of academic excellence and evangelistic passion that became a hallmark of GBS at the time. Among these were James D. Robertson (1928) and Leslie D. Wilcox (1927), both of whom would go on to render invaluable service to GBS as faculty members and as academic deans. Another graduate that illustrated this rare blend was Charles Webb Carter (1928), whose unique career along with his wife's led to their designation as "missionaries extraordinary."[23]

This title reflects, not a claim to superiority, but recognition of the non-traditional elements of the Carters' ministry, much of which can be traced back to the influence of GBS. Charles began college at Dakota Wesleyan University but rejected its promotion of Darwinian thought and left there after a year, also leaving the Methodist Episcopal Church and joining the Wesleyan Methodist Church. After a semester at Faith Home Bible School, a small holiness institution in Mitchell, South Dakota, he went to GBS in 1925 "under the advice" of his conference president, a GBS alumnus. While appreciative of the classroom instruction he received on the Hilltop, and "much impressed and edified by the spiritual atmosphere of the campus," the greatest impact GBS had on Carter was through his "personal work among the poor and underprivileged people of the slums of the city"—at times in "extremely dangerous" conditions. He received extensive experience in "city mission preaching" and was rewarded with several converts, later suggesting that "this practical ministry was of much value . . . when [he] became a missionary in the jungles of Africa."[24]

This ministry began in October 1928, as Charles arrived to begin the first of three terms in Sierre Leone, West Africa, along with his new bride, Elizabeth (Hutchinson), whom he had married on June 6 in a double wedding ceremony conducted by M. G. Standley, along with fellow GBS students Garnett Phillipe and Elma Stephenson (who served as missionaries in China and India under OMS). The young couple was assured of their alma mater's support, with a send-off including a substantial offering taken at Charles' graduation under the direction of Minnie Knapp.[25]

As in inner city Cincinnati, the Carters witnessed numerous conversions during their ministry in West Africa, defying the conventional wisdom of veteran missionaries who suggested that the Carters focus their evangelistic efforts on children, because there was little hope of seeing adult Africans convert to Christianity.[26] One of the most dramatic conversions under Charles' ministry was that of Alamami Duray, "one of the most noted kings of all West Africa," who was reputed to be "a very shrewd and evil man who . . . had made a human sacrifice at the opening of the planting season every year during his long reign." Smitten by conviction under Charles' preaching, Duray "threw himself in prostration before God and repented and accepted Christ."[27] Undoubtedly, such conversions furthered the cause of revival that was promoted throughout the Carters' missionary efforts.

During furloughs, Charles pursued further studies, receiving the A.B. and the Th.B. from Marion College (now Indiana Wesleyan University) and the M.A. from the Winona Lake School of Theology in 1933. His mission work developed an educational focus as he returned to administer and teach at a seminary in Sierre Leone, further whetting his appetite for scholarly pursuits. This leaning was satisfied when he was invited to teach at Marion College in 1946, where he served as Chair of the Division of Religion and Philosophy from 1946 to 1957 and as Scholar-in-Residence from 1971 to 1990. In addition, he served on the faculty of Taylor University from 1959 to 1971 and lectured and served as "missionary-evangelist" during sabbaticals in several countries including Taiwan, Japan, India, and the Philippines. Meanwhile, he pursued further studies, earning the M. A. and Th. M. from Butler University and a B. D. from Asbury Theological Seminary, which also honored him with a D.D. in 1968.[28]

Dr. Carter's scholarly bent also led him to author and edit an amazing array of about thirty books and numerous articles. Among the works he edited are *A Contemporary Wesleyan Theology* (two volumes) and *The Wesleyan Bible Commentary* (six volumes).[29] In addition, he was a charter member of the Wesleyan Theological Society and the first editor of the *Wesleyan Theological Journal* (1965-1972).[30] His own writings reflect an emphasis undoubtedly encouraged at GBS during his student days—the work of the Holy Spirit—whether in biblical studies as in his commentary on Acts co-authored with Ralph Earle, or in systematic theology as in his *The Person and Ministry of the Holy Spirit: A Wesleyan Perspective*, or in relation to application as in *The Bible Gift of Tongues* or *From Revival to Evangelism*.[31] Throughout all these works, an emphasis on practical theology reflects the dual commitment to scholarly pursuit and soul-winning zeal imbibed at GBS, not only by Charles Carter, but also by numerous fellow students.

Intensifying the Missions Thrust: From the Dakotas to Japan and Beyond

While the careers already noted of students and other GBS constituents throughout this period make apparent the continued fervor of soul-winning passion at the school, the intensity of this passion should also be observed in the careers of several other students and in initiatives undertaken by them, often with key support from the GBS administration. Some of these would focus on evangelism at home; others would take the message of full salvation to foreign lands; all displayed the ingenuity and tenacity inspired on the Mount of Blessings.

Among these noteworthy students were some who, like Charles Carter, gave outstanding service to the Wesleyan Methodist Church. One of these was the conference president who had recommended that Carter attend GBS—John Franklin Simpson, who had himself attended GBS from 1910 to 1913.[32] His wife Lovenah Ida (Reisdorph), whom he married in 1916, was also a student at GBS (1913-1915), where they began their courtship.[33] Simpson quickly rose to leadership in the WMC, giving exemplary guidance to the Dakota Conference as its president from 1920 to 1928 and from 1940 to 1957. During this time, he received denomination-wide recognition for his work among young people, which included helping to establish the denominational young people's society as well as one of the first conference-level youth societies.[34]

Simpson also established a reputation for challenging the Dakota Conference to undertake "daring adventures of faith in pioneer church extension work and in missions,"[35] with one of the most ambitious of these beginning in 1948 with the establishment of a work in the Philippines. This involved initially sponsoring a Filipino preacher who had become a Wesleyan Methodist under Simpson's influence while living in the Dakotas. Since the denominational board was unprepared to support the work at the time, the conference undertook support for this project for over a decade, until the denominational Department of World Missions could assume responsibility for it. Meanwhile, Simpson began a series of missionary travels to the Philippines in 1956, resulting in his election as President of the Wesleyan Methodist Connection of the Philippines. He gave over a decade of dedicated service in this capacity "without salary from the Mission" and inspired other leaders to follow his example of adaptable, sacrificial servanthood.[36]

Another prominent Wesleyan Methodist leader who joined Simpson in the Philipine mission work was his wife's brother, Rufus D. Reisdorph. Like Charles Carter, Reisdorph interspersed educational pursuits among his many ministerial duties, following his graduation at GBS (1919) with studies at Marion College, Miltonvale College, Vanderbilt University, and Iliff University, completing the A. B. and M. A. degrees.[37] His early ministry was devoted to evangelism, but he was elected to the presidency of the Dakota Conference in 1928, following Simpson in that position and retaining it until Simpson would return to it in 1940.[38]

About that time, Reisdorph went from conference leadership to denominational administration, where he served in various positions for about twenty years, interrupted by a stint as a chaplain in the U. S. Army during World War II (1943-1946). His first denomination-wide position was as Sunday School Secretary and Editor (1939-1943; 1947-1959). His "vigorous efforts" in this role were rewarded with dramatic results including Sunday school enrollment almost doubling from 1938 to 1958. He also served as president of Miltonvale College (1946-1948) and in several "key assignments" including membership on the general conference committee on denominational reorganization and as chairman of the publicity and public relations committee to solicit contributions toward new denominational headquarters at Marion, Indiana. His success in these and numerous other undertakings made him a natural choice for general superintendent, an office which he held from 1959 to 1963.

Throughout his ministry, Reisdorph and his wife Ruby devoted significant energy to promoting missions, both in "missionary evangelism" throughout England, France, Sierra Leone, the Belgian Congo, Burundi-Ruanda, Kenya, East Africa, Egypt, Palestine, Lebanon, India, Ceylon, Australia, the Philippines, Formosa, Japan, Colombia, Jamaica, Haiti, and Puerto Rico, and in representing world missions throughout the United States. After this productive career which the general conference recognized as going "beyond the call of duty" and which many would have considered justification for retirement, the Reisdorphs instead continued their devoted service unabated, giving several years as missionaries in the Philippines.[39] In his later years, Reisdorph continued to recognize the impact GBS had on his ministry, asserting that "those who have submitted to the process of God's Bible School can not disassociate their labors from her influence. Personally, I am indebted to her for clear teachings in the Way of Holiness, and also my first opportunity to bear that witness."[40]

The continued missions thrust at GBS involved not only sending students out to evangelize but also providing an open door for international students, many of whom were seeking refuge from oppressive conditions in their native land. One of them was a roommate of John Franklin Simpson, a young Italian named Anthony Catanese.[41] Although Catanese' staunchly Catholic family initially opposed his attendance at GBS, where he experienced entire sanctification, he faithfully witnessed to them until his father commited one of his brothers to Anthony's care, so that he too attended GBS where he was converted. In addition, Anthony "found an open door" in an Italian church in Cincinnati to proclaim to other immigrants the message of full salvation that had transformed his own life.[42]

Similarly, Krikor Gayjikian, an Armenian who fled his home country after escaping two Turkish massacres of his people, found refuge first with relatives in Cincinnati, and then at GBS, to which he was introduced through the ministry of Lew Standley and George Street Mission. School leadership, particularly Minnie Knapp and Nettie Peabody, strove heroically to educate this young man who was practically illiterate in English, with Peabody devoting many hours outside class to tutoring him.[43] This investment in Krikor during his attendance at GBS from 1913 to 1920 was amply rewarded, with Krikor gaining enough proficiency to preach the gospel, to share his personal testimony, and to recount the sufferings of his people with great poignancy and notable success. His writing skills were also developed by 1920 to the point that he was able to write a book sharing his life's story and his burden for Armenia, thus disseminating his message even further.[44] These successes marked the launching of a long, productive career in both foreign and home missions. After his ordination in the Pilgrim Holiness Church, Krikor and his wife Osanna, along with their five children, served for eight years as missionaries among Armenians in Syria and Lebanon. In 1940, they returned to Cincinnati, where Krikor began Lighthouse Mission, which he operated for over three decades, until his death in 1972.[45]

While such students as Anthony Catanese and Krikor Gayjikian brought foreign missions home to the GBS campus in a vivid and direct way, giving teachers like Nettie Peabody the opportunity to conduct cross-cultural missions on the Hilltop, the student who may have done most to fan the flames of missions passion at the school during the Standley administration was an American—Alice Minnie White.[46] During her childhood in Indiana, White showed a predilection for spiritual things, early desiring to be in "Gospel Work." A visit in 1911 to the GBS camp meeting inclined her to become a student there, but it was not until a camp meeting conducted by John T. Hatfield near her home in September 1914 that she received "her call to preach and a call to prepare at God's Bible School." In typical fashion, her resultant elation erupted in exuberant praise, so that "her shouting broke up the service."

White, then twenty years of age, eagerly enrolled that fall at GBS in the two-year Bible School course, expressing frequently her desire to be a "flaming evangelist." Her enthusiastic attitude quickly endeared her to the campus family, with her praises amplified by a "loud, booming voice and a shout few could equal." Her immersion in campus work, especially in kitchen duties, was such that she did not graduate with her certificate until June 1919. Following graduation, she entered evangelistic work, excitedly pursuing her dream. However, after only three meetings, she sensed God speaking to her about returning to work on the Hilltop, a call verified when she received a letter from the school trustees requesting her to return to the school as a staff member. She complied and began an astoundingly varied tenure of service that found her involved in numerous facets of ministry on the campus, helping to make it truly a "Mount of Blessings" to many of the students who encountered her beaming face and encouraging words as she served them in the dining room, counseled them as Dean of Women, served with them during Thanksgiving Dinners, taught them in prayer class, distributed clothing from "The Poor Barrel," and handed out mail in the mailroom.[47] By 1925, she had already earned the title with which many students would affectionately refer to her throughout the remainder of her career—"Mother" or "Mom" White.[48]

In addition to campus activities, White also engaged in a variety of soul-winning activities off campus, particularly at George Street Mission, where her leadership skills came into play as she was given charge of the mission during the summer of 1920, allowing Lew Standley to take a leave of absence.[49] Likewise, she served as pulpit supply at Cincinnati's First Pilgrim Holiness Church between pastors during the summer of 1927.[50] However, White's legacy was to be not one of pulpit ministry so much as one of intercession for and promotion of missions.

Perhaps her greatest memorial was an organization that developed under her leadership—the Missionary Prayer Band. Combining White's dual passion for prayer and missions, this organization evolved from a prayer meeting that she conducted in the early 1920s with two other young ladies in which they focused on the needs of missionaries. These meetings eventuated in a regular Saturday evening prayer meeting that drew many students, several of whom received missionary calls themselves while in attendance.[51] "Returned missionaries" also frequently spoke before the Missionary Prayer Band, presenting "slides and moving pictures of different mission fields" to better inform students as to developments there.[52]

Many students turned to "Mom" White for advice concerning their call and went on to yield invaluable service in mission fields around the world. For example, Helen Hammer (Dotson) sought such counsel and went as a missionary to Haiti, where she served admirably for several years under the leadership of G. T. Bustin.[53] Indeed, like Nettie Peabody, "Mom" White found that she had reached many more fields through the students she served than she ever could have done personally. In addition, her prayers for numerous mission works continued to support them even after she was forced by poor health to retire from GBS in 1964. Furthermore, her role as a prayer warrior would not only bless the farflung mission outposts on foreign soil, but would make its mark on the Mount of Blessings itself in ways that would continue to unfold long after her death on December 7, 1967.

One of the most ambitious mission endeavors in which the GBS family participated during White's student days found the school cooperating with the Oriental Missionary Society in one of the greatest undertakings in the annals of Asian missions. Known as the Great Village Campaign, this endeavor to place Scripture portions and other gospel literature in every home in Japan remains legendary in GBS and OMS lore.[54] The roots of this massive effort went back to 1908, when a group of "earnest Christian women" in the "homeland" caught the vision for reaching the rural areas of Japan during a meeting with Lettie Cowman.[55] It was calculated that the cost of doing this through literature was relatively inexpensive, with a Japanese New Testament costing only two and one/half cents and the average expense of supplying a Testament to each home in a typical village estimated at five dollars per village. These women decided to undertake the financial support of such an outreach, forming a "Japanese Village Band" in which each member was "responsible to underwrite the cost of evangelizing a village." The concept quickly gained popularity, and the campaign to supply every home in Japan with Christian literature was underway by 1909, with the Cowmans, fellow missionary Lizzie Pearce, Juji Nakada, and three other Japanese initiating the seemingly endless task.[56]

The powerful impetus of this campaign bore testimony to the continued vitality among GBS and OMS constituents of two foundational themes of these organizations. Of course, one was the mission impulse, which was radicalized by Charles Cowman's and E. A. Kilbourne's understanding of the Great Commission as literally mandating the evangelization of every person—"The command is to 'go to EVERY creature'."[57] Lettie Cowman wrote of her husband that "the words *To every creature*," literally took possession of him and burned like fire in his bones."[58]

While this zeal provided the rationale for the ambitious *scope* of the Great Village Campaign, the campaign's *urgency* was fueled by another foundational plank in radical holiness ideology—premillennial eschatology. The conviction that "every sign of the times sends out the warning note that the Coming of the Lord is at our very doors" drove participants in the campaign, and their supporters, to increase the intensity of their efforts, especially as the war clouds looming over Europe erupted in 1914 as the First World War.[59]

By that time, numerous other American missionaries and Japanese soul-winners had joined the campaign, with the entire force of OMS in Japan engaged in some way in this all out effort to reach every Japanese home with the gospel message, going beyond simply distributing literature (which was considered to be "not so much evangelism as seed sowing")[60] to one-on-one witnessing and conducting open air services. "By the end of 1915, the bands had reached an estimated 24,000,000 Japenese with about 30,000,000 remaining."[61] However, it became clear that if they were to accomplish their goal of reaching every Japanese home by the end of 1917, they would need additional assistance, both in finances and in laborers.

Financially, a tremendous boon to the cause came in 1915 with a $15,000 contribution from the Stewart Foundation, a California benevolence directed by W. E. Blackstone, best-selling dispensationalist author.[62] This donation provided the funding to underwrite the expenses of additional volunteers from the United States. Charles Cowman turned for assistance in this regard to Edward Oney, a GBS graduate who had been assisting since June 1914 with the Great Village Campaign. In response, Oney returned to America in March 1916 to solicit recruits from his alma mater.

Oney's appeal garnered nine other volunteers: one other alumnus—Harry Woods, and eight current students—Lewis Hiles, John Orkney, Rollie Poe, William Miller, Vernie B. Stanley, Everette Williamson, Paul Haines, and William Thiele. On December 24, 1917, these young men bade farewell to the campus family in a special service in God's Tabernacle. It took about a month to complete their journey to the "Land of the Rising Sun" where they disembarked at Yokohoma on January 20, 1917. Joining a force led by twenty men, they were "immediately deployed" by Ernest Kilbourne, who assigned each to lead a small group of native workers.[63]

Altogether comprising a force of almost sixty, the reinforced village bands trudged over the Japanese countryside covering an estimated twenty to thirty miles daily, reaching approximately two hundred homes and about one thousand souls per day, with even larger numbers in towns and cities.[64] Numerous hardships attended their way, including inclement weather, poor food, the bites of mosquitos and fleas, and harassment by unsympathetic villagers.[65] However, they pushed onward, and by November 1, the *Revivalist* reported that one million homes remained to be reached.[66] By the year's end, the bands were in the last stages of completing the campaign—with finalization reached in June 1918.

The magnitude of its accomplishment still defies imagination—with only about one hundred workers (including about sixty native workers), gospel literature was distributed to "10,300,000 homes at a cost in excess of $100,000."[67] While the primary task was "seed sowing," immediate fruit was produced, with estimates of between seven and eight thousand converts coming to Christ during the campaign and an inestimable number of others following.[68]

Undoubtedly, the final heroic thrust of this ambitious effort to reach "every creature" was largely successful because of the dedicated contribution of the "ten splendid young men" from GBS who "gladly" bore the hardships of the campaign "for Jesus' sake," prompting Charles Cowman to exult: "Every man of them went out to Japan with the victory; every man of them kept the victory; and every man of them still shouts the victory."[69] Indeed, "most of them went on to distinguished careers in Christian service"[70], with several serving as pastors, evangelists, and administrators in the United States, including Rollie Poe—United Methodist pastor, William Miller—Nazarene evangelist, and Edward Oney—who became a Nazarene pastor highly regarded as "an effective church planter" in West Virginia, where he eventually served as district superintendent.⁷¹ Some also returned to the mission field, with several going back to Asia with OMS, including John Orkney, Paul Haines, William Thiele, William Miller, and Harry Woods, and some serving with other agencies, such as Everette Williamson who ministered in Japan for six years with the Evangelical Church and Lewis Hiles who served in the Caribbean and in South America with the Pilgrim Holiness Church for several years before returning to America to pastor in Oklahoma.⁷²

Flush with victory in Japan, the Cowmans and Kilbournes launched a similar campaign in Korea, where OMS would experience its greatest success. Here, such GBS alumni as William Thiele would again help to lead the charge, and the GBS family proved so supportive that one area of the Korean work became known as "God's Revivalist Province."⁷³

Much of this support for missions during this period was due to the ardent fervor for outreach that continued to be exemplified by the school's trustees. Their efforts included George Kulp's and Mrs. Knapp's appeals for offerings in special services and "farewell tours" for students ranging from Irene Blyden to Krikor Gayjikian, as well as Mrs. Knapp's own missions tour throughout the Caribbean in 1918, the reports of which were published in the *Revivalist* and later as a book entitled *Diary Letters*.⁷⁴ Furthermore, M. G. Standley's passionate plea for "personal work," such as the address he gave during the 1928 Nazarene General Assembly in Columbus, Ohio, served to stoke the flames of holiness evangelism at home and abroad.⁷⁵ In addition, the trustees' commitment ensured that the GBS camp meeting would remain distinguished among holiness camps for its mission emphasis, as recognized by special resolutions presented to the trustees in honor of their support by representatives of "seven different Holiness [mission] Societies" during the 1924 camp meeting.⁷⁶ This zeal would also figure largely in several advances made on the Mount of Blessings itself.

Building a Memorial to the Faithfulness of God and His People

During its second decade, the expansion of the school's physical plant was primarily through acquisitions of existing buildings near the campus. Most notable was the purchase on March 14, 1918, of an old mansion located at 1811 Young Street for only $7,000, a significant bargain considering its original value had been set at $40,000. This spacious building with its fourteen rooms provided much needed additional dormitory facilities for ladies. Later, it served as faculty and staff housing before becoming home to the school's music division, a function it would serve into the next century.⁷⁷

However, it was apparent as the school entered its third decade that growth by acquisition of existing structures was falling far short in meeting the demands of escalating enrollment, which reached 337 by the 1919-1920 school year.[78] Thus, in its issue for July 15, 1920, the *Revivalist* announced "A Mighty Challenge to the Faith of God's Revivalist Family"—unveiling an architectural drawing of the most ambitious campus building project since the construction of the first Girls' Dormitory (the "Ten Weeks Building").[79] The proposed structure was of impressive dimensions—195 feet long, 40 feet wide, and 6 stories tall—to be constructed of fire-proof, reinforced concrete covered with brick. In addition to providing space for ninety rooms in which one hundred eighty students could be housed, the building was to be multi-purpose. Its basement (first two floors) would serve as a "House of Pure Books"—giving ample space for a bookstore and the equipment of Revivalist Press. Another floor was envisioned to supply facilities needed to accommodate the academic advance led by John Franklin Knapp, with a library, science laboratory, and additional class rooms.[80]

With an estimated cost of $200,000, the "new building" certainly provided a tremendous challenge to the GBS/Revivalist constituency. However, with creativity and alacrity the trustees solicited their support, procuring the services of Charles L. Slater as "field agent" for the fund raising campaign. The *Revivalist* reported progress on this campaign by means of a large thermometer displaying various faith-building Scripture texts, such as "My God shall supply all your need," alongside key milestone figures.[81] "By September 16, 1920, the thermometer registered $20,000 in cash and $40,000 in pledges"; it registered $67,500 by the following January and over $100,000 by November 3, 1921.[82]

Much of the enthusiasm fostered by this campaign was generated among students and alumni, with the appeal to them likened to that of "a mother-in-need to her faithful children."[83] Their response was overwhelmingly positive, with gifts and pledges from current students during the camp of 1921 reaching over one thousand dollars. However, the campaign was broadened by the trustees' decision to make the new facility a "Memorial Building"—in a sense giving tribute to the founding vision of Martin Wells Knapp but more generally "a tribute to the trust, devotion, and self-denial of the some *two hundred thousand readers of God's Revivalist*" and especially "A TRIBUTE TO THE FAITHFULNESS OF A PRAYER-HEARING AND PRAYER-ANSWERING GOD."[84] In effect then, the "God's Revivalist Memorial Building," as it was named, was to serve as a memorial to the entire Revivalist Movement and its God.

This recognition of the inestimable contribution of the Revivalist "family" to the work of God's Bible School powerfully evoked the support of the school's entire constituency throughout the building campaign. Appropriately, the funds for the building thus came, not from just a few large donations, but from hundreds of small contributions, making the building a true memorial to the generosity of God's people. Such gifts were encouraged by various plans devised by the trustees, including one to supply rooms with "plain and simple" furnishings "as becometh godliness" at the cost of $750.00 per room.[85] A donation to furnish an entire room entitled the donor to "name a room after any godly person, relative, or friend," with a name plate to be affixed to the door of the room furnished in their honor.[86] Supporters of lesser means could still help with one massive aspect of the project—providing the 300,000 bricks required. At a cost of thirteen cents each, even children in the Do-Without Band could afford to supply a few bricks. The response to this appeal was phenomenal, with more than $6,000 received in only three weeks during February 1922.[87]

Another method of fund raising that appealed to supporters with more substantial financial resources was that of selling annuities, introduced with the announcement:

> The Trustees are prepared to guarantee a good rate of interest for life to persons who want to put their money to work for God, and who, at the same time, require an income from it. An ironclad contract is entered into whereby the offering thus received shall, twice each year, as long as the giver lives, draw a regular interest.[88]

Although this was apparently the first time the school employed this instrument for fund raising, it would not be the last. Indeed, its practice would have significant ramifications for many years to come.

Perhaps the point at which the excitement generated by the campaign surfaced most dramatically was at the laying of the cornerstone on Saturday, June 18, 1921, during the annual camp meeting. Enthusiasm reached a fever pitch during a midnight prayer meeting led by J. F. Knapp that actually began about eleven o'clock the previous evening and extended until two o'clock, Saturday morning. During this time, two "voluntary gifts" totaling about $1,500 were given, and Knapp rejoiced in this evidence that "the saints [had] prayed through, and God [had] answered from Heaven." Between two to three hours later, Rev. and Mrs. Standley led a "great march" throughout the campus, accompanied by "the Orchestra, the Chorus, and many students" who sang "the Awakening Chorus."[89] (No rising bell was needed that morning!) During the 6 a. m. meeting, several ministers spoke briefly about the heroes of faith in Hebrews 11, followed by more fervent prayer. About 8 a. m., the cornerstone was brought to the platform, displaying on one side the words "God Preeminent"—the motto of the Class of 1921, which had payed for the stone—and on another the words "A Memorial to God's Faithfulness."[90]

The entrance of the large cornerstone, likened by observers to "*The Ark of the Covenant*,"[91] precipitated a torrent of praise, worship, and sacrificial giving that defies description. Scheduled services were forgotten as things flowed with the momentum of the occasion—"Everything moved along in the Spirit." It seemed that everyone had "a burning desire to give 'something'." Many followed the example of "one young man who desired to give something but had no money to give" and so "presented a good suit of clothes."[92] The cornerstone itself became a receptacle for many such gifts, with "fountain pens, valise, watches, shawls, shoes, a fine auto robe, suits, Bibles, jewelry, all [going] on the ark" as the congregation sang, "The ark is coming up the road." Others committed to selling baked goods and livestock to provide additional funds for the new building with the endorsement of evangelist John Norberry.[93] Consequently, "the slogan 'Sell Something!' was adopted for the entire day."[94] To this, President Standley added his "oft repeated and Scriptural advice"—"SELL THAT THOU HAST, AND GIVE!,"[95] himself contributing "a valuable set of books from his library, and [laying] it in the Cornerstone." Ultimately, the cornerstone was "more than running over with evidences of real self-denial," reinforcing—along with the inscriptions engraved on its sides—the function of the cornerstone as a monument to "the self-sacrifice of God's people."[96]

By the time the cornerstone was "borne aloft" to the excavation site with the Trustees leading the way and the congregation singing "The Ark Is Coming Up The Road" and other songs, "the whole neighborhood was intensely interested" in the proceedings. These began with a Scripture reading from Nehemiah by John Norberry and an invocation given by Will Huff. Several school leaders and camp workers participated in the sealing of the stone, now holding a copper box containing a Bible signed by the 1923 camp workers, a list of Revivalist subscribers, and other significant papers. As he "laid his trowelful, Charles Slater underscored the connection of the building project with the school's larger mission to reach souls, declaring "On behalf of world-wide missions I lay this mortar!" Likewise, in the dedicatory prayer that followed, George Kulp prayed "that from the Building young people [would] go, filled with the Spirit, bearing the glad tidings of full salvation to all the world . . ."[97]

In fact, the entire campaign to raise funds for the construction of God's Revivalist Memorial Building was cast in terms of the passion to reach "Souls! Souls! Souls! All for souls."[98] The appeal to this underlying impetus continued to prove remarkably effective, for by the time the building was dedicated on June 10, 1923, during camp meeting, only ten percent remained to be paid on the expenses for furnishing and finishing the building.[99] Meanwhile, the *Revivalist* updated readers as to progress on the building itself, with final touches being completed by April 1924, the *Revivalist* proclaiming that "GOD GETS ALL THE GLORY THAT IT IS DONE."[100]

Twin Giants: Indebtedness and Renewed Court Action

Enthusiasm ran high on the Mount of Blessings. Only fifteen thousand dollars was yet owed on God's Revivalist Memorial Building, and the removal of this indebtedness by June 1924 through a "BLOT OUT" campaign[101] encouraged school leaders to begin envisioning their next large building project—a new tabernacle to replace the deteriorating building that had been erected under Martin Wells Knapp's direction in 1901.[102]

The planned replacement for the old wood structure was on a much grander scale than its predecessor, as reflected by an impressive architect's sketch appearing in *God's Revivalist* and in the April 1, 1925 edition of Cincinnati's *Daily Times-Star*. The proposed structure of 95 feet by 140 feet would serve as another multi-purpose building, including "a combination tabernacle, gymnasium, and dining room," with several classrooms, a library, and a balcony overlooking the auditorium, which was planned to seat 2,000 persons.[103] The magnitude of the project, initially estimated to exceed $100,000 in cost, provided yet another illustration of the demands for expanded facilities made by the school's continued growth and of the ambitious vision of M. G. Standley.

However, before work on the new tabernacle could begin—in fact, before the campaign for the Memorial Building had even been completed—ominous signs of impending challenges were already emerging even as enrollment and facilities expanded. In fact, many (though not all) of these challenges could be viewed as the natural outflow of expansion, and included growing indebtedness, increased burdens on personnel—especially the trustees, and the development of tensions among campus leaders.

One of the actions taken to cope with additional administrative pressures was the expansion of the number of trustees, beginning with the addition of John Franklin Knapp in 1920. This move was placed squarely in the context of the trustees' growing burden, with the Standleys and Minnie Knapp basing their appeal to the Court of Common Pleas on the contention "that the original trustees [were] unable without assitance to carry on the work, and that it [was] necessary to appoint an additional Trustee . . ." Interestingly, at this point there appeared to be no mention to the court of another factor that made John Franklin a logical choice to become a fourth administrative trustee—the wishes of Martin Wells Knapp himself. In fact, this may have been because, in this light, John Franklin's appointment as trustee appeared long overdue, since the same document in which Martin Wells Knapp provided for his three immediate successors as trustees also reputedly indicated that his "son, John Franklin Knapp, shall be added to that number when he shall reach his majority, if in the judgment of said Trustees he shall be considered worthy and called to that office."[104] For reasons not entirely clear, it appears that the Standleys and Minnie Knapp decided to wait until institutional demands necessitated putting John Franklin in that post, rather than simply installing him when he reached age twenty-one according to his father's request.[105]

Regardless, John Franklin, at age thirty-two, was finally consecrated as the fourth trustee on June 13, 1920, during camp meeting, although he was not officially recognized as such by the court until that November.[106] His appointment was apparently received with popular acclaim and garnered the support of such influential holiness leaders as George Kulp, who presented the charge during John Franklin's consecration service.[107] Later, in language reminiscent of W. B. Godbey's prayer "that Johnnie shall rise up and be 'Brother Knapp' number two!," Kulp suggested that on John Franklin's "shoulders the mantle of his sainted father has so evidently descended."[108]

On the surface, it appeared that "the gifts, grace, wisdom, and education that fit [John Franklin] for leadership" provided a perfect complement to the zeal, vision, and spiritual depth of M. G. Standley, with evangelist J. B. McBride concluding that both were "God's chosen men for the place they occupy."[109] Indeed, the academic progress made under John Franklin's leadership seemed to bear this out. However, beneath the surface, "friction" between the new trustee and the other three trustees appeared as early as John Franklin's first board meeting after his official appointment by the court. The point of controversy then, and one that would frequently recur, was finances.[110]

Financial and other pressures were such that by 1925, in an attempt to alleviate their burdens even further, the existing trustees again presented to the court appeals for the appointment of additional trustees.[111] As a consequence, the court approved two new trustees—George B. Kulp, whose appointment was effective June 16, 1925, and F. M. Messenger, who took office December 22, 1925.[112] Both men were natural choices in light of their associations with the school since its founding days and in view of their significant contributions to its finances—Kulp as principle fund raiser during camp meeting for many years and Messenger as likely the largest donor during the school's first several decades.[113] In addition, they represented key elements of the school's constituency, with Kulp cementing the Pilgrim Holiness connection and Messenger, far removed from his early associations with the Metropolitan Church Association which he had left in 1913, now serving as chairman of the General Board of the burgeoning Nazarene denomination and as associate pastor of the historic First Church of the Nazarene of Chicago.[114]

The high esteem with which both new trustees were regarded throughout the holiness movement, especially due to Kulp's sacrificial lifestyle during his many years as general superintendent and due to Messenger's rare business acumen prominently showcased in the success of Messenger Publishing Company, lent a much needed sense of stability to the school's administration and finances. It was apparently hoped that this factor would inspire increased confidence among constituents and thus spark even greater contributions, with the suggestion after Kulp's appointment,

> And how could the members of God's Revivalist family better testify their appreciation of this splendid addition to their Trustees, than by sending at once a substantial offering on the pressing financial needs which have already fallen heavily upon the shoulders of our dear Brother Kulp, and which must be met at once if the work is to go on?[115]

Indeed, the condition expressed in the last few words of that appeal was far from an idle statement, as the financial pressures bearing upon the school had reached crisis proportions. Complex factors, which remain difficult to sort out, had contributed to this development, and included irregular financial practices, unabated expansion, and unexpected crises. With regard to business procedures, neither M. G. Standley as a spiritual visionary or J. F. Knapp as a progressive educator possessed the business acumen or training necessary to standardize the school's financial procedures.[116] In addition, the continual push to expand the horizons of Revivalist ministries, which included some forty missionaries looking to the school for regular support as late as 1925,[117] kept GBS and its related enterprises at the breaking point of their resources, with practically no allowance for unanticipated expenses. This meant that what may have otherwise been relatively minor setbacks grew to become significant threats to the well-being of God's Bible School.

For instance, the issue of quarters for Hope Cottage became an urgent question. In 1919, the home had been relocated from the campus proper to a house near Milford, Ohio, a move bearing several implications. First, this made the old building available for Bible School purposes, helping to alleviate the school's growing pains. In addition, the administration felt that the rescue home residents would benefit more from a rural environment. Furthermore, the new home was purchased from a member of the school family, John Franklin Knapp, "for the nominal sum of only $5,500"—a bargain considering the house was located on a spacious plot of ten acres.[118]

This facility functioned well until November 30, 1923 (the day after Thanksgiving), when it was ravaged by fire, leaving only "a single chimney swaying in the wind."[119] This proved a serious set-back from which Revivalist ministries could not easily recover. In fact, it was not until the following June that a new facility was procured, this time "a large brick building with eight large rooms and four small rooms located on six acres of land" that also included a garden and an orchard. Situated about ten miles north of Cincinnati, the building and property cost $9,250.[120]

The *Revivalist* announced on June 26, 1924, that the mortgage on the newest Hope Cottage ($4,000), funds for its furnishing and remodeling ($2,000), and the deficit for the 1923-24 school year ($25,000), left the school with a pressing need of $31,000.[121] While school functions, such as the Thanksgiving Dinner, continued as usual throughout the following school year, the previous year's "heavy deficit" along with general maintenance on the campus and the necessity of purchasing new equipment for the school laundry presented a serious burden for school leadership.[122] By the following summer, the situation had accelerated to the point that the *Revivalist* depicted it as "a threatening peril to God's Bible School and Revivalist work" and candidly acknowledged that "The ALARMING DEFICIT at the close of the School year is beyond any precedent in the past and THREATENS TO SWAMP THE INSTITUTION." Supporters were implored to "PRAY! PRAY! PRAY!" and to assist with this crushing load as their means would permit—through outright offerings or by making loans of $100 or more for one to five years or by investing in annuities for even longer periods. Those who had invested in Liberty Bonds during World War I were encouraged to cash in these and to put the proceeds "to work for God." Investors were assured that they would "be able to see just how every cent of the money thus donated [was] being expended at any time . . ."[123] In addition, the prices for

Revivalist Press books were slashed—many going at cost—in an unprecedented "Great Money Raising Sale" admittedly forced by "the pressing financial needs of God's Bible School."[124]

Regardless these appeals and extreme measures, the financial woes of the school increased. In March 1927, Bessie Standley noted that the "pressing needs" included the mortgage on the orphanage, which then stood at $5,800.[125] This, with other obligations, coalesced to form an ominous "giant of debt" of around $125,000 that held GBS in its grip, threatening to bring Revivalist ministries to a close.[126]

To further complicate circumstances, another "giant" was looming on the horizon, proving a formidable menace in its own right. This was the spectre of additional litigation against the trustees, a threat that apparently increased in tandem with the school's financial woes. A dizzying array of issues coalesced to eventuate renewed court action regarding the governance of the school. The trigger was a lawsuit by a contractor who claimed breach of contract after the school was forced to abandon the initial agreement for him to superintend the construction of the new tabernacle, the original plans for which were necessarily downscaled as projected estimates of its cost soared to $200,000 or more. Although GBS paid the contractor $3,500 to compensate for income he may have lost, this was too little or too late to keep the case out of court by November 1927.[127]

This lawsuit afforded opportunity for others with grievances concerning school leadership to present their complaints to the Court of Common Pleas, the result being another full-blown trial concerning the legitimacy and fidelity of the school's trusteeship. Among the complicating factors were the tensions that had developed among various members of the Knapp, Standley, and Queen families. John Franklin Knapp had married Dollie Queen, a sister to Bessie Standley. Another brother-in-law, Orville F. Green, was a key employee in Revivalist Press, where he worked as a printer from 1911 until the summer of 1927. In addition, several other family members became employees of the school and/or residents on the campus during its second and third decades. Among these was Jay Meagan, a member of the music faculty and director of the GBS band, who was married to Dorothea, the oldest daughter of M. G. and Bessie Standley, who would herself become prominent in school affairs as her parents became advanced in age.

Resultant friction brought to the surface again an issue that had been dealt with in the initial court case placing GBS under the court's jurisdiction twenty years before—the status of the Knapp family's claim to the work left behind by Martin Wells Knapp. The original court settlement preserving GBS, *God's Revivalist*, and related ministries as a public trust, while entitling Knapp's heirs to some copyrights, printing plates, and royalties for his writings, was called into question. On the one hand, Minnie Knapp steadfastly "refused to touch any of the money from the books or royalties, and gave her share, which was one third of what the Court allowed the heirs, back to the Institution."[128] On the other hand, it appears that some of the heirs, including some who had married into the Knapp family and their descendents, were convinced that their rightful property had been unfairly amalgamated with institutional interests.

This dispute became part of a larger controversy over the compensation and benefits received by the trustees, particularly the Standleys and John Franklin Knapp, including housing privileges, monetary remuneration, automobile allowances, and trustee accounts with the institution.[129] In addition, John Franklin Knapp continued to question various business practices currently or previously employeed by the Standleys, including petty cash expenditures, bookkeeping, lack of minutes for trustee meetings (before he became trustee), and the school's sale of annuities to supporters.[130] He protested the latter, not out of objection to the practice in principle, but out of concern that adequate "financial reserve" was not backing the annuities and growing doubt as to their legality.[131]

Furthermore, both M. G. Standley and John Franklin Knapp had pursued personal business ventures that overlapped with their interests at GBS, leading to questions of propriety if not legality. For example, Standley had helped establish the Certigraph Company, with the purpose of manufacturing a "pocket" printing machine for various applications such as inventory recording.[132] In the process of establishing the company, he apparently utilized at least one employee of Revivalist Press and encouraged GBS constituents to purchase stock in the enterprise.[133] These practices were understandable in light of Standley's intention to "spend nine-tenths" of the money made "in the education and preparation of preachers of the Gospel and missionaries," ostensibly at GBS.[134] However, the Certigraph Company ultimately failed, casting aspersions on Standley's business judgment, regardless of his noble motive. Similarly, John Franklin Knapp's connection with the *Christian Home Magazine*, a periodical promoting Christian moral and political views, which he founded with the assistance of F. M. Messenger, created questions since it was considered the personal property of Knapp, even though it was produced for a time on the GBS campus and was advertised in the *Revivalist*, where it was offered to subscribers along with *Sparkling Waters* and *God's Revivalist* in a three-paper promotion.[135]

As agitation over such concerns increased, it became clear that the deeper issue that threatened to dash the GBS/Revivalist family against the rocks of division was that of leadership—who should continue at the helm of the school, M. G. and Bessie Standley or John F. and Dolly Q. Knapp? The situation deteriorated to the point that the working relationship all but dissolved between John Franklin Knapp and the Standleys and Minnie Knapp, although John Franklin presented a united front with the other trustees in public appeals to constituents for support of the school as late as March 1927.[136] However, he soon concluded that the ongoing "friction" necessitated a change and presented to the other trustees the idea that he should enter "field work" on behalf of the institution, to which the trustees agreed, voting unanimously (with one abstention—likely himself) in October 1927 to employee him as a field agent for two years.[137]

While John Franklin would retain for a short time the titles of "principal of the high school and secretary of the board of trustees,"[138] arrangements on campus including having an acting principal perform the day-to-day duties of the position effectively removed him from campus responsibilities.[139] By the following year, he had been replaced altogether as principal by Noah Douthit, a 1904 GBS alumnus.[140] In addition, Knapp resigned the pastorate of the McHenry Methodist Episcopal Church in Cincinnati's Northside, a position he had served for several years concurrent with his responsibilities at GBS, further freeing him to engage in "interdenominational" evangelistic work.[141]

Although John Franklin pursued this combination of evangelistic meetings and GBS field work beginning about November 1927, this apparent attempt at a Barnabas/Paul resolution (Acts 15:39) to the tensions between him and the other trustees would ultimately prove ineffectual, largely due to agitation ongoing among constituents by disaffected parties including family members who remained on campus.[142] Some of these even intruded on meetings of the trustees to the point that the latter resorted to conducting several meetings off campus at a secret location (the Gibson Hotel).[143]

Tensions reached a high point after Oliver F. Green and Reverend Henry W. Bromley (who was also married to a sister of Bessie Standley) joined with John Franklin Knapp in forming a publishing company, the United Religious Press, located a short distance from GBS on Mt. Auburn. The removal during the summer of 1927 of several items, including printing plates that were considered the property of John Franklin Knapp, from the GBS campus to the new printing establishment, became the pivotal issue around which Knapp's detractors rallied.[144]

By late 1927, it became apparent that, while the trustees themselves may have been able to ameliorate their differences, the continual agitation instigated by others had created an impass which could only be resolved by drastic action. Thus, M. G. Standley tendered his resignation as chairman of the board of trustees, and F. M. Messenger was elected as his successor. However, even this measure failed to satisfy the Standleys' opponents, and the likelihood of forthcoming litigation led Messenger to resign his chairmanship only two weeks after his election. Although he and George Kulp subsequently further distanced themselves from the quagmire by resigning as trustees altogether, it was not before Messenger had moved to reinstate Standley as chairman of the board.[145]

As 1927 drew to a close, GBS was deeply enshrouded by one of the darkest clouds in its history. However, it was against this dismal setting that some of the most dramatic victories of the school would be realized. The resultant recovery underscores several outstanding aspects of the school's history—first, dependence on God's providential care; second, the loyalty of the school's constituency; and third, the inspiration and genius of M. G. Standley's leadership.

The Campaign to "Owe No Man Anything, But To Love One Another"

At this point, M. G. Standley made one of the most brilliant decisions of his entire administration—one that he credited to divine direction—and launched what became perhaps the most dramatic campaign in the history of GBS: an all-out effort to eliminate the school's indebtedness. He thus shared with *Revivalist* readers in December 1927, how he had "told Mrs. Standley and Mrs. Knapp and some of the workers that [he] was sure that God would have [them] put this burden on the friends who have prayed for this work and who have wonderfully helped by their means . . .."[146]

The campaign was cast in terms of a battle to free the school from the clutches of "Giant Debt," with the objective that by the campaign's end, Revivalist ministries would indeed "owe no man anything, but to love one another" (Romans 13:8). This scripture provided the slogan for the campaign, and its last phrase tactfully reflected the fact that indebtedness was not the only giant which the school's supporters sought to defeat. In effect, the campaign against the Giant Debt was only one front of a two-pronged offensive designed also to counter negative agitation and potentially unfavorable outcomes from pending litigation.

To be sure, the aspect of the campaign seeking to rescue GBS from the Standley's detractors was more discrete and focused than that combating indebtedness, but just as crucial for the school's stability. In December 1927, about a week after he had shared the school's financial burden with *Revivalist* readers, M. G. Standley also sent a "Sealed Message" to numerous key supporters, explaining the circumstances leading up to renewal of litigation.[147] As a result, a flood of letters published in special supplements in the *Revivalist* during the campaign indicated not only support for debt elimination but also moral support for the Standleys' and Minnie Knapp's leadership. Accordingly, the supplement section was often entitled, "Our Hearts Are With You!" In addition, as a "silent protest" against gossip, supporters were encouraged to wear buttons emblazoned with the motto, "Speak Evil of No Man," which could be purchased for five cents apiece through the *Revivalist*.[148]

The sheer volume of the *Revivalist* supplements throughout the first half of 1928 helps to indicate just how successful was M. G. Standley's appeal to the vast coalition that had been forged under his leadership over the course of the previous quarter century.[149] Like the campaign to raise funds for the Revivalist Memorial Building, this new campaign appealed with remarkable success to every facet of the school's constituency, including other school leaders, alumni, numerous leaders throughout the holiness movement, the majority of the school's creditors, and even the children who read the *Revivalist* and *Sparkling Waters*.

Long-time campus leaders like Nettie Peabody, Alice White, Belle Staples, and, of course, Minnie Knapp, gave tremendous support through their endorsement of the plan to put fundraising for a new tabernacle on hold until indebtedness was eliminated, with several of them leading the way by asking that their previous contributions for the Building Fund instead be applied to "burying the debt."[150] In addition, Alice White's prayer band and her kitchen crew bathed the campus in prayer, and the *Revivalist* reported special promises that "Mom" White and others had received regarding the campaign.[151]

Although George Kulp, then in his eighties, apparently faded from involvement with GBS after his resignation as trustee, F. M. Messenger remained a stalwart supporter.[152] In fact, it is doubtful than any single individual, with the exception of M. G. Standley himself, did more to rally the faithful to support the campaign than did Messenger, who helped to give it an early boost with a personal donation of one thousand dollars.[153] Even though his wife died during the height of the campaign (May 7, 1928), he had already traveled from his home in Chicago to visit the Hilltop by the following week, radiating encouragement to the campus family and reflecting his commitment to the cause.[154] In addition, he penned numerous front-page articles in the *Revivalist* encouraging constituents to continue their liberal giving, which he praised as "almost Pentecostal" in its proportions.[155]

Truthfully, the array of alumni rallying behind the campaign for the school was overwhelming. G. C. Bevington led the way, donating to the cause one thousand copies of his popular book, *Remarkable Incidents and Modern Miracles Through Prayer and Faith*.[156] His supportive letters were joined by a plethora of articles and letters of support from such prominent alumni as R. G. Finch, Fred T. Fuge, John Franklin Simpson, and Charles Slater.[157] Several of these emphasized the positive impact of GBS on the holiness movement through its contributions to numerous other ministries, as when E. A. Kilbourne highlighted the OMS-GBS connection.[158] Many others expressed similar sentiments to Richard and Irene (Blyden) Taylor, who wrote, "If I were a patriarch I'd stand up and bless you; and if I were a millionaire I would send you all the money you need . . . and endow you. But neither of these is in my power; but what is in my hand, I give, and that is *importunate prayer*."[159]

Support also outpoured from prominent evangelists and other holiness leaders, ranging from John and Bona Fleming to Paul S. Rees and from Rev. and Mrs. Joseph H. Smith to Rev. and Mrs. R. Wingrove Ives.[160] Especially noteworthy was the support from such Nazarene leaders as Bud Robinson, E. O. Chalfant, and Charles A. Gibson, the latter then serving as district superintendent in Ohio, making him host of the Nazarene General Assembly in 1928. In a photograph featured on the front page of the *Revivalist* for May 17, 1928, these three men appeared with M. G. Standley, sending a powerful message of their solidarity with the Standleys and Minnie Knapp. Chalfant and Robinson contributed articles strongly promoting the campaign, with the latter opining that "no greater calamity to my way of thinking, could come to the nation than to have this School close." He then hastened to add confidently, "But I am sure it will not. . . . We believe that God is going to see these good people through; that every dollar of the money will be sent in, and that before the close of the Camp Meeting every bill will be met. We believe that God will be glorified and that the devil will be defeated."[161]

Here Robinson reflected the terms in which many of the school's constituents viewed its current difficulties. They saw it as a spiritual struggle with far greater significance than mere financial problems or administrative tensions. They saw behind the school's troubles satanic opposition which in turn found an ally in human carnality. Thus, E. E. Shelhamer wrote in anticipation of his participation in the 1928 camp meeting, "Hope the smell of court rooms and carnality will not linger around the 'Hill' up until Camp. Let us pray God to blow from the four winds of Heaven and clear the atmosphere."[162] Some found in this spiritual conflict connections with larger cultural trends and the decline of vital Christianity. For example, in her powerful plea for the preservation of the Hilltop institutions that had done so much to call people "Back to the Bible," Lettie Cowman put the campaign in the context of such issues as the Modernist-Fundamentalist controversy and a loss of "the secret forces of Pentecost," as education and eloquence had replaced tarrying in prayer. However, she had confidence that as GBS had, "for a quarter of a century . . . stood foursquare to all the winds that blow"—"It MUST not, it will not fail!"[163]

Remarkably, many supporters anticipated that the outcome of the assault on GBS by the forces of darkness would be positive. George W. Fuller, financial secretary at Asbury College, predicted that the devil would "see utter defeat when the smoke of battle" cleared, leaving *"God's Bible School . . . stronger than ever."* Indeed, he contended that "the devil . . . surely made a mistake in starting such a fight against the School, as it . . . turned loose *a volume of prayer all over the country,*" unintentionally enlisting "thousands *for* the School."[164] Similarly, in April 1928, J. L. Glascock exulted, "I have been encouraged in this thought that while the enemies of this school have thought to do it evil, the trials imposed by them have been a blessing."[165] In fact, it appears that these positive assessments were largely correct for, as debt was eliminated, optimism for the school's future rose, dispelling much of the criticism of the administration and helping to assure constituents that, as M. G. Standley and F. M. Messenger put it, "God is with us."[166]

This effect, as well as an answer to the prayers of thousands, also reflected the genius of M. G. Standley's leadership. His untiring efforts to see the "Giant Debt" defeated, which included negotiating in less than thirty days the renewal of numerous promissory notes amounting to around thirty thousand dollars, set an inspiring example for others who loved the school.[167] In addition, his general approach in articles and admonitions throughout the campaign was positive, focusing on soliciting support and looking forward to future progress rather than attacking adversaries and looking back at past difficulties.[168] This buoyant leadership style had an inspiring impact and further endeared M. G. Standley and his colleagues to loyal constituents. In specific details of the campaign, Standley continued to demonstrate the creativity and passion that had long marked his administration. His successful appeal to the wide range of constituents described above stemmed from his concerted efforts to keep all supporters abreast of developments, to make each one realize the importance of his/her own contribution—no matter how small, and to keep everyone focused on the campaign's ultimate goal.

Shortly after introducing the campaign, Standley announced that upon elimination of the indebtedness, monuments commemorating the debts' burials would be erected—one on the GBS campus, the other on the orphanage property—both bearing plaques inscribed with the campaign's slogan.[169] While pressing toward this ultimate goal, Standley gave weekly updates on the front page of the *Revivalist*, sharing new plateaus of giving that had been reached and stoking excitement as various milestones were reached.

A remarkable feature of the campaign that reflects its grassroots appeal was the involvement of readers of the *Revivalist*'s "Children's Page" and/or *Sparkling Waters*. Beginning in February 1928, M. G. Standley presented their own special aspect of the campaign to the children, giving them their own "giant" to defeat—the $5,500 debt on the orphanage.[170] To accommodate the small amounts of change they might collect toward the effort, young readers were sent coin-cards that would hold ten dimes when filled, which Standley likened to David's sling. Captivating student-drawn cartoons, depicting the "great big giant, GOLIATH-DEBT" as it menaced the orphanage, pulled at young heart-strings, and donations to "slay the giant" soon began pouring into the Mount of Blessings.[171] In fact, the response was so enthusiastic that the debt hanging over the orphanage was quickly dispatched, with M. G. Standley announcing that as of March 13, the "GIANT, GOLIATH-DEBT, that has hung over God's Orphanage so long, has been slain!"[172]

This milestone was marked by a cartoon in *Sparkling Waters* and the *Revivalist* depicting children from "God's Revivalist Regiment" and "Sparkling Waters Army" rejoicing over the body of the slain "Giant Debt" and exulting "WE'VE KILLED HIM! WE'VE KILLED HIM!"[173] This artistic rendering may not have been far from the actual hilarity that filled the air on Saturday afternoon, March 17, as a crowd gathered at the orphanage property to conduct a "funeral ceremony" for the "Giant" debt during which its mortgage note was laid to rest in the inexpensive monument that had been made from boulders gathered throughout the countryside. From there, they journeyed to Hope Cottage, for which the mortgage had also been paid, and erected a monument similar to that on the orphanage grounds.[174] These victories M. G. Standley viewed as indicators of better things to come—as the "earnest" of the school's "Jubilee Year"—by which he meant, not its fiftieth anniversary, but its year of release from the bondage of debt.[175] Thus, on Sunday, April 1, a "Jubilee Service" was held in the school tabernacle, both to offer thanksgiving for the debts already paid and to provide a "glorious foretaste" of an even more auspicious "GREAT JUBILEE" anticipated to celebrate the culmination of the campaign during camp meeting.[176]

Such celebration certainly fueled the zeal of supporters to—as Bud Robinson put it—"go over the top, and make the shore landing!"[177] Coin "slings," filled by children and adults, continued to make an important contribution as young and old combined forces for a final assault against the debt that still loomed over the school, depicted in a new cartoon as a towering giant threatening the Mount of Blessings itself with a club bearing the inscription "Debt Slaves."[178] By April 23, with only about four weeks until camp meeting would begin, over $84,000 in cash and pledges had been received, but a little over $35,000 remained for the indebtedness to be cleared.[179] Over the next few weeks, the campaign reached fever-pitch intensity. The week of May 7-13 proved crucial in the campaign's success. Designated by the trustees as "self-denial" or "Do-Without" week and promoted by such stalwart school workers as E. G. Marsh, it was launched on campus with a Monday morning chapel sermon from the irrepressible Bud Robinson and marked on Friday morning by fasting and prayer.[180] By the following Wednesday the grand total raised had surpassed $93,000.[181] While optimism was building, the question still remained concerning the "Giant Debt"—"Will he be killed by camp?"[182]

Perhaps no camp meeting has ever begun with such an atmosphere of anticipation. M. G. Standley reported that "From the very beginning it looked as if we were at high tide, but no, it kept rising, and again and again it looked as though we had struck the climax."[183] Remarkably, however, the focus during camp was not put on the school's financial needs, with Joseph H. Smith exclaiming over the fact that "less prominence and less pressure was given to money matters than in any meeting of the size we ever remember attending. The spiritual interests were all absorbing." In addition, the trustees determined that the campaign for the indebtedness would not interfere with the customary missionary offering, with the result that donations for missions reached over $5,000, well surpassing the previous year's offering.[184]

In confidence that the debt would be eliminated, on Thursday, May 31, a monument was erected, with fifteen stones left off the top, "each stone representing a $1,000."[185] Sunday, June 3, was designated as "Bible School Day" and it began on a high note with the crowd giving a great shout "when the first thousand was given on the last $15,000 due." Pledges continued to pour in from all over the tabernacle so that soon only $7,000 was still needed to reach the goal, with the congregation standing "with hearts filled with joy and praise" and singing the *Gloria Patri*.[186] Following this, evangelist C. H. Babcock, who had been scheduled to preach, indicated that he felt the giving should continue—"that God wanted to slay the giant then." Other camp participants concurred, including F. M. Messenger and Joseph H. Smith, both of whom again gave substantial offerings.[187] Within moments, the goal had been met and "the cry rang out, 'We've cut off the Giant's head—we've gone over the top—the debt has been cleared'."[188]

What followed was one of the most euphoric scenes ever witnessed on the Mount of Blessings. M. G. Standley likened it to Armistice Day—celebrating victory in World War I—"only this was in the power and demonstration of the Spirit"—"it just looked as if the waters that had been pent up . . . burst forth in one great gush until it seemed to sweep everything before it! Some were shouting, some crying, some jumping and others waving their handkerchiefs in the air."[189] Edwin and Hazel Kilbourne reported, "Shouts of hallelujahs could be heard for blocks around. The great audience wept and shouted and laughed until the entire hilltop echoed and re-echoed the praises of God. Sister Standley had the platform, running back and forth weeping and praising God. Brother Standley stood with his head in his hands, seemingly unable to move for a few moments."[190]

A triumphal march soon ensued, with the crowd making its way to the "Ebenezer Monument" that awaited its crown of fifteen stones. The jubilant tumult was so great that E. E. Shelhamer, unable to get there in time from his third floor room in the main building, straddled his window and joined the praise.[191] The Standleys, Kilbournes, and others placed the final stones on the monument, marking, as C. H. Babcock explained it, God's answer to the "great praying by the thousands who love *God's Revivalist* and God's Bible School and Missionary Training Home."[192] Then, the throng, led by the orchestra, extended their triumphant march down the streets surrounding the campus, stopping at each corner "to offer thanksgiving in prayer and praise and song while the residents stood at the windows and in the doorways and wondered what it was all about."[193] After returning to the campus, they circled the main building "and stopped in a great ring and had the final note of Dedication"—a prayer delivered by F. M. Messenger.[194] M. G. Standley summed it up, "I shall never forget that scene. It was the greatest day we ever had on the 'Mount of Blessings,' and the greatest day I ever saw."[195]

Pressing Forward

While the victory over the "Giant Debt" ended so dramatically, the resolution of litigation in the Court of Common Pleas was—much like the original case in 1907—rather anti-climatic. Perhaps the most remarkable feature of the trial was the fact of its repeated postponement, so that the case was not heard until the July 1928 term of the court. This delay was attributed to answered prayer by the Standleys and their supporters, who rejoiced that it allowed sufficient time for the successful conclusion of the campaign to eliminate indebtedness. In fact, it appears that the judge allowed for the trial's delay on at least one occasion because of the tremendous progress of the campaign, with the comment "that litigation did not pay debts, and that he was not disposed to do anything that would injure the Institution."[196]

This concern for the future stability and success of GBS and its related ministries seemed to dominate Judge Thomas Darby's decisions in the case. Although detractors on both sides had apparently questioned in particular the validity of the appointment as trustees of the Standleys and/or John Franklin Knapp and in general the place of the Court of Common Pleas to authorize the appointment of trustees, the Court asserted its authority and declared the trusteeship of the Standleys, Mrs. Knapp, and John Franklin Knapp to be valid.[197] Also, as in its 1907 decision, the court denied the motion to place the school in receivership and dismissed allegations of misconduct on the part of any of the trustees as lacking sufficient evidence.[198]

The Court's judgment apparently sought to effect reconciliation between the disaffected trustees. Perhaps this decision was swayed by testimony that had made clear the benefits that the Standleys and John Franklin Knapp had each contributed to the school and by the high esteem in which most of the school's creditors apparently held M. G. Standley.[199] Regardless, the aftermath favored the Standleys' leadership, leaving them in a much stronger position than that of John Franklin Knapp, who would continue to work for the school serving as field representative from 1930 until he was forced to resign his duties after "he suffered a severe illness with ulcers of the stomach"[200] and "heart trouble"[201] in 1934. Although he would remain a trustee at GBS until about three weeks before his death on May 27, 1943, Knapp would never again have the influence on the Hilltop that he had before the trial when he had led the school's academic advance. His later years were devoted to pioneering a Nazarene church in Covington, Kentucky, a congregation he pastored until his death on May 27, 1943.[202] Posterity would remember him as "an excellent preacher, a splendid teacher, a gifted writer and an efficient, untiring worker."[203]

With the successful rout of the giants of indebtedness and litigation behind the Standleys, once more vindicating their leadership, they and the school's supporters were eager to press forward, as if the recent challenges GBS had weathered only served to increase their vigor. Thus, M. G. Standley challenged *Revivalist* readers, "But we are not going to stop here; we are going to keep praying . . . We want to dress up our buildings and fix up the grounds . . . We want to make it look as though God lived at God's Bible School and God's Orphanage. So let us march on to greater things!"[204]

Constituents were additionally heartened to embrace this challenge by the administration's new commitment to continue in the spirit of the campaign to "Owe no man anything, but to love one another"—or, as M. G. Standley put it, to "trust [God] to supply our needs AS WE GO."[205] In fact, Charles Slater suggested that this sentiment be added in a new motto to compliment the School's historic commitment to Biblical Christianity: "It is the prayer and deepest wish of all present, and we are sure of all the great *Revivalist* Family, that the motto of this great Institution from henceforth will be, as it now is "BACK TO THE BIBLE," and additional: **PAY AS WE GO!**"[206]

Among the initiatives proposed during and following the exhilarating days of the debt campaign's conclusion was the establishment of a new rescue mission—an idea proposed by J. L. Glascock and enthusiastically endorsed by M. G. Standley.[207] Another vision that was reborn as the campaign neared a close was the construction of a new tabernacle. While M. G. Standley led in marshalling support for "God's House of Prayer,"[208] those lending their voices in favor of this enterprise included "Bud" Robinson, E. E. Shelhamer, and Joseph H. Smith.[209] By October 29, 1929, the enthusiastic response of constituents to the theme "Take Every Man a Beam!" (see II Kings 6:2) had garnered $9,710 toward the project.[210]

This was just one area that signaled brighter days to come. M. G. Standley accordingly viewed the school's past successes, particularly in the campaign of 1928, as only the foundation of even greater things to come:

> He has wonderfully blessed us in the past and demonstrated His power, but this last year God has worked so marvelously in our midst that we cannot help but see that the foundation that He has been laying is an evidence of the great superstructure, which we believe will testify to the world of His mighty workings! . . . how could we be true to our God and not *go forward* and even believe for greater things! If Jesus tarries, we ought to expect greater School years and greater Camp Meetings with greater demonstrations of the power of the Holy Ghost! . . . [and] to expect Him to do greater things, to help us to reach out and do more for Him, not only on the *"Mount of Blessings,"* but in the home and foreign missionary fields.[211]

Even a visionary like M. G. Standley would have hardly been able to anticipate to what extent these aspirations would be realized over the next two decades. In fact, though the Great Depression and other daunting challenges lay just around the corner, the following decades would prove to be the time of the most ambitious expansion of the ministries of GBS, bringing it to the height of its influence during its first century. This story of how the flames of holy fire blazed higher and spread further would require another volume.

Notes

[1] "Pressing Forward," *Revivalist* (Nov. 9, 1911), 1.
[2] Cited in Larry D. Smith, "M. G. Standley (1911-1950): Strong, Aggressive Leadership," *Revivalist Centenary Commemorative Edition* (Sept. 2000), 9.
[3] *Court Records on Case no. 136432 for Hamilton County, Ohio, Court of Common Pleas, (Filed June 5, 1929)*, 136.
[4] Ibid and Standley, *My Life*, 141.
[5] See Millie M. Lawhead, "Echoes from the National Holiness Convention," *Revivalist* (June 25, 1925), 13 and *Court Records on Case no. 136432 for Hamilton County, Ohio, Court of Common Pleas, (Filed June 5, 1929)*, 185.
[6] Day, 74-75.
[7] Day, 74. Day cites the November 23, 1916 "Bible school Notes":

> The Academic Course fully complies with the requirements of the National Board in obtaining credits for admission to college. The time required for this course is four years. One completing the Academic work here, will be able to take up College work, as the Course answers to the requirements of Class, First, of the State Schools.

[8] For a complete listing of the "Academic Course of Study" when the high school began in 1914, see Day, 76. See Sidney Collett, *All About The Bible: Its Origin—Its Language—Its Translation—Its Canon—Its Symbols—Its Inspiration—Its Alleged Errors and Contradictions—Its Plan—Its Science—Its Rivals* Twentieth Ed. (New York: Fleming H. Revell Co., c. 1934). This work was popular among holiness educators, remaining in the Nazarene course of study for ministers from 1914 to 1944. See Bassett, "The Fundamentalist Leavening . . ." 71-72.
[9] Day, 78. For correspondence from Vernon M. Riegal, state Director of Education, accompanying the certificate, see Appendix B in Day, 154.
[10] *Court Records on Case no. 136432 for Hamilton County, Ohio, Court of Common Pleas, (Filed June 5, 1929)*, 136.
[11] Ibid.
[12] Susan Elmera McNeill Westhafer, "Conservatory of Gospel Music," in Moser and Smith, 22.
[13] Day, 77.
[14] Ibid, 83.
[15] Ibid, 77.
[16] Ibid, 79. See the course requirements for this program in Day, 80-82.
[17] Ibid, 83.
[18] "Our Specialty," *Revivalist* (Sept. 21, 1916), 1, 14.
[19] For example, see the description of the school's various ministries in "God's Bible School and Missionary Training Home," *Revivalist* (Jan. 4, 1912), 7-10.
[20] "God's Bible School and Missionary Training Home," *Revivalist* (Sept. 27, 1917), 12 and "God's Bible School and Missionary Training Home," *Revivalist* (June

4-11, 1925), 13.

[21] Day, 84 and "God's Bible School and Missionary Training Home," *Revivalist* (Sept. 8, 1921), 12.

[22] "God's Bible School and Missionary Training Home," *Revivalist* (June 4-11, 1925), 13.

[23] See Charles W. Carter, *Missionaries Extraordinary: The Life and Labors of Charles and Elizabeth Carter*, Rev. ed. (N.p., Charles W. Carter, 1993).

[24] Ibid, 23-40. Also, see "Charles Carter at God's Bible School," *Revivalist* (Dec. 1996), 12-13 and Charles R. Wilson, "Charles W. Carter," in *Handbook of Evangelical Theologians*, Walter A. Elwell, ed. (Grand Rapids: Baker Books, 1993), 209-218.

In his memoirs, Carter commended GBS for adhering to the philosophy of "service in training and outreach to the lost world of mankind with the Gospel of Christ" (39).

[25] *Missionaries Extraordinary*, 41-42. Also, see Mrs. M. W. Knapp, "Bible School Notes," *Revivalist* (July 12, 1928), 11-12 and Moser and Smith, 156.

[26] Ibid, 48-50.

[27] McLeister and Nicholson, 399.

[28] See "Charles W. Carter (1905-1996)," *WTJ* Vol. 32 No. 2 (Fall 1997), 218; " 'Distinguished Alumnus' Dr. Charles W. Carter Receives Heavenly Award October 21," *Revivalist* (Dec. 1996), 12; and "Charles W. Carter," in *Handbook of Evangelical Theologians*, 210.

[29] *A Contemporary Wesleyan Theology: Biblical, Systematic, and Practical* (Grand Rapids: Zondervan, 1983) and *The Wesleyan Bible Commentary* (Grand Rapids: Eerdmans, 1965).

[30] See William C. Kostlevy, "The Wesleyan Theological Society: An Historical Overview," c. 16 in Callen and Kostlevy, eds. *Heart of the Heritage*, 359-361, originally in *WTJ* Vol. 30 No. 1 (Spring 1995), 212-215.

[31] Charles W. Carter and Ralph Earle, *The Evangelical Bible Commentary: The Acts of the Apostles* (Grand Rapids: Zondervan, 1959); Charles W. Carter, *The Person and Ministry of the Holy Spirit: A Wesleyan Perspective*, Rev. ed. (Grand Rapids: Baker Book House, 1977); *The Bible Gift of Tongues* (Syracuse, NY: The Wesley Press, 1951); *From Revival to Evangelism or The Effects of Spiritual Renewal* (Salem, OH: Schmul, 1986).

[32] *Missionaries Extraordinary*, 38.

[33] *50 Years of Profiles in Faith* (N. P.: n. p., n. d.), n. p. This booklet located in the GBS archives gives a brief sketch of the lives of John Franklin and Lovenah (Reisdorph) Simpson. Also, see Moser and Smith, 81 and 87.

[34] McLeister and Nicholson, 467 and 602.

[35] Ibid, 602.

[36] *Profiles* and McLeister and Nicholson, 454-455.

[37] McLeister and Nicholson, 188 and 513.

[38] Virgil A. Mitchell, "Wesleyan Methodists Chart A New Course, 1935-1968," c. 7 in Caldwell, 294 and McLeister and Nicholson, 602.

[39] Ibid, 294-296 and McLeister and Nicholson, 189.

[40] R. D. Reisdorph, "Where Former Students Now Labor," *Revivalist* (Dec. 28, 1972), 6.

[41] See Moser and Smith, 69 and "Archives," *Revivalist* (Oct. 1997), 16 for a photo

of Simpson and Catanese in their dorm room, the only known extant photograph of an early GBS dormitory room.

⁴² See "Anthony Catanese" in Moser and Smith, 76.

⁴³ Krikor Gayjikian, *Martyred Armenia and The Story of My Life* (Cincinnati: God's Revivalist Press, 1920), 42.

⁴⁴ Ibid. Also, see Mrs. M. W. Knapp, "Bible School Notes," *Revivalist* (June 27, 1929), 11.

⁴⁵ See Moser and Smith, 89-90, 92. Gayjikian died on November 13, 1972, when he was struck by an automobile. See Barry D. Walker, "Rev. Krikor Gayjikian Fatally Injured Enroute to Church," *Revivalist* (Jan. 11, 1973), 6.

⁴⁶ For a helpful overview of White's life which largely informs this work, see Dorothy Walters, "Her Labors, Not In Vain," *Revivalist* (Jan. 18, 1968), 3-4. Also, see Moser and Smith, 332.

⁴⁷ See Moser and Smith, 189 on White's involvement in the Thanksgiving Dinners in the 1930s.

⁴⁸ "Reports by Some of the Preachers, Missionaries, and Workers," *Revivalist* (July 9, 1925), 4-5. This name was evidently first used by two "motherless boys" in whom White took a great deal of interest in making sure they were provided with clothes and other necessities (Walters, "Her Labors," 3).

⁴⁹ "Bible School Notes," *Revivalist* (July 22, 1920), 12.

⁵⁰ Mrs. M. W. Knapp, "Bible School Notes," *Revivalist* (Sept. 29, 1927), 9.

⁵¹ To get a glimpse into the passion of this organization under White's leadership, see *Unveiling the Missionary World* Comp. by God's Bible School Missionary Prayer Band, Alice M. White, Director (Cincinnati: God's Bible School and Missionary Training Home, 1936).

⁵² Day, 104.

⁵³ Helen Hammer Dotson, *Along Life's Trail: Autobiography of Helen Hammer Dotson* (N. P., n. p.: n. d.), 31. Also see 24 and 61 on White's "mothering" influence on Hammer. After serving under Bustin's group, Evangelical Bible Mission, Hammer also served with the Wesleyan Methodist Church and the Holiness Pilgrim Church mission.

Hammer initially attended GBS in 1924, graduating in 1926. She returned in the 1940s to take the "Ten Weeks Course." It was after this course that she went to Haiti. See "Helen Dotson Remembers GBS in the 1920's," *Revivalist* (Sept. 1997), 12-13.

⁵⁴ Moser and Smith, 96-99, 102; Day, 103; Robert D. Wood, *In These Mortal Hands*, c. VII, 88-108; and Lettie Cowman, *Missionary Warrior*, c. XXIII, 209-335.

⁵⁵ Wood (88-89) suggests that this meeting took place in England. However, Lettie Cowman's article "Japanese Village Work and How It Began," *Revivalist* (March 11, 1909), 8-9, indicates that it took place in America.

⁵⁶ Wood, 89.

⁵⁷ Ibid, 100.

⁵⁸ Cowman, *Missionary Warrior*, 300.

⁵⁹ Wood, 100. Also, see 98.

⁶⁰ Ibid, 105.

[61] Ibid, 100.

[62] Considering the impetus given the campaign by belief in Christ's imminent return, it was fitting that such significant funding came from the foundation directed by Blackstone, a Methodist minister and leading Christian Zionist. His book, *Jesus Is Coming*, first appeared in 1878 and was among recommended "Books on the Second Coming" listed in *God's Revivalist* for October 31, 1901 (7). In 1908, Fleming H. Revell (brother-in-law of Dwight L. Moody) began publishing it, with sales surpassing 386,000 in 25 languages by 1916. It did much to advance the premillennial dispensationalist agenda across a wide spectrum of evangelicals, with both R. A. Torrey and J. Wilbur Chapman testifying that the book significantly impacted their own understanding of the Second Coming (Wood, 101).

[63] Day, 103; Wood, 104.

[64] Wood, 105.

[65] Ibid, 106-108; Moser and Smith, 98, 102.

[66] Charles and Lettie Cowman, "One Million Homes Still to Be Reached," *Revivalist* (Nov. 1, 1917), 10.

[67] Wood, 108.

[68] See William Kostlevy, "OMS International (OMS)" in *Dictionary*, 220-221; Wood, 108; and Moser and Smith, 102.

[69] Moser and Smith, 102. See also, Davison, Smith, and Plank, *Discover GBS!*, 9-10.

[70] Ibid.

[71] Wood, 103.

[72] On the subsequent careers of all ten men, see Wood, 102-104 and Moser and Smith, 99. Miller and Hiles were not the only ones who gave service both on foreign fields and in the United States.

[73] See Charles C. Cowman, "God's Revivalist Province in Korea," *Revivalist* (Aug. 5, 1920), 10 and William Thiele, "Village Work In God's Revivalist Province, Korea," *Revivalist* (May 17, 1923), 10. Actually, this area consisted of two Korean provinces, South Choong Chong and North Chulla. The OMS work in these provinces was superintended by GBS alumni William Thiele and William Miller, respectively.

[74] Mrs. M. W. Knapp, *Diary Letters: A Missiona[r]y Trip through the West Indies and to South America* (Cincinnati: God's Revivalist Office, 1918). Also, see "Sister Knapp's Diary Letter," *Revivalist* (Jan. 31, 1918), 5 and Moser and Smith, 94, which includes a photo from this trip.

[75] Mrs. M. W. Knapp, "Bible School Notes," *Revivalist* (July 12, 1928), 11-12. She reported of Standley's message, "God mightily stirred the hearts of those present, and pastors, missionaries and friends will go out to do and dare for God, we feel, as never before."

[76] C. W. Troxel, "That Missionary Day," in "A Great Spiritual Feast—the Camp of 1924," *Revivalist* (July 17, 1924), 1-2.

[77] Day, 58, 60.

[78] "Thermometer for Returns in the Two Hundred Thousand Dollar Campaign," *Revivalist* (July 22, 1920), 5.

[79] "A Mighty Challenge to the Faith of God's Revivalist Family," *Revivalist* (July

15, 1920), 8-9.

[80] Day, 61.

[81] "Thermometer for Returns . . .," *Revivalist* (July 22, 1920), 5. Another chart was also utilized, that appeared more like a ladder with a drawing of the new building at the top. See *Revivalist* (July 28, 1921), 11 and *Revivalist* (Aug. 18, 1921), 8.

[82] Day, 61.

[83] "An Open Letter to the Students of God's Bible School," *Revivalist* (Feb. 23, 1922), 8.

[84] "An Easter Memorial Day," *Revivalist* (April 14, 1921), 2 (original emphasis).

[85] "Stewards of Faith: An Adventure in Sanctified Faith and Stewardship," *Revivalist* (July 15, 1920), 7.

[86] Day, 61.

[87] J. F. K. [John Franklin Knapp], "Answered Prayer: February a Banner Month for 'Brick': More than $6,000 Received in Three Weeks," *Revivalist* (March 9, 1922). See also, "Brick! Brick!! Brick!!! Great Forward Movement Started Monday, March 13, 1922," *Revivalist* (March 23, 1922), 8.

[88] "The Zeal of Thine House Hath Eaten Me Up," *Revivalist* (Oct. 6, 1921), pp. 8-9.

[89] S. V. Williams, "Saturday, June 18," *Revivalist* (July 28, 1921), 5.

[90] B. Trunick, "A Wonderful Memory," *Revivalist* (July 14, 1921), 8.

[91] S. V. Williams, "Saturday, June 18," 5 (original emphasis).

[92] Mr. and Mrs. A. E. Rassman, "Saturday, June 18," *Revivalist* (July 28, 1921), 4. For an earlier example of similar generosity by a student named Sarah Bachman, see Moser and Smith, 120-125.

[93] S. V. Williams, "Saturday, June 18," 5-6.

[94] Rassman, "Saturday, June 18," 4.

[95] S. V. Williams, "Saturday, June 18," 5 (original emphasis).

[96] B. Trunick, "A Wonderful Memory," *Revivalist* (July 14, 1921), 8.

[97] S. V. Williams, "Saturday, June 18," 6-7.

[98] "Brick! Brick!! Brick!!! Great Forward Movement Started Monday, March 13, 1922," *Revivalist* (March 23, 1922), 8.

[99] Day, 61; "Thousands of Dollars Would Be Wasted," *Revivalist* (June 28, 1923), 8; "The Great Revivalist Camp of 1923," *Revivalist* (July 19, 1923), 1-3.

[100] "Now for the Final Leap of Faith," *Revivalist* (April 3, 1924), 8 (original emphasis).

[101] Ibid (original emphasis). See "The 'Blot Out' Campaign," *Revivalist* (May 29, 1924), 8 and similar updates throughout *Revivalist* (June 26, 1924), 8.

[102] For a photograph of the original tabernacle shortly before its demolition in 1931, see Moser and Smith, 166.

[103] "Tabernacle for God's Bible School," *The Daily Time-Star* (April 1, 1925), Section D, 15. Also, see "The Proposed New Tabernacle for God's Bible School," *Revivalist* (June 4-11, 1925), 8 and Moser and Smith, 172.

[104] *Court Records on Case no. 136432 for Hamilton County, Ohio, Court of Common Pleas, (Filed June 5, 1929), Decision.* Some unsubstantiated reports went even further, suggesting that Martin Wells Knapp had even higher aspirations for John Franklin. For example, Glenn Black states, "I have heard, yet have not verified such, that it

was Knapp's desire for his son, John, to ultimately lead the school at the appropriate timing." However, as editor Black noted, "This never materialized" (Three Women Served As Administrators At God's Bible School From 1901-1911," *Revivalist* (Aug. 4, 1983), 11).

[105] It may have been that the trustees were simply waiting for John Franklin to complete his studies at the University of Cincinnati, from which he graduated in 1920.

[106] The space of a few months between John Franklin's "consecration" as trustee and actual approval by the court has led to some confusion as to the date of his trusteeship. In addition, he was listed as a trustee in the *Revivalist* as early as August 1920, although the Standleys and Minnie Knapp did not file the application requesting John Franklin's addition as trustee until September 21, 1920. See *Court Records... (Filed June 5, 1929), Decision*; "Obituary," *Revivalist* (June 17, 1943), 7; Day, 77-78; and Glenn Black, "John F. Knapp: Preacher—Teacher—Writer," *Revivalist* (Nov. 17, 1983), 7.

[107] Day, 77-78.

[108] George B. Kulp, "The Lord God Omnipotent Reigneth," *Revivalist* (July 21, 1921), 4.

[109] J. B. McBride, "Sunday, June 4," in "A Glorious and Victorious Camp: The Story as Told by a Number of the Workers," *Revivalist* (July 13, 1922), 4.

[110] *Court Records... (Filed June 5, 1929)*, 193-194, et. al.

[111] Although the Revivalist announced these appointments to be made upon the "unanimous" request or petition of the existing trustees, M. G. Standley reported later that they were made over the "vehement protests" of Minnie Knapp. Perhaps she feared that the additions would increase rather than decrease the mounting tensions among the trustees. See "Extraordinary Announcement," *Revivalist* (June 25, 1925), 1; "Pray For Our New Co-Worker," *Revivalist* (Jan. 7, 1926), 1; and Standley, *My Life*, 142.

[112] Day, 79.

[113] See "Extraordinary Announcement," *Revivalist* (June 25, 1925), 1, for Kulp's introduction as trustee. On Messenger's support of GBS, see *Court Records... (Filed June 5, 1929)*, 300-302, et. al. M. G. Standley indicated that his donations had surpassed $20,000 by 1928 ("His Gift Is Different," *Revivalist* (Jan. 19, 1928), 1-2).

[114] "Pray for Our New Co-Worker," *Revivalist* (Jan. 7, 1926), 1. This article is signed by Mrs. M. W. Knapp, Mrs. M. G. Standley, Rev. M. G. Standley, Rev. J. F. Knapp, and Rev. G. B. Kulp.

[115] "Extraordinary Announcement," *Revivalist* (June 25, 1925), 1. This article is signed Mrs. M. W. Knapp, Mrs. M. G. Standley, Rev. M. G. Standley, and Rev. J. F. Knapp.

[116] This becomes apparent in the testimony of J. F. Knapp in *Court Records... (Filed June 5, 1929)*, 181-284. John Franklin (262) admitted with regard to bookkeeping, "I am exceedingly ignorant, and it was a very great trial to me when I came into the institution to have to engage in this financial work. I wanted to attend to the educational work." Also, note F. M. Messenger's assessment of M. G. Standley as a business man—"while I never questioned his motives, his methods of business were not the best" (334).

¹¹⁷ See "Foreign Missionary Work As Carried On By God's Bible School and Revivalist," *Revivalist* (Dec. 31, 1925), 13. Here it was emphasized, "Remember that when you send money to God's Revivalist Office for the foreign field, every dollar that you send goes in full to that field. Nothing is taken out for the necessary bookkeeping, correspondence, or other items of expense."

¹¹⁸ "The New Hope Cottage—Better Than Ever," *Revivalist* (June 19, 1924), 8. See *Court Records . . . (Filed June 5, 1929)*, 357-358.

¹¹⁹ "A Sad Catastrophe to 'Hope Cottage'—God's Revivalist Rescue Home," *Revivalist* (Dec. 13, 1923), 8-9. This article is duplicated in Moser and Smith, 140-141. Day (60) mistakenly gives December 23, 1923, as the date of the fire.

¹²⁰ Day, 60.

¹²¹ "The 'Blot Out' Campaign," *Revivalist* (June 26, 1924), 8.

¹²² "What About Thanksgiving?" *Revivalist* (Nov. 6, 1924), 8.

¹²³ "A Threatening Peril . . ." *Revivalist* (July 2, 1925), 14 (original emphases). Day (63-64) says that four financial plans, including (1) the "Annuity Contract," (2) the "Loan" plan, (3) the "Estate Note" plan, and (4) "the 'Gift' plan (whereby money was given outright)" were "inaugurated in 1930." However, these plans were all essentially in place by at least 1925 during the campaign to eliminate indebtedness.

¹²⁴ See advertisements in *Revivalist* (July 2, 1925), 8-9 and 15. Also, see "Additional Books which are Going At Cost in the Great Money Raising Sale," *Revivalist* (July 9, 1925), 15 and advertisements throughout several following issues.

¹²⁵ Mrs. M. G. Standley, "Pressing Needs," *Revivalist* (March 3, 1927), 11.

¹²⁶ Day, 62. Also, see Moser and Smith, 154-155.

¹²⁷ See M. G. Standley, "How Strangely and Wonderfully God Works At Times!" *Revivalist* (July 5, 1928), 1-2 and "Note of Explanation," *Revivalist* (July 5, 1928), 3. The lawsuit was filed the day before Thanksgiving although the trial was postponed until well into the next year. See Standley, *My Life*, 144-145.

¹²⁸ M. G. Standley, "I Was Surprised," *Revivalist* (January 12, 1928), 9.

¹²⁹ See the testimony presented in *Court Records . . . (Filed June 5, 1929)*.

¹³⁰ Ibid, 195-198, 230-232.

¹³¹ Ibid, 231.

¹³² Ibid, 303.

¹³³ Ibid, 162-164.

¹³⁴ Ibid, 325. Here F. M. Messenger indicates that Standley was "very enthusiastic" about the possibilities that Certigraph success would mean for GBS.

¹³⁵ Ibid. Apparently, before it became dissociated from GBS, the school "received the receipts from the magazine" and in turn paid Knapp's salary for running it. on explanation of benefits (255). See offer in *Revivalist* (March 19, 1925), 14-15.

¹³⁶ See J. F. Knapp, "Holy Ground," *Revivalist* (March 3, 1927), 8. At this point, he was still attempting to raise funds for a new tabernacle.

¹³⁷ *Court Records . . . (Filed June 5, 1929)*, 217-219 and 94.

¹³⁸ Ibid, 95 and 219.

¹³⁹ Ibid, 136.

¹⁴⁰ Day, 79.

¹⁴¹ Ibid, 185-186, 221.

¹⁴² See F. M. Messenger's testimony, Ibid, 335-337.

¹⁴³ Ibid, 273-274, 310-312.

¹⁴⁴ Ibid, 165-170, 274-284. In addition to conflict of interest, it was indicated that some of the items removed may have been, in fact, school property—although if this were so, it may not have been known to Knapp at the time of their removal, since he was apparently not involved in the actual removal of some of the items.

¹⁴⁵ See Standley, *My Life*, 142-143 and *Court Records . . . (Filed June 5, 1929)*, 329-341.

¹⁴⁶ M. G. Standley, "Bear Ye One Another's Burdens, and So Fulfil the Law of Christ," *Revivalist* (Dec. 15, 1927), 1, 5.

¹⁴⁷ M. G. Standley, "How Strangely and Wonderfully God Works At Times!" *Revivalist* (July 5, 1928), 1-3.

¹⁴⁸ Advertisement, *Revivalist* (May 10, 1928), 11. In anticipation of demand, large quantities were offered at discount prices. Although not specifically mentioned, context undoubtedly brought these buttons to reflect on the purveyors of negative rumors about the school.

¹⁴⁹ Bessie Standley reported that 50,000 letters of support were received from December 26, 1927, until June 1, 1928. See Mrs. M. G. Standley, "Continuation of Great Things!" *Revivalist* (June 28, 1928), 1-2. Of course, only a fraction of these appeared in the *Revivalist* supplements. It was explained concerning letters from children: "We get so many letters that we cannot publish them all, so we put them in a basket and shake them up well, then draw out enough to fill the page" ("The Soldier's Report," Supplement to the *Revivalist* (May 31-June 7, 1928), 7).

¹⁵⁰ "How Some of Our Workers See It," *Revivalist* (Jan. 19, 1928), 5, 12. Also, see Standley, "Bear Ye One Another's Burdens, . . ." *Revivalist* (Dec. 15, 1927), 1, 5. See such articles as Nettie Peabody, "Adversity," *Revivalist* (March 15, 1928), 8, and "God Answers," *Revivalist* (April 5, 1928), 10, which, while not directly addressing the tumultuous conditions confronting GBS, reflect her perspective on such situations.

¹⁵¹ See "Bible School Notes," *Revivalist* (April 14, 1927), 8 and "LATEST NEWS! APRIL 30, 1928," *Revivalist* (May 10, 1928), 1.

¹⁵² Various factors may have reduced Kulp's involvement at GBS. One was likely the illness of his wife during the time of the campaign. See his letter published in M. G. Standley, "LATEST NEWS? MARCH [2]5, 1928," *Revivalist* (April 12, 1928), 1.

¹⁵³ See M. G. Standley, "His Gift Is Different," *Revivalist* (Jan. 19, 1928), 1-2.

¹⁵⁴ See boxed announcement, *Revivalist* (May 17, 1928), 2; M. G. Standley, "Another of God's Beautiful Saints Gone Home!" *Revivalist* (May 24, 1928), 8; and M. G. Standley, "LATEST NEWS! NOON, MAY 16, 1928," *Revivalist* (May 24, 1928), 1.

¹⁵⁵ F. M. Messenger, "They Gave Themselves," *Revivalist* (March 1, 1928), 1-2. Also, see his articles, "The Great Debt," *Revivalist* (Jan. 12, 1928), 1, 12; "Don't Rob Yourself of This Great Opportunity," *Revivalist* (Jan. 26, 1928), 1; "God With Us," *Revivalist* (March 29, 1928), 1; and "Will God Fail Us?" *Revivalist* (May 10, 1928), 1.

¹⁵⁶ See M. G. Standley, "LATEST NEWS! NOON, MAY 16, 1928," *Revivalist*

(May 24, 1928), 1; M. G. Standley, "A Restaurant With Birds and Squirrels as Waiters," *Revivalist* (May 31-June 7, 1928), 7, 14; and Advertisement, *Revivalist* (May 31-June 7, 1928), 8. Also, see the letters from Bevington in "God is Working, Hallelujah!" *Revivalist* (Jan. 26, 1928), 5 and "Our Hearts Are With You! Supplement to *Revivalist* (Feb. 23, 1928), 1.

157 In addition to the *Revivalist* supplements, see Charles Slater, "God's Bible School and Its Debt," *Revivalist* (Jan. 26, 1928), 3 and R. G. Finch, "A Soul Refiner! A Spiritual Dynamo!" *Revivalist* (Feb. 9, 1928), 1-2.

158 E. A. Kilbourne, "The Oriental Missionary Society," *Revivalist* (Feb. 2, 1928), 1. This was one of the last articles by Kilbourne in the *Revivalist*, as he died a few months later.

159 "God Is Working, Hallelujah!" Supplement to *Revivalist* (Feb. 9, 1928), 1 (original emphasis).

160 For example, see John and Bona Fleming, "NOT DOWN BUT THROUGH" in "Our Hearts Are With You," *Revivalist* (Feb. 16, 1928), 8; As Bro. Joseph H. Smith Sees It," *Revivalist* (March 15, 1928), 1; the letter to Bessie Standley from Mrs. Joseph H. Smith, "Our Hearts Are With You!" Supplement to *Revivalist* (May 24, 1928), 1; and the letters from Paul S. Rees and the Ives in "Our Hearts Are With You!" Supplement to *Revivalist* (March 22, 1928), 1.

161 "A Letter from Brother Bud Robinson," *Revivalist* (May 17, 1928), 1, 4. Also, see "Uncle Bud Robinson Sees by Faith With Us Our Jubilee Year!" *Revivalist* (March 29, 1928), 2; E. O. Chalfant, "Why Pay the Debt?" *Revivalist* (May 17, 1928), 2; "Testimony of Brother E. O. Chalfant: Nazarene Superintendent of Chicago Central District," *Revivalist* (May 24, 1928), 3; and "Testimony of Chas. A. Gibson: Superintendent of the Nazarene Church of Ohio," *Revivalist* (May 24, 1928), 3-4.

162 Letter from E. E. Shelhamer in "Our Hearts Are With You!" Supplement to *Revivalist* (April 19, 1928), 1.

163 Mrs. Charles E. Cowman, "Back to the Bible," *Revivalist* (March 22, 1928), 1-2 (original emphasis).

164 See his letter in "Our Hearts Are With You!" Supplement to *Revivalist* (March 15, 1928), 1 (original emphases).

165 See "The Jubilee Service in God's Bible School Tabernacle," *Revivalist* (April 19, 1928), 5.

166 M. G. Standley, "God Is With Us," *Revivalist* (May 24, 1928), 1 and F. M. Messenger, "God With Us," *Revivalist* (March 29, 1928), 1.

167 M. G. Standley, remarks in "The Dedicatory Service at the Monument," reported by R. R. and A. E. *Revivalist* (June 21, 1928), 10. Also, see M. G. Standley, *My Life*, 143-144.

168 See Standley's message, "Be Thou an Example of the Believers," *Revivalist* (Feb. 2, 1928), 2-6, 12 (preached in Tabernacle, Sunday afternoon, Jan. 22), and his articles "What Do These Feeble Jews? (What do these feeble Revivalist folk?)," *Revivalist* (Feb. 9, 1928), 2, 9; "No Weapon That Is Formed Against Thee Shall Prosper," *Revivalist* (Feb. 23, 1928), 1-2; and "Some Feats of Faith That Seem Discouraging," *Revivalist* (March 8, 1928), 1-2.

[169] See the illustration of the monument planned for the orphanage property in Sister Embury, "Children's Page," *Revivalist* (February 16, 1928), 7 and a photograph of it, *Revivalist* (April 5, 1928), 10.

[170] Ibid and M. G. Standley, "I Am But a Little Child," *Revivalist* (Feb. 16, 1928), 2.

[171] M. G. Standley, "The People Had a Mind to Work," *Revivalist* (March 1, 1928), 4-5; M. G. Standley, "Welcoming God's Revivalist Family's Children in Our Army to Kill the Giant, Goliath-Debt," *Revivalist* (March 8, 1928), 4, 9; and Day, 62.

[172] M. G. Standley, "Latest News! Noon, March 13, 1928," *Revivalist* (March 22, 1928), 1.

[173] This cartoon by J. Payton appears in M. G. Standley, "The Giant Is Slain," *Revivalist* (March 22, 1928), 4, an article duplicated from *Sparkling Waters*.

[174] M. G. Standley, "Latest News! Noon, March 21, 1928," *Revivalist* (March 29, 1928), 1; R. R. and A. E., "The Giant Debt Hanging Over God's Orphanage Is Buried," *Revivalist* (March 29, 1928), 2-3, 7-8; M. G. Standley, "Oh, It Was a Great Sight!" *Revivalist* (March 29, 1928), 4-5; and J. W. Harris, "A Funeral Occasion," *Revivalist* (April 5, 1928), 10.

[175] M. G. Standley, "The 'Earnest' of Our Jubilee Year," *Revivalist* (March 29, 1928), 1, 9 and "A Sabbath of Jubilee," *Revivalist* (April 12, 1928), 1.

[176] "LATEST NEWS! MARCH [2]5, 1928," *Revivalist* (April 12, 1928), 1 and R. R. and A. E., "The Jubilee Service in God's Bible School Tabernacle," *Revivalist* (April 12, 1928), 3-5 and "The Jubilee Service . . ." *Revivalist* (April 19, 1928), 2-6.

[177] "UNCLE BUD ROBINSON SEES BY FAITH WITH US OUR JUBILEE YEAR!" *Revivalist* (March 29, 1928), 2.

[178] Cartoon by J. Payton with article, M. G. Standley, "Forward March Against This Great Giant," *Revivalist* (April 5, 1928), 11. Also, see Children's Page, *Revivalist* (May 10, 1928), 7 and Children's Page, *Revivalist* (May 24, 1928), 7.

[179] See M. G. Standley, "LATEST NEWS! APRIL 23, 1928," *Revivalist* (May 3, 1928), 1.

[180] See M. G. Standley, "LATEST NEWS! APRIL 23, 1928," *Revivalist* (May 3, 1928), 1; M. G. Standley, "A 'DO-WITHOUT-WEEK' AND A 'TIME OF FASTING AND PRAYER,' *Revivalist* (May 3, 1928), 2; and letter from Mrs. M. W. Knapp on "Self-Denial Week," in Supplement to *Revivalist* (May 10, 1928), 1. This supplement also contains articles by C. H. Babcock, Belle Staples, Lettie Cowman, Charles Slater, E. G. Marsh, and an excerpt from John Wesley on "Self-Denial." Other similar articles or letters appeared in the same *Revivalist* issue, written by Bud Robinson, Nettie Peabody, C. W. Ruth, and J. W. Harris.

[181] See M. G. Standley, "LATEST NEWS! NOON, MAY 16, 1928," *Revivalist* (May 24, 1928), 1.

[182] Caption under cartoon on Children's Page, *Revivalist* (May 24, 1928), 7.

[183] M. G. Standley, "The Latest And Best News," *Revivalist* (June 14, 1928), 1-2.

[184] Joseph H. Smith, "A Day of Jubilee," *Revivalist* (June 21, 1928), 4.

[185] Standley, "The Latest and Best News."

[186] Edwin and Hazel Kilbourne, "The Last Day of the Feast," *Revivalist* (June 21, 1928), 13.

[187] Standley, "The Latest and Best News."

188 Kilbourne, "The Last Day of the Feast."

189 Standley, "The Latest and Best News," 2.

190 Kilbourne, "The Last Day of the Feast."

191 See the photograph in *Revivalist* (June 21, 1928), 5. Several other photographs in this and the following issue of the *Revivalist* document the celebration.

192 C. H. Babcock, "A Glorious Camp Meeting," *Revivalist* (June 21, 1928), 3.

193 Kilbourne, "The Last Day of the Feast."

194 Charles L. Slater, "J-u-b-i-l-e-e D-a-y!" *Revivalist* (June 21, 1928), 9, and "The Dedicatory Service at the Monument," *Revivalist* (June 21, 1928), 10-11, 8.

195 M. G. Standley, "The Lord Hath Done Great Things for Us; Whereof We Are Glad" *Revivalist* (June 21, 1928), 8. Others concurred in this assessment, including Charles Slater ("J-u-b-i-l-e-e D-a-y!")—"June 3, 1928, has gone down in history as the greatest day that was ever known at the 'Mount of Blessings,' God's Bible School, Cincinnati, Ohio!"

196 M. G. Standley, "The Lord God Omnipotent Reigneth!" *Revivalist* (March 22, 1928), 3. See "Latest News" updates in several *Revivalist*s throughout the spring and summer of 1928 for reports on the trial's postponement.

197 See *Court Records... (Filed June 5, 1929)*, 5, and Decision.

198 Ibid, Decision.

199 Standley reported, "By January 31 when the trial was set we had succeeded in getting our creditors to sign a petition protesting against a receivership—nearly ninety per cent had answered protesting!" (Remarks in "The Dedicatory Service at the Monument," reported by R. R. and A. E. *Revivalist* (June 21, 1928), 10).

200 Glenn Black, "John F. Knapp...."

201 M. G. Standley, "Devout Men Carried Him to His Burial," *Revivalist* (June 17, 1943), 2 and "Obituary," *Revivalist* (June 17, 1943), 7.

202 See Glenn Black, "John Franklin Knapp...." His resignation as trustee was accepted on May 3, 1943, due to doctors' orders for him to have "a complete severance from all obligations and responsibilities" (Day, 94-95). On Knapp's pioneer work in establishing the Eastside Church of the Nazarene in Covington, Kentucky, see the file on Knapp in the Charles and Lettie Cowman Archives at GBS, which includes a brief history of the church's founding by Daisy Hampton and an article on "John Franklin Knapp" by R. D. Grubbs, a personal friend. The latter also recounts Grubb's memories of the circumstances surrounding Knapp's death resulting from heart trouble. Funeral services were conducted at the Eastside Church of the Nazarene and at GBS, in the latter of which E. E. Shelhamer, Andrew Johnson, and John Paul participated and Fred T. Fuge delivered "a marvelous message" (Standley, "Devout Men..." *Revivalist* (June 17, 1943), 2. Glenn Black, "John Franklin Knapp..." reproduces a portion of Fuge's sermon, a transcript of which appears in "If A Man Die, Shall He Live Again," *Revivalist* (June 17, 1943), 5-7.

203 Glenn Black, "John Franklin Knapp..."

204 M. G. Standley, "The Lord Hath Done Great Things for Us; Whereof We Are Glad," *Revivalist* (June 21, 1928), 8.

205 M. G. Standley wrote, "We covenant with God that if He will lift us out of this debt, we will fast, and pray, and trust Him to supply our needs AS WE GO" ("I

Was Surprised," *Revivalist* (Jan. 12, 1928), 9 original emphasis).

[206] Slater, "J-u-b-i-l-e-e D-a-y!" *Revivalist* (June 21, 1928), 9 (original emphases). For a similar sentiment, see J. L. Glascock's message recorded in "The Jubilee Service in God's Bible School Tabernacle: Sunday Afternoon, April 1, 1928," *Revivalist* (April 19, 1928), 4-5.

[207] See the messages by J. L. Glascock and M. G. Standley in "The Jubilee Service . . ." *Revivalist* (April 19, 1928), 4-6. Although this project did not materialize, GBS students and workers remained active in urban outreach through various store-front missions and other ministries.

[208] M. G. Standley, "'Mine House . . . A House of Prayer," *Revivalist* (Oct. 10, 1929), 1.

[209] "Uncle Buddie" Robinson, "Memories of the Old Tabernacle," *Revivalist* (Sept. 5, 1929), 1-2; E. E. Shelhamer, "A Pressing Need," *Revivalist* (July 11, 1929), 1; and Joseph H. Smith, letter reprinted in "Arise and Build," in Supplement to *Revivalist* (Nov. 7, 1929), 1.

[210] M. G. Standley, "Take Every Man a Beam!" *Revivalist* (Nov. 7, 1929), 8.

[211] M. G. Standley, "This Is the Lord's Doing, And it Is Marvelous in Our Eyes!" *Revivalist* (June 21, 1928), 1-2 (original emphasis).

Appendix A

Dedicatory Prayer by Seth Rees, September 27, 1900

A call was made for those who wished to dedicate themselves to the Lord to come forward. Two responded. Then we kneeled at a table upon which lay the Holy Bible and Brother Rees offered the following prayer:

Mighty God, the God of David, the God of the temple who came in and filled it with His glory, we bow before Thee to-night, we worship Thee, we adore Thee, we extol Thee, we give Thee all the glory that we know how to give Thee. Teach us how to do it. We feel to thank Thee for this hour. We thank Thee for the developments that have come to this movement from year to year. O God, we thank Thee that during past years, Thou hast poured out such blessings upon this movement, and hast brought us to this hour! We come here thanking and praising Thee for leading us to this hour. Now, Lord, Thou hast evidently not only purchased this property but Thou hast planned for its payment and for its improvement and the work; and, O Lord, it gives us great pleasure to-night to give this property to Thee! Brother and Sister Knapp, and all who are concerned here are delighted that Thou hast accepted it, and here, in the presence, not only of those who are here; but in the presence of angels we give this property to Thee for the interests of Thy kingdom, to be held for Thee until Jesus comes, for the spreading of Thy truth, for a place where the fire can fall from heaven upon human souls, for a place where sinners may become so convicted for sin, that they will rush to the Savior, and a place where Thy people may receive such power as to send them out with more than multiplied energy to minister Thy truth all over the world. O God, we give this property to Thee asking that Thy power and Thy glory may come into it just now and abide forever! Keep it from all danger, from fire, from blasting storms, from all kinds of evil, and keep it free from sin, and make it a place where sin will be rebuked. Let this be a place where the fire shall fall from heaven upon the hearts of those who shall go into the slums, into the highways, into the saloons, and into the homes of the wealthy that surround it. Lord, as we give this property to Thee, we do it with a burning desire that this shall be made such a place where fire will fall that hundreds of revivals will be kindled. We give it to Thee, not only for a Bible-school, but for a camp-meeting, and not only for camp-meetings, but for conventions, where God's people may come from all over this land and get mighty things of God. Now, Lord, here are some souls who have come to present themselves, and who say from this very day of their consecration they want to be Yours, and want to be considered the Lord's property. O God, sanctify them wholly to-night! Let this be the night when fire shall fall out of the skies, and when they shall receive a mighty incentive to go out and spread this truth. Lord, we want to pray for these young people, these precious boys and girls who have left their homes to come to this place to fill up on the Word. It may be that some of them have never been away from home before. Save them from being homesick. We pray Thee that the Spirit of the Lord may so settle down upon them that they may be in the Divine order. Mighty God, we pray Thy blessings upon these boys and girls! We commend them to Thee. We ask Thy special blessing upon Brother and Sister Knapp. Thou knowest we love them. We trust Thee to cover them all over with blessings; we trust Thee to cover them with Thine Almighty Arm. Bless their sacrifice. They have sacrificed the blessings of domestic life, and we pray Thee to repay them a hundred-fold. Bless Sister Knapp in body and give her energy for this work. Thou alone canst do it. We trust Thee to do it. Thou alone dost know and understand how much there is resting upon her and we trust Thee to give her the needed strength and grace. Take care of those who have come, those who ought to come, and those who are going to come, and at last bring us, with a great concourse of people who have been saved, sanctified, healed, and finally glorified, to Thyself, and unto the King Eternal and Infinitely Wise we give all the glory and honor. Amen!

Appendix B

Bibliographical Essay

As would be expected, school publications, especially *God's Revivalist and Bible Advocate*, provide the core of primary source materials. Many other religious periodicals reflecting on God's Bible School and the *Revivalist* also provide valuable primary and secondary material. Among these are the *Christian Witness and Advocate of Bible Holiness*, *The Guide to Holiness*, *The Michigan Christian Advocate*, *The Missionary Revivalist*, *The Pentecostal Herald* (later, simply *The Herald*), *The Preacher's Magazine*, and *The Way of Faith and Neglected Themes*.

Reports concerning the school which appeared in the Cincinnati newspapers supply helpful, and often vivid, insights from an outside perspective. The three major newspapers during the twentieth century were the *Cincinnati Enquirer*, the *Cincinnati Post*, and the *Cincinnati Times-Star*. The *Times-Star* bears particular significance for GBS history due to the affiliation of the Taft family, which owned it, with the school.[1]

Biographical works treating significant individuals in the school's history present important primary and secondary material. Such biographies include A. M. Hills, *A Hero of Faith and Prayer; or, Life of Rev. Martin Wells Knapp*;[2] Lettie B. Cowman, *Missionary Warrior: Charles E. Cowman*; the *Autobiography of Rev. W. B. Godbey, A.M.*; Paul Rees, *Seth Cook Rees: The Warrior Saint*; and Meredith G. Standley, *My Life As I Have Lived It For Christ and Others*.

Another important source of information is the growing collection of correspondence, memoirs, and records in the school archives. Now included in this collection is data from the Hamilton County Court of Clerks office from the lengthy period during which the school was held in receivership as a public charitable trust by the Court of Common Pleas. All of these materials have been appreciably augmented by personal interviews and written questionnaires of principle participants and representative alumni. Warm vignettes and frank assessments gave invaluable assistance in clarifying character traits and interactions between pivotal individuals. The author interviewed the following in connection with this project: Dr. and Mrs. Michael Avery, Rev. Glenn Black, Mr. and Mrs. P. Lewis Brevard, Dr. Samuel Deets, Dr. Kenneth Farmer, Dr. and Mrs. Robert England, Sr., Dr. and Mrs. Bence Miller, Dr. Leonard Sankey, Dr. and Mrs. Kenneth Stetler, Rev. Edsel Trouten, and Mr. Garan Wolf, I. Several interviews conducted by Larry Smith and Kevin Moser for *God's Clock Keeps Perfect Time* also proved helpful to this project: Dr. Wesley Duewel, Mr. Ted Henschen, Mr. and Mrs. Richard Sparks, and Rev. Chester Wilkins. Questionnaires for this work were completed by Dr. V. O. Agan, Dr. Mark Eckart, Mr. Donald Hubbard, Rev. Melvin Schaper, Rev. Daniel Stetler, and Mr. George Vernon, III.

Several secondary sources also inform the work. These include histories of the holiness movement and its denominations and other institutions.[3] Of obvious significance is Lloyd Day's master's thesis, *A History of God's Bible School in Cincinnati: 1900-1949*[4] and the centenary picture-book prepared by Kevin M. Moser and Larry D. Smith, *God's Clock Keeps Perfect Time: God's Bible School's First 100 Years: 1900-2000*.[5] Glenn Black's well-researched articles on "Our Heritage" in the 1983-84 *Revivalist*s also provide helpful material and insightful assessment. Two other especially helpful works are Donald Dayton's *Theological Roots of Pentecostalism* , a seminal work which provides a helpful paradigm for understanding early Pentecostalism and the radical holiness movement, and William Kostlevy's *Holy Jumpers: Evangelicals and Radicals in Progressive Era America*, a groundbreaking work which brilliantly elucidates the dynamic development of the radical holiness movement led by Martin Wells Knapp and his associates.[6]

Notes

[1] Charles P. Taft [Sr.] was the principal owner and editor of the *Times-Star* until his death on December 31, 1929, when he was succeeded by his nephew, Hulbert Taft, as editor-in-chief and president of the company. In 1943, the newspaper became the *Cincinnati Times-Star* and retained that title until its consolidation with the *Cincinnati Post* in July, 1958.

In the years before the purchase of the newspaper by Taft, the *Daily Times* was a general paper of usual scope and content. Under the Tafts the *Times-Star* was oriented in the Republican spirit (History, Microfilm, *Cincinnati Times-Star*, The Cincinnati Historical Society).

[2] Although this work uses Newby's reprint of Hill's biography, his book has gone through several editions, the most recent being released while this work was in process (Winesburg, OH: Manna Ministries, 2000).

[3] A recent history that provides a concise rendering of events related to the development of the *Revivalist* and God's Bible School is Robert Black and Keith Drury, *The Story of the Wesleyan Church* (Indianapolis: Wesleyan Publishing House, 2012). Note especially pages 96-114.

[4] While Day's work provides a helpful overview of the first fifty years of the school, it tends to focus on academic developments and to avoid discussions of theological, sociological, and even administrative factors. This is understandable considering the area of his master's degree: education.

[5] This book not only contains a beautiful photographic chronology of the school's history but is augmented by anecdotes of events that put the photographs in perspective.

[6] Also, see William Kostlevy, "The Burning Bush Movement: A Wisconsin Utopian Religious Community," *Wisconsin Magazine of History* vol. 83 no. 4 (Summer 2000), 227-257.

www.ingramcontent.com/pod-product-compliance
Lightning Source LLC
Chambersburg PA
CBHW030333240426
43661CB00052B/1615